# LIVING LITURGY™

# LIVING ✛ LITURGY™

## Spirituality, Celebration, and Catechesis for Sundays and Solemnities

### Year B • 2018

*Brian Schmisek*
*Diana Macalintal*
*Jay Cormier*

**LITURGICAL PRESS**
Collegeville, Minnesota

www.litpress.org

ISSN 1547-089X

ISBN 978-0-8146-4722-6   ISBN 978-0-8146-4747-9 (ebook)

# ✝ CONTENTS

# CONTRIBUTORS

**Brian Schmisek** is professor and dean of the Institute of Pastoral Studies at Loyola University Chicago. Prior to coming to Chicago in 2012, he was the founding dean of the School of Ministry at the University of Dallas. His published works include *Ancient Faith for the Modern World: A Brief Guide to the Apostles' Creed* (ACTA), *A Greek Reader for Chase & Phillips* (Wipf & Stock), *Resurrection of the Flesh or Resurrection from the Dead: Implications for Theology* (Liturgical Press), many other books coauthored for biblical study, and articles.

**Diana Macalintal** has served as a liturgist, musician, author, speaker, and composer for the last twenty-five years, and her work can be found in *Give Us This Day* and many other publications. She is the author of *The Eucharist Catechist's Guide* (Saint Mary's Press), as well as *The Work of Your Hands: Prayers for Ordinary and Extraordinary Moments of Grace* and *Joined by the Church, Sealed by a Blessing: Couples and Communities Called to Conversion Together* (Liturgical Press). Macalintal is a cofounder of TeamRCIA.com with her husband, Nick Wagner.

**Jay Cormier** is editor of *Connections*, a monthly newsletter for homilists and preachers. He is an adjunct professor of humanities and communications at St. Anselm College in Manchester, New Hampshire, and leads preaching and liturgy workshops for clergy and laity. Cormier has contributed to *America, U.S. Catholic, Worship*, and *Give Us This Day*; and is the author of *The Deacon's Ministry of the Word* and previous editions of *Waiting in Joyful Hope: Daily Reflections for Advent and Christmas* and *Not by Bread Alone: Daily Reflections for Lent* (Liturgical Press).

## Renewal

There comes a time when a family needs to move to a new home, whether across the country or simply down the street. Some externals certainly change, maybe the number of bedrooms, or the size of the kitchen. Decorations may be different; we might want new artwork for the walls or even some new furniture. But ultimately it is the same family in a slightly different context. That image comes to mind when this family of *Living Liturgy*™ readers and users encounters the 2018 edition. On behalf of the new authorship team, we want to express our humility and gratitude for being asked to contribute to this worthwhile endeavor. We respect the work of past teams who developed this material to what it is over a period of nearly twenty years. Sr. Joyce Ann Zimmerman, CPPS, director of the Institute for Liturgical Ministry (now closed, unfortunately), and Sr. Kathleen Harmon, SNDdeN, were with this project from the beginning, when the 2000 edition of *Living Liturgy*™ was released in September 1999. Each brought strong liturgical backgrounds informed by a living and vibrant faith. And Sr. Joyce Ann's insight that the paschal mystery is the central principle of both liturgy and life is something we were keen to retain in this resource for the larger parish community. In addition to familiar features, you the readers, the family of *Living Liturgy*™, will find some new things in this 2018 edition, the nineteenth volume. Allow us a brief tour.

## Artwork

Like a new home, some of the first things you might notice about this 2018 edition is a new "look and feel." Liturgical Press sought various artists who offered suggestions for change and eventually three were chosen: Deborah Luke, Tanja Butler, and Ned Bustard. The artwork is new and original, commissioned especially for this edition. It should go without saying that we hope you like it. Many other features of the book remain the same.

## Reflecting on the Gospel and Living the Paschal Mystery

As a result of some focus group feedback and consultation with regular users, we learned that the most frequented part of the book is "Reflecting on the Gospel," followed by "Living the Paschal Mystery," true to Sr. Joyce Ann's insight. So it is with a sense of care and concern that Brian Schmisek has written these pieces. He wrote many informed by the Catholic social tradition of the church, and all are infused with what Pope Francis calls "the joy of love."

## Focusing the Gospel, Model Prayers, and Homily Points

The survey of current users also indicated that pages 2–3 of the material each week were widely used. Jay Cormier wrote these sections. His work is informed by his own diaconal ministry that includes teaching and preaching. He incorporated a new layout, retaining "Focusing the Gospel" and adding direct comments about each reading including the psalm. He also proposed reflection questions intended to appeal to a broader audience. The feedback we received indicated that these kinds of questions would be better suited to how the books are actually used. So we hope these are beneficial.

## Liturgy

As the name of the book certainly implies, liturgy is a primary focus, and we are fortunate to have Diana Macalintal's experienced voice heard in this section. Not only does she recommend certain musical selections, but she includes liturgical advice and wisdom gained from her years of service in a variety of roles. She is well versed in the style and substance of liturgy and we have confidence that you will find her comments informative and helpful.

## Purpose

The three new authors for this book, Brian, Jay, and Diana, retained its original and primary purpose: "to help people prepare for liturgy and live a liturgical spirituality (that is, a way of living that is rooted in liturgy), opening their vision to their baptismal identity as the Body of Christ and shaping their living according to the rhythm of paschal mystery dying and rising. The paschal mystery is the central focus of liturgy, of the gospels, and of this volume." As indicated above, we are privileged to follow in the footsteps of previous teams of authors. In the past, there were different voices added at different times: Christopher W. Conlon, SM; Thomas A. Griesen; Thomas L. Leclerc, MS; and John W. Tonkin. But the two constant team members were Sr. Joyce Ann and Sr. Kathleen. If our work carries on their task and is found meaningful for a new generation of parish communities, we will be gratified. We look forward to the feedback of the *Living Liturgy*™ family as you encounter and use this material, living into it as you might a new home with a well-loved and supportive family.

SEASON OF ADVENT

## ✛ SPIRITUALITY

**GOSPEL ACCLAMATION**
Ps 85:8

R̸. Alleluia, alleluia.
Show us Lord, your love;
and grant us your salvation.
R̸. Alleluia, alleluia.

### Gospel

Mark 13:33-37; L2B

Jesus said to his disciples:
"Be watchful! Be alert!
You do not know when the
time will come.
It is like a man traveling
abroad.
He leaves home and places his
servants in charge, each with
his own work,
and orders the gatekeeper to be
on the watch.
Watch, therefore;
you do not know when the lord of the
house is coming,
whether in the evening, or at
midnight,
or at cockcrow, or in the morning.
May he not come suddenly and find you
sleeping.
What I say to you, I say to all:
'Watch!'"

### Reflecting on the Gospel

We are plunged into the First Sunday of Advent with a reading from Mark 13. Jesus speaks about the coming end time, encouraging Peter, James, John, and Andrew (and us) to be watchful, to be prepared, and to recognize the signs of the times. The passage concludes this ominous chapter with the key word "watch" that occurs in each but one verse. "Watch" is an appropriate word with which to begin our Advent season. We are to be prepared for the Lord's coming, not knowing precisely when that will be. We, like the gatekeeper, keep watch in the evening, at midnight, at dawn, and in the morning. Like the early disciples, we know not when he comes, but that he is coming. Many novelists have written books using this chapter to discern precisely when the end time will be. Though Scripture clearly states that nobody knows the day or hour, these charlatans claim to know the month and year, and you can too if you buy their books!

Today we read this passage from Mark 13 not as a code book to discern the exact "when" of the end time, while wondering what the "desolating abomination standing" is and when that might occur. Rather, we recognize that Mark wrote at a time when the early Christians expected Jesus' imminent return. The four apostles in the story were likely dead by the time of this writing. It might have seemed that Jesus was not coming back as he had promised. So the readers of Mark's gospel were given a new promise, "this generation will not pass away until all these things have taken place" (Mark 13:30, NABRE). These early Christians saw in the events of their time "nation . . . ris[ing] against nation," "earthquakes," and "famines," as the "beginnings of the labor pains" signifying the end was near (13:8, NABRE). But unfortunately, we know these kinds of cataclysmic events happen with some regularity. That generation did in fact pass away. The early Christians did not imagine we would be reading this gospel two thousand years hence.

Still, we can discern the signs of our own times and recognize the Lord's coming, perhaps not in an apocalyptic sense, but in the Christmas incarnation. That is, Jesus, the Word of God, comes to us in flesh and blood. Jesus is the incarnation of God, and he comes to us sacramentally in the Eucharist. Each generation seems to say the end is near. While we are looking to the sky for signs of the end time, the Lord is in our midst in weakness and vulnerability. Do we see Jesus present in that disguise? Or is it easier and "more fun" to be caught up with a code book, discerning the end time and seeking the "abomination standing"? Instead, we see that God is in our midst. The key word for this Sunday is "watch." But we may also say, "recognize."

### Living the Paschal Mystery

Many times we are impressed by big events, fireworks, theme parks, light shows, and more. We mark special events with parties, celebrations, dinners, family, friends, and loved ones. While these are natural tendencies, Christianity is also about finding meaning in the small, seemingly inconsequential events in our lives. Changing a diaper is a routine task for parents, but it is also an act of charitable love. Preparing a meal for a family gathering can be tedious and time-consuming, but it too is an act of charitable love. Being fully present to another can be difficult for us who are accustomed to checking mobile devices several times an hour, but it is an act of charitable love. Most of us are not going to do grandiose acts of charity for which we are praised and thanked on the evening news. But it is our everyday tasks done with intention and meaning that can make the difference between routine and a day filled with self-giving love.

## Focusing the Gospel
*Mark 13:33-37*
We begin a new liturgical year at the end of time. Jesus' brief parable of the master's return is a call to realize the trust God has placed in us in the present to create his kingdom of justice and peace to transcend all time. Jesus counters the conventional fears of the apocalypse with "signs" of hope and new beginnings.

## Focusing the First Reading
*Isa 63:16b-17, 19b; 64:2-7*
Today's first reading is a prayer of hope as the Jewish community returns home. The long night of the Babylonian exile is over; the Jewish exiles make their way back to what is left of Jerusalem. Now begins the hard work of restoration. In this reading from Trito-Isaiah, the prophet acknowledges the people's sinfulness that led to their nation's collapse and seeks God's mercy as their "Father" as they begin the work of rebuilding. In the beautiful image of God as "potter," the people of Israel ask God to recreate and reform them into a people and nation worthy of the covenant.

## Focusing the Responsorial Psalm
*Ps 80:2-3, 15-16, 18-19*
Psalm 80 is a plea to God for help in the wake of disaster. The devastated nation cries to God as their "shepherd," their once and future protector, to come down and restore the "vine" (a treasured symbol of Israel) that God planted at Israel's deliverance from Egyptian slavery and now seeks to reestablish its covenant of justice and mercy with God.

## Focusing the Second Reading
*1 Cor 1:3-9*
In the opening words of his first letter to the church at Corinth, the apostle Paul reminds his readers that the Lord's return at the end of time—a return that Paul's Christian community expected at any moment—was not a cause for fear and despair but a reason for hope. "The day of the Lord" is the fulfillment of God's covenant with his people, a covenant made whole and complete in Christ Jesus.

---

**PROMPTS FOR HOMILISTS, CATECHISTS, AND RCIA TEAMS**

In what experiences of your life have you come to realize the preciousness and limits of time?

Have you ever "missed" the good and affirming in your life through inattention or distraction?

What has been your most difficult experience of waiting—and how were you able to persevere to its fulfillment?

How can this Advent season be a time of restoration, of re-creation?

3

## Model Penitential Act

*Presider:* In the hope of this Advent season, let us begin this Eucharist by acknowledging our sins, ever confident of the mercy and grace of God to restore and heal. *[pause]*

Come, Father and Redeemer forever: Lord, have mercy.

Come, Savior and Shepherd, and gather us in God's peace: Christ, have mercy.

Come, Spirit of grace, and restore us to hope: Lord, have mercy.

## Homily Points

• Advent urges us to "stay awake" and not sleep through the opportunities life gives us to discover God in our midst. Advent calls us to "watch," to pay attention to the signs of God's unmistakable presence in our lives, to live life expectantly not as a death sentence but as a gift from God. The disciple's life is centered in such "watchfulness," in "attentiveness" to the love of God in every joy and sorrow, every pain and trauma, every victory and setback before us.

• Our lives are an Advent, a prelude, to the life of God to come. While confronting us with the reality that our lives are finite and fragile, these Sundays of Advent also assure us of the mercy of God, who is with us in the midst of all the struggles of our everyday Advent journey to the dwelling place of God. Advent challenges us to see our lives not as a disjointed set of experiences and circumstances but as a pilgrimage to the dwelling place of God—a journey in which every moment, every step is a new revelation of God's presence in our midst. God is both the road we travel and the destination of our pilgrimage.

• Waiting is a reality of the human condition. It is often in waiting that love is realized: In waiting for someone, our own everyday business becomes almost meaningless as we anticipate, worry, and prepare for his or her return. In waiting, we realize our own powerlessness, our deepest hopes and needs, and the gift the person we are awaiting is to us. Our lives are Advents of waiting: to be healed, to make things better, to complete and move on. Our experiences of such waiting are fulfilled in the Messiah Jesus, who makes our lives whole, who brings healing to those difficult times we all experience.

## Model Universal Prayer (Prayer of the Faithful)

*Presider:* "No ear has ever heard, no eye has ever seen" greater wonders than what God has done for us. With confidence, then, let us pray.

*Response:* Lord, hear our prayer.

That our ministries of compassion and care may reveal God's presence in our midst . . .

That all nations and peoples may work together to protect and nurture the "vine" of justice and peace that God has planted . . .

That this Advent season may be a time of restoring the lost and forgotten and healing the broken and shattered . . .

That Christ will bring into his Father's presence the souls of our deceased relatives and friends *[especially . . . ]* . . .

*Presider:* You, O Lord, are the Potter and we are the clay, the work of your hands. Shape us in your ways of justice and mercy, form us in your peace, and craft us in your love. We ask these things in the name of Jesus, Emmanuel. **Amen.**

## COLLECT

Let us pray.

*Pause for silent prayer*

Grant your faithful, we pray, almighty God,
the resolve to run forth to meet your Christ
with righteous deeds at his coming,
so that, gathered at his right hand,
they may be worthy to possess the heavenly Kingdom.
Through our Lord Jesus Christ, your Son,
who lives and reigns with you in the unity of the Holy Spirit,
one God, for ever and ever. **Amen.**

## FIRST READING
Isa 63:16b-17, 19b; 64:2-7

You, Lord, are our father,
    our redeemer you are named forever.
Why do you let us wander, O Lord, from your ways,
    and harden our hearts so that we fear you not?
Return for the sake of your servants,
    the tribes of your heritage.
Oh, that you would rend the heavens and come down,
    with the mountains quaking before you,
while you wrought awesome deeds we could not hope for,
    such as they had not heard of from of old.
No ear has ever heard, no eye ever seen,
    any God but you
    doing such deeds for those who wait for him.
Would that you might meet us doing right,
    that we were mindful of you in our ways!
Behold, you are angry, and we are sinful;
    all of us have become like unclean people,
    all our good deeds are like polluted rags;
we have all withered like leaves,
    and our guilt carries us away like the wind.
There is none who calls upon your name,
    who rouses himself to cling to you;
for you have hidden your face from us
    and have delivered us up to our guilt.
Yet, O Lord, you are our father;
    we are the clay and you the potter:
    we are all the work of your hands.

## RESPONSORIAL PSALM

Ps 80:2-3, 15-16, 18-19

R℣. (4) Lord, make us turn to you; let us see
your face and we shall be saved.

O shepherd of Israel, hearken,
from your throne upon the cherubim,
shine forth.
Rouse your power,
and come to save us.

R℣. Lord, make us turn to you; let us see
your face and we shall be saved.

Once again, O LORD of hosts,
look down from heaven, and see;
take care of this vine,
and protect what your right hand has
planted,
the son of man whom you yourself
made strong.

R℣. Lord, make us turn to you; let us see
your face and we shall be saved.

May your help be with the man of your
right hand,
with the son of man whom you yourself
made strong.
Then we will no more withdraw from you;
give us new life, and we will call upon
your name.

R℣. Lord, make us turn to you; let us see
your face and we shall be saved.

## SECOND READING

1 Cor 1:3-9

Brothers and sisters:
Grace to you and peace from God our
Father
and the Lord Jesus Christ.

I give thanks to my God always on your
account
for the grace of God bestowed on you in
Christ Jesus,
that in him you were enriched in every
way,
with all discourse and all knowledge,
as the testimony to Christ was
confirmed among you,
so that you are not lacking in any
spiritual gift
as you wait for the revelation of our
Lord Jesus Christ.
He will keep you firm to the end,
irreproachable on the day of our Lord
Jesus Christ.
God is faithful,
and by him you were called to
fellowship with his Son, Jesus
Christ our Lord.

### About Liturgy

**What matters most:** Despite our expectation that Advent is a quieter time, this first Sunday of the new liturgical year is a flurry of activity in parishes. We switch out old missalettes, worship aids, and liturgical calendars. The environment committee replaces the green from the last week of Ordinary Time with violet bunting and Advent wreaths. Lectors search for the correct place in the Lectionary, and ushers recruit volunteers to light the Advent wreath. No one who coordinates liturgy is dozing off this time of year because there's too much to do! Yet, we might miss the point of today's readings. In the busyness of liturgy preparation, are we missing God's presence?

We must certainly do the hard work of preparing the liturgy well, so that everyone is ready to fully participate. But we cannot let the work be what matters most. The work is there to train our eyes so that we will see God, who will surprise us when we least expect. As good servants, let us continue to do our work well so that when God arrives unannounced, we will be ready. But as clay in God's hands, let's remember that, ultimately, this is the work of God, who shapes and reshapes our plans, calling us to attend first to his presence. Let's make a new liturgical year's resolution to pay attention to what matters most: God present in the most unplanned of situations and in the most unlikely of persons we will meet this year.

### About Initiation

**The Rite of Acceptance:** Sometimes RCIA teams plan a Rite of Acceptance into the Order of Catechumens for this day, intending to connect the beginning of a new liturgical year with the beginning of formal preparation for baptism. The intent is good, but the timing is bad. By connecting the rite to the beginning of the liturgical year, it unintentionally makes people think that the catechumen's journey will end at the high point of the year, Easter, or it might imply that, like the school year, we're beginning a "new year of RCIA." However, the process of conversion is ongoing and the length of a person's formation cannot be predetermined. Also, there are already many other liturgical elements that are unique to this Sunday and season. Let Advent be the focus, and schedule the Rite of Acceptance for Ordinary Time instead.

### About Liturgical Music

**The sound of Advent:** Advent has a sobriety that is about intense focus on what matters most. It calls us to strip away extraneous practices or bad habits and return to the core of our ministry. Advent's music needs to reflect this joyful anticipation and humble repentance. Remember that the way you perform and prepare the music is as important as the music you choose. If you regularly use SATB arrangements, consider going back to the song's core and sing in unison. If you employ lots of instruments, try some music *a cappella*. Before diving right into learning notes, do "breaking open the hymn" faith-sharing on the text you will sing.

**Repetition is good:** Because it's short, Advent is a good time to explore using seasonal music, which will be used for all four Sundays. This gives a musical unity to the season, and the repetition helps the assembly know the music "from the heart" if not "by heart." The Lectionary provides two seasonal psalm options for Advent: Psalm 25 ("To you, O Lord, I lift my soul") and Psalm 85 ("Lord, show us your mercy and love"). Consider using one of these psalms for the responsorial psalm or perhaps as the Communion song each week. If possible, use the same service music for both Advent and Christmas, but vary the way you perform it so that Advent's sound is simpler while Christmas pulls out all the stops.

**DECEMBER 3, 2017**

# FIRST SUNDAY OF ADVENT

**GOSPEL ACCLAMATION**
cf. Luke 1:28

R̸. Alleluia, alleluia.
Hail, Mary, full of grace, the Lord is with you;
blessed are you among women.
R̸. Alleluia, alleluia.

## Gospel  Luke 1:26-38; L689

The angel Gabriel was sent from God
    to a town of Galilee called Nazareth,
    to a virgin betrothed to a man named
        Joseph,
    of the house of David,
    and the virgin's name was Mary.
And coming to her, he said,
    "Hail, full of grace! The Lord is with
        you."
But she was greatly troubled at what was
        said
    and pondered what sort of greeting
        this might be.
Then the angel said to her,
    "Do not be afraid, Mary,
    for you have found favor with God.
Behold, you will conceive in your womb
        and bear a son,
    and you shall name him Jesus.

*Continued in Appendix A, p. 261.*

*See Appendix A, p. 261, for the other readings.*

## Reflecting on the Gospel

"What's the immaculate conception again?" a confused confirmation student asked the catechist. The unfortunate reply was a struggling attempt to explain the biological process of sperm and egg uniting that results in conception. "And that's how Jesus was conceived?" was the hesitant second question. "No, no," the catechist clarified. This is all about Mary.

Unfortunately there's a great deal of confusion on the part of Catholics regarding this solemnity, which commemorates Mary's own conception without original sin. Part of the confusion comes from the choice of gospel reading for today's liturgy where we hear about Mary's "yes" to the angel Gabriel. Basically, the gospel readings for the immaculate conception speak of Mary conceiving in her womb and bearing a son. Of course, that is the story of what is known as the feast of the Annunciation (Mar. 25), which is exactly nine months prior to the birth of Jesus, otherwise known as the feast of the Nativity (Dec. 25). The feast of the Immaculate Conception (Dec. 8) is precisely nine months prior to the feast of the Nativity of Mary (Sept. 8). So we can excuse those fellow Catholics who might be confused by the issue of the immaculate conception. It *is* a bit confusing and can require some explanation.

Moreover, the commemoration of the immaculate conception has a fairly recent history, with the dogma being officially proclaimed by Pope Pius IX in 1854. Prior to that, the commemoration had a varied and complex path with divisions between East and West over what the theological implications of Mary's conception, and any "original sin," were.

Nothing in the Scriptures tells us about the conception of Mary. That was a post–New Testament development with legends concerning Anne and Joachim, Mary's purported parents. The primary reason there is nothing in the New Testament about Mary's conception is that the New Testament authors were focused squarely on Jesus. Even the feast of the Immaculate Conception ultimately says more about Jesus and the power of the incarnation than it does about Mary.

The gospel we read today tells us about Mary, full of grace, saying yes to God. By that yes, she cooperated with God for the salvation of humanity. For a moment, human salvation hung in the balance, dependent upon the "yes" from a human. Her affirmation of God's desire led to the birth of the Messiah and our eternal life. She was truly special, which is part of the reason the church commemorates her own conception. Heady ideas and a complex history of theology surround this solemnity. It's easy to get "lost in the weeds," so to speak; but, like Mary, let's keep our hearts focused on God and our "yes" to him.

## Living the Paschal Mystery

Some ancient peoples thought the world rested on a turtle. But what did that turtle rest on? The answer: another turtle. Our dying and rising with Christ begins with the annunciation to Mary. And before there was Mary we had Anne and Joachim, Mary's parents. What about Anne and Joachim's parents? Like the ancient Greeks, we can push the questions too far.

The Scriptures tell us of the power of the Most High overshadowing Mary and she conceived by the Holy Spirit. Not content to leave it at that, early Christians wanted to know precisely how Mary was conceived. The Christian imagination knows no bounds.

Today we can ponder how much of God's plan of salvation is dependent upon human beings—not only Mary in her moment of "yes," but it is also dependent upon us. We first heard the gospel because somebody preached. Somebody said "yes" to God, which allows us to say "yes." Where are the moments in our daily lives where we need to say yes to what God has in store for us? It will likely not be a visit from an angel, but something more sublime. May we have eyes to see and ears to hear.

## Focusing the Gospel

Luke's annunciation story is filled with Old Testament imagery (e.g., the announcement by the angel parallels the announcements of the births of many key figures in salvation history, such as Isaac and Samuel; the "overshadowing" of Mary recalls the cloud of glory covering the tent of the ark and temple in Jerusalem).

Mary is mystified by the angel's greeting. How is she the highly favored one? What has she done that this should happen to her? Her motherhood is the call of God, Gabriel tells her—and Mary's yes is the generous response of a woman of faith. From the beginning, Mary is the model of the disciple of the Christ she will bring into the world.

## Model Penitential Act

*Presider:* With the faith and trust of Mary, let us place our hearts before God, confident of his mercy and forgiveness. *[pause]*

Son of God and child of Mary: Lord, have mercy.

Redeemer of nations and Lord of justice: Christ, have mercy.

The Word and grace of God made like us, for us: Lord, have mercy.

## Model Universal Prayer (Prayer of the Faithful)

*Presider:* To God, the Father who has blessed us in Christ with every blessing, let us pray.

*Response:* Lord, hear our prayer.

That our ministries of prayer and charity may "give birth" to God's love and peace in our own Nazareths . . .

That the nations and peoples of the world may seek to raise up the dignity of every person as a son or daughter of God . . .

That Mary's faithful humility may inspire us to become generous and compassionate servants to the poor, the forgotten, and the desperate . . .

That all parents may see in Mary a model of loving patience and selfless devotion . . .

*Presider:* In loving trust and faith, O God, your daughter Mary accepted your will for her to bring into the world your Son, the Messiah. May the prayers we offer to you today and our work to bring them to fulfillment bring the light and peace of Mary's child into our own time and place. We make these prayers to you in the name of your Son, Jesus the Christ. **Amen.**

### COLLECT

Let us pray.

*Pause for silent prayer*

O God, who by the Immaculate Conception of
   the Blessed Virgin
prepared a worthy dwelling for your Son,
grant, we pray,
that, as you preserved her from every stain
by virtue of the Death of your Son, which you
   foresaw,
so, through her intercession,
we, too, may be cleansed and admitted to your
   presence.
Through our Lord Jesus Christ, your Son,
who lives and reigns with you in the unity of
   the Holy Spirit,
one God, for ever and ever. **Amen.**

### FOR REFLECTION

• What was the most important yes you have ever given? What causes you to be reluctant in giving your complete and trusting yes to the call of God?

• When have you encountered "Gabriel" in your life, "announcing" to you God's call to do something surprising and unexpected, something that challenged your confidence or stretched your abilities?

## Homily Points

• In her yes to God, Mary our sister becomes a model and inspiration for our yes to God. Today's solemnity calls us to realize the yes God is asking of us: to bring his justice and compassion into our own time and place, to "give birth" to his Christ in our midst in our everyday acts of generosity, caring, and forgiveness.

• Gabriel appears in our busy days in the form of the forgotten and hurting, asking us to put aside our agenda in order to be the compassion of God for that "messenger" at our door. God calls us to "die" to our own doubts, fears, and comfort in order to embrace the new life of his Son's resurrection. Like Mary, we think of all the reasons why this doesn't make sense—but in these everyday annunciations God changes the course of history.

## ✝ SPIRITUALITY

**GOSPEL ACCLAMATION**
Luke 3:4, 6

℟. Alleluia, alleluia.
Prepare the way of the Lord, make straight his paths:
all flesh shall see the salvation of God.
℟. Alleluia, alleluia.

## Gospel

Mark 1:1-8; L5B

The beginning of the gospel of Jesus Christ the Son of God.

As it is written in Isaiah the prophet:
*Behold, I am sending my messenger ahead of you;*
*he will prepare your way.*
*A voice of one crying out in the desert:*
*"Prepare the way of the Lord, make straight his paths."*
John the Baptist appeared in the desert proclaiming a baptism of repentance for the forgiveness of sins.
People of the whole Judean countryside
and all the inhabitants of Jerusalem were going out to him
and were being baptized by him in the Jordan River
as they acknowledged their sins.
John was clothed in camel's hair, with a leather belt around his waist.
He fed on locusts and wild honey.
And this is what he proclaimed:
"One mightier than I is coming after me.
I am not worthy to stoop and loosen the thongs of his sandals.
I have baptized you with water;
he will baptize you with the Holy Spirit."

### Reflecting on the Gospel

The church gives us the opening verses of Mark's gospel for the Second Sunday of Advent. As a lion, Mark pounces on his subject matter. A one-line intro is followed by a mishmash of Scripture quotes attributed to Isaiah. In actuality, Mark combines Malachi 3:1a with Isaiah 40:3 and applies both to the enigmatic figure of John the Baptist. It's as though Mark doesn't have the time for precise details. He charges in. This is why Mark is often portrayed as a lion.

With John the Baptist's unkempt appearance and fiery, apocalyptic preaching, he gathered crowds of those acknowledging their sins and seeking forgiveness. In the first of perhaps many theological quandaries created by the presence of John the Baptist, he proclaimed a "baptism of repentance for the forgiveness of sins." The problem is created when Jesus comes forward to be baptized. Of course, for modern Christians (and even some ancient Christians) the question naturally arises, why would Jesus need to be baptized as he is without sin? Such questions seem to be beyond the scope of Mark's quick narrative. They are left for others like Luke and Matthew to address, each in his own way. In the Gospel of John of course there is simply no baptism of Jesus at all, but only John the Baptist testifying to Jesus.

But in the Gospel of Mark, the first canonical gospel written, the reader is carried forward swiftly. John the Baptist proclaims, "One mightier than I is coming after me." This person will baptize with the Holy Spirit. In these short verses the stage is set for Jesus. Mark has no infancy narrative such as Matthew or Luke would have it. There is no dramatic, cosmic prologue attuned to the opening words of Genesis as the Gospel of John would have it. Instead, Mark charges in, immediately quoting Scripture before introducing John the Baptist. We readers are swept up in the story.

Perhaps it is appropriate that we read these opening verses on the Second Sunday of Advent with our busy lives, shopping lists, and details to which we must attend. The gospel, and especially its opening, seems to lend itself to our frenetic pace. Still there is the proclamation that something, someone, is coming. He is mightier than John the Baptist, mightier than our concerns for the season, mightier than our lists of things to get done. He will baptize with the Holy Spirit and our lives will never be the same.

### Living the Paschal Mystery

It's cliché now to talk about how busy the Christmas season is. Still, each year it approaches us as though we had no idea it was coming. Instead, the image of a pregnant mother is appropriate. Ready or not, the baby is coming! Those weeks or days immediately prior to the birth are spent "nesting," making last-minute preparations for the new life that will be in our midst. Once here, our lives are never the same. A child changes us.

The same is the case with Christmas. The infant child Jesus will change our worlds. Though we have had time to ponder the meaning of this birth, the knowledge that it is at least two weeks away can also give us comfort. We have many things to attend to before that day. As we go about our Christmas routines, checking off lists, ensuring we have purchased just the right gifts, delivering food and presents, we are reminded that this child is coming. Ready or not.

## Focusing the Gospel

*Mark 1:1-8*

John's brief appearance in Mark's gospel begins a new era in the history of salvation. Mark's details about John's appearance recall the austere dress of the great prophet Elijah (2 Kgs 1:8). Some of the Jews in Jesus' time believed that Elijah would return from heaven to announce the long-awaited restoration of Israel as God's kingdom. For Mark and Matthew, this expectation is fulfilled in John the Baptist. In the Baptist's proclamation of Jesus as the Messiah, the age of the prophets is fulfilled and the age of the Messiah begins. John's baptism with water is an act of hope and expectation in the Messiah's baptism in the very Spirit and life of God.

## Focusing the First Reading

*Isa 40:1-5, 9-11*

Today's first reading is the beginning of the second section of Isaiah, often called the "Book of Consolation." The prophet (Deutero-Isaiah) is sent by God to announce to a broken people that their long night of exile at the hands of the Babylonians is at an end and that they will soon begin the journey home and the hard work not only of rebuilding their nation but also restoring their covenant with God. But, the prophet assures them, God will be with them as their healer, protector, and "shepherd." The gospel writers will invoke Isaiah's image of the prophet/herald in their accounts of John the Baptist.

## Focusing the Responsorial Psalm

*Ps 85:9-10, 11-12, 13-14*

The exiles have returned to God's city of Jerusalem and begin the hard work of rebuilding both their nation and identity as the people of God. The psalmist sings of the promise of a restored Israel, a people God brings home to Jerusalem. In Psalm 85, the singer imagines a new and thriving Israel, the kingdom of God, built on justice, kindness, truth, and mercy. God promises peace, the Old Testament ideal of shalom: not just the absence of conflict but a wholeness in relationships between God and his people, among neighbors, and with the land itself.

## Focusing the Second Reading

*2 Pet 3:8-14*

In today's second reading, the Second Letter of Peter echoes many of the Advent themes from last Sunday's readings, especially the section from 1 Corinthians. Peter confronts the notion that somehow Christ's return has been "delayed" (remember that the first generation of Christians expected that Christ's return was imminent). This "delay" is a gift of time for repentance and reconciliation with God and one another. Treating time as a gift from God and our lives as experiences of grace marks our identity as an Advent people.

---

**PROMPTS FOR HOMILISTS, CATECHISTS, AND RCIA TEAMS**

Who are the "prophets" among us who proclaim the presence of God in our midst?

How do we balance the gospel's seeming opposing messages of warning and hope?

What are the wastelands of our community and society that we can transform into a "highway" for God's justice?

How can we make the traditional and practical preparations for the coming Christmas holiday experiences of "grace"?

## Model Penitential Act

*Presider:* God, our Shepherd and Father, has gathered us here at his table. In hope, then, let us begin by asking forgiveness for our sins and failings. *[pause]*

Come, Lord, comfort your broken people: Lord, have mercy.

Come, Lord, restore our land in your justice and peace: Christ, have mercy.

Come, Lord, make your dwelling in our midst: Lord, have mercy.

## Homily Points

• The word *prophet* comes from the Greek word meaning "one who proclaims." Not all prophets wear camel skins and eat locusts—there are prophets among us right now who proclaim in their ministries, in their compassion and their kindness, in their courageous commitment to what is right that Jesus the Messiah has come. In the baptismal call to become prophets of the God who comes, we are to do the work of transforming the wastelands around us into harvests of justice and forgiveness, to create highways for our God to enter and recreate our world in charity and peace. To be a prophet of God's justice begins with embracing God's vision of what the world can and should become and then giving one's self totally to the work of realizing that vision.

• These days of Advent are a microcosm of our lives: we work to become, we struggle to change, we adjust to the new. The completion of a "straightened path" leads to new directions to travel; the discovery of God reveals new possibilities for our lives; the waters of baptism recreate us in the Spirit of God's compassion and grace. Our own baptisms call us to take up the Advent work of John the Baptist: to straighten the crooked roads of our lives, to transform "deserts" barren of love into places of welcome and reconciliation, to gather up the lost and forgotten, to proclaim the coming of God's Christ in our midst. "Make straight in the wasteland a highway for our God!"

## Model Universal Prayer (Prayer of the Faithful)

*Presider:* In the hope of this Advent season, let us pray.

*Response:* Lord, hear our prayer.

For those who serve our church as bishops, priests, deacons, ministers, teachers, and catechists, that they may proclaim the comforting and healing mercy of God . . .

For all the nations and peoples of the world, that we may work together to create a highway of peace for all to travel and transform wastelands into a new earth where justice dwells . . .

For the sick, the suffering, and the dying, that they may know the embrace of God in our comfort and care for them . . .

For our church and parish community, that our ministries and work together may herald the good news of God's presence in our midst . . .

*Presider:* Hear these prayers, O God. May your glory be revealed in our work to bring these prayers for mercy, justice, and peace a reality in our own deserts and cities. In Jesus' name, we pray. **Amen.**

## COLLECT

Let us pray.

*Pause for silent prayer*

Almighty and merciful God,
may no earthly undertaking hinder those
who set out in haste to meet your Son,
but may our learning of heavenly wisdom
gain us admittance to his company.
Who lives and reigns with you in the unity
    of the Holy Spirit,
one God, for ever and ever. **Amen.**

## FIRST READING
Isa 40:1-5, 9-11

Comfort, give comfort to my people,
    says your God.
Speak tenderly to Jerusalem, and proclaim
    to her
    that her service is at an end,
    her guilt is expiated;
indeed, she has received from the hand of
    the LORD
    double for all her sins.

    A voice cries out:
In the desert prepare the way of the LORD!
    Make straight in the wasteland a
        highway for our God!
Every valley shall be filled in,
    every mountain and hill shall be made
        low;
the rugged land shall be made a plain,
    the rough country, a broad valley.
Then the glory of the LORD shall be
        revealed,
    and all people shall see it together;
    for the mouth of the LORD has spoken.

Go up onto a high mountain,
    Zion, herald of glad tidings;
cry out at the top of your voice,
    Jerusalem, herald of good news!
Fear not to cry out
    and say to the cities of Judah:
    Here is your God!
Here comes with power
    the Lord GOD,
    who rules by his strong arm;
here is his reward with him,
    his recompense before him.
Like a shepherd he feeds his flock;
    in his arms he gathers the lambs,
carrying them in his bosom,
    and leading the ewes with care.

## RESPONSORIAL PSALM
Ps 85:9-10, 11-12, 13-14

℟. (8) Lord, let us see your kindness, and
    grant us your salvation.

I will hear what God proclaims;
    the Lord—for he proclaims peace to his
      people.
Near indeed is his salvation to those who
    fear him,
    glory dwelling in our land.

R̸. Lord, let us see your kindness, and
    grant us your salvation.

Kindness and truth shall meet;
    justice and peace shall kiss.
Truth shall spring out of the earth,
    and justice shall look down from heaven.

R̸. Lord, let us see your kindness, and
    grant us your salvation.

The Lord himself will give his benefits;
    our land shall yield its increase.
Justice shall walk before him,
    and prepare the way of his steps.

R̸. Lord, let us see your kindness, and
    grant us your salvation.

## SECOND READING
2 Pet 3:8-14

Do not ignore this one fact, beloved,
    that with the Lord one day is like a
      thousand years
    and a thousand years like one day.
The Lord does not delay his promise, as
    some regard "delay,"
    but he is patient with you,
    not wishing that any should perish
    but that all should come to repentance.
But the day of the Lord will come like a
    thief,
    and then the heavens will pass away
      with a mighty roar
    and the elements will be dissolved by
      fire,
    and the earth and everything done on it
      will be found out.

Since everything is to be dissolved in this
    way,
    what sort of persons ought you to be,
    conducting yourselves in holiness and
      devotion,
    waiting for and hastening the coming
      of the day of God,
    because of which the heavens will be
      dissolved in flames
    and the elements melted by fire.
But according to his promise
    we await new heavens and a new earth
    in which righteousness dwells.
Therefore, beloved, since you await these
    things,
    be eager to be found without spot or
      blemish before him, at peace.

## About Liturgy

*Roaring like a lion:* Have you ever seen an ambo, gospel book, or another item in your church decorated with four winged creatures? Take a closer look. You'll probably find a human, a lion, a bull, and an eagle. These are traditional symbols of the four evangelists: Matthew (human), Mark (lion), Luke (bull), John (eagle). The symbols refer to the four living creatures who surround the throne of God in Revelation (4:6-7). Several early Christian writers assigned different pairings, but St. Jerome in the late fourth century gave us our current tradition. He did not provide specific reasons for the pairings, but some have connected each creature with how each gospel begins. Today's gospel from the beginning of Mark combines Isaiah's messenger "crying out in the desert" with John the Baptist proclaiming a message of repentance. This is why some will say that Mark is symbolized with the roaring lion. Matthew's gospel begins with the genealogy of Jesus, thus the human figure; Luke starts with Zechariah in the temple, where oxen or calves are sacrificed, thus the bull; and John's opening prologue of the Word coming down from heaven reminds us of the soaring eagle high above.

These symbols are good mnemonics for remembering how each gospel begins, but perhaps there's a deeper meaning to these fantastical creatures. The living creatures around God's throne serve only one purpose: to constantly praise God night and day. The gospels are not history books about events in the past. They are the *living* Word that has but one message, that God is wildly in love with us. For those with faith to hear this message, the gospels cannot be entirely analyzed and explained simply by rational thought, because, like any relationship with a person we love, the gospels embody the irrational, beyond-what-we-can-imagine kind of love God has for us through the person of Jesus.

When we proclaim the gospels and listen to them with the ear of our hearts with that kind of love in mind, we too might roar into the desert-places of our world the glad tidings that God is crazy in love with us.

## About Liturgical Music

*In praise of introductions:* John the Baptist is often called the precursor or forerunner of Jesus. As musicians, we shouldn't dismiss that role too quickly. John the Baptist had to prepare God's people to do the work God would call them to do, that is, follow Jesus in his mission. Musicians, especially those who play the instruments that serve as the primary musical accompaniment to the assembly's singing, must do the same in the short musical introductions they provide to the assembly's song. When they do this well, three things happen. First, they ground the assembly in both the tempo and the pitch they are about to sing. Second, they give the assembly confidence in knowing exactly when to begin singing. And third, they enhance the liturgical "flow" and honor the role of the assembly by attending to the pace of the ritual. This last point is most evident in the acclamations throughout the Mass that are responses to a dialogue. Here's one real example of what not to do. Before the new translation of the Mass, a priest once said, "Let us proclaim the mystery of faith." There was a long uncomfortable silence while the assembly waited for the organist to begin. The priest finally broke the silence by saying, with a chuckle, "Or not."

Don't be timid in your musical intros, especially with the acclamations. When an acclamation is meant to be a response to a statement or invitation, imagine you are responding in the conversation with your musical intro. This will help you be ready so that you do not stall or hurry the flow of the ritual.

**DECEMBER 10, 2017**
# SECOND SUNDAY OF ADVENT

## ✛ SPIRITUALITY

**GOSPEL ACCLAMATION**
Isa 61:1 (cited in Luke 4:18)

R̸. Alleluia, alleluia.
The Spirit of the Lord is upon me,
because he has anointed me
    to bring glad tidings to the poor.
R̸. Alleluia, alleluia.

### Gospel   John 1:6-8, 19-28; L8B

A man named John was sent from God.
He came for testimony, to testify to the
    light,
    so that all might believe through him.
He was not the light,
    but came to testify to the light.

And this is the testimony of John.
When the Jews from Jerusalem
        sent priests and Levites to
        him
    to ask him, "Who are you?"
    he admitted and did not deny it,
    but admitted, "I am not the
        Christ."
So they asked him,
    "What are you then? Are you Elijah?"
And he said, "I am not."
"Are you the Prophet?"
He answered, "No."
So they said to him,
    "Who are you, so we can give an answer
        to those who sent us?
What do you have to say for yourself?"
He said:
    "I am *the voice of one crying out in the
        desert,*
    *'make straight the way of the Lord,'*
    as Isaiah the prophet said."
Some Pharisees were also sent.
They asked him,
    "Why then do you baptize
    if you are not the Christ or Elijah or the
        Prophet?"
John answered them,
    "I baptize with water;
    but there is one among you whom you do
        not recognize,
    the one who is coming after me,
    whose sandal strap I am not worthy to
        untie."
This happened in Bethany across the Jordan,
    where John was baptizing.

### Reflecting on the Gospel

On this "Gaudete" (Rejoice) Sunday, other readings and the gospel acclamation may speak more directly to joy or glad tidings than the gospel, which gives us its version of the story of John. Of course, he is often referred to as John the Baptist in Matthew, Mark, and Luke, but not in this gospel. Here he is clearly and simply called a "man" (John 1:6), and when he is named, it is merely "John" without modifier (e.g., 1:6, 15, 19, 26, 28, 32). In this way, and in many others in this gospel, he is distinguished from Jesus.

The Fourth Gospel states clearly and unequivocally that John was not the light, but was sent from God to testify to the light (John 1:8). John admits that he is not the Messiah; he is not Elijah. (In both Matthew [11:14] and Mark [9:13], John is considered the Elijah figure, said to be so by Jesus himself.) In the Fourth Gospel, John is not even the prophet. His role is to cry out in the desert, "make straight the way of the Lord." Such a deflection away from any attention or claims to himself seems to reflect the interests of the evangelist more than the historical situation of the time. Indeed, there are other clues in the Fourth Gospel and other New Testament writings that tell us that John continued to have a following years, perhaps decades, after his death. Today we recognize that John prepared the way for Jesus.

This first chapter of the Fourth Gospel reminded the early Christian community that John was merely a precursor, a forerunner, to Jesus the Messiah. We have heard these stories so often, and frequently from the Synoptic point of view. When we read the Fourth Gospel on its own terms we see that John says he baptizes with water. We might expect him to say, "but the one coming after me baptizes with the Holy Spirit" as we hear in the Synoptics. Instead, John says, "I baptize with water; / but there is *one among you whom you do not recognize.*" There is nothing in this gospel about Jesus baptizing with the Holy Spirit. Instead, Jesus is the Lamb of God who takes away the sin of the world. Even the use of the term sin in the singular rather than the plural is deliberate. Rather than merely taking away individual sins, Jesus takes away the cosmic force of sin. The Fourth Gospel reflects a different but congruent theological thought world than the Synoptics. The differences in details may seem minute but they point to profound theological emphases.

Once John points the way to Jesus, once he testifies to the Lamb of God, John in effect disappears from the gospel (there are some minor passing references). His role is basically confined to chapter 1 of the Fourth Gospel, and it consists in testifying to Jesus.

### Living the Paschal Mystery

When we see how John gave testimony to Jesus we recognize him as a model for ourselves. John is not the center of attention. When he receives attention he deflects it to Jesus. John will not even claim the title of prophet. He is merely a pointer to Jesus. After accomplishing his role John recedes into the background so that the one who is already in their midst might be made more fully known.

Where do we find Jesus in our midst? Are we pointing to that reality, and testifying to it? Once having done so, do we then recede into the background?

## Focusing the Gospel

*John 1:6-8, 19-28*

Today's gospel is the Fourth Gospel's portrait of John's baptismal ministry. In a scene unique to the Fourth Gospel, a delegation of priests and Levites from the city confront John about his preaching and baptizing. John responds that he is not Elijah, the great prophet who was expected to return in the last days of time to announce the coming of the Messiah; John claims to be only the "voice of one crying out in the desert." But, John says, the Messiah they have waited for has already come and is "among you."

There is serenity about this portrait of John: there are no descriptions of wearing camel hair and eating locusts or wild honey; there are no rantings to repent or angry confrontations with official Jerusalem. The Baptist of the Fourth Gospel is a figure of peace and humility. John preaches that God has revealed himself to his people through the incarnation of his Word, Jesus the Christ, and John has been called to testify (to witness) to this revelation as standing "among you whom you do not recognize."

Forms of "baptism" were common in the Judaism of gospel times. But John's baptism was distinctive: his baptism at the Jordan was a rite of repentance and *metanoia*—a conversion of heart and spirit. John's ministry fulfilled the promise of Ezekiel (Ezek 36:25-26): at the dawn of a new age, the God of Israel would purify his people from their sins with clear water and instill in them a new heart and spirit.

## Focusing the First Reading

*Isa 61:1-2a, 10-11*

Today's first reading is the prophet Isaiah's proclamation of his mission to the exiles returning to Jerusalem in the sixth century BC, after decades of slavery in Babylon. It is the beginning of a new era of hope for Israel: Judah, condemned to exile because of the injustice of its economic and social systems, will be restored by the Spirit to a new commitment to justice for the poor. In Luke's gospel, Jesus himself reads these words at the beginning of his preaching and healing ministry (Luke 4:16-20).

## Focusing the Responsorial Psalm

*Luke 1:46-48, 49-50, 53-54 (Isa 61:10b)*

Today's response to the first reading is not from the psalms but a weaving of Mary's song of praise in Luke's gospel upon her greeting from Elizabeth with images from the prophet Isaiah's canticle of hope for the returning exiles (Isa 61, today's first reading). Both Mary's song and Isaiah's prophecy celebrate that God is recreating humankind in his goodness and mercy.

## Focusing the Second Reading

*1 Thess 5:16-24*

Paul's exhortation to rejoice gives this Third Sunday of Advent its traditional name *Gaudete Sunday*. Today's second reading is the conclusion of what scholars recognize as the oldest surviving documents of Christianity, Paul's first letter to the Christian church at Thessalonica (written around 51 AD). The apostle Paul has spoken sternly to the Thessalonian community about their passivity as they await the Lord's return. He concludes his letter urging them to embrace the joy that is experienced in following the Spirit's prompting to create the ideals of Christian community: joy, thanksgiving, wise discernment, seeking and maintaining the common good.

---

**PROMPTS FOR HOMILISTS, CATECHISTS, AND RCIA TEAMS**

What signs can you point to of the Word of God's compassion in the midst of your parish/community?

Who have been the "prophets" you have known in your life who "proclaimed" to you the reality of God's love and mercy?

What images of light and darkness speak to you this Advent?

As you read the opening verses of Isaiah 61, what do you sense the Spirit of God is "sending" you to do?

## Model Penitential Act

*Presider:* With joy in God's constant love and hope in his limitless mercy, let us call to mind our sins. *[pause]*

Come, Savior of the nations: Lord, have mercy.

Come, Light of wisdom and peace: Christ, have mercy.

Come, Spirit that sends us forth to do the work of God: Lord, have mercy.

## Homily Points

• In our own individual Advents of poverty and despair, in our struggle to find meaning and purpose in this life we have been given, God is with us. Advent faith calls us to approach God not in fear but in joy: not a Pollyanna, happy-face, sugarcoated denial of anything bad or unpleasant, but a constant awareness that God is always present to us. That despite the heartaches, there is always healing; that despite our forgetting and abandoning God, God neither forgets nor abandons us; that despite the cross, there is the eternal hope of resurrection.

• Light is the opening image of today's gospel: John proclaims Jesus as the light who will shatter the darkness that envelops our world, the light who illuminates our vision with compassion and justice. In our own baptisms, that light is ignited within us, melting the winter cold of despair and self-absorption and opening our eyes to see God's goodness in our midst. We are called to "testify" to the light we have seen in the compassion and forgiveness of others, to become the means to straighten the roads we travel that have been made crooked and dangerous by injustice and greed. We have been entrusted by God to transform our deserts into God's vineyard of mercy and peace.

• The coming of Christ calls us to the work of making a straight road for him, of transforming the barren deserts around us into harvests of justice and peace, of making the light of his presence in our midst known to all. As God gives himself so completely and unreservedly to us in the birth of his own Son, may we find our life's joy and fulfillment in giving completely and unreservedly of ourselves to others.

## Model Universal Prayer (Prayer of the Faithful)

*Presider:* In the joy of God's Spirit embracing us and our community, let us offer our prayers for God's people.

*Response:* Lord, hear our prayer.

That, in our church and parish's ministries of compassion and care, we may bring glad tidings and proclaim the Lord's favor to all . . .

That God's justice, liberty, and peace may "spring up" before all nations . . .

That Christ the light of God may be the health and hope of the sick and dying, the addicted and recovering . . .

That the joy and peace of this holy season may illuminate every home in our community in every season of the year . . .

*Presider:* Gracious God, hear our prayers. May your Spirit come upon us to transform our lives and our world from barrenness to harvest, from sickness to wholeness, from division to completeness, from death to life. In Jesus' name, we pray. Amen.

## COLLECT

Let us pray.

*Pause for silent prayer*

O God, who see how your people
faithfully await the feast of the Lord's
     Nativity,
enable us, we pray,
to attain the joys of so great a salvation
and to celebrate them always
with solemn worship and glad rejoicing.
Through our Lord Jesus Christ, your Son,
who lives and reigns with you in the unity
     of the Holy Spirit,
one God, for ever and ever. **Amen.**

## FIRST READING

Isa 61:1-2a, 10-11

The spirit of the Lord God is upon me,
     because the Lord has anointed me;
he has sent me to bring glad tidings to the
          poor,
     to heal the brokenhearted,
to proclaim liberty to the captives
     and release to the prisoners,
to announce a year of favor from the Lord
     and a day of vindication by our God.

I rejoice heartily in the Lord,
     in my God is the joy of my soul;
for he has clothed me with a robe of
          salvation
     and wrapped me in a mantle of justice,
like a bridegroom adorned with a diadem,
     like a bride bedecked with her jewels.
As the earth brings forth its plants,
     and a garden makes its growth spring
          up,
so will the Lord God make justice and
          praise
     spring up before all the nations.

## RESPONSORIAL PSALM

Luke 1:46-48, 49-50, 53-54

R⁊. (Isa 61:10b) My soul rejoices in my God.

My soul proclaims the greatness of the
    Lord;
    my spirit rejoices in God my Savior,
for he has looked upon his lowly servant.
    From this day all generations will call
      me blessed:

R⁊. My soul rejoices in my God.

The Almighty has done great things for
    me,
    and holy is his Name.
He has mercy on those who fear him
    in every generation.

R⁊. My soul rejoices in my God.

He has filled the hungry with good things,
    and the rich he has sent away empty.
He has come to the help of his servant
    Israel
    for he has remembered his promise of
      mercy.

R⁊. My soul rejoices in my God.

## SECOND READING

1 Thess 5:16-24

Brothers and sisters:
Rejoice always. Pray without ceasing.
In all circumstances give thanks,
    for this is the will of God for you in
      Christ Jesus.
Do not quench the Spirit.
Do not despise prophetic utterances.
Test everything; retain what is good.
Refrain from every kind of evil.

May the God of peace make you perfectly
    holy
    and may you entirely, spirit, soul, and
      body,
    be preserved blameless for the coming
      of our Lord Jesus Christ.
The one who calls you is faithful,
    and he will also accomplish it.

## About Liturgy

*Liturgy doesn't lie:* In today's gospel, John the Baptist testifies to the light "so that all might believe through him." In other words, he was to tell the truth about the light.

At the midway point of Advent, today's liturgical texts overflow with joy. "Rejoice" appears in the first and second readings and the responsorial psalm, and the gospel acclamation speaks of "glad tidings." This Sunday is obviously meant to communicate the joy of our faith in Christ the Light.

Now take a look around you at Mass at the faces of those present, especially of the liturgical ministers and other parish leaders. Do their faces "testify" to the light, to that joy? Or do they look like the Christians Pope Francis described as those who "have expressions like they're going to a funeral procession rather than going to praise God" (homily in Casa Santa Marta, May 31, 2013)?

As liturgical ministers, we must not give in to what Pope Francis calls the "disease of a lugubrious face" that "weakens our service to the Lord" and conveys an untruth in the liturgy (address to the Roman Curia, December 22, 2014). If we are homilists, lectors, or music ministers, when we say "rejoice," let us mean it and, more importantly, *look* it! Our faces and demeanor need to be a silent proclamation to the truth of Christ—a proclamation that can be even more powerful than our words. If ushers, let us radiate joy with a sincere greeting not just to those we know by name but most of all to those we do not recognize. To those who arrive late, may our attitude convey to them that in Christ's eyes, latecomers are as richly blessed as those who come early. If we are Communion ministers, let us use the most of our few seconds with each person to express joy through our eyes and faces, testifying to our love for the Body and Blood of Christ in our hands as well as in the person before us.

Of course we all know this, but sometimes we may not be aware of what our faces actually communicate. So it may be useful to ask someone to take video of you as you minister (and throughout the liturgy) so that you can assess how well you are silently conveying the joy of your faith.

At every Sunday liturgy, and most especially on this Gaudete "Rejoice" Sunday, let us testify to the truth of Christ the Light who radiates through our faces, words, and actions.

*A "short" Advent:* In 2017, the Fourth Sunday of Advent falls on December 24, which makes this coming week the last week of Advent! This means there are only three full weeks of Advent this year. Be aware of this as you schedule liturgical preparations, especially for environment ministers and music ministers, who will need to make a quick changeover from Advent to Christmas next Sunday.

## About Liturgical Music

*Rejoice! Rejoice!:* "O Come, O Come, Emmanuel" is a musical staple of Advent, and the season feels incomplete without it. The verses of this song come from the antiphons of Evening Prayer from the Liturgy of the Hours from December 17 to 23. The final weeks of Advent are the perfect time to include this hymn at every liturgical gathering. However, take care to be authentic witnesses to the message of this text. Sometimes we tend to think that Advent's sound is quiet, slow, and contemplative—and at times it is. Yet when the first words of the refrain of this song are "Rejoice! Rejoice!" we should make the sound of our music match the message. Therefore, be careful to avoid falling into the trap of singing this piece too slowly or timidly. Experiment with a livelier tempo, and consider adding more joyful accompaniment and instrumentation so that these words truly may usher in the joyful anticipation of these last days of the season.

## ✝ SPIRITUALITY

**GOSPEL ACCLAMATION**
Luke 1:38

℟. Alleluia, alleluia.
Behold, I am the handmaid of the Lord.
May it be done to me according to your word.
℟. Alleluia, alleluia.

### Gospel  Luke 1:26-38; L11B

The angel Gabriel was sent from God
  to a town of Galilee called Nazareth,
  to a virgin betrothed to a man named
    Joseph,
  of the house of David,
  and the virgin's name was Mary.
And coming to her, he said,
  "Hail, full of grace! The Lord is with you."
But she was greatly troubled at what was
  said
  and pondered what sort of greeting this
    might be.
Then the angel said to her,
  "Do not be afraid, Mary,
  for you have found favor with God.

"Behold, you will conceive in your womb
  and bear a son,
  and you shall name him Jesus.
He will be great and will be called Son of
  the Most High,
  and the Lord God will give him the throne
    of David his father,
  and he will rule over the house of Jacob
    forever,
  and of his kingdom there will be no end."
But Mary said to the angel,
  "How can this be,
  since I have no relations with a man?"
And the angel said to her in reply,
  "The Holy Spirit will come upon you,
  and the power of the Most High will over-
    shadow you.
Therefore the child to be born
  will be called holy, the Son of God.
And behold, Elizabeth, your relative,
  has also conceived a son in her old age,
  and this is the sixth month for her who
    was called barren;
  for nothing will be impossible for God."
Mary said, "Behold, I am the handmaid of
  the Lord.
May it be done to me according to your word."
Then the angel departed from her.

### Reflecting on the Gospel

For the fourth and final Sunday of Advent we are brought back to the Gospel of Luke, and its beautiful story of the annunciation. This story is markedly different from that in Matthew, where Joseph learns of Mary's pregnancy in a dream. In Luke, the angel Gabriel (which means "God is my strength") appears to Mary. Gabriel's greeting is repeated each time we pray the Hail Mary and so we are reminded of this scene. As anyone might be, Mary is "greatly troubled." How often does an angel bear greetings? Upon hearing the news Mary wonders how this can be. In fact, many people today wonder the same. A virgin birth? How was Jesus conceived? The response given to us is the same as that given to Mary: "The Holy Spirit will come upon you, / and the power of the Most High will overshadow you." Nothing is impossible for God. This is an act of God so that the child, Jesus, will rightly be called "the Son of God." His kingdom will last forever; he will be the Son of the Most High. Many church fathers spoke of how in that moment the entire plan of God hung in the balance, awaiting Mary's "yes." Human salvation, a free gift from God, depends upon human cooperation. In other words, God's gift is not forced but available to be freely accepted. Saint Bernard of Clairvaux wrote, "The angel awaits an answer; it is time for him to return to God who sent him. We too are waiting, O Lady, for your word of compassion." We then hear Mary's "fiat," the Latin rendering of "let it be done." And again, according to the church fathers, all heaven rejoices.

Though we celebrated the Annunciation on March 25, precisely nine months prior to Christmas, we read this gospel now, during the Fourth Sunday of Advent, because the incarnation was, in a certain way, dependent upon Mary's response. Later theologians saw in her "yes" a counter to Genesis 3, so that Mary could be called the new Eve. Her response to God was not to step outside the circle of obedience, as we saw in Genesis 3, but to accept God's design and to cooperate. As the response in Genesis led ultimately to human sinfulness and death, Mary's response leads to grace and new life. Perhaps we are not too surprised to learn that of all the gospels it is Luke that has the most to say about women. In Luke's story of the birth of Jesus, Mary plays a central role, setting the stage for centuries of theological reflection.

### Living the Paschal Mystery

It can sometimes be difficult to comprehend the human cooperation required for salvation. There can be a tremendous theological emphasis on the graciousness of the gift. Our salvation is not earned, but human cooperation is required. We have many opportunities throughout the day to say "fiat" or "let it be done." There are countless occasions of God's grace breaking into our daily life. When we cooperate with that grace, extraordinary things happen. Though we are not receiving visits from angels with messages of a virgin birth, we do have opportunities to recognize the working of God in the world.

## Focusing the Gospel

*Luke 1:26-38*

Today's gospel on this Sunday before Christmas is Luke's account of the angel Gabriel's appearance to Mary.

God begins the "Christ event" with Mary, a simple Galilean Jewish girl who is at the very bottom of the social ladder of her time; the God who created all things makes the fulfillment of his promise dependent upon one of the most dispossessed and powerless of his creatures. Yet God exalts her humility, her simplicity, her trust in his love and mercy; in Mary, God reveals his "favor" for the poor, the rejected, the abandoned, and the forgotten among us today.

Luke's annunciation story is filled with Old Testament imagery (e.g., the announcement by the angel parallels the announcements of the births of many key figures in salvation history, such as Isaac and Samuel; the "overshadowing" of Mary recalls the cloud of glory covering the tent of the ark and temple in Jerusalem). Mary's yes to Gabriel's words set the stage for the greatest event in human history: the conception and subsequent birth of our Savior.

## Focusing the First Reading

*2 Sam 7:1-5, 8b-12, 14a, 16*

"House" is the keyword of today's first reading. At last installed in his own palace in his new capital, King David begins the planning of an equally magnificent house for the ark of the covenant. But the prophet Nathan prophesies that God has another "house" in mind: David, as a father as well as a king, will be the beginning of this "house" or dynasty, fulfilling the hopes of Israel since the exodus—and from this "house" will come God's promised Son of David.

## Focusing the Responsorial Psalm

*Ps 89:2-3, 4-5, 27, 29 (2a)*

The psalmist takes up the theme of God's favor toward David in today's responsorial psalm. Psalm 89 is a song of thanksgiving for what God has done for Israel from its beginning in the Sinai to the raising up of David as king, and a profession of hope in what is to come for God's people.

## Focusing the Second Reading

*Rom 16:25-27*

Today's second reading is the conclusion of Paul's letter to the Romans, the apostle's theological treatise on baptism and justification by faith. Paul concludes his letter to the Christians at Rome praising God for the final and complete revelation of his Word in the gospel: Jesus.

### PROMPTS FOR HOMILISTS, CATECHISTS, AND RCIA TEAMS

When have your plans been "interrupted" or your perspective been changed by a moment of revelation?

Have you ever encountered Gabriel, the messenger of God, in an unexpected situation?

In what ways can a family home be transformed into a "house" of God?

How is Mary a model of discipleship?

What have you learned from the poor, the troubled, the sick, and the desperate about the mystery of God's love?

## Model Penitential Act

*Presider:* As we await the dawning of the Lord, let us begin our celebration of these sacred mysteries by asking forgiveness for our sins and failings. *[pause]*

You are Father of all peoples and nations: Lord, have mercy.

You reveal your love to us in the child born of Mary: Christ, have mercy.

You send your Spirit upon us that we may be prophets of your peace: Lord, have mercy.

## Homily Points

• Mary's life was a series of annunciations: God constantly calling her to be the reflection of his compassion, to be a source of persevering faith, to mirror in her motherhood of Christ his loving providence for all his children. Throughout our own lives we too experience "annunciations": God calling us to the work of "giving birth" to his compassion and peace. As Mary realizes, discerning God's will demands time and thoughtfulness; in God's "annunciations" to us, we have a great deal to process. Gabriel may come in the form of an invitation, a plea, a concern for another's well-being. Like Mary, we think of all the reasons why this doesn't make sense—but it is in these everyday annunciations that God changes the course of history.

• Both David and Mary are called by God to create a "house" for him. While David is thinking in terms of a magnificent temple, God envisions a nation of justice and compassion. Mary, an unmarried teenager, possesses the faith and trust in God to respond to this extraordinary vision with an uncompromising yes to make a place in her home and heart for God to dwell. David and Mary take up the challenge of Advent: to make room for this Child in the midst of the hectic commerce of our professions and careers, in the quiet desperation of our pain and anguish; at our kitchen tables, on our soccer fields, in our classrooms and conference rooms; in our wallets and checkbooks, in our calendars and day planners—to make room for him when he is welcome and when his presence is embarrassing and inconvenient.

• The mystery of the incarnation is relived every time we echo Mary's "yes" to God's call to bring his Christ into our world; when we accept, as did Mary, God's asking us to make the gospel Jesus alive in our own time and place. In the Advents of our lives, God calls us to bring his Christ into our own time and place, to put aside our own doubts and fears to say, as Mary does, *I am your servant, O God. Be it done to me according to your word.*

## Model Universal Prayer (Prayer of the Faithful)

*Presider:* The Lord is with us. In confidence, let us pray.

*Response:* Lord, hear our prayer.

That our church and parish may give birth to God's Christ in our worship and work together . . .

That the reign of God's peace may be established forever among all the peoples and nations of the world . . .

That the kindness and grace of God may be revealed in our care and concern for the sick, the poor, the despairing, and the forgotten . . .

That those who do not celebrate Christ's birth may also know the joy and peace of God's love in their midst . . .

*Presider:* O God, whose mercy is without limit and kindness is endless, hear our prayers as we eagerly await your coming into our homes and hearts in the birth of your Son, our Lord Jesus Christ. **Amen.**

**COLLECT**

Let us pray.

*Pause for silent prayer*

Pour forth, we beseech you, O Lord,
your grace into our hearts,
that we, to whom the Incarnation of Christ
   your Son
was made known by the message of an
   Angel,
may by his Passion and Cross
be brought to the glory of his
   Resurrection.
Who lives and reigns with you in the unity
   of the Holy Spirit,
one God, for ever and ever. **Amen.**

**FIRST READING**
2 Sam 7:1-5, 8b-12, 14a, 16

When King David was settled in his
   palace,
   and the LORD had given him rest from
      his enemies on every side,
   he said to Nathan the prophet,
   "Here I am living in a house of cedar,
   while the ark of God dwells in a tent!"
Nathan answered the king,
   "Go, do whatever you have in mind,
   for the LORD is with you."
But that night the LORD spoke to Nathan
   and said:
   "Go, tell my servant David, 'Thus says
      the LORD:
   Should you build me a house to dwell
      in?'

"'It was I who took you from the pasture
   and from the care of the flock
   to be commander of my people Israel.
I have been with you wherever you went,
   and I have destroyed all your enemies
      before you.
And I will make you famous like the great
   ones of the earth.
I will fix a place for my people Israel;
   I will plant them so that they may dwell
      in their place
   without further disturbance.
Neither shall the wicked continue to afflict
   them as they did of old,
   since the time I first appointed judges
      over my people Israel.
I will give you rest from all your enemies.
The LORD also reveals to you
   that he will establish a house for you.
And when your time comes and you rest
   with your ancestors,
   I will raise up your heir after you,
      sprung from your loins,
   and I will make his kingdom firm.

I will be a father to him,
and he shall be a son to me.
Your house and your kingdom shall
endure forever before me;
your throne shall stand firm forever.'"

## RESPONSORIAL PSALM
Ps 89:2-3, 4-5, 27, 29

R&#8359;. (2a) For ever I will sing the goodness of
the Lord.

The promises of the LORD I will sing
forever;
through all generations my mouth shall
proclaim your faithfulness.
For you have said, "My kindness is
established forever";
in heaven you have confirmed your
faithfulness.

R&#8359;. For ever I will sing the goodness of the
Lord.

"I have made a covenant with my chosen
one,
I have sworn to David my servant:
forever will I confirm your posterity
and establish your throne for all
generations."

R&#8359;. For ever I will sing the goodness of the
Lord.

"He shall say of me, 'You are my father,
my God, the Rock, my savior.'
Forever I will maintain my kindness
toward him,
and my covenant with him stands firm."

R&#8359;. For ever I will sing the goodness of the
Lord.

## SECOND READING
Rom 16:25-27

Brothers and sisters:
To him who can strengthen you,
according to my gospel and the
proclamation of Jesus Christ,
according to the revelation of the
mystery kept secret for long ages
but now manifested through the
prophetic writings and,
according to the command of the
eternal God,
made known to all nations to bring
about the obedience of faith,
to the only wise God, through Jesus
Christ
be glory forever and ever. Amen.

## About Liturgy

*The gradual nature of seasons:* Our secular calendar marks the days one season ends and another begins. Yet in our daily life, that line is not as sharply defined. Fall colors gradually turn to winter cold as, day by day, the temperatures drop and we add, one by one, another layer of clothing. We naturally experience the change in the seasons gradually. Our experience of the liturgical seasons should be the same.

Hispano-Latino cultures understand well this gradual shift in liturgical seasons. The tradition of *Las Posadas* ("the inns") and the Filipino custom of *Simbang Gabi* ("church in the night") are joyful celebrations of light and color, prayer and music, fiesta and food during the nine days leading up to Christmas. The growing anticipation of Advent and the delight of Christmas harmonize together during these transitional days, and those who celebrate them are not afraid to let elements of one season flow into the other.

Does this mean we shouldn't worry that Christmas began in October on our commercial calendars? Of course not. We should continue to celebrate each season fully with their unique characteristics at their proper times. Yet we should also take care to not be so rigid when we hear a stray Christmas carol in Advent or see Christmas trees all around us that we fail to embody in our words and actions the promised joy of either liturgical season.

Especially this year, when the Fourth Sunday of Advent is also Christmas Eve, we can take a cue from nature and these novenas and allow a little bit of Christmas to infiltrate the final days of Advent. For example, during the last week of Advent, daily incorporate environmental elements of Christmas into your worship space, such as bare evergreen wreaths, red holly berries, and white swaths of fabric along with your Advent violet, so that on the last Sunday of Advent, Christmas is on the brink of burgeoning all about us. Most of all, let your joyful attitude during these busy days be your best expression of the true meaning of both seasons.

## About Liturgical Music

*Mary and the liturgy:* Pope Paul VI called Advent "that time which is particularly apt for the cult of the Mother of God" *(Marialis Cultus* 4), and this last Sunday of Advent turns our focus specifically to Mary. This may seem to be an invitation to plan Marian hymns for this Sunday. However, our liturgical focus, even when it is filtered through the lens of Mary, is always centered on her Son, Jesus. In 2001, the Vatican Congregation for Divine Worship and the Discipline of the Sacraments issued a directory, which is a kind of handbook, on popular piety and the liturgy. Two statements from that document can guide us in appropriate use of Marian texts, especially for Sunday Mass.

First, the Vatican reminds us that in the Eastern churches, "all Marian mysteries are Christological mysteries since they refer to the mystery of our salvation in Christ" (101). Second, the directory gives us the fundamental principle that all Marian piety should derive from our worship of Christ since our faith "originates in Christ, finds full expression in Christ, and through him, in the Holy Spirit leads to the Father" (186).

Therefore, if you choose to incorporate Marian songs on this Sunday, choose those with texts that are based on Scripture and focus on our salvation through Christ and praise of the Father. A communal song that sets the words of the *Magnificat* is perfect for this final day of Advent. Also, don't be afraid to anticipate Christmas cheer by selecting more energetic music. "Soon and Very Soon" by Andraé Crouch is a simple way to musically bridge the anticipation of Advent and the exuberance of Christmas.

**DECEMBER 24, 2017**
# FOURTH SUNDAY OF ADVENT

# SEASON OF CHRISTMAS

The Lord entered her, and became a servant;

the Word entered her, and became silent within her;

thunder entered her, and his voice was still;

the Shepherd of all entered her;

he became a Lamb in her, and came forth bleating.

—St. Ephrem the Syrian

# ✠ SPIRITUALITY

## The Vigil Mass

**GOSPEL ACCLAMATION**
R̸. Alleluia, alleluia.
Tomorrow the wickedness of the
    earth will be destroyed:
the Savior of the world will reign
    over us.
R̸. Alleluia, alleluia.

## Gospel

Matt 1:1-25; L13ABC

**The book of the genealogy of
    Jesus Christ,
    the son of David, the son of
        Abraham.**

**Abraham became the father of
    Isaac,
    Isaac the father of Jacob,
    Jacob the father of Judah and his
        brothers.
Judah became the father of Perez and
        Zerah,
    whose mother was Tamar.
Perez became the father of Hezron,
    Hezron the father of Ram,
    Ram the father of Amminadab.
Amminadab became the father of
        Nahshon,
    Nahshon the father of Salmon,
    Salmon the father of Boaz,
    whose mother was Rahab.
Boaz became the father of Obed,
    whose mother was Ruth.
Obed became the father of Jesse,
    Jesse the father of David the king.**

**David became the father of Solomon,
    whose mother had been the wife of
        Uriah.
Solomon became the father of Rehoboam,
    Rehoboam the father of Abijah,
    Abijah the father of Asaph.**

*Continued in Appendix A, p. 262, or
Matt 1:18-25 in Appendix A, p. 262.*

*See Appendix A, p. 263, for the other readings.*

## Reflecting on the Gospel and Living the Paschal Mystery

*To the point:* We are connected to one another, even through the generations, in ways we don't always see. Therefore, our choices matter and can change lives. Yet we need not act out of fear, for God rejoices in us. God is at work, even in our weakness. So trust in the slow but steady work of God.

*To ponder and pray:* Christmas is a season for traditions. We return to familiar rituals of our childhood. We renew the bonds of friendship through customs of gathering and greeting. And we create new traditions as a way of giving something of ourselves with hope for the future.

Whether new or old, strictly followed or merely done out of habit, our traditions tie us together from person to person and from one generation to the next. They are the common thread between the past, through the present, into the future.

When adults prepare to enter into the Christian family through baptism, the Christian community gathers around them and celebrates the *traditio*—the handing on or presentation of the Creed. The essence of our faith that has been handed on to us from our ancestors all the way from Abraham and culminating in Jesus is this: God is with us.

Like the dawn breaking forth or a burning torch at night, this Christmas message of Emmanuel cannot be hidden. It will not stay silent. It will sing and rejoice and be pronounced directly by the mouth of God into our darkest night. God is with us in the turmoil of our lives, the grudges that endure from one generation to the next, and the hopelessness that comes from our persistent failure to be the people we know we could be. Into that world, God breathes this message, like a midwife or spouse breathes with a woman about to give birth: "Do not be afraid. I am with you." In our fractured homes, our divided neighborhoods, and our broken planet, God binds up all our wounds and knits us together, for we are forsaken no longer. Whether saint or sinner, strong in faith or barely hanging on, God calls each of us "My Delight," for God is not swayed by human merit. God is not regulated by societal conventions and norms. God does not draw with straight lines through history, nor does God choose perfect people to reveal his message through the ages. For God acts with grace.

What we see in the genealogy of Jesus proclaimed today is God's grace at work in human history. Unpredictable, creative, generative, and surprising grace that embraces the unknown and chooses the unexpected. Grace that chose Rahab, a prostitute and a protector; David, a king and an adulterer; Jacob, a thief; and Ruth, a foreigner. Grace that is at times inconvenient, sometimes imperceptible, always persistent. In everything, we must trust in the slow but steady work of God.

This Christmas, we receive the message handed down by tradition and teaching from our ancestors that according to his promise God is with us, never to abandon us. We are all part of this lineage of grace. Abraham fathered Isaac, Jesse fathered David, Jesus called Peter and Paul, Paul called Lydia, and someone called you to announce this message. Together let us keep our tradition and hand on the grace and blessings that we have received from God.

## ✝ SPIRITUALITY

## Mass at Midnight

### GOSPEL ACCLAMATION
Luke 2:10-11

℟. Alleluia, alleluia.
I proclaim to you good news of great joy:
today a Savior is born for us,
Christ the Lord.
℟. Alleluia, alleluia.

### Gospel

Luke 2:1-14; L14ABC

In those days a decree went out from
    Caesar Augustus
  that the whole world should be
    enrolled.
This was the first enrollment,
  when Quirinius was governor of Syria.
So all went to be enrolled, each to his
    own town.
And Joseph too went up from Galilee
    from the town of Nazareth
  to Judea, to the city of David that is
    called Bethlehem,
  because he was of the house and fam-
    ily of David,
  to be enrolled with Mary, his betrothed,
    who was with child.
While they were there,
  the time came for her to have her child,
  and she gave birth to her firstborn son.

*Continued in Appendix A, p. 263.*

*See Appendix A, p. 264, for the other readings.*

### Reflecting on the Gospel and Living the Paschal Mystery

*Key words and phrases:* good news of great joy / that will be for all the
people; a savior . . . who is Christ and Lord; on earth peace to those on whom
his favor rests

*To the point:* The birth of Jesus is a preview of the kingdom of God that
Jesus will proclaim in Luke's gospel. The foundation of the kingdom of God
is justice for the poor and vulnerable among us. Tonight's gospel redefines the
world's understanding of peace as more than the absence of discord but the
reality of justice, mercy, and reconciliation.

*To ponder and pray:* The gospel for the Mass at Midnight is Luke's familiar
story of the birth of Jesus in a stable at Bethlehem during a census mandated
by the Roman emperor. Luke's account of Jesus' birth introduces two themes
that he will develop throughout his narrative.

First, the story of Jesus' birth mirrors the kingdom of God that the adult
Jesus will preach. It is a kingdom that is the antithesis of the "kingdoms" of
the Caesars of the world. While the world's power brokers enforce their rule by
military and economic power, the kingdom of God is a "kingdom" of human
hearts in which compassion, mercy, and justice are the rule. Earthly kingdoms
are defined by culture and classes, but the kingdom of God embraces all.

Nowhere is the difference between these two "kingdoms" clearer than in the
use of the word *peace* in tonight's gospel.

Luke places Jesus' birth during the reign of Caesar Augustus, who ruled
from 27 BC to AD 14. Augustus's long reign was hailed as the *pax Augusta*,
a period of peace throughout the vast Roman world. But Rome's peace was
not anything like "goodwill" as sung by the angels. It was a "peace" that was
enforced by intimidation and brutality. Roman "peace" was the absence of division and discord. It brutally suppressed any challenge to imperial rule. Even the
Roman author Tacitus said of the Romans, "They rob, kill, and steal all in the
false name of empire. Where they create desolation, they call it peace."

But the peace of Christmas is a very different understanding of peace: a
peace that brings together heaven and earth, angels and mortals, shepherds and
kings, society's dismissed outcasts and ruling elite. The *pax Christi* is not just
the absence of strife but the presence of compassion and forgiveness; Christ's
peace is built on justice for every human being, especially the vulnerable and
the powerless. Christ's peace is the very foundation of the kingdom of God:
peace that is not fearful passivity but loving perseverance that enables reconciliation and healing; peace that is not imposed but celebrated in mutual respect
and generosity; peace that is not the province of the powerful but the responsibility of all "those on whom his favor rests." The Jesus of Luke's gospel will
proclaim this vision of peace throughout his preaching and healing ministry.

A second theme of Luke's gospel is the inclusiveness of this kingdom of God.
Throughout Luke's gospel, it is the poor, the lowly, the outcast, and the sinner
who first embrace Jesus' message of reconciliation and forgiveness. Jesus shows
compassion and care to the poor, the infirm, and grieving who approach him; he
includes into his company Gentiles, tax collectors, Samaritans, and women. The
announcement of the Messiah's birth to shepherds—who were among the least
regarded—is in keeping with Luke's theme that the poor are especially blessed
of God. The shepherds are the first of the many saints in Luke's gospel whose
lives are transformed by their encounters with Jesus, the "grace of God [who]
has appeared" this night (Titus 2:11-14, tonight's second reading).

# ✠ SPIRITUALITY

## Mass at Dawn

### GOSPEL ACCLAMATION
Luke 2:14

R̸. Alleluia, alleluia.
Glory to God in the highest,
and on earth peace to those
on whom his favor rests.
R̸. Alleluia, alleluia.

### Gospel

Luke 2:15-20; L15ABC

When the angels
      went away from
      them to heaven,
   the shepherds
      said to one
      another,
   "Let us go, then, to
      Bethlehem
   to see this thing
      that has taken
      place,
   which the Lord
      has made known to us."
So they went in haste and found Mary
      and Joseph,
   and the infant lying in the manger.
When they saw this,
   they made known the message
   that had been told them about this
      child.
All who heard it were amazed
   by what had been told them by the
      shepherds.
And Mary kept all these things,
   reflecting on them in her heart.
Then the shepherds returned,
   glorifying and praising God
   for all they had heard and seen,
   just as it had been told to them.

*See Appendix A, p. 264, for the other readings.*

## Reflecting on the Gospel and Living the Paschal Mystery

*Key words and phrases:* haste, Mary and Joseph, infant lying in the manger, glorifying and praising God

*To the point:* The "manger" is not so much a pretty scene as it is a radical foreshadowing of Jesus' role as "food for the world."

*To ponder and pray:* Having heard the good news from the angels of heaven, the shepherds quickly make their way to find the infant Jesus. He was in "swaddling clothes" (2:12), an ancient and still used practice of wrapping an infant in garments that restrict the movement of the limbs. We can imagine a newborn wrapped, as they typically are, to resemble something akin to a burrito!

The shepherds find Jesus in a stable. As we know, Mary and Joseph could find no room at the inn and were reduced to having their baby in a stable, dirty with animal droppings, feed, animal bedding, and various creatures that we might expect in such a place. This was a far cry from palatial stables seen on TV during the Kentucky Derby. The ancient stable was often unkempt, certainly not a place for a newborn, or even a family. It would be more akin to a "chicken coop" or perhaps a "doghouse" today. The point is, there is no pageantry surrounding his place of birth. The family is one of migrants, on the move, without access to something as basic as a bed, or as sanitary as a bathroom. Modern depictions of the stable of Jesus' birth are often so sanitized that we can miss the scandal of such a place. But it is precisely the scandalous conditions of his birth that is such a critical piece of the story.

This "king" is not born in a palace, but in a stable. The reversal is a common gospel theme, especially for Luke. It was prefigured in Mary's canticle (Luke 1:46-55) when she said, "He has thrown down the rulers from their thrones / but lifted up the lowly" (NABRE). The one who has no place to lay his head has been lifted up by God. In short, God's ways are not our ways.

Jesus comes to us as one who is lowly. The infant wrapped in blankets that restrict his movement is laid in a manger. A manger, of course, is not simply a pretty place to lay a baby. In fact, a manger is a "feed-box." Such a depiction is quite deliberate on Luke's part. Jesus will be bread for the world, food for the world as is foreshadowed by his being laid in a feed-box. Jesus is the nourishment that will sustain the world, as echoed in the multiplication of the loaves (Luke 9:10-17). The manger foreshadows the Passover meal at which Jesus will say, "This is my body, which will be given for you" (Luke 22:19, NABRE). After the resurrection, the disciples will come to know Jesus in the "breaking of the bread" (Luke 24:35). The next generation of Christians too will know Jesus in the breaking of bread (Acts 2:46; 20:7), for Jesus is food for the world.

This morning's story, then, is not so much about a cute baby, but about the incarnate God choosing to be born in lowly and migrant conditions, placed in a feed-box, foreshadowing the nourishing, life-giving role he would have for centuries to come. The story should cause us to reconsider how we think of the lowly, for they will be lifted up. God's ways are not our ways. We may look to and admire the powerful, the moneyed, the purveyors of influence. God, on the other hand, casts down those from their lofty places and instead lifts up those who have little to no standing in this world. The birth of Jesus signals a major reversal that was foretold by Mary herself. May we be ready for the upheaval that reversal will bring.

## ✠ SPIRITUALITY

### Mass during the Day

**GOSPEL ACCLAMATION**
℟. Alleluia, alleluia.
A holy day has dawned upon us.
Come, you nations, and adore the Lord.
For today a great light has come upon the earth.
℟. Alleluia, alleluia.

### Gospel

John 1:1-18; L16ABC

**In the beginning was the Word,**
**and the Word was with God,**
**and the Word was God.**
**He was in the beginning with God.**
**All things came to be through him,**
**and without him nothing came to be.**
**What came to be through him was life,**
**and this life was the light of the**
**human race;**
**the light shines in the darkness,**
**and the darkness has not overcome it.**

**A man named John was sent from God.**
**He came for testimony, to testify to the**
**light,**
**so that all might believe through him.**
**He was not the light,**
**but came to testify to the light.**
**The true light, which enlightens everyone,**
**was coming into the world.**
**He was in the world,**
**and the world came to be through him,**
**but the world did not know him.**
**He came to what was his own,**
**but his own people did not accept him.**

**But to those who did accept him**
**he gave power to become children of**
**God,**
**to those who believe in his name,**
**who were born not by natural**
**generation**
**nor by human choice nor by a man's**
**decision**
**but of God.**

*Continued in Appendix A, p. 265, or*
John 1:1-5, 9-14 *in Appendix A, p. 265.*

*See Appendix A, p. 265, for the other readings.*

### Reflecting on the Gospel and Living the Paschal Mystery

*Key words and phrases:* the Word became flesh; the light shines in the darkness

*To the point:* The Word of God is incarnate in the person of Jesus, the light of the world. The darkness has not, and will not, overcome this light.

*To ponder and pray:* In grand Johannine (Gospel of John) language we hear the words, "And the Word became flesh" as the pinnacle of this gospel reading. The central mystery of Christian faith is summed up in this pithy statement about the incarnation. The eternal, limitless, powerful God undergoes change to become human in a particular time, limited and powerless. The Word of God, whose tent was pitched among us, now dwells with us as a fellow human being. The audacity of such a claim is staggering.

The prologue of the Gospel of John sets the stage for the reader, who knows the identity of Jesus. This reading opens the gospel, and seems to recall another important writing by beginning, "In the beginning." As such, the author may be purposefully writing "Scripture" by echoing those simple words of Genesis 1:1. Now we hear more to that story of beginnings. There was the Word, and the Word was made flesh. The gospel reaches its climax and conclusion when, twenty chapters later, a human being proclaims what the reader knows to be true about Jesus: "My Lord and my God!" (John 20:28, NABRE).

Some may find it odd to have this reading on Christmas morning. For, in this gospel we have no nativity scene, no shepherds, and no angels. Instead, there is a clear and decisive focus on Jesus, the Word made flesh. In this gospel, like no other, the emphasis is on Jesus and his identity. The author of the Fourth Gospel has been called simply, The Theologian, for his Christology is interwoven tightly with theology. The two cannot be separated. The Fourth Gospel writer is often depicted as an eagle, for the eagle soars above the clouds. In classical terms, the Christology of the Fourth Gospel is "high" like the eagle.

The prologue gives us another image by which to understand this mystery: the light shone in the darkness. Once the light appears, there is no longer darkness. Darkness does not and cannot overcome the light. Such a simple metaphor is profound, and is also indicative of the Fourth Gospel, with its use of other theologically rich yet simple metaphors: bread, life, and water. The symbolic language of this gospel will become the source of centuries of theological contemplation. It's the source for our contemplation today.

The church gives us this reading on Christmas precisely because it expresses the fundamental mystery of faith, not in a story as we might expect, but in rich and lofty theological terms. Christian faith is ultimately an adult faith. It demands an adult response, a wholly determined and decisive "yes" to what God has done in the incarnation. The image of the infant is absent in favor of dense theological ideas that deserve our thought and contemplation.

Today we are confronted with the central claim of Christian faith. Do I believe that the Word of God became flesh, with all its weakness, needs, desires, and proclivity to selfishness? Or do I believe that the Word of God pretended to become flesh, so that Jesus was a mere puppet in the hands of God? Christian faith holds in tension the divine and the human, incarnate. The eternal enters time. The immortal becomes mortal. And the divine, human. In so doing, humanity is raised to divinity. This is the mystery of faith we profess, especially on this day.

## Model Penitential Act

*Presider:* Dear friends in Christ, rejoice! The Lord has come! Let us open our hearts to welcome him with his reconciling peace and forgiveness. *[pause]*

Light of God who dawns upon us: Lord, have mercy.
Child of Bethlehem, born in holy simplicity in our midst: Christ, have mercy.
Word of God who makes your dwelling among us: Lord, have mercy.

## Model Universal Prayer (Prayer of the Faithful)

*Presider:* The grace of God has appeared this night/day. In peace, then, let us pray.

*Response:* Lord, hear our prayer.

That our parish's prayer and ministries may proclaim the glad tidings of Christ's birth . . .

That all nations and peoples may rejoice in the dawning of the Sun of Justice . . .

That the poor, the sick, the addicted, and the dying may see the salvation of our God . . .

That the faith of Mary and the righteousness of Joseph may inspire all parents, guardians, and caregivers . . .

*Presider:* Hear these prayers, O God, that we make this Christmas night/day in the name of our blessed hope, your Son and our Savior, Jesus Christ. **Amen.**

---

### COLLECT

*(from the Mass during the Day)*

Let us pray.

*Pause for silent prayer*

O God, who wonderfully created the dignity
     of human nature
and still more wonderfully restored it,
grant, we pray,
that we may share in the divinity of Christ,
who humbled himself to share in our humanity.
Who lives and reigns with you in the unity of
     the Holy Spirit,
one God, for ever and ever. **Amen.**

---

### FOR REFLECTION:

• How is Christmas a feast for the poor? How can we make the poor, the forgotten, and the rejected part of our Christmas celebration?

• In what concrete ways can you transform "peace" in your family and community from an absence of conflict into God's peace of generosity, forgiveness, and humility?

---

### Homily Points

• The miracle of Christmas continues to take place in the Bethlehems of our own hearts. In the emptiness of our souls, God forgives us, reassures us, exalts us, lifts us up, loves us. Amid the pain and anguish of a broken people, Christ came with new hope and transforming joy. In the middle of our own dark nights of pain and anguish, God comes and transforms them into holy nights of his peace. This Christmas night, the compassion of God transforms all of our nights and days in the brightness of heavenly peace.

• Simple shepherds—and not the world's powerful and elite—are the first to behold the birth of humanity's Savior, the Christ who would portray himself as the Good Shepherd whose love and compassion for humanity would know neither end nor limitation. The shepherds are everyone of everyday life, albeit at life's harder edges. Throughout his gospel, Luke raises up the faithful poor, the desperate souls who continue to hope in God's goodness, who recognize and welcome Christ in their midst.

## ✠ SPIRITUALITY

**GOSPEL ACCLAMATION**
Col 3:15a, 16a

℟. Alleluia, alleluia.
Let the peace of Christ control your hearts;
let the word of Christ dwell in you richly.
℟. Alleluia, alleluia.

### Gospel

Luke 2:22-40; L17B

**When the days were completed
    for their purification
    according to the law of
        Moses,
    the parents of Jesus took him
        up to Jerusalem
    to present him to the Lord,
    just as it is written in the law
        of the Lord,
    *Every male that opens the
        womb shall be conse-
        crated to the Lord,*
    and to offer the sacrifice of
    *a pair of turtledoves or two young
        pigeons,*
    in accordance with the dictate in the
        law of the Lord.**

**Now there was a man in Jerusalem whose
        name was Simeon.
This man was righteous and devout,
    awaiting the consolation of Israel,
    and the Holy Spirit was upon him.
It had been revealed to him by the Holy
        Spirit
    that he should not see death
    before he had seen the Christ of the
        Lord.
He came in the Spirit into the temple;
    and when the parents brought in the
        child Jesus
    to perform the custom of the law in
        regard to him,
    he took him into his arms and blessed
        God, saying:
    "Now, Master, you may let your
        servant go
    in peace, according to your word,**

*Continued in Appendix A, p. 266, or*
Luke 2:22, 39-40 *in Appendix A, p. 266.*

### Reflecting on the Gospel

Luke tells us a rather unique story, often referred to as "The Presentation of the Lord" or simply "The Presentation." While still an infant, Jesus is taken to the temple by his parents. There they meet two people about whom we know nothing other than what this story tells us: the righteous and devout Simeon, and the prophetess Anna. It is typical of Luke to pair his stories, one with a male character followed by one with a female character. We see that here with Simeon and Anna. In this way, and in many others, Luke shows a concern for women.

Simeon's canticle begins in English with the words, "Now, Master, you may let your servant go / in peace." The gospel was written in Greek and later translated into Latin. This verse thus began in Latin, "Nunc dimittis servum tuum, Domine . . ." This is why it is often referred to today as the *Nunc Dimittis*. The promise to Simeon, that he would not see death until he had seen the Messiah of the Lord, was fulfilled. Simeon will exit but not before uttering a final prophecy to Mary. In this way Luke highlights the role of Mary, a woman. Luke's gospel more than any other focuses on Mary, from the annunciation, to the birth, the presentation, Jesus' earthly ministry, and in the days following Jesus' ascension, including Pentecost. Mary's role is prominent in Luke's gospel.

Immediately after Simeon exits the scene, the eighty-four-year-old widow prophetess Anna steps to the fore. Her worship is punctuated with fasting and prayer, much like the early Christians we will hear about in Luke's second volume, the Acts of the Apostles. She gives thanks to God and speaks about the child, foreshadowing again the lives of the early Christians. It is significant that Luke includes this story of the prophetess. How many women prophets do we recall from the Old Testament? They are often men (Ezekiel, Jeremiah, Isaiah, etc.). Yet, for Luke, not even Simeon is called a prophet. Instead Anna is a prophetess, foreshadowing the equality women enjoy in the ideal Christian life.

Finally, the gospel reading concludes with some fairly innocuous sounding words: "The child grew and became strong, filled with wisdom; / and the favor of God was upon him." How many of us imagine Jesus as a toddler, or as a young boy? Would he have had to ask questions? to learn? Certainly so. Jesus was fully human. To be so meant he had to learn. He grew and became strong. He reached maturity. He was not a divine puppet on the human stage, but he was a real human being, born into a family, and raised to maturity.

This gospel story, unique to Luke, reminds us of the equality of women and men, the relationship of the family, and the importance of human development as a place for God's favor.

### Living the Paschal Mystery

Family life is the heart of faith life for so many of us, including Jesus himself. It is the family where we first experience unconditional love. This experience then becomes one image or model upon which we imagine God's love. For this reason, but not only for this reason, the experience of family is sacred.

After the experience in the temple, Jesus, Mary, and Joseph returned home and lived as a family. They did not live in the temple. Instead, it was in the daily routine of living, in a small town away from the activity of Jerusalem, that Jesus grew and became strong with God's favor upon him.

We are reminded, then, of the sacredness of our own homes and family life. God's presence and favor is in the caring for children, self-sacrificing for their benefit and well-being. God's grace is in the relationships we share in which we experience and express unconditional love.

## Focusing the Gospel
*Luke 2:22-40 or 2:22, 39-40*

In today's gospel, the faithful Joseph and Mary bring their son to the temple for his presentation to the Lord, a ritual required by the law. The book of Exodus taught that a family's firstborn son "belonged" to the Lord who saved them when the firstborn sons of the Egyptians were destroyed at the first Passover (Exod 13:15). The prophet Simeon and the prophetess Anna are idealized portraits of the faithful "remnant" of Israel awaiting the Messiah's coming. Simeon's canticle (prayed by the church every night in the Liturgy of the Hours at the day's final hour of Compline) praises God for the universal salvation that will be realized in Jesus. In Simeon's ominous prophecy, the shadow of the cross to come falls upon the Holy Family.

Anna, as an elderly widow, is considered among the most vulnerable and poor of society. Her encounter with the child typifies the theme woven throughout Luke's gospel: the exaltation of society's poorest and most humble by God.

Every family can identify with the stories of Jesus' birth and childhood (which were later additions to Matthew and Luke's gospels, drawn from the many stories about Jesus' life that were part of the early Christian oral tradition that had developed). Life for the family of Joseph, Mary, and Jesus is harsh: they are forced from their home; they are innocent victims of the political and social tensions of their time; they endure the suspicions of their own people when Mary's pregnancy is discovered; their child is born under the most difficult and terrifying of circumstances; they experience the agonizing anxiety of searching for their missing child. And yet, through it all, their love and faithfulness to one another do not waver. We experience such love within our own families and households as we confront the many tensions and crises that threaten the stability, peace, and unity that are the joys of being a family.

## Focusing the First Reading
*Gen 15:1-6; 21:1-3*

The historic roots of the ritual that takes place in the temple in today's gospel are the focus of today's first and second readings and the responsorial psalm. God calls the elderly Abram to be the patriarch of a new nation, a people united to God in a covenant of goodness and justice. The birth of Isaac to Sarah and Abraham is the beginning of this new tribe that God will make his own.

## Focusing the Responsorial Psalm
*Ps 105:1-2, 3-4, 6-7, 8-9 (7a, 8a)*

The covenant God has made with Abraham for "a thousand generations" is celebrated in this hymn. The singer/composer of Psalm 105 calls the descendants of Abraham to remember all that God has done for them and to celebrate his continued presence in their midst.

## Focusing the Second Reading
*Heb 11:8, 11-12, 17-19*

For the writer of the letter to the Hebrews, the faithfulness of Abraham that enables him not to withhold his beloved son Isaac prefigures God's giving of his own Son and God's raising him from the dead.

---

**PROMPTS FOR HOMILISTS, CATECHISTS, AND RCIA TEAMS**

What rituals and customs in your family best reflect the spiritual dimension of Christmas?

If you are a parent, how do you most identify with Joseph and Mary in today's gospel?

What have you learned about yourself from raising, teaching, or working with children?

What has been the hardest situation your family has had to deal with? How were you able to cope with it?

Who are the Simeons and Annas in your life and community?

## Model Penitential Act

*Presider:* Let us prepare to celebrate these sacred mysteries by calling to mind our sins and failings, trusting in the mercy and forgiveness of God, the Father of us all. *[pause]*

Father of all families and peoples: Lord, have mercy.

Christ Jesus, light of God's salvation: Christ, have mercy.

Spirit that binds us in love as families and communities: Lord, have mercy.

## Homily Points

• Today's feast of the Holy Family reminds us that being a family is a journey of changes and challenges—and that it is the love of spouses and parents and children and brothers and sisters that enables us to negotiate and survive those changes, to confront and conquer those challenges. Our belonging to a family means that we reflect for one another the selfless, limitless, and unconditional love of Christ, both in good times and bad. The Holy Family is a model for our own families as we struggle together to adapt and change and to deal with the many tensions and crises that threaten the stability, peace, and unity that are the joys of being a family.

• Every family is part of a bigger story: the experience of those who came before us had a great deal to do with shaping us into the people we have become, that the traditions and cultures and journeys of our ancestors have enabled us to form our own values and the values we now pass on to our children. As their parents had done for them, Mary and Joseph bring their newborn son to the temple to present him to the Lord, to incorporate him into the life and traditions of their cherished faith. We seek to give our own children the best that we have, as well. In baptism, we incorporate our little ones into the life of the risen Christ; within our home, we try to guide them in learning the gospel values of compassion, love, forgiveness, justice, and peace that we have embraced.

• While parents are the first and principal teachers of their children, children can be their parents' best teachers of love and generosity. Children reveal to us the wonder of creation and move us to gratitude for everyone and everything God has made; children also help us realize our own capacity to love and our ability to be the means of God's compassion and forgiveness for others to an extent we may not be aware of.

## Model Universal Prayer (Prayer of the Faithful)

*Presider:* Let us now offer our prayers to God for all our brothers and sisters in Christ.

*Response:* Lord, hear our prayer.

For our church and parish community, that Christ's peace may reign in our life together . . .

For families in crisis, for families in mourning, for families estranged and separated, that Christ may be present to them in the loving support of neighbors and friends . . .

For the sick, the suffering, and the dying, that they may know the peace and hope of the newborn Savior in our compassion and care . . .

For our children and young people, that they may learn and grow in wisdom and grace within the joy of a loving family . . .

*Presider:* Hear the prayers of your family gathered around your table, O Lord. As Jesus taught us to call you "Father," may we learn to respect and love one another as brothers and sisters. We offer these prayers to you in the name of your Son, Jesus, the Christ. **Amen.**

### COLLECT

Let us pray.

*Pause for silent prayer*

O God, who were pleased to give us
the shining example of the Holy Family,
graciously grant that we may imitate them
in practicing the virtues of family life and
    in the bonds of charity,
and so, in the joy of your house,
delight one day in eternal rewards.
Through our Lord Jesus Christ, your Son,
who lives and reigns with you in the unity
    of the Holy Spirit,
one God, for ever and ever. **Amen.**

### FIRST READING

Gen 15:1-6; 21:1-3

The word of the LORD came to Abram in a
    vision, saying:
  "Fear not, Abram!
    I am your shield;
    I will make your reward very great."
But Abram said,
  "O Lord GOD, what good will your gifts
    be,
  if I keep on being childless
  and have as my heir the steward of my
    house, Eliezer?"
Abram continued,
  "See, you have given me no offspring,
  and so one of my servants will be my
    heir."
Then the word of the LORD came to him:
  "No, that one shall not be your heir;
  your own issue shall be your heir."
The Lord took Abram outside and said,
  "Look up at the sky and count the stars,
    if you can.
Just so," he added, "shall your descendants
    be."
Abram put his faith in the LORD,
  who credited it to him as an act of
    righteousness.

The LORD took note of Sarah as he had
    said he would;
  he did for her as he had promised.
Sarah became pregnant and bore
    Abraham a son in his old age,
  at the set time that God had stated.
Abraham gave the name Isaac to this son
    of his
  whom Sarah bore him.

## RESPONSORIAL PSALM

Ps 105:1-2, 3-4, 6-7, 8-9

R⁂. (7a, 8a) The Lord remembers his
   covenant for ever.

Give thanks to the LORD, invoke his name;
   make known among the nations his
      deeds.
Sing to him, sing his praise,
   proclaim all his wondrous deeds.

R⁂. The Lord remembers his covenant for
   ever.

Glory in his holy name;
   rejoice, O hearts that seek the LORD!
Look to the LORD in his strength;
   constantly seek his face.

R⁂. The Lord remembers his covenant for
   ever.

You descendants of Abraham, his servants,
   sons of Jacob, his chosen ones!
He, the LORD, is our God;
   throughout the earth his judgments
      prevail.

R⁂. The Lord remembers his covenant for
   ever.

He remembers forever his covenant
   which he made binding for a thousand
      generations
which he entered into with Abraham
   and by his oath to Isaac.

R⁂. The Lord remembers his covenant for
   ever.

## SECOND READING

Heb 11:8, 11-12, 17-19

Brothers and sisters:
By faith Abraham obeyed when he was
      called to go out to a place
   that he was to receive as an inheritance;
   he went out, not knowing where he was
      to go.
By faith he received power to generate,
   even though he was past the normal age
   —and Sarah herself was sterile—
   for he thought that the one who had
      made the promise was trustworthy.
So it was that there came forth from one
      man,
   himself as good as dead,
   descendants as numerous as the stars
      in the sky
   and as countless as the sands on the
      seashore.

*Continued in Appendix A, p. 266.*

*See Appendix A, pp. 266–267, for optional
readings.*

### About Liturgy

**Called to be holy:** On this feast of the Holy Family, we reflect on the meaning of being "holy." To be holy is to be consecrated, that is, set aside for a purpose. We find facets of that purpose in today's gospel: to be a family who lives by God's law; to be a man who keeps his eyes open for Christ, no matter how long he has to wait; to be a woman who speaks a word of hope to those who have lost hope. Next week, we will see an image of that purpose in the wise men who follow the signs of the times in search of Christ. Finally, at the end of the Christmas season, we will see the fullness of that purpose in Christ as he is baptized in the Jordan. He will embody in his very life Isaiah's invitation to all who thirst.

Because this feast coincides this year with New Year's Eve, this reflection on holiness and Simeon's canticle found in today's gospel might inspire you to end the last day of 2017 with a simple liturgy called "Compline" or Night Prayer. This liturgy from the Liturgy of the Hours is the last liturgy celebrated at the end of each day. The basic structure begins with a brief examination of conscience followed by a penitential act similar to what is said at Mass, and a psalm or two with a brief Scripture reading. The liturgy concludes with the singing or recitation of the Canticle of Simeon, also called the *Nunc Dimittis*. As we let go of the old year, Simeon's words invite us to reflect back on it to reveal how our eyes have seen God's salvation. Celebrating this simple liturgy after the last Mass on this last day of the year may be a welcomed way for New Year's Eve revelers prayerfully to consecrate the coming year to our common call to holiness.

**Called to be family:** Some parishes use this feast day to bless families since the feast itself focuses on Jesus' family. Yet the Christmas season can also be a time of great sadness for parishioners and visitors who are estranged or separated from family, who are unable to conceive a child of their own, or are single and feeling lonely. Such a public blessing of families on this day may deepen those wounds. Today's readings give us a bigger image of what it means to be family, even for those who are single, widowed, or childless, for all who have been consecrated to God are united into the one family of Christ. The *Book of Blessings* gives us several ways to bless families and their domestic churches. Consider helping households, regardless of their makeup, pray for God's blessings in their homes by giving them prayers and rituals to celebrate at home with all those whom they call family.

### About Liturgical Music

**The Christmas season:** For a liturgist or pastoral musician, some of the most disappointing things to see this time of year are barren Christmas trees discarded onto the sidewalk waiting to be recycled the day after Christmas. Christmas isn't over until the Baptism of the Lord at least a week away! Help catechize your parishioners and visitors to let them know that Christmas is more than just one day. Be sure to continue using your Christmas Mass settings and acclamations on this day and through Epiphany and Baptism of the Lord next week. Though the shopping malls have moved on to Valentine's Day and Easter, continue using Christmas hymns and songs as gathering and dismissal songs. If you don't want to use all Christmas carols for today's Mass, two traditional hymns can help reflect today's feast: "Of the Father's Love Begotten" is a Christmas song that harkens to Simeon and Anna's announcement of God's salvation; and "For the Beauty of the Earth" presents a beautiful image of kinship and familial love.

**DECEMBER 31, 2017**

# THE HOLY FAMILY OF JESUS, MARY, AND JOSEPH

**GOSPEL ACCLAMATION**
Heb 1:1-2

℟. Alleluia, alleluia.
In the past God spoke to our ancestors through
    the prophets;
in these last days, he has spoken to us through
    the Son.
℟. Alleluia, alleluia.

## Gospel

Luke 2:16-21; L18ABC

**The shepherds went in haste to
    Bethlehem and found Mary
    and Joseph,
  and the infant lying in the
    manger.
When they saw this,
  they made known the message
    that had been told them about
    this child.
All who heard it were amazed
  by what had been told them by
    the shepherds.
And Mary kept all these things,
  reflecting on them in her heart.
Then the shepherds returned,
  glorifying and praising God
  for all they had heard and seen,
  just as it had been told to them.**

**When eight days were completed for
    his circumcision,
  he was named Jesus, the name given
    him by the angel
  before he was conceived in the
    womb.**

*See Appendix A, p. 267, for the other readings.*

## Reflecting on the Gospel

We often begin the secular New Year with resolutions, promises, and good intentions. We annually commit ourselves to make some changes for our own self-betterment or that of others. We hope (and pray!) that these changes last. At the same time, it is important to recognize the good that we regularly do, and so we recommit to that too. There are many good habits we have developed through the course of our lives and we do not want to lose sight of them.

Though this is New Year's Day in the secular calendar, according to the liturgical calendar this is the solemnity of Mary, the Holy Mother of God. In a sense we begin the New Year by reminding ourselves of some of the basics. How appropriate for Catholics that we begin the year by honoring Mary, and especially so that we refer to her as "Theotokos," "God-bearer," or more typically, "Mother of God." Like many Marian titles, this one says more about Jesus than it does about Mary. In the early church there were some who objected to such a title; they preferred to call Mary "Christotokos" or "Christ-bearer." Others who were perhaps more avant-garde used the more provocative "Theotokos" or "God-bearer." By this latter title, they meant that Jesus was the incarnation of God from the moment of his conception so that Mary could be called not merely bearer of the Christ, but bearer of God. For even in Mary's womb, Jesus was the incarnation of God.

After much debate and even some condemnations, the church settled on this title of "God-bearer" as ultimately it spoke to the identity of Jesus. And therefore to call Mary the "Mother of God" meant not that Mary was divine, but that Jesus was. As this unique title only developed in the Christian tradition centuries after the New Testament, there is by definition no gospel story that would use the title. Instead, for today's gospel, we have the story of the nativity, the birth of Jesus. In particular, we have the story of the shepherds finding the infant Jesus lying in a manger. The church gives us this delicate scene today to remind us that Mary was not merely the mother of the Christ, but even at the moment he was lying in the manger, Jesus was divine. Mary bore the divine within her womb and gave birth to Jesus. As such, she can be called the Mother of God. We begin the secular New Year with this reminder of a basic element of our faith, the incarnation. No resolutions are needed.

## Living the Paschal Mystery

By becoming human, Jesus divinized humanity. Because of that, we can never look at our neighbor the same way again, for each person is a locus of the divine. Each human being, not only the infant Jesus, is worthy of respect and honor. The Son of God humbled himself to become human, being born of a human. No longer is the divine other-worldly, or beyond our reach. The divine has come to us, as one of us, born of a woman. Our faith teaches us that humanity is therefore sacred. How we treat one another is often a more accurate reflection of our relationship with God than how we behave before God when worshiping at church. We often have great reverence and respect for the divine presence in the Eucharist. What would our world, or even our parish, look like if we showed that same reverence and respect for the divine presence in our neighbor?

## Focusing the Gospel

Today's solemnity is the oldest feast of Mary in the church, honoring her by the theologically sophisticated title, "Mother of God." Today's gospel recounts the visit of the shepherds to Jesus' Bethlehem birthplace. Luke includes this touching detail: "And Mary kept all these things, / reflecting on them in her heart." Mary, the model of faithful discipleship in her yes to God's call to give birth to his Christ, is also a model for us on what it means to become a person of discerning prayer and reflection.

Jesus is given the name *Yeshua* (Joshua), "The Lord saves." The rite of circumcision, eight days after his birth, unites Mary's child with God's chosen people and makes him an heir to the promises God made to Abraham—promises to be fulfilled in the Child himself.

## Model Penitential Act

*Presider:* With the faith and trust of Mary, let us place our hearts before God, confident of his mercy and forgiveness. *[pause]*

Lord of graciousness and mercy: Lord, have mercy.
Son of God and child of Mary: Christ, have mercy.
The Word and grace of God made like us, for us: Lord, have mercy.

## Model Universal Prayer (Prayer of the Faithful)

*Presider:* As the gift of a New Year dawns, let us come before the Lord in prayer for the peace and safety of all people.

*Response:* Lord, hear our prayer.

That our prayer and work as a church in this New Year reveal God's mercy and compassion in our midst . . .

That all nations may seek to protect the worth of all human beings as children of God . . .

That this New Year may be, with our outreach and help, a new beginning for the poor, the struggling, and the forgotten . . .

That the light of God's peace may shine upon all our deceased relatives and friends *[especially . . . ]* . . .

*Presider:* Abba, "Father," hear the prayers we make for ourselves and for all members of our human family. With the faith and trust of Mary, may we make your gift of this New Year a time of reconciliation and grace, a season of peace and mercy for all your sons and daughters. We make these prayers in the name of Mary's child, your Son, Jesus the Christ. **Amen.**

### COLLECT

Let us pray.

*Pause for silent prayer*

O God, who through the fruitful virginity of
    Blessed Mary
bestowed on the human race
the grace of eternal salvation,
grant, we pray,
that we may experience the intercession of her,
through whom we were found worthy
to receive the author of life,
our Lord Jesus Christ, your Son.
Who lives and reigns with you in the unity of
    the Holy Spirit,
one God, for ever and ever. Amen.

### FOR REFLECTION

• In what real, concrete ways can you give "birth" to God in the year ahead?

• How is the Mary of the gospels a wise, compelling companion for us on our journey through the year ahead?

• What is the most difficult memory of 2017 that you would like to heal in 2018?

## Homily Points

• On this first day of the New Year, we honor Mary under her most ancient title, Theotokos, "God-bearer." God seeks to be born in our loveless stables and forgotten caves; in Bethlehems of anger and hopelessness; in the Nazareths of our homes, schools, and workplaces. In baptism into the life of Mary's child, we are called to be "God-bearers": to give birth to God in every life he comes to enter and transform in his light and love.

• All time is a gift of God, who gives us his grace to make our own time something good and holy. We believe that God has sanctified all time in his work of creation and his re-creation of the world in Christ. The God who makes all things new in Christ enables us to make this truly a New Year for each one of us: a time for renewal in God's love, establishing God's peace in our lives, becoming people of compassion, making this New Year truly a "year of our Lord."

## ✛ SPIRITUALITY

**GOSPEL ACCLAMATION**
Matt 2:2

℟. Alleluia, alleluia.
We saw his star at its rising
and have come to do him homage.
℟. Alleluia, alleluia.

### Gospel

Matt 2:1-12; L20ABC

**When Jesus was born in Bethlehem of Judea,**
  **in the days of King Herod,**
  **behold, magi from the east arrived in Jerusalem, saying,**
  **"Where is the newborn king of the Jews?**
**We saw his star at its rising**
  **and have come to do him homage."**
**When King Herod heard this,**
  **he was greatly troubled,**
  **and all Jerusalem with him.**
**Assembling all the chief priests and the scribes of the people,**
  **he inquired of them where the Christ was to be born.**
**They said to him, "In Bethlehem of Judea,**
  **for thus it has been written through the prophet:**
  *And you, Bethlehem, land of Judah,*
    *are by no means least among the rulers of Judah;*
  *since from you shall come a ruler,*
    *who is to shepherd my people Israel."*

*Continued in Appendix A, p. 268.*

*Continued in Appendix A, p. 268.*

### Reflecting on the Gospel

Today's gospel gives us the classic and familiar story of the "visit of the magi." We have heard it so often that we may sometimes miss critical, and perhaps not so critical, elements in the story. For example, we are never told how many wise men, or magi, there are. We also note that verse 1 states simply that Jesus was born. Not until several verses later do we learn about Herod ascertaining from the magi when the star appeared. He then sent them to search for the *child* (not infant). That one word, child, rather than infant, is a clue that the star had appeared sometime earlier. And then we learn that Herod ordered male children up to the age of two to be killed. So it seems Matthew had in mind that the visit of the magi happened while Jesus was a child about the age of two.

In our own minds we have likely harmonized Matthew's nativity account with Luke's so that we place Luke's angels together with Matthew's magi in the crèche! But in Matthew's telling, there is no census that brings the family from Nazareth to Bethlehem, no manger, no animals, and no shepherds. According to Matthew Jesus was born at home in Bethlehem, where Joseph and Mary lived. We may be forgiven for combining Matthew and Luke's versions of the stories. Even the nativity scenes in our home have harmonized these narratives too!

Ultimately, the importance of what Matthew and Luke are telling us rests not in details about how the family moved from Bethlehem to Nazareth, or whether Jesus was born in a home or a stable. Instead, Matthew provides a theological insight into the person of Jesus and the activity of God. The magi are not Jews. They are Gentiles. They worship Jesus. As such they prefigure the Gentile mission that the risen Jesus will inaugurate in the closing verses of this gospel (Matt 28:16-20). That is to say, Matthew "bookends" his gospel with a story of Gentiles (the magi) coming to worship Jesus at the beginning, and the risen Jesus' own command to his disciples to "make disciples of all nations [Gentiles], baptizing them in the name of the Father, and of the Son, and of the holy Spirit" (NABRE). Ultimately the Gentiles are coheirs with the Jews of the promises of God. We cannot limit God's mercy. It knows no bounds, and includes all!

### Living the Paschal Mystery

It's likely been some time since we've put away our Christmas decorations. Or if we are purists, our decorations have remained up until today. The very timing of the Epiphany, or the visit of the magi, tells us that we've moved on from the Christmas event. We are no longer in the manger. Our lives have begun to go in other directions. The infant is growing up to be a child and is walking. Ordinary Time quickly approaches. And now we have a visit from strangers who have come to see the cause of our celebration. We call to mind that time, and perhaps we relive some of its joy. But as with the magi, danger unfortunately lurks. They go home another way, aware of skulking peril. This too, along with Herod's massacre of the innocents, foreshadows the violent end that Jesus will ultimately face.

And so living the paschal mystery is a combination of joy in new life with an awareness of death. But death will be overcome by life. How many of us might prefer to dwell with the baby Jesus in a manger, or sit with the Holy Family when all is calm and peaceful. But that is not the life we lead. Though these periods of calm, serenity, and joy punctuate our lives, we are aware of the pressing journey. We navigate our paths aware of danger and peril. We rely on God and our own sense to steer us toward safety, all the while aware of a specter of malevolence. For we, like the Gentile magi, worship a child who will face a violent end, only to be raised to new life. It is the paschal mystery.

## Focusing the Gospel

*Matt 2:1-12*

Matthew's story of the magi serves as a preview of what is to come as his gospel narrative unfolds. First, the reactions of the various parties to the birth of Jesus mirror the effects Jesus' teaching will have on those who hear it. Herod is threatened by the Jesus of the poor who comes to overturn the powerful and rich. The chief priests and scribes greet with haughty indifference the news of the birth of the Jesus who comes to give new life and meaning to their rituals and laws. But the magi—nonbelievers in the eyes of Israel—possess the humility of faith and the openness of mind and heart to seek and welcome the Jesus who will establish the second covenant between God and the new Israel.

Second, the gifts of the astrologers indicate the principal dimensions of Jesus' life and mission: *Gold* is a gift fitting for a king, a ruler, one with power and authority; gold was a symbol of divinity. This Child comes to transform our perspective of wealth to treasure again the things of God—compassion, forgiveness, and peace are the coin of the realm of the newborn King. *Frankincense* comes from a small tree found only in Arabia and parts of northern Africa. The hardened resin of the plant was used as a medicine for many ailments: to stop bleeding and to heal wounds; as an antidote for poisons and as a salve for bruises, ulcerations, and paralyzed limbs. This Child comes to restore and heal not just the physical ailments of those he will encounter in his gospel journey, but to heal us of our fears and doubts, to bridge the chasms that separate us from one another and from God. *Myrrh* was an expensive extract from the resin of the myrrh tree. It, too, was used as a medicine but, more significantly, it was used in embalming the dead. Only royalty and the very wealthy were embalmed; myrrh, therefore, was a gift reserved for kings. This Child comes to recreate us in the life of God: his death will be the defeat of death, his cross will be his—and our—glory. The three gifts of the magi are a gospel in themselves. They honor the Child who is himself a gift from the God whose love is beyond our comprehension, whose goodness knows neither limit nor condition.

## Focusing the First Reading

*Isa 60:1-6*

The exiled Jews are returning to Jerusalem from Babylon to rebuild their nation and their way of life. But Isaiah envisions more for the city than just the rebuilding of its capital: Jerusalem will be a light for all nations, a gathering place where not only returning Jews but all peoples of every land will be welcomed, a city of joy that mirrors for all the world the justice and peace of God.

## Focusing the Responsorial Psalm

*Ps 72:1-2, 7-8, 10-11, 12-13 (11)*

This royal psalm envisions the king as the vicar of God, the embodiment of the justice and peace of the Creator, the premier leader of the world, to whom all nations and peoples come for wisdom and guidance. In the light of today's feast, this "divine kingship" is perfected in the Child born of Mary. (Could Matthew have had Psalm 72 in mind in composing his story of the magi?)

## Focusing the Second Reading

*Eph 3:2-3a, 5-6*

This letter is a synthesis of Paul's theology of the church. In today's reading, the apostle writes that the church transcends national and cultural identities: in Christ, Jew and Gentile form one body and share equally in the promise of the resurrection.

---

**PROMPTS FOR HOMILISTS, CATECHISTS, AND RCIA TEAMS**

What "epiphanies" have you experienced in your life that have been most revealing and instructive?

What star have you followed that led you to discovering the "holy"? What star have you followed that led you to emptiness and disappointment?

What do you see as the largest wall separating you from someone else, the deepest chasm between your family or community or church or nation and others?

What was the most satisfying and rewarding gift you gave this Christmas? What made it so?

35

## Model Penitential Act

*Presider:* The light of Christ has dawned, shattering the night of sin and despair. With humility and hope, let us begin our Eucharist celebrating the Epiphany of the Lord by seeking his forgiveness for our sins and failings. *[pause]*

> Holy Light, the grace of God in our midst: Lord, have mercy.
>
> Holy Light, that shatters the darkness of sin: Christ, have mercy.
>
> Holy Light, that leads us to the dwelling place of God: Lord, have mercy.

## Homily Points

• Our journeys through life are filled with "epiphanies": manifestations of the compassion and peace of God in the love and generosity of family and friends, of teachers and coaches, of mentors and counselors. In times of both great joy and accomplishment and of turmoil and disappointment, the love of God is manifested to us in the most hidden kindnesses, in the barely visible light, in unexpected moments of grace. In these everyday epiphanies, God is manifested in the queries of the "magi" who come into our lives searching for Jesus, in the "stars" we follow that lead us to lives of compassion and generosity, in the gifts of ourselves that we put to the service of our families, church, and community.

• The Epiphany of the Lord is a story about seeking and finding the God within us and around us. Like the magi's journey in search for the newborn King of the Jews, our lives are a constant search for meaning, for purpose, for God and the things of God. Mirroring our own journeys, the story of the magi challenges us to consider the "stars" we follow in the course of our lives as we seek to make our lives all that God has created them to be, to fix our lives on the constant, eternal values of peace, compassion, mercy, justice, and forgiveness that are God with us.

• In Matthew's gospel, it is "Gentile" astrologers who discover the newborn "King of the Jews," while the people of the covenant (Herod, the chief priests and scribes) remain oblivious to his presence or seek to eliminate him from their midst. In Christ, God is present in all of human history; God is not the property of one nation or people; no religious group holds title to the blessings of God. The Epiphany calls us to a new vision of the world that sees beyond the walls and borders we have created and to walk by the light that has dawned for all of humankind, a light by which we are able to recognize all men and women as our brothers and sisters under the loving providence of God, the Father of all.

## Model Universal Prayer (Prayer of the Faithful)

*Presider:* Christ our Light has dawned upon the world. In joyful hope, then, let us pray.

*Response:* Lord, hear our prayer.

That all churches and faith communities may honor and respect one another as coheirs and sharers of God's promise . . .

That all nations and their leaders may walk by the light of God's justice and peace . . .

That the light of Christ may burn away the darkness and hopelessness of illness, poverty, and distress for all our suffering brothers and sisters . . .

That our church and parish may be a haven of safety and a place of welcome for all who seek God . . .

*Presider:* Father, may your holy light illuminate the roads we walk on our journeys to you, as we seek to realize the hope of these prayers, prayers that we offer for all peoples in the name of your Christ. **Amen.**

## COLLECT

Let us pray.

*Pause for silent prayer*

O God, who on this day
revealed your Only Begotten Son to the
    nations
by the guidance of a star,
grant in your mercy
that we, who know you already by faith,
may be brought to behold the beauty of
    your sublime glory.
Through our Lord Jesus Christ, your Son,
who lives and reigns with you in the unity
    of the Holy Spirit,
one God, for ever and ever. Amen.

## FIRST READING

Isa 60:1-6

Rise up in splendor, Jerusalem! Your light
    has come,
    the glory of the Lord shines upon you.
See, darkness covers the earth,
    and thick clouds cover the peoples;
but upon you the LORD shines,
    and over you appears his glory.
Nations shall walk by your light,
    and kings by your shining radiance.
Raise your eyes and look about;
    they all gather and come to you:
your sons come from afar,
    and your daughters in the arms of their
      nurses.

Then you shall be radiant at what you see,
    your heart shall throb and overflow,
for the riches of the sea shall be emptied
    out before you,
    the wealth of nations shall be brought
      to you.
Caravans of camels shall fill you,
    dromedaries from Midian and Ephah;
all from Sheba shall come
    bearing gold and frankincense,
    and proclaiming the praises of the LORD.

## RESPONSORIAL PSALM

Ps 72:1-2, 7-8, 10-11, 12-13

℟. (cf. 11) Lord, every nation on earth will adore you.

O God, with your judgment endow the king,
  and with your justice, the king's son;
he shall govern your people with justice
  and your afflicted ones with judgment.

℟. Lord, every nation on earth will adore you.

Justice shall flower in his days,
  and profound peace, till the moon be no more.
May he rule from sea to sea,
  and from the River to the ends of the earth.

℟. Lord, every nation on earth will adore you.

The kings of Tarshish and the Isles shall offer gifts;
  the kings of Arabia and Seba shall bring tribute.
All kings shall pay him homage,
  all nations shall serve him.

℟. Lord, every nation on earth will adore you.

For he shall rescue the poor when he cries out,
  and the afflicted when he has no one to help him.
He shall have pity for the lowly and the poor;
  the lives of the poor he shall save.

℟. Lord, every nation on earth will adore you.

## SECOND READING

Eph 3:2-3a, 5-6

Brothers and sisters:
You have heard of the stewardship of God's grace
  that was given to me for your benefit,
  namely, that the mystery was made known to me by revelation.
It was not made known to people in other generations
  as it has now been revealed
  to his holy apostles and prophets by the Spirit:
  that the Gentiles are coheirs, members of the same body,
  and copartners in the promise in Christ Jesus through the gospel.

## About Liturgy

**Go and search:** Today's solemnity brings a rich tradition of customs for the parish and the home church. From the proclamation of the date of Easter to the chalking of the door at one's home; from the sharing of the *rosca de reyes* or "king cake" in Hispanic and Latino cultures, in which a coffee bean or baby figurine is hidden, to the blessing of water in the Orthodox Church reminding us of the epiphanies at the Jordan and at Cana—all these traditions call us to "go and search" for Christ in our daily lives throughout the year.

**Blessing the home:** One such tradition that has become popular for parishes to do on this day is to bless chalk for each household to take home. The household uses the chalk to inscribe over the main door of the home the customary initials of the wise men, C M B, for Caspar, Melchior, and Balthasar, along with the numerals of the new year. Thus, for this year, they would write "20 C + M + B 18" above their door. This is a way for the family to bless their home and to remember that every time they pass through that door, they are to search for Christ and pay him homage as the wise men did.

At the end of Mass today, you might consider blessing chalk, invoking God's grace and protection upon those who will use the chalk to mark their homes. Then invite family members to take one piece of chalk home along with instructions for marking their door and a prayer they might say together as a family that reminds them to be like the wise men each day, always searching for Christ, giving him praise, and being changed with every encounter to follow him with more joy and hope throughout the coming year.

Also consider encouraging priests, deacons, and parish lay leaders to assist families in blessing their homes using the rite for Blessing of Homes During the Christmas and Easter Seasons found in the *Book of Blessings*.

## About Liturgical Music

**Proclaiming the date of Easter:** On this day, the church has an ancient tradition of ritually announcing the dates of Easter and the other important feasts of the coming year. Every year, the date of Easter depends on the solar and lunar calendars. Easter Sunday is always the first Sunday after the first full moon that happens after the spring equinox. Because other feasts, like Ash Wednesday and Pentecost, depend on the date of Easter, those dates also change every year.

In an age of Google and iPhones, it seems strange to make a public announcement about the date of Easter and other important feasts in the church year. Couldn't we just look them up on the internet? Yet, the ritual proclamation of these dates on the solemnity of the Epiphany is another way of teaching us that the mystery of Christ is revealed to us gradually throughout the entire year within every gathering of the faithful. Christ's saving mission is manifested most clearly in the paschal feast of Easter, but the feasts and seasons and, indeed, each day of the year reveal yet another facet of this paschal mystery in our daily lives. Our call is to be open each day to seeing Christ revealed among us in new and unexpected ways.

You can find this sung proclamation, officially called "The Announcement of Easter and the Moveable Feasts," in Appendix I of the Roman Missal. The announcement is sung after the proclamation of the gospel reading, and it can be led by the deacon or the cantor. You will want to look ahead and insert the correct days and months into the appropriate sections for each feast.

ORDINARY
TIME I

## ✚ SPIRITUALITY

R⁊. Alleluia, alleluia.
We have found the Messiah:
Jesus Christ, who brings us truth and grace.
R⁊. Alleluia, alleluia.

## Gospel

John 1:35-42; L65B

John was standing with two
   of his disciples,
   and as he watched Jesus
   walk by, he said,
   "Behold, the Lamb of
   God."
The two disciples heard
   what he said and fol-
   lowed Jesus.
Jesus turned and saw them
   following him and said to them,
   "What are you looking for?"
They said to him, "Rabbi"—which
   translated means Teacher—,
   "where are you staying?"
He said to them, "Come, and you will
   see."
So they went and saw where Jesus was
   staying,
   and they stayed with him that day.
It was about four in the afternoon.
Andrew, the brother of Simon Peter,
   was one of the two who heard John
   and followed Jesus.
He first found his own brother Simon
   and told him,
   "We have found the Messiah"—which
   is translated Christ.
Then he brought him to Jesus.
Jesus looked at him and said,
   "You are Simon the son of John;
   you will be called Cephas"—which is
   translated Peter.

### Reflecting on the Gospel

Now that we are in Ordinary Time it might be surprising to read from the Gospel of John. After all, we are in "Year B" when we read primarily from Mark. Even so, we begin with the Gospel of John, the author of which is also known as "The Theologian." And the theology in this gospel can also be called Christology, for what he says about Jesus he says about God. The two are in a close, dynamic relationship so that Jesus can say, "The Father and I are one" (John 10:30). In today's story we have the calling of the first disciples, only one of whom is named, Andrew the brother of Simon Peter. The other disciple has traditionally been understood to be the "beloved disciple" or "the disciple whom Jesus loved," even though he is not named such here. Only later, beginning with the Last Supper, do we have that name (13:23-26; 19:25-27; 20:2-10; 21:7; 21:20-23; 21:24). But if this unnamed disciple from chapter 1 is the same as the beloved disciple from later chapters, then the "eyewitness" (John 19:35) of the Fourth Gospel would have been present with Jesus from the beginning of his ministry. Andrew and the unnamed disciple evangelize Simon, Andrew's brother, by saying they have found the Messiah. They bring Simon to Jesus. And before Simon can say a word, Jesus names him "Cephas," the Aramaic term for "Rock," translated into Greek as "Petros," from which we get the name "Peter." This story of Jesus naming Simon "Peter" is much different than that in the Synoptics, where Jesus names him "Peter" only after Simon confesses Jesus as the Messiah (Matt 16:16; Mark 8:29; Luke 9:20). The Gospel of John, with its intense emphasis on Jesus, does not allow the possibility of Simon's name change to be associated with his confession, or absolutely anything else Simon has done. In fact, this seems to be why the Gospel of John places this story in the first chapter, immediately after the call of the first disciples. Moreover, Andrew, rather than his brother Simon, is the one who says Jesus is the Messiah. Simon merely hears the news and comes to meet Jesus. In the Gospel of John, Jesus exercises authority not dependent upon human beings. In this case, we see clearly Johannine theology with its overriding emphasis on Jesus. For this reason and many others the author of this gospel has been named "The Theologian."

### Living the Paschal Mystery

The gospel story about Peter reminds us that Jesus takes the initiative with us, his disciples. He sees who we truly are and calls us by name, even to the point of giving us a new name! Once we are known by Jesus, there is no need to "perform" or "meet targets." We may rest in the knowledge that we are known by him. Like Simon Peter, we each have a destiny, a purpose, and meaning. Like Andrew, we also have a mission, and that is to proclaim Jesus to others. Only by Andrew's proclamation did Simon learn about Jesus. And Andrew learned about Jesus only by John the Baptist's testimony.

   In our own lives we recognize that we learned about Jesus from someone else, whether a parent, grandparent, teacher, or friend. We too tell another about Jesus. In this way Christian faith is passed from one generation to the next. Evangelization is a hallmark of Christian identity from the beginning, as we see in today's gospel. May we have zeal for evangelization that comes from the surety that we are known personally by Jesus.

## Focusing the Gospel

*John 1:35-42*

In John's proclamation of Jesus as the "Lamb of God," the age of the prophets ends and the era of the Messiah begins.

Jesus' invitation to Andrew, "Come, and you will see," so moves Andrew that he invites his brother Simon Peter to come and see for himself. This is the first of three episodes in John's gospel in which Andrew introduces someone to Christ: Andrew brings to Jesus the lad with the five barley loaves and a couple of dried fish (John 6:8-9) and it is Andrew who asks Jesus to meet with the Greeks who approach Andrew—"Sir, we would like to see Jesus" (John 12:21).

## Focusing the First Reading

*1 Sam 3:3b-10, 19*

Today's first reading also recounts a call from God: the beginning of the work of Samuel, Israel's first great prophet. There are two parallels to today's gospel: The priest Eli serves in the same role as Andrew does in today's gospel, facilitating the young Samuel's meeting with the Lord. Like John the Baptist, Samuel serves as a "bridge" figure between Israel's era of the judges and the era of the kings.

## Focusing the Responsorial Psalm

*Ps 40:2, 4, 7-8, 8-9, 10 (8a, 9a)*

The antiphon to today's responsorial psalm mirrors the response of the young Samuel to the Lord's call (first reading). The psalm is a song of thanksgiving from one who has been rescued by God and now sings the "new song" of hope and mercy of God that he has experienced. The psalmist stands before the Lord ready to speak his word. For the psalmist, the perfect offering for God's blessing is not a ritual sacrifice but obedience and trust.

## Focusing the Second Reading

*1 Cor 6:13c-15a, 17-20*

The second readings for the first fourteen Sundays of Ordinary Time in Year B of the Lectionary cycle are taken from Paul's two letters to the Christian community he founded at Corinth. Corinth was considered the gateway between the East and West of antiquity, a city of ethnic and cultural diversity. Corinth also had a well-earned reputation for licentiousness and moral depravity—in some part a reaction to the classic exaltation of the ascetic and scorn of the physical. Greek dramatists often portrayed Corinthians as loud, drunk, and depraved; in Greek, the word "Corinthian" was often employed as an adjective for immoral and corrupt. In his two years living and preaching in Corinth, Paul came to know the city and its notoriety well.

Paul's First Letter to the Corinthians is a series of admonitions on living the moral and ethical dimensions of the Gospel he taught. In today's pericope, Paul exhorts Corinthian Christians not to fall back on their old ways. Remember, Paul writes, the dignity of the human body as "a temple of the Holy Spirit." Our "bodies" are not our own but "purchased" for us by God so that we may be reflections of his Spirit in our world (Corinth was a marketplace for the buying and selling of slaves, so Paul's "purchasing" metaphor would have been clear to his readers). God has a claim on them; their freedom was "bought" by Christ.

### PROMPTS FOR HOMILISTS, CATECHISTS, AND RCIA TEAMS

Have you ever been the means of "inviting" someone to "behold" God's love in their lives? Has someone ever been an Andrew or John the Baptist for you?

When have you heard the voice of God inviting you to make a new beginning?

Think about ways in which God provides opportunities for new beginnings that overcome the pain of broken relationships or the trauma of change.

Where and when do we hear the voice of God calling us like the young Samuel to the work of the prophet?

## Model Penitential Act

*Presider:* Let us begin our celebration of these sacred mysteries by calling to mind our sins. *[pause]*

Lord Jesus, you are both Teacher and Word: Lord, have mercy.

Lord Jesus, the Anointed One of God: Christ, have mercy.

Lord Jesus, the Lamb of God sacrificed for us: Lord, have mercy.

## Homily Points

• In today's gospel, the first disciples are invited to "come and see" what is before them, to realize who is in their midst. The same invitation is extended to us, Jesus' disciples in the here and now. The challenge of discipleship/prophecy is to discern and respond to that call within our own lives, in the context of our own experiences. Jesus calls us to "come and see": to realize the presence of God in the goodness and generosity around us. And Jesus calls us to follow him: to focus our attention on the needs of others rather than our own wants, to find purpose in bringing joy into the lives of others rather than in the pursuit of the things the world deems as important.

• Early in the Fourth Gospel, John the Baptist leaves the stage, exhorting his followers—and us—to "Behold, the Lamb of God." The word *behold* means much more than just to "look." One "beholds" something in wonder, attentiveness, and awe. John calls us not just to "see" Jesus in our midst, but to "behold" his presence: to put aside our fears, stop our constant busyness, and open our whole being to Jesus' presence in our midst transforming our lives and world. In the person of Jesus, God becomes one of us, taking on our humanity in all its messiness, embarrassments, and disappointments, and shows us how to deal with it all with generosity, compassion, and grace. John calls us to open our hearts and consciences to see and hear Christ working, healing, and teaching in our midst; to embrace and be embraced by that love of God moving and animating this story of his Son living among us.

• Regardless of our social standing or lifestyle, regardless of where or how we live, God is present in every moment of our lives. Whether we are movers and shakers on Wall Street or live from paycheck to paycheck, we can make God's reign a reality in our own time and place through our faithfulness to the Gospel values of servanthood, reconciliation, justice, and peace. We are called to bring others to Jesus, to show others all that God has done for us and help them realize their own gifts and potential to greatness. As John and Andrew and Philip introduced the Messiah to their followers and family, we are called to point to the Messiah in our selflessness and our commitment to reconciliation, justice, and peace.

## Model Universal Prayer (Prayer of the Faithful)

*Presider:* To God, the Giver of all life and the Lord of peace, let us pray.

*Response:* Lord, hear our prayer.

That Pope N. and the pastors and teachers of our church may proclaim, with courage and conviction, as did Samuel and John the Baptist, the presence of God among us . . .

That all nations and peoples may live in peace and cooperation, working together to protect the dignity and rights of every member of the human family . . .

That, in our compassion and mercy, we may bring God's healing and love to the sick, the suffering, the addicted, and the dying . . .

That our young people and students may hear God calling them to live lives of selfless service to others . . .

*Presider:* Hear, O Lord, these prayers we offer. May your Spirit dwelling within us and in the midst of this community help us to make these prayers a reality—prayers we ask in the name of Jesus, your Christ. **Amen.**

**COLLECT**

Let us pray.

*Pause for silent prayer*

Almighty ever-living God,
who govern all things,
both in heaven and on earth,
mercifully hear the pleading of your
    people
and bestow your peace on our times.
Through our Lord Jesus Christ, your Son,
who lives and reigns with you in the unity
    of the Holy Spirit,
one God, for ever and ever. **Amen.**

### FIRST READING
1 Sam 3:3b-10, 19

Samuel was sleeping in the temple of the
    Lord
    where the ark of God was.
The Lord called to Samuel, who answered,
    "Here I am."
Samuel ran to Eli and said, "Here I am.
    You called me."
"I did not call you," Eli said. "Go back to
    sleep."
So he went back to sleep.
Again the Lord called Samuel, who rose
    and went to Eli.
"Here I am," he said. "You called me."
But Eli answered, "I did not call you, my
    son. Go back to sleep."

At that time Samuel was not familiar with
    the Lord,
    because the Lord had not revealed
        anything to him as yet.
The Lord called Samuel again, for the
    third time.
Getting up and going to Eli, he said, "Here
    I am. You called me."
Then Eli understood that the Lord was
    calling the youth.
So he said to Samuel, "Go to sleep, and if
    you are called, reply,
    Speak, Lord, for your servant is
        listening."
When Samuel went to sleep in his place,
    the Lord came and revealed his
        presence,
    calling out as before, "Samuel, Samuel!"
Samuel answered, "Speak, for your
    servant is listening."

Samuel grew up, and the Lord was with
    him,
    not permitting any word of his to be
        without effect.

## RESPONSORIAL PSALM

Ps 40:2, 4, 7-8, 8-9, 10

R⁊. (8a and 9a) Here am I, Lord; I come to
do your will.

I have waited, waited for the LORD,
and he stooped toward me and heard
my cry.
And he put a new song into my mouth,
a hymn to our God.

R⁊. Here am I, Lord; I come to do your will.

Sacrifice or offering you wished not,
but ears open to obedience you gave me.
Holocausts or sin-offerings you sought not;
then said I, "Behold I come."

R⁊. Here am I, Lord; I come to do your will.

"In the written scroll it is prescribed for
me,
to do your will, O my God, is my delight,
and your law is within my heart!"

R⁊. Here am I, Lord; I come to do your will.

I announced your justice in the vast
assembly;
I did not restrain my lips, as you, O
LORD, know.

R⁊. Here am I, Lord; I come to do your will.

## SECOND READING

1 Cor 6:13c-15a, 17-20

Brothers and sisters:
The body is not for immorality, but for the
Lord,
and the Lord is for the body;
God raised the Lord and will also raise
us by his power.

Do you not know that your bodies are
members of Christ?
But whoever is joined to the Lord becomes
one Spirit with him.
Avoid immorality.
Every other sin a person commits is
outside the body,
but the immoral person sins against his
own body.
Do you not know that your body
is a temple of the Holy Spirit within
you,
whom you have from God, and that you
are not your own?
For you have been purchased at a price.
Therefore glorify God in your body.

### About Liturgy

**Ordinary Time:** This Sunday begins Ordinary Time, which is not really a season but the time between liturgical seasons. Though the Sundays we celebrate during these weeks may be simpler in solemnity compared to the Christmas or Easter seasons, "ordinary" does not necessarily describe the quality of this time. Rather, we call these weeks ordinary because they are "ordinal," a word that refers to putting things into an order. In Ordinary Time, the church counts the weeks between the liturgical seasons and orders our days through the lens of the ordinary ways we encounter Christ in daily life.

During the Christmas season, we celebrated three manifestations of Christ: on Christmas Day in Bethlehem; to the magi on Epiphany; and in the Jordan on the Baptism of the Lord. Today the manifestation continues with John the Baptist recognizing Christ as he walks by. What a fitting way to enter into this "ordinary" time where every person who walks by us just may well be Christ in disguise.

Note that Lent this year begins in exactly one month on February 14. So you have little time after the end of Christmas to finalize your plans.

### About Initiation

**Rite of Acceptance:** Today's gospel is the same one assigned for the Rite of Acceptance into the Order of Catechumens, the first public ritual celebrated by those who are unbaptized and formally entering into a period of formation. The Rite of Christian Initiation of Adults (RCIA 18) recommends that parishes set aside two or three dates during the year when the rite might be celebrated in case there are inquirers ready to take this first public step. This Sunday's readings fit the meaning of this ritual well, which symbolizes God's call to a person and that person's response to God's initiative.

Remember, however, that if you celebrate this rite today, the person who becomes a catechumen through this rite normatively must remain within the catechumenate for at least one year before he or she could be considered ready for baptism. This is because a person who is just beginning to know and enter into an intimate relationship with Christ can only encounter the fullness of the mystery of Christ as it is unfolded during the course of one full liturgical year. Therefore, in ordinary cases, anyone who celebrates this rite today should not be baptized at this coming Easter Vigil. See the United States National Statutes for the Catechumenate (6) for more information.

### About Liturgical Music

**Music suggestions:** The first reading today reminds us of the well-loved song by Dan Schutte, "Here I Am, Lord." This certainly would be a fitting piece for the assembly to sing today. However, take care to not schedule this setting as today's responsorial psalm. Although the refrain of Schutte's song is similar to the antiphon for today's assigned psalm (Ps 40), the verses do not reflect the verses in the Lectionary. An option to the prescribed psalm of the day is any other fitting psalm as found in other ritual books or one of the common psalms for Ordinary Time found in the Lectionary. See the *General Instruction of the Roman Missal* 61 for more information on these options.

Because this period of Ordinary Time is so short, if you plan to use a different Mass setting than the one you used for Christmas, consider singing the same Mass setting you will use for Lent during the next month. This will give your assembly a bit more continuity. If you choose to do this, you can distinguish these Ordinary Time weeks from those of Lent by simply changing your instrumentation. For example, in Ordinary Time, use a fuller arrangement of the Mass setting; then in Lent, consider singing the setting *a cappella* or with sparser instrumentation.

**JANUARY 14, 2018**
# SECOND SUNDAY IN ORDINARY TIME

## ✝ SPIRITUALITY

**GOSPEL ACCLAMATION**
Mark 1:15

R̸. Alleluia, alleluia.
The kingdom of God is at hand.
Repent and believe in the Gospel.
R̸. Alleluia, alleluia.

### Gospel

Mark 1:14-20; L68B

After John had been arrested,
   Jesus came to Galilee
      proclaiming the
      gospel of God:
   "This is the time of
      fulfillment.
The kingdom of God
   is at hand.
Repent, and believe in
   the gospel."

As he passed by the Sea of Galilee,
   he saw Simon and his brother
      Andrew casting their nets into
      the sea;
   they were fishermen.
Jesus said to them,
   "Come after me, and I will make you
      fishers of men."
Then they abandoned their nets and
   followed him.
He walked along a little farther
   and saw James, the son of Zebedee,
      and his brother John.
They too were in a boat mending their
   nets.
Then he called them.
So they left their father Zebedee in the
   boat
   along with the hired men and
      followed him.

### Reflecting on the Gospel

Cycle B means we are reading primarily from the Gospel of Mark, even though last week we read from the Gospel of John, and heard about the call of the first disciples, Andrew, and an unnamed disciple. This week we have a different version, Mark's version, of the call of the first disciples. Though Andrew is still part of the story, we do not have the "unnamed disciple" from the Gospel of John.

There are some significant differences between last week's story and this. For one, in last week's story Andrew and his companion were initially followers of John the Baptist. After the Baptist pointed out Jesus, they began to follow him.

In Mark's story Jesus is walking along the Sea of Galilee when he calls the brothers Simon and Andrew. They abandon their nets and follow him. He then calls the brothers James and John, sons of Zebedee. All four become Jesus' followers that day, whereas Zebedee is left holding the net!

The sons of Zebedee are critical figures in the Synoptic stories as opposed to the Gospel of John. In fact, we only hear of the "sons of Zebedee" in the epilogue of the Gospel of John (chap. 21), but nowhere in the first twenty chapters. Even in John 21 we don't learn their names. They are merely the sons of Zebedee.

But the image Mark paints for us is different. He gives us their names and depicts them as giving themselves in complete dedication to following Jesus. All is abandoned in their pursuit of him.

In this story we also hear something of the preaching of Jesus, which to a certain degree echoed that of John the Baptist. Jesus' preaching will be developed and expanded throughout the Gospel of Mark, but at this early stage it is centered around the twofold command, "Repent, and believe."

The story is certainly idealized for dramatic effect; we only need to look at the Gospel of John to see another version of Andrew and Peter being called by Jesus. But what is Mark telling us by narrating the story the way he does? Certainly that these first disciples left everything in a single-minded pursuit of Jesus. As such, they represent the ideal. Still, as we will learn throughout this gospel, the disciples did not often live up to that ideal. And perhaps this is another lesson of Mark's story. Our beginnings can be filled with such idealism, promise, and pure-hearted devotion. Only later will "reality" begin to sink in and our failings and shortcomings become apparent, as they no doubt will with the disciples.

### Living the Paschal Mystery

Think back to the first time you fell in love, not a crush, but a true love. The emotional, spiritual, intellectual connection was undoubtedly strong and probably seemed like it would last forever. That's also the way the love songs often sing of it. Yet, those initial stages inevitably recede and the grind of daily life looms larger. At that point the love may have developed into something deeper, stronger. Or perhaps it died out altogether and is now only a happy memory.

Something similar often happens with a faith life, and the disciples were not immune to this. Today we hear the story about how they started out strong, abandoning everything to follow Jesus. We know that Simon Peter will eventually confess Jesus as the Christ. And later, Peter will deny three times that he even knows him. The relationship that starts out with such promise, even reaching soaring heights, can truly crash and burn. This happened with the disciples; it can happen with us.

Our faith life might start out strong. It might need to be rekindled from time to time. We might need to go to the well of that initial experience of falling in love to draw sustenance and inspiration. And yet, there may be times when we effectively hang it up or abandon it, as Peter did. In those times we know that Jesus still sought Peter. Peter was forgiven and brought back into the fold. There will be another example later in this gospel of a disciple who abandoned Jesus and did not seek forgiveness. His end was not like Peter's. Our living relationship with Christ is not a one-time exhilarating moment, but, like all relationships, it is a lifelong give and take, wax and wane, love and be loved.

## Focusing the Gospel
*Mark 1:14-20*

Jesus began his ministry by calling simple fishermen to be his most trusted co-workers. Although the Twelve were hardly scholars or men wise in the ways of the world, Jesus saw beyond their gruff simplicity to call forth from them their faith, sincerity, and goodness. As Mark's gospel unfolds each Sunday this year, the first disciples will misunderstand Jesus (if not miss the point entirely), desert him, and even deny and betray him—but Jesus maintains his trust in them.

In this rabbi from Nazareth, the day of the Messiah has dawned; but newness demands change: a "turning away" (the original meaning of the word *repentance*) from business as usual to a complete trust in the life and love of God. Simon and Andrew's "abandoning" of their nets and James and John's "abandoning" of their father in today's gospel illustrate the total trust and commitment Jesus wants of those who would be his disciples.

## Focusing the First Reading
*Jonah 3:1-5, 10*

At first, Jonah (of the three-days-in-the-belly-of-the-whale fame) wants no part of being God's prophet. When first sent by God to Nineveh, Jonah refuses to go, believing that the city deserved to be destroyed. He resents God's mercy to the hated capital city of Assyria. But, in his near tragic ocean voyage to escape God, Jonah comes to realize that any individual, tribe, or nation (not just Israel) can *turn* ("repent") to the Lord and be reconciled in God's kindness and peace—even the wicked Ninevites.

## Focusing the Responsorial Psalm
*Ps 25:4-5, 6-7, 8-9 (4a)*

We can imagine a repentant Jonah praying Psalm 25 in the wake of his disastrous attempt to escape God's call to be his prophet to the Ninevites. The psalmist prays for wisdom that he might humbly walk the path God has set him on. The psalm acknowledges (as Jonah comes to realize) that God extends his mercy and salvation to all who turn to him.

## Focusing the Second Reading
*1 Cor 7:29-31*

Paul and the first Christians believed that Jesus' return at the end of time was imminent—they fully expected Jesus to appear in their lifetimes. For Paul and his contemporaries, time was growing short; much needed to be done to prepare for Christ's return. Despite the near alarmist urgency of today's second reading, Paul writes of the impermanence of our relationships and possessions in this world, a world that "is passing away."

---

**PROMPTS FOR HOMILISTS, CATECHISTS, AND RCIA TEAMS**

What "fishing nets" must we "abandon" if we are to follow Jesus?

Who are Jesus' most unlikely disciples among us today?

How have Jesus' teachings on forgiveness, compassion, and healing been the beginnings of new possibilities in your life?

What do you find to be the most difficult aspect of "following" Jesus?

### Model Penitential Act

*Presider:* As we prepare to celebrate this Eucharist, let us begin by calling to mind our sins and failings, in the certain hope of God's forgiveness. *[pause]*

You show the humble your way: Lord, have mercy.

You guide the poor and brokenhearted to justice: Christ, have mercy.

You remember us all in your love and kindness: Lord, have mercy.

### Homily Points

• Being the "fisher" that Jesus calls us to be does not require us to cast our nets very far. The values we instill in our children, the help we offer to neighbors and friends, our contributions to our church and community realize the vision Jesus articulates in today's gospel. To follow Christ means "abandoning our nets" of self-interest to embrace the needs of others and taking the difficult path of humility and selflessness. If we are going to be "fishers of men," we have to cast our nets into waters that are turbulent and unfamiliar, that threaten the safety and security of our small boats.

• In the liturgical year ahead, we will hear Jesus speak often of the "kingdom of God." The challenge for many of us will be to redefine that kingdom from what we hope and expect it to be and what God calls it to be. The word "repent" (*metanoia*) is more accurately translated as a change of heart and perspective. Jesus calls us to abandon our "fishing nets" of self-interest to seek, instead, happiness and peace for others; he shows us a bigger world than our own little Galilees and invites us to follow him in establishing the reign of God through forgiveness, reconciliation, and generosity. In Jesus, the time for hope in God's justice and forgiveness has come; the light of God's peace illuminates our incomplete and hidden understanding of authentic happiness and peace.

• When Jesus began his ministry, he did not go to the ranks of "professional" religious to be his coworkers; he entrusted his Gospel to good, hardworking fishermen. In doing so, Jesus underscores that his call to discipleship is extended to every one of us, regardless of occupation. That is the challenge of Jesus' call to discipleship: to use our skills and knowledge for the common good rather than for personal profit or fame; to seek reconciliation and forgiveness when the rest of the world demands vengeance; to see Christ in the faces of those who have been written off by society; to embrace the role of servant when the conventional wisdom dictates "me first."

### Model Universal Prayer (Prayer of the Faithful)

*Presider:* To the God of mercy, let us pray.

*Response:* Lord, hear our prayer.

That the church's bishops, priests, deacons, ministers, and teachers may proclaim the mercy of God to all . . .

That the world's nations and peoples may come together to establish God's kingdom of peace and justice on earth . . .

That we may imitate the compassion of Christ the Healer in our outreach to the poor and forgotten and in our care for the sick, the suffering, and the dying . . .

That our worship and work together as a parish may be the means for others to come to God . . .

*Presider:* Timeless and eternal God, hear our prayers. Help us to realize that your gift of time is not the end or limit of this life but the pathway to the complete and perfect life of the Risen One, in whose name we offer these prayers. **Amen.**

---

**COLLECT**

Let us pray.

*Pause for silent prayer*

Almighty ever-living God,
direct our actions according to your good
   pleasure,
that in the name of your beloved Son
we may abound in good works.
Through our Lord Jesus Christ, your Son,
who lives and reigns with you in the unity
   of the Holy Spirit,
one God, for ever and ever. **Amen.**

**FIRST READING**

Jonah 3:1-5, 10

The word of the LORD came to Jonah,
   saying:
   "Set out for the great city of Nineveh,
   and announce to it the message that I
      will tell you."
So Jonah made ready and went to Nineveh,
   according to the LORD's bidding.
Now Nineveh was an enormously large
   city;
   it took three days to go through it.
Jonah began his journey through the city,
   and had gone but a single day's walk
      announcing,
   "Forty days more and Nineveh shall be
      destroyed,"
   when the people of Nineveh believed
      God;
   they proclaimed a fast
   and all of them, great and small, put on
      sackcloth.

When God saw by their actions how they
   turned from their evil way,
   he repented of the evil that he had
      threatened to do to them;
   he did not carry it out.

## RESPONSORIAL PSALM
Ps 25:4-5, 6-7, 8-9

R̸. (4a) Teach me your ways, O Lord.

Your ways, O LORD, make known to me;
  teach me your paths,
guide me in your truth and teach me,
  for you are God my savior.

R̸. Teach me your ways, O Lord.

Remember that your compassion, O LORD,
  and your love are from of old.
In your kindness remember me,
  because of your goodness, O LORD.

R̸. Teach me your ways, O Lord.

Good and upright is the LORD;
  thus he shows sinners the way.
He guides the humble to justice
  and teaches the humble his way.

R̸. Teach me your ways, O Lord.

## SECOND READING
1 Cor 7:29-31

I tell you, brothers and sisters, the time is
  running out.
From now on, let those having wives act
  as not having them,
  those weeping as not weeping,
  those rejoicing as not rejoicing,
  those buying as not owning,
  those using the world as not using it
  fully.
For the world in its present form is
  passing away.

## About Liturgy

**Hearing is believing:** Have you ever noticed how central hearing is in the Scriptures? God's first act was to speak. Who was meant to hear? If the Creator creates by speaking and our Savior is the "Word made flesh," then we have been created to hear what God speaks and to proclaim what we have heard. Yet we've become so tied to our visual sense. Much of our time is spent looking, scanning, scrolling, watching. We've lost the art of listening with the "ear of our heart," as St. Benedict instructed. Our faith is handed down from ear to heart and back out through our mouths to repeat the cycle for any who would listen. Perhaps today's readings are *calling* us to close our eyes, turn off the screens, put away the missalette, and just listen. Listen to what Jonah *announces*. Hear what Jesus *proclaims*. Attend to his *call* to follow.

**Proclaiming is different than reading:** One way we can attune our ears is to practice liturgical hearing and proclamation. The spoken and sung word in ritual is symbolic. It resists being didactic or pragmatic, because the exchange of words is not about exchanging information but about opening hearts to one another and to Christ, the Logos. Liturgical hearing and proclamation is a form of communion—common union—because if we really hear what has been proclaimed, our hearts will be moved to respond by opening our lives to others and putting into action what we have heard. For when God speaks, something new is created: new faith, courage, hope, wisdom, life. Here are some ways to practice liturgical hearing and proclamation:

1. Read and pray with the Sunday readings during the week before coming to church.
2. Avoid the temptation to read along as the lector or psalmist proclaims the Scripture. Just actively listen and respond.
3. If you're a lector or psalmist, commit each week to doing one thing to help you believe what you will read or sing on Sunday. Work on one thing this year to improve your proclamation skills.
4. Attend to what you say from the moment you arrive at church to the moment you leave. Your words have great power to build up or destroy a person's faith.
5. At liturgy, communicate with your actions and body language, not just your words.

## About Liturgical Music

**Introducing bilingual music:** For most in the United States, having people who live within your parish boundaries who speak languages other than English is simply a reality. Though some may say that there aren't any Spanish-speakers, for example, in their parish, as soon as you provide a liturgy or pastoral service in Spanish, you'll discover that the adage is true: If you build it, they will come.

How do you introduce music in another language when most, if not all, of your music ministers do not speak it? The most important step is to remember that this is not about language but about relationship. Sharing one another's languages is a tool for entering into deeper friendship and love for one another. A second step is to explore common repertoire. Today's gospel is a great invitation to try a beloved song in Spanish, "Pescador de Hombres," meaning "fisher of men," by Cesáreo Gabaráin (OCP). In English, this song is known as "Lord, You Have Come." In your English-speaking choir, learn the melody and English text. Then, if you know a music minister from your Spanish-speaking community, invite him or her to teach your English-speaking choir just the Spanish words of the refrain. Better yet, go to the Spanish Mass and listen to the assembly sing it and join in with them. When you begin to sing the Spanish text at your English Mass, don't feel you have to sing the entire song in Spanish. Like relationship-building, let it be a gradual and long-term process. The goal is not perfection but communion.

## ✠ SPIRITUALITY

**GOSPEL ACCLAMATION**
Matt 4:16

R̸. Alleluia, alleluia.
The people who sit in darkness have seen a great
    light;
on those dwelling in a land overshadowed by
    death,
light has arisen.
R̸. Alleluia, alleluia.

### Gospel  Mark 1:21-28; L71B

Then they came to Capernaum,
    and on the sabbath Jesus entered the
        synagogue and taught.
The people were astonished at his teaching,
    for he taught them as one having authority
        and not as the scribes.
In their synagogue was a man with an unclean
        spirit;
    he cried out, "What have you to do with us,
        Jesus of Nazareth?
Have you come to destroy us?
I know who you are—the Holy One of God!"
Jesus rebuked him and said,
    "Quiet! Come out of him!"
The unclean spirit convulsed him and with a
        loud cry came out of him.
All were amazed and asked one another,
    "What is this?
A new teaching with authority.
He commands even the unclean spirits and
        they obey him."
His fame spread everywhere throughout the
        whole region of Galilee.

### Reflecting on the Gospel

Having called his first four disciples, Jesus goes to the village of Capernaum on the Sea of Galilee, where he begins to teach in the synagogue. He is confronted by evil, a man with an unclean spirit. There is a foreshadowing here as we know that in the end, Jesus will lose his life in a confrontation with evil. What the reader knew from the beginning of Mark's gospel, namely, that Jesus was the Messiah, the Son of God (1:1), the man with the unclean spirit shouts out, "I know who you are—the Holy One of God!" No human being, only the spirits, call Jesus this during his earthly ministry. The only human being to call him "the Son of God" will be the centurion, and only after he has witnessed Jesus die on the cross (15:39). Jesus' mission necessarily involves a confrontation with evil, suffering, and death, only after which his true identity as "Son of God" can be proclaimed by a human being.

As we have it in this story, Jesus commands the evil spirit to come out of the man, and it obeys, though not without dramatic theatrics. The assembled people were understandably amazed. And, not surprisingly, Jesus' reputation spread.

As we will learn later in the gospel, Jesus' wonder-working will be tempered with suffering and ultimately death. We have here not the lilies-of-the-field Jesus but the Jesus who encounters, battles, and is victorious over evil.

The term "authority" is used twice in this story. Jesus' teaching is not like the others, for he teaches with authority. As if to demonstrate the authority Jesus wields, even the unclean spirit obeys him. If any wondered about his teaching authority, they need look no further than the man from whom the unclean spirit was expelled.

It is significant too that the disciples were with Jesus during this encounter. We see that no sooner had the disciples been called by Jesus to be his followers than did they encounter evil. The disciples are in relationship with Jesus, and as such they witness the opposition he faces. Later they will encounter similar opposition. Even though the gospel does not tell the story, we, like those in Mark's community, know that many of Jesus' disciples lost their lives too in confrontations with evil.

### Living the Paschal Mystery

Perhaps we do not like to hear it, but the Christian life (and, in fact, any life) is riddled by encounters with evil. We learn in today's gospel that Jesus is more powerful than that. Jesus has authority and by that authority he can dispel what is oppositional and troublesome. Once we become followers of Jesus we will still encounter challenges and hostility. Some might wish to think that becoming Christian inoculates one from having those encounters. But the gospel (and our own lived experience) tells a different story.

Even though we will continue to face such encounters, we are comforted in knowing that Jesus has authority over all. A preacher once phrased it this way: "Rest assured in your baptism." By that he meant that our baptism configures us to Christ, who will be with us. Of course, this doesn't mean that we disregard precautions, or that we walk around in a state of naïveté. Remember that Jesus himself was killed. It does mean that we have an ally, the author of life. Once we know this, we can rest assured. Even death itself is not the final word.

### Focusing the Gospel

*Mark 1:21-28*

For the Jews of Jesus' time, the scribes were the voices of authority, the final arbiters of the law. Their status was centered in their ability to read and write, a skill possessed by less than 10 percent of the population. Their interpretation of the law was considered absolute.

"Unclean spirits" (the phrase Mark uses for "demons") are encountered several times in Mark's gospel. Any condition or behavior that could not be explained or understood, such as disease, mental illness, or bizarre or criminal behavior, was considered the physical manifestations of the evil one—"demons" or "unclean spirits."

Both the unclean spirits and the skeptical scribes are silenced in today's gospel. Jesus' casting out the unclean spirit from the possessed man silences the demons of hatred and division that plague humanity. In his compassionate outreach to the poor and sick, Jesus "silences" the scribes by redefining their understanding of authority: whereas the "authority" of the scribes' words is based solely on their perceived status and learnedness, the authority of Jesus is born of compassion, peace, and justice. The casting out of the demons and his curing of the sick are manifestations of the power and grace of his words.

Note that the people of the Bible viewed these deeds differently than we might. Even the Gospel of Mark uses the term "mighty deed" rather than "miracle." While we, in our high-tech, scientific approach to the world, might dismiss miracles as some kind of disruption or "overriding" of the laws of nature, the contemporaries of Jesus saw these mighty deeds as signs of God's immediate activity in his creation. While we ask, *How could this happen?* they asked, *Who is responsible for this happening?* Those who witnessed Jesus' healings saw these mighty deeds as God directly touching their lives.

## Focusing the First Reading

*Deut 18:15-20*

Today's first reading, from the book of Deuteronomy, recounts God's promise to raise up a successor to Moses—a promise Christians saw as ultimately fulfilled in Jesus. But Moses cautions the Israelite tribes to listen with careful and wise discernment to those who claim to speak with the authority of the prophetic office, to be clear in their own minds and hearts that a "prophet" speaks the authentic word of God with humility and integrity.

## Focusing the Responsorial Psalm

*Ps 95:1-2, 6-7, 7-9 (8)*

For more than twenty-five hundred years, Psalm 95 has invited God's people to worship at the beginning of the day (it is still the first psalm sung each morning in the Liturgy of the Hours). The first verses sung today praise God for his continued saving action in our midst; the final verses are a painful reminder to Israel of its revolt against God in the wilderness during the exodus and the consequences of their lack of trust in God's word.

## Focusing the Second Reading

*1 Cor 7:32-35*

Keeping in mind the social mores regarding marriage and family life in Paul's time as well as the expectation of the first Christians that the Parousia would happen in their lifetimes, today's reading from 1 Corinthians reminds the Christians of Corinth that the business of life—including our relationships—should be free from anxiety. Whether married or unmarried (and Paul believes that the unmarried should remain so), their undivided attention should be on the coming of the Lord.

---

**PROMPTS FOR HOMILISTS, CATECHISTS, AND RCIA TEAMS**

Who have you known in your life who possesses or possessed an "authority" based, not on fame or power of wealth, but on their heroic and committed sense of justice, compassion, and charity?

What "unclean spirits" do we hear "speaking" today that can be silenced or driven out, not by anger and retribution, but by the example of Jesus' compassionate outreach?

Who are the prophets in our midst today: those men and women of faith in whose mouths God places his Word?

### Model Penitential Act

*Presider:* Let us begin our celebration of these sacred mysteries by confessing our failings and sins, confident of God's mercy and grace. *[pause]*

Lord Jesus, you reconcile us to God and to one another: Lord, have mercy.

Lord Jesus, you shepherd us in the ways of God: Christ, have mercy.

Lord Jesus, you drive out the unclean spirits of sin that possess us: Lord, have mercy.

### Homily Points

• True authority is empowered by persuasion, not coercion; effective leadership is a matter of articulating a shared goal rather than warning of the consequences of failure. Jesus' "authority" inspires rather than enforces; he sees his call to "lead" as a trust, as a responsibility to serve others by revealing the God who calls us to compassion and mercy for the sake of his kingdom of peace. To possess the authority of the gospel Jesus is to become men and women of empathy, compassion, and selflessness for those we are called to teach, to guide, and to serve.

• The "unclean spirit" that Jesus casts out of the poor man in today's gospel is the voice of evil that sometimes speaks within us: the voice of revenge, self-centeredness, self-righteousness, greed, anger. The fear of letting go, those narrow attitudes and perceptions we cling to are the "unclean spirits" we all possess—or possess us: "unclean spirits" that disable us from extending compassion and kindness, "unclean spirits" that scare us from making the moral and ethical decision, "unclean spirits" that limit our perception to our own wants and needs. In our own acts of compassion and generosity, we can speak with the voice of Christ to drive out the unclean spirits that possess our minds and hearts and dispossess us of the things of God.

• Scribes were experts in the finer points regarding application of Mosaic law. Because they possessed the ability to read and write (unlike most of the population), they were well-regarded by others and indeed themselves! Oftentimes they focused on the finer points to such a degree that they missed the larger point. Today we might say they missed the forest for the trees. This can be a temptation for each of us who is well-versed in a given subject. We can become experts in trivial detail. We are reminded that Jesus was able to see the bigger picture and make that the focus of his teaching and preaching.

### Model Universal Prayer (Prayer of the Faithful)

*Presider:* With thanks for his many blessings to us and confident of his continued grace, let us offer our prayers to our Father in heaven.

*Response:* Lord, hear our prayer.

For Pope N. and the bishops, priests, and ministers of the church, that they lead and serve with the authority of Jesus' compassion and humility . . .

For the leaders of nations and officers of governments, that they may lead and act with the authority of their own dedication and commitment to the justice and wisdom of God . . .

For the sick, the suffering, the troubled, and the dying, that the love of Christ may drive out from their lives the "unclean spirits" of anxiety, despair, and suffering . . .

For married couples and their families in our community, that the peace of Christ may dwell in their homes and hearts . . .

*Presider:* Father of mercy, hear these prayers and instill in us your Spirit that, in imitating your Son's humble generosity and reconciling peace, we may bring these prayers to reality. In Jesus' name, we pray. **Amen.**

**COLLECT**

Let us pray.

*Pause for silent prayer*

Grant us, Lord our God,
that we may honor you with all our mind,
and love everyone in truth of heart.
Through our Lord Jesus Christ, your Son,
who lives and reigns with you in the unity
    of the Holy Spirit,
one God, for ever and ever. **Amen.**

**FIRST READING**

Deut 18:15-20

Moses spoke to all the people, saying:
    "A prophet like me will the LORD, your
        God, raise up for you
    from among your own kin;
    to him you shall listen.
This is exactly what you requested of the
        LORD, your God, at Horeb
    on the day of the assembly, when you
        said,
    'Let us not again hear the voice of the
        LORD, our God,
    nor see this great fire any more, lest we
        die.'
And the LORD said to me, 'This was well
        said.
I will raise up for them a prophet like you
        from among their kin,
    and will put my words into his mouth;
    he shall tell them all that I command
        him.
Whoever will not listen to my words
        which he speaks in my name,
    I myself will make him answer for it.
But if a prophet presumes to speak in my
        name
    an oracle that I have not commanded
        him to speak,
    or speaks in the name of other gods, he
        shall die.'"

## RESPONSORIAL PSALM

Ps 95:1-2, 6-7, 7-9

R̸. (8) If today you hear his voice, harden not your hearts.

Come, let us sing joyfully to the LORD;
  let us acclaim the rock of our salvation.
Let us come into his presence with thanksgiving;
  let us joyfully sing psalms to him.

R̸. If today you hear his voice, harden not your hearts.

Come, let us bow down in worship;
  let us kneel before the LORD who made us.
For he is our God,
  and we are the people he shepherds, the flock he guides.

R̸. If today you hear his voice, harden not your hearts.

Oh, that today you would hear his voice:
  "Harden not your hearts as at Meribah,
    as in the day of Massah in the desert,
  where your fathers tempted me;
    they tested me though they had seen my works."

R̸. If today you hear his voice, harden not your hearts.

## SECOND READING

1 Cor 7:32-35

Brothers and sisters:
I should like you to be free of anxieties.
An unmarried man is anxious about the things of the Lord,
  how he may please the Lord.
But a married man is anxious about the things of the world,
  how he may please his wife, and he is divided.
An unmarried woman or a virgin is anxious about the things of the Lord,
  so that she may be holy in both body and spirit.
A married woman, on the other hand, is anxious about the things of the world,
  how she may please her husband.
I am telling you this for your own benefit,
  not to impose a restraint upon you,
  but for the sake of propriety
  and adherence to the Lord without distraction.

### About Liturgy

**Reclaiming authority:** We need to reclaim a few words in our church today. "Traditional" doesn't mean old or stodgy; it means being connected to something bigger than oneself. "Hierarchy" is not code for "whatever Father wants"; it describes how we all matter and must all do our part. And "authority" isn't about power. It's about being authentic and true to one's self and the community. It requires integrating one's experience into the current situation and speaking prophetically with wisdom, prudence, compassion, and courage. Authority is not lauded over others but is shared to draw the community together to act with confidence and hope only if necessary.

Our leaders and all who participate in the liturgy have authority, not because of any title or degree. We have authority when what we say and do together is "of God" through Christ in the Spirit, flowing from our baptismal rights and responsibilities. We have authority when we know where we have come from as a universal church and a local community and have listened to the wisdom of both those who have come before us and those who are the young church, called to be prophets for today. We have authority when we do not choke our communities with rigid rubricism but we use the tradition and rubrics to attend with creativity and compassion to the needs of real people seeking real hope for the real demons from which they suffer.

Most of all, we have authority when all we say and do is done with the abundant and merciful love of God, the author of love, who spoke with human love through Jesus, and who continues to speak through us, the people of God.

**Preaching with authority:** Clergy have a grave responsibility here, as their liturgical preaching affects how the laity will, in turn, proclaim Christ to the world. Today's readings show how homilists can preach with greater authority. Moses announced to the people that one of their own would rise up to speak in God's name. Jesus, one like us yet never sinned, spoke with authority directly to the demons of his day. Homilists cannot stand apart from the people to whom they preach, speaking as if they were a separate class. Those who preach with authority must know the community, understand their pain and suffering, share their joys and griefs, and speak in their language in ways that move their hearts. In other words, the homilist begins with the people and "interprets peoples' lives" through the Scriptures (*Fulfilled in Your Hearing*, 52), or as Pope Francis says, they must be "shepherds living with the smell of the sheep" (Chrism Mass homily, March 28, 2013).

When homilists speak from their genuine concern and knowledge of their assembly's lives, then the assembly will, at the end of every Mass, be able to "go and announce the Gospel of the Lord."

### About Liturgical Music

**Singing with authority:** Bono, the lead singer for the rock band U2, made headlines in early 2016 when he said he wished that modern Christian music would be more honest like the psalms. He's right. The psalms run the gamut of human emotion: rage, anger, joy, hopeless despair, unwarranted hope. Why should our other liturgical songs not have the same authenticity?

Composers and those who select the music for our assemblies each week have the great opportunity and responsibility to help us sing with the authority of Jesus, who commanded even demons to obey him. Seek out strong texts and sturdy melodies, and don't shy away from challenging lyrics. One hymn to consider for this week that places our power within the authoritative power of Christ is Marty Haugen's "God Is Still Speaking" (GIA Publications).

**JANUARY 28, 2018**
# FOURTH SUNDAY IN ORDINARY TIME

## ✝ SPIRITUALITY

**GOSPEL ACCLAMATION**
Matt 8:17

℟. Alleluia, alleluia.
Christ took away our infirmities
and bore our diseases.
℟. Alleluia, alleluia.

### Gospel

Mark 1:29-39; L74B

On leaving the synagogue
  Jesus entered the house of Simon
      and Andrew with James and
      John.
Simon's mother-in-law lay sick with
  a fever.
They immediately told him about
  her.
He approached, grasped her
  hand, and helped her up.
Then the fever left her and she
  waited on them.

When it was evening, after sunset,
  they brought to him all who were ill
      or possessed by demons.
The whole town was gathered at the
  door.
He cured many who were sick with
  various diseases,
  and he drove out many demons,
  not permitting them to speak because they knew him.

Rising very early before dawn, he left
  and went off to a deserted place,
      where he prayed.
Simon and those who were with him
  pursued him
  and on finding him said, "Everyone is
      looking for you."
He told them, "Let us go on to the
  nearby villages
  that I may preach there also.
For this purpose have I come."
So he went into their synagogues,
  preaching and driving out demons
      throughout the whole of Galilee.

### Reflecting on the Gospel

Sometimes when children are excited and tell stories of their latest adventures, they can skip over details, jumping from one tale to the next. "And then" is a common conjunction joining these hurried sentences that quickly moves the narrative forward, often in fits and starts. The excitement definitely carries the story. The listener (maybe even a parent!) is often left wondering exactly what happened. There are a number of questions left unanswered, but one thing is clear: "This was exciting!"

Something similar is happening in the first chapter of Mark, indeed some would say it happens throughout the entire Gospel of Mark! We see this excitement and hurried storytelling on prominent display in today's reading. Though we have only a few verses, there are at least three distinct vignettes.

The action begins in Capernaum, where Jesus has been preaching in the synagogue. He and his new disciples (for they were called by Jesus only a few verses earlier) go to the house of the brothers Simon and Andrew. There Simon's mother-in-law is healed. Too many bad jokes have already been told about healing Simon's "mother-in-law," and the preacher is advised against adding to the list. Still, a few things are clear: Simon (Peter) had a wife; and the extended family, including at least his brother and his mother-in-law, lived under the same roof. This is family togetherness that many middle-class people in the United States may no longer experience.

This particular home must have been a welcoming place. Not only was it the location of such an extended family, but James and John were also with them that day. And by evening it seemed the entire town was at the door! Jesus cured many of the townspeople before leaving early the next day.

Though Capernaum formed something of a base for his Galilean ministry, Jesus still needed to get away from time to time as the last short story in today's reading reminds us. But even a few moments of solitude were nearly beyond reach as Jesus tells his disciples that he came for one purpose: to preach.

The action and excitement covered in this brief period is palpable. In one sense it covers only twenty-four hours before concluding with a sentence that says he went throughout the whole of Galilee preaching and driving out demons. Jesus has a purpose and his followers are witness to it. It's as though there is no time to spare, not even a predawn moment to himself, for that is filled with prayer.

Excitement fills the air with the wonders Jesus does.

### Living the Paschal Mystery

At times our busied lives can seem frenetic, simply moving from one activity to the next with barely a moment in between. We imagine "the good old days" when things weren't so harried. It's true that technology has perhaps increased our attention (or lack thereof) to many details, but time marches along at the same pace it always has for us. Years, months, days, and even hours and minutes may seem to move more quickly than before, but in reality it's been moving at a constant pace for many centuries. Most of us feel the pressure of time because we are driven by a purpose. There are things we need to do. And today we hear of Jesus driven by the same. He has something to accomplish. He has a purpose. Though he wakes before dawn to have some time to himself, even that sacred moment quickly vanishes in the midst of the day's activities. Simply being busy or having things to accomplish is not a bad thing. In fact, it can be the opposite. Today we have a chance to reflect on what motivates us. For what purpose are we driven? Are we taking time to pray, brief as it may be? Even when we do find a moment of solitude, the needs of others come before our own needs.

## Focusing the Gospel
*Mark 1:29-39*

Today's gospel is the second of three miracles in the first chapter of Mark's gospel: the casting out of the unclean spirit (last Sunday's gospel), the curing of Peter's mother-in-law (today's gospel), and the cleansing of the leper (next Sunday's gospel). Of note in today's gospel is the Greek word that Mark uses to describe the woman's cure. The Lectionary text reads that Jesus "helped her up"—but a more accurate translation of the Greek is Jesus "raised her up." Mark will use the same word to describe Jesus' resurrection. The English text then reads that Simon's mother-in-law "waited" on them, but the Greek is more accurately rendered as she "served" them. The life of the Risen One, who comes "not to be served but to serve," is one of compassionate and selfless giving and service to others. Throughout his gospel, Mark portrays Jesus as somewhat uncomfortable with his growing renown as a miracle worker. He clearly values time away from the crowds to be alone to pray—even though that time is cut short by the needs of those around him.

Jesus works miracles not out of any need of his own for the adulation of the masses but out of an extraordinary sense of compassion and love for those who come to him in crisis or pain. The miracles he works are not to solicit acclaim for himself but to awaken faith and trust in the word of God, to restore in humankind God's vision of a world united as brothers and sisters under his providence ("For this purpose have I come"). Jesus' compassion for those who come to him breaks down stereotypes and defenses that divide, segregate, and marginalize people; his ministry is not to restore bodies to health but to restore spirits to wholeness.

## Focusing the First Reading
*Job 7:1-4, 6-7*

The brokenness and despair, the alienation of estrangement from God that is the lot of many souls is movingly portrayed in this brief reflection by Job. The Jesus of the gospel enters such broken and defeated lives to restore them to hope and meaning.

## Focusing the Responsorial Psalm
*Ps 147:1-2, 3-4, 5-6*

The first third of Psalm 147, today's responsorial, is a hymn of praise to the God who heals those broken in body or spirit, the God who brings home the scattered and exiled, the God who lifts up the poor and powerless.

## Focusing the Second Reading
*1 Cor 9:16-19, 22-23*

In a sophisticated metropolitan city like Corinth, freedom of thought and the exercise of one's rights were highly valued; to surrender one's freedom was considered anathema to the citizens of Corinth. But, in today's excerpt from his First Letter to the Corinthians, Paul writes that he places his freedom at the service of others, as did Christ: we are to make oneself "weak" for the sake of the "weak," to become a "slave" to others for the sake of the Gospel.

---

**PROMPTS FOR HOMILISTS, CATECHISTS, AND RCIA TEAMS**

Have you known someone who, despite the pain and trauma he or she has endured, still manages to live a life of purpose and joy?

Is there a "demon" that you struggle to "cast out" of your life?

In what realistic and authentic ways can and should the Gospel influence such public arenas as politics, business, education, sports, and family life?

How would you respond to Job's lament in today's first reading?

Do you have a "deserted place" in your life where or when you are alone with God?

## Model Penitential Act

**Presider:** Let us open our hearts to the healing mercy of God by humbly acknowledging our sins and failings. *[pause]*

Lord Jesus, you lift up the sinner and grasp the falling: Lord, have mercy.

Lord Jesus, you heal the sick and brokenhearted: Christ, have mercy.

Lord Jesus, you reveal to us the hope of the kingdom of God: Lord, have mercy.

## Homily Points

• Traumatic experiences, emotional disasters, and shattered dreams trap us, enslave us, cripple us; such "demons" so drain us of hope that we may easily surrender to them. In today's gospel, Jesus drives out the demons that have destroyed the lives of those possessed. Healing was a central part of Jesus' ministry: he sought to restore the sick, the suffering, the desperate, and the lost. Jesus' healings reveal the kingdom of God as a present reality: where no one should go hungry, be imprisoned or enslaved by the tragedies of life, or be left to stumble and fall alone in the darkness. Christ calls us to the work of driving out "demons" that divide our families, sever friendships, and rend our spirits in hopelessness by the power of our own compassion, forgiveness, and understanding.

• In today's gospel, the evangelist Mark includes the short but important detail that Jesus, in the midst of his demanding preaching and healing ministry, seeks out a "deserted," out-of-the-way place to pray. We all need that deserted place in our lives where we can reconnect with God. That "deserted" place may be a set time for prayer every day or a walk in the woods, a quiet corner of our home, a book by an insightful spiritual writer, or some quiet activity like gardening or baking bread—whatever renews within us a sense of gratitude for the blessings of God's presence.

• What drives Jesus' teaching and healing ministry is compassion that uncovers the basic humanity we share with all God's children; compassion that enables us to open our hearts to others, to see one another as more than just the labels and numbers we assign to them; compassion that makes us not only feel the pain of others but compels us to seek to heal that pain. In imitating Christ's compassion, we can work our own "miracles" of charity and generosity through which our families and communities can be restored to hope and trust in the God who loves us. In our compassion and empathy, we reveal the love of God present in the midst of our families and communities.

## Model Universal Prayer (Prayer of the Faithful)

**Presider:** Let us now join our hearts and voices in prayer for our human family.

**Response:** Lord, hear our prayer.

For Pope N. and for the bishops, priests, and ministers of our church, that they may proclaim to the world the Gospel of compassion and reconciliation . . .

For President N. and the leaders of the world's nations, that the Spirit of God will inspire them to work for peace and justice among all peoples . . .

For those suffering from depression; for the victims of physical, emotional, and substance abuse; for those grieving and in despair, that God will cast out the "demons" of fear and brokenness and spark within them a light of hope . . .

For our parish, that we may be a source of healing and reconciliation in our community . . .

**Presider:** O Lord, you have walked among us; you know our pain and our brokenness. May these prayers we offer begin the mending of our relationships with one another and the healing of our hearts in your hope and peace. In Jesus' name, we pray. **Amen.**

## COLLECT

Let us pray.

*Pause for silent prayer*

Keep your family safe, O Lord, with
    unfailing care,
that, relying solely on the hope of
    heavenly grace,
they may be defended always by your
    protection.
Through our Lord Jesus Christ, your Son,
who lives and reigns with you in the unity
    of the Holy Spirit,
one God, for ever and ever. **Amen.**

## FIRST READING

Job 7:1-4, 6-7

Job spoke, saying:
    Is not man's life on earth a drudgery?
        Are not his days those of hirelings?
    He is a slave who longs for the shade,
        a hireling who waits for his wages.
    So I have been assigned months of
            misery,
        and troubled nights have been
            allotted to me.
    If in bed I say, "When shall I arise?"
        then the night drags on;
    I am filled with restlessness until the
            dawn.
    My days are swifter than a weaver's
            shuttle;
        they come to an end without hope.
    Remember that my life is like the wind;
        I shall not see happiness again.

## RESPONSORIAL PSALM

Ps 147:1-2, 3-4, 5-6

R̸. (cf. 3a) Praise the Lord, who heals the
brokenhearted.
*or:*
R̸. Alleluia.

Praise the LORD, for he is good;
sing praise to our God, for he is gracious;
it is fitting to praise him.
The LORD rebuilds Jerusalem;
the dispersed of Israel he gathers.

R̸. Praise the Lord, who heals the
brokenhearted.
*or:*
R̸. Alleluia.

He heals the brokenhearted
and binds up their wounds.
He tells the number of the stars;
he calls each by name.

R̸. Praise the Lord, who heals the
brokenhearted.
*or:*
R̸. Alleluia.

Great is our Lord and mighty in power;
to his wisdom there is no limit.
The LORD sustains the lowly;
the wicked he casts to the ground.

R̸. Praise the Lord, who heals the
brokenhearted.
*or:*
R̸. Alleluia.

## SECOND READING

1 Cor 9:16-19, 22-23

Brothers and sisters:
If I preach the gospel, this is no reason for
me to boast,
for an obligation has been imposed on
me,
and woe to me if I do not preach it!
If I do so willingly, I have a recompense,
but if unwillingly, then I have been
entrusted with a stewardship.
What then is my recompense?
That, when I preach,
I offer the gospel free of charge
so as not to make full use of my right in
the gospel.

Although I am free in regard to all,
I have made myself a slave to all
so as to win over as many as possible.
To the weak I became weak, to win over
the weak.
I have become all things to all, to save at
least some.
All this I do for the sake of the gospel,
so that I too may have a share in it.

### About Liturgy

***The purpose of healing:*** When we pray for those who are sick and ask God for healing, we are doing an act of mercy. However, the hoped-for healing is not the end-goal of our prayer or of God's action. Jesus says it plainly in today's gospel. His purpose is to preach the good news. When we or our loved ones get sick, good news is knowing that we are not alone, especially when we are at our most helpless. Sickness prevents us from doing the things we normally do. We can't enjoy the ordinary pleasures of life, and we are separated from our circle of friends and colleagues. Illness disconnects us from life and from our community, and it isolates us from the world.

Remembering the sick, praying for them, and visiting them restores that connection. It brings the people who are sick, even if they are not physically present, back into the hearts and minds of the community. And when a cure is not possible, we can still continue to preach Jesus' good news for our loved ones—that they will never be alone in their suffering. Christ is present, and we, the hands and feet of Christ, are present, too.

When recovery of health does happen, our mission to preach the good news does not end. The final purpose of healing is praise of God and service to God's people, because when the person returns to the community "with their health restored, / they may give [God] thanks in the midst of [the] Church" (Roman Missal, Mass for the Sick, Collect). This is our service, our sacrifice and offering of praise. Like Simon's mother-in-law, who, when she was healed, waited on others, we, too, use the blessing of healing to serve those in need and to continue to preach the good news of Christ.

***Celebrating the anointing of the sick:*** Whenever anyone of the baptized is in danger of death from sickness or old age, it is fitting to celebrate the sacrament of anointing of the sick. This sacrament is most often celebrated individually outside of Mass in a health care facility or a sick person's home. However there is an option to celebrate it within Mass at a church for a diocesan or parish gathering where there may be a large number of people desiring the sacrament. (See *Pastoral Care of the Sick*, 108–10, 131–48.)

The ritual Mass for anointing of the sick is permitted on Sundays in Ordinary Time, which means you have the option to use the anointing of the sick readings in the Lectionary along with the ritual Mass from the Roman Missal. The presider, who is a priest or a bishop, wears white vestments.

Because of the appropriateness of this Sunday's readings, you might consider celebrating this sacrament within one of the regular parish Sunday Masses. Be sure to discern this well and with all the liturgical staff involved before deciding this. Also, catechize the assembly well beforehand so that they can discern their need for the sacrament, since "only those whose health is seriously impaired by sickness or old age are proper subjects for the sacrament" (108).

### About Liturgical Music

***Music suggestions:*** The hymns for this Sunday should focus not only on healing but also on discipleship and praise, which is our response to God's healing. Two newer, contemporary compositions you might consider are "Christ in Me Arise" by Trevor Thomson (Spirit & Song) and "A Gift of Love" by Rufino Zaragoza, OFM (OCP). Thomson's piece has a haunting Irish quality with text that harkens back to St. Patrick's Lorica. The second piece is actually a Vietnamese hymn, which Br. Zaragoza translated into English. Pedro Rubalcava also provided Spanish text. Both pieces speak of our call to mission, having heard God's word and received God's healing.

**FEBRUARY 4, 2018**

# FIFTH SUNDAY IN ORDINARY TIME

## ✚ SPIRITUALITY

**GOSPEL ACCLAMATION**
Luke 7:16

℟. Alleluia, alleluia.
A great prophet has arisen in our midst,
God has visited his people.
℟. Alleluia, alleluia.

### Gospel

Mark 1:40-45; L77B

A leper came to Jesus and
    kneeling down begged
    him and said,
"If you wish, you can
    make me clean."
Moved with pity, he
    stretched out his
    hand,
    touched him, and
        said to him,
"I do will it. Be made
    clean."
The leprosy left him immediately,
    and he was made clean.
Then, warning him sternly, he
    dismissed him at once.

He said to him, "See that you tell no
    one anything,
    but go, show yourself to the priest
    and offer for your cleansing what
        Moses prescribed;
    that will be proof for them."

The man went away and began to
    publicize the whole matter.
He spread the report abroad
    so that it was impossible for Jesus to
        enter a town openly.
He remained outside in deserted
    places,
    and people kept coming to him from
        everywhere.

### Reflecting on the Gospel

After many weeks we have come to the conclusion of the first chapter of the Gospel of Mark. What a whirlwind it has been. From the opening sentence announcing the Gospel of Jesus Christ, son of God, to John the Baptist, the calling of disciples, casting out demons, healing the sick, including Simon's mother-in-law, preaching in synagogues, and now concluding with the healing of someone with a skin disease, the story has been like riding a roller coaster. We reach new heights and move swiftly from episode to episode.

Though our English Bibles refer to the person cured as a "leper," the term means anyone with a skin disease. An entire chapter in the book of Leviticus (13) is dedicated to diagnosing and treating skin diseases, which were broadly categorized in the ancient world as "leprosy." Verses 45-46 of that chapter in Leviticus discuss how the person with the disease is to behave, namely, by crying "unclean, unclean" before approaching others, and living apart from the community for as long as the infection lasts.

So the healing performed by Jesus is not merely a healing of the skin disease, though it is certainly that. By telling the man to show himself to the priest, Jesus is, in effect, setting up the situation so the man will be brought back into community. Once the priest declares the infection gone, the afflicted person may return as a full-fledged member of the people, without having to cry out "unclean, unclean" as he goes about his business.

It is for this reason, among others, that scholars and preachers say that Jesus' ministry was about inclusion. He ministered to those on the margins, or even outside of the community, like this person with a skin disease, and Jesus made them whole. Once whole, the excluded persons could be welcomed back.

Interestingly, even though Jesus warned the man sternly and ordered him not to tell anyone (aside from the priest), the cured man publicized the matter widely! And this publicity affected Jesus' ministry so that he was no longer able to enter towns openly. It's as though Jesus were being stalked by the ancient equivalent of the paparazzi. He was not even left alone in the "deserted places" outside the villages.

By the end of the first chapter of Mark the stage has been set. What will happen to this wonder-worker? Will his fame spread beyond the backwater of Galilee? Who else on the margins or outskirts of society will he embrace? What kind of whirlwind will this be?

### Living the Paschal Mystery

Sometimes the news is so good we can't keep it to ourselves. This might happen when someone is getting married, or having a baby, or is out of the hospital after a long illness. Our joy cannot be contained and so it was with the man afflicted with a skin disease. Even though Jesus himself told him to keep it quiet, that was simply not possible. He told everyone! The news spread throughout the region, and Jesus was left to live with the consequences. Why was the cured man so joyful? Not only because the affliction was cured, but now he was able to be restored to the community. No longer would he have to shout "unclean, unclean" before approaching anyone. Now he was whole and an integral part of the people.

Whom do we see excluded today? What is today's equivalent of an ancient skin condition? Are there groups or individuals who are effectively preceded with shouts of "unclean!"? Jesus' desire is not merely to heal the man's skin, but to restore him to the group. In effect, the healing of the leper was as much for the community as it was for the leper. The community had rejected this person and would not accept him with that condition. If we want to be like Jesus we can find those on the margins and bring them into the fold. We may not have the power to heal physical ailments, but we can certainly reach out to the marginalized and draw them close.

### Focusing the Gospel

*Mark 1:40-45*

The cleansing of the leper is a climactic moment in Mark's gospel. By just touching the leper Jesus challenges one of the strictest proscriptions in Jewish society (today's first reading provides the context for understanding the social and religious revulsion of lepers).

The leper is one of the heroic characters of Mark's gospel (along with such figures as the poor widow who gives her only penny to the temple and the blind Bartimaeus). The leper places his entire trust in Jesus. For him, there is no doubt: this Jesus is the Messiah of hope, the Lord of life. His request for healing is more than a cry for help—it is a profession of faith: "you can make me clean."

Jesus' curing of the leper shocked those who witnessed it. Jesus did not drive the leper away, as would be the norm (the leper, according to the Mosaic law, had no right to even address Jesus); instead, Jesus stretched out his hand and touched him. Jesus did not see an unclean leper but a human being in desperate need.

Consider what Jesus does after healing the leper. He sends the cleansed leper to show himself to the priest "and offer for your cleansing what Moses prescribed." This leper's healing is a sign to the Jewish establishment, represented by the priest: that the Messiah has come and is present among you.

### Focusing the First Reading

*Lev 13:1-2, 44-46*

As noted above, today's first reading, from the book of Leviticus, sets forth how "lepers"—those suffering from any kind of skin disease—are to be treated under the law.

### Focusing the Responsorial Psalm

*Ps 32:1-2, 5, 11 (7)*

The second of the seven penitential psalms, Psalm 32 expresses the joy of forgiveness and of being reconciled to God and the community. The psalmist sings his gratitude for the grace to confront one's sins and the faith to trust in God's mercy to recreate one's life in God's peace.

### Focusing the Second Reading

*1 Cor 10:31–11:1*

A great debate raged in the church of Corinth: After animal sacrifices were offered before Greek idols, the meat often found its way into the marketplace. The more scrupulous believers saw eating such pagan offerings as an affront to the one true God; others thought that eating such meat was harmless and did nothing to undermine a Christian's faithfulness. In today's second reading, Paul writes that the matter is too trivial to risk dividing the church. In all things, Paul counsels, respect one another's viewpoints and perspectives while focusing together on the faith they share in the God revealed to them by Christ Jesus.

---

**PROMPTS FOR HOMILISTS, CATECHISTS, AND RCIA TEAMS**

Who are the "lepers" in our own "villages" who frighten us and cause us to run away, lest somehow we become "contaminated"?

Have you ever felt like a "leper"—segregated, isolated, estranged, misunderstood?

What does it mean to act out of compassion?

Have you ever "wished" to act in a certain way, but did not? Have you ever found yourself in a situation in which God's presence was unmistakably clear, but you were reluctant or even afraid to acknowledge that presence?

## Model Penitential Act

*Presider:* To prepare ourselves to offer these sacred mysteries, let us call to mind our sins, trusting in the forgiveness of God. *[pause]*

O God, you are the source of all that is good: Lord, have mercy.

O God, in you we are healed and made whole: Christ, have mercy.

O God, in you we are recreated in forgiveness and hope: Lord, have mercy.

## Homily Points

• Our attitudes and perceptions often reduce others to the status of "lepers": those whose beliefs and lifestyles we fear, who don't "fit" our image of class and sophistication, whose politics or religion or race or identity differ from our own. The Christ who heals lepers comes to heal us of our debilitating sense of self that blinds us to the sacredness and dignity of those we segregate as "lepers," to heal us of our own "leprosy" so that we are able to realize again that God extends his compassion and grace even to the likes of us. Before God, no one is a leper, no one is beyond the reach of God's mercy and compassion; all of us are made in the sacred image of the God of justice, peace, and reconciliation.

• "If you wish, you can make me clean." The leper's request of Jesus is a challenge to each of us. We can transform our lives and world in the goodness of God—if we wish. Jesus' compassion makes it possible for us to perform our own miracles of healing and reconciliation: to restore to health and community those considered "lepers," to bring God's grace to the brokenhearted, lost, and despairing. We possess the means to transform our lives and world—what is required is the desire and determination to do so: to heal the broken, restore lepers to wholeness, reconcile with those from whom we are estranged.

• In today's gospel, Jesus is so moved by the plight of the leper that he risks the possibility of contracting the disease (and the censure of the community), not only curing him of his illness but inviting him to rejoin his human and religious family. Jesus works his wonders not to solicit acclaim for himself but to awaken faith in God's providence, to restore God's vision of a world where humanity is united as brothers and sisters in the love of God. Jesus calls us to let our own "miracles" of charity, mercy, forgiveness, and justice be "proof" of our committed discipleship to the Gospel and our trust in God who is the real worker of wonders in our midst.

## Model Universal Prayer (Prayer of the Faithful)

*Presider:* To the God of healing reconciliation, let us offer our prayers.

*Response:* Lord, hear our prayer.

That all who serve the church may be imitators of the humble generosity and love of Christ . . .

That respect for all, a commitment to peace and justice, and care for the good earth we all share may be the heart of all relations between nations and peoples . . .

That God's spirit of compassion may inspire the work of those who care for the sick, the suffering, and the dying and those who are the first responders in times of disaster and catastrophe . . .

That married people and those engaged to be married may reflect, in the sacrament of their life together, God's love for all his people . . .

*Presider:* Hear our prayers, O God, for all the family of humankind. Mend our broken relationships with one another; heal us of the leprosy of selfishness and injustice; make us clean and whole in your love and compassion. We offer these prayers in the name of Jesus, the Healing Christ. **Amen.**

## COLLECT

Let us pray.

*Pause for silent prayer*

O God, who teach us that you abide
in hearts that are just and true,
grant that we may be so fashioned by
     your grace
as to become a dwelling pleasing to you.
Through our Lord Jesus Christ, your Son,
who lives and reigns with you in the unity
     of the Holy Spirit,
one God, for ever and ever. **Amen.**

## FIRST READING

Lev 13:1-2, 44-46

The Lord said to Moses and Aaron,
     "If someone has on his skin a scab or
          pustule or blotch
     which appears to be the sore of leprosy,
     he shall be brought to Aaron, the priest,
     or to one of the priests among his
          descendants.
If the man is leprous and unclean,
     the priest shall declare him unclean
     by reason of the sore on his head.

"The one who bears the sore of leprosy
     shall keep his garments rent and his
          head bare,
     and shall muffle his beard;
     he shall cry out, 'Unclean, unclean!'
As long as the sore is on him he shall
          declare himself unclean,
     since he is in fact unclean.
He shall dwell apart, making his abode
          outside the camp."

## RESPONSORIAL PSALM

Ps 32:1-2, 5, 11

℟. (7) I turn to you, Lord, in time of
    trouble, and you fill me with the joy
    of salvation.

Blessed is he whose fault is taken away,
    whose sin is covered.
Blessed the man to whom the LORD
    imputes not guilt,
    in whose spirit there is no guile.

℟. I turn to you, Lord, in time of trouble,
    and you fill me with the joy of
    salvation.

Then I acknowledged my sin to you,
    my guilt I covered not.
I said, "I confess my faults to the LORD,"
    and you took away the guilt of my sin.

℟. I turn to you, Lord, in time of trouble,
    and you fill me with the joy of
    salvation.

Be glad in the LORD and rejoice, you just;
    exult, all you upright of heart.

℟. I turn to you, Lord, in time of trouble,
    and you fill me with the joy of
    salvation.

## SECOND READING

1 Cor 10:31–11:1

Brothers and sisters,
whether you eat or drink, or whatever you
        do,
    do everything for the glory of God.
Avoid giving offense, whether to the Jews
        or Greeks or the church of God,
    just as I try to please everyone in every
        way,
    not seeking my own benefit but that of
        the many,
    that they may be saved.
Be imitators of me, as I am of Christ.

## About Liturgy

*We have more power than we think:* I visited a parish in another state. In the sanctuary was a banner that read, "All are welcome. All belong." At Mass, I sat behind a lovely family of a mom and her two sons, one about seven years old, the other still an infant. At times during the Mass, the infant seemed to be singing, loudly. He wasn't crying or wailing. He was just very happy and vocal about it. He squirmed like all infants are supposed to do, but mom was great. She was attentive to both her children, doing her best to teach them good behavior, obviously loving them and sharing her faith with them. She bounced her baby in one arm and with the other held open the hymnal for her older son. Her finger followed the notes as they both sang. She did the same with the readings. She was actively teaching her children (and all of us) how to fully participate in the liturgy, how to hand on our faith to the next generation, and how to be joyful in the presence of the community and of God.

After Mass, I told her how beautiful it was to see her with her children at church. Just then, a gentleman who had been sitting on the other side of the church came up to her and scolded her for not taking her baby to the cry room. He was not in the mood for a discussion and left after his criticism. The mom shrugged it off, and I tried to reassure her that her baby had been no trouble at all.

However, at the coffee and donuts gathering after Mass, I saw her sobbing at a table alone with her children. Five other parishioners had come up to her, not being as mean as the first, but all in one way or another letting her know that the "proper thing" would have been for her to take her baby out during the Mass. She herself was not a parishioner but lived in the neighboring city. I doubt that parish will have her baby bothering them again.

"If you wish, you can make me clean," said the leper to Jesus. And all it took for the leper to be welcomed back into the community was one person's will: "I do will it. Be made clean." We don't need a miracle or more hospitality ministers or a banner to help us make our churches welcoming communities where all are indeed welcomed and all truly belong. We simply need to will it and to do it, each one of us, every single Sunday.

## About Initiation

*Rite of Sending:* If you have catechumens ready to be baptized this Easter, today may be a good time to celebrate the optional Rite of Sending Catechumens for Election. Part of this rite is the signing of the Book of Elect. If the signing of the book will take place at the diocesan Rite of Election, you omit that signing here. If you have baptized candidates who will be confirmed and will receive Eucharist this Easter, you can celebrate the optional Rite of Sending the Candidates for Recognition by the Bishop and for the Call to Continuing Conversion. Note, however, that you do not celebrate this optional parish rite if your diocese does not celebrate a combined Rite of Election and Call to Continuing Conversion.

## About Liturgical Music

*A last Alleluia:* This last Sunday before Lent is an excellent time to break out all the Alleluias, not just during the gospel acclamation but also in the hymns that begin and conclude the Mass. Every hymnal collection has a variety of songs that highlight our alleluias. One good example is "Alleluia! Sing to Jesus," sung to the tune of Hyfrydol. Another song that could fit for the preparation of gifts is "Let All Mortal Flesh Keep Silence" (Picardy), especially the final verse.

**FEBRUARY 11, 2018**

# SIXTH SUNDAY IN ORDINARY TIME

# SEASON OF LENT

**GOSPEL ACCLAMATION**
See Ps 95:8

If today you hear his voice,
harden not your hearts.

## Gospel    Matt 6:1-6, 16-18; L219

Jesus said to his disciples:
   "Take care not to perform righ-
      teous deeds
   in order that people may see them;
   otherwise, you will have no
      recompense from your
      heavenly Father.
When you give alms,
   do not blow a trumpet before you,
   as the hypocrites do in the
      synagogues and in the streets
   to win the praise of others.
Amen, I say to you,
   they have received their reward.
But when you give alms,
   do not let your left hand know what
      your right is doing,
   so that your almsgiving may be secret.
And your Father who sees in secret will
   repay you.

"When you pray,
   do not be like the hypocrites,
   who love to stand and pray in the
      synagogues and on street corners
   so that others may see them.
Amen, I say to you,
   they have received their reward.
But when you pray, go to your inner room,
   close the door, and pray to your Father in
      secret.
And your Father who sees in secret will
   repay you.

"When you fast,
   do not look gloomy like the hypocrites.
They neglect their appearance,
   so that they may appear to others to be
      fasting.
Amen, I say to you, they have received their
   reward.
But when you fast,
   anoint your head and wash your face,
   so that you may not appear to be fasting,
   except to your Father who is hidden.
And your Father who sees what is hidden
   will repay you."

*See Appendix A, p. 268, for the other readings.*

## Reflecting on the Gospel

Though today is the secular "holiday" of Valentine's, it falls on Ash Wednesday. It would seem foolish to overlook the juxtaposition of these two events. Valentine's Day is for lovers, friends, admirers, and crushes. Ash Wednesday reminds us that we too shall pass; to dust we shall return. And yet our faith tells us these bonds of love, which we celebrate on Valentine's Day, are everlasting. The relationships we form, the love we share, lasts beyond this earthly life, which has a definite end, and which is marked by the ashes on our foreheads.

Today we seem to do the opposite of the Gospel injunction, wearing ashes, by which people see we have been to Mass. Of course, that isn't the purpose of the ashes, but that's the result. The ashes on our foreheads mark us as Mass-goers on this unique day. But what if we went to Mass today only to wash off the ashes immediately afterwards? What would people think if they did not see ashes on our foreheads? Would they wonder if we had been to Mass? Might we be judged as shirking a Catholic ritual, though certainly not a holy day of obligation?

Jesus reminded his followers, and he therefore reminds us, that our good deeds, prayers, almsgiving, and fasting ought to be done in secret. There is a temptation in religion to appear to be "doing it right," which can easily slip into self-righteousness. That self-righteousness can be fed by others who look and admire at the external appearances of holiness. Ostentatious acts of good deeds, almsgiving, prayer, and fasting can be admired as markers of holiness. But Jesus tells us that it is better for the one practicing these essential aspects of faith to do so quietly, even secretly. In so doing there will be no admiration from others. There will be no acclaim. There will be no external attention. Instead, one's heavenly Father is the audience, nobody else. God alone knows our hearts and our actions. We do not need to justify ourselves before anyone but God.

The ashes remind us of our end, when we will be face-to-face with our Maker, who indeed knows our hearts and our actions. At that point, we stand alone with the bonds of love we have created throughout our lives. How appropriate that we celebrate Valentine's Day and Ash Wednesday today.

## Living the Paschal Mystery

Though not a holy day, we know that many Catholics attend Mass today and wear their ashes at their places of work. Today many who are culturally Catholic attend Mass. How welcoming are we to those who attend today and perhaps not again until Easter or even Christmas? The desire to attend Mass today, and connect with something elemental in the human experience, our own knowledge of our own personal death, is to be respected and admired. Rather than convey a self-righteous attitude on this day (or, frankly, any day), it would be good to be especially attentive to new faces and fresh experiences at Mass.

The sacramental (with a small *s*) practice of smearing ashes on one's head carries profound mythic sensibilities and taps into something deep within the human spirit. Ashes can be made only from fire, the utter and nearly complete consummation of a thing. All that remains are carbon compounds and other trace particles. The symbolism of smearing this substance on a human head cannot be underestimated. This is a large part of why so many attend services today. Our Catholic sacramentals connect with something deep in the human spirit, almost pagan. For Christians, we recall how fragile life is. The refining fire of the Spirit of God purifies all, leaving only a remnant.

Today we ponder this elemental mystery of faith. We have been graced into existence for only a short while. We will return to the earth from which we came. But something of God remains; something eternal grasps for the infinite.

### Focusing the Gospel

The readings for this first day of the Lenten journey to Easter call us to *turn*.

In Hebrew, the word for repentance is to *turn*, like the turning of the earth to the sun at this time of year, like the turning of soil before spring planting. The Lenten journey that begins on this Ash Wednesday calls us to repentance: to turn away from those things that separate us from God and re*turn* to the mercy, justice, and reconciliation of the Lord.

In today's gospel, from his Sermon on the Mount, Jesus instructs his listeners on the Christian attitude and disposition toward prayer, fasting, and almsgiving. Such acts are meaningful only if they are outward manifestations of the *turning* that has taken place within our hearts.

### Model Universal Prayer (Prayer of the Faithful)

*Presider:* This is the "acceptable time"; the day of salvation has come! In confidence, then, let us pray.

*Response:* Lord, hear our prayer.

That those preparing for baptism and for reception into the church may discover, during their Lenten pilgrimage, the depth of God's mercy and love for them . . .

That these next forty days may be a time for transforming deserts of division and conflict into springs of reconciliation and community . . .

That our prayers and sacrifices this Lent may be the source of new hope and new beginnings for the poor, the suffering, the rejected, and the forgotten . . .

That, in our parish's work and worship together, we may be "ambassadors for Christ" and signs of God's loving presence in the midst of our community and neighborhoods . . .

*Presider:* Merciful God, look upon us as we enter these forty days of Lent, bearing on our heads the marks of ashes. May our fasting be a hunger for justice; may our alms be the means of peace and reconciliation; may our prayers be the hopes we are prepared to work and sacrifice for. In Jesus' name, we pray. **Amen.**

### COLLECT

Let us pray.

*Pause for silent prayer*

Grant, O Lord, that we may begin with holy fasting
this campaign of Christian service,
so that, as we take up battle against spiritual evils,
we may be armed with weapons of self-restraint.
Through our Lord Jesus Christ, your Son,
who lives and reigns with you in the unity of the Holy Spirit,
one God, for ever and ever. **Amen.**

### FOR REFLECTION

• In what ways do we *need* an experience or season like Lent?

• How can fasting be a positive, optimistic experience, rather than simply an act of self-denial or self-mortification?

### Homily Points

• Spring is the season for turning: Earth completes its spring "turning" toward the sun and we will soon begin "turning" ground for the year's planting. The Lenten springtime is also a spiritual "turning." Lent calls us to *conversion*, from the Latin word for *turning*: away from whatever unjustly steals our time and energy and re*turn* to the embrace of family and friends; away from idols of wealth and re*turn* to the things of God. These ashes are signs of such *conversion*: our promise to transform the ash heaps of destruction into lights of hope and fires of compassion.

• The word *sacrifice* comes from the Latin words "to make holy." We might think of sacrifice as denying ourselves something as a sign of mortification, but real sacrifice—denying ourselves so that another may be enriched—is generosity that reveals the presence of God. The point of sacrifice is not our own hardship or humiliation; it is not about self-abnegation and mortification. Sacrifice is about "making holy" by bringing together, lifting up, making right.

## ✝ SPIRITUALITY

**GOSPEL ACCLAMATION**
Matt 4:4b

One does not live on bread alone,
but on every word that comes forth from the
    mouth of God.

### Gospel

Mark 1:12-15; L23B

**The Spirit drove Jesus out into
    the desert,
    and he remained in the desert
        for forty days, tempted by
        Satan.
He was among wild beasts,
    and the angels ministered to
        him.**

**After John had been arrested,
    Jesus came to Galilee proclaim-
        ing the gospel of God:
"This is the time of fulfillment.
The kingdom of God is at hand.
Repent, and believe in the gospel."**

### Reflecting on the Gospel

Upon making a commitment, how often do we start out with strong intentions, firm will, and fortitude? Perhaps nothing represents that more in our modern culture than a New Year's resolution. We see and hear ads for gym memberships and diet plans flooding the internet and the airwaves during those first few weeks of January. So many of us are resolute in those weeks. But once a hurdle is in our path we can quickly stumble. Sometimes we can make a commitment to exercise daily, and that routine is manageable for a few days, or even a few weeks. But we also face other priorities in the midst of our goal to exercise daily. Pretty soon, exercising is a long-gone wish.

Jesus faced something much more profound than a New Year's resolution or an intention to exercise daily. Upon being baptized and starting his ministry, he was immediately faced with temptation. He was driven into the desert, a place of no consolation, no respite, and no refreshment. The experience of knowing he is God's Son gives way to isolation and solitude in a harsh environment.

As a human being, Jesus knew temptation; the gospel is clear about that. But for many Christians it can be difficult to imagine that Jesus was truly tempted, for he was also divine. And yet as he was fully human he was truly tempted. Despite these real temptations, he overcame them. Mark does not tell us much about this period, unlike Luke, for example, with the many scenes of Jesus conversing with Satan. Mark is intent to tell us in sparse text, without wasting a word, that Jesus was tempted by Satan. Jesus was fully human and experienced temptation as we do.

As Jesus was tempted we too will be tempted. Perhaps even our profound experience of faith and trust in God is tested. But after this period of testing Jesus returns to Galilee, his home, and proclaims the Gospel. In this he is a model for us, who will not live without temptation. We might have an experience of desolation that God is not with us in our trials. But like Jesus we can undergo this experience and emerge stronger, with the courage to proclaim the Gospel.

### Living the Paschal Mystery

Our lives are filled with many competing priorities. Sometimes we call these "distractions" or temptations. But it is important for us to wisely discern between distractions/temptations and merely competing priorities. Family responsibilities, for example, are hardly temptations, but they can sometimes pull us in directions we do not enjoy or that are not always life-giving. Perhaps this is why they are called "responsibilities." Life-giving activities are from the Spirit of God. Pursuits that pull us away from who we are called to be are better called "temptations." This is where the example of Jesus can be so powerful.

Jesus was, and was called to be, the Son of God. Mark tells us about this experience at Jesus' baptism. Yet immediately after his baptism, Jesus was in the desert for forty days, being tempted, only to return to his home, true to his mission, to preach the Gospel.

Often we know who we are called to be. Even in the midst of temptation, or desolation, we know who we are and what we ought to do. Following Christ does not mean a life on easy street without trials or perils. Quite the opposite.

The Christian life is beset by obstacles, temptations, and pitfalls. As Jesus did, we are called to proclaim the Gospel, whether we do that at home, in our workplace, or with friends.

### Focusing the Gospel

*Mark 1:12-15*

Every year the Lenten season begins in the desert. Mark's brief account of Jesus' forty days in the desert takes place immediately after Jesus' baptism. Driven by the Spirit, Jesus' going to the desert is an act of obedience to the Father. This is a time for contemplation and discernment regarding the tremendous task before him.

The word "Satan" comes from the Hebrew word for "adversary." Satan serves as Jesus' adversary, tempting him along another path. And this was in the truest sense, a "temptation" for Jesus, who was not merely play-acting. But Jesus never succumbed to the adversary's temptation. Thus, Mark's portrait of Jesus in the desert is that of God's son and Messiah overcoming temptation and re-emerging to preach the gospel.

### Focusing the First Reading

*Gen 9:8-15*

Today's first reading recounts God's covenant with Noah. The first Christians saw in the Noah tale an image of baptism: a new world, free from sin, cleansed by the flood waters and God makes a covenant with humanity. After their forty days and nights adrift in the ark, Noah and his family begin the task of reestablishing God's creation.

### Focusing the Responsorial Psalm

*Ps 25:4-5, 6-7, 8-9*

Covenant and journey are the themes of today's responsorial psalm. Humankind's covenant with God, reestablished in the faithfulness of Noah and his clan, is centered in God's compassion and justice. The psalm also praises God as the source of true wisdom: God is the guide and teacher who marks our life's journey by way of justice and humility.

### Focusing the Second Reading

*1 Pet 3:18-22*

In Christ, God has again raised up his beloved sons and daughters from the tombs of their sins. The writer of the First Letter of Peter picks up the baptismal theme of the Noah story: God again restores life through water and recreates our fallen world through Christ.

**PROMPTS FOR HOMILISTS, CATECHISTS, AND RCIA TEAMS**

What form does "Satan" most powerfully take in your life?

How can you bring a sense of stillness to your life this Lent?

What would you like to recreate and transform in your life this Lent?

What temptation do you find hardest to resist?

## Model Penitential Act

*Presider:* Called by the Spirit to the Lenten desert with Christ, let us ask for the mercy of God for our sins. *[pause]*

    *Confiteor:* I confess . . .

## Homily Points

• The same Spirit that "drove" Jesus into the desert drives us into our own "deserts" to rediscover God. Lent calls us to our interior deserts, to that place within us where we can turn off the noise and shut out the fears and tensions of our lives to realize God's grace. It is only in such stillness that we can realize the many manifestations of God's love in our midst, a love that is difficult to see in all the distractions demanding our attention and hard to hear in all the noise screaming at us. In the stillness of the Lenten desert, we rediscover what it means to be people of faith, what values we want our lives to stand for, what path we want our lives to take on our journey that inevitably leads to God and Easter resurrection.

• Lent calls us to face our mortality, to realize that our lives are all too brief and fragile. As Jesus was led to the desert to confront the mission before him, we are called to the desert of our hearts and spirits to confront what we are making of this time we have been given, what we want our lives to stand for, what we want to leave to those we love. Lent calls us into the deserts of our hearts to turn away from the attitudes and behaviors that mire our lives in selfishness, unhappiness, and disappointment and turn toward the values of God we seek to embrace.

• While the "Spirit" of God calls us to the work of reconciliation, justice, and generosity, "Satan" dissuades us from taking on God's work by focusing, instead, on our own temptations. Our Lenten desert experience with Jesus is a time to confront the "temptations of Satan": those things (however common in the scheme of life) that can too easily displace the things of God in our lives. This First Sunday of Lent is a call to "repent": to change our lives' focus and direction and recreate those wants and attitudes that doom our resolve to realize the kingdom of God in our lives.

## Model Universal Prayer (Prayer of the Faithful)

*Presider:* To the God of reconciliation and peace, let us pray.

*Response:* Lord, hear our prayer.

For our church, that, in our prayer and work, we may be signs of God's love . . .

For all the nations and peoples of the earth, that they may work together to protect the gifts of God's creation for the peaceful use of all . . .

For the sick, the suffering, the recovering, and the dying, that the limitless compassion of God will restore them to health and hope . . .

For those who are preparing for baptism and the Easter sacraments, that these forty days may be a time of discovering the love and mercy of God in their lives . . .

*Presider:* Hear the prayers we offer to you, O Lord. During these holy days of Lent, may we dedicate ourselves to the work of making these prayers a reality. We ask these things of you in the name of Jesus, our Redeemer. **Amen.**

---

**COLLECT**

Let us pray.

*Pause for silent prayer*

Grant, almighty God,
through the yearly observances of holy
    Lent,
that we may grow in understanding
of the riches hidden in Christ
and by worthy conduct pursue their
    effects.
Through our Lord Jesus Christ, your Son,
who lives and reigns with you in the unity
    of the Holy Spirit,
one God, for ever and ever. **Amen.**

**FIRST READING**
Gen 9:8-15

God said to Noah and to his sons with
    him:
"See, I am now establishing my covenant
    with you
    and your descendants after you
    and with every living creature that was
        with you:
    all the birds, and the various tame and
        wild animals
    that were with you and came out of the
        ark.
I will establish my covenant with you,
    that never again shall all bodily
        creatures be destroyed
    by the waters of a flood;
    there shall not be another flood to
        devastate the earth."
God added:
"This is the sign that I am giving for all
        ages to come,
of the covenant between me and you
    and every living creature with you:
I set my bow in the clouds to serve as
        a sign
of the covenant between me and the
        earth.
When I bring clouds over the earth,
    and the bow appears in the clouds,
I will recall the covenant I have made
between me and you and all living
        beings,
so that the waters shall never again
        become a flood
to destroy all mortal beings."

**RESPONSORIAL PSALM**

Ps 25:4-5, 6-7, 8-9

R̸. (cf. 10) Your ways, O Lord, are love
and truth to those who keep your
covenant.

Your ways, O LORD, make known to me;
teach me your paths,
guide me in your truth and teach me,
for you are God my savior.

R̸. Your ways, O Lord, are love and truth
to those who keep your covenant.

Remember that your compassion, O LORD,
and your love are from of old.
In your kindness remember me,
because of your goodness, O LORD.

R̸. Your ways, O Lord, are love and truth
to those who keep your covenant.

Good and upright is the LORD,
thus he shows sinners the way.
He guides the humble to justice,
and he teaches the humble his way.

R̸. Your ways, O Lord, are love and truth
to those who keep your covenant.

**SECOND READING**

1 Pet 3:18-22

Beloved:
Christ suffered for sins once,
the righteous for the sake of the
unrighteous,
that he might lead you to God.
Put to death in the flesh,
he was brought to life in the Spirit.
In it he also went to preach to the spirits
in prison,
who had once been disobedient
while God patiently waited in the days
of Noah
during the building of the ark,
in which a few persons, eight in all,
were saved through water.
This prefigured baptism, which saves you
now.
It is not a removal of dirt from the body
but an appeal to God for a clear
conscience,
through the resurrection of Jesus Christ,
who has gone into heaven
and is at the right hand of God,
with angels, authorities, and powers
subject to him.

## About Liturgy

**Lenten environment:** Many of us have gotten it into our Catholic imagination that Lent is about the desert. One reason for this is today's gospel reading, which, on the First Sunday of Lent, is always about Jesus' temptation in the desert. But beyond that reference, nothing else about Lent implies desert or dryness, much less cacti or sand.

The Constitution on the Sacred Liturgy says that Lent has a twofold nature: "[By] the recalling of Baptism or the preparation for it, and Penance . . . the church prepares the faithful for the celebration of Easter, while they listen more attentively to God's word and devote more time to prayer. Accordingly . . . more use is to be made of the baptismal features which are part of the Lenten liturgy" (109). Join this directive with today's first reading about Noah and the flood and the second reading connecting that flood with the saving waters of baptism, and we get something that looks a lot more like spring with its thunderstorms and new buds bending under the weight of that water.

That image of new life in need of extra care from sudden storms is what this First Sunday of Lent is about as the church makes a covenant with its most vulnerable—the elect. The promise we give them is that they too will be saved, like Noah, by the flood of God's grace in the waters of baptism at the upcoming Easter Vigil. We, the church, will be their ark of safety during these last few weeks of temptation, doubt, and second thoughts.

We who are baptized are to be examples for these elect of ongoing conversion and renewal, of repentance and deeper commitment to living out the vows of our baptism. This is why we must make more use of the baptismal features that are proper to the Lenten liturgy in order to help us remember our own baptismal vows for the sake of those who are preparing to make those vows for the first time. Therefore, get rid of the sand and cacti. Make sure all your fonts are overflowing with water. Preach about baptism and what it means to live as baptized people who face daily temptations with the courage and faith of Jesus.

## About Initiation

**Rite of Election:** In every diocese today, bishops will elect those who are ready to be initiated at the next Easter Vigil. If you have catechumens in your parish who will be declared elect, be sure to highlight them in the community's prayer throughout Lent. In addition to the Lenten rites for the elect (the three scrutinies, the two presentations, and the preparation rites on Holy Saturday), make sure to include intercessions at every Mass for the elect, enthrone the Book of the Elect by the baptismal font, and continue to celebrate the dismissal of catechumens with the elect as they enter this final period of preparation and intense prayer.

## About Liturgical Music

**What Lent sounds like:** A bit like the misconception that Lent is about the desert, sometimes we have made Lenten music to be about all things soft and quiet. However, the season of Lent began with the trumpet blast in the first reading of Ash Wednesday. Rather than striving for a meditative or contemplative atmosphere in Lent, let us hear Lent as a call to intense focus and clearheaded sobriety. Lent challenges us to strip away whatever has become routine or meaningless and to let go of whatever we cling to that keeps us safe in our comfort zones. Perhaps this Lent is calling your choir to push itself to sing *a cappella* so that the focus is clearly on the power of the human voice. Or perhaps your choir might sing more in unison with the assembly to renew the assembly's sense of its own voice as primary.

**FEBRUARY 18, 2018**
# FIRST SUNDAY OF LENT

## SPIRITUALITY

**GOSPEL ACCLAMATION**
cf. Matt 17:5

From the shining cloud the Father's voice is
    heard:
This is my beloved Son, listen to him.

### Gospel

Mark 9:2-10; L26B

**Jesus took Peter, James, and John**
    **and led them up a high**
        **mountain apart by**
        **themselves.**
**And he was transfigured**
    **before them,**
    **and his clothes became**
        **dazzling white,**
    **such as no fuller on earth**
        **could bleach them.**
**Then Elijah appeared to them along with**
    **Moses,**
    **and they were conversing with Jesus.**
**Then Peter said to Jesus in reply,**
    **"Rabbi, it is good that we are here!**
**Let us make three tents:**
    **one for you, one for Moses, and one for**
        **Elijah."**
**He hardly knew what to say, they were so**
    **terrified.**
**Then a cloud came, casting a shadow**
    **over them;**
    **from the cloud came a voice,**
    **"This is my beloved Son. Listen to**
        **him."**
**Suddenly, looking around, they no longer**
    **saw anyone**
    **but Jesus alone with them.**

**As they were coming down from the**
    **mountain,**
    **he charged them not to relate what**
        **they had seen to anyone,**
    **except when the Son of Man had risen**
        **from the dead.**
**So they kept the matter to themselves,**
    **questioning what rising from the dead**
        **meant.**

### Reflecting on the Gospel

Mountains have always been a place for human beings to seek the transcendent. Mountains were considered the realm of the gods from antiquity. We recall the ancient Greeks and Mount Olympus, the home of Zeus. In the Old Testament we know of Mount Sinai and Moses' encounter with God there. In today's gospel we hear of another encounter with the divine on a mountain, the place of the transcendent. This encounter takes place not in front of the crowds, the disciples, or even the Twelve. This encounter is special; it is unique. For this special event, Jesus takes Peter and the sons of Zebedee.

The language of this encounter is steeped in symbolism, beginning with the mountain itself, but including the white garments, the cloud, the voice from heaven, and the figures alongside Jesus. The garments Jesus wears are turned "dazzling white, / such as no fuller on earth could bleach them." Modern ears may wonder about the word "fuller," which is not commonly used today. The word comes from Latin, via Old English, and refers to one who cleans cloth, especially wool. In any case, Jesus' garments were made *really* white. The symbolism should be clear. He is pure.

Moses and Elijah, appearing alongside Jesus, represent the Law and the Prophets. Jesus fulfills both; his ministry is in continuity with Moses and Elijah. He is not doing anything contrary to either. Rather than rest in the moment, and simply take in the wonderment of it all, Peter breaks into the scene with an idea to make three tents, which would be places of worship, commemorating this event. His response is so often typical of our own. He wants to preserve the occasion, mark it in some way. But no sooner had he voiced this proposal than God himself, the voice from heaven, speaks in a way reminiscent of Jesus' baptism. At Jesus' baptism the voice from heaven was heard by Jesus alone: "You are my beloved Son; with you I am well pleased" (Mark 1:11, NABRE). Now the three disciples, not present at Jesus' baptism, hear the voice too. And with that, the episode ends. The three disciples are left alone with Jesus to come down from the mountain, struggling to understand what this experience and Jesus' own admonition meant.

When considering the symbolism associated with this mountaintop experience, we can relate it to our own lives when we have an experience of the transcendent.

### Living the Paschal Mystery

Mountaintop experiences are rare, and we cannot stay there, as much as we would like. The Scriptures give us a glimpse into that reality. Without warning Jesus was transfigured. The encounter with the divine often happens that way, without warning. And it seems that as soon as we have the encounter, it is over, and we are left to descend the mountain. We can share Peter's desire to commemorate the event. It seems natural to erect a monument or some marker so that we may return to this place of encounter again and again. But that is not to be. The three are left wondering what the experience means, and what Jesus' saying about rising from the dead might mean. Of course, this experience and Jesus' saying will become clear in hindsight, after the crucifixion and exaltation.

And this is a model for us of how the paschal mystery is lived. We have peak experiences followed by moments of wonder and discernment. The Christian life is not one grand, never-ending peak experience. In fact, such experiences may be rare, even as they were for the disciples. And the Christian life is not all wonder and discernment, as meaning develops gradually and in light of unfolding events. We stay faithful to Jesus and accompany him in the peak experiences, and also in the struggle to discern meaning.

### Focusing the Gospel
*Mark 9:2-10*

Today's gospel is Mark's account of the transfiguration of Jesus (read each year in the Roman rite on the Second Sunday of Lent). In the vision witnessed by Peter, James, and John on the mountain, Jesus fulfills both the Law (Moses) and the Prophets (Elijah). This story is a watershed moment in Jesus' relationship with his disciples. In this extraordinary vision, Peter, James, and John perceive the divinity that exists within Jesus, a divinity that is affirmed by the voice heard in the cloud. Though overwhelmed by fear, the three disciples realize that they have entered a new chapter in their journey with Jesus.

Throughout Israel's history, God revealed his presence to Israel in the form of a cloud (for example, the column of cloud that led the Israelites in the desert during the exodus [Exod 15]). On the mountain of the transfiguration, God again speaks in the form of a cloud, claiming the transfigured Jesus as his own Son.

As they make their way down the mountain, Jesus urges the three not to tell anything of what they had just seen. Whatever they would say would only confirm the popular misconceptions and false expectations of an all-powerful Messiah who comes to avenge Israel's humiliation and restore Judaism's political fortunes. The mission of Jesus the Messiah is to proclaim the kingdom of God through the cross and resurrection, concepts Peter and the others still do not grasp.

### Focusing the First Reading
*Gen 22:1-2, 9a, 10-13, 15-18*

Today's first reading is a preview of the Easter Vigil: the story of Abraham and Isaac is the second of the Old Testament readings assigned for the night watch of Jesus' resurrection. For Christians, the story beautifully parallels the sacrifice of Christ on the altar of the cross. While God's demand of Abraham seems cruel, it is important to understand that human sacrifice was common in the desert religions of Abraham's time, and even into the times of the kings. The distraught Abraham is doing what was expected of him by his time and culture. Abraham's faith and trust in this one God became the basis of a new relationship between humankind and our Creator: a relationship built not only on faith, but also on compassion, justice, and freedom.

### Focusing the Responsorial Psalm
*Ps 116:10, 15, 16-17, 18-19 (116:9)*

One can hear the relieved Abraham offering today's responsorial psalm. Even in the midst of his anguish and suffering, at a time when his faith was tested to the limit, the psalmist continues to trust in the Lord (as the devastated Abraham did). The psalmist recommits himself to the service of the God who has saved him and will fulfill his "vow": his public offering of thanksgiving for the saving work of God in his life.

### Focusing the Second Reading
*Rom 8:31b-34*

In his letter to the Romans, his great treatise on baptism, the embattled Paul offers a hymn celebrating the great love of God "who did not spare his own Son / but handed him over for us all." With Christ as our intercessor at God's right hand, Paul preaches, who on earth do we need to fear or cower before?

---

**PROMPTS FOR HOMILISTS, CATECHISTS, AND RCIA TEAMS**

In what ways can the "divinity" that exists within us make a difference to others?

When are we confronted by both the Christ of the transfiguration and the Christ of the crucifixion?

What has been the hardest thing that God has asked of you—and how was your trust rewarded?

What have you learned from your own experiences of suffering, anguish, and pain that had a profound and lasting effect on your life?

## Model Penitential Act

*Presider:* Confident of God's constant mercy, let us begin our prayer by calling to mind our sins. *[pause]*

    *Confiteor:* I confess . . .

## Homily Points

• On the mount of the transfiguration, Peter, James, and John realize for the first time the divinity possessed by Jesus. That same spirit, that same "divinity," shines within and through them and us, as well. The Spirit of God dwells within us, enabling us to realize our own potential for generosity, compassion, and gratitude—and, in the light of Christ's transfiguration, to recognize that same goodness in others.

• In Mark's story of the transfiguration, Peter does not know what to say or how to react to the incredible scene he has witnessed. All he can offer is the weak suggestion of setting up three booths or shrines to commemorate the event (similar to the custom of building such structures as part of the Jewish feast of Tabernacles or Booths). But the transfigured Christ asks more of us than memorials of wood and stone, brick and mortar: He seeks to be a living presence that illuminates human hearts and transforms human history. He asks those who follow him to mirror that presence in their own lives of "transfiguring" despair into hope, sadness into joy, anguish into healing, estrangement into community.

• The transfiguration is a vision that holds glorious promise—but a vision that will only be realized at a heavy price. Accepting the God of blessing and joy is one thing, but when God asks us to give readily and humbly and sacrificially to others, to forgive others without limit or condition, we hesitate and begin to back away. The weeks ahead call us to descend the mountain with the "transfigured" Jesus and to take up our crosses—be they physical, emotional, economic, or intellectual—and realize the sacred goodness and value within each one of us to bring the glory of Easter into our lives and the lives of those we love.

## Model Universal Prayer (Prayer of the Faithful)

*Presider:* As the apostle Paul writes, "If God is for us, who can be against us?" With confidence, then, let us offer God our needs.

*Response:* Lord, hear our prayer.

For our church, that, in our prayer and work together, "the earth shall find blessing" in us . . .

For all nations and peoples, that they may work together to recreate our world in the justice and peace of God . . .

For the sick, the suffering, and the dying, that they may know, in our care and compassion for them, the healing presence of the risen One . . .

For parents and guardians in our community, that their children may discover in their love and care for them the loving providence of God . . .

*Presider:* Father, hear the prayers we make before you. May your Spirit of compassion and peace "transfigure" us and our world into the image of Jesus, the risen Christ, in whose name we offer these prayers. **Amen.**

**COLLECT**

Let us pray.

*Pause for silent prayer*

O God, who have commanded us
to listen to your beloved Son,
be pleased, we pray,
to nourish us inwardly by your word,
that, with spiritual sight made pure,
we may rejoice to behold your glory.
Through our Lord Jesus Christ, your Son,
who lives and reigns with you in the unity
    of the Holy Spirit,
one God, for ever and ever. **Amen.**

**FIRST READING**
Gen 22:1-2, 9a, 10-13, 15-18

God put Abraham to the test.
He called to him, "Abraham!"
"Here I am!" he replied.
Then God said:
    "Take your son Isaac, your only one,
        whom you love,
    and go to the land of Moriah.
There you shall offer him up as a
      holocaust
    on a height that I will point out to you."

When they came to the place of which
      God had told him,
    Abraham built an altar there and
      arranged the wood on it.
Then he reached out and took the knife to
      slaughter his son.
But the LORD's messenger called to him
      from heaven,
    "Abraham, Abraham!"
"Here I am!" he answered.
"Do not lay your hand on the boy," said the
      messenger.
"Do not do the least thing to him.
I know now how devoted you are to God,
    since you did not withhold from me
      your own beloved son."
As Abraham looked about,
    he spied a ram caught by its horns in
      the thicket.
So he went and took the ram
    and offered it up as a holocaust in place
      of his son.

Again the LORD's messenger called to
      Abraham from heaven and said:
    "I swear by myself, declares the LORD,
    that because you acted as you did
    in not withholding from me your
      beloved son,
    I will bless you abundantly
    and make your descendants as
      countless
    as the stars of the sky and the sands of
      the seashore;

your descendants shall take possession
of the gates of their enemies,
and in your descendants all the nations
of the earth
shall find blessing—
all this because you obeyed my
command."

## RESPONSORIAL PSALM

Ps 116:10, 15, 16-17, 18-19

℞. (116:9) I will walk before the Lord, in
the land of the living.

I believed, even when I said,
"I am greatly afflicted."
Precious in the eyes of the LORD
is the death of his faithful ones.

℞. I will walk before the Lord, in the land
of the living.

O LORD, I am your servant;
I am your servant, the son of your
handmaid;
you have loosed my bonds.
To you will I offer sacrifice of
thanksgiving,
and I will call upon the name of the
LORD.

℞. I will walk before the Lord, in the land
of the living.

My vows to the LORD I will pay
in the presence of all his people,
in the courts of the house of the LORD,
in your midst, O Jerusalem.

℞. I will walk before the Lord, in the land
of the living.

## SECOND READING

Rom 8:31b-34

Brothers and sisters:
If God is for us, who can be against us?
He who did not spare his own Son
but handed him over for us all,
how will he not also give us everything
else along with him?

Who will bring a charge against God's
chosen ones?
It is God who acquits us. Who will
condemn?
Christ Jesus it is who died—or, rather, was
raised—
who also is at the right hand of God,
who indeed intercedes for us.

### About Liturgy

*Penitential lifestyle:* Have you ever had to make a very difficult decision, and you finally made your choice and gathered up all the courage you had to go through with your decision? Then at the very last minute someone tells you to do something different and causes you to doubt your decision! Wouldn't you be a bit annoyed? Wouldn't you just want to go ahead with your choice and be done with it?

I imagine that's a bit of what Abraham went through in today's reading. It's obvious that Abraham displayed great faith by unquestioningly following God's irrational command to slaughter his son. However, the nineteenth-century philosopher and theologian Søren Kierkegaard points out that Abraham's true obedience was shown in that last moment when God called out to him to stop. At that moment, Abraham obeyed just as unreservedly and immediately as he had done at the first command. Without questioning why God had made him go through all the anxiety of preparing for such a terrible act, without wondering why, when he had almost fulfilled God's will, he was commanded to do just the opposite. Without hesitation, Abraham obeyed quickly and willingly. Kierkegaard says that Abraham was able to do this only through an intimate relationship with God.

Lent is a time when we can strengthen our intimate relationship with God through acts of penance so that we can have this kind of unreserved faith. However, just as a relationship cannot grow unless we tend to it daily, we must commit to a penitential *lifestyle* that we nourish with more intense disciplines in this penitential season. The *Catechism of the Catholic Church*, 1435–37, gives us practices we can do daily to live this penitential lifestyle: "gestures of reconciliation, concern for the poor, the exercise and defense of justice and right, by the admission of faults to one's brethren, fraternal correction, revision of life, examination of conscience, spiritual direction, acceptance of suffering, endurance of persecution for the sake of righteousness. Taking up one's cross each day" (1435). We also turn more readily to God when we celebrate the Eucharist, read Scripture, pray the Liturgy of the Hours and the Lord's Prayer, do spiritual exercises and pilgrimages, and make sacrifices.

### About Initiation

*Penitential rite:* Part II of the RCIA provides an optional rite for those already baptized who are preparing to be received or to celebrate confirmation and Eucharist. Although this rite is parenthetically called "scrutiny," it is different than what is celebrated with the unbaptized elect on the third, fourth, and fifth Sundays of Lent. RCIA 463 cautions that those scrutinies for the elect should not be combined with this penitential rite for the baptized. A better recommendation is to omit this optional rite for the baptized and instead encourage them to participate in the parish's regularly scheduled penitential liturgies and reconciliation services.

### About Liturgical Music

*Music suggestions:* Today's readings give us many options for songs that correspond directly to the Scripture texts of the day. One traditional hymn text is "'Tis Good, Lord, to Be Here" by Robinson and Bird, which you might consider using as a song of praise after Communion or as a song for sending forth. Brian Wren's text set by Ricky Manalo, CSP, in "Transfiguration" (OCP) gives the assembly a way to place themselves with the disciples on that holy mountain. Grayson Warren Brown's strong hymn "If God Is for Us" (OCP) sets today's second reading to a powerful gospel melody that may work well as a gathering or song during the preparation of gifts.

## SPIRITUALITY

**GOSPEL ACCLAMATION**
John 3:16

God so loved the world that he gave his only Son,
so that everyone who believes in him might have
      eternal life.

### Gospel    John 2:13-25; L29B

Since the Passover of the Jews was near,
   Jesus went up to Jerusalem.
He found in the temple area those who sold
      oxen, sheep, and doves,
   as well as the money changers seated there.
He made a whip out of cords
   and drove them all out of the temple
         area, with the sheep and oxen,
   and spilled the coins of the money
      changers
   and overturned their tables,
   and to those who sold doves he said,
   "Take these out of here,
   and stop making my Father's house a
         marketplace."
His disciples recalled the words of Scripture,
*Zeal for your house will consume me.*
At this the Jews answered and said to him,
   "What sign can you show us for doing this?"
Jesus answered and said to them,
   "Destroy this temple and in three days I
         will raise it up."
The Jews said,
   "This temple has been under construction
         for forty-six years,
   and you will raise it up in three days?"

*Continued in Appendix A, p. 269.*

*Year A readings may be used, see Appendix A,
pp. 269–271.*

### Reflecting on the Gospel

Today we depart from the Gospel of Mark and enter into the Gospel of John. The story of Jesus driving out the money changers happens during Holy Week in the Synoptic Gospels, but early in Jesus' ministry in John's gospel. In fact, we are in chapter 2, and Jesus is already in Jerusalem. Rather than a ministry in Galilee followed by a momentous journey to Jerusalem as we have the story in the Synoptic gospels, here in John's gospel Jesus goes back and forth to Jerusalem throughout his ministry.

At the time of Jesus, the temple had become in some senses a place of commodification. Oxen, sheep, and doves were sold to be sacrificed. It wasn't enough for one to bring one's own animals. They had to pass an inspection, and were "pre-certified," so to speak, guaranteed to be without blemish and therefore worthy of sacrifice. Of course, there might have been a markup for this quality assurance. For a nice price you could buy a worthy sacrifice. How quickly and easily does religion seem to fall into a trap of commodification? Similar things have happened in our own church history—the selling of indulgences comes to mind.

The challenge of commodification of religion is not limited to Jesus' day, or the annals of church history. Commodification of God's grace happens today too. The unholy alliance of money and the access to religion that it buys were scandalous then, and should be scandalous today. Jesus responds to this scandal as the Scriptures foretold (Ps 69:9). He is zealous, passionate for his Father's house, which has been turned into a bazaar.

Those with the vested interest in the status quo are upset. But Jesus replies with his parabolic riddle-speech. "Destroy this temple and in three days I will raise it up." Of course, he is referring to the temple of his own body. But the stakeholders do not see the deeper meaning of his speech. They see only literal realities and they know that the temple took nearly half a century to build. To them, Jesus must have seemed a wild-eyed zealot, off his rocker and half-baked. He was dangerous, a threat to business and religious interests, and would have to be stopped.

But for Jesus, the temple is holy, not worthy of profanation, neither the Father's house nor Jesus' own self. The example Jesus gives us today demands consideration. We must recoil at every instance of commodified religion, or a selling of God's grace. God's presence is not to be bartered; it is not a commodity. God's grace is freely given to all.

### Living the Paschal Mystery

The gospel tells us something today that we often overlook. The temple is not only a physical place in Jerusalem, but metaphorically it is Jesus' very self. By extension, the human body is a place of God's presence. To be holy is not merely to go to the physical temple to purchase a "pre-certified and quality assured" sacrifice. If the human being is a dwelling place of God, then true worship becomes how we treat ourselves, and how we treat the other. But treating another kindly, patiently, and with love is much more difficult to commodify. It seems easier to say, "buy this" and all will be well with you and God. But God's grace is not dependent on somebody else, what they sell us, in deed or in word. Rather, our relationship with God is dependent upon how we treat the other, who is a dwelling place of God in our midst. It can be difficult to die to our preconceived notions of God, to let go of the idea of an accountant God who takes stock of each and every sacrifice, ensuring it is without blemish. Instead, Jesus invites us to a relationship with God based on Jesus himself, the enfleshment of God. If Jesus is the incarnation of God, if humanity is a dwelling place for the divinity, then proper worship becomes how we treat our neighbor.

## Focusing the Gospel

*John 2:13-25*

The temple is the focus of today's gospel. While Matthew, Mark, and Luke place Jesus' cleansing of the temple immediately after his Palm Sunday entrance into Jerusalem, John places the event early in his gospel, following Jesus' first sign at Cana. The Synoptic Gospels recount only one climactic journey to Jerusalem, but the Jesus of the Fourth Gospel makes several trips to the holy city.

Pilgrims to the temple were expected to make a donation for its upkeep. Because Roman currency was considered "unclean," Jewish visitors had to change their money into Jewish currency in order to make their temple gift. Money changers, whose tables lined the outer courts of the temple, charged exorbitant fees. Visitors who wished to have a sacrifice offered on the temple altar would sometimes have to pay fifteen to twenty times the market rate for animals purchased inside the temple. Vendors could count on the cooperation of the official temple "inspectors" who, as a matter of course, would reject as "unclean" or "imperfect" animals brought in from outside.

Jesus' angry toppling of the vendors' booths and tables is a condemnation of the injustice and exploitation of the faithful in the name of God. So empty and meaningless has their worship become that God will establish a new "temple" in the resurrected body of the Christ.

Of course, the leaders and people do not appreciate the deeper meaning of Jesus' words, just as those who witnessed any of his miracles understand the true nature of his messianic mission. As the writer of the Fourth Gospel observes, only after Jesus' resurrection will they understand that Jesus was speaking of the sanctuary of his own body.

## Focusing the First Reading

*Exod 20:1-17*

The Israelites' encounter with God during their exodus experience transformed them from a nomadic tribe into a nation. On Mount Sinai, God gives to Moses his "law": the ethical and moral principles that will form them as God's people, a nation of justice and mercy and light for all nations. The "law" here is seen not merely as a series of proscriptions but as a treaty whereby God binds himself, or enters into covenant, as the protector of his servant Israel.

## Focusing the Responsorial Psalm

*Ps 19:8, 9, 10, 11 (John 6:68c)*

The wisdom of God's law is praised in this short poem. For the psalmist, the law of God is not a restriction but the source of wisdom that empowers and liberates its adherents to live lives of meaning and purpose. The antiphon is Peter's reply to Jesus at the conclusion of John 6. After Jesus calls himself the "Bread of Life," many abandon him but Peter steadfastly remains, confessing his faith in Jesus' words as the source of "everlasting life."

## Focusing the Second Reading

*1 Cor 1:22-25*

For the Jews, who expect signs, and for the Greeks, who seek wisdom, a crucified Messiah makes no sense. A crucified King is both folly and a sign of contradiction. But Paul argues to the Christians at Corinth that God's apparent failure manifests power and what looks foolish is truly wisdom; that the absurdity of the cross reflects the wisdom of God who upends the world's expectations: humility and service reveal true power and authority.

---

**PROMPTS FOR HOMILISTS, CATECHISTS, AND RCIA TEAMS**

How can anger be channeled into a positive emotion?

Have you ever struggled to "drive out" of your life some attitude, situation, or set of circumstances that deadened you to the real joy and purpose of life?

In what ways does your parish realize Jesus' vision of "my Father's house" in today's gospel?

How is your community a sign of Christ crucified?

When have you discovered God's "law" as "everlasting life"?

How has a particular ministry in your parish been an experience of unexpected grace for both those who serve and those served?

### Model Penitential Act

*Presider:* God has invited us to this house of prayer to offer and receive the gift of the Eucharist. Let us begin by placing our hearts in God's peace and asking his forgiveness for our sins and failings . . . *[pause]*

    *Confiteor:* I confess . . .

### Homily Points

• In the temple precincts of our lives are "money changers"—fear, ambition, addictions, selfishness, prejudice—that distort the meaning of our lives and debase our relationships with God and with one another. Other "money changers" might be any attempt to buy or sell God's grace and favor. What Jesus does in the temple in today's gospel we must do in the "temples" of our lives: drive out any commodification of God; drive out the useless, meaningless, and destructive that desecrate the sacred place within us where God dwells. Our relationship with God is not to be bartered. It is a free gift, given by the divine.

• Anger is a very powerful emotion that can get the better of us—or bring out the best in us. Jesus' anger compels him to act to restore the temple to what it was intended to be: a house of prayer for all people. The Lenten season challenges us to consider what makes us angry enough to change ourselves and our attitudes and perspectives, in order to restore and recreate our lives and world in the compassion and justice of God. To raise one's voice against injustice, to stand up to the powerful on behalf of the weak, to demand accountability of those who exploit and abuse others is to imitate the courageous vision of Jesus, who threw out the money changers who had defiled his Father's temple with their attempt to sell access to God.

• In today's gospel, Jesus drives out those money changers and vendors who have distorted the meaning of the temple; he then redefines the temple from a place of stone and mortar to a community of persons centered in his own resurrected body. Jesus' cleansing of the temple challenges us to take a look at our own parish "temple" with Lenten eyes: to realize that Christ has called us to make our own churches houses of God's compassion, mercy, and peace; to refocus all we do here—from our music to doughnuts after Mass, from preparing children for First Communion to bringing Communion to the homebound, from RCIA to the quilters. Rather than barter access to God, the parish is a place where we celebrate God's presence in our midst.

### Model Universal Prayer (Prayer of the Faithful)

*Presider:* Gathered in this holy place, let us now raise our hearts and voices in prayer to God.

*Response:* Lord, hear our prayer.

That the church may be a place of welcome and care for all . . .

That God's mercy may be at the heart of all laws and public policies . . .

That couples and families experiencing difficult times in their lives together may realize anew the presence of Christ in their homes and hearts . . .

That the works of charity and service of our parish community may be living signs of the risen One in our midst . . .

*Presider:* We come before you, O God, with open and humble hearts. Give us the vision to seek you in all things, so that our lives may be made complete in your joy and made whole in your compassionate love. Hear these prayers we ask of you in the name of Jesus, our Redeemer. **Amen.**

### COLLECT

Let us pray.

*Pause for silent prayer*

O God, author of every mercy and of all goodness,
who in fasting, prayer and almsgiving
have shown us a remedy for sin,
look graciously on this confession of our lowliness,
that we, who are bowed down by our conscience,
may always be lifted up by your mercy.
Through our Lord Jesus Christ, your Son,
who lives and reigns with you in the unity of the Holy Spirit,
one God, for ever and ever. **Amen.**

### FIRST READING

Exod 20:1-17

In those days, God delivered all these commandments:
  "I, the LORD, am your God,
  who brought you out of the land of Egypt, that place of slavery.
You shall not have other gods besides me.
You shall not carve idols for yourselves
  in the shape of anything in the sky above
  or on the earth below or in the waters beneath the earth;
  you shall not bow down before them or worship them.
For I, the LORD, your God, am a jealous God,
  inflicting punishment for their fathers' wickedness
  on the children of those who hate me,
  down to the third and fourth generation;
  but bestowing mercy down to the thousandth generation
  on the children of those who love me
  and keep my commandments.

"You shall not take the name of the LORD, your God, in vain.
For the LORD will not leave unpunished
  the one who takes his name in vain.

"Remember to keep holy the sabbath day.
Six days you may labor and do all your work,
  but the seventh day is the sabbath of the LORD, your God.
No work may be done then either by you,
  or your son or daughter,
  or your male or female slave, or your beast,
  or by the alien who lives with you.

In six days the LORD made the heavens and
the earth,
   the sea and all that is in them;
   but on the seventh day he rested.
That is why the LORD has blessed the
   sabbath day and made it holy.

"Honor your father and your mother,
   that you may have a long life in the land
   which the LORD, your God, is giving you.
You shall not kill.
You shall not commit adultery.
You shall not steal.
You shall not bear false witness against
   your neighbor.
You shall not covet your neighbor's house.
You shall not covet your neighbor's wife,
   nor his male or female slave, nor his ox
   or ass,
   nor anything else that belongs to him."

*or*

Exod 20:1-3, 7-8, 12-17

In those days, God delivered all these
   commandments:
   "I, the LORD, am your God,
   who brought you out of the land of
      Egypt, that place of slavery.
You shall not have other gods besides me.

"You shall not take the name of the LORD,
   your God, in vain.
For the LORD will not leave unpunished
   the one who takes his name in vain.

"Remember to keep holy the sabbath day.
Honor your father and your mother,
   that you may have a long life in the land
   which the LORD, your God, is giving you.
You shall not kill.
You shall not commit adultery.
You shall not steal.
You shall not bear false witness against
   your neighbor.
You shall not covet your neighbor's house.
You shall not covet your neighbor's wife,
   nor his male or female slave, nor his ox
   or ass,
   nor anything else that belongs to him."

**RESPONSORIAL PSALM**
Ps 19:8, 9, 10, 11

**SECOND READING**
1 Cor 1:22-25

*See Appendix A, p. 269.*

## About Liturgy

*Scrutinies in Year B:* "How come we always have to do Year A at the scrutinies? The assembly is missing out on hearing the readings for Year B. Besides, we've already written new scrutiny rites for the Year B readings. Can't we use those?"

I hear those comments every year we aren't in the Year A cycle of the Lectionary, but read the "scrutiny gospels" nonetheless. (Recall that the readings we hear every Sunday are structured on a three-year rotation. In Year A, we hear primarily from Matthew's gospel; in Year B, from Mark; and in Year C, from Luke. John's gospel is interspersed throughout each year.) For the next three Sundays, we will hear from John's gospel. However, these episodes in Year B are not the Johannine readings prescribed for the celebration of the scrutinies that take place on the third, fourth, and fifth Sundays of Lent.

The RCIA is very clear: "In every case the ritual Masses 'Christian Initiation: The Scrutinies' are celebrated and in this sequence: for the first scrutiny the Mass with the gospel of the Samaritan woman; for the second, the Mass with the gospel of the man born blind; for the third, the Mass with the gospel of Lazarus" (146).

Just as the scrutinies themselves are meant to be a series of rites spanning over an extended period of time, so too are these three gospel readings meant to be "digested" little by little with time in between each set. This is because the readings in their assigned sequence reflect the very purpose of the scrutinies. That is, little by little, these readings with their rites uncover what is weak and sinful and strengthen what is good and upright in the elect. Through them, "the elect are instructed gradually about the mystery of sin, from which the whole world and every person longs to be delivered" (RCIA 143). Furthermore, these readings are intended "to enlighten the minds and hearts of the elect with a deeper knowledge of Christ the Savior" (RCIA 139) because these gospels ask the elect, Could he possibly be the Messiah? Do you believe in the Son of Man? Do you believe this (the resurrection)?

Though well-intentioned and creative, when we compose new scrutiny texts to match the readings from Year B or C, we sever ourselves and our elect from the rich history and wisdom of the church, which over the centuries has understood the unique power of these three Johannine gospel readings. Remember that although you may be tired of hearing these Year A readings year after year on these three Sundays, this will be the only time your elect will ever hear these readings in their lifetime as members of the chosen ones of God and subjects of the rite.

Note that there is no directive given in the RCIA whether or not these Year A readings should be used at all the Sunday Masses even if your elect are not present at all of them. The Introduction to the Lectionary (97) gives the option any year to use the Year A readings for these Sundays. It is your call. Your homilists may appreciate having to prepare only one homily each Sunday if you do use the Year A readings at all your Masses this year.

## About Liturgical Music

*Universal prayer:* One of the main elements of the scrutinies is the intercessions over the elect. These intercessions are similar in format to the general intercessions for Mass. Whether or not you have a scrutiny today, you might consider chanting the intercessions (universal prayer), both petition and people's response, during the Lenten season. Your deacon, who normatively announces the intercessions, can intone each petition on a single note, while the cantor chants the invitation to the response. Keep it simple, and do this *a cappella.*

## ✠ SPIRITUALITY

**GOSPEL ACCLAMATION**
John 3:16

God so loved the world that he gave his only Son,
so everyone who believes in him might have
    eternal life.

### Gospel

John 3:14-21; L32B

Jesus said to Nicodemus:
  "Just as Moses lifted up the
      serpent in the desert,
  so must the Son of Man be
      lifted up,
  so that everyone who believes
      in him may have eternal
      life."

For God so loved the world that
    he gave his only Son,
  so that everyone who believes in him
      might not perish
  but might have eternal life.
For God did not send his Son into the
    world to condemn the world,
  but that the world might be saved
      through him.
Whoever believes in him will not be
    condemned,
  but whoever does not believe has
      already been condemned,
  because he has not believed in the
      name of the only Son of God.
And this is the verdict,
  that the light came into the world,
  but people preferred darkness to
      light,
  because their works were evil.
For everyone who does wicked things
    hates the light
  and does not come toward the light,
  so that his works might not be exposed.
But whoever lives the truth comes to
    the light,
  so that his works may be clearly seen
      as done in God.

*Year A readings may be used, see Appendix A,
pp. 271–273.*

### Reflecting on the Gospel

In our modern American culture, Sundays are often punctuated with football. We know that Mass attendance can even be influenced by the time of the local game. The excitement, joy, and anticipation of the game can even distract otherwise intent Mass-goers! More than a few times we have heard homilies incorporating a reference to Sunday football. It's become something of a national religion practiced in varying degrees by fans. Some time ago, in the end zones of various football games, dedicated believers displayed a simple message: "John 3:16." For those who were not familiar with their Scriptures, many went to look it up later in the day, and perhaps that was something of the point. And it is that verse that appears in today's gospel.

This Fourth Sunday of Lent is traditionally called "*Laetare* Sunday," from the Latin meaning "to rejoice" or "to be joyful." Though it might appear to be a football term (Rejoice Sunday), the term comes from the Introit (Isa 66:10); it's unrelated to football! Still, it might seem odd to "rejoice" in Lent, but that exhortation is a reminder, or rather a foreshadowing, of Easter. It is as though Easter itself is breaking into the Lenten season this Sunday.

For the gospel we continue from last week with another reading from John that includes the famous passage cited in football end zones. The first two Sundays of Lent we heard Mark (the temptation of Jesus, and the transfiguration of Jesus). Last week was John's version of Jesus overturning the money changers in the temple. Today we have Jesus and Nicodemus, a story unique to this gospel.

The passage that many use to sum up the gospel is simply this: "For God so loved the world that he gave his only Son." The profundity of this statement can be lost by its pithiness. We proclaim a God of love, not a God of condemnation. And this love results in God sending his only Son, Jesus. The starting point of our theology is, then, love.

Though many today and throughout history seem to prefer a God of judgment, a God of condemnation, today we are reminded that our God is love. And God's love is eternal, expressed in a never-ending life he wants for each of us, where the relationships and bonds we create in this life are never broken. On this Laetare Sunday, where we read John 3:16, may the joy experienced by those at a football game remind us of the joy we have at Easter, when the promise of eternal life is fulfilled.

### Living the Paschal Mystery

The gospel addresses eternal life quite clearly as God's intention for us. But prior to that famous passage (John 3:16), we hear Jesus tell Nicodemus that the Son of Man must be lifted up (crucified). Only by means of death is eternal life opened. Unique to this gospel, Jesus' death is often referred to in metaphorical ways, like "lifted up" or even "glorified." For the Gospel of John, Jesus on the cross was a moment of glory, almost devoid of explicit suffering. For example, John never mentions the scourging of Jesus. Even Jesus' final words from the cross, "I thirst," can be taken more as metaphorical or symbolic than a literal expression of suffering.

Ultimately, John does not focus on Jesus' pain, or "how much it hurt." Instead, the cross is glory and the path to eternal life. For his followers, belief in Jesus is the means by which they receive eternal life. As we journey through Lent, it might be fruitful for us too to focus on Jesus and our belief in him. He represents and is himself the incarnation of God's love for the world. As followers of Jesus how do we represent God's love for the world?

### Focusing the Gospel

*John 3:14-21*
Nicodemus is a Pharisee, and like so many others who heard Jesus, he is fascinated by this Worker of wonders and extraordinary Teacher. He arranges to meet Jesus at night, so as not to attract undue attention.

Jesus teaches Nicodemus about the Son of Man and how eternal life comes to those who believe in the Son of Man. This is a radical notion unheard of in Judaism of the time. Jesus invokes the image of Numbers 21:4-9: As God directs, Moses lifts up the image of a serpent on a pole to heal those who suffer from a deadly plague caused by the bite of serpents. The Son of Man, too, will be "lifted up" and become the means by which eternal life comes to those who believe in him. God gave his only son to the world in an act of love, the ultimate act of self-gift.

### Focusing the First Reading

*2 Chr 36:14-16, 19-23*
Today's first reading is a watershed moment in Judah's history. Prophet after prophet called the leaders of the southern kingdom to return to the moral anchor of their covenant with God, but Judah's unfaithfulness has led to their destruction and seventy years of exile from Jerusalem. But God uses an unlikely source—Cyrus, the king of Persia—as the means for rebuilding Jerusalem and the Jewish nation and reestablishing the Jews' covenant with God.

### Focusing the Responsorial Psalm

*Ps 137:1-2, 3, 4-5, 6 (6ab)*
Psalm 137 is the soul-wrenching lament of refugees forced from their beloved city into slavery. The exiles of Jerusalem vow to remember the land they left behind and to never lose hope in the Lord who does not forget them.

### Focusing the Second Reading

*Eph 2:4-10*
In his eloquent letter to the Ephesians, Paul echoes Jesus' words to Nicodemus: that we owe our salvation not to anything we have done or accomplished but only to the great mercy and grace of God.

**PROMPTS FOR HOMILISTS, CATECHISTS, AND RCIA TEAMS**

How does living a faith based on trust and gratitude differ from living a faith based on condemnation and fear?

How do Jesus' words to Nicodemus challenge attitudes and perspectives of others?

Have you ever felt that, at some point in your life, you were traveling through a "strange land" in your life? How did you find your way "home"?

How have you unexpectedly experienced the mercy of God?

In what ways do we prefer "darkness" to "light"?

## Model Penitential Act

*Presider:* As we prepare to celebrate these sacred mysteries, let us ask forgiveness for our sins and failings from God—God who is rich in mercy and compassion. *[pause]*

　　*Confiteor:* I confess . . .

## Homily Points

• In his encounter with Nicodemus, Jesus challenges him, and us, to rethink our understanding and vision of God: to see God as a living entity who is present in every encounter, every moment, every heart—especially when God seems most absent, when we feel no reason for hope or joy. Jesus reveals a much bigger God than we can imagine: a God who does not condemn but loves, who does not punish but lifts up, who does not destroy but reconciles. God is not about death but about life. Redemption begins with God; reconciliation and healing are God's work, filled with possibilities that are as limitless as they are undeserved.

• God's Son comes as a "light" to enable humankind to realize the great love and mercy of God. We meet God—the loving parent, the compassionate physician, the good and wise friend—in the person of Jesus, in whom we discover our identity as children of God and participants with God in the work of re-creation. God so loves us that, by his grace, he recreates our darkest nights into the morning light of hope; by his wisdom, he transforms our Good Friday despair into Easter joy; by his compassion, he heals our broken spirits into hearts made whole.

• Jesus' meeting with Nicodemus is one of the most hopeful episodes in the gospels. In his questioning, Nicodemus is welcomed by Jesus with understanding and compassion. To Nicodemus—and to all of us—Jesus reveals a God of life and restoration who constantly seeks our healing and reconciliation with him and with one another. The God Jesus reveals to Nicodemus is not the God of condemnation and destruction but the God of forgiveness, mercy, compassion, and eternal life. God is detached neither from us nor the universe he set into motion. God is the Father of creation who constantly seeks to create and nurture life, to heal the brokenhearted, to raise up those who have fallen down and are pushed aside.

## Model Universal Prayer (Prayer of the Faithful)

*Presider:* "God so loved the world that he gave his only Son," not to condemn the world, but that we "might have eternal life." In confidence, then, let us pray.

*Response:* Lord, hear our prayer.

For those in the church who are persecuted for their faith and beliefs, that their perseverance may be a witness to the world of God's mercy and peace . . .

For those separated from their families and homes by war, famine, or catastrophe, that, under God's providence, they may be reunited quickly and safely . . .

For those lost in the darkness of illness, depression, and addiction, that they may see the light of Christ in our care and outreach to them . . .

For our parish community, that we may manifest in our prayer and work together the mercy and compassion of God . . .

*Presider:* May our prayers be the stones of our temple of praise to you, O Lord; may our acts of compassion and selflessness build us into the body of Christ, your beloved Son, in whose name we offer these prayers. **Amen.**

## COLLECT

Let us pray.

*Pause for silent prayer*

O God, who through your Word
reconcile the human race to yourself in a
　　wonderful way,
grant, we pray,
that with prompt devotion and eager faith
the Christian people may hasten
toward the solemn celebrations to come.
Through our Lord Jesus Christ, your Son,
who lives and reigns with you in the unity
　　of the Holy Spirit,
one God, for ever and ever. **Amen.**

## FIRST READING
2 Chr 36:14-16, 19-23

In those days, all the princes of Judah, the
　　priests, and the people
　　added infidelity to infidelity,
　　practicing all the abominations of the
　　　　nations
　　and polluting the Lord's temple
　　which he had consecrated in Jerusalem.

Early and often did the Lord, the God of
　　their fathers,
　　send his messengers to them,
　　for he had compassion on his people
　　　　and his dwelling place.
But they mocked the messengers of God,
　　despised his warnings, and scoffed at
　　　　his prophets,
　　until the anger of the Lord against his
　　　　people was so inflamed
　　that there was no remedy.
Their enemies burnt the house of God,
　　tore down the walls of Jerusalem,
　　set all its palaces afire,
　　and destroyed all its precious objects.
Those who escaped the sword were
　　carried captive to Babylon,
　　where they became servants of the king
　　　　of the Chaldeans and his sons
　　until the kingdom of the Persians came
　　　　to power.
All this was to fulfill the word of the Lord
　　spoken by Jeremiah:
　　"Until the land has retrieved its lost
　　　　sabbaths,
　　during all the time it lies waste it shall
　　　　have rest
　　while seventy years are fulfilled."

In the first year of Cyrus, king of Persia,
  in order to fulfill the word of the LORD
    spoken by Jeremiah,
  the LORD inspired King Cyrus of Persia
  to issue this proclamation throughout
    his kingdom,
  both by word of mouth and in writing:
  "Thus says Cyrus, king of Persia:
  All the kingdoms of the earth
  the LORD, the God of heaven, has given
    to me,
  and he has also charged me to build him
    a house
  in Jerusalem, which is in Judah.
  Whoever, therefore, among you belongs to
    any part of his people,
  let him go up, and may his God be with
    him!"

**RESPONSORIAL PSALM**
Ps 137:1-2, 3, 4-5, 6

R℣. (6ab) Let my tongue be silenced, if I
    ever forget you!

By the streams of Babylon
  we sat and wept when we remembered
    Zion.
On the aspens of that land
  we hung up our harps.

R℣. Let my tongue be silenced, if I ever
    forget you!

For there our captors asked of us
  the lyrics of our songs,
and our despoilers urged us to be joyous:
  "Sing for us the songs of Zion!"

R℣. Let my tongue be silenced, if I ever
    forget you!

How could we sing a song of the LORD
  in a foreign land?
If I forget you, Jerusalem,
  may my right hand be forgotten!

R℣. Let my tongue be silenced, if I ever
    forget you!

May my tongue cleave to my palate
  if I remember you not,
if I place not Jerusalem
  ahead of my joy.

R℣. Let my tongue be silenced, if I ever
    forget you!

**SECOND READING**
Eph 2:4-10

*See Appendix A, p. 271.*

### About Liturgy

***Rejoicing and mourning:*** So much of our Scriptures, especially the psalms, speak of human emotion and run the whole gamut from exultant rejoicing to resigned grief. On this *Laetare* (or "rejoice") Sunday, we have similar contrasts. We get the name for this Sunday from the entrance antiphon: "Rejoice, Jerusalem, and all who love her. / Be joyful, all who were in mourning; / exult and be satisfied at her consoling breast" (Isa 66:10-11). Like *Gaudete* Sunday in Advent, this midpoint to the Lenten penitential season gives us a little breather. We are halfway through our Lenten observance! Therefore, the rubrics in the Mass call for rose or violet vestments, and instrumental music as well as flowers at the altar may be used on this day.

However, Psalm 137 assigned for today stands in stark contrast to this mid-season rejoicing: "Let my tongue be silenced, if I ever forget you! / By the streams of Babylon / we sat and wept when we remembered Zion." What do we make of these extremes in emotion, and how does it inform our liturgical preparation? Is liturgy about feelings, and are liturgists meant to direct an assembly's emotions? Our faith is wonderfully incarnational and human, and we teach that in Jesus' incarnation, all human feeling and experience is transformed by his divinity. Yet, the liturgy itself is dispassionate, not because it is devoid of emotion but because it is rooted in the constancy of God who, out of passionate love for humankind, "gave his only Son, / so that everyone who believes in him might not perish / but might have eternal life." Gabe Huck said it well when he wrote about liturgy and feelings:

> Liturgy is not about how we feel. It is about who we are and whose we are. Much is made today of feelings and of the individual's great importance. When Christians enter upon their liturgy, however, all of that must be balanced with something else. The liturgy is what the church does. If I do the liturgy, I do it as a baptized member of this community of baptized persons. In a sense, I play a role that is only partly mine now, the role of a member of God's reign. The liturgy does not exist so that I can get my feelings expressed. Rather, it rehearses me in the feelings I ought to have. . . .
>
> We can begin to glimpse how the liturgy is filled not simply with emotion but with passion. Look at the words we sing in the psalms and hear in the scripture, look at the lives we celebrate on feasts, look hardest at the very core of the Eucharist. In the Eucharistic Prayer we speak as passionate people about creation and sin and God's relentless love. The climax of Catholic liturgy is the eating and drinking of Christ's body and blood, a deed that holds and little by little reveals a multitude of human passions. (*Hymnal for Catholic Students: Leader's Manual* [LTP and GIA, 1989], 21)

### About Liturgical Music

***Music suggestions:*** Much of our liturgical music today can fall into an overreliance on emotions. Emotion in our music is not a bad thing and can certainly draw us into deep prayer. However, there is also great value in the kind of stoicism that a sturdy hymn tune and text can give to a worshiping assembly made up of a variety of people bringing with them their different feelings and emotions to prayer. GIA Publications provides a useful resource called *Hymns for the Gospels* (2001), a collection of familiar and new hymn tunes set to texts indexed by scriptural verse. For today's gospel, we find Carl Daw's "God Our Author and Creator" set to the familiar tune BEACH SPRING, and Herman Stuempfle's "Alone and Filled with Fear" set to FRANCONIA.

## SPIRITUALITY

**GOSPEL ACCLAMATION**
John 12:26

Whoever serves me must follow me, says the Lord;
and where I am, there also will my servant be.

### Gospel

John 12:20-33; L35B

Some Greeks who had come to
    worship at the Passover Feast
came to Philip, who was from
    Bethsaida in Galilee,
and asked him, "Sir, we would
    like to see Jesus."
Philip went and told Andrew;
    then Andrew and Philip went and
    told Jesus.
Jesus answered them,
    "The hour has come for the Son
    of Man to be glorified.
Amen, amen, I say to you,
    unless a grain of wheat falls to the
    ground and dies,
    it remains just a grain of wheat;
    but if it dies, it produces much fruit.
Whoever loves his life loses it,
    and whoever hates his life in this world
    will preserve it for eternal life.
Whoever serves me must follow me,
    and where I am, there also will my
    servant be.
The Father will honor whoever serves
    me.

"I am troubled now. Yet what should I
    say?
'Father, save me from this hour'?
But it was for this purpose that I came to
    this hour.
Father, glorify your name."
Then a voice came from heaven,
    "I have glorified it and will glorify it
    again."

*Continued in Appendix A, p. 274.*

*Year A readings may be used, see Appendix A,
pp. 274–276.*

### Reflecting on the Gospel

"The end is near!" says the placard held by the one who firmly believes in the approaching apocalypse. Many claim to know when a disaster will strike, or when God will send his judgment upon the earth. Some look for signs and discern meaning from natural events. An earthquake might mean the foundations of the world are being shaken, in preparation for God's judgment. Terrible and violent storms are understood as God's anger poured out on an unrepentant people. God's activity is often discerned (rightly or wrongly) by interpreting events in daily life.

In today's gospel two Greeks (certainly not Jews) approach not Jesus but Philip, which, by the way, is a Greek name. Up to this point in Jesus' ministry, according to the Gospel of John, Jesus has never, not once, interacted with a Gentile. Luke, of course, paints a different picture, but today we are reading from the Gospel of John.

Philip listens to the request of these two Greeks who want to see Jesus and, in turn, goes to Andrew (another Greek name!) to enlist his help with this unorthodox request. Together the disciples intercede for the Greek interlocutors. Jesus rightly perceives this to be the conclusion of his ministry. If even the Greeks (that is, Gentiles) are now coming to see him, the end is near! Death is at the ready. Jesus then begins an eloquent teaching on the necessity of death for bearing fruit, and no mention is made that the Greeks ever met Jesus. Instead, they serve merely as a narrative tool to usher in the final days of Jesus.

It's true that the ancients did not have the knowledge about biology that we have today. Upon hearing the metaphor of a seed dying to produce much fruit, many in a modern audience might dispute the analogy. For we know that a seed does not truly die, but the soil, moisture, and light cause an organic change. Still we do not want to lose the message in spite of the metaphor. Only by his death will Jesus' ministry truly bear fruit. That is the necessary next step. His death is necessary because this is the purpose for which Jesus came. There is no sidestepping or dodging this inevitable end, which is ratified by a voice from heaven. The end is near.

### Living the Paschal Mystery

In this Lenten Sunday preceding Palm Sunday we share a sense of impending doom. But we are also reminded of the necessity of death for something to bear fruit. If the seed stays on the countertop, it will never bear fruit. But once "dead" and planted in the ground, the seed produces. The paschal mystery is presented for us in a simple, agrarian, even if scientifically outdated, image.

Do we allow ourselves to die to our own desires, wants, and agenda? From today's gospel reading, it seems Jesus was not quite ready for this moment. But the arrival of the Greeks was a clarion signal that the end was near. Even for Jesus there was no fighting this eternal purpose. This was the reason he came into the world. His example of letting go serves as a model for us. We are not the masters of our own fate. We are not in ultimate control of our own destiny. The illusion that we are somehow planning our own destiny is simply that, an illusion. There are greater forces at work. We are called to discern those forces so we can recognize them when they face us. For Jesus it was the request from two Greeks. What are the signs that encourage us to let go of our own desires and submit to something greater? When we die to ourselves we will see fruit that bears eternal life.

### Focusing the Gospel
*John 12:20-33*

Today's gospel is a pivotal moment in John's narrative. Jesus' words about the coming of his "hour" mark the end of John's "book of signs" and prefaces of the "book of glory": the passion, death, and resurrection of Jesus.

The annual Passover feast is about to begin; many Jews (including some Greeks) have arrived in Jerusalem for the festival. Meanwhile, Jesus' conflict with the Jewish establishment has escalated to a dangerous level. The events that will lead to Jesus' condemnation and death are now in motion. Jesus obediently accepts his fate and is prepared for the outcome.

Jesus compares his "glorification" to a grain of wheat that is buried and dies to produce its potential crop. The death and ultimate harvest of the grain of wheat are the fate and glory of anyone who would be Jesus' disciple.

The "voice" may have only been heard by Jesus. While those around heard thunder, Jesus heard what was called a *bat qol* ("daughter of a voice"): in Jewish tradition, individuals and groups sometimes heard a "voice" from heaven revealing to them God's teaching or will for them. The *bat qol* that Jesus "hears" in today's gospel is a call to all the world that a new Passover was about to begin.

### Focusing the First Reading
*Jer 31:31-34*

In today's first reading, the prophet Jeremiah prophesies a "new covenant" that will be written not on stone (as was the law of Moses) but on human hearts and spirits. Jeremiah's vision will be realized in Jesus' vision of the kingdom of God, a kingdom established on justice, mercy, and peace.

### Focusing the Responsorial Psalm
*Ps 51:3-4, 12-13, 14-15 (12a)*

The image of God recreating hearts, of renewing human souls, that Jeremiah writes of in today's first reading is echoed in the antiphon and verses selected from Psalm 51, today's responsorial psalm.

### Focusing the Second Reading
*Heb 5:7-9*

The theology in the second reading is sophisticated and subtle. The letter to the Hebrews praises Jesus for his obedience to the will of God his Father. In his suffering, the son learns obedience and is thereby perfected. For us who obey him, he is the source of eternal salvation.

---

**PROMPTS FOR HOMILISTS, CATECHISTS, AND RCIA TEAMS**

How have you experienced the dying and the harvest of the grain of wheat in your life?

What is the most powerful or authoritative "law" that God has written on your heart?

When have you found it most difficult to be obedient to God?

When have you lost something that, in time, turned out to be a gain?

Have you ever experienced the presence of Jesus in the love and support of someone?

## Model Penitential Act

*Presider:* Let us begin our celebration of the Eucharist by calling to mind our sins, confident of the never failing mercy of God. *[pause]*

   *Confiteor:* I confess . . .

## Homily Points

• It is in our most challenging experiences that we discover what we are capable of; it is during our darkest nights that we find the light of possibility. To transform our lives in order to become the people we are meant to be begins by "dying" to those ambitions, prejudices, and fears we cling to and embrace the values, wisdom, and grace that give meaning and purpose to our lives. Jesus readily acknowledges that such change is hard; the struggle to change is, in its own way, an experience of death—but such transformation is necessary if such resurrection can be experienced. The gospel of the grain of wheat is Christ's assurance to us of the great things we can do and the powerful works we can accomplish by dying to self and rising to the love and compassion of Jesus, the Servant Redeemer.

• Life demands change, risk, and a certain amount of "dying" to our fears, despair, and sense of self; but if we are willing to risk loving and allowing ourselves to be loved, Jesus promises us the harvest of the gospel grain of wheat. In our willingness to nurture healing and forgiveness, in our openness to God's grace and the compassion of others, there will always be possibilities for new beginnings, second chances, constant plantings, and unlimited bounties. Only by loving is love returned; only by reaching out beyond ourselves do we learn and grow; only by giving to others do we receive; only by dying do we rise to new life.

## Model Universal Prayer (Prayer of the Faithful)

*Presider:* Let us join our prayers with those of the obedient Christ Jesus for the needs of all God's sons and daughters.

*Response:* Lord, hear our prayer.

That all who serve the church as bishops, priests, deacons, ministers, and teachers may imitate the humble obedience of Christ Jesus . . .

That the wisdom and justice of God may be the foundation of all laws and public policies of the world's governments, corporations, and institutions . . .

That those who are entombed by illness, violence, addiction, or fear may be raised up to a new life of hope and fulfillment . . .

That, in our common life together, our church and parish community may proclaim the life and love of God . . .

*Presider:* God of life, Source of love, accept the offering of our prayers. Bless us always with the hope of the grain of wheat, so that we may seek to die to ourselves for the sake of others, and one day rise to the new life of the eternal springtime of your Son, our Lord and risen Savior, Jesus Christ. **Amen.**

### COLLECT

Let us pray.

*Pause for silent prayer*

By your help, we beseech you, Lord our
   God,
may we walk eagerly in that same charity
with which, out of love for the world,
your Son handed himself over to death.
Through our Lord Jesus Christ, your Son,
who lives and reigns with you in the unity
   of the Holy Spirit,
one God, for ever and ever. **Amen.**

### FIRST READING

Jer 31:31-34

The days are coming, says the LORD,
   when I will make a new covenant with
      the house of Israel
   and the house of Judah.
It will not be like the covenant I made with
      their fathers
   the day I took them by the hand
   to lead them forth from the land of
      Egypt;
   for they broke my covenant,
   and I had to show myself their master,
      says the LORD.
But this is the covenant that I will make
   with the house of Israel after those
      days, says the LORD.
I will place my law within them and write
   it upon their hearts;
   I will be their God, and they shall be my
      people.
No longer will they have need to teach
      their friends and relatives
   how to know the LORD.
All, from least to greatest, shall know me,
      says the LORD,
   for I will forgive their evildoing and
      remember their sin no more.

## RESPONSORIAL PSALM

Ps 51:3-4, 12-13, 14-15

R̂. (12a) Create a clean heart in me, O God.

Have mercy on me, O God, in your
    goodness;
    in the greatness of your compassion
      wipe out my offense.
Thoroughly wash me from my guilt
    and of my sin cleanse me.

R̂. Create a clean heart in me, O God.

A clean heart create for me, O God,
    and a steadfast spirit renew within me.
Cast me not out from your presence,
    and your Holy Spirit take not from me.

R̂. Create a clean heart in me, O God.

Give me back the joy of your salvation,
    and a willing spirit sustain in me.
I will teach transgressors your ways,
    and sinners shall return to you.

R̂. Create a clean heart in me, O God.

## SECOND READING

Heb 5:7-9

In the days when Christ Jesus was in the
    flesh,
    he offered prayers and supplications
      with loud cries and tears
    to the one who was able to save him
      from death,
    and he was heard because of his
      reverence.
Son though he was, he learned obedience
    from what he suffered;
    and when he was made perfect,
    he became the source of eternal
      salvation for all who obey him.

## About Liturgy

*Memorizing readings:* Some people have a great gift for memorizing texts. I've seen some excellent priests proclaim the gospel reading (every Sunday!) from memory, never straying from the approved translation or paraphrasing it in their own words. Perhaps they have a photographic memory. Whereas for me, I need to take many hours in contemplation and repetition with a reading in order to memorize it well until it becomes a part of me.

Today's first reading from Jeremiah speaks eloquently of God writing his covenant not on tablets of stone but on his people's hearts so that "[n]o longer will they have need to teach their friends and relatives / how to know the Lord." In this way, God's law becomes something that we do not so much memorize as internalize. In other words, being in right relationship with God means being in a relationship of love, not of fear.

This intimate relationship with God through Scripture is something that lectors can nurture if they practice a discipline of memorizing at least parts of their readings each week. The purpose of this is not to proclaim the readings from memory, although there may be appropriate times when a lector might do this. The goal, rather, is to become so intimately familiar with the text that the lector no longer "thinks" about reading the text but merely speaks it *from the heart.*

Even if a lector, deacon, or priest memorizes a complete reading and is able to proclaim it without using the Lectionary or Book of Gospels, there is still symbolic value to the reader standing at the ambo with the open book. Even if they never look at the book, by proclaiming the reading *from the book,* they communicate that this is not their word but God's, handed down from generation to generation and from heart to heart.

## About Initiation

*Preparation rites for Holy Saturday:* This is a good time to remind your elect, their godparents, and any other parishioners who have been significant in the faith journey of the elect about the preparation rites for Holy Saturday. These rites, celebrated on Holy Saturday during the day, are the final liturgical prayers for the elect as they await the beginning of the Easter Vigil where they will make their baptismal promises and be initiated into the death and resurrection of Christ. Even if they do not participate in these rites, inform your parishioners with an announcement at Mass or in the bulletin so that they can at least pray in solidarity with and for the elect in the days ahead.

## About Liturgical Music

*Music suggestions:* Here are several lovely pieces that go well with today's focus on the disciple's self-sacrifice in imitation of Jesus' sacrifice in love for us. "You Shall Be My People" by Michael Philip Ward (WLP) contemplates God's covenant with his people and opens with a nice complement to the plea in Psalm 51 that God give us a new heart. Steve Warner's "Christ Has No Body Now But Yours" (WLP), inspired by text from St. Teresa of Ávila, moves us out into being Christ's disciples in the world. Finally, a longtime favorite by David Haas is "Deep Within" (GIA), which focuses again on the text from today's first reading.

**MARCH 18, 2018**
# FIFTH SUNDAY OF LENT

# ST. JOSEPH, SPOUSE OF THE BLESSED VIRGIN MARY

## GOSPEL ACCLAMATION
Ps 84:5

Blessed are those who dwell in your house,
O Lord;
they never cease to praise you.

## Gospel

Luke 2:41-51a; L543

Each year Jesus' parents went
to Jerusalem for the feast of
Passover,
and when he was twelve years old,
they went up according to festival
custom.
After they had completed its days, as
they were returning,
the boy Jesus remained behind in
Jerusalem,
but his parents did not know it.
Thinking that he was in the caravan,
they journeyed for a day
and looked for him among their
relatives and acquaintances,
but not finding him,
they returned to Jerusalem to look for
him.
After three days they found him in the
temple,
sitting in the midst of the teachers,
listening to them and asking them
questions,
and all who heard him were astounded
at his understanding and his answers.
When his parents saw him,
they were astonished,
and his mother said to him,
"Son, why have you done this to us?
Your father and I have been looking for
you with great anxiety."
And he said to them,
"Why were you looking for me?
Did you not know that I must be in my
Father's house?"
But they did not understand what he said
to them.
He went down with them and came to
Nazareth,
and was obedient to them.

*or Matt 1:16, 18-21, 24a in Appendix A, p. 277.*

*See Appendix A, p. 277, for the other readings.*

## Reflecting on the Gospel

There is no manual given to first-time parents informing them about how to raise their little bundle of joy. For better or worse, often parents simply fall back on the way they were raised. If our parents were lenient, we tend to be lenient. If our parents were strict, we tend to be strict. It takes a conscious effort to recognize and then break out of these patterns, should that be what we want to do. Something similar happens with marriage. The most prominent model for marriage many people have is their own parents. We tend to fall into patterns there too, again, for better or worse.

Though we know precious little about Joseph, we can be confident that he married Mary, staying true to her in the difficult circumstances of an unwed pregnancy, and the child who was not his own. From this alone we can surmise that Joseph must have been noble and courageous. And by the time of Jesus' public ministry Joseph is no longer on the scene. This lacuna is usually interpreted to mean that Joseph had passed away by that time. But between the birth of Jesus and his public ministry, Luke gives us the story of finding Jesus in the temple. This happened when Jesus was a preteen, only twelve years old. Joseph and Mary's response to finding Jesus in the temple after three days gives us a brief insight into their roles as parents. Perhaps significantly, it is Mary who speaks on their behalf in their collective astonishment. Joseph listens in silence, though Mary is clear that they were both looking for Jesus "with great anxiety." This episode was certainly worthy of remembrance not only because they found him in the temple, but quite likely because of the anxiety it produced in Joseph and Mary.

It goes without saying that Joseph and Mary's parenting had an influential role on Jesus. The story concludes by saying that Jesus was obedient to them. His actions during his adult ministry were no doubt greatly influenced by how he was raised in their home. He likely modeled the behavior he saw in his home. Though we have no words from Joseph in the gospels the impact of a father on a son (or daughter, for that matter) is profound. Today we spend some time considering the role of Joseph in the life of Jesus and Mary. Joseph was at times courageous and noble, but at other times also astonished, and even filled with anxiety. But true to his vocation as father and spouse, he lived a life worthy of emulation.

## Living the Paschal Mystery

So often we can think of the lives of the saints as beyond us. With respect to Joseph and Mary, for example, how can we compare? Is anyone today raising a Son of God who is the Messiah?! Still, God's activity in the world did not conclude two thousand years ago. One of the lessons from today's gospel is to be reminded of the holiness of family life. Sanctity is found in familial relationships: husband, father, spouse, parent, mother, wife. Moreover, those family relationships are not always "neat and tidy." Joseph is sometimes called the foster father of Jesus as a way to indicate that Jesus was not Joseph's biological son. Joseph married a pregnant Mary even though he knew the child was not his. But God is nevertheless active; he does not demand our perfection before dealing with us as humans. God is present in the everyday messy situations of our lives.

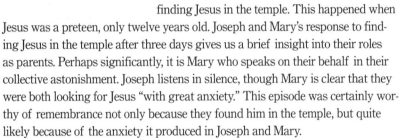

We do not need to become capital *S* Saints in order to follow God's will for us in this life. When we are true to our vocation of spouse, parent, uncle, aunt, friend, responding in typical human ways including courage, nobility, astonishment, and even anxiety, we are living God's will for ourselves.

### Focusing the Gospel

There are two options for today's gospel reading. Joseph's "righteousness" and devotion to Mary and the child are central to both.

Luke's story of the twelve-year-old Jesus' disappearance in Jerusalem is every parent's worst nightmare. For three days Mary and Joseph frantically look for the boy, finally finding him in the temple with the teachers. Every parent and guardian can understand the anxiety and fear suffered by Mary and Joseph in their desperate search for their missing boy.

In Matthew's account of Jesus' birth, Joseph, a descendent of David, is formally engaged to Mary, a legally binding arrangement. When she is found to be pregnant, the "righteous" Joseph plans to divorce her quietly rather than subject her to the full fury of Jewish law. Visited by God's angel in a dream, Joseph responds with faith and trust in God's plan and takes into his home Mary and the child. In acknowledging the child and naming him *Jesus* ("Savior"), Joseph becomes, in the eyes of the law, the legal father of Jesus. Thus, through Joseph, Isaiah's prophecy is fulfilled in Jesus: the virgin has given birth to a son, one who is a descendent of David's house. Jesus is truly *Emmanuel*, "God is with us."

### Model Penitential Act

*Presider:* Let us begin our eucharistic celebration on this solemnity of St. Joseph, the husband of Mary and guardian of Jesus, by asking God's mercy and grace for our sins and failing. *[pause]*

O God, Father of all peoples and nations: Lord, have mercy.
Lord Jesus, Savior and Redeemer: Christ, have mercy.
Holy Spirit, the love of God moving in our midst: Lord, have mercy.

### Model Universal Prayer (Prayer of the Faithful)

*Presider:* In the spirit of St. Joseph's righteousness and compassion, let us offer our prayers.

*Response:* Lord, hear our prayer.

That the church's work and worship may establish the house of God in all communities . . .

That the peace and justice of God's reign may be realized in a spirit of cooperation and respect among all nations and peoples . . .

That, in the loving support of family and friends, Christ may be present to families in crisis and households experiencing hardship or grief . . .

That fathers and mothers may see in Joseph's example a model of loving compassion and patience for the children God has entrusted to their care . . .

*Presider:* God our Father, hear our prayers on this day when we remember Joseph, to whom you entrusted the care of your Son. May we be inspired by his devotion, goodness, and integrity. In embracing his faith in your Word and his care for your Word made flesh, may we become Josephs for one another: brothers and sisters of your compassion and love. In Jesus' name, we pray. **Amen.**

**COLLECT**
Let us pray.

*Pause for silent prayer*

Grant, we pray, almighty God,
that by Saint Joseph's intercession
your Church may constantly watch over
the unfolding of the mysteries of human
    salvation,
whose beginnings you entrusted to his
    faithful care.
Through our Lord Jesus Christ, your Son,
who lives and reigns with you in the unity of
    the Holy Spirit,
one God, for ever and ever. **Amen.**

**FOR REFLECTION**

• What are the most important and lasting things that parents give their children?

• When have you had to make the choice between being "right" and being compassionate?

• Of all the stories of Joseph in Scripture, which one most resonates with you, that recalls a time when you experienced the emotions that Joseph felt?

### Homily Points

• Though Joseph is considered to be Jesus' "foster father," make no mistake: Jesus must have learned a great deal about integrity and compassion from his "dad." When the adult Jesus taught about placing the difficult values of the heart above the technicalities of law, when he revealed God as our Father and our belonging to one another as brothers and sisters, when he spoke of the blessedness of the poor and humble, when he preached about love so great as to give one's life for another, the memories of his "dad" must have been close to his heart.

• Parenthood is one of life's most fulfilling experiences, but it is also terrifying and demanding, filled with pain, doubt, and anxiety. Yet to be a parent is to be a coworker with God, the Father of all, whose love for his sons and daughters knows no limit. In Joseph and Mary's struggles, we realize that the light of God's love shines in our own families as we confront those same tensions and crises.

## ✝ SPIRITUALITY

**GOSPEL ACCLAMATION**
Phil 2:8-9

Christ became obedient to the point of death,
even death on a cross.
Because of this, God greatly exalted him
and bestowed on him the name which is above
        every name.

***Gospel*** at the procession with palms

Mark 11:1-10; L37B (John 12:12-16 may also
be read.)

**When Jesus and his disciples drew near
        to Jerusalem,
    to Bethphage and Bethany at the Mount
        of Olives,
    he sent two of his disciples and said to
        them,
    "Go into the village opposite you,
    and immediately on entering it,
    you will find a colt tethered on which
        no one has ever sat.
Untie it and bring it here.
If anyone should say to you,
    'Why are you doing this?' reply,
    'The Master has need of it
    and will send it back here at once.'"
So they went off
    and found a colt tethered at a gate
        outside on the street,
    and they untied it.**

*Continued in Appendix A, p. 278.*

***Gospel*** at Mass   Mark 14:1–15:47; L38B
or Mark 15:1–39; L38B *in Appendix A,
pp. 278–281.*

### Reflecting on the Gospel

How quickly praise can turn to derision. We see it in business, politics, even with friends and family. One minute somebody is singing praises, the next it's insults and scorn. The gospel readings display that very juxtaposition today. We come into church singing "Hosanna!" and fifteen minutes later we cry, "Crucify him!"

The people wanted an earthly king to shake off Roman occupation and achieve political independence. But how quickly they turned on Jesus when they realized that he would not fulfill their plans. God had something else in store.

As Jesus did not meet the expectations of the crowd, or even his disciples, they turned and fled. One disciple ran so fast he ran out of his clothes (Mark 14:51-52)! Peter, of course, denied he even knew Jesus. The crowd chose to have an insurrectionist released to them rather than Jesus. By the time Jesus was on the cross the only remaining friends were some women and Joseph of Arimathea, though it seems Jesus wouldn't have known about Joseph's act of courage. The women were said to have ministered to him and followed him when he was in Galilee. Though the women lacked the "disciple" title, they were clearly his followers, offering a ministry of presence up to and during his death and subsequent burial. They stand in contrast to the behavior of the "real" disciples (those who bear the name) who denied Jesus, or simply fled the scene.

The entire passion narrative in Mark shows the confusion, bewilderment, and misunderstanding that punctuated the horrific scene of Jesus' crucifixion. The crowds believe Jesus is calling for Elijah, the chief priests and scribes mock Jesus as one who cannot save himself, Pilate acquiesces to the crowd's demands and participates in a miscarriage of justice. The centurion alone (a Gentile) is the only one to face the crucified after death and proclaim faith in him. Peter (a Jew) confessed Jesus as Christ (Mark 8:29) and now the centurion (a Gentile) confesses Jesus as Son of God, only after his death. To be the Christ, the Son of God, necessarily means suffering and death. To have come down from the cross would have been to deny Jesus' own identity as Christ and Son of God. Rather than a political military leader commanding armies in a revolution, Jesus is the crucified Son of God, Messiah. God's plans are not our own.

### Living the Paschal Mystery

We are fickle human beings, often in search of entertainment. We are designed by eons of evolution to look toward the future rather than the past. Palm Sunday is our conscious effort to root ourselves in our past, the very foundation of our faith, the paschal mystery. This week we celebrate the most ancient and fundamental mysteries of faith. Without this effort to reach our touchstone we would likely be fleeting from one moment to the next, seeking to fulfill various desires and cravings. Being in touch with the paschal mystery reminds us that this life has meaning beyond the here and now. We have a future that is eternal. The love, relationships, and bonds we create in this life will endure. The passion and death of Jesus necessarily result in his resurrection, which gives us a promise and foretaste of that eternal life. Rather than seek the next best thing, upon entering this Holy Week we recall that our faith is rooted in the past, and our destiny is eternal.

### Focusing the Gospel

*The Blessing and Procession of Palms: Mark 11:1-10 or John 12:12-16*
It was the custom for pilgrims to enter Jerusalem on foot. Only great kings and rulers would "ride" into the city, and usually on great steeds. In *Mark's* gospel, Jesus, the King of the new Jerusalem, chooses to ride into the city not on a majestic stallion (associated with war) but on the back of a young colt (a sign of

humility and peace) in what was likely a conscious effort on Jesus' part to call to mind the prophecy of Zechariah five centuries before (see Zech 9:9).

The story of Jesus' entry into the city is essentially the same in all four gospels. The entire narratives of Mark, Matthew, and Luke all lead to Jesus' coming to Jerusalem; but in *John's* shorter account, Jesus' Palm Sunday entry is actually his third trip to Jerusalem. In the Fourth Gospel, Jesus is enthusiastically welcomed by the crowds, many of whom had heard about his raising of Lazarus. John specifically refers to Zechariah's prophecy. The crowd's welcome of Jesus with *Hosannas* ("God save us") and palm branches is taken from the concluding verses of Psalm 118.

*The Passion: Mark 14:1–15:47*
Mark portrays the anguish of Jesus, abandoned by friends and disciples and resigned to his fate. He submits to arrest; he offers no response to the false accusations made against him; he makes no reply to Pilate. When asked if he is the Messiah, Jesus replies, "I am," and speaks of his glory to come; to Pilate's question as to whether he is "the king of the Jews," he says only, "You say so." Jesus' response to the chief priests contrasts the different understandings the rulers of Judaism have of the Messiah; Jesus' answer to Pilate shows the great chasm between the "peace" of Roman rule and the "peace" of God's kingdom.

Mark pointedly portrays the disciples' failure to provide any support to Jesus. The "last" disciple who flees naked into the night when Jesus is arrested is a powerful symbol in Mark's gospel of the disciples who left family and friends behind to follow Jesus but now leave everything behind to get away from him.

### Focusing the First Reading
*Isa 50:4-7*
Isaiah preached hope and perseverance to the Jews who were exiled from Jerusalem and their homeland by the Assyrians seven hundred years before Christ. Isaiah is the prophet of "Emmanuel," the first major prophet to envision what Jesus will call the "kingdom of God." In four passages, known as the Servant Songs, Isaiah describes this figure who will restore Israel's covenant with God. The first reading for Palm Sunday is the third of these songs. The prophet portrays the servant-redeemer as a devoted teacher of God's word who is ridiculed and abused by those who are threatened by his teaching.

### Focusing the Responsorial Psalm
*Ps 22:8-9, 17-18, 19-20, 23-24 (2a)*
Psalm 22, Jesus' last cry of abandonment, is today's response. The psalms were the song book of Judaism and faithful Jews would know its hymns by heart. Onlookers would have immediately recognized the words to this lament cried by Jesus as he hung outside the city gates. Several of the horrific images in the psalm's verses that are sung on Palm Sunday mirror the sufferings endured by Jesus, but the psalm concludes with hope and trust in God's providence.

### Focusing the Second Reading
*Phil 2:6-11*
In his letter to the Christian community at Philippi (in northeastern Greece), Paul quotes what many scholars believe was the text of an early Christian hymn in praise of Jesus' "attitude" of humility and obedience. As Christ totally and unselfishly "emptied himself" to accept crucifixion for our sakes, to follow Jesus requires us to "empty" ourselves of our wants and needs for the sake of others.

**PROMPTS FOR HOMILISTS, CATECHISTS, AND RCIA TEAMS**

How is Christ's "attitude," as articulated in St. Paul's hymn in today's reading from Philippians, the antithesis of the world's "attitude"?

Has a cross you have had to take up been the means of new life and resurrection?

When have you felt abandoned by God, but discovered him again in your life?

How do we experience "redemption" in our time and place?

How and why do the crowds change from welcoming Jesus with palms today to calling for his crucifixion five days from now?

### Model Penitential Act *(used only with the simple entrance)*

*Presider:* Today we begin our celebration of the Lord's paschal mystery. Our Holy Week journey with Jesus begins with his entry into Jerusalem to shouts of "Hosanna" and the joyful waving of palm branches. In the days ahead, the joy of this moment will be darkened by betrayal and death. Let us begin our Palm Sunday liturgy by placing our hearts in the love of God, who, in his Son, takes up the cross in order to bring us to Easter resurrection. *[pause]*

*Confiteor:* I confess . . .

### Homily Points

• Holy Week confronts us with the powerful symbol of the cross. No other word or object so definitively and completely symbolizes the love of God for us, his own. No other symbol confronts us with the very worst we fail to see in ourselves, that part of us that enables us to rationalize the crucifixions we execute. By the cross, we are reconciled with God; by the cross, our lives are transformed in the perfect love of Christ; by the cross, Jesus' spirit of humility and compassion become a force of hope and re-creation in our hurting and despairing world.

• Jesus enters Jerusalem for the final and climactic chapter of his messiahship, when God will vindicate his son's teachings on selfless love, his exaltation of humble service, his revelation of God as the Father of reconciliation and compassion. In the passion of his Christ, God redeems our own Jerusalems: from despair to hope, from coldness to compassion, from alienation to community. We who have been baptized in the death and resurrection of Jesus have been entrusted with his work of redemption, of recreating our Jerusalems into cities of peace and the kingdom of God.

• Throughout our lives, we find ourselves crying the psalm that Jesus utters on the cross: "My God, my God, why have you abandoned me?" In his passion account, Mark portrays a Jesus who is utterly alone, abandoned by all. Yet, amid the darkness, a light glimmers: a new temple rises from the shreds of the old temple curtain; an unexpected voice proclaims, "This is indeed the Son of God"; a group of faithful, compassionate women begin the work that will lead to their becoming the first witnesses of an extraordinary event. Easter is the very promise of God that in suffering comes healing, in struggle comes strength, in the cross comes resurrection.

### Model Universal Prayer (Prayer of the Faithful)

*Presider:* Let us join our hearts and voices in prayer to God our Father, in the name of Jesus, the humble and obedient Servant of God.

*Response:* Lord, hear our prayer.

That the church's worship and ministries may mirror the love of Christ Jesus, the obedient servant of God . . .

That the world's governments may be dedicated to the cause of peace . . .

That we may imitate the attitude of the humble and obedient Jesus by "emptying" ourselves for the sake of the poor, the hungry, the homeless, and the forgotten . . .

That the love of Christ and our church community may embrace the RCIA catechumens and candidates as they prepare for the Easter sacraments . . .

*Presider:* Father of endless love and compassion, hear the prayers of your family gathered around your altar. May we imitate your Son by taking up our crosses with joyful obedience, seeking your justice in all things; may we embrace his example of loving humility, praising you in the compassionate care we extend to one another. In his name, we offer you these prayers. **Amen.**

---

**COLLECT**

Let us pray.

*Pause for silent prayer*

Almighty ever-living God,
who as an example of humility for the
    human race to follow
caused our Savior to take flesh and submit
    to the Cross,
graciously grant that we may heed his
    lesson of patient suffering
and so merit a share in his Resurrection.
Who lives and reigns with you in the unity
    of the Holy Spirit,
one God, for ever and ever. **Amen.**

**FIRST READING**
Isa 50:4-7

The Lord God has given me
    a well-trained tongue,
that I might know how to speak to the
    weary
    a word that will rouse them.
Morning after morning
    he opens my ear that I may hear;
and I have not rebelled,
    have not turned back.
I gave my back to those who beat me,
    my cheeks to those who plucked my
      beard;
my face I did not shield
    from buffets and spitting.

The Lord God is my help,
    therefore I am not disgraced;
I have set my face like flint,
    knowing that I shall not be put to
      shame.

**RESPONSORIAL PSALM**
Ps 22:8-9, 17-18, 19-20, 23-24

℟. (2a) My God, my God, why have you
    abandoned me?

All who see me scoff at me;
    they mock me with parted lips, they
      wag their heads:
"He relied on the Lord; let him deliver him,
    let him rescue him, if he loves him."

℟. My God, my God, why have you
    abandoned me?

Indeed, many dogs surround me,
a pack of evildoers closes in upon me;
they have pierced my hands and my feet;
I can count all my bones.

R̶. My God, my God, why have you
abandoned me?

They divide my garments among them,
and for my vesture they cast lots.
But you, O Lᴏʀᴅ, be not far from me;
O my help, hasten to aid me.

R̶. My God, my God, why have you
abandoned me?

I will proclaim your name to my brethren;
in the midst of the assembly I will
praise you:
"You who fear the Lᴏʀᴅ, praise him;
all you descendants of Jacob, give glory
to him;
revere him, all you descendants of
Israel!"

R̶. My God, my God, why have you
abandoned me?

**SECOND READING**
Phil 2:6-11

Christ Jesus, though he was in the form
of God,
did not regard equality with God
something to be grasped.
Rather, he emptied himself,
taking the form of a slave,
coming in human likeness;
and found human in appearance,
he humbled himself,
becoming obedient to the point of
death,
even death on a cross.
Because of this, God greatly exalted him
and bestowed on him the name
which is above every name,
that at the name of Jesus
every knee should bend,
of those in heaven and on earth and
under the earth,
and every tongue confess that
Jesus Christ is Lord,
to the glory of God the Father.

## About Liturgy

*Reviewing some basics:* As we enter into the holiest days of the liturgical year, it is easy to do what I call "planning by memory." That is, we prepare liturgy by doing what we remember because "that's how we've always done it." So it's always good to go back and reread the rites, introductions, rubrics, and directives as we make our preparations. The Roman Missal gives you not only the texts to be used but also the specific rubrics (directions) and instructions for each liturgy. Also, an extremely helpful yet little-read Vatican document is *Paschale Solemnitatis* (On Preparing and Celebrating the Paschal Feasts), which gives extensive instructions on Holy Week and the Triduum liturgies.

There are three ways to begin Palm Sunday Mass. You may be surprised to discover that the way most of us begin this Mass—everyone starting outside, blessing palm branches, reading a gospel, then processing into the church—is only to be done once on this day at the main Mass of the parish. At all the other Masses, a less elaborate form is used. See the specific descriptions for each form in the Roman Missal, Palm Sunday, 1–18. The general liturgical principle here is that more is not always better. Multiplying symbols, in this case formal processions, can sometimes lead to making the symbol less significant overall. We will find this principle highlighted throughout Holy Week. If you use either of the first two forms of procession, the usual introductory rites are omitted and you end the procession with the collect.

At the proclamation of the passion gospel, the usual candles, incense, greeting by the deacon or priest, and signing of the book are omitted (Roman Missal, Palm Sunday, 21). During the gospel reading, the assembly's normative posture is standing, showing reverence for Christ present in the Word. You may think letting the assembly be seated for this long reading is a pastoral accommodation. However, unless the majority of your assembly really cannot physically handle standing for the duration of the reading, it is more pastoral to ask the assembly to remain standing *as they are able*. This keeps the assembly in an active posture, not only by their stance but also by giving them a choice to do what is best for them to show reverence to the Word and to be attentive to that Word. It also gives permission to those who do need to sit down, for whatever reason, to do so. The general liturgical principle here is to always ask for the norm while allowing exceptions for those unable to fulfill the norm. Don't get into the habit of making the exception the norm.

## About Liturgical Music

*Music suggestions:* Whether you do the first or second form of the processions for this day, you will need processional music that is either known by heart by the assembly or quickly learned without the need for worship aids. Call-and-response or responsorial forms always work well for this purpose. Also rely more on music that can be sung without musical accompaniment than on trying to set up amplification for guitars or other instruments outdoors. However, several people with hand drums spread throughout the procession also helps to keep everyone together singing.

"The Children of Jerusalem" by Cyprian Consiglio, OSB Cam (OCP) has a short memorable refrain. The verses can be led by a cantor with the assembly joining in on repeated phrases. "Palm Sunday Procession" by Christopher Willcock (OCP) uses an ostinato refrain. "Sing Hosanna to Our King" by John Angotti (WLP) is a bit more contemporary and may need some harmonies to fill out the refrain. "Palm Sunday Processional" by Rory Cooney (GIA) is in a litany form that can be easily learned by the assembly.

# EASTER TRIDUUM

Prayer is the wall of faith,

our shield and weapons

against the foe who studies us from all sides.

Hence, let us never set forth unarmed.

Let us be mindful

of our guard-duty by day

and our vigil by night.

Beneath the arms of prayer

let us guard the standard of our general,

and let us pray as we await the bugle call of the angel.

—Tertullian, On Prayer, 29

## Reflecting on the Triduum

These three days are the backbone of our faith. We commemorate and celebrate the paschal mystery par excellence. Jesus' Last Supper, betrayal, suffering, death, and ultimate resurrection are the featured acts in these most holy of days. Indeed there is so much to commemorate we cannot do it in only one day, or even two. This triad of days reaches into the depths of our existence with such elemental symbols as fire, water, light, darkness, and, of course, bread and wine.

We let these symbols speak to us on an existential level. As we stand outside the church building, gathered around a fire before the Easter Vigil, we are reminded of our ancestors in faith, and perhaps even the ancestors in the evolution of our species who gathered around fires for 700,000 years seeking warmth, light, companionship, safety, and food. These images and symbols have new meaning because of Christ, who becomes for us warmth, light, companionship, safety, and even food.

We begin our Triduum with the celebration of Holy Thursday, combining the Passover meal of the Synoptics with the washing of the feet in John's gospel. Jesus gave us a prime example of service in washing the feet of his disciples, and in becoming the bread and wine shared by them. The master who serves is a radical departure from ancient or even modern models of power. This is not merely "servant-leadership" but a Master who literally serves, and not merely dinner, or serving at table, but much more than that. The Master is performing the menial task of washing another's feet. What CEO today cleans up after a lowly subordinate? Or washes a subordinate's dishes? But the example Jesus gives is much more profound than that. The act of washing another's feet is personal, tactile, and lowly. If Jesus acts this way, how are we to act?

Then we learn this act of service is only a precursor to a paramount act of self-denial when Jesus is crucified. Liturgically, this is commemorated not with a Mass, but with readings from Scripture, veneration of the cross, and distribution of Communion. Not until the Easter Vigil will we truly celebrate the resurrection, scarcely forty-eight hours after we celebrated Holy Thursday; but in so doing, it's as though the church cannot contain its joy. We must celebrate at the earliest possible moment, after sundown, thereby marking a new day. The vigil is marked by fire, candles, light in the darkness, singing, the Gloria and an Alleluia, and the celebration of the Eucharist.

These sacred rites mark us as Christian; they form our identity. They touch something deep within. We will never exhaust these rites. Let us return to them now, enter into them, and drink deeply from their well.

## Living the Paschal Mystery

As we prepare to enter into the celebration of these most holy days, we recall that images of the paschal mystery abound. Each cycle of the seasons, with autumn, winter, spring, then summer, gives us a profound and yet entirely common experience of the paschal mystery. How appropriate, then, that we celebrate Easter in the spring, when new life abounds after a winter hibernation, or even a winter death. Trees bud forth, lilies bloom, tulips break through the ground, babies are born to all manner of creatures. Life itself is renewed on the face of the earth by nature and its seemingly never-ending regenerative cycle. And so we celebrate the author of life, who underwent death only to live again. Death may appear eternal but only life truly is. We celebrate the living in this three-day ritual, not the dead; life rather than death. Our hope of eternal life is based entirely on this mystery we celebrate.

### TRIDUUM

"Triduum" is an odd-sounding word that comes from the Latin term for "three days." These most sacred days begin Holy Thursday evening through Friday evening (day one), include Friday evening through Saturday evening (day two), and conclude with the Easter Vigil and Easter Sunday (day three). We recall that though the modern world (like the ancient Romans) starts a day at midnight, the Jewish day starts at sundown. (And a day for the ancient Greeks started at sunrise!)

These "three days" are the most sacred of the year. And the pinnacle liturgical celebration of the Triduum is the Easter Vigil (General Norms for the Liturgical Year and the Calendar, 19). Parishes sometimes begin this only an hour after sundown. It's as though the church can't wait to celebrate Easter.

### SOLEMN PASCHAL FAST

Even though Lent officially ends with the Holy Thursday liturgy, that does not mean our Lenten fast ends too. Rather, the church keeps a solemn paschal fast on Good Friday and we are encouraged to keep it on Saturday as well, in anticipation of Communion at the Easter Vigil. Only then is our fast complete and the Easter season begun.

"But the paschal fast must be kept sacrosanct. It should be celebrated everywhere on Good Friday, and where possible should be prolonged through Holy Saturday so that the faithful may attain the joys of Easter Sunday with uplifted and receptive minds" (Constitution on the Sacred Liturgy, 110).

## GOSPEL ACCLAMATION
John 13:34

I give you a new commandment, says the Lord:
love one another as I have loved you.

## Gospel   John 13:1-15; L39ABC

Before the feast of Passover, Jesus knew
that his hour had come
to pass from this world to the Father.
He loved his own in the world and he
loved them to the end.
The devil had already induced Judas, son
of Simon the Iscariot, to hand him
over.
So, during supper,
fully aware that the Father had
put everything into his
power
and that he had come from God
and was returning to God,
he rose from supper and took off
his outer garments.
He took a towel and tied it around
his waist.
Then he poured water into a basin
and began to wash the disciples' feet
and dry them with the towel around his
waist.
He came to Simon Peter, who said to him,
"Master, are you going to wash my
feet?"
Jesus answered and said to him,
"What I am doing, you do not
understand now,
but you will understand later."
Peter said to him, "You will never wash
my feet."
Jesus answered him,
"Unless I wash you, you will have no
inheritance with me."
Simon Peter said to him,
"Master, then not only my feet, but my
hands and head as well."
Jesus said to him,
"Whoever has bathed has no need
except to have his feet washed,
for he is clean all over;
so you are clean, but not all."

*Continued in Appendix A, p. 282.*
*See Appendix A, p. 282, for the other readings.*

## Reflecting on the Gospel and Living the Paschal Mystery

*To the point:* Liturgically we celebrate the "institution of the Eucharist" but the gospel reading is about Jesus washing the feet of his disciples as a model of service. The church gives us this reading from the Gospel of John on Holy Thursday to remind us of the Christian call to imitate the master who served. For the Christian, service is required. It is not something we do only when we feel so moved. Rather, it is a fundamental and constitutive element of our identity. We act this way, in service, because of the example Jesus himself gave us. Of course, if his life and death were not example enough, we have this further action on his part during the Last Supper. So in addition to healing the sick, curing the lame, making the blind see, we have one further example par excellence. It's as though Jesus is preemptively responding to later followers who might say, "Sure, Jesus made the blind see, but I can't do that." Or, "Sure, Jesus made the leper whole, but I can't do that." And Jesus gave us another example, one that each person could do. Jesus bent down, and washed the feet of his disciples, even though they called him "Master." Such an example reverberates through the centuries. As human beings, we typically enjoy the status that comes with power and privilege. We enjoy sitting in places of honor. We enjoy getting bumped up to first class on a flight. We enjoy having a fine meal at a restaurant. And these things are all well and good. But Jesus reminds us that those with true power are servants of others without power. Jesus reminds us that to be the master is to be the servant. In so doing, Jesus overturns cultural and societal norms. How many servants are praised and admired? If we become a servant like Jesus what will happen to our prestige, power, and honor? What would people think of us if we stooped so low to be of service to those "beneath us"? Yet, this is precisely what Jesus asks of his disciples. This is not to be a "once-off," or "one-and-done" kind of service for show, so we can be admired for how much we serve. Instead, this is to be our way of being.

We can imagine what Jesus' followers, and the crowds, and even his enemies thought of him when he was serving others to the point of being crucified. Jesus certainly did not appear to be one with power, prestige, or honor at that point. Yet, that is precisely where these acts of self-service lead, and it is where they will lead us. We will pour ourselves out to the point of complete and utter self-emptying. And at that point, God will raise us up like he did Jesus.

*To ponder and pray:* Over this and each Triduum we recall the ultimate mystery of faith. The death and resurrection of Jesus. There could be no resurrection without a death. And the death was humiliating, shameful, and complete. In some ways it can be difficult to imagine that this poor Galilean who died at the hands of an occupying force still has followers today. His message completely upended cultural and societal norms. How many of us really want to follow Jesus to the cross? It seems much easier to admire him from afar.

In preparation for his death Jesus celebrates supper one last time with his disciples. He gives them a lesson they will never forget. In John's gospel we do not have the institution of the Eucharist (for we had the bread of life discourse in chapter 6). Instead, in John's gospel we have an outward sign instituted by Jesus Christ to give grace: the washing of the feet. Up to the thirteenth century the washing of the feet was listed among one of more than thirty sacraments. And of course, this evening we see this ritual commemorated again in the liturgy. This fundamental element of our identity is not something for liturgy only. It is to be lived every day of our lives.

## Model Penitential Act

*Presider:* This evening we begin the Easter Triduum: our solemn remembrance of the passion, death, and resurrection of the Lord, our celebration of Jesus' "passing over" from death on the cross to the life of the resurrection. On this first night of the Triduum, we remember Jesus' Last Supper with his disciples. Tonight Jesus gives his commandment to wash each other's feet in a spirit of humility and service to one another. Let us begin this evening's Mass of the Lord's Supper by placing our hearts in the presence of God, seeking his mercy as we acknowledge our failure to realize Jesus' commandment to love one another as he has loved us. *[pause]*

Lord Jesus, the Lamb of the new Passover feast: Lord, have mercy.
Lord Jesus, bread blessed and broken for us: Christ, have mercy.
Lord Jesus, teacher and model of humble service: Lord, have mercy.

## Model Universal Prayer (Prayer of the Faithful)

*Presider:* In peace, let us pray.

*Response:* Lord, hear our prayer.

For our church and all the people of God, that we may follow the example of Christ who washed the feet of his disciples . . .

For the nations and peoples of the world, that Christ's peace and justice may reign forever . . .

For the sick and dying, the addicted and imprisoned, the suffering and desperate, that the peace and healing of Christ may be theirs . . .

For those preparing for baptism and the Easter sacraments, that they may rise from death to life in the Easter Christ . . .

For our deceased brothers and sisters, that they may live forever in the light of Christ . . .

*Presider:* Hear the prayers we offer you this night, O God, as we gather to celebrate your Son's Passover. By your grace, make us bread for one another and "footwashers" in the spirit of your Son, our Lord Jesus Christ, in whose name we pray. **Amen.**

### COLLECT
Let us pray.

*Pause for silent prayer*

O God, who have called us to participate
in this most sacred Supper,
in which your Only Begotten Son,
when about to hand himself over to death,
entrusted to the Church a sacrifice new for all
     eternity,
the banquet of his love,
grant, we pray,
that we may draw from so great a mystery,
the fullness of charity and of life.
Through our Lord Jesus Christ, your Son,
who lives and reigns with you in the unity of
     the Holy Spirit,
one God, for ever and ever. **Amen.**

### FOR REFLECTION

• In what ways can we "wash the feet" of another in the spirit of Jesus' humility and compassion?

• In what concrete ways is our parish/community formed and inspired by "remembering" Jesus' passion, death, and resurrection?

## Homily Points

• Jesus speaks to us in the pages of the gospel book, in the basin, pitcher, and towel, in the eucharistic bread and wine. We find our identity as Christ's disciples in the memory of this night, which challenges us to make the memory of Jesus' love for all humanity live again in our acts of healing forgiveness and compassionate generosity. In our imitating his simple but eloquent act of washing others' feet, we become the story we remember.

• We loath being vulnerable, but this night confronts us with our need for love and forgiveness, our belonging to one another as children of the same God. Tonight, Christ asks us to take up the towel, pitcher, and basin and take off our robes of pride, and bend down to wash the dirty, tired feet of another. Then, he invites us to sit down and, with equal humility and gratitude, welcome the healing water from another's pitcher washing our feet.

## GOSPEL ACCLAMATION
Phil 2:8-9

Christ became obedient to the point of death,
even death on a cross.
Because of this, God greatly exalted him
and bestowed on him the name which is above
    every other name.

## Gospel   John 18:1–19:42; L40ABC

Jesus went out with his disciples
    across the Kidron valley
  to where there was a garden,
  into which he and his disciples
    entered.
Judas his betrayer also knew the place,
  because Jesus had often met there
    with his disciples.
So Judas got a band of soldiers and guards
  from the chief priests and the
    Pharisees
  and went there with lanterns,
    torches, and weapons.
Jesus, knowing everything that was going
    to happen to him,
  went out and said to them, "Whom are
    you looking for?"
They answered him, "Jesus the Nazorean."
He said to them, "I AM."
Judas his betrayer was also with them.
When he said to them, "I AM,"
  they turned away and fell to the ground.
So he again asked them,
  "Whom are you looking for?"
They said, "Jesus the Nazorean."
Jesus answered,
  "I told you that I AM.
So if you are looking for me, let these
    men go."
This was to fulfill what he had said,
  "I have not lost any of those you gave me."
Then Simon Peter, who had a sword,
    drew it,
  struck the high priest's slave, and cut
    off his right ear.
The slave's name was Malchus.
Jesus said to Peter,
  "Put your sword into its scabbard.
Shall I not drink the cup that the Father
    gave me?"

*Continued in Appendix A, pp. 283–284.*
*See Appendix A, p. 285, for the other readings.*

### Reflecting on the Gospel and Living the Paschal Mystery

*To the point:* The longest reading from any gospel in a liturgical context takes place today, when there is no eucharistic liturgy. Today we feast on two brilliant chapters from the Fourth Gospel. We are not surprised to learn that the author of the Fourth Gospel has been called "the Theologian." Among his rhetorical tools, he uses irony, betrayal, and sophistication to reflect his high Christology, perhaps an early Mariology and sacramental theology, and a unique theological perspective concerning the day on which Jesus was crucified. Unlike what we read in the other gospels, this is explicitly said to be based on eyewitness testimony.

Those disciples whom Jesus called do not seem up to the task. Judas betrays him outright, and Peter folds when the going gets tough. Only one unnamed disciple, and he was known to the high priest, is true to Jesus. It is this unnamed disciple who is thought to be the "eyewitness" (19:35) on which this gospel was based. It is this same disciple who will run with Peter on Easter Sunday morning to find the empty tomb. But during the trial of Jesus, Peter falters under questioning from a maid.

Pilate, the symbol of Roman imperial power and justice, is portrayed as feckless. In a bit of irony, he says to the author of life, "Do you not know that I have the power to release you / and I have power to crucify you?" But the ultimate irony is the placard placed above the crucified Jesus, "the King of the Jews." Though this was done by Pilate in a mocking tone, it proclaims reality. Jesus is a king, the King of Kings.

The theology of Jesus' death in the Gospel of John is bound up in the calendar. Unlike the Synoptic Gospels that portray the Last Supper as a Passover meal, the Gospel of John says that the Last Supper was on the day of preparation for the Passover, in effect one day earlier than the Synoptics would have it. In the two chapters of John we read today it is clear that the Passover will take place on the Sabbath, the day after the crucifixion. For the Gospel of John, the day of the crucifixion is the day of preparation. This is theologically significant because in the Gospel of John, Jesus is the Lamb of God. The lambs for Passover were slaughtered on the day of preparation beginning around noon (see John 19:14). The theology conveyed by this gospel is sophisticated and subtle. Counterintuitively, it's easy to miss this gospel's theology if we are too familiar with the readings. But today we gnaw on the word of God (see John 6). We allow it to sink in and penetrate our very being. The Word made flesh will be consumed, as well as heard.

*To ponder and pray:* Each gospel writer has a unique theological point of view. Each has something to say about Jesus. The church in her wisdom preserves all four, with their different voices and blending melodies. We do not need to reconcile each gospel with the other. Each is true with respect to theology, even if they differ over seemingly important details such as whether Jesus was crucified on Passover or the day of preparation. For the Synoptics, Jesus being crucified on Passover allows them to develop the theology of the Last Supper as a reinterpretation of the Passover meal, something not found in John. For John, Jesus being crucified on preparation day allows him to develop the theology of Jesus as Lamb of God, a title not found in the Synoptics. The richness of our Christian theology means we can hold multiple perspectives simultaneously. The theology about Jesus is more nuanced, sophisticated, and complex than one evangelist alone can convey.

### Music Suggestions

The basic answer to the question, "Were you there?" is no. None of us living today was there at Golgotha, watching the events that took place on that cross. But all of us can say that we are *here*, in *this* time, in *this* place, witnessing the passion and death of Jesus in the lives of the suffering of so many in this world. During the Triduum, and especially on Good Friday, we have to resist the temptation of leaping back in time to recreate what happened in the past. Instead, the liturgical act of remembering is called *anamnesis* or "memorial." This is more than just remembering or recreating a past event. We call to mind what God has done for us in order to help us see God still acting in the events of today. In this memorial, we can glimpse a foretaste of what God has promised us will be in the fullness of time. The United States bishops said it well when they described the purpose of the homily in their 1982 document, Fulfilled in Your Hearing: The Homily in the Sunday Assembly:

> Since the purpose of the homily is to enable the gathered congregation to celebrate the liturgy with faith, the preacher does not so much attempt to explain the Scriptures as to interpret the human situation through the Scriptures. In other words, the goal of the liturgical preacher is not to interpret a text of the Bible as much as to draw on the texts of the Bible as they are presented in the lectionary to interpret people's lives. (52)

We can do the same when we select music for today's liturgy. What songs and texts will help us "interpret people's lives" today through the lens of what happened on that cross long ago? John's gospel account, which we proclaim every Good Friday, gives us a clue. The overarching tone of the passion in John's gospel, although focused on Jesus' death, is always about God's victory over death. Good Friday is "good" because of the resurrection. Therefore, what we sing today needs to present the entire picture of both death *and* resurrection, suffering *and* triumph.

"O Sacred Head" by Bob Hurd (OCP) takes the poetic text of Bernard of Clairvaux that describes the event of the cross, reframes it with the suffering of our sisters and brothers today, and calls us to action now with the promise of resurrection always before us. Tony Alonso's "We Should Glory in the Cross" (WLP) unites the entrance antiphon for Holy Thursday with a litany of ways we glory in Christ's cross today.

**COLLECT**

Let us pray.

Remember your mercies, O Lord,
and with your eternal protection sanctify your
    servants,
for whom Christ your Son,
by the shedding of his Blood,
established the Paschal Mystery.
Who lives and reigns for ever and ever.
**Amen.**

*or:*

O God, who by the Passion of Christ your
    Son, our Lord,
abolished the death inherited from ancient sin
by every succeeding generation,
grant that just as, being conformed to him,
we have borne by the law of nature
the image of the man of earth,
so by the sanctification of grace
we may bear the image of the Man of heaven.
Through Christ our Lord.
**Amen.**

**FOR REFLECTION**

• Where is the crucifixion of Jesus taking place now, in our own time and place?

• Where do we see the brokenness of Christ in our church and community?

• What does humankind most thirst for this Good Friday?

### Homily Points

• "Truth" stands before us in the figure of the suffering, ridiculed, crucified Jesus, in a God who loves us to a degree we cannot begin to fathom. Good Friday calls us to embrace the "truth" of a God of unconditional love and that love's power to recreate our lives and world.

• The "goodness" of this day is that our God who created us came to live, suffer, and die among us. But God refuses to let death be the victor. Good Fridays take place throughout the year, when generous love transforms disappointment and pain into hope and love. This "Good" Friday is not the end of the Christ story. It is the turning point from the gallows to resurrection.

## Gospel

Mark 16:1-7; L41B

When the sabbath was over,
Mary Magdalene, Mary, the mother
of James, and Salome
bought spices so that they might go
and anoint him.
Very early when the sun had risen,
on the first day of the week, they
came to the tomb.
They were saying to one another,
"Who will roll back the stone for
us
from the entrance to the tomb?"
When they looked up,
they saw that the stone had been
rolled back;
it was very large.
On entering the tomb they saw a
young man
sitting on the right side, clothed in
a white robe,
and they were utterly amazed.
He said to them, "Do not be
amazed!
You seek Jesus of Nazareth, the
crucified.
He has been raised; he is not here.
Behold the place where they laid him.
But go and tell his disciples and Peter,
'He is going before you to Galilee;
there you will see him, as he told
you.'"

*See Appendix A, pp. 286–291, for the other
readings.*

### Reflecting on the Gospel and Living the Paschal Mystery

*To the point:* The Gospel of Mark was the first to be written. At sixteen chapters, it is the shortest gospel. It also has the shortest concluding chapter, which we read this evening. (And yet, we do not read the final verse of this shortest chapter, Mark 16:8. That awkward ending is omitted today.) We remember Mark as one who gets right to the point. There is no need for extraneous detail. Indeed, in the original ending of the gospel there is not even a resurrection appearance! The women find the tomb empty, and in the following verse (the one omitted), they run away afraid! Other copyists and editors, including other gospel writers, thought this was no way to end a gospel, which is part of the reason we have multiple endings to the Gospel of Mark (see notes in the NABRE for more).

But in today's story the women come to the tomb, a place of repose for the dead. The tomb itself has been sealed with a massive stone, and so the women contemplate how they will be able to move it. Both the tomb and its stone are stark reminders to the reader that Jesus was crucified. He was then left as dead. It's not as though he merely passed out from exhaustion on the cross. No. Jesus truly died, a claim that will be repeated in the New Testament and even in later creeds, including the ones we proclaim today.

But upon their arrival, the women find the stone, that exclamation point on the tomb, has been moved. The tomb is empty. Shockingly, a white-robed young man (who will be called an angel by Luke and Matthew, but is a "young man" in Mark) announces to the women that Jesus has been raised! They are to announce this good news to Peter and the disciples. As such, St. Augustine referred to Mary Magdalene in particular as *apostola apostolorum*, "the apostle to the apostles," for she was sent to preach the Easter message to those whom Jesus has called, the apostles themselves.

Death has no hold on the author of life. The tombstone cannot seal God's son. He has been raised from death to new life!

*To ponder and pray:* We are told that the women were amazed. We likely would share their amazement. And yet they are told not to be amazed. Jesus had risen from the dead, and they were *not* to be amazed. What Jesus had predicted at least three times earlier in the gospel he has now accomplished. He rose on the third day. Though it can be a natural reaction to be amazed at the work of God, we are to expect that he will do what he says he will. We can rely on the promises of God, who raises from the dead.

The first to witness the effect of this resurrection were the women, whose testimony would not count in Jewish court. Still, these were the ones with the motivation, love, care, and concern to visit the tomb. Mark does not say anything about the male disciples being there. Rather, they would meet Jesus in Galilee, where they first were called. It seems their long journey would bring them back to the beginning. Only now Galilee will be so much different, not because it has changed, but because the disciples have changed. They will not be able to go back to the way things were, but they are going back to the beginning nonetheless. And so it can appear to us as we live the spiritual life. So many of our conclusions circle back to where we began. But we are never the same, having been transformed by our experience of the risen Christ.

## Model Universal Prayer (Prayer of the Faithful)

*Presider:* In the radiance of this holy night, let us pray.

*Response:* Lord, hear our prayer.

For our church and parish family, that, in our work and worship together, we may proclaim the good news of Easter's empty tomb . . .

For the nations and peoples of the world, that the peace of the risen Christ may reign forever . . .

For all those who are suffering, that they may be freed from their infirmities and recreated and healed in the life of the risen Christ . . .

For all who have been baptized and welcomed into our church this Easter, that their lives may be transformed in the joy and hope of this night . . .

For all who have died in the peace of Christ *[especially . . . ]*, that they may be brought by Christ into the dwelling place of God . . .

*Presider:* Father of life, Author of love, in raising your Son from the grave all of creation has been reborn. May the life and love manifested in the paschal mystery be a constant and lasting reality in our lives. We ask this through Christ, our risen Lord. **Amen.**

---

**COLLECT**

Let us pray.

*Pause for silent prayer*

O God, who make this most sacred night radiant with the glory of the Lord's Resurrection, stir up in your Church a spirit of adoption, so that, renewed in body and mind, we may render you undivided service. Through our Lord Jesus Christ, your Son, who lives and reigns with you in the unity of the Holy Spirit, one God, for ever and ever. **Amen.**

---

**FOR REFLECTION**

• Tonight's vigil centers around four symbols: fire (light), story (Scripture), water (baptism), bread (Eucharist). What does each of these symbols teach us about the paschal mystery?

• The risen Christ "is going before you to Galilee; / there you will see him, as he told you," the angel reassures the women. How do we "see" the risen Christ today in our own "Galilees"?

## Homily Points

• The compassion and love of the women would not be blocked by a stone, for it had been moved. We, like the women on Easter morning, often prepare to be confronted by "stones"—metaphorical stones of social conventions, profit and power, humiliation and ridicule. But Christ's resurrection is the complete victory of love over the "stones" of sadness and hatred. With Easter faith we see these stones have been removed so we can experience the risen Christ, who overcomes all barriers.

• Easter is a belief in the living presence of Christ breathing new life and hope into our minds and spirits. Easter is a light to guide us along this path of stones we stumble along. It is Easter whenever love pulls us out of our tombs of hopelessness. It is Easter whenever love illuminates our winter hearts and exhausted spirits to behold that we are embraced by God in the embrace of one another. Easter is a promise made at the empty tomb of Christ to be fulfilled one day in the shadow of our own.

℟. Alleluia, alleluia.
Christ, our paschal lamb, has been sacrificed;
let us then feast with joy in the Lord.
℟. Alleluia, alleluia.

## Gospel

John 20:1-9; L42ABC

On the first day of the week,
   Mary of Magdala came to the tomb
      early in the morning,
   while it was still dark,
   and saw the stone removed from the
      tomb.
So she ran and went to Simon Peter
   and to the other disciple whom Jesus
      loved, and told them,
   "They have taken the Lord from the
      tomb,
   and we don't know where they put
      him."
So Peter and the other disciple went
   out and came to the tomb.
They both ran, but the other disciple ran faster than Peter
   and arrived at the tomb first;
   he bent down and saw the burial
      cloths there, but did not go in.
When Simon Peter arrived after him,
   he went into the tomb and saw the
      burial cloths there,
   and the cloth that had covered his
      head,
   not with the burial cloths but rolled
      up in a separate place.
Then the other disciple also went in,
   the one who had arrived at the tomb
      first,
   and he saw and believed.
For they did not yet understand the
   Scripture
   that he had to rise from the dead.

*or*

Mark 16:1-7; L41B *in Appendix A, p. 292,*

*or, at an afternoon or evening Mass*
Luke 24:13-35; L46 *in Appendix A, p. 292.*

*See Appendix A, p. 293, for the other readings.*

## Reflecting on the Gospel and Living the Paschal Mystery

***To the point:*** Mary of Magdala was the first to discover the empty tomb and her reaction might be described as fear and unknowing. She reported the events to Peter and the Beloved Disciple, but she misunderstood the meaning. She thought somebody had taken Jesus' corpse. Only when the Beloved Disciple and Peter saw the empty tomb for themselves did the Beloved Disciple believe. But they still did not understand that Jesus had to rise from the dead.

***To ponder and pray:*** Easter morning must have been a confusing, even frightening, time. Jesus had just been killed by the state, an imperial occupying power. Most of the disciples had scattered. Now when Mary of Magdala comes to pay her final respects, she finds the tomb empty. It might be hard for us to imagine, but apparently the early disciples did not understand that Jesus was to rise from the dead. Though they had been with Jesus during his earthly ministry, they were unprepared for this victorious act of God over death itself. To us, the resurrection of Jesus is a central point of faith. For them, it seems to have been wholly unexpected. The gospels are remarkably candid about this embarrassing fact.

But are we ready for God to conquer death in our lives? Or is this something wholly unexpected as well? Each of us has experienced loss, and sometimes it can be comforting to hold on to this loss. We want to visit the tomb. We remember the way things were. We see the burial garments are left in the tomb, as a symbol of a past that is no longer present. The disciples will never experience Jesus in the same way. His earthly ministry is over. Something new is in store and it is something wholly unexpected. With respect to our own personal losses, those moments will never be the same. God will bring something new, wholly unexpected from those crises.

In this as in the other gospel accounts, the first indications of Jesus' resurrection were the discovery of the empty tomb. The appearances of the risen Jesus came later. Initially the women discovered the tomb empty, pondered its meaning, and reported to the remaining disciples. Only the Beloved Disciple, likely the "eyewitness" behind the Fourth Gospel, was one who believed upon finding the tomb empty. No other disciple did. But for most disciples, the empty tomb was not enough. Thus the risen Jesus appears.

We see similar movements of faith in our own lives. We find our own empty tombs, signifiers of something greater. But often we do not grasp the full meaning until later, until something equivalent to a resurrection appearance. Let us be attentive to the empty tomb signs and experiences in our lives that leave us pondering, wondering how God is acting in the world. It could be that we will experience a resurrection, new life from death, meaning from loss.

## Model Penitential Act

*Presider:* On this Easter morning, God raises us up from the tombs of our sins and failings. In the risen Christ, we are recreated in the love of God. And so, with humility and joy, let us begin our Easter Eucharist by asking God's forgiveness and peace. *[pause]*

Risen Lord, the Anointed One of God: Lord, have mercy.
Risen Lord, the Paschal Lamb sacrificed for us: Christ, have mercy.
Risen Lord, the cornerstone of God's kingdom: Lord, have mercy.

## Model Universal Prayer (Prayer of the Faithful)

*Presider:* "This is the day the Lord has made." In the gladness of this Easter day, let us pray.

*Response:* Lord, hear our prayer.

For our church and parish family, that all our ministries may proclaim the good news of the empty tomb . . .

For the nations and peoples of the world, that the peace and mercy of God may reign throughout the earth . . .

For the sick and dying, the suffering and imprisoned, the addicted and despairing, that the victorious Christ may break the chains of their suffering and pain . . .

For all who have been baptized and welcomed into our church this Easter, that they may walk anew in the light of the risen One . . .

For our deceased brothers and sisters *[especially . . . ]*, that God may raise them up to the new life of his risen Son:

*Presider:* Father of life, Author of love, in raising your Son from the grave, all of creation has been reborn. May the life and love manifested in the paschal mystery be a constant and lasting reality in our lives. We ask this through Christ, our risen Lord. **Amen.**

---

**COLLECT**

Let us pray.

*Pause for silent prayer*

O God, who on this day,
through your Only Begotten Son,
have conquered death
and unlocked for us the path to eternity,
grant, we pray, that we who keep
the solemnity of the Lord's Resurrection
may, through the renewal brought by your Spirit,
rise up in the light of life.
Through our Lord Jesus Christ, your Son,
who lives and reigns with you in the unity of
    the Holy Spirit,
one God, for ever and ever. **Amen.**

---

**FOR REFLECTION**

• Where is the risen Lord present among us? How is the good news of the risen One proclaimed in the faithfulness and compassionate charity of people in your life?

• When have you seen seemingly misplaced compassion, forgiveness, or reconciliation "vindicated"?

---

## Homily Points

• Easter calls us out of the darkness that shrouds our lives into the light of possibility, of healing, of re-creation. In his rising from the dead, Christ enables us to bring into our own lives all that he taught and lived throughout his life: the love, compassion, generosity, humility, and selflessness that ultimately triumphs over hatred, bigotry, prejudice, despair, greed, and death.

• We sometimes find ourselves stuck in a Good Friday world: our problems batter us, overwhelm us, strain our ability to cope and make it all work. But in raising his Son from the dead, God vindicates the Gospel of his Christ: that good conquers evil, that love transforms hatred, that light shatters the darkness. Our lives are filled with experiences of resurrection, when the despair and desperation of our Good Fridays are transformed into Easter hope by the compassion and mercy of those who have embraced the good news of Easter morning.

SEASON OF EASTER

## ✠ SPIRITUALITY

**GOSPEL ACCLAMATION**
John 20:29

R7. Alleluia, alleluia.
You believe in me, Thomas, because you have
    seen me, says the Lord;
blessed are those who have not seen me, but still
    believe!
R7. Alleluia, alleluia.

## Gospel   John 20:19-31; L44B

On the evening of that first day of the
    week,
    when the doors were locked, where the
        disciples were,
    for fear of the Jews,
    Jesus came and stood in their midst
    and said to them, "Peace be with you."
When he had said this, he showed them
    his hands and his side.
The disciples rejoiced when they saw the
    Lord.
Jesus said to them again, "Peace be with
    you.
As the Father has sent me, so I send
    you."
And when he had said this, he breathed
    on them and said to them,
    "Receive the Holy Spirit.
Whose sins you forgive are forgiven them,
    and whose sins you retain are retained."

Thomas, called Didymus, one of the
    Twelve,
    was not with them when Jesus came.
So the other disciples said to him, "We
    have seen the Lord."
But he said to them,
    "Unless I see the mark of the nails in
        his hands
    and put my finger into the nailmarks
    and put my hand into his side, I will
        not believe."

Now a week later his disciples were again
    inside
    and Thomas was with them.
Jesus came, although the doors were locked,
    and stood in their midst and said,
        "Peace be with you."

*Continued in Appendix A, p. 293.*

### Reflecting on the Gospel

Have you ever heard news that seemed too good to be true? Maybe that a friend was visiting, or that something special was in store for you? Perhaps the news was so good or unexpected, we needed "to see it to believe it." We might be reminded of the motto of Missouri, the "show me" state. There is a healthy skepticism we bring to the table. We don't want to get our hopes up only to be disappointed. We want proof, demonstrable proof. This is precisely Thomas's reaction on hearing the news about Jesus' resurrection.

Though the disciples had been witness to the risen Lord on Easter Sunday evening, Thomas was absent, and so he functions as a disciple for all of us. In a sense, we stand in the person of Thomas. We were not present that Easter Sunday evening. And perhaps, like Thomas, we reply, "seeing is believing." The beatitude that Jesus speaks to Thomas is meant for each of us: "Blessed are those who have not seen and have believed."

The church gives us this reading on the Second Sunday of Easter, as that is when Thomas had his experience of the risen Lord. Though we are not given the opportunity to put our finger in the nail marks (and the gospel doesn't say that Thomas did that), we, like Thomas, may condition our belief on seeing.

The gift Jesus gives his disciples is "peace." It is not a peace that the world gives, that is, merely an absence of war. But the peace Jesus gives is a serenity in the face of life. The gift is a sense of calm knowing that Jesus is "my Lord and my God," and that there is nothing in this life that can separate him from me. The reader of this gospel recalls Jesus' prayer to the Father in the garden, about not losing a single one who has been given to Jesus. In this gospel, Jesus calls us friends. And it is a friendship that can never be broken; its hallmark is "peace."

### Living the Paschal Mystery

Perhaps it is something in the human condition that we do not automatically believe good news, or news that might seem too good to be true. That can be a natural defense mechanism. But today we learn that God wants to surprise us with joy. He wants us to live in the life of the resurrection. Rather than be skeptics, he wants us to be joyful in the knowledge that his love is greater than even death.

Our own experiences of loss can be transformed with the power of God's love. The marks of loss will always be there, as Jesus' body was marked with the signs of the cross; but something greater is in store. We can never take away the experience of loss, the experience of death, and the experience of tragedy. But those experiences can be made new. Being made new does not mean that the loss was OK. Rather, in spite of the loss, in spite of the transgressions, and in spite of death itself, God has another reaction. He raises to new life. God transforms pain, loss, and abandonment into life, peace, and wholeness. This is the ultimate paschal mystery that is lived out in our daily lives countless times with relationships, friendships, family, work, and even the cycles of nature. Every fall and winter is succeeded by spring and summer. New life abounds, and because of this we celebrate.

## Focusing the Gospel

*John 20:19-31*

The gospel for the Second Sunday of Easter (for all three years of the Lectionary cycle) is what we might call act 2 of John's Easter drama, if act 1 was the discovery of the empty tomb. Scene 1 takes place on Easter night. The terrified disciples are huddled together, realizing that they are marked men because of their association with the executed Jesus. The risen Jesus appears in their midst with his greeting of "peace." The writer of the Fourth Gospel clearly has the Genesis story in mind when he describes Jesus as "breathing" the Holy Spirit on his disciples: just as God created man and woman by breathing life into them (Gen 2:7), the risen Christ recreates humankind by breathing the new life of the Holy Spirit upon the surviving company of apostles.

In scene 2, the disciples excitedly tell the just-returned Thomas what they had seen. Thomas responds to the news with understandable skepticism. Thomas had expected the cross (see John 11:16 and 14:5)—and no more.

The climactic third scene takes place one week later, with Jesus' second appearance to the assembled community—this time with Thomas present. He invites Thomas to examine his wounds and to "believe." Christ's blessing in response to Thomas's profession of faith exalts the faith of every Christian of every age who "believes without seeing." All Christians of every place and time who embrace the Spirit of the risen One possess a faith that is no less than that of the first disciples.

## Focusing the First Reading

*Acts 4:32-35*

On the Sundays of the Easter season, the first reading is taken from the Acts of the Apostles, Luke's chronicle of the founding and growth of the church. Acts has been called the "Gospel of the Holy Spirit" because it recounts how the Spirit of God was at work forming this small group of followers on the fringes of Judaism into "the Way" whose members were eventually called "Christian" (Acts 11:26). Today's brief reading is one of several "snapshots" Luke includes of the idealized community, united in heart and mind, committed to charity and sharing what they had with one another.

## Focusing the Responsorial Psalm

*Ps 118:2-4, 13-15, 22-24 (1)*

As on Easter Sunday, today's responsorial psalm is taken from Psalm 118, the great festival psalm that has become the Easter psalm of the church.

## Focusing the Second Reading

*1 John 5:1-6*

In this Year B of the Lectionary cycle, the second readings on the Sundays of the Easter season are taken from the first letter attributed to John. This epistle echoes many of the themes of the Fourth Gospel. This brief circular letter (not addressed to a specific church) is more of a homily than an epistle. It appeals to Christians of the Johannine community to remain faithful to the love that unites them in Christ Jesus—a unity that is being undermined by conflicting teachers. In today's reading, the writer reminds his brothers and sisters that their identity is centered in believing that Jesus is the Christ, loving God, and following the commandments. Reborn in the risen Christ, they are now begotten by God the Father, and should live their lives accordingly.

---

**PROMPTS FOR HOMILISTS, CATECHISTS, AND RCIA TEAMS**

Have you ever been swallowed up in Thomas-like skepticism and cynicism? How was that "doubt" transformed into hope and trust?

In what ways is your parish community like—or can become like—the first Christian community portrayed in today's first reading?

How can we "breathe" new life into our relationships with others?

In what "non-sacramental" ways can individuals forgive and "retain" sins?

## Model Rite for the Blessing and Sprinkling of Water

*Presider:* Dear friends, we will use this water to remind us of our baptisms. Let us ask God to bless this water and bless all of us, so that, by his grace, we may be recreated in Easter peace. *[pause]*

[*continue with* The Roman Missal, *Appendix II*]

## Homily Points

• The "peace" Christ gives his new church on Easter night is not the mere absence of conflict. Christ's "gift" is hard work: the peace of the Easter Christ is to honor one another as children of the same Father in heaven, to build bridges and find solutions rather than assigning blame or extracting punishment, to develop relationships that are just, ethical, and moral. Christ's Easter peace honors humility and cherishes reconciliation; it transforms, recreates, and renews; it is born of wisdom, integrity, and thanksgiving. Christ calls us to "breathe" such hard-won and demanding peace into our own homes and communities.

• We possess the grace to forgive, to make our own small "sacraments" of reconciliation and peace. We can also "retain" sins: we can be advocates for what is right and just, insisting that fair and just practices be followed in commerce and public policy—and we can also "retain" anger and grudges that can be deadly not just to the person who has wronged us but to ourselves as well, isolating us in graves of bitterness and anger. The Easter Christ calls us to take up his work of forgiveness and transforming reconciliation, work that often begins with being humble and gracious enough to take that first difficult step to offer or seek forgiveness.

• In today's gospel, Jesus appears to his disciples and shows them his hands and his side; later he invites the doubting Thomas to touch the marks from the nails and the gash from the soldier's lance. We all have scars from our own Good Fridays that remain despite our small experiences of resurrection. Our "nail marks" remind us that all pain, grief, ridicule, suffering, disappointments, and anguish are transformed into healing and peace in the love of God we experience from others and that we extend to them. Jesus tells Thomas and his brothers not to be afraid of the nail marks, the scars, the fractured bones, the crushed spirit, and the broken heart. Compassion, forgiveness, justice—no matter how clumsily offered—can heal and mend.

## Model Universal Prayer (Prayer of the Faithful)

*Presider:* In peace, let us pray.

*Response:* Lord, hear our prayer.

For all who serve our church, that they may bear witness to the resurrection of Jesus and the great favor of God for all his people . . .

For the nations and peoples of the world, that they may seek to share the blessings of God's creation with the poor and provide a safe haven to the displaced . . .

For those who are suffering loss, grieving, in despair, that they may see signs of God's love in our care and concern for them . . .

For our parish, that we may be "of one heart and mind" in our generosity and compassion . . .

*Presider:* Hear the prayers of this community, O God, whom you gather at your table to remember in the "breaking of bread" your Son's passion, death, and resurrection. May his peace and spirit enable us to be your ministers of reconciliation and forgiveness in our homes and communities. In Jesus' name, we pray. **Amen.**

---

**COLLECT**

Let us pray.

*Pause for silent prayer*

God of everlasting mercy,
who in the very recurrence of the paschal feast
kindle the faith of the people you have made your own,
increase, we pray, the grace you have bestowed,
that all may grasp and rightly understand
in what font they have been washed,
by whose Spirit they have been reborn,
by whose Blood they have been redeemed.
Through our Lord Jesus Christ, your Son,
who lives and reigns with you in the unity of the Holy Spirit,
one God, for ever and ever. **Amen.**

**FIRST READING**

Acts 4:32-35

The community of believers was of one heart and mind,
and no one claimed that any of his possessions was his own,
but they had everything in common.
With great power the apostles bore witness
to the resurrection of the Lord Jesus,
and great favor was accorded them all.
There was no needy person among them,
for those who owned property or houses would sell them,
bring the proceeds of the sale,
and put them at the feet of the apostles,
and they were distributed to each according to need.

**RESPONSORIAL PSALM**

Ps 118:2-4, 13-15, 22-24

℟. (1) Give thanks to the Lord for he is good, his love is everlasting.
*or:*
℟. Alleluia.

Let the house of Israel say,
"His mercy endures forever."
Let the house of Aaron say,
"His mercy endures forever."
Let those who fear the LORD say,
"His mercy endures forever."

℟. Give thanks to the Lord for he is good, his love is everlasting.
*or:*
℟. Alleluia.

I was hard pressed and was falling,
   but the Lord helped me.
My strength and my courage is the Lord,
   and he has been my savior.
The joyful shout of victory
   in the tents of the just.

R̸. Give thanks to the Lord for he is good,
   his love is everlasting.
   *or:*
R̸. Alleluia.

The stone which the builders rejected
   has become the cornerstone.
By the Lord has this been done;
   it is wonderful in our eyes.
This is the day the Lord has made;
   let us be glad and rejoice in it.

R̸. Give thanks to the Lord for he is good,
   his love is everlasting.
   *or:*
R̸. Alleluia.

## SECOND READING

1 John 5:1-6

Beloved:
Everyone who believes that Jesus is the
      Christ is begotten by God,
   and everyone who loves the Father
      loves also the one begotten by him.
In this way we know that we love the
      children of God
   when we love God and obey his
      commandments.
For the love of God is this,
   that we keep his commandments.
And his commandments are not
      burdensome,
   for whoever is begotten by God
      conquers the world.
And the victory that conquers the world is
      our faith.
Who indeed is the victor over the world
   but the one who believes that Jesus is
      the Son of God?

This is the one who came through water
      and blood, Jesus Christ,
   not by water alone, but by water and
      blood.
The Spirit is the one that testifies,
   and the Spirit is truth.

### About Liturgy

*Easter Sunday all season long:* The Sundays of the Easter season are meant to be continuations of Easter Sunday, so the fifty days of Easter reflect the mystery of dying and rising that we celebrated in its fullness at the Triduum. However, it's the liturgical ministers who often feel pretty dead after the intensity of all the Triduum and Easter Sunday liturgies. Even the lilies that had been so glorious just last week are starting to look a little droopy and over the next several Sundays will drop out altogether, one by one. You'll want to help your ministers pace themselves so that all eight Sundays of the Easter season are the best Sundays of the year. One way to help keep that Easter focus is to practice mystagogy. This is a prayerful breaking open of the Easter mysteries, especially focusing on the liturgical symbols of Easter. This discipline, which begins with encountering the risen Christ in the sacraments, is meant to give us "a new perception of the faith, of the Church, and of the world" (RCIA 245). Today, for example, you might focus on the sign of peace and the peace that the risen Christ gave to his disciples in the Upper Room. Christ's offering of peace did three things in today's gospel: it eased the disciples' fear, gave them the power to forgive, and strengthened their belief. When we share the sign of peace at Mass, let us call to mind that this simple rite is more than just a pleasant greeting. It can change a person's life, especially ours, if we share it with those who are afraid, those we need to forgive, and those who need encouragement in their faith.

### About Initiation

*Getting neophytes to "come back" for mystagogy:* One of the most common concerns among RCIA teams is how to make sure people come back after they are baptized at the Easter Vigil. The best way to do this is first to make sure that, from the beginning of their formation, we avoid using language that implies their journey is over at baptism. Remember, this is Christian *initiation*—it is just the beginning! Second, encourage the neophytes (and their godparents) to be present at Sunday Mass at every Sunday in the Easter season. The Sunday Masses of the Easter season—and not more classes or other RCIA gatherings—are the principal place for mystagogy and post-baptismal catechesis. If they are at Mass, they are "coming back" for mystagogy.

### About Liturgical Music

*Music for the Easter season:* The Easter season can be challenging for choirs that are already feeling tired from the rehearsals and liturgies of Lent and Triduum, and many will be looking forward to a break. But don't make that an excuse to let the musical energy slowly lag during these next weeks until Pentecost. Schedule more festive organ or piano instrumentals for the dismissal song, since singing a song at the end of Mass is optional! Make more use of seasonal music for some parts of the liturgy, such as the gathering song, the responsorial psalm, or Communion. For example, keep singing some of the traditional hymns that you sang on Easter Sunday as your gathering song for the next three Sundays. Your assembly will appreciate being able to sing something familiar to begin the Mass. Psalm 118 and Psalm 66 are two seasonal psalms for the Easter season that you can sing as the responsorial psalm. For Communion, choose two or three settings of Psalm 34 ("Taste and see . . .") that your assembly already knows, and schedule each of them for a few weeks this season. Then for your rehearsals, spend more time in fellowship, celebration, and ongoing formation with your choir before the summer.

**APRIL 8, 2018**
# SECOND SUNDAY OF EASTER
## (or of DIVINE MERCY)

**GOSPEL ACCLAMATION**
John 1:14ab

The Word of God became flesh and made his
    dwelling among us;
and we saw his glory.

## Gospel    Luke 1:26-38; L545

The angel Gabriel was sent from God
    to a town of Galilee called Nazareth,
    to a virgin betrothed to a man named
        Joseph,
    of the house of David,
    and the virgin's name was Mary.
And coming to her, he said,
    "Hail, full of grace! The Lord is with
        you."
But she was greatly troubled at what was
        said
    and pondered what sort of greeting this
        might be.
Then the angel said to her,
    "Do not be afraid, Mary,
    for you have found favor with God.
Behold, you will conceive in your
        womb and bear a son,
    and you shall name him Jesus.
He will be great and will be called
        Son of the Most High,
    and the Lord God will give him the throne
        of David his father,
    and he will rule over the house of Jacob
        forever,
    and of his Kingdom there will be no end."
But Mary said to the angel,
    "How can this be,
    since I have no relations with a man?"
And the angel said to her in reply,
    "The Holy Spirit will come upon you,
    and the power of the Most High will over-
        shadow you.
Therefore the child to be born
    will be called holy, the Son of God.
And behold, Elizabeth, your relative,
    has also conceived a son in her old age,
    and this is the sixth month for her who
        was called barren;
    for nothing will be impossible for God."
Mary said, "Behold, I am the handmaid of
        the Lord.
May it be done to me according to your
        word."
Then the angel departed from her.

*See Appendix A, p. 294, for the other readings.*

## Reflecting on the Gospel

*Surprised by Joy* is the title of a classic work by C. S. Lewis wherein he describes his journey from atheism to theism, and then theism to Christianity. The appropriate title captures something essential about Christianity, the sheer joy that *should* accompany it. Saint Paul writes in his letter to the Philippians, "Rejoice in the Lord always. I shall say it again: rejoice!" (4:4, NABRE). Often young couples, even when the news is unexpected, are filled with joy upon finding out they will have a baby, a new life. Joy is a hallmark of Christianity, and a marked facet of the human experience.

The joy that accompanies a new birth was Mary's experience, though certainly mixed with being "greatly troubled." She was definitely not expecting such news. She faced the unusual visitor bearing the quixotic announcement with a wholehearted openness. "May it be done to me according to your word." The first four English words, "may it be done" are encapsulated in the four-letter Latin term, *fiat*. (Though Mary certainly did not speak Latin, and the Scriptures were not written in Latin, the Latin term comes to us by way of the Vulgate, the Latin translation of the Scriptures by St. Jerome.) A simple, open, and wholehearted reply from Mary opened the way for human salvation. Not only she but all humanity is "surprised by joy" by the angel's announcement and by Mary's response.

Mary is sometimes referred to as the first disciple, for she followed the will of God and brought Jesus, God's son, into the world. Her *fiat*, her words, "May it be done to me according to your word," echoes the prophets of the Old Testament, and foreshadow Jesus' own disposition toward his agony and definitive death on the cross. Mary and ultimately Jesus allow their own will to conform to God. In that way, Mary is the first disciple, and serves as a model for us.

There is great joy in the Christian life, a joy like that which results from a birth announcement. That joy animates our lives, allowing us to speak our own *fiat* to God and God's will.

## Living the Paschal Mystery

If we could have spoken to the young woman Mary immediately after the annunciation, what would she have said? How would she have described the experience? Would she know that her decision would impact us over two thousand years later, and an entire continent and a vast ocean away? The ripple effects of her *fiat* grew into mighty waves and continued to wash over the entire world ever since, even to today.

And what about the decisions we make in our daily lives? What will be their ripple effects? Those ripple effects from Mary's fiat are perhaps easier to discern. That child impacts our lives in tremendous ways. What about other decisions in our daily lives? What are the unforeseen consequences of our actions? It seems only natural in such a world to conform our will to that of God and entrust our goodwill intentions to Divine Providence. There is so much we simply do not control. Once our *fiat* is proclaimed life seems to take on a will of its own and moves beyond preconfigured borders. May we be attentive to the workings of God in our lives so that we too may be "surprised by joy."

## Focusing the Gospel

Today, about nine months before Christmas, we celebrate Mary's acceptance of God's plan for her to give birth to Christ. The annunciation story in Luke's gospel is filled with Old Testament imagery: the announcement by the angel parallels the announcements of the births of many key figures in salvation history, such as Isaac and Samuel; the "overshadowing" of Mary recalls the cloud of glory covering the tent of the ark and temple in Jerusalem.

God begins the "Christ event" that was prefigured in the Scriptures with Mary, a simple Jewish girl who is at the bottom of the social ladder; the God who created all things makes the fulfillment of his promise dependent upon a vulnerable and powerless human being. Yet God exalts her humility, simplicity, and trust in his love and mercy. God's "favor" belongs to the Marys of every place and time: the poor, powerless, and people on the margins of society. Mary's yes to Gabriel's words set the stage for God's great intervention in human history.

## Model Penitential Act

*Presider:* With the faith and trust of Mary, let us place our hearts before God, confident of his mercy and forgiveness. *[pause]*

Christ Jesus, Son of God and child of Mary: Lord, have mercy.
Christ Jesus, Redeemer of all nations and Lord of justice: Christ, have mercy.
Christ Jesus, the Word and grace of God made like us, for us: Lord, have mercy.

## Model Universal Prayer (Prayer of the Faithful)

*Presider:* Emmanuel: "God is with us." In confidence, let us pray.

*Response:* Lord, hear our prayer.

That the church may give birth to God's Christ in worship and work together . . .

That God's kingdom of justice and peace may be established forever among all peoples and nations of the world . . .

That our care and concern for the sick, the poor, the despairing, and the forgotten may be a sign of God's love in our midst . . .

That all parents and guardians of children may see in Mary a model of loving patience and selfless devotion . . .

*Presider:* O God, hear our prayers. As you called Mary to give birth to your Christ, let your Spirit dwell in our homes and communities and churches, enabling us to bring to birth your Word of compassion and peace in our world. In Jesus' name, we pray. **Amen.**

**FOR REFLECTION**

• Have you ever experienced an "annunciation" of God calling you, in the simple, ordinary course of your days, to do something you did not feel capable of doing or were afraid to take on?

• How can we make our homes, in all their messiness, dwelling places for God's Son?

## Homily Points

• God calls all of us to the vocation of prophet, the ministry of charity, the work of forgiveness. Gabriel may come to us in the form of an invitation, a plea, a concern for another's well-being. It is in these everyday annunciations that God's kingdom is realized in our time and place. In her faith and trust in God's goodness, Mary is a model of discipleship to all of us, as we struggle to respond to God's "annunciations."

• Creating a home requires more than the tangibles of wood and brick; a home is built of the intangibles of love and forgiveness. Creating a home is not just erecting a solid structure and installing security systems; a home is a safe place where all are accepted and loved. Creating a home is not just maintaining a shelter but a sense of loving family. That is what God asks Mary and Joseph to do for his beloved Christ, and that is what God asks of us in creating our own homes: to make places of acceptance and forgiveness, where the love of Mary's Son dwells always for our own families.

## ✝ SPIRITUALITY

**GOSPEL ACCLAMATION**
cf. Luke 24:32

℟. Alleluia, alleluia.
Lord Jesus, open the Scriptures to us;
make our hearts burn while you speak to us.
℟. Alleluia, alleluia.

### Gospel    Luke 24:35-48; L47B

The two disciples recounted what had taken
    place on the way,
    and how Jesus was made known to them
    in the breaking of bread.

While they were still speaking about this,
    he stood in their midst and said to them,
    "Peace be with you."
But they were startled and terrified
    and thought that they were seeing a ghost.
Then he said to them, "Why are you troubled?
And why do questions arise in your hearts?
Look at my hands and my feet, that it is I
    myself.
Touch me and see, because a ghost does not
    have flesh and bones
    as you can see I have."
And as he said this,
    he showed them his hands and his feet.
While they were still incredulous for joy
    and were amazed,
    he asked them, "Have you anything here
    to eat?"
They gave him a piece of baked fish;
    he took it and ate it in front of them.

He said to them,
    "These are my words that I spoke to you
        while I was still with you,
    that everything written about me in the
        law of Moses
    and in the prophets and psalms must be
        fulfilled."
Then he opened their minds to understand
    the Scriptures.
And he said to them,
    "Thus it is written that the Christ would
        suffer
    and rise from the dead on the third day
    and that repentance, for the forgiveness
        of sins,
    would be preached in his name
    to all the nations, beginning from
        Jerusalem.
You are witnesses of these things."

### Reflecting on the Gospel

The student teacher was eager to receive some comments after his first experience in the classroom. The mentor offered a gentle critique: "When some students don't understand the lesson, it isn't enough simply to repeat it more loudly." But the student teacher's experience can be our own many times. My explanation was so good! They'll understand it if I repeat it again . . . But instead of repeating something over and over, more loudly each time, it might be good to try another example or another explanation instead. Or it might be worth the effort to appeal to a different style of learner. Perhaps the first approach to the lesson appealed to the visual learners. The second could be pitched to the auditory learners.

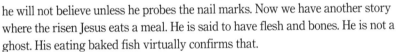

Now that we are in the third week of Easter, we hear yet another story of a resurrection appearance of Jesus. There are a number of different Easter stories that appeal to us on a variety of levels. Initially, the story was the finding of the empty tomb. Then, we had a story of the appearance of Jesus to the disciples without Thomas, followed by one with Thomas. Thomas says he will not believe unless he probes the nail marks. Now we have another story where the risen Jesus eats a meal. He is said to have flesh and bones. He is not a ghost. His eating baked fish virtually confirms that.

If we didn't understand with the empty tomb, if we didn't understand when Jesus appeared to even Thomas, now there is another appearance where he graphically demonstrates that he is present amongst them. Of course, each of the three stories we are referring to are from different gospel writers: the empty tomb (Mark), the appearance to Thomas (John), and now the risen Jesus eating fish (Luke). But these texts are given to us on successive Sundays to confirm for us that Jesus truly rose from the dead.

Moreover, today's gospel passage begins with a line that should not be neglected: the disciples recounted "how Jesus was made known to them / in the breaking of bread." Of course, the Emmaus story precedes this in the Gospel of Luke. And Luke is telling his audience that the "breaking of bread" is the way Jesus is made known to the community. No longer is Jesus appearing to his assembled followers. That ended with the ascension. Instead, the community will now come together and experience Christ in the breaking of bread, or in what we call Eucharist.

So in addition to the empty tomb, and the appearances, this is yet another way this resurrected Lord is made known to us. By hearing a variety of different stories, we might, like the disciples, come gradually to accepting the risen Christ.

### Living the Paschal Mystery

Each time we celebrate the Eucharist, the risen Christ is made known to us as he was made known to the disciples on the road to Emmaus. We may wish for a resurrection appearance where Jesus would eat baked fish, but those appearances are complete. After the ascension, the primary way we come to know him is through the breaking of bread. The risen Lord is flesh and bones, a true human being, raised to new life by the power of God. We participate in that new life by consuming the bread broken and shared. The breaking symbolizes the death. And the sharing symbolizes the community united in the one loaf. The bread is nourishment and life-giving, as is Jesus himself. It is no wonder that the early Christians, like us, find Jesus made known in the breaking of bread.

## Focusing the Gospel

*Luke 24:35-48*

Today's gospel is the conclusion of Luke's account of Jesus' first post-resurrection appearance to his disciples. The two disciples who met Jesus on the road to Emmaus have returned to Jerusalem to confirm the women's story of the resurrection. As they are excitedly telling what happened, Jesus appears.

Luke goes to great lengths in his Easter accounts to make clear that the resurrection was neither the fantasy of crazy zealots nor a plot concocted by the disciples who somehow managed to spirit the body of Jesus away (according to Luke's account, the disciples had not gone near the tomb themselves; they had not even imagined any kind of "resurrection"). In the details he presents here, Luke is countering the arguments forwarded to explain away the resurrection account. There can be no mistake: The resurrection of Jesus Christ is a reality, a reality in which all of the Scriptures find their ultimate fulfillment. What the disciples see is not a ghost but the physical presence of Jesus risen from the dead. Christ is present with us, and he is present with God in glory.

For Luke, the power of Jesus' resurrection is realized in the way it "opens" one's heart and mind to understanding the deeper meaning of God's word and to fully embracing the Spirit of God. In our faith and trust in the risen Christ, we become "witnesses" of the mercy and forgiveness of God.

## Focusing the First Reading

*Acts 3:13-15, 17-19*

Invoking the name of Jesus, Peter and John have just cured a crippled man at the gate of the temple. The man's jumping about on his newly restored limbs and his loud praising of God has drawn a crowd. Today's first reading is Peter's address to those who have gathered. Peter's sermon is a stinging indictment of the Jewish establishment that plotted Jesus' death, making specific mention of how the priests and scribes deceived them in demanding the release of the murderer Barabbas instead of the innocent Jesus (Luke 23:18-25). But Peter goes on to proclaim the mercy and forgiveness of God, inviting his hearers to embrace the life of the Servant Jesus, in whom the promises of their ancient faith are fulfilled.

## Focusing the Responsorial Psalm

*Ps 4:2, 4, 7-8, 9 (7a)*

Psalm 4 is an evening meditation, a prayer before retiring for the night. The psalmist ends his day by giving thanks for the "wonders" of the day past and placing his trust in the mercy of God to forgive his failings and ease his anxieties as he retires.

## Focusing the Second Reading

*1 John 2:1-5a*

The writer of the First Letter of John proclaims the mercy and forgiveness of God, reminding his community that in Jesus Christ we have an "Advocate" before God. To "know" Jesus (and not just know *about* Jesus) is to "keep his commandments," chief among which is to "love one another." It is no more complicated than that.

**PROMPTS FOR HOMILISTS, CATECHISTS, AND RCIA TEAMS**

When have you witnessed love that persevered in the most difficult and trying circumstances—and, in the end, that perseverance was rewarded?

What have you learned from your own experiences of suffering and despair?

Have you known someone who has been able to transform the suffering and injustice they encountered into hope and justice for others?

When was the last time you confronted your own "ignorance" about something or someone?

## Model Rite for the Blessing and Sprinkling of Water

*Presider:* Dear friends, this water will be used to remind us of our baptisms. Let us ask God to send his Spirit upon this water and upon us, so that we may be faithful to the baptism we received. *[pause]*

   [*continue with* The Roman Missal, *Appendix II*]

## Homily Points

• The risen One walks among us in "flesh and bone": he is our family and friends who offer their love to us and receive the love we yearn to give; he is the poor and troubled who challenge us to imitate his compassion and servanthood. As the risen Jesus appears to the eleven disciples as "flesh and bone," Jesus call us to be "flesh and bone" witnesses of his resurrection, to be "flesh and bone" compassion and justice to all. In calling us to be "witnesses" of his resurrection, Jesus asks us to live his Gospel of peace and reconciliation in the simplicity of our everyday lives, in the complexities of our workplaces, in the struggle to realize our hopes and dreams for ourselves and our families.

• Just as the risen Jesus asks the eleven disciples if they have "anything here to eat," he seeks the same from us today in the cries and pleas of the poor and needy in our midst. In imitating his humility and compassion, we, in turn, "feed" our own hunger for fulfillment, for purpose, for God. To become witnesses of Christ's resurrection is to embrace his peace in our own lives and work, joyfully bringing that peace into the lives of others, both for them and for ourselves.

• Easter is a second creation, a second beginning for all of us. In Christ, God has recreated the world, God has restarted life, including our own, so we may live in the compassion, justice, and peace of the Gospel. Easter faith transforms our vision to realize God's hand in every moment, transforms our attitudes to realize the need for God's compassion and forgiveness in every human encounter from politics to child rearing, transforms our spirits to realize that there is always reason to hope even in the face of life's most painful and traumatic moments. The Gospel of the risen One is a light in which we see God's love as the force that animates every molecule and cell, the bonding agent that unites all of us as sons and daughters of God.

## Model Universal Prayer (Prayer of the Faithful)

*Presider:* The risen Christ is among us. In joyful hope, then, let us pray.

*Response:* Lord, hear our prayer.

That the church may faithfully witness to the risen Jesus' Gospel of compassion and peace . . .

That all who lead nations and cities, who serve as judges and legislators, may seek the wisdom and justice of God in their work for their people . . .

That the light of God's countenance may shine upon the sick, the dying, the imprisoned, and the suffering . . .

That our parish's catechists may bring their students to the joy of realizing the limitless and unconditional love of God for them . . .

*Presider:* Father of life, hear our Easter prayers. In our work to make these prayers a reality, may your love be perfected in us—love revealed in the resurrection of your Christ, in whose name we offer these prayers. **Amen.**

### COLLECT

Let us pray.

*Pause for silent prayer*

May your people exult for ever, O God,
in renewed youthfulness of spirit,
so that, rejoicing now in the restored glory
   of our adoption,
we may look forward in confident hope
to the rejoicing of the day of resurrection.
Through our Lord Jesus Christ, your Son,
who lives and reigns with you in the unity
   of the Holy Spirit,
one God, for ever and ever. **Amen.**

### FIRST READING

Acts 3:13-15, 17-19

Peter said to the people:
"The God of Abraham,
   the God of Isaac, and the God of Jacob,
   the God of our fathers, has glorified his
      servant Jesus,
   whom you handed over and denied in
      Pilate's presence
   when he had decided to release him.
You denied the Holy and Righteous One
   and asked that a murderer be released
      to you.
The author of life you put to death,
   but God raised him from the dead; of
      this we are witnesses.
Now I know, brothers,
   that you acted out of ignorance, just as
      your leaders did;
   but God has thus brought to fulfillment
   what he had announced beforehand
   through the mouth of all the prophets,
   that his Christ would suffer.
Repent, therefore, and be converted, that
   your sins may be wiped away."

## RESPONSORIAL PSALM

Ps 4:2, 4, 7-8, 9

R̸. (7a) Lord, let your face shine on us.
*or:*
R̸. Alleluia.

When I call, answer me, O my just God,
you who relieve me when I am in
distress;
have pity on me, and hear my prayer!

R̸. Lord, let your face shine on us.
*or:*
R̸. Alleluia.

Know that the LORD does wonders for
his faithful one;
the LORD will hear me when I call
upon him.

R̸. Lord, let your face shine on us.
*or:*
R̸. Alleluia.

O LORD, let the light of your countenance
shine upon us!
You put gladness into my heart.

R̸. Lord, let your face shine on us.
*or:*
R̸. Alleluia.

As soon as I lie down, I fall peacefully
asleep,
for you alone, O LORD,
bring security to my dwelling.

R̸. Lord, let your face shine on us.
*or:*
R̸. Alleluia.

## SECOND READING

1 John 2:1-5a

My children, I am writing this to you
so that you may not commit sin.
But if anyone does sin, we have an
Advocate with the Father,
Jesus Christ the righteous one.
He is expiation for our sins,
and not for our sins only but for those
of the whole world.
The way we may be sure that we know
him is to keep
his commandments.
Those who say, "I know him," but do not
keep his commandments
are liars, and the truth is not in them.
But whoever keeps his word,
the love of God is truly perfected in
him.

## About Liturgy

*From altar to table:* Let us continue our mystagogical reflection on the symbols of Easter. We see in today's gospel the risen Christ ask for something to eat, and he eats what is prepared for him as a sign that he is not an apparition. He's not a ghost or something the disciples imagined. He is truly present! He proves this at an ordinary dinner table, just as he proved it to the disciples on the road to Emmaus in the section just before today's reading from Luke's gospel.

What does this mean, then, about our own dinner tables? If the risen Christ has shown himself not only at the altar in the Eucharist but also in such ordinary places as a diner on the road or at a home dinner table, should we not treat the tables wherever we eat as sacred spaces as well? Whenever we prepare food and place it before some-one to eat in our homes, do we see Christ present there, too?

This Easter season, honor the tables where you eat and the opportunity to see Christ present there. Use a tablecloth on your kitchen or dining table if you don't already use one. Use your special-occasion plates, utensils, and glasses, for Easter is truly a special occasion! Commit to eating at least one meal at home each week, on Sunday if pos-sible. Light candles, turn off the TV, set aside all electronic devices, and put on some nice music for these meals. Every time you eat, know that Christ is there with you.

## About Liturgical Music

*The gospel procession:* One of the biggest liturgical "sins" a music leader might commit is to end a piece of music before the ritual it is meant to accompany is over. This reveals that the music leader is not paying attention to the ritual or does not understand the purpose of that particular piece of music.

These are the ritual moments in Mass that dictate the length of music that accom-pany them: the rite of sprinkling, gospel procession, preparation of gifts, Lamb of God, and Communion. Each of these moments has some action taking place, and the music accompanies that action. Let's consider an example of one of these ritual moments.

The Alleluia or gospel acclamation not only gives praise to Christ present in the Word but also accompanies the deacon's (or priest's) procession from the altar, where the Book of Gospels was placed at the beginning of Mass, to the ambo, where he pro-claims the gospel reading. Sometimes, the deacon might show the Book of Gospels in a ritual way to the assembly, or he might take a longer route than usual from altar to ambo, or he just might walk at a different pace than other deacons. Whatever happens, the music leader needs to watch and pay attention and be ready to repeat the Alleluia refrain a few more times, or even repeat the gospel verse, if necessary, in order to ac-company the entire procession from beginning to end.

Another point about the gospel acclamation that you should know in case your celebrant is a bishop: After the gospel is proclaimed, the deacon or priest presents the bishop with the Book of Gospels. The bishop kisses the book before the deacon or priest enthrones it in a suitable place. You will want to signal the assembly to remain standing during this short ritual. The easiest way to do that is simply to repeat the singing of the Alleluia refrain a few more times (without the gospel verse) as this ritual happens.

**APRIL 15, 2018**
# THIRD SUNDAY OF EASTER

✠ S P I R I T U A L I T Y

**GOSPEL ACCLAMATION**
John 10:14

R♡. Alleluia, alleluia.
I am the good shepherd, says the Lord;
I know my sheep, and mine know me.
R♡. Alleluia, alleluia.

## Gospel

John 10:11-18; L50B

Jesus said:
"I am the good shepherd.
A good shepherd lays down his life for
the sheep.
A hired man, who is not a shepherd
and whose sheep are not his own,
sees a wolf coming and leaves the
sheep and runs away,
and the wolf catches and scatters
them.
This is because he works for pay and
has no concern for the sheep.
I am the good shepherd,
and I know mine and mine know me,
just as the Father knows me and I
know the Father;
and I will lay down my life for the
sheep.
I have other sheep that do not belong to
this fold.
These also I must lead, and they will
hear my voice,
and there will be one flock, one
shepherd.
This is why the Father loves me,
because I lay down my life in order to
take it up again.
No one takes it from me, but I lay it
down on my own.
I have power to lay it down, and power
to take it up again.
This command I have received from my
Father."

### Reflecting on the Gospel

In the early church, before Jesus was depicted as suffering and dying on the cross, he was depicted as "the Good Shepherd." This image was central to early Christian identity. We see paintings and even statues of Jesus as the Good Shepherd. The cross seems to have been too painful or too inappropriate to be an effective way to portray Jesus. The Good Shepherd conveyed the Christian message much more clearly.

Today we celebrate "Good Shepherd" Sunday as we read this famous gospel story from John. We are no longer in the realm of resurrection appearance stories, but now we have entered the world of Jesus' "I AM" parabolic discourse. In John, Jesus doesn't preach in parables, "The kingdom of God is like . . . a shepherd, a gate, a vineyard, etc." Instead, we hear Jesus say, "I AM the good shepherd," or in another passage, "I AM the gate," or "I AM the vine," etc. Some scholars call this an "I AM" Christology of the Fourth Gospel because it is used so frequently here, as opposed to the Synoptics. It is true that the Gospel of John has an intense emphasis on the person of Jesus, reflected in a high Christology. The joke is that if you ask Jesus in the Gospel of John how he's doing, he'll take two chapters to say he and the Father are just fine.

The image of a shepherd is certainly one rooted in antiquity. There are not as many shepherds today as there were then. And the site of a shepherd was much more common in that culture than it is today. Yet, even though most of us probably do not know any shepherds, or even seen any recently, we are all familiar with the image. Even Pope Francis spoke about shepherds shortly after he became pope. He spoke about how he wanted priests to have "the smell of the sheep" on them. This kind of graphic, even smelly, analogy offended some people. One person responded, "That sounds gross! Did he actually say that?" But it is precisely the image Francis meant to convey about whom he wanted as priests, and the language stems from this gospel story about Jesus himself being the Good Shepherd.

Interestingly, Jesus makes a distinction in this discourse about himself as the "good shepherd" and a "hired man" who works for money. The latter has no real concern for the sheep. He is in it only for the pay. Jesus, on the other hand, loves the sheep and has concern for them. He lays down his life for the sheep. The hired hand will run away at the first sign of danger. The result of his running away is that the sheep are scattered. As we consider this in our own time we can see the many Christians, many of us, who have been scattered. As we listen for the voice of the Good Shepherd and come to him, we will be reunited.

### Living the Paschal Mystery

Though the imagery in today's gospel may be foreign to our everyday experience, it rings true nonetheless. In some ways the story's setting sounds similar to a fairy tale with the shepherd, the hired hand, a wolf, and scattered sheep. But of course, the lessons from this gospel are much more profound than a fairy tale. This gospel tells us that the kingdom of God is not merely like a shepherd and his sheep; but rather, Jesus himself is the Good Shepherd who lays down his life for the sheep. The sheep know his voice. The Good Shepherd smells like the sheep. We can ask ourselves how we attune ourselves to the voice of the Good Shepherd. Where do we hear him calling? Have we been scattered, or are we attentive to the voice and near the Shepherd?

Jesus lays down his life for his sheep but takes it up again. The process does not conclude with the laying down, but culminates in the taking up. And thus we have the paschal mystery.

## Focusing the Gospel

*John 10:11-18*

Jesus' figure of the Good Shepherd is not an idyllic, serene image. Palestinian shepherds were tough, earthy characters who fearlessly swung their staffs (more like clubs than walking sticks) against poachers and wolves.

While the shepherd/sheep metaphor is found throughout Scripture, Jesus' vow to lay down his life for his sheep is something new and likely shocking to his audience. Of course, the image becomes clear in light of the resurrection. But ancient shepherds did not sacrifice their own lives for sheep, even if the sheep were their own! Jesus lays down his life for us, his sheep, and is therefore rightly called the Good Shepherd.

## Focusing the First Reading

*Acts 4:8-12*

In chapter 3 of Acts, Peter and John cure a crippled man in the temple precincts and Peter explains to the crowd who had witnessed the healing just who this Jesus is in whose name that healed the man (last Sunday's first reading). The two are quickly hauled before an angry Sanhedrin who demands an explanation for these rantings about the resurrection of the executed Jesus. Peter responds that in healing the man in the name of Jesus, God manifests the same power he revealed in raising Jesus from the dead. The healing of the crippled man is a sign of God's salvation of all who believe.

## Focusing the Responsorial Psalm

*Ps 118:1, 8-9, 21-23, 26, 28, 29 (22)*

The antiphon in today's responsorial psalm, Psalm 118, is quoted by Peter in his sermon in the first reading. The first Christian community prayed the images and the refrain, "for his mercy endures forever," of Psalm 118 as a thanksgiving for God's great love manifested in raising Jesus from the dead.

## Focusing the Second Reading

*1 John 3:1-2*

A common theme among Hellenistic religions was that to truly know and understand someone or something was to strive to act "like" them. In today's second reading, the writer of the First Letter of John teaches that to "know" God is to love one another as he loves us as his sons and daughters. To "know" God's love makes us more than just faithful adherents but transforms us into "children" of the God that Jesus revealed as "Father."

---

**PROMPTS FOR HOMILISTS, CATECHISTS, AND RCIA TEAMS**

Who have you known in your life who exemplifies the model of the Good Shepherd?

Who are those who daily "lay down" their lives for others?

What does the image of the Good Shepherd reveal about the role of leadership and authority?

Who are the "wolves" who force us to run away from our responsibilities as "shepherds"?

Why are certain "Sanhedrins" in our time and place so threatened by the idea of the resurrection of Jesus?

## Model Rite for the Blessing and Sprinkling of Water

*Presider:* Dear friends, we will use this water to remind us of our baptisms into the life of the risen Christ. Let us ask God to bless this water and bless all of us, so that, by his grace, we may be recreated in Easter peace. *[pause]*

[*continue with* The Roman Missal, *Appendix II*]

## Homily Points

• To be a disciple of Jesus is not simply to be a "hired hand" who acts only to be compensated, who is concerned only with his or her own welfare. Christ the Good Shepherd calls us to approach our lives, not with the limited, unfeeling, money-centered self-interest of the hired hand, but with Jesus' sense of loving, compassionate concern for all men, women, and children. In embracing the gospel attitude of humility and compassion for the sake of others, in "laying down" our own lives for our brothers and sisters, we will one day "take up" our lives again in the Father's Easter promise.

• The Gospel of the Good Shepherd is a lesson in leadership that is centered in the servanthood of Jesus. To act in the interest of those in our care, to "freely" place our own stature at the service of others, is to embrace the model of Christ the Good Shepherd. Christ calls each one of us to realize that the gifts, talents, and abilities that God has entrusted to us are not for our own profit or aggrandizement but to fulfill our vocations as "good shepherds": to seek out and bring back the lost, scattered, and forgotten; to enable people to move beyond their fears and doubts and realize their own gifts and talents; to bring the peace and justice of God into our own relationships and communities.

• Our lives are filled with noise and distractions and calamities that drown out the voice we desperately strain to hear: the voice of calm, the voice of reason, the voice of assurance, the voice of unconditional and unqualified love. Such is the voice of Jesus the Good Shepherd who speaks to us in the quiet of our hearts, in the unqualified love of family and friends, in the cries of those who call out to us in need. Grace is to hear the Easter Christ's voice of mercy, justice, and reconciliation amid the demanding and conflicting voices that shout at us every day of our lives.

## Model Universal Prayer (Prayer of the Faithful)

*Presider:* In the name of Jesus, the Good Shepherd, let us offer to the Father our prayers.

*Response:* Lord, hear our prayer.

For all who teach, counsel, and minister in our church, that they may be inspired in their service by the example of Jesus, the Good Shepherd . . .

For all who lead, manage, and govern, that they may exercise their responsibilities in the Good Shepherd's spirit of selflessness and sacrifice . . .

For police officers, firefighters, emergency personnel, military members, and all who risk their lives every day for our safety and protection, that God will be with them in their generous and selfless service . . .

For our parish community, that together we may live the Gospel of the Good Shepherd in a spirit of peace and concern for one another . . .

*Presider:* Hear, O God, the prayers of your children gathered at your table. Open our hearts and spirits to hear the voice of your Son leading us to the fulfillment of your kingdom. We make these prayers in the name of your Son, Jesus the Good Shepherd. **Amen.**

---

### COLLECT

Let us pray.

*Pause for silent prayer*

Almighty ever-living God,
lead us to a share in the joys of heaven,
so that the humble flock may reach
where the brave Shepherd has gone before.
Who lives and reigns with you in the unity
　　of the Holy Spirit,
one God, for ever and ever. **Amen.**

### FIRST READING

Acts 4:8-12

Peter, filled with the Holy Spirit, said:
　　"Leaders of the people and elders:
　　If we are being examined today
　　about a good deed done to a cripple,
　　namely, by what means he was saved,
　　then all of you and all the people of
　　　　Israel should know
　　that it was in the name of Jesus Christ
　　　　the Nazorean
　　whom you crucified, whom God raised
　　　　from the dead;
　　in his name this man stands before you
　　　　healed.
He is *the stone rejected by you, the*
　　*builders,*
*which has become the cornerstone.*
There is no salvation through anyone else,
　　nor is there any other name under
　　　　heaven
　　given to the human race by which we
　　　　are to be saved."

### RESPONSORIAL PSALM

Ps 118:1, 8-9, 21-23, 26, 28, 29

℟. (22) The stone rejected by the builders
　　has become the cornerstone.
　　*or:*
℟. Alleluia.

Give thanks to the LORD, for he is good,
　　for his mercy endures forever.
It is better to take refuge in the LORD
　　than to trust in man.
It is better to take refuge in the LORD
　　than to trust in princes.

℟. The stone rejected by the builders has
　　become the cornerstone.
　　*or:*
℟. Alleluia.

I will give thanks to you, for you have
        answered me
    and have been my savior.
The stone which the builders rejected
    has become the cornerstone.
By the LORD has this been done;
    it is wonderful in our eyes.

R︎. The stone rejected by the builders has
        become the cornerstone.
    *or:*
R︎. Alleluia.

Blessed is he who comes in the name of
        the LORD;
    we bless you from the house of the
        LORD.
I will give thanks to you, for you have
        answered me
    and have been my savior.
Give thanks to the LORD, for he is good;
    for his kindness endures forever.

R︎. The stone rejected by the builders has
        become the cornerstone.
    *or:*
R︎. Alleluia.

## SECOND READING
1 John 3:1-2

Beloved:
See what love the Father has bestowed
        on us
    that we may be called the children of
        God.
Yet so we are.
The reason the world does not know us
    is that it did not know him.
Beloved, we are God's children now;
    what we shall be has not yet been
        revealed.
We do know that when it is revealed we
    shall be like him,
    for we shall see him as he is.

## ✝ CATECHESIS

### About Liturgy
*United under one Shepherd:* We continue our Easter mystagogical reflection by breaking open the eucharistic prayer, specifically the section in which we pray for the pope and the local bishop, who are our shepherds under Christ, the Good Shepherd.

We call this part of the eucharistic prayer the intercessions. Here we pray for church members, living and dead. We ask God to remember his church, "spread throughout the world" (Eucharistic Prayer II). Then we recall by name the pope and the bishop of the diocese in which the Mass takes place. We do this not as a simple courtesy of prayer but as an expression and sign of our unity as a church that is called to be one, holy, catholic, and apostolic. We do not make this prayer alone on our own initiative. We pray it in union with all God's people throughout history who have been called by the voice of the Shepherd.

Our unity is not some abstract connection or idea but is marked by specific persons recognized as shepherds for the people of God. This is why we remember by name the current pope and the local ordinary (the head bishop of the diocese), then in general all the clergy. Every pastor of a parish (a priest or the one designated by the local bishop to serve in that leadership role) promises obedience to the local bishop; and every bishop promises to be of one mind with the bishops of the world, including the pope, preserving communion within the Catholic Church. Then having remembered those who are living, we recall those who have gone before us: our beloved dead and all the saints, with whom we are united in the communion of saints.

Communion is the sign of our unity of mind and action, in obedience to the one Shepherd. This unity is a reality that is present when the church gathers to pray under the leadership of its ministers. Yet it is also a truth we must strive to live daily with the help of the Holy Spirit who binds us together in love. The next time you pray the eucharistic prayer and name the pope and your bishop, pray for true and lasting unity among all Christians and for charity and respect for all who shepherd us.

### About Liturgical Music
*In praise of unison singing:* Sometimes, singing in unison is seen by choir members as something boring or uninteresting. Indeed, one purpose of the choir is to "enrich the celebration by adding musical elements beyond the capabilities of the congregation alone" (Sing to the Lord, 28). Thus, choral members enhance the beauty of liturgical song by adding harmonies to the song of the assembly. However, the same paragraph of Sing to the Lord also says, "The choir must not minimize the musical participation of the faithful. The congregation commonly sings unison melodies, which are more suitable for generally unrehearsed community singing. This is the primary song of the Liturgy."

Because music ministers are first assembly members before they are choir members, they should readily and regularly sing in unison with the assembly this primary song of the liturgy. These are times when unison singing by all would be appropriate and desired: when an assembly is still learning a new song; during the first few repetitions of the antiphon of the responsorial psalm or of other refrains; more often during Lent and Advent to contrast the more festive seasons of Easter and Christmas; in later stanzas of hymns to reenergize the voice of the assembly.

## ✠ SPIRITUALITY

**GOSPEL ACCLAMATION**
John 15:4a, 5b

℟. Alleluia, alleluia.
Remain in me as I remain in you, says the Lord.
Whoever remains in me will bear much fruit.
℟. Alleluia, alleluia.

### Gospel

John 15:1-8; L53B

**Jesus said to his disciples:**
   **"I am the true vine, and my Father**
      **is the vine grower.**
   **He takes away every branch in me**
      **that does not bear fruit,**
      **and every one that does he prunes so**
         **that it bears more fruit.**
**You are already pruned because of the**
      **word that I spoke to you.**
**Remain in me, as I remain in you.**
**Just as a branch cannot bear fruit on**
      **its own**
      **unless it remains on the vine,**
      **so neither can you unless you remain**
         **in me.**
**I am the vine, you are the branches.**
**Whoever remains in me and I in him**
      **will bear much fruit,**
      **because without me you can do**
         **nothing.**
**Anyone who does not remain in me**
      **will be thrown out like a branch and**
         **wither;**
      **people will gather them and throw**
         **them into a fire**
      **and they will be burned.**
**If you remain in me and my words**
      **remain in you,**
      **ask for whatever you want and it will**
         **be done for you.**
**By this is my Father glorified,**
      **that you bear much fruit and become**
         **my disciples."**

### Reflecting on the Gospel

Grapes that are native to the United States are good for only one thing, grape juice. They do not produce good wine. On the other hand, many grapes native to Europe, Sangiovese, for example, one of the primary grapes that is used for Chianti, are excellent for producing wine. There are stories of nineteenth-century Italian immigrants coming to California with their grapevine cuttings, so they would be able to plant their own native grapes in this New World and have wine. They tended these cuttings onboard ships and then across the Appalachian range, the Great Plains, and the Rocky Mountains before finally settling on the West Coast. These grapevine cuttings were precious reminders of the land, culture, and people the immigrants left behind; and these same cuttings, properly trans-planted, cared for, and pruned, would provide life and happiness in this, the New World. And it turned out that California's climate, Napa Valley in particular, was ideal for growing grapes that would produce some of the world's best wines.

We can imagine something of this when Jesus says that he is the Vine. In typical Johannine fashion, we have here no parable about the kingdom of God being like a vine-yard. For the Fourth Gospel, Jesus *is* the Vine! He goes a step further to say that the Father is the vine grower. For us and our image above, perhaps the Father is the immigrant who brings the precious vine to the New World, ready to plant in fertile soil.

Jesus reminds us of the vine grower's role. Not only does the vine grower ensure its viability, but he prunes branches to produce fruit, and cuts away those that do not produce any fruit. In a stark vision of the end time, Jesus takes yet another step to say that those branches that have been cut away will be thrown into the fire to be burned. Such apocalyptic images are rare in this gospel, though they appear more frequently in Matthew. As vine grower, the Father tends his precious vine much like the immigrant bringing native cut-tings to the New World. Once transplanted, the real work begins.

Where are we in the metaphor? We are the branches, fully aware that no branch can produce fruit on its own. We must remain attached to the vine to bear fruit. So as not to be lopped off, we remain in Jesus.

This agrarian image is ancient, but easily applicable and comprehended. Anyone with experience in gardening or observing nature grasps the symbol-ism here. The metaphor is simple yet sublime, and seems to be evidence of a good Teacher.

### Living the Paschal Mystery

The image used in today's gospel is polyvalent. It can be understood in a num-ber of ways. For one, Jesus says that the branches that do bear fruit are pruned, to bear more. We can reflect on that to wonder why these fruit-bearing branches need to be pruned at all! Isn't it enough to cut off the branches that do not bear fruit? No, for the vine grower, merely producing fruit is not enough. He knows that the branch can produce more. And anyone with gardening experience would agree.

And so we at times have the experience of being pruned. We can wonder why. Things seem to be going well. Life is in order. Good things are happening.

And yet, we are pruned. We die to parts of ourselves regularly. And this dying is essential if we are to produce more fruit. The vine grower, the Father, knows what he is doing. Our task is simply to remain on the vine, and to produce fruit. Our being pruned is a natural and healthy, though perhaps painful, experience that is necessary for us to grow into the people we are to become. This process of being pruned, of dying to self, is essential for the Christian life, and it is directed, even carried out by the Father. It is the paschal mystery. The result of which is producing fruit.

## Focusing the Gospel

*John 15:1-8*

As he takes his physical leave, Jesus promises that he will always "remain" with the community of disciples. In this reading from his Last Supper discourse, Jesus appropriates the Old Testament image of the vine as a symbol of his constant connectedness to his church. From the music of the psalms to the engravings on the temple pediments, vines were a symbol of Yahweh's many blessings to Israel. Jesus is the vine that connects us to him as his disciples, and thus connected to one another as church.

## Focusing the First Reading

*Acts 9:26-31*

Chapter 9 of the Acts of the Apostles tells the story of the conversion of Saul (*Saul* is his original Hebrew name; later, as he begins his mission among the Gentiles, he will choose to be known by his Latin name *Paul*.) The Christians at Jerusalem are afraid of Paul, who had been their fiercest persecutor. Barnabas, one of the most trusted members of the Jerusalem community, serves as mediator between Paul and the wary community, enabling Paul to tell the story of his conversion and begin his work as teacher and missionary.

## Focusing the Responsorial Psalm

*Ps 22:26-27, 28, 30, 31-32 (26a)*

Psalm 22 was the psalm Jesus prayed on the cross according to Matthew and Mark's gospels ("My God, my God, why have you abandoned me?" [Ps 22:2, NABRE]); but the final third of the psalm (today's responsorial) takes a dramatic turn from lament to thanksgiving: despite the horrors that have befallen him, the psalmist is confident that, in the end, God will be his salvation. We can also imagine these words being prayed by Paul in today's first reading, as God calls him from his old life as oppressor of the Gospel to a new life as evangelizer of the risen Jesus.

## Focusing the Second Reading

*1 John 3:18-24*

Echoing the Fourth Gospel's teachings on love, the writer of the epistle attributed to John urges his hearers to remain faithful to the sacred commandment to love one another in the spirit of Jesus Christ. The letter echoes the theme of today's gospel: that in our love for others we "remain" in Christ.

---

**PROMPTS FOR HOMILISTS, CATECHISTS, AND RCIA TEAMS**

How does our connectedness to Christ make our parish more than just another charitable or humanitarian organization?

What are the signs that an individual or a church is in need of "pruning"? What in your life or church needs to be "gathered and thrown into a fire"?

Consider Paul's conversion and the fear and distrust of the Jerusalem church when he seeks to become part of the community he has persecuted. Have you ever experienced a negative reaction from others when you have sought to change or move on to a new approach or position?

Have you known, in your life and work, a mediator like Barnabas?

## Model Rite for the Blessing and Sprinkling of Water

*Presider:* Dear friends, in the waters of baptism we were recreated in the life of the Easter Christ. We begin our Eucharist by using water to remember our baptisms, asking that the Spirit that came upon us then may continue to fill us with God's grace and Christ's peace. *[pause]*

   [*continue with* The Roman Missal, *Appendix II*]

## Homily Points

• In Jesus' image of the vine and branches, we realize that we are connected to one another as church, we belong to one another as family, we are branches of the same vine planted by the Father, the vine grower. In Christ, we are sustained in God's grace throughout time and space; despite our different races and creeds, our nationalities and cultures, we are branches that draw life from the same root. On the night before he died (the setting of today's gospel), Jesus reminds his disciples of every time and place that, in his love, we are "grafted" to one another in ways we do not completely realize or understand. As branches of Christ the Vine, we are part of something greater than ourselves, something that transforms and transcends the fragileness of our lives.

• Our lives can become strangled by fear and complacency. The demands on our lives that render us unable to love and accept love can be the overgrowth that isolates us from others, that mires us in cynicism and loneliness. When this happens we can be assured that the Father, the vine grower, will "prune" away the excess and the useless, the dysfunctional and the broken in order that we might produce more fruit.

• Our place at God's table in eternity, our worthiness to be called disciples of Christ is determined not by titles, not by our facility to talk about our beliefs, not by our self-imagined greatness, but by our belief in Jesus the Christ, and our remaining in him. We are united to him as a branch to the vine. As the branch is pruned to bear more fruit, so should anyone who remains in Christ expect to be "pruned" to bear more fruit as well.

## Model Universal Prayer (Prayer of the Faithful)

*Presider:* Confident that "God is greater than our hearts," let us offer our prayers.

*Response:* Lord, hear our prayer.

For all Christian churches and communities, that they may be faithful to the love and peace of God both "in deed and in truth" . . .

For the world's nations and governments, peoples and tribes, that they may realize the dignity shared by all human beings as sons and daughters of God, the vine grower . . .

For the persecuted, displaced, and imprisoned; for the estranged or separated; for the rejected and marginalized, that we may be inspired by the example of Barnabas, enabling them to be reconciled with their families and communities and serving as advocates for their return to home and church . . .

For our parish community, that we may be a rich and vibrant branch of Christ the Vine . . .

*Presider:* Hear our Easter prayers, O Lord. May your words forever be a part of us; may your peace forever reign over us; may your love forever unite us as your children. We ask these things in the name of your Son, the risen One. **Amen.**

---

**COLLECT**

Let us pray.

*Pause for silent prayer*

Almighty ever-living God,
constantly accomplish the Paschal
   Mystery within us,
that those you were pleased to make new
   in Holy Baptism
may, under your protective care, bear
   much fruit
and come to the joys of life eternal.
Through our Lord Jesus Christ, your Son,
who lives and reigns with you in the unity
   of the Holy Spirit,
one God, for ever and ever. **Amen.**

**FIRST READING**   Acts 9:26-31

When Saul arrived in Jerusalem he tried to
      join the disciples,
   but they were all afraid of him,
   not believing that he was a disciple.
Then Barnabas took charge of him and
      brought him to the apostles,
   and he reported to them how he had
      seen the Lord,
   and that he had spoken to him,
   and how in Damascus he had spoken
      out boldly in the name of Jesus.
He moved about freely with them in
      Jerusalem,
   and spoke out boldly in the name of the
      Lord.
He also spoke and debated with the
      Hellenists,
   but they tried to kill him.
And when the brothers learned of this,
   they took him down to Caesarea
   and sent him on his way to Tarsus.

The church throughout all Judea, Galilee,
      and Samaria was at peace.
It was being built up and walked in the
      fear of the Lord,
   and with the consolation of the Holy
      Spirit it grew in numbers.

**RESPONSORIAL PSALM**

Ps 22:26-27, 28, 30, 31-32

℟. (26a) I will praise you, Lord, in the
      assembly of your people.
   *or:*
℟. Alleluia.

I will fulfill my vows before those who fear
      the LORD.
   The lowly shall eat their fill;
they who seek the LORD shall praise him:
   "May your hearts live forever!"

℟. I will praise you, Lord, in the assembly
      of your people.
   *or:*
℟. Alleluia.

All the ends of the earth
  shall remember and turn to the LORD;
all the families of the nations
  shall bow down before him.

R̦. I will praise you, Lord, in the assembly
    of your people.
  *or:*
R̦. Alleluia.

To him alone shall bow down
  all who sleep in the earth;
before him shall bend
  all who go down into the dust.

R̦. I will praise you, Lord, in the assembly
    of your people.
  *or:*
R̦. Alleluia.

And to him my soul shall live;
  my descendants shall serve him.
Let the coming generation be told of the
    LORD
  that they may proclaim to a people yet
    to be born
  the justice he has shown.

R̦. I will praise you, Lord, in the assembly
    of your people.
  *or:*
R̦. Alleluia.

### SECOND READING

1 John 3:18-24

Children, let us love not in word or speech
  but in deed and truth.

Now this is how we shall know that we
    belong to the truth
  and reassure our hearts before him
  in whatever our hearts condemn,
  for God is greater than our hearts and
    knows everything.
Beloved, if our hearts do not condemn us,
  we have confidence in God
  and receive from him whatever we ask,
  because we keep his commandments
    and do what pleases him.
And his commandment is this:
  we should believe in the name of his
    Son, Jesus Christ,
  and love one another just as he
    commanded us.
Those who keep his commandments
    remain in him, and he in them,
  and the way we know that he remains
    in us
  is from the Spirit he gave us.

## About Liturgy

*Being witnesses for one another:* We know well that to be disciples we are to be witnesses for Christ. Yet we are also called to be witnesses for one another, speaking on behalf of the work that Christ is doing in others. We see how that happened in today's first reading when Barnabas testified to the apostles and gave witness to Saul's own conversion.

In the liturgy, we give a similar kind of witness for one another at significant moments. In the process of conversion to Christ, sponsors, godparents, and other members of the assembly give public witness at the Rite of Election to the work God has done in a catechumen's life. In the Order of Celebrating Matrimony, the assembly stands as witness to the covenantal love God has already made with the couple, who now enters that same covenant of love with each other. At confirmation and at ordination, the candidates are presented to the celebrant by a member of the assembly who testifies to the candidates' readiness for the sacrament. And every time we offer intercessions, we are "exercising the office of [our] baptismal Priesthood" (*General Instruction of the Roman Missal*, 69), giving witness for one another before God to the needs of the church, the world, those who suffer, and the local community.

By being witnesses for one another, we offer encouragement and hope and we help one another recognize and strengthen the good work that God continues to do in the world through each one of us. Since it was God who first chose us and called us to be one with him in baptism, bearing witness for one another is also bearing witness to Christ.

## About Liturgical Music

*To be in the assembly of God's people:* The antiphon of today's responsorial psalm says, "I will praise you, Lord, in the assembly of your people." This gives us an opportunity to reflect on what it means to be *in the assembly* of God's people as music ministers.

Sing to the Lord speaks of the placement of the music ministers within the assembly: "The placement of the choir should show the choir members' presence as a part of the worshiping community, yet serving in a unique way" (98). How this is done will be different in each church, depending on architecture, acoustics, and size of the choir and the musical instruments involved. Yet the general principle is always that the choir is first and foremost participating members of the worshiping assembly. For this reason, Sing to the Lord reminds music ministers, "When not engaged in the direct exercise of their particular role, music ministers, like all ministers of the Liturgy, remain attentive members of the gathered assembly and should never constitute a distraction" (96). It also gives directives for where specific members of the music ministry exercise their responsibilities. For example, the cantor leads the assembly in singing, therefore should generally be in front of the assembly and visible to them. However, when the assembly is able to sing on their own, the cantor does not need to be visible (97). Another example is the psalmist, who, like the lectors, is called to proclaim the Scripture. Therefore, the psalmist leads the responsorial psalm from the ambo (97), although another location visible to the assembly is also allowed.

**APRIL 29, 2018**
# FIFTH SUNDAY OF EASTER

## ✝ SPIRITUALITY

**GOSPEL ACCLAMATION**
John 14:23

R7. Alleluia, alleluia.
Whoever loves me will keep my word, says the Lord,
and my Father will love him and we will come to him.
R7. Alleluia, alleluia.

## Gospel

John 15:9-17; L56B

Jesus said to his disciples:
"As the Father loves me, so I also love you.
Remain in my love.
If you keep my commandments, you will remain in my love,
just as I have kept my Father's commandments
and remain in his love.

"I have told you this so that my joy may be in you
and your joy might be complete.
This is my commandment: love one another as I love you.
No one has greater love than this,
to lay down one's life for one's friends.
You are my friends if you do what I command you.
I no longer call you slaves,
because a slave does not know what his master is doing.
I have called you friends,
because I have told you everything I have heard from my Father.
It was not you who chose me, but I who chose you
and appointed you to go and bear fruit that will remain,
so that whatever you ask the Father in my name he may give you.
This I command you: love one another."

## Reflecting on the Gospel

When we are young we learn a list of "dos" and "don'ts." Don't cross the street without looking both ways. Do show respect for your elders. Don't misbehave. Do treat people the way you would like to be treated. Lend a hand in cleaning the dishes after a meal. The list is seemingly endless. Some grade-school children learn the list well and follow all the rules. And some of these might even become a little self-righteous with the way they follow the rules in the midst of many others who do not. There is a comfort that can come from following the rules, doing what is expected, keeping the list. But there also comes a time when we grow out of childhood, internalize the purpose of the rules, and live as adults.

Even the Old Testament had a list, which today we refer to as the Ten Commandments. Honor your father and mother. Do not covet another's belongings. Here again, learning the list and following it is rather easy and straightforward. It's literally a checklist as to how to be good and honorable in God's sight. And too often we encounter (or have become ourselves) those who are a bit smug in the way they keep the rules and follow the list, much like proud grade-school children who find comfort and validation in mere obedience.

But Jesus gives us a command in today's gospel that supersedes all others. It is simply this: "love one another." Of course, with a command like this, it can be seductive to return to a checklist! How much easier would it be to maintain a checklist, such as, going to church, celebrating the sacraments, fasting on Ash Wednesday and Good Friday. But the command issued by Jesus is much more difficult. A command to love knows no bounds, knows no checklist. It can be much easier to simply attend church once a week, and again on days of obligation, than it can be to "love." By this command Jesus invites us to an adult spirituality, no longer satisfied by keeping a list. We are not children who need to be told to help with cleaning up after dinner. We do this naturally out of love. And we likely do much more.

There is no box to check for "love." Love does not count the cost or put a limit on what price is too high. Love can always do more. Love is based on a personal relationship with another that is not transactional but self-giving. As Jesus says in the gospel, his love for his friends reaches the point of laying down his own life for them. There is no boundary to what love calls us to do. And for that reason, we might prefer a list of dos and don'ts. But that is not what we receive from Jesus. We receive from him a command simple but demanding: "love one another."

## Living the Paschal Mystery

The Christian life, modeled on Jesus, is about a freedom to love to the point of laying down one's life for the other. A relationship with Jesus necessarily involves a relationship with his friends. And these friends are called to love not only Jesus and the Father but, perhaps more importantly, one another. How much simpler the spiritual life would be if we only had to focus on loving Jesus, or loving God. But to be a friend of Jesus means we must love his other friends as well. This kind of love is not simply a checklist of good deeds, but a dying to self that puts the other first. This love is self-sacrificial and demands we put our own wants, needs, and desires aside to serve and love the other. But, some might respond, others have so many needs there is no way we can meet them all. We would die trying. "Precisely," is the answer we might expect. The Christian life is one that demands a kind of heroism of daily self-sacrifice, daily dying to one's self. This is the paschal mystery given to us by Jesus himself. For when we give ourselves to the point of no return, God is there to raise us up to new life.

## Focusing the Gospel

*John 15:9-17*

Chapters 13 through 17 of John's gospel, Jesus' Last Supper discourse, might be called Jesus' last will and testament to his fledgling disciples.

Continuing last Sunday's theme of the vine and branches, Jesus speaks of the love of God as the bonding agent between himself and his disciples, and the disciples and one another. The model of love for the faithful disciple—"love one another as I love you"—is total, limitless, and unconditional. The love manifested in the life and teachings of the gospel Jesus and the resurrection of Christ creates an entirely new relationship between God and humanity: In Christ, we are not "slaves" of a distant divine Creator but "friends" of God who hears the prayers and cries made to him in Jesus' name. That love becomes the source of our lives' joy; in that love, we realize the meaning and purpose of our lives. As "friends of God," we are called to reflect that love to the rest of the world.

## Focusing the First Reading

*Acts 10:25-26, 34-35, 44-48*

Cornelius, a Roman centurion, was a religious man, the kind of Gentile whom the Jews called a "God fearer." Cornelius has a dream in which an angel instructs him to send for Peter. Peter's meeting with Cornelius is a revelation, both for the officer and the apostle: Peter begins to understand that God calls all men and women—not just religious Jews—to himself. This is a critical development in the growth of the new church, which has been wrestling with the tensions between its deeply ingrained Jewish identity and practices and what that might mean for the mission to the Gentiles.

## Focusing the Responsorial Psalm

*Ps 98:1, 2-3, 3-4 (2b)*

Psalm 98 is one of a series of consecutive psalms (95–100) inviting the hearer to join in praising God as savior/deliverer, king/sovereign, and judge/lawgiver. Today's responsorial psalm is inspired by some great military victory or act of deliverance by God: some scholars suggest that these psalms may have been composed for the rededication of the temple following Israel's return from Babylonian exile.

## Focusing the Second Reading

*1 John 4:7-10*

The author of the Johannine epistles writes eloquently of the love of God revealed in his only Son. In today's second reading, the writer speaks of love as being of God to the point that he says those who love know God. He does not state this the other way around, as though knowing God necessarily leads to love. Instead, for this author, everyone who loves knows God.

---

**PROMPTS FOR HOMILISTS, CATECHISTS, AND RCIA TEAMS**

What does it mean to be a "friend" of God, as opposed to simply believing in the existence of God?

Who is your best friend, and what makes him or her so? Has that friendship ever been tested?

How have your ideals and beliefs about love changed throughout your life?

How do we know that God loves us?

How has Christ "chosen" us—and for what?

## Model Rite for the Blessing and Sprinkling of Water

*Presider:* Dear friends, we will use this water to remind us of our baptisms. May God send his Spirit upon it and upon us, so that the Word of God may continue to recreate us in God's love. *[pause]*

    [*continue with* The Roman Missal, *Appendix II*]

## Homily Points

• Jesus asks us to love one another as he has loved us: to put others before ourselves, to seek our joy in bringing joy to others, to honor and cherish others simply because they are sons and daughters of the God of mercy and compassion. *Love one another*—with no qualifications, conditions, or limitations. *Love one another*—without judgment, measurements, or expectations of a return. *Love one another*—even the undeserving, the mean-spirited, the ungrateful, and the unreasonable. Such love can be overwhelmingly demanding, but such love can be the source of "complete" joy and fulfillment, love that is no less than an experience of Easter resurrection.

• The night before he died, in his last words to his disciples, Jesus calls them "friends," a friendship based on acceptance, openness, and love. In inviting us to be his friends, Jesus defines exactly what friendship is. True friendship is a holy relationship, a covenant centered on love. It does not demand but seeks to give; it always sees and lifts up the good in one another; it is a relationship that can be depended upon for support and trusted for its integrity.

• Christ transforms creation's relationship with its Creator: God, as revealed by Christ, is not the distant, aloof, removed architect of the universe; he is not the cruel taskmaster; he takes no delight in the destruction of the wicked. Christ reveals to us a God who is present in all things in the form of creative, reconciling, energizing, healing love. All that God has done in the first creation of Genesis and the re-creation of Easter has been done out of his limitless, unfathomable love. Such love invites us to seek out God's presence, not out of fear or some perverted sense of self-loathing, but out of grateful joy at what God has done for us, God's friends in the risen Christ.

## Model Universal Prayer (Prayer of the Faithful)

*Presider:* God's love has been revealed in our midst in his Son, the risen Christ. With confidence, then, let us offer our prayers to God in Jesus' name.

*Response:* Lord, hear our prayer.

That the sacrifice of those in our church who have given their lives for others may be a sign of God's love recreating our world . . .

That a spirit of humility and service may guide the world's leaders of churches, governments, businesses, and institutions . . .

That we may bring healing and hope to the poor, sick, and suffering through our faithful keeping of Jesus' commandment to love one another as he has loved us . . .

That our parish's work and worship may reflect the complete and unconditional love of God in our midst . . .

*Presider:* O God of unfathomable love, hear our Easter prayers. Make us worthy to be your "friends," in our compassion and support for our friends here, in our seeking what is right and acceptable in your eyes, in our faithfulness to your commandment to love one another as you love us. We ask these things through Christ Jesus, our brother and friend. **Amen.**

**COLLECT**

Let us pray.

*Pause for silent prayer*

Grant, almighty God,
that we may celebrate with heartfelt
    devotion these days of joy,
which we keep in honor of the risen Lord,
and that what we relive in remembrance
we may always hold to in what we do.
Through our Lord Jesus Christ, your Son,
who lives and reigns with you in the unity
    of the Holy Spirit,
one God, for ever and ever. **Amen.**

**FIRST READING**

Acts 10:25-26, 34-35, 44-48

When Peter entered, Cornelius met him
    and, falling at his feet, paid him
      homage.
Peter, however, raised him up, saying,
    "Get up. I myself am also a human
      being."

Then Peter proceeded to speak and said,
    "In truth, I see that God shows no
      partiality.
Rather, in every nation whoever fears him
    and acts uprightly
    is acceptable to him."

While Peter was still speaking these
    things,
    the Holy Spirit fell upon all who were
      listening to the word.
The circumcised believers who had
    accompanied Peter
    were astounded that the gift of the Holy
      Spirit
    should have been poured out on the
      Gentiles also,
    for they could hear them speaking in
      tongues and glorifying God.
Then Peter responded,
    "Can anyone withhold the water for
      baptizing these people,
    who have received the Holy Spirit even
      as we have?"
He ordered them to be baptized in the
    name of Jesus Christ.

## RESPONSORIAL PSALM

Ps 98:1, 2-3, 3-4

℟. (cf. 2b) The Lord has revealed to the
    nations his saving power.
    *or:*
℟. Alleluia.

Sing to the LORD a new song,
    for he has done wondrous deeds;
his right hand has won victory for him,
    his holy arm.

℟. The Lord has revealed to the nations
    his saving power.
    *or:*
℟. Alleluia.

The LORD has made his salvation known:
    in the sight of the nations he has
        revealed his justice.
He has remembered his kindness and his
    faithfulness
    toward the house of Israel.

℟. The Lord has revealed to the nations
    his saving power.
    *or:*
℟. Alleluia.

All the ends of the earth have seen
    the salvation by our God.
Sing joyfully to the LORD, all you lands;
    break into song; sing praise.

℟. The Lord has revealed to the nations
    his saving power.
    *or:*
℟. Alleluia.

## SECOND READING

1 John 4:7-10

Beloved, let us love one another,
    because love is of God;
    everyone who loves is begotten by God
        and knows God.
Whoever is without love does not know
    God, for God is love.
In this way the love of God was revealed
    to us:
    God sent his only Son into the world
    so that we might have life through him.
In this is love:
    not that we have loved God, but that he
        loved us
    and sent his Son as expiation for our sins.

*Or, where the Ascension is celebrated on
Sunday, the second reading and gospel for
the Seventh Sunday of Easter may be used
on this Sunday.*

1 John 4:11-16, p. 133.

John 17:11b-19, p. 130.

### About Liturgy

***Love is more than a good feeling:*** Today's gospel message seems pretty simple: love one another. The challenge, however, is what Christ adds to that command: "love one another as I love you." It's the "as I love you" part that's tricky because look at how Jesus loved us: even unto death. Loving one another that way is much more difficult. For the majority of us, following Christ's command will not call us to actual martyrdom. However, we are all called to show this sacrificial kind of love. We see what this love looks like in the church's description in the Rite of Christian Initiation of Adults, 75.2, of how catechumens learn to live as Christians by learning to live in community:

> As they become familiar with the Christian way of life and are helped by the example and support of sponsors, godparents, and the entire Christian community, the catechumens learn to . . . practice love of neighbor, even at the cost of self-renunciation. Thus formed, " . . . they pass from the old to a new nature made perfect in Christ. Since this transition brings with it a progressive change of outlook and conduct, it should become manifest by means of its social consequences . . . Since the Lord in whom they believe is a sign of contradiction, the newly converted often experience divisions and separations, but they also taste the joy that God gives without measure" (quoting *Ad Gentes* 14).

Loving one another is much more than simply a feel-good moment. Just ask any married couple, parent, or person living in community! In order to love one another, we must, each day, give up our own wants and needs; sometimes we have to sacrifice our own comfort; many times we need to die to our own point of view and deeply held preconceptions if we want to love others as Jesus loved us to the cross.

Every Sunday, we have another opportunity to practice this kind of love. In the assembly, we are called to love especially those we do not know, those whose faith may be tepid or merely cultural, those who don't look like us, speak like us, vote like us, or even pray like us. We exercise this kind of love in many ways. Greeting those around us and making room for others in our pews is one way. Speaking intentionally and looking one another in the eye at the sign of peace is another. Opening our hearts and our mouths to try to sing and pray in our neighbor's language and style of music, even if it is unfamiliar to us, is yet another. If we can learn to love those who worship with us, we will have a greater chance at showing that sacrificial love to those most in need in the world.

### About Liturgical Music

***How we love one another in our music:*** Singing in a choir is a gift and blessing, especially when it is a ministry we share in faith for a worshiping community. It's even more wonderful when we like the people we minister with and share the same tastes in music. But what happens when there's conflict among choir members? Or how about when a choir director chooses music that seems very different in style than you're used to?

We can do as the US bishops reminded all music ministers: "Each Christian must keep in mind that to live and worship in community often demands a personal sacrifice. All must be willing to share likes and dislikes with others whose ideas and experiences may be quite unlike their own" (Music in Catholic Worship, 17). Even in our music and music-making, we are called to love one another as Christ loved us.

**MAY 6, 2018**
# SIXTH SUNDAY OF EASTER

## SPIRITUALITY

**GOSPEL ACCLAMATION**
Matt 28:19a, 20b

℟. Alleluia, alleluia.
Go and teach all nations, says the Lord;
I am with you always, until the end of the world.
℟. Alleluia, alleluia.

**Gospel**   Mark 16:15-20; L58B

**Jesus said to his disciples:**
   **"Go into the whole world**
   **and proclaim the gospel to every**
      **creature.**
**Whoever believes and is baptized will be**
      **saved;**
   **whoever does not believe will be**
      **condemned.**
**These signs will accompany those who**
      **believe:**
   **in my name they will drive out demons,**
   **they will speak new languages.**
**They will pick up serpents with their**
      **hands,**
   **and if they drink any deadly thing, it**
      **will not harm them.**
**They will lay hands on the sick, and they**
      **will recover."**

**So then the Lord Jesus, after he spoke to**
      **them,**
   **was taken up into heaven**
   **and took his seat at the right hand of God.**
**But they went forth and preached**
      **everywhere,**
   **while the Lord worked with them**
   **and confirmed the word through**
      **accompanying signs.**

### Reflecting on the Gospel

Many people associate snake charmers with Asia, in particular India and its surrounding region. The snake seems to be hypnotized by the music played by its handler. Crowds gather around, amazed at such a thing. How can this poisonous reptile be made so seemingly docile? The snake charmers are special, perhaps magical!

In today's gospel we hear an odd-sounding statement about those who are baptized; they will be able to pick up snakes, drink poison without being harmed, and heal the sick by laying hands on them. Aside from a few fundamentalist churches, virtually no Christians take this passage literally. And even those churches who handle snakes and practice faith healings do not drink poison! What are we to make of this? Though it might be easier to gloss over this strange verse, it will likely be in our minds as we hear it at this Mass. The notes in the New American Bible make clear that Mark's gospel ended at 16:8. But it seems that some copyists did not like the ending to be one where all the disciples run away because they were afraid! And so we have a multiplicity of endings attested to by different manuscripts. What we refer to as Mark 16:9-20 is one such ending, and it is certainly considered canonical, inspired, and authoritative, but it was not part of the "original" gospel. It was written by a later author, probably someone who wanted to address certain issues in their community.

Among other things, Mark 16:9-20 answers the question of the Gentile mission, or why there are so many Gentiles in a movement that was initially Jewish. The answer is that Jesus gave them the command, "Go into the whole world / and proclaim the gospel to every creature." In a sense, this is Mark's version of Matthew's more elegant Great Commandment (Matt 28:19-20). The Markan gospel passage, and the gospel itself, concludes with an echo of 1 Timothy 3:16 and Luke 24:15, namely that Jesus was "taken up" into heaven. This episode answers the question, where is Jesus now? He is in heaven, seated at the right hand of God.

And between this version of the great commission and the "taking up" into heaven we have the verse about snake handling, drinking poison, and healing the sick. This corresponds well to a story in Acts 28:3-9 about Paul spending the winter in Malta. There he was bitten by a snake but suffered no ill effects, and he healed their sick by laying hands on them. So this later ending to Mark's gospel seems to allude to this other New Testament story. And it is for this reason too that scholars believe the addition to Mark's gospel is late. More than anything else, the gospel today tells us that Jesus is with God in heaven. There is really nothing magical about that at all.

### Living the Paschal Mystery

Some Bible stories can appear odd to modern readers. We have to remind ourselves that these vignettes were written about two thousand years ago by people who lived in the ancient world. Signs and wonders for them can sometimes seem like "magic" or "snake charming" today. For example, for one to claim today that one drank poison with no ill effect, or handled snakes without suffering harm, would more likely demonstrate one's strangeness rather than one's Christian identity. It can be challenging to discern theological meaning from some of the Bible's stories. And yet, we are to do just that. We do not read the Bible literally, but we read it as thinking Christians, with the guidance of the church, our community of fellow believers. To assist us with this endeavor, the church provides us with translations of the Bible that include extensive notes. Part of our living the paschal mystery is to encounter the Scriptures as thinking adults. And we are grateful to have so many resources for us in today's age for that very task.

## Focusing the Gospel

*Mark 16:15-20*

Scholars call today's gospel the "longer ending" of Mark's text. In style and substance, these six verses are very unlike the rest of Mark's text; scholars recognize that these verses were added sometime later to "complete" Mark's account to include the tradition of the ascension of Jesus. (The "signs" that "accompany those who believe" are somewhat incongruous; earlier in Mark's narrative, Mark 8:11-12, Jesus rebukes the Pharisees for seeking such signs.) This ending reflects the traditional post-resurrection stories of Jesus commissioning his new church to continue his presence on earth through their proclamation of the Good News.

## Focusing the First Reading

*Acts 1:1-11*

Today's readings include two accounts of Jesus' return to the Father: the first reading is the beginning of the Acts of the Apostles, Luke's "Gospel of the Holy Spirit." Jesus' ascension begins volume two of Luke's work on the life of Jesus and the beginnings of Christianity. The words and images in today's first reading evoke the Old Testament accounts of the ascension of Elijah (2 Kgs 2) and the forty years of the exodus: Luke considers the time that the risen Lord spent with his disciples a sacred time, a "desert experience" for the apostles to prepare them for their new ministry of preaching the Gospel of the resurrection. (Acts alone places the ascension forty days after Easter; in Luke's first telling [Luke 24:50-53], perhaps before he planned to write Acts of the Apostles, he indicates that the ascension takes place on the day of Easter. Like the original ending in Mark, neither Matthew nor John has an account of the ascension.)

Responding to their question about the restoration of Israel, Jesus discourages his disciples from speculating on what God alone knows. Greater things await them as his "witnesses."

The two men in white ("Men of Galilee, / why are you standing there looking at the sky?") chide the eleven disciples to change focus: to look not at the sky but straight ahead to the mission that Jesus has entrusted to them.

## Focusing the Responsorial Psalm

*Ps 47:2-3, 6-7, 8-9 (6)*

Psalm 47 is one of several psalms called the "enthronement psalms," songs that celebrate the Lord as King. The verses of the psalm imagine God assuming his throne for all eternity, to the acclaim of all nations. The Christian community saw Jesus' triumphant return to the Father in the images of this psalm.

## Focusing the Second Reading

*Option 1: Ephesians 1:17-23*

The letter to the Ephesians (attributed to Paul and certainly inspired by him, but probably not actually written by him) celebrates the union of all men and women in and with Christ, as members of his mystical body. In the letter's opening, the apostle prays that the Christian community at Ephesus may be united in the great "hope" they share in the risen Christ, whom the Father has made sovereign over all creatures and head of the church.

**PROMPTS FOR HOMILISTS, CATECHISTS, AND RCIA TEAMS**

Most of us are neither teachers nor preachers. So how do we fulfill Jesus' commission to be his "witnesses" in our own Jerusalems?

What emotions and feelings do you imagine the disciples experienced as they walked down the mountain and returned to Jerusalem?

Who are Jesus' "apostles" to the small, hidden places on earth?

In Mark's gospel, Jesus says that these "signs will accompany those who believe": driving out demons, speaking new languages, picking up serpents with their hands, not being harmed by drinking "any deadly thing," healing the sick. How do we figuratively experience these "signs"?

### Model Rite for the Blessing and Sprinkling of Water

*Presider:* Dear friends, in baptism we have been called to be witnesses of Christ Jesus. Let us ask God to send his Spirit upon this water that we will use to remember our baptisms—and may that same Spirit again descend upon us, sending us forth to realize the hope of our call. *[pause]*

[*continue with* The Roman Missal, *Appendix II*]

### Homily Points

• Jesus' ascension is both an ending and a beginning. The resurrection appearances of Jesus are at an end; his revelation of the kingdom of God is complete; the promise of the Messiah is fulfilled. Now begins the work of his disciples to teach what they have learned and to share what they have witnessed. It is not a promising start. Like any beginning or transition in life, it is a moment of great uncertainty, confusion, and apprehension. Christ places his church in the hands of a company of illiterate fishermen and otherwise unremarkable people—and yet, what began with those followers of Jesus has grown and flourished through the centuries to this parish family of ours. The church Jesus leaves to them is rooted not in buildings or wealth or systems of theology but in faith nurtured in the human heart, a faith centered in wisdom and trust that is empowering and liberating, a faith that gives us the strength and freedom to be authentic witnesses of the risen One, who is present among us.

• On the mount of the ascension, Jesus calls us to be his "witnesses," to tell others about the good that God has worked in the Easter mystery. Jesus asks us to be witnesses of God's presence in our midst, to be agents of hope, to be prophets of compassion and peace. We who have heard the story of Jesus and beheld his presence in the reconciling love we have experienced in our own lives are now called to bring that love into the lives of others and into the lives we share as families, as the church, as humankind. We are called to continue Jesus' work to teach, to witness, and to heal in our own small corners of the world, to hand on the story that has been handed on to us about Jesus and his Gospel of love and compassion.

### Model Universal Prayer (Prayer of the Faithful)

*Presider:* The risen Christ now sits at God's right hand until the end of time. In confidence and hope, then, let us offer our prayers.

*Response:* Lord, hear our prayer.

That Pope N. and the bishops, priests, deacons, and ministers of our church may continue the great mission entrusted by Christ to the disciples . . .

That every nation, power, and dominion of the earth may give praise to God through their work together for justice and peace for all peoples . . .

That the poor, the sick, the suffering, and the needy may come to know, in our outreach to them, "the one hope" to which God has called us . . .

That our parish family may be witnesses of the risen Christ in our own community and "to the ends of the earth" . . .

*Presider:* Father, in raising the Lord Jesus from the grave you have given hope to us and to all humanity. Hear the prayers we make to you in the name of Jesus your Christ, the source and life of that hope, who lives and reigns with you forever and ever. **Amen.**

**COLLECT**

Let us pray.

*Pause for silent prayer*

Gladden us with holy joys, almighty God,
and make us rejoice with devout
thanksgiving,
for the Ascension of Christ your Son
is our exaltation,
and, where the Head has gone before in
glory,
the Body is called to follow in hope.
Through our Lord Jesus Christ, your Son,
who lives and reigns with you in the unity
of the Holy Spirit,
one God, for ever and ever. **Amen.**

**FIRST READING**
Acts 1:1-11

In the first book, Theophilus,
    I dealt with all that Jesus did and taught
    until the day he was taken up,
    after giving instructions through the
        Holy Spirit
    to the apostles whom he had chosen.
He presented himself alive to them
    by many proofs after he had suffered,
    appearing to them during forty days
    and speaking about the kingdom of
        God.
While meeting with them,
    he enjoined them not to depart from
        Jerusalem,
    but to wait for "the promise of the
        Father
    about which you have heard me speak;
    for John baptized with water,
    but in a few days you will be baptized
        with the Holy Spirit."

When they had gathered together they
        asked him,
    "Lord, are you at this time going to
        restore the kingdom to Israel?"
He answered them, "It is not for you to
        know the times or seasons
    that the Father has established by his
        own authority.
But you will receive power when the Holy
        Spirit comes upon you,
    and you will be my witnesses in
        Jerusalem,
    throughout Judea and Samaria,
    and to the ends of the earth."
When he had said this, as they were
        looking on,
    he was lifted up, and a cloud took him
        from their sight.

While they were looking intently at the
    sky as he was going,
    suddenly two men dressed in white
        garments stood beside them.
They said, "Men of Galilee,
    why are you standing there looking at
        the sky?
This Jesus who has been taken up from
    you into heaven
    will return in the same way as you have
        seen him going into heaven."

## RESPONSORIAL PSALM
Ps 47:2-3, 6-7, 8-9

R℣. (6) God mounts his throne to shouts of
    joy: a blare of trumpets for the Lord.
*or:*
R℣. Alleluia.

All you peoples, clap your hands,
    shout to God with cries of gladness,
for the LORD, the Most High, the awesome,
    is the great king over all the earth.

R℣. God mounts his throne to shouts of joy:
    a blare of trumpets for the Lord.
*or:*
R℣. Alleluia.

God mounts his throne amid shouts of joy;
    the LORD, amid trumpet blasts.
Sing praise to God, sing praise;
    sing praise to our king, sing praise.

R℣. God mounts his throne to shouts of joy:
    a blare of trumpets for the Lord.
*or:*
R℣. Alleluia.

For king of all the earth is God;
    sing hymns of praise.
God reigns over the nations,
    God sits upon his holy throne.

R℣. God mounts his throne to shouts of joy:
    a blare of trumpets for the Lord.
*or:*
R℣. Alleluia.

## SECOND READING
Eph 1:17-23

*or* Eph 4:1-13

*or* Eph 4:1-7, 11-13

*See Appendix A, pp. 294–295.*

---

### About Liturgy
*Moveable feasts:* Why do some places celebrate Ascension on Thursday while others move it to the following Sunday? The Acts of the Apostles gives us the tradition of placing the Ascension forty days after Christ's resurrection. This is how we get the tradition of Ascension Thursday, or the fortieth day after Easter.

So how did we get an option for Ascension Sunday? The Code of Canon Law, canon 1246 §1, lists the holy days of obligation, including Ascension. In §2 of that same canon, conferences of bishops are given permission to omit certain days from this universal list or transfer their observance to a Sunday. In 1999, the US bishops allowed individual ecclesiastical provinces in the United States to decide whether Ascension should be moved from Thursday to the following Sunday. (An ecclesiastical province is a group of local dioceses under the jurisdiction of an archdiocese.) Only the ecclesiastical provinces of Boston, Hartford, New York, Newark, Philadelphia, and Omaha decided to retain the tradition of observing Ascension on Thursday, while everywhere else in the US, the solemnity was moved to Sunday.

Regardless of when your province celebrates the Ascension, the more important issue is what we believe Christ's ascension means for us. We can imagine that scene with the disciples staring up into the sky. Some religious paintings and sculptures even depict this event showing only Jesus' feet dangling from beneath the clouds! Yet, if all we understand about ascension is that Jesus went up to heaven, we miss the point. In a homily in 2009 on the solemnity of the Ascension, Pope Benedict XVI explained that "this word Heaven does not indicate a place above the stars but something far more daring and sublime: it indicates Christ himself, the divine Person who welcomes humanity fully and for ever."

Ascension isn't so much about where Jesus went but about where Jesus sends us. Just as Christ commissioned his own disciples to go to all the nations, our memorial of Christ's ascension moves us out into the whole world to proclaim the Gospel. As Christ is one in union with the Father, Ascension draws us closer in union with Christ who is found most clearly not up in the sky but here in our neighbor and in those most in need.

*Mother's Day:* If the Ascension is celebrated on Sunday, May 13, Mother's Day coincides with it. See the comments under Catechesis: About Liturgy given for the Seventh Sunday of Easter.

### About Initiation
*End of the period festivities:* The final period of the RCIA is the period of mystagogy and postbaptismal catechesis, which coincides with the Easter season. RCIA 249 invites us to mark the close of this period with a celebration for the neophytes held near Pentecost Sunday. There are no specific guidelines for what this celebration looks like other than the inclusion of "festivities in keeping with local custom."

### About Liturgical Music
*Music suggestions:* On this solemnity and during the final weeks of Easter, focus on songs of commissioning and discipleship. "Lord, You Give the Great Commission" with text by Jeffery Rowthorn set to ABBOT'S LEIGH (Hope Publishing) is a sturdy hymn that works well as a dismissal song. Another traditional hymn with more contemporary lyrics is "Church of God, Elect and Glorious" set to the joyful HYFRYDOL (Hope Publishing). Tom Kendzia's "The Eyes and Hands of Christ" (OCP) is a simple but strong processional that would work well as a Communion procession or dismissal song. John Angotti's "I Send You Out" (WLP) is perfect for this day and for the last few weeks of the Easter season.

**MAY 10, 2018 (Thursday) or MAY 13, 2018**
# THE ASCENSION OF THE LORD

## ✝ SPIRITUALITY

### GOSPEL ACCLAMATION
cf. John 14:18

R̸. Alleluia, alleluia.
I will not leave you orphans, says the Lord.
I will come back to you, and your hearts will
    rejoice.
R̸. Alleluia, alleluia.

### Gospel

John 17:11b-19; L60B

Lifting up his eyes to heaven,
    Jesus prayed, saying:
"Holy Father, keep them
        in your name that you
        have given me,
    so that they may be one
        just as we are one.
When I was with them I
        protected them in your
        name that you gave me,
    and I guarded them, and none of
        them was lost
    except the son of destruction,
    in order that the Scripture might be
        fulfilled.
But now I am coming to you.
I speak this in the world
    so that they may share my joy
        completely.
I gave them your word, and the world
        hated them,
    because they do not belong to the
        world
    any more than I belong to the world.
I do not ask that you take them out of
        the world
    but that you keep them from the evil
        one.
They do not belong to the world
    any more than I belong to the world.
Consecrate them in the truth. Your
        word is truth.
As you sent me into the world,
    so I sent them into the world.
And I consecrate myself for them,
    so that they also may be consecrated
        in truth."

### Reflecting on the Gospel

Do you remember the first time you received the keys to the car? That might have been as a teenager. Or do you recall giving a set of car keys to your teenage child for the first time? What trepidation! But what pride and joy as well. Receiving the keys to the car marks a milestone. One is no longer a child but not quite an adult. The awesome responsibility of driving a car might be missed by some and embraced by others. As parents we want to ensure that our children know the obligations that accompany driving. We hope beyond hope that nothing bad happens, that there is no accident. Each of us probably gave a stern yet encouraging talk to these budding adolescents who were yearning only to get behind the wheel and go! And ultimately, we hand over the keys to the car while hoping and praying that all are safe from harm.

In today's gospel Jesus is praying a final prayer to the Father prior to his own arrest and ultimate crucifixion. What must have been going through his mind at that time? He was definitely concerned for his friends, those whom the Father had given and entrusted to Jesus. He prays for them, not that they be taken out of the world, but that they are kept from evil, safe from harm, while living in it. Jesus protected his friends while he was with them, but he will be with them no longer. He will not be able to keep them from evil, or even keep them safe. They are being sent into the world as Jesus was sent. Almost as a concerned parent, Jesus makes his prayer to the Father.

Jesus' desire for his friends is that they may share his joy completely. We too are those who are the objects of this prayer. We are Jesus' friends and he wants our joy to be complete. He knows that the world is a tough, sometimes violent place. He will lose his life in a contest with violence. And yet, he does not take us out of the world. He gives us the ability to live in it, while asking the Father to keep us from the evil one. Moreover, he consecrates himself to us. As we are his followers, indeed his very friends, we are consecrated in truth. This final prayer and petition tells us a great deal about Jesus, his relationship with the Father, and his relationship with us. How fortunate we are to have him as our advocate.

### Living the Paschal Mystery

It can be difficult to say good-bye. Relationships, friendships, and bonds of love enter a new phase when we say good-bye. We may never see our loved ones again, or in the same way. People will develop, grow, and change. And we give them the freedom to do so. Jesus gives us this same freedom today. He knows he is returning to the Father, leaving those who were entrusted to him on their own. Yet, he will promise (in another reading) to send another advocate, the Spirit. But as for Jesus, he will no longer be with them, his friends. If dying on the cross were not enough, Jesus also knew that he was letting go of friendships. He knew the end was in store, and so he placed these relationships in prayer with the Father.

This can be a model for us as we enter new phases of relationships, or when we say good-bye to those we love. At some point we turn it over to the Father, entrusting them and the relationship to his care. Though the relationship may be buffeted by storms, in the meantime it is Jesus' prayer and our own that we will be safe, and the relationships will be secure and last the test of time. Giving over this trust to the Father can be an exercise in humility, knowing that we are not in control. When we turn over control like this, it can seem that we are dying to our own wishes and desires. But in letting go, we are giving new life.

## Focusing the Gospel
*John 17:11b-19*

In John's account of the Last Supper, after Jesus' final teachings to his disciples before his passion, he addresses his Father in prayer. Today's gospel is from chapter 17 of John's gospel, where Jesus prays for his disciples and the mission before them and commends them to God's protection. Jesus prays that they may persevere despite the world's "hatred" of them for they are not of the world. He prays that they may share the "joy" of Jesus completely and "be consecrated in [the] truth."

## Focusing the First Reading
*Acts 1:15-17, 20a, 20c-26*

After Jesus' ascension, the eleven apostles return to Jerusalem. Peter calls upon the community, which Luke numbers at about 120 (no doubt including women as Acts 1:14, the verse immediately prior to what is proclaimed today, indicates), to restore the number of apostles to the sacred biblical number of twelve (see Luke 22:29-30) that Jesus himself had established during his earthly ministry. Nominating two of the company—Barsabbas and Matthias—to serve with the eleven as "witness[es] to his resurrection," they prayerfully place the final selection in the hands of God.

Though it may seem odd to us, drawing lots was a common biblical process of election between equal or like things (for example, the distribution of the land of Canaan among the tribes of Israel [Num 26:55]; Zechariah's designation to offer incense in the temple sanctuary [Luke 1:9]). The use of lots was considered an act of faith in God's judgment instead of subjecting important decisions to the vagaries of human manipulation or prejudice. Of course, we do not use this process of decision making today!

To the reader/hearer of antiquity, what is important in this story is not how Matthias is chosen but that the number of apostles is restored to twelve as Jesus had intended. These twelve will preach to assembled Israel (the people of the twelve tribes) on the feast of Pentecost. After that point, for example, when James is martyred, there is no further effort to reconstitute the twelve apostles. The purpose of the reconstituted twelve has been accomplished on Pentecost.

## Focusing the Responsorial Psalm
*Ps 103:1-2, 11-12, 19-20 (19a)*

The verses from Psalm 103 that make up today's responsorial psalm are a hymn of thanksgiving for God's constant mercy and his care of the poor and humble. Today's psalm takes up Ascension Thursday's theme of the Lord's universal sovereignty. The Hebrew word translated here as "soul" (*nephesh*) might be more accurately translated as "life" or "living being": the use of the word "soul" in the psalm is a call to give praise to God with the very being that propels and animates our lives.

## Focusing the Second Reading
*1 John 4:11-16*

The final selection for this Easter season from the First Letter of John celebrates the Spirit of God's love that binds us to God and to one another. "No one has ever seen God," but God remains in us in our love for one another.

 **CELEBRATION**

### Model Rite for the Blessing and Sprinkling of Water

*Presider:* Dear friends, this water will be used to remind us of our baptisms. May the Spirit of God come down upon this water and upon all of us, consecrating us in God's truth and grace. *[pause]*

[*continue with* The Roman Missal, *Appendix II*]

### Homily Points

• We have heard God's word and we realize the truth of that word: its call to justice, its charge to forgive and seek reconciliation, its grounding in humility and gratitude. But we have become quite adept at finding ways to justify and rationalize our putting aside truth when it conflicts with our own interests and wants. We are called to honor, regardless of the cost, the holiness of truth—truth that is rooted in the reality of God's love and in the sacredness of every person as created in the image and life of God. The Gospel challenges us to recognize the prejudices, biases, ambitions, and hatreds that exist within each one of us and to realize how they affect the decisions we make and what we uphold as "truth."

• Discovering and proclaiming the "truth" often comes at a price. A world that is more than willing to bend, shape, rework, edit, manipulate, and rationalize life's challenges, difficulties, and inconveniences to fit its own concept of what the truth should be often fails to appreciate or welcome the prophet/disciple's uncompromised, honest proclamation of God's truth. Facing the truth can be painful; admitting the truth can be costly. But it is in embracing the truth and paying the price for proclaiming it that we can begin to transform our lives, our communities, our world.

• In calling us to discipleship, Jesus seeks more from us than just having a baptismal certificate or taking a seat at Mass each week. He sends us forth to take on his work of healing, of reconciliation, of bringing others to God. By imitating his simple compassion, Christ promises that we can begin to transform the lives of the hurting, the lost, and the despairing. By becoming advocates for justice in our own time and place, we can begin to change the unjust attitudes and perspectives that demean and hurt all members of society. By seeking reasons to hope despite the cynicism and negativity that surround us, we give the world reason to hope.

### Model Universal Prayer (Prayer of the Faithful)

*Presider:* Let us now join our prayers with Jesus' eternal prayer to the Father for all God's people, in every time and place.

*Response:* Lord, hear our prayer.

For all who serve the church as bishops, priests, ministers, and catechists, that they may proclaim the peace and hope of the risen Christ . . .

For the nations and peoples of the world, that God's reconciling love and peace may dwell in every land . . .

For the sick, the suffering, the recovering, and the dying, that the God of compassion may restore them to health and hope . . .

For our parish community, that the love of God may remain in us as we carry on our ministries of charity and reconciliation . . .

*Presider:* Gracious God, hear the prayers of the people your Son has gathered before you. Consecrate us in your Word so that we may speak your truth in justice and mirror your never-failing love in works of reconciliation. We offer these prayers to you in the name of your Son, the risen Jesus. **Amen.**

**COLLECT**

Let us pray.

*Pause for silent prayer*

Graciously hear our supplications, O Lord,
so that we, who believe that the Savior of
    the human race
is with you in your glory,
may experience, as he promised,
until the end of the world,
his abiding presence among us.
Who lives and reigns with you in the unity
    of the Holy Spirit,
one God, for ever and ever. **Amen.**

**FIRST READING**
Acts 1:15-17, 20a, 20c-26

Peter stood up in the midst of the brothers
    —there was a group of about one
        hundred and twenty persons
    in the one place—.
He said, "My brothers,
    the Scripture had to be fulfilled
    which the Holy Spirit spoke beforehand
    through the mouth of David,
        concerning Judas,
    who was the guide for those who
        arrested Jesus.
He was numbered among us
    and was allotted a share in this
        ministry.

"For it is written in the Book of Psalms:
    *May another take his office.*

"Therefore, it is necessary that one of the
    men
    who accompanied us the whole time
    the Lord Jesus came and went among
        us,
    beginning from the baptism of John
    until the day on which he was taken up
        from us,
    become with us a witness to his
        resurrection."
So they proposed two, Judas called
    Barsabbas,
    who was also known as Justus, and
        Matthias.
Then they prayed,
    "You, Lord, who know the hearts of all,
    show which one of these two you have
        chosen
    to take the place in this apostolic
        ministry
    from which Judas turned away to go to
        his own place."
Then they gave lots to them, and the lot
    fell upon Matthias,
    and he was counted with the eleven
        apostles.

## RESPONSORIAL PSALM

Ps 103:1-2, 11-12, 19-20

℟. (19a) The Lord has set his throne in
    heaven.
    *or:*
℟. Alleluia.

Bless the LORD, O my soul;
    and all my being, bless his holy name.
Bless the LORD, O my soul,
    and forget not all his benefits.

℟. The Lord has set his throne in heaven.
    *or:*
℟. Alleluia.

For as the heavens are high above the
    earth,
    so surpassing is his kindness toward
        those who fear him.
As far as the east is from the west,
    so far has he put our transgressions
        from us.

℟. The Lord has set his throne in heaven.
    *or:*
℟. Alleluia.

The LORD has established his throne in
    heaven,
    and his kingdom rules over all.
Bless the LORD, all you his angels,
    you mighty in strength, who do his
        bidding.

℟. The Lord has set his throne in heaven.
    *or:*
℟. Alleluia.

## SECOND READING

1 John 4:11-16

Beloved, if God so loved us,
    we also must love one another.
No one has ever seen God.
Yet, if we love one another, God remains
    in us,
    and his love is brought to perfection in
        us.

This is how we know that we remain in
    him and he in us,
    that he has given us of his Spirit.
Moreover, we have seen and testify
    that the Father sent his Son as savior of
        the world.
Whoever acknowledges that Jesus is the
    Son of God,
    God remains in him and he in God.
We have come to know and to believe in
    the love God has for us.

God is love, and whoever remains in love
    remains in God and God in him.

## About Liturgy

*One last week of Easter:* We've had seven Sundays of Easter so far. How are you doing with keeping the energy and joy of Easter Sunday all season long? With the end of the season in sight, and everyone beginning to focus on graduations, vacations, and summer activities, it can be difficult to keep your focus on the Easter mysteries. But you still have one more week to reinvigorate your Easter spirit! Here are a few simple ways to do that:

*Take an Easter walk:* Take a walk around your neighborhood, in your garden, at the park, or even at the local shopping center. Look for signs of new life all around you. Remember the neophytes—those who were baptized this Easter—who are "new plants" in the household of God.

*Remember your baptism:* Search for photos and other mementos of your own baptism, for example, your baptismal gown or certificate. Place these in a prominent spot in your home this week.

*Make bathing a time of renewal:* Whenever you shower or bathe, recall how the neophytes were bathed in the font. Make it a special time of prayer by giving thanks to Christ, the Water of Life.

*Write a thank-you note:* "Eucharist" means "thanksgiving" in Greek. Each day this last week of Easter, write a thank-you note or email to someone you appreciate but don't often thank in a special way. Say a prayer for him or her as you seal the envelope or hit "send."

*Mother's Day:* Today the United States honors Mom. The month of May is also a special time the church remembers Mary, our Mother. However, we need to remember that Sunday is focused on giving thanks to the Father through Christ. Just as we ensure our liturgical focus is on the Son of Mary, and not on Mary herself, we can make sure that whatever we do to honor mothers on this day is framed as thanksgiving to God for the life we have been given through our mothers. You will also want to be attentive to those for whom this day is not a joyful one. Any intercessions for mothers should also include prayers for those who have been like mothers to us, for those unable to become mothers, for mothers who have lost children, and mothers separated from us by distance, division, or death.

## About Liturgical Music

*Singing songs about Mary:* During the month of May, and especially today, Mother's Day, would it be a good idea to include songs about Mary in the Sunday Mass? Many music ministers do, but before you break out the "Ave Marias," ask yourself these three questions: (1) Does the song give praise to God, or is it mostly praising Mary? (2) Is it a song that everyone can sing, or is it a solo or ensemble piece? (3) Does the placement of the song fit the purpose and action of that part of the Mass?

If the song focuses on God, can be sung by all, and fits the purpose of that part of the Mass, then you are probably good to go. One example of a piece like this is almost any well-known setting of the *Magnificat*, such as "Canticle of the Turning" by Rory Cooney (GIA); "Magnificat" by David Haas (GIA); "Mary's Song" by Millie Rieth (OCP); or "Holy Is His Name" by John Michael Talbot (Birdwing Music). These work because the focus remains squarely on praise of God. By using Mary's own words from Scripture, she stands with us and we with her in thanksgiving and praise to God.

## ✠ SPIRITUALITY

**GOSPEL ACCLAMATION**

R⁊. Alleluia, alleluia.
Come, Holy Spirit, fill the hearts of your faithful
and kindle in them the fire of your love.
R⁊. Alleluia, alleluia.

### Gospel   John 20:19-23; L63B

On the evening of that first day of the
    week,
    when the doors were locked, where the
        disciples were,
    for fear of the Jews,
    Jesus came and stood in their midst
    and said to them, "Peace be with you."
When he had said this, he showed them his
    hands and his side.
The disciples rejoiced when they saw the
    Lord.
Jesus said to them again, "Peace be with
    you.
As the Father has sent me, so I send you."
And when he had said this, he breathed
    on them and said to them,
    "Receive the Holy Spirit.
Whose sins you forgive are forgiven them,
    and whose sins you retain are retained."

or John 15:26-27; 16:12-15

Jesus said to his disciples:
    "When the Advocate comes whom I will
        send you from the Father,
    the Spirit of truth that proceeds from the
        Father,
    he will testify to me.
And you also testify,
    because you have been with me from the
        beginning.

"I have much more to tell you, but you
    cannot bear it now.
But when he comes, the Spirit of truth,
    he will guide you to all truth.
He will not speak on his own,
    but he will speak what he hears,
    and will declare to you the things that are
        coming.
He will glorify me,
    because he will take from what is mine
        and declare it to you.
Everything that the Father has is mine;
    for this reason I told you that he will take
        from what is mine
    and declare it to you."

### Reflecting on the Gospel

When Christians think of Pentecost, we often have the image of the disciples in the Upper Room, with the tongues of fire descending upon each before they preach to Jerusalem. But that is Luke's story in the Acts of the Apostles and he definitely has a flair for storytelling. In his telling of the Spirit's descent, he places the event on the feast of Pentecost, a Jewish feast celebrated fifty days after Passover. Moreover, Luke has made the ascension forty days after Passover, which makes a nice bridge to this feast of Pentecost only ten days later. He tends to objectify the supernatural, for example, he portrays the Spirit at Pentecost as tongues of fire descending on each disciple. And because he is such a good storyteller, it is his stories we remember.

But today we have John's version of the handing on of the Spirit. Interestingly, this event happens not on Pentecost, as Luke would have it, but on Easter Sunday evening! This is the same evening on which the risen Jesus appeared to the assembled disciples without Thomas. So we get our liturgical timetable from Luke, but our theology today comes from the Gospel of John.

The risen Jesus appears in the midst of the disciples, despite the locked doors. This means not that Jesus walks through walls, as so many preachers would have it, but that he appears from his heavenly glory. For if he walked through a wall, where was he immediately prior to that? No, after the resurrection, Jesus is with his Heavenly Father, and comes from there at will. Jesus comes to be with the disciples and give them the gift of peace, and also the gift of the Holy Spirit by breathing upon them. This earthy, rather sacramental way of gifting the disciples with the Spirit is much different than Luke would have it. For him, the Spirit is a gift of God. In John's gospel, the Spirit is a gift of the Father, but given directly by Jesus.

Not only do the disciples receive the Spirit but also the ability to forgive sins. By his death and resurrection Jesus has conquered the cosmic power of sin, with a capital S. Now it is the disciples' role, and our own, to continue this mission by forgiving individual sins, almost as a "mop-up" operation after the major victory has been won. The same Spirit has been given to us, and it is our mission to forgive individual sins each time someone sins against us. Forgiveness is not limited to sacramental confession. As Christians, we are to forgive. It is a hallmark of our identity, given to us by Jesus himself.

### Living the Paschal Mystery

It can be a true challenge to forgive on a daily basis. There are so many opportunities for slights, annoyances, oversights, and sometimes even deliberate harm. Something in our human nature wants to learn and remember when these things happen to us. And while we will probably never forget such experiences, we are to forgive. In so doing we continue the victory Jesus won on Easter Sunday. By our forgiving others, we advance the glorious reign of peace. This is our task, and we have the Holy Spirit to help us. Forgiving means letting go, so that the matter does not consume us from within. Forgiving does not mean the matter was OK. When we forgive we do so as much for our benefit as for the one we are forgiving. By forgiving we are simultaneously conforming ourselves more perfectly to Christ, and dying to ourselves and our earthly cares and desires.

## Focusing the Gospel

*John 20:19-23*

The reading for today's gospel is the Easter night appearance of the risen Jesus before his ten disciples (remember Thomas is not present). In the Fourth Gospel, Easter night is the Pentecost event. Jesus appears even though they are hiding behind "locked doors" and greets them with "Peace"—the peace he spoke of in his final words to them at the Last Supper. As God "breathed" life into Adam in the Genesis story of creation, Jesus "breathes" the Holy Spirit upon the disciples, giving life to the new creation of the church of the resurrection. In the resurrection, the Spirit replaces their sense of self-centered fear and confusion with the "peace" of understanding, enthusiasm, and joy and shatters all barriers among them to make of them a community of hope and forgiveness.

## Focusing the First Reading

*Acts 2:1-11*

Pentecost ("Fiftieth" in Greek) was the Jewish festival of the harvest (also called the feast of Weeks), celebrated fifty days after Passover, when the firstfruits of the corn harvest were offered to the Lord. One of the three great pilgrimage feasts (hence the presence in Jerusalem of so many "devout Jews from every nation"), Pentecost also commemorated Moses' receiving the law on Mount Sinai. For the church, the new Israel, Pentecost becomes the celebration of the Spirit of God's compassion, peace, and forgiveness: the Spirit of God that gave meaning and authority to the Law and the Prophets now "breathes" into the young church's universal mission of proclaiming the Gospel (the planting of a new harvest?).

Luke employs many words and images that evoke the revelation at Mount Sinai: thunder, wind, "shaking" of the house (see Exod 19:16-19). God frequently revealed his presence in fire (the pillar of fire in the Sinai) and in wind (the wind that sweeps over the earth to make the waters subside at creation). The Hebrew word for spirit, *ruah*, and the Greek word for spirit, *pneuma*, also refer to the movement of air, not only as wind but also of life-giving breath (as God's "breath" gives life to the "clay" as man in Gen 2 and revives the dry bones in Ezek 37). Through his life-giving "breath," the Lord begins the era of the new Israel on Pentecost. The list of nations represented among the pilgrims is a clear sign that the Spirit of God transcends old understandings of salvation and embraces all the human family.

## Focusing the Responsorial Psalm

*Ps 104:1, 24, 29-30, 31, 34 (30)*

Invoking many images of the creation story in Genesis, Psalm 104 is a hymn of praise to God the Creator, whose "Spirit" sets all of creation in motion, whose "breath" animates all life.

## Focusing the Second Reading

*1 Cor 12:3b-7, 12-13*

Appealing for unity among the badly splintered Corinthian community, Paul reminds the church there that the Holy Spirit's presence in their midst should bring together the different gifts (*charismata*) that each of them possesses. No one has merited such gifts; they are all derived from the same source: the goodness and compassion of God. God gives these charisms to individuals for the good of the entire "body," the people of God.

---

**PROMPTS FOR HOMILISTS, CATECHISTS, AND RCIA TEAMS**

The Spirit of God reveals itself in today's readings in the forms of fire and wind (Acts 2) and breath (Ps 104, gospel). What other images can help us understand the Spirit of God working within and around us?

How does the presence of God's Spirit make your parish "different" from other groups and organizations?

When have you sensed the Spirit prompting you to a specific act or moved you to act beyond your fears or doubts or out of your "comfort zone"?

What is the Spirit calling your community to take on or embrace this Pentecost?

What "truth" have you been struggling with? What do you "hear" the Spirit saying to you?

## Model Rite for the Blessing and Sprinkling of Water

*Presider:* Dear friends, we will use this water to celebrate and renew our baptisms. Let us ask God to send the Spirit of Pentecost upon this water so that, through it, we may be recreated in the love of God. *[pause]*

  *[continue with* The Roman Missal, *Appendix II]*

## Homily Points

• God's *ruah*, life-giving Spirit, is the source of Easter peace and Pentecost direction. It is the Spirit of God that brings two people together as spouses, forges strong and lasting friendships, and transforms a group of disparate persons into a community of faith. We cooperate with the *ruah* of God to recreate our world in the love of the God who became one of us, died for us, and rose for us. The Spirit empowers us to put aside our fears to be God's agents of peace and reconciliation in our own time and place. God's *ruah* transforms us and recreates us in that unique and mysterious love that binds God the Father and God the Son and binds us to God and to one another.

• The real miracle of Pentecost (Acts 2) is one of listening: God's Spirit overcomes the barriers of language and perception, opening not only the crowds' minds but their hearts to hear the word of God spoken by Peter and the Twelve. The Spirit enables us to discern the voice of God in the context of God's compassion and peace, to hear what God actually speaks and not what we want or hope to hear. As on Pentecost, God's Spirit continues to speak in the midst of the busyness, pain and despair of our lives, inviting us to embrace the life and love of God in our homes and hearts.

• In the Pentecost moment, the church comes into being. As that first gathering of Jesus' friends experienced his Spirit in wind and fire, that same Spirit "speaks" to us. Through the Spirit, God has formed us into a community, an instrument for bringing his life and love into our world. Today we celebrate the presence of God's life-giving breath (*ruah*) infusing the church with the music of his divinity. In Jesus' breathing upon the disciples on Easter night the new life of the Spirit, the community of the resurrection—the church—takes flight. That same Spirit continues to "blow" through today's church to give life to our mission to preach the Gospel to every nation, to proclaim forgiveness in God's name, to immerse all of humanity into the love of God manifested in Jesus' resurrection.

## Model Universal Prayer (Prayer of the Faithful)

*Presider:* Gathered in this place, we have come to celebrate God's Spirit dwelling among us. Let us give voice to that Spirit in the prayers we now offer.

*Response:* Lord, hear our prayer.

That the Spirit of God may inspire us to joyfully use our gifts and talents for the common good of the one Body of Christ . . .

That the Advocate, the Spirit of truth, may guide our pope, our president, and all leaders of our church and nation in the truth of God's justice and peace . . .

That God's Spirit of compassion and healing will bring light and hope to the sick, the suffering, and the dying . . .

That the Spirit of God will make each one of us ministers of peace and forgiveness in our homes, schools, and workplaces . . .

*Presider:* Father of life, hear our prayers. Recreate us in your Holy Spirit so that we may be a source of forgiveness and a community of hope for our hurting world. We make these prayers in the name of Jesus, the risen Christ. **Amen.**

### COLLECT

Let us pray.

*Pause for silent prayer*

O God, who by the mystery of today's
  great feast
sanctify your whole Church in every
  people and nation,
pour out, we pray, the gifts of the Holy Spirit
across the face of the earth
and, with the divine grace that was at work
when the Gospel was first proclaimed,
fill now once more the hearts of believers.
Through our Lord Jesus Christ, your Son,
who lives and reigns with you in the unity
  of the Holy Spirit,
one God, for ever and ever. **Amen.**

### FIRST READING

Acts 2:1-11

When the time for Pentecost was fulfilled,
  they were all in one place together.
And suddenly there came from the sky
  a noise like a strong driving wind,
  and it filled the entire house in which
    they were.
Then there appeared to them tongues as
  of fire,
  which parted and came to rest on each
    one of them.
And they were all filled with the Holy Spirit
  and began to speak in different tongues,
  as the Spirit enabled them to proclaim.

Now there were devout Jews from every
  nation under heaven staying in
  Jerusalem.
At this sound, they gathered in a large
  crowd,
  but they were confused
  because each one heard them speaking
    in his own language.
They were astounded, and in amazement
  they asked,
  "Are not all these people who are
    speaking Galileans?
Then how does each of us hear them in
  his native language?
We are Parthians, Medes, and Elamites,
  inhabitants of Mesopotamia, Judea and
    Cappadocia,
  Pontus and Asia, Phrygia and
    Pamphylia,
  Egypt and the districts of Libya near
    Cyrene,
  as well as travelers from Rome,
  both Jews and converts to Judaism,
    Cretans and Arabs,
  yet we hear them speaking in our own
    tongues
  of the mighty acts of God."

## RESPONSORIAL PSALM

Ps 104:1, 24, 29-30, 31, 34

℟. (cf. 30) Lord, send out your Spirit, and
    renew the face of the earth.
    *or:*
℟. Alleluia.

Bless the Lord, O my soul!
    O Lord, my God, you are great indeed!
How manifold are your works, O Lord!
    The earth is full of your creatures.

℟. Lord, send out your Spirit, and renew
    the face of the earth.
    *or:*
℟. Alleluia.

If you take away their breath, they perish
    and return to their dust.
When you send forth your spirit, they are
    created,
    and you renew the face of the earth.

℟. Lord, send out your Spirit, and renew
    the face of the earth.
    *or:*
℟. Alleluia.

May the glory of the Lord endure forever;
    may the Lord be glad in his works!
Pleasing to him be my theme;
    I will be glad in the Lord.

℟. Lord, send out your Spirit, and renew
    the face of the earth.
    *or:*
℟. Alleluia.

## SECOND READING

1 Cor 12:3b-7, 12-13

*or*

Gal 5:16-25

## SEQUENCE

*See Appendix A, p. 295.*

## About Liturgy

***Speaking in our own tongues:*** The solemnity of Pentecost is a wonderful expression of the diversity of gifts the Spirit gives the church. One of these gifts is diversity itself, expressed in the many languages of the world in which God's mighty acts are proclaimed. So is Pentecost the day to include as many different languages as we can in the liturgy? Not necessarily so. Diversity, like any gift, needs to be appreciated by nurturing the relationships it brings. A parish cannot simply celebrate a "multicultural" Mass one day without having carefully built up the relationships needed to draw forth the variety of gifts from the cultures that make up the parish. If your worshiping assemblies haven't already "crossed borders" by incorporating various languages into the liturgy spoken by native speakers from the parish, then start to build those relationships by beginning outside of liturgy. Meals and parties are perfect opportunities for encouraging these cross-cultural relationships. Once you've established caring and trusting relationships among the various cultures of your community, then together discern how best to express the gifts that each culture brings to the liturgy. Most of all, remember that diversity is not expressed by spoken language alone. Visual arts, music (sung and instrumental), and especially gracious hospitality can do more to express our unity in diversity than a multitude of languages.

***A word about birthdays:*** It has become a bit common for some to view Pentecost as the church's "birthday." In some ways, Luke's account of Pentecost feels a little like a birth in which the Spirit inaugurates the church's public witness to the world. Yet to use the cultural symbols of our chronological anniversaries of birth, such as birthday cakes and "Happy Birthday" songs, to express the kairotic mystery of Christ's mission misses the point. If there is any birthday metaphor to this day, it is found in Christ *breathing* the Spirit's life into the disciples in that Upper Room, in the same way the Creator breathed the Spirit into the nostrils of the first human, in the same way the Spirit breathed over the waters in the beginning, in the same way Jesus on the cross breathed his last and handed over his spirit.

We might understand this birth of the church better in light of what we understand about the sacraments of initiation. Because the Holy Spirit is present from the beginning, the Spirit is given first to a person at baptism, and that gift is sealed by the anointing of confirmation, and strengthened for mission by the Eucharist. As we read in the General Introduction of Christian Initiation: "Thus the three sacraments of Christian initiation closely combine to bring us, the faithful of Christ, to his full stature and to enable us to carry out the mission of the entire people of God in the Church and in the world" (2).

## About Liturgical Music

***Pentecost sequence:*** Today and Easter Sunday are the two times during the year when we are required to include a sequence in the Sunday Mass. This hymn is an elaborate prelude to the Alleluia before the gospel reading. You can find the text for today's sequence, *Veni Sancte Spiritus*, in the Lectionary, but you can use other approved translations of this text. Ideally, the assembly also sings the sequence, either in its entirety or antiphonally, alternating between cantor and assembly, schola and assembly, left side and right side, or women and men. One setting that works very well because the tune is so familiar and fitting for the season is Jerome Siwek's adaptation to the tune O FILII ET FILIAE (WLP). To reflect the excitement of that first Pentecost, begin singing each succeeding stanza on the last note of the previous stanza; and on the last note of the last stanza, have your cantor intone the Alleluia to the same tune as the entire assembly stands for the gospel acclamation.

ORDINARY
TIME II

## ✚ SPIRITUALITY

**GOSPEL ACCLAMATION**
Rev 1:8

℟. Alleluia, alleluia.
Glory to the Father, the Son, and the Holy Spirit;
to God who is, who was, and who is to come.
℟. Alleluia, alleluia.

### Gospel

Matt 28:16-20; L165B

The eleven disciples went to Galilee,
  to the mountain to which Jesus
    had ordered them.
When they all saw him, they
    worshiped, but they doubted.
Then Jesus approached and said to
    them,
  "All power in heaven and on earth
    has been given to me.
Go, therefore, and make disciples of all
  nations,
  baptizing them in the name of the
    Father,
  and of the Son, and of the Holy
    Spirit,
  teaching them to observe all that I
    have commanded you.
And behold, I am with you always, until
    the end of the age."

### Reflecting on the Gospel

We have all heard of the shamrock, which, according to legend, was used by St. Patrick to represent the Holy Trinity to the native Irish in the early fifth century. Three leaves on one sprig, representing three persons in one God. That story has been repeated countless times, and the image of the shamrock has become forever linked with the Trinity, and with the Irish. But, of course, God is more than a sprig, and the relationship between the persons of the Trinity is more complex and subtle than three leaves. Earlier church fathers used the image of the sun to speak of the Trinity, with the sun itself representing the Father, the light representing the Son, and the heat representing the Spirit. This image does more than the shamrock to convey the subtlety at work in such a sophisticated concept of "three persons, one God." But still, the metaphor of the sun with its light and heat is still just that, a metaphor. Though *trinitas* is a Latin word and therefore not found in the New Testament, which was written in Greek, there are many "triadic" texts that speak of Father/God, Son, Spirit. Passages like the one for today would be considered "triadic," and they would give rise to full-blown trinitarian theology in later centuries.

The gospel scene is after Easter, but in Galilee. According to Matthew, this is the first and only appearance of the risen Jesus to his disciples (only eleven now in a somber reminder of Judas's fate). Still, the disciples doubt. They receive the command that has been referred to as "the Great Commandment": "Go, therefore, and make disciples of all nations, / baptizing them in the name of the Father, / and of the Son, and of the Holy Spirit." The Gospel of Matthew, which restricted the use of the term disciple to the Twelve during Jesus' ministry, now shows that following the resurrection, there will be disciples in all nations. Matthew's baptismal formula for making a disciple is the same as what Christians use today. Based on this "Great Commandment," Christianity has become a worldwide religion. From a mountaintop in Galilee, those initial disciples made other disciples by baptism, who made still more disciples by baptism, and so on, until our very day. Discipleship founded on baptism into the life of the Trinity is much more powerful than a shamrock, or even the sun.

### Living the Paschal Mystery

When questioned about the Trinity, many catechists or others resort to, "It's a mystery. We can't understand it." While that may be true, it doesn't mean we don't think about it. A mystery of faith is in some ways similar to the mystery of the universe. We plumb its depths. We examine it from various angles. We ask questions. We discuss. We debate. And we find that we have not exhausted the topic; rather, it has exhausted us. And we return to it again later, learning more with each engagement. Dismissing any consideration of the Trinity solely because it is a mystery does us a disservice as rational yet faith-filled Christians. Many theologians have sought to express various aspects of this mystery through the centuries, and many more will continue to do so into the future.

Part of our living the mystery is to know that we will never fully comprehend or understand all of what it means for God to be a Trinity. In the same manner, we will never fully comprehend or understand the entirety of the universe. But we can approach each mystery with humility and a sense of wonder and respect. Jesus is the incarnate God. He called God Father, and promised to send the Spirit who would remind his disciples about Jesus. Each of us has been baptized into the life of the Trinity and will continue to let that meaning unfold each day of our ongoing lives.

## Focusing the Gospel
*Matt 28:16-20*
Ordinary Time resumes with the solemnity of the Holy Trinity. The feast originated in France in the eighth century and was adopted by the universal church in 1334. The solemnity focuses on the essence of our faith: the revelation of God as Father, the perfection of his creation in Jesus the Son, the fullness of the love of God poured out on us in the Holy Spirit.

By tradition, today's gospel takes place at the mount of the ascension, even though Matthew does not tell the story of the ascension. The risen Jesus commissions his fledgling church to teach and baptize in the name of the Holy One who reveals himself as Father, Son, and Spirit. In the Trinity we find our identity as the people of God.

## Focusing the First Reading
*Deut 4:32-34, 39-40*
Moses reminds Israel during their exodus journey that God is first encountered in God's act of creation, and then in God's redemption of the Israelites from Egyptian captivity and leading them to nationhood in the exodus. In today's first reading, from the book of Deuteronomy (the "law book" of the Torah), Moses exhorts the Israelites to remain faithful to the commandments on which their covenant with God is established.

## Focusing the Responsorial Psalm
*Ps 33:4-5, 6, 9, 18-19, 20, 22 (12b)*
Psalm 33 praises God who put all of creation into motion by his Word. The verses selected for today's responsorial psalm mirror Moses' exhortation (first reading) that God creates and maintains all life, including and especially humankind, to reflect his vision of justice and kindness.

## Focusing the Second Reading
*Rom 8:14-17*
The Spirit of God is that unique love that exists between God the Father and God the Son. In that same Spirit, God "adopts" us as his own, enabling us to cry out to God as "Father" and to one another as brothers and sisters, children of the same God.

---

**PROMPTS FOR HOMILISTS, CATECHISTS, AND RCIA TEAMS**

How have you experienced the presence of God in the ordinary and every day? How would you explain this presence to nonbelievers?

What are the implications for society if God is not just Creator but "Father"?

How can we "teach" others about God without the use of theological language or jargon?

## Model Penitential Act

*Presider:* To God, our Father and Redeemer, let us ask his forgiveness for our sins and failings. *[pause]*

God the Father, Creator of all that is good: Lord, have mercy.
God the Son, the Light and Word of God made human for us: Christ, have mercy.
God the Spirit, the love of God in our midst: Lord, have mercy.

## Homily Points

• Today's solemnity of the Trinity celebrates the many ways God makes his presence known in our midst, in the many manifestations of his love in our lives and our world. God is the very love that creates, nurtures, and preserves: love that is Father/Maker, Son/Beloved, Spirit/Sustainer. We are all held and cared for in that love, a love too perfect and complete for us to even begin to understand. God's love becomes fully human for us in the person of Jesus, who taught us that God loves us like a father loves his beloved sons and daughters and, in his resurrection, shows that God's love for us extends beyond this world but well into the next. In the gift of his Spirit, we experience the fullness of God's love in one another.

• God calls us, not as the all-powerful Creator demanding homage from the lowly objects he created, but as a compassionate parent welcoming and loving one's own children; God invites us to a relationship with him not based on fear and judgment but centered in love, mercy, and trust. The core of all of Jesus' teachings is the revelation of God as Father to humanity: our God seeks a relationship with humankind as a loving parent who welcomes his own children back home.

• We have all been called, as Christ's disciples in this time and place, to teach what we have seen and heard, to pass on to others "all that I have commanded you" through our imitation of Christ the Teacher's compassion, forgiveness, and servanthood. The risen Christ calls us to a new awareness of God's loving presence in every moment and experience of our lives; to mirror, as Jesus' disciples, the Gospel of reconciliation and justice; to embrace and be embraced by God's Spirit of love and mercy enabling us to live our lives in humble, joyful gratitude.

## Model Universal Prayer (Prayer of the Faithful)

*Presider:* The risen Christ has promised that he is always with us. In confidence, then, let us pray.

*Response:* Lord, hear our prayer.

That all who serve our church as pastors, ministers, teachers, and counselors may, through their selfless work, make disciples of all nations . . .

That the nations and peoples of the world may glorify the Creator through the responsible care and just sharing of the gifts of God's creation . . .

That the God of compassion may restore to health and hope the sick, the suffering, the recovering, the imprisoned, and the dying . . .

That all families may prosper in their love for one another and their trust in the constant love of God . . .

*Presider:* Hear the prayers we offer to you, O God of compassion and mercy, O God who redeems us and restores us to life, O God who lives in us and through us. We offer these prayers, O Father, in your Spirit of love, in the name of your Son, Christ Jesus. **Amen.**

## COLLECT

Let us pray.

*Pause for silent prayer*

God our Father, who by sending into the world
the Word of truth and the Spirit of sanctification
made known to the human race your wondrous mystery,
grant us, we pray, that in professing the true faith,
we may acknowledge the Trinity of eternal glory
and adore your Unity, powerful in majesty.
Through our Lord Jesus Christ, your Son,
who lives and reigns with you in the unity of the Holy Spirit,
one God, for ever and ever. **Amen.**

## FIRST READING

Deut 4:32-34, 39-40

Moses said to the people:
"Ask now of the days of old, before your time,
ever since God created man upon the earth;
ask from one end of the sky to the other:
Did anything so great ever happen before?
Was it ever heard of?
Did a people ever hear the voice of God
speaking from the midst of fire, as you did, and live?
Or did any god venture to go and take a nation for himself
from the midst of another nation,
by testings, by signs and wonders, by war,
with strong hand and outstretched arm, and by great terrors,
all of which the LORD, your God,
did for you in Egypt before your very eyes?
This is why you must now know,
and fix in your heart, that the LORD is God
in the heavens above and on earth below,
and that there is no other.
You must keep his statutes and commandments that I enjoin on you today,
that you and your children after you may prosper,
and that you may have long life on the land
which the LORD, your God, is giving you forever."

## RESPONSORIAL PSALM
Ps 33:4-5, 6, 9, 18-19, 20, 22

℟. (12b) Blessed the people the Lord has
    chosen to be his own.

Upright is the word of the LORD,
  and all his works are trustworthy.
He loves justice and right;
  of the kindness of the LORD the earth
    is full.

℟. Blessed the people the Lord has chosen
    to be his own.

By the word of the LORD the heavens were
  made;
  by the breath of his mouth all their
    host.
For he spoke, and it was made;
  he commanded, and it stood forth.

℟. Blessed the people the Lord has chosen
    to be his own.

See, the eyes of the LORD are upon those
  who fear him,
  upon those who hope for his kindness,
to deliver them from death
  and preserve them in spite of famine.

℟. Blessed the people the Lord has chosen
    to be his own.

Our soul waits for the LORD,
  who is our help and our shield.
May your kindness, O LORD, be upon us
  who have put our hope in you.

℟. Blessed the people the Lord has chosen
    to be his own.

## SECOND READING
Rom 8:14-17

Brothers and sisters:
Those who are led by the Spirit of God are
    sons of God.
For you did not receive a spirit of slavery
    to fall back into fear,
  but you received a Spirit of adoption,
  through whom we cry, "Abba, Father!"
The Spirit himself bears witness with our
    spirit
  that we are children of God,
  and if children, then heirs,
  heirs of God and joint heirs with Christ,
  if only we suffer with him
  so that we may also be glorified with
    him.

### About Liturgy
*The sign of the cross:* Homilists often dread preparing the homily for this Sunday's solemnity because it is so easy to get caught up in trying to explain either a mathematical conundrum or a complex theological mystery. The problem here is not so much the content of the homily but the intent. One cannot "explain" the mystery of the Trinity, not because it is unknowable or difficult. Rather, this mystery is one that we know in our bones because it has been marked upon us from the beginning of our life of faith. The mystery of it is that no matter how much we try to describe what the Trinity is, we could never fully communicate the depth of its meaning because the Trinity is ultimately about relationship. Like any relationship with a loved one, we can only understand it fully by entering into it with our hearts.

That was the crux of one of the best homilies I've heard on the Trinity. It was memorable because the homilist focused on only one thing: the sign of the cross. What else is this simple gesture but the Trinity expressed in a way that even children could understand?

When we make the sign of the cross on our bodies, we recall that everything we do begins and ends with God. We mark ourselves with a sign that identifies who we are and whose we are. It is a sign that physically encompasses our entire being, reminding us that we are drawn into the life and love of the Trinity, a life-giving and self-sacrificing relationship between Father and Son in the love of the Spirit. The sign of the cross consecrates and gives purpose to anyone and anything we bless with that sign, for the work of the Trinity is to bring blessing to all creation; and all creation is made for being in relationship with the Creator. We first learn the significance of this sign (and thus the meaning of the Trinity) usually from our parents or family and friends who have shared with us their faith. Here, then, we learn that being in a loving relationship with God is not an abstract idea but is a relationship we first encounter through the love of another person for us. By loving others, we embody and deepen our understanding of the meaning of the Trinity.

### About Initiation
*Sacramentals:* Making the sign of the cross is one of the many sacramentals we have in our Catholic tradition. These are rituals that recall or prepare us for the grace of a sacrament. Catechumens—those who are unbaptized who have celebrated the Rite of Acceptance into the Order of Catechumens—are marked with the sign of the cross at the Rite of Acceptance. Therefore, even though they are not yet baptized, they are encouraged to sign themselves with the cross as preparation for their initiation into the death and resurrection of Christ. Related to this, there is no prohibition for catechumens to use holy water, even though they are not yet baptized, since the use of holy water in signing themselves is a way of strengthening their desire for the sacrament.

### About Liturgical Music
*Attend to the text:* Many of the songs that are appropriate for this day are hymns of praise of the Trinity. Since the verses or stanzas of these songs usually focus on one person of the Trinity, you will want to be sure to sing all the necessary verses or stanzas. Otherwise, you might end up leaving out an important member of the Trinity! Also include any final verse that serves as a concluding doxology. Songs structured like this are best used for the gathering or concluding song when you are not constrained by a liturgical action that may require you to end the song early.

## ✝ SPIRITUALITY

### GOSPEL ACCLAMATION
John 6:51

℟. Alleluia, alleluia.
I am the living bread that came down from
    heaven,
says the Lord; / whoever eats this bread will live
    forever.
℟. Alleluia, alleluia.

### Gospel   Mark 14:12-16, 22-26; L168B

On the first day of the Feast of Unleavened
    Bread,
  when they sacrificed the Passover lamb,
  Jesus' disciples said to him,
  "Where do you want us to go
  and prepare for you to eat the Passover?"
He sent two of his disciples and said to
    them,
  "Go into the city and a man will meet you,
  carrying a jar of water.
Follow him.
Wherever he enters, say to the master of
    the house,
  'The Teacher says, "Where is my guest
    room
  where I may eat the Passover with my
    disciples?"'
Then he will show you a large upper room
    furnished and ready.
Make the preparations for us there."
The disciples then went off, entered the
    city,
  and found it just as he had told them;
  and they prepared the Passover.

While they were eating,
  he took bread, said the blessing,
  broke it, gave it to them, and said,
  "Take it; this is my body."
Then he took a cup, gave thanks, and gave
    it to them,
  and they all drank from it.
He said to them,
  "This is my blood of the covenant,
  which will be shed for many.
Amen, I say to you,
  I shall not drink again the fruit of the
    vine
  until the day when I drink it new in the
    kingdom of God."
Then, after singing a hymn,
  they went out to the Mount of Olives.

### Reflecting on the Gospel

A middle schooler looked over the menu of the fine restaurant. The waiter had given her a cloth napkin. That's how she knew it was a "fine" restaurant. As she read the headings of the menu there were some strange-sounding titles: antipasti, vegetali, pesci, carni. But under the carni heading there were some familiar dishes. But to be sure, she finally asked her mother, "What's carni?" "It's plural for 'meats,' but literally, 'carne' means 'flesh,'" was the reply. That would do. She loved meat, even though she didn't like to think of it as flesh.

The graphic image of "body and blood" comes from the ancient world where the body is flesh and "blood is life" (Deut 12:23). The bread and wine of the eucharistic banquet become the Body and Blood of Christ, in a *transubstantive* way.

The gospel reading for today is Mark's version of the Last Supper, which for him was in the context of the Passover meal. Even the singing of the hymn, which Mark is certain to include, is an integral part of the Passover to this very day. But according to the Synoptic Gospels (Matthew, Mark, and Luke) Jesus gave new meaning to the Passover meal. The bread that he takes, blesses, breaks, and shares is his Body. The cup of thanksgiving that is shared is his covenantal Blood. Anyone who has been to a Jewish Seder meal likely has a profound appreciation for these symbols of bread and wine, and how they were appropriated in the Christian tradition. The Passover meal, which commemorated the people's delivery from Egypt, would now commemorate Jesus' death and ultimate delivery from death to resurrection. Our participation in consuming the bread and wine is a participation in the life, death, and subsequent resurrection of Jesus.

We who gather around the table of the Eucharist (which is a Greek word meaning "thanksgiving") are fed by Christ and become one in him. The eucharistic feast actually causes the unity, which is why it is scandalous to have disunity at such a meal, as Paul reminded the Corinthians. The celebration of the Body and Blood of Christ is much more than the celebration of something to be revered. By necessity, the solemnity of the Body and Blood of Christ causes the unity shared by Christians by their participation in the eucharistic feast. That unity was Jesus' own desire expressed by his prayer to the Father. May we be instruments of that unity by our own share in that same Eucharist.

### Living the Paschal Mystery

Catholicism is a sacramental faith. We are an earthy people, needing to touch, taste, see, smell, and feel. Is it any wonder that the way we connect with the incarnation of God is to consume the Body and Blood of that incarnation? Rather than merely listen to the word of God, we consume that Word of God made flesh. The sacramental reality reaches something deep within. Our faith is not simply a head trip, or the summary of what can be learned in books. Our faith is something we experience with our senses. We taste bread; we drink wine. By consuming this sacramental meal we participate in the life of Christ and his paschal mystery.

The very word "incarnation" has "carne" (flesh) in its root. We can say that the "incarnation" of the word of God is the "enfleshment" of the Word of God. The graphic nature of the image might repulse us. But we are not disembodied spirits upon this earth. We are earthy, organic omnivores. Our sustenance comes from consumption, and our spiritual sustenance comes from consumption as well. The bread and wine, our sacramental meal, is our living the paschal mystery.

## Focusing the Gospel

*Mark 14:12-16, 22-26*
Today's celebration of the Body and Blood of the Lord originated in the Diocese of Liege in 1246, under the title of the feast of Corpus Christi. In the reforms of Vatican II, Corpus Christi was joined with the feast of the Precious Blood (July 1) to become the solemnity of the Body and Blood of the Lord. Today's solemnity focuses on Jesus' gift of the Eucharist, the "source and summit" of our life together as the church. Today's gospel is Mark's account of the Last Supper. Jesus gives new meaning to the ancient Passover ritual.

## Focusing the First Reading

*Exod 24:3-8*
The ancient Israelites believed that life itself was contained in blood—blood, therefore, belonged to God alone (which is why even today a devout Jew will never eat any meat that is not completely drained of blood). As such, blood was revered as life and as a means of purification. In today's reading from Exodus, Moses returns to the Israelite camp from Sinai where the Lord gave Moses the law. To affirm their unanimous acceptance of the law, the people sacrifice animals to God. During the ritual, Moses splashes half of the sacrificed animals' blood on the altar, a symbol of God, and then sprinkles the other half on the people, as a sign of their belonging to God through this covenant.

## Focusing the Responsorial Psalm

*Ps 116:12-13, 15-16, 17-18 (13)*
Psalm 116 is also the responsorial psalm for Holy Thursday. The latter part of Psalm 116 is the prayer of someone desperately ill and facing death. Yet despite his distress, the psalmist expresses his trust in God and gratefully acknowledges the many blessings he has experienced. With confidence in God's continued mercy, the psalmist continues to offer public acts of praise and thanksgiving to the Lord, "tak[ing] up" the "cup of salvation" in humility and hope.

## Focusing the Second Reading

*Heb 9:11-15*
This understanding of the sacredness of blood is key to the theology of the letter to the Hebrews. The crucified Jesus is both priest and victim, whose own blood cleanses us of our sins (as the blood of sacrificed animals cleansed the Israelites in their worship [first reading]) and seals a new covenant between God and those he calls in Christ.

### PROMPTS FOR HOMILISTS, CATECHISTS, AND RCIA TEAMS

How can we be "Eucharist" to another? How can we bring the Eucharist from our church into the world?

How do our own family rituals at dinnertime and around the family table reflect the Eucharist?

What ministries and projects of our parish are especially inspired by or connected to our celebration of the Eucharist?

The word Eucharist means "thanksgiving." How can our sharing of the Body and Blood of the Lord be an act of thanksgiving, even when we gather under the most painful of circumstances?

## Model Penitential Act

*Presider:* To prepare ourselves to offer this sacrament of the Body and Blood of the Lord, let us begin by calling to mind our sins, asking the constant mercy of God, who invites us to this table. *[pause]*

You are the Bread of Life and cup of blessing: Lord, have mercy.

You are both gift and giver, priest and offering: Christ, have mercy.

You make of us one, holy, thankful people in this Eucharist: Lord, have mercy.

## Homily Points

• The gift of the Eucharist comes with an important "string" attached: it must be shared. In sharing the Body of Christ, we become the Body of Christ. We become what we receive; what we consume now consumes us. If we partake of the one bread and one cup, then we must be willing to become Eucharist for others—to make Christ's love real for all. Our coming to the eucharistic table is more than just reliving the memory of Christ's great sacrifice for our redemption: in sharing his "body" in the bread of the Eucharist we reenter the inexplicable love of God who gives us eternal life in his Son, the risen Christ; in drinking his "blood" in the wine of the Eucharist we take his life into the very core of our beings.

• When we gather here at this table, we take bread and wine to remember Jesus: the wise teacher, the worker of wonders, the very love of God. We come to the Eucharist to celebrate his presence among us and recommit ourselves to following his example of compassion and justice; in doing so, we rediscover our identity as his disciples and reaffirm our baptismal commitment to become his body and blood for others. At Christ's table, we are always welcome. In celebrating Jesus' great gift of the Eucharist, we make our parish family's table a place of reconciliation and compassion—and we make all our family tables places of love and safety where Christ is present in our service and care for one another.

• This meal is the living sign of our covenant with God. In this sacrament, bread and wine are transformed by the Spirit of God into the Body and Blood of Christ; in turn, the sacrament we receive transforms us into sacraments and signs of God's love for our families and communities. As the Eucharist makes us a church of reconciliation, so it makes us reconcilers; as the Eucharist animates the church with Christ's life, so it animates our lives in God's love and compassion. This bread and cup also makes of us a community with those all over the world: from gatherings around the altars of magnificent cathedrals, to those huddled around scraps of bread on dirt floors. Regardless of the venue and circumstances, the risen One welcomes us all and all we are—we come with all our joys and sorrows to be nourished at the great banquet of his Body and Blood.

## Model Universal Prayer (Prayer of the Faithful)

*Presider:* Let us ask God's blessings upon his holy people.

*Response:* Lord, hear our prayer.

That the sacrament of Christ's Body and Blood may be the heart and spirit of our life together as the people of God, the church . . .

That the world's nations and governments may enter into a covenant centered in God's justice and peace, enabling them to work together for the good of all peoples . . .

That the suffering may know, in our compassion, the healing presence of Jesus . . .

That our parish may welcome the poor, the lost, the struggling, and the forgotten . . .

*Presider:* Hear our prayers, O God. May the bread and wine of the Eucharist transform us into the bread of generosity and the wine of joy for our hurting world. We ask these things in the name of Jesus, the Bread of Life. **Amen.**

## COLLECT

Let us pray.

*Pause for silent prayer*

O God, who in this wonderful Sacrament
have left us a memorial of your Passion,
grant us, we pray,
so to revere the sacred mysteries of your
    Body and Blood
that we may always experience in
    ourselves
the fruits of your redemption.
Who live and reign with God the Father
in the unity of the Holy Spirit,
one God, for ever and ever. **Amen.**

## FIRST READING

Exod 24:3-8

When Moses came to the people
    and related all the words and
        ordinances of the LORD,
    they all answered with one voice,
    "We will do everything that the LORD
        has told us."
Moses then wrote down all the words of
    the LORD and,
    rising early the next day,
    he erected at the foot of the mountain
        an altar
    and twelve pillars for the twelve tribes
        of Israel.
Then, having sent certain young men of
    the Israelites
    to offer holocausts and sacrifice young
        bulls
    as peace offerings to the LORD,
Moses took half of the blood and put it
    in large bowls;
    the other half he splashed on the altar.
Taking the book of the covenant, he read
    it aloud to the people,
    who answered, "All that the LORD has
        said, we will heed and do."
Then he took the blood and sprinkled it on
    the people, saying,
    "This is the blood of the covenant
    that the LORD has made with you
    in accordance with all these words of
        his."

## RESPONSORIAL PSALM

Ps 116:12-13, 15-16, 17-18

℟. (13) I will take the cup of salvation, and
    call on the name of the Lord.
*or:*
℟. Alleluia.

How shall I make a return to the Lᴏʀᴅ
    for all the good he has done for me?
The cup of salvation I will take up,
    and I will call upon the name of the
        Lᴏʀᴅ.

℟. I will take the cup of salvation, and call
    on the name of the Lord.
*or:*
℟. Alleluia.

Precious in the eyes of the Lᴏʀᴅ
    is the death of his faithful ones.
I am your servant, the son of your
        handmaid;
    you have loosed my bonds.

℟. I will take the cup of salvation, and call
    on the name of the Lord.
*or:*
℟. Alleluia.

To you will I offer sacrifice of
        thanksgiving,
    and I will call upon the name of the
        Lᴏʀᴅ.
My vows to the Lᴏʀᴅ I will pay
    in the presence of all his people.

℟. I will take the cup of salvation, and call
    on the name of the Lord.
*or:*
℟. Alleluia.

## SECOND READING

Heb 9:11-15

## OPTIONAL SEQUENCE

*See Appendix A, p. 296.*

### About Liturgy

***The difference between Eucharist and Communion:*** We often use these words interchangeably, yet there is a significant difference between Eucharist and Communion. While Eucharist can refer to the consecrated bread and wine, it also describes the entire liturgical action of the Mass. More importantly, Eucharist describes the heart of the Mass—the eucharistic prayer. In this "center and high point of the entire celebration" (GIRM, 78), we do more than ask the Holy Spirit to consecrate the bread and wine. In this prayer, the church's intention is that "the faithful not only offer this unblemished sacrificial Victim but also learn to offer their very selves, and so day by day to be brought, through the mediation of Christ, into unity with God and with each other" (ibid., 79). The eucharistic prayer calls us to a life of sacrifice for one another, and we embody that sacrifice not only in the prayer but in the sharing of Communion.

Communion refers specifically to the Body and Blood of Christ and generally to the part of the Mass that begins with the Communion rite (Lord's Prayer to the prayer after Communion). Communion can be distributed outside of Mass, as in a Communion service. Although the consecrated hosts shared at a Communion service are the same Blessed Sacrament as the hosts shared at Eucharist, what is missing is the unique offering of the assembly's sacrifice of praise that is intended in the eucharistic prayer. The sacrifice of the assembly and their offering of praise are not directly and ritually connected to the hosts they receive at a Communion service. This disconnect also occurs when we distribute Communion from the tabernacle to the assembly at Mass.

These distinctions may seem subtle. Unfortunately, through years of habitually distributing Communion from the tabernacle at Mass or overuse of Communion services, we have taught people that getting Communion rather than participating in the sacrifice of Christ is the primary goal of the Eucharist.

### About Initiation

***Who gets dismissed?:*** Once they become catechumens, those who are unbaptized are normally dismissed from Mass before the Creed. However, those who are baptized and are preparing for confirmation and Eucharist or for reception into the full communion of the Catholic Church are not dismissed. Nowhere in the RCIA is there an option or a directive for dismissing the baptized along with the catechumens. All the baptized have the right and duty to pray the prayers of the faithful. These include the Creed, the universal prayer (general intercessions), and the eucharistic prayer. Even though they cannot yet share in Communion, the baptized who are preparing for the sacraments still must stay to pray these important prayers that belong to all the baptized.

### About Liturgical Music

***Songs for adoration:*** Although the celebration of the Eucharist certainly has elements of adoration of Christ in the Word and sacrament, the music for Mass is essentially different than those more appropriate for eucharistic adoration. The difference, however, is usually very subtle and is found mostly in the texts or the musical structure.

Music more appropriate for sharing in Communion are usually those whose texts are based on the psalms or other Scripture readings or have verbs related to taking, eating, and drinking. These usually also are antiphonal rather than hymn form. Music more appropriate for adoration has text that is predominantly praise-oriented and speaks of seeing or being in the presence of God. These are not strict distinctions, and songs can serve both purposes. You will want to be attentive, however, and be sure the songs you choose match the ritual actions the liturgy intends.

**JUNE 3, 2018**

# THE MOST HOLY BODY AND BLOOD OF CHRIST (CORPUS CHRISTI)

℞. Alleluia, alleluia.
Take my yoke upon you, says the Lord;
and learn from me, for I am meek and humble
    of heart.
℞. Alleluia, alleluia.

*or*

1 John 4:10b

℞. Alleluia, alleluia.
God first loved us
and sent his Son as expiation for our sins.
℞. Alleluia, alleluia.

## Gospel

John 19:31-37; L171B

**Since it was preparation day,**
    **in order that the bodies might not**
        **remain on the cross on the**
        **sabbath,**
    **for the sabbath day of that week**
        **was a solemn one,**
    **the Jews asked Pilate that their legs**
        **be broken**
    **and they be taken down.**
**So the soldiers came and broke the legs**
    **of the first**
    **and then of the other one who was**
        **crucified with Jesus.**
**But when they came to Jesus and saw**
    **that he was already dead,**
    **they did not break his legs,**
    **but one soldier thrust his lance into**
        **his side,**
    **and immediately blood and water**
        **flowed out.**
**An eyewitness has testified, and his**
    **testimony is true;**
    **he knows that he is speaking the**
        **truth,**
    **so that you also may come to believe.**
**For this happened so that the Scripture**
    **passage might be fulfilled:**
    *Not a bone of it will be broken.*
**And again another passage says:**
    *They will look upon him whom they*
        *have pierced.*

*See Appendix A, p. 297, for the other readings.*

## Reflecting on the Gospel

"I love you with all my heart," the child's mother said upon sending her little girl to her first day of kindergarten. We all know that the familiar expression "with all my heart" means "completely," "without limit," or "with all I am." The heart has long been a symbol for love, as we see on Valentine's Day. Heart-shaped boxes of chocolate, heart-shaped sugar candies with emblazoned sayings like "be mine," even heart-shaped pizzas are on special at enterprising pizzerias! The heart is the poetic seat of emotion and love. How different, though how much more accurate, it would be to say the seat of emotion and love is the brain! But no, it's the heart that we associate with love.

Today we celebrate the divine love that Jesus himself has for humanity. It's not simply that God loves humanity, but today we take special note of Jesus' love for humanity. Quite appropriately, the gospel reading we have today is a graphic display of that love. The crucified, dead body of Jesus on the cross is pierced. Blood and water flow out of his side, symbolically representing (among other things) Jesus' death (blood) and the handing on of the spirit (water). But later theologians also see in this symbolism the humanity and divinity of Jesus, or the sacraments of baptism and Eucharist. As the images are symbolic, they are polyvalent, and open to interpretation.

At the very least, we see in the death of Jesus the great love he had for humanity. God's love became incarnate in the person of Jesus. And what was the human response? We killed it. Even so, that is not the last word. We know there will be a resurrection. God's love knows no bounds. God's love is not conquered even by death.

It is a rare thing, as the early Christians recognized (see Rom 5:7-8), for a person to die for a loved one. Sometimes a parent sacrifices one's life for a child. There are occasions when soldiers will die for another, or a police officer will be killed in the line of duty. But as Paul notes in his letter to the Romans, Christ died for us while we were still sinners. There was no guarantee we would accept the gift. That didn't matter. The love Jesus had for us was so strong that he faced death on the cross. He loves us "with all his heart," "completely," and "without limit."

## Living the Paschal Mystery

The blockbuster movie *Saving Private Ryan* is bookended with its opening and closing scenes of a World War II veteran at a cemetery. The movie is in effect a flashback, with the audience witnessing and the veteran remembering how many soldiers died so that he would live. In the closing scene at the cemetery he becomes overwhelmed with emotion, recalling the sacrifice the others made so he could live. He turns to his wife and asks if he's lived a good life. He wants to know that his life was somehow worthy of the cost, or at least not spurning of the cost.

That powerful cinematic moment captures something of what we might imagine when considering the gift of our own lives. Each of us has been given a divine gift of life itself. And even if we haven't had friends or others sacrifice their own lives for us, it was God who loved us into existence and Jesus his Son who gave himself for us. The Sacred Heart is a metaphor for that love of Christ. How we live our lives is our gift in return. We do not want to have spurned this precious gift of life. We want our lives to be in some ways worthy of, or perhaps reflective of, the cost. For to whom much has been given, much is expected.

## Focusing the Gospel

Today's gospel takes place at Golgotha, the site of Jesus' crucifixion. With Passover beginning at sundown (we are in the Johannine timeline here rather than the Synoptic), there was little time to properly dispose of the bodies of the executed criminals. Breaking the legs of those crucified was done to hasten the process of suffocation, but Jesus was already dead. Instead, a soldier thrust his lance into the side of Jesus and blood and water gushed forth. In the Fourth Gospel, Jesus is portrayed as the perfect Passover lamb; hence, the bones are not broken, as the law prescribes for the Passover lamb. Church fathers saw Jesus as both the priest and the offering of the new Passover sacrifice that seals a new covenant between God and humankind redeemed in Christ. They saw the blood and water flowing from Jesus' side as signs of the Eucharist and baptism, the life sources of the church. The first generations of Christians also considered the blood and water flowing from the physical body of Jesus as the release of the Spirit of God into the church as the Body of Christ.

## Model Penitential Act

*Presider:* Humbled by God's limitless mercy, let us begin our celebration of these sacred mysteries by seeking God's forgiveness for our sins and failings. *[pause]*

Father of compassion and forgiveness: Lord, have mercy.

Healer of broken hearts and spirits: Christ, have mercy.

Spirit of God that speaks and moves in the depths of every heart: Lord, have mercy.

## Model Universal Prayer (Prayer of the Faithful)

*Presider:* Let us now pray for all who are embraced in God's heart of mercy and love.

*Response:* Lord, hear our prayer.

That our church's ministers may preach, with humility and compassion, the "riches" of Christ and bring to light the wisdom of God . . .

That the selflessness and humility of Jesus the Sacred Heart may inspire the leaders of nations and governments in their service to their peoples and constituencies . . .

That Christ will raise up those whose bodies are broken and lives are sacrificed for the victims of injustice, violence, and poverty . . .

That the work and worship of our church and parish may reflect the love of God for all his holy ones . . .

*Presider:* Hear our prayers, O God. May our hearts be made whole in the compassion and peace of the Sacred Heart of your Son, Christ Jesus, in whose name we offer these prayers. **Amen.**

### COLLECT
Let us pray.

Grant, we pray, almighty God,
that we, who glory in the Heart of your
   beloved Son
and recall the wonders of his love for us,
may be made worthy to receive
an overflowing measure of grace
from that fount of heavenly gifts.
Through our Lord Jesus Christ, your Son,
who lives and reigns with you in the unity of
   the Holy Spirit,
one God, for ever and ever. **Amen.**

*or:*

O God, who in the Heart of your Son,
wounded by our sins,
bestow on us in mercy
the boundless treasures of your love,
grant, we pray,
that, in paying him the homage of our devotion,
we may also offer worthy reparation.
Through our Lord Jesus Christ, your Son,
who lives and reigns with you in the unity of
   the Holy Spirit,
one God, for ever and ever. **Amen.**

### FOR REFLECTION

• When have you risked everything for the love of another?

• What do the elements of blood and water reveal about the love of God made human?

## Homily Points

• People of biblical times spoke of the heart as our emotional center, as the seat of understanding and wisdom. In the "heart" of Jesus, the compassion and love of God is revealed, we experience the "water" of God's life-giving reconciliation and resurrection, and we are enriched and animated in the wisdom and grace of God.

• Jesus' sacrificial love is freely given, risks brokenness, and embraces everyone. To risk our own "hearts" is the call of discipleship: love that does not see itself as a hardship, but as a gift; that seeks its joy in the good of the beloved; that is expressed in humble generosity in caring for those we love. Such is the love of Jesus, the "Sacred Heart."

## ✝ SPIRITUALITY

**GOSPEL ACCLAMATION**
John 12:31b-32

R̸. Alleluia, alleluia.
Now the ruler of this world will be driven out,
   says the Lord;
and when I am lifted up from the earth, I will
   draw everyone to myself.
R̸. Alleluia, alleluia.

*Gospel*   Mark 3:20-35; L89B

Jesus came home with his disciples.
Again the crowd gathered,
   making it impossible for them even to eat.
When his relatives heard of this they set
   out to seize him,
   for they said, "He is out of his mind."
The scribes who had come from Jerusalem said,
   "He is possessed by Beelzebul,"
   and "By the prince of demons he drives
      out demons."

Summoning them, he began to speak to
   them in parables,
   "How can Satan drive out Satan?
If a kingdom is divided against itself,
   that kingdom cannot stand.
And if a house is divided against itself,
   that house will not be able to stand.
And if Satan has risen up against himself
   and is divided, he cannot stand;
   that is the end of him.

*Continued in Appendix A, p. 297.*

### Reflecting on the Gospel

Today we have a story about Jesus' family. In between this story there is another about scribes from Jerusalem attributing Jesus' power to Beelzebul, a name for the devil. Mark often uses this literary device of "sandwiching" one story within another (referred to as a Markan "sandwich"). The gospel begins with a snippet that is unique to Mark: Jesus' relatives come to get him, saying, "He is out of his mind." This is hardly the image we have of Jesus' own family. But, we are reminded that in Mark, the first canonical gospel that was written, there is no infancy narrative, no annunciation to Mary or Joseph's dream that he should take Mary as his wife. If we had only Mark's gospel, our image of the Holy Family would be quite different. For this story begins with the claim that Jesus is out of his mind, and concludes with Jesus' semi-rebuke to his family: "Here are my mother and my brothers. / For whoever does the will of God / is my brother and sister and mother."

This gospel passage tells us something about the persecuted Markan Christian community of the late first century. For that community especially, bonds of faith in Jesus were stronger than blood relationships. Many of the early Christians left family to join this band of believers. Remaining family members may have looked down on Christians almost as we regard cult members today. The early Christians were misunderstood by society, persecuted, and even killed. They found consolation with other Christians and their common faith in Jesus. Nonbelieving family members thought this new religion was strange. Jesus is the prime example of one misunderstood by his family, who thinks he is out of his mind. They come to bring him home, perhaps believing he is an embarrassment. Rather than acquiesce to their demands, he demonstrates that his believers have a bond stronger than blood.

Wrapped in this story about Jesus' family is another about scribes from Jerusalem who attribute his power to the devil. Not surprisingly, Jesus disputes that. He has been engaged in a battle with evil since the beginning of his ministry. He is not fighting on behalf of evil. A house divided against itself cannot stand. To attribute Jesus' activity to the devil is a sin against the Holy Spirit that will not be forgiven.

The stakes are high. Jesus seems to be getting it from all sides. His family, who raised him, and the scribes, who are experts in the law, do not understand him. He is thought to be out of his mind by some and by others to be possessed by a demon. Neither is very flattering! But Jesus stays true to who he is and counters each assault. The community he is forming is something new, based not on familial relations, but stronger than family.

### Living the Paschal Mystery

Today's passage gives us a rather unique perspective on the identity of Jesus vis-à-vis his contemporaries. Often we are so imbued with stories from other gospels and preaching from years of attending Mass, that it can be challenging to hear a gospel story on its own terms, unencumbered by other material. But today's gospel reminds us that Jesus did not have it easy. Are we expecting the same? Today self-righteous Christians may think they are persecuted for their faith when in fact they might simply be obnoxious. Jesus was misunderstood not because of obnoxious behavior, aloofness, or one-upmanship, but because he enjoyed the company of "sinners." He ate with those who were considered of ill repute. He engaged those who were said to be with demons. He did not fast but enjoyed great dinner parties. His behavior embarrassed his family and those who preferred cultural norms that kept certain people on the margins. It's one thing to admire Jesus. It's quite another to act as he did. Many of us are admirers of Jesus. But do I act as he did? Am I willing to face embarrassment to do what he did?

## Focusing the Gospel

*Mark 3:20-35*

A central theme of Mark's gospel is how Jesus' hearers (especially the Twelve) fail to comprehend the deeper meaning of his words and actions. The wild charges made by the scribes and the apologies offered by his family in today's gospel indicate just how misunderstood Jesus was by those closest to him. The Jesus who cast out demons and cured the sick is charged with being possessed himself. The scribes cannot grasp the single-minded dedication of Jesus to the will of God without the filters of their interpretations and direction; hence, he must be an agent of Satan, the prince of demons. (Remember that whatever the people of gospel Palestine could not understand or explain was considered the work of "demons.") "How can Satan drive out Satan?" Jesus responds. In Jesus' analogy, Satan is the "plunderer" who can only succeed if he "ties up" the property owner, but if the property owner is "strong" in faith, Satan will fail.

Jesus' remarks on "blasphem[ing] against the Holy Spirit" contrast between "unclean spirits" (Satan) and the "holy spirit" (God's spirit of justice and mercy). Everyone, in whom God has "breathed" life, possesses the spirit of God. To deny that spirit, to reject the natural state of goodness possessed by all, is "blasphemy."

The scene ends with the arrival of his family. Apologizing for his exorbitant claims about himself and his challenging their most cherished traditions and revered institutions, his family attempts to bring Jesus home. Jesus responds by redefining family as a relationship centered, not in blood, but in the doing of the will of God.

## Focusing the First Reading

*Gen 3:9-15*

Today's first reading is the Genesis story of God's censure of the serpent for destroying the harmony between the Creator and creation by "deceiving" Adam and Eve into selfishness and disobedience. The serpent convinces Adam and Eve that to "eat" of the tree of the knowledge of good and evil they will become "like God"—but their selfish act of disobedience causes alienation between themselves and God, and even creation. God's vision for humanity has been betrayed. Jesus the Redeemer and Healer will restore that vision and harmony between God and humankind and humankind and creation.

## Focusing the Responsorial Psalm

*Ps 130:1-2, 3-4, 5-6, 7-8 (7bc)*

In this penitential psalm, the psalmist cries out to God from "the depths." The psalmist does not ask for justice but forgiveness, suggesting he may have brought this time of "iniquities" on himself. But the psalmist sings of his unwavering hope in God's constant mercy.

## Focusing the Second Reading

*2 Cor 4:13–5:1*

Paul exhorts the Corinthian community to remain focused on the things of God and not of the earth ("what is seen is transitory"), to remember that faith ultimately triumphs over misery and death. The God who raised Jesus from the dead will also raise us and bring us into his presence.

**PROMPTS FOR HOMILISTS, CATECHISTS, AND RCIA TEAMS**

When have you experienced your family, community, parish, etc., putting aside individual interests for the sake of the common good?

What is the "craziest" thing that Jesus says in the gospels?

When have you lost hope in the possibility of forgiveness, of mercy, of justice?

Have you ever faced the sudden realization (as Adam and Eve do in the first reading) that you have done something wrong—that you were suddenly "naked"?

## Model Penitential Act

*Presider:* Let us begin our celebration of these sacred mysteries by asking the healing forgiveness of God for our sins and failings. *[pause]*

Father of compassion and forgiveness: Lord, have mercy.

Lord Jesus, our Redeemer and Savior: Christ, have mercy.

Spirit of God's enduring hope and love: Lord, have mercy.

## Homily Points

• In the humanity we share, we are bound to one another in a way that not only transcends things that divide us but can become even stronger in the wake of loss and suffering. Jesus comes as the means of unity among God's people, to reconcile humanity to God and to one another, to instill a deeper appreciation of our sacred dignity as being made in God's image. Jesus destroys the barriers created by race, culture, wealth, and social status in order to realize the Father's vision of one human family. We are called, as the church of the new covenant, to seek the humanity we all share that comes from God, the Father of all and the Giver of everything that is good.

• Sometimes we act out of a self-centeredness that is of "Satan" and not out of the compassionate spirit of Jesus—and, without fail, the "house" we have built out of such selfishness collapses in anger and hurt. If a house is to stand, it must be constructed out of forgiveness, humility, and generosity; to build it of cheaper materials, to compromise the integrity of the structure by placing one's own interest over that of the family, is to invite disaster. Jesus' life is testimony to the reality that the "power" of "Beelzebub" cannot heal or restore or recreate—only the Spirit of God can bring about such transformation.

• Jesus was considered "insane" by many of his hearers. This strange rabbi from Nazareth appears with the crazy idea that love will triumph over hatred, light will shatter the darkness, life will conquer death. This "crazy" Jesus seeks to heal us of what is, in fact, our own "insanity"—the "insanity" of allowing pettiness, pride, anger, prejudice, and self-centeredness to alienate us from one another; the lunacy of constantly grabbing as much as we can as fast as we can while many people on this planet have nothing. Jesus invites us to become "alive" in his "insane, lunatic" sense of community, joy, and reconciliation.

## Model Universal Prayer (Prayer of the Faithful)

*Presider:* Trusting that God is attentive to the cries of his people, let us offer our prayers.

*Response:* Lord, hear our prayer.

That our church may be a family of faith, bound together by Jesus' spirit of humble service . . .

That all peoples of the world may be united in their common pursuit of God's justice and peace . . .

That, in our compassion, we may lift up those mired in the depths of illness, addiction, and despair . . .

That families in crisis may find joy in their life together through the healing presence of Christ . . .

*Presider:* O Lord, may the prayers we offer with one voice make us one in heart and spirit, as well. Grant these prayers that we make to you in the name of Christ Jesus, the Lord. **Amen**.

## COLLECT

Let us pray.

*Pause for silent prayer*

O God, from whom all good things come,
grant that we, who call on you in our need,
may at your prompting discern what is
    right,
and by your guidance do it.
Through our Lord Jesus Christ, your Son,
who lives and reigns with you in the unity
    of the Holy Spirit,
one God, for ever and ever.

## FIRST READING   Gen 3:9-15

After the man, Adam, had eaten of the tree,
    the Lord God called to the man and
        asked him, "Where are you?"
He answered, "I heard you in the garden;
    but I was afraid, because I was naked,
    so I hid myself."
Then he asked, "Who told you that you
        were naked?
You have eaten, then,
    from the tree of which I had forbidden
        you to eat!"
The man replied, "The woman whom you
        put here with me—
    she gave me fruit from the tree, and so
        I ate it."
The Lord God then asked the woman,
    "Why did you do such a thing?"
The woman answered, "The serpent
    tricked me into it, so I ate it."

Then the Lord God said to the serpent:
    "Because you have done this, you shall
        be banned
        from all the animals
        and from all the wild creatures;
        on your belly shall you crawl,
            and dirt shall you eat
            all the days of your life.
    I will put enmity between you and the
        woman,
        and between your offspring and hers;
    he will strike at your head,
        while you strike at his heel."

## RESPONSORIAL PSALM

Ps 130:1-2, 3-4, 5-6, 7-8

℟. (7bc) With the Lord there is mercy, and
    fullness of redemption.

Out of the depths I cry to you, O Lord;
    Lord, hear my voice!
Let your ears be attentive
    to my voice in supplication.

℟. With the Lord there is mercy, and
    fullness of redemption.

If you, O Lord, mark iniquities,

LORD, who can stand?
But with you is forgiveness,
 that you may be revered.

R̸. With the Lord there is mercy, and
 fullness of redemption.

I trust in the LORD;
 my soul trusts in his word.
More than sentinels wait for the dawn,
 let Israel wait for the LORD.

R̸. With the Lord there is mercy, and
 fullness of redemption.

For with the LORD is kindness
 and with him is plenteous
 redemption;
and he will redeem Israel
 from all their iniquities.

R̸. With the Lord there is mercy, and
 fullness of redemption.

### SECOND READING
2 Cor 4:13–5:1

Brothers and sisters:
Since we have the same spirit of faith,
 according to what is written, *I
 believed, therefore I spoke,*
 we too believe and therefore we
 speak,
 knowing that the one who raised the
 Lord Jesus
 will raise us also with Jesus
 and place us with you in his presence.
Everything indeed is for you,
 so that the grace bestowed in
 abundance on more and more
 people
 may cause the thanksgiving to
 overflow for the glory of God.
Therefore, we are not discouraged;
 rather, although our outer self is
 wasting away,
 our inner self is being renewed day
 by day.
For this momentary light affliction
 is producing for us an eternal weight
 of glory
 beyond all comparison,
 as we look not to what is seen but to
 what is unseen;
 for what is seen is transitory, but
 what is unseen is eternal.
For we know that if our earthly dwelling,
 a tent,
 should be destroyed,
 we have a building from God,
 a dwelling not made with hands,
 eternal in heaven.

## About Liturgy

*A house divided:* Some people think that when you work for the Catholic Church, everything is harmonious and pleasant and everyone gets along. But just like any human organization, there can be problems and challenges. Just talk about liturgy and your preferences about it with other liturgically minded Catholics and, soon enough, a debate will break out, and once in a while, that debate can get nasty.

All of us have our preferences when it comes to what we think makes liturgy meaningful and prayerful. We each have a liturgical sensibility and style that works for us and helps us enter more deeply into prayer. But our preferences and sensibilities have to find their appropriate place within the challenging, but often rewarding, task of discerning what is best for the assembly. The United States bishops said it well in their 1972 document on music in the liturgy (which today is replaced by a newer document, Sing to the Lord, whose arrival also came with some debate as well). They said, "Each Christian must keep in mind that to live and worship in community often demands a personal sacrifice. All must be willing to share likes and dislikes with others whose ideas and experiences may be quite unlike their own" (Music in Catholic Worship, 17).

We can plan liturgy well and authentically for an assembly only when we collaborate with others who have responsibility for various aspects of the liturgy. That collaboration will surely raise disagreements at times. Those moments are opportunities for each of us to embrace sacrifice and to remind one another of our common goal: the praise of God and the sanctification of humanity through the full, conscious, and active participation of all the faithful. Let us remember that we're all on the same team when it comes to doing the holy work of communal prayer. We do not need to be a house divided against itself if we can treat one another with compassion and remind ourselves that "in my Father's house there are many dwelling places" (John 14:2, NABRE).

## About Initiation

*Other Christians becoming Catholic:* For some of our Christian sisters and brothers, the decision to become Catholic is relatively easy and they find much support from family and friends. Perhaps they have been married to a Catholic for many years, raised their children Catholic, and been attending Mass and participating in the Catholic parish throughout. However, for some others, the decision to leave the denomination of their childhood is filled with grief and anguish. Some may have family members who believe they are out of their minds, as Jesus' own relatives thought of him in today's gospel reading. Some may have even been estranged from loved ones because of their decision.

The Rite of Christian Initiation of Adults reminds us that for Christians choosing to become Catholic, "no greater burden than necessary is required for the establishment of communion and unity" (RCIA 473). This, however, does not always relieve the pain that some will experience. Let us honor each person's unique path and discernment and give each of them the support they need to find peace within their chosen and given families.

## About Liturgical Music

*Summer music:* As we enter into summer Ordinary Time, be aware that many in your assemblies may be visitors coming in for graduations, weddings, and family vacations. Use these Sundays to strengthen your base repertoire. These are the solid standards that generally every Catholic would know. Think of the songs that your assembly sings best on its own. You may be tired of them, but the assembly sings them with gusto. Remember that the assembly is the primary music minister. If they're not singing, even if they're just visiting, we're not doing our job of helping them participate fully in the liturgy.

**JUNE 10, 2018**
## TENTH SUNDAY IN ORDINARY TIME

## SPIRITUALITY

**GOSPEL ACCLAMATION**
R⁷. Alleluia, alleluia.
The seed is the word of God, Christ is the sower.
All who come to him will live forever.
R⁷. Alleluia, alleluia.

### Gospel

Mark 4:26-34; L92B

Jesus said to the crowds:
 "This is how it is with
 the kingdom of God;
 it is as if a man were to
 scatter seed on the
 land
 and would sleep and rise
 night and day
 and through it all the
 seed would sprout
 and grow,
 he knows not how.
Of its own accord the land
 yields fruit,
 first the blade, then the ear,
 then the full grain in the ear.
And when the grain is ripe, he wields
 the sickle at once,
 for the harvest has come."

He said,
 "To what shall we compare the
 kingdom of God,
 or what parable can we use for it?
It is like a mustard seed that, when it is
 sown in the ground,
 is the smallest of all the seeds on the
 earth.
But once it is sown, it springs up and
 becomes the largest of plants
 and puts forth large branches,
 so that the birds of the sky can dwell
 in its shade."
With many such parables
 he spoke the word to them as they
 were able to understand it.
Without parables he did not speak to
 them,
 but to his own disciples he explained
 everything in private.

### Reflecting on the Gospel

Parables are a genre that seem to be relegated to the gospels; not many people speak in parables today. But for Jesus, this was a routine way of teaching. Jesus' parables have many meanings and people have differing interpretations of them. Some parables in Mark that are left ambiguous are explained in Matthew's gospel. Other parables in Mark are simply enigmatic. We don't find them in any other gospel and, frankly, we don't know what Jesus might have meant. The first parable in today's gospel falls into that latter category. The "seed growing secretly" has been interpreted in a variety of ways. Interestingly, neither Matthew nor Luke reproduced it in their gospels. Because of its polyvalent meaning, many scholars say that this parable in particular is rooted in the sayings of the historical Jesus.

In some ways we are familiar with the gospel image of seed being scattered, such as the parable of the sower and seed, wherein the seed represents God's word. This parable is found in Mark 4:1-20 with parallels in Matthew and Luke. But today's gospel tells a different story. God's kingdom is likened to a man scattering seed upon the ground, and the seed grows without the man knowing how. But when the grain is ripe, the man comes with the sickle. The parable of the mustard seed, which follows immediately, is more familiar to us. Here too God's kingdom is likened to something, but in this case a mustard seed. The parable refers to it as the smallest seed of all, but it produces the greatest of all shrubs. Perhaps the meaning of this parable is more self-evident than that which preceded it. In any case, neither parable is explained.

We are told that Jesus spoke to the crowds in parables, but he explained them to his disciples privately. We might wonder why Jesus would not explain the parables to the crowds. Our somewhat disturbing answer comes in the same chapter, where Jesus tells his disciples, "The mystery of the kingdom of God has been granted to you. But to those outside everything comes in parables, so that / 'they may look and see but not perceive, / and hear and listen but not understand, / in order that they may not be converted and be forgiven'" (Mark 4:11-12, NABRE). It may seem strange that Jesus would not want those on the outside to be converted and forgiven. But like other Markan passages, this tells us a great deal about the community for whom Mark wrote, and its sense of being persecuted. The disciples whom Jesus called formed bonds stronger than family. They were chosen to live in relationship with him and one another. Though he taught in enigmatic parables, he explained all to his disciples. Those on the outside understood the words, but not the hidden meaning of the parables.

### Living the Paschal Mystery

At a Catholic Biblical Association meeting, one scholar said, "At some point we are going to have to address the strangeness, the oddness of Jesus." We have domesticated Jesus to such a point that sometimes his message, what it meant at the time, is lost to nice explanations and tidy clarifications. But truthfully, Jesus was someone who spoke in riddle-like speech we call parables. Perhaps he did not want his meaning to be grasped by larger audiences. Or perhaps that is merely a reflection of the Markan community that preserved some of these parables. In any case, these enigmatic sayings that Mark preserved needed a solution. They needed to be explained or simply dropped from the story. There are examples of each of these two kinds of solutions in Matthew and Luke. Though it can be difficult, it might not be bad to recognize that Jesus was perceived as eccentric. Such an image can challenge our catechetical Jesus. Let's allow him to speak with his own voice in the Scriptures, without wrapping up all the loose ends. His words have power and meaning, especially to a believing audience. Once that power is unleashed it becomes life-giving. But if it remains domesticated it loses its potential efficacy.

## Focusing the Gospel
*Mark 4:26-34*

Farming is a matter of hard work and patient faith: all the farmer can do is plant the seed and nurture it along with water and care; God's unseen hand in creation transforms the tiny seed into a great harvest. Today's gospel parables of the seed that grows by itself (a parable unique to Mark's gospel) and the mustard seed, then, are calls to patience, hope, and readiness. The mustard seed—that tiny speck containing the chemical energy to create the great tree— is a natural parable for the greatness that God raises up from small beginnings. The faith of the sower is centered in a spirit of trust and gratitude that God makes all things work together for good.

Jesus may have been making a coded reference to the Zealots, a Jewish sect that sought the political restoration of Israel. Some Zealots were terrorists, employing murder and insurrection to destabilize the Roman government. The Zealots dreamed of a Messiah who would restore the Jewish nation. Jesus, however, calls them to see their identity as God's people not in terms of political might but of interior faith and spiritual openness to the love of God.

## Focusing the First Reading
*Ezek 17:22-24*

Ezekiel's allegory of the cedar crest speaks of the "replanting" of the kingdom of Israel in the wake of the Babylonian occupation and destruction. From this small, humble "branch," God will reestablish his people as a "majestic cedar" of peace and justice for the world.

## Focusing the Responsorial Psalm
*Ps 92:2-3, 13-14, 15-16 (see 2a)*

The planting theme of today's Liturgy of the Word continues in today's responsorial Psalm 92. Palm trees were considered symbols of God's providence, trees that give both food and shelter from the burning desert sun and fierce storms. The "just" of God are like the magnificent cedar trees of Lebanon; their compassion and generosity of heart will continue into a graceful old age and then flourish anew in the house of God in eternity.

## Focusing the Second Reading
*2 Cor 5:6-10*

This body of ours is not our home, Paul writes to the secular-focused Corinthian community; this "life" is not the beginning and end of our existence. We make our way to our true "home" by walking in the light of Christ. At the end of our journey, we will face the question, Did we come anywhere close to accomplishing in our "bodies" the good that Jesus did in his body?

---

**PROMPTS FOR HOMILISTS, CATECHISTS, AND RCIA TEAMS**

Have you seen examples of "small seeds" someone unconsciously "planted" that resulted in an unexpected harvest for the good of others?

Has your life ever been changed by a simple, small "mustard-seed-like" act of kindness or care?

What does gardening and the planting and nurturing of seeds teach us about everyday life?

## Model Penitential Act

*Presider:* To prepare ourselves to celebrate these sacred mysteries, let us place our hearts before God, seeking his mercy for our sins and failings. *[pause]*

Lord God, you bring to fruition every seed and plant: Lord, have mercy.

Lord God, you breathe your life into every soul: Christ, have mercy.

Lord God, you embrace all of us in your love: Lord, have mercy.

## Homily Points

• Christ calls us to embrace the faith of the gospel farmer and the hope of the mustard seed: to be willing to plant whatever "seeds" of gospel hope and compassion that we possess, wherever and whenever we can, in the certain knowledge that it will, in some way, result in a harvest of God's life and love. We may never realize what that seed has harvested, but it is from such seeds that the reign of God will flourish.

• We often dismiss whatever and whomever we consider too "small" to matter, too powerless to make a difference, too insignificant to contribute anything useful. But we are all mustard seeds, possessing within ourselves the ability to accomplish Godlike things if we are encouraged and inspired to do so. The "mustard seed" faith that Jesus calls us to embrace is to honor that "spark" of God within every human being that enables everyone to contribute to the building of God's kingdom in our midst. Mustard seed faith is centered in the conviction that, in the smallest acts of compassion and generosity, we can transform the most barren stretches of our lives into great gardens of hope.

• Mark notes at the end of today's reading that Jesus taught in parables "as they were able to understand." Jesus did not speak of God in detached doctrines or impersonal legalisms, but sought to reveal the presence of God's love in the ordinary joys and struggles and sorrows of his listeners' lives. In the parables of our own seeds sown, of lost sheep found, of prodigals safely home, may we realize the reality of God in all the messiness and doubts of the lives we live every day.

## Model Universal Prayer (Prayer of the Faithful)

*Presider:* To the God who lifts up the lowly, exalts the humble, and blesses the poor with every good thing, let us pray.

*Response:* Lord, hear our prayer.

That our church may be the "cedar" tree planted by God, providing the "shade" of welcome and safety in the branches of our prayer and work . . .

That all nations may work together for responsible use of creation by all the human family . . .

That the efforts of those who serve the poor and oppressed may reap an abundant harvest of compassion and justice . . .

That our Father in heaven will bless and guide all fathers, stepfathers, and guardians in the holy vocation of fatherhood . . .

*Presider:* Accept these prayers, O God, and, with the faith of the mustard seed, may our smallest acts of kindness and justice bring your kingdom to reality in our own time and place. In Jesus' name, we pray. **Amen.**

**COLLECT**

Let us pray.

*Pause for silent prayer*

O God, strength of those who hope in you,
graciously hear our pleas,
and, since without you mortal frailty can
    do nothing,
grant us always the help of your grace,
that in following your commands
we may please you by our resolve and our
    deeds.
Through our Lord Jesus Christ, your Son,
who lives and reigns with you in the unity
    of the Holy Spirit,
one God, for ever and ever. **Amen.**

**FIRST READING**

Ezek 17:22-24

Thus says the Lord GOD:
    I, too, will take from the crest of the
        cedar,
        from its topmost branches tear off a
            tender shoot,
    and plant it on a high and lofty
        mountain;
        on the mountain heights of Israel I
            will plant it.
    It shall put forth branches and bear
        fruit,
        and become a majestic cedar.
    Birds of every kind shall dwell beneath
        it,
        every winged thing in the shade of
            its boughs.
    And all the trees of the field shall know
        that I, the LORD,
    bring low the high tree,
        lift high the lowly tree,
    wither up the green tree,
        and make the withered tree bloom.
    As I, the LORD, have spoken, so will I do.

## RESPONSORIAL PSALM
Ps 92:2-3, 13-14, 15-16

℞. (cf. 2a) Lord, it is good to give thanks
    to you.

It is good to give thanks to the LORD,
    to sing praise to your name, Most High,
to proclaim your kindness at dawn
    and your faithfulness throughout the
        night.

℞. Lord, it is good to give thanks to you.

The just one shall flourish like the palm
    tree,
    like a cedar of Lebanon shall he grow.
They that are planted in the house of the
    LORD
    shall flourish in the courts of our God.

℞. Lord, it is good to give thanks to you.

They shall bear fruit even in old age;
    vigorous and sturdy shall they be,
declaring how just is the LORD,
    my rock, in whom there is no wrong.

℞. Lord, it is good to give thanks to you.

## SECOND READING
2 Cor 5:6-10

Brothers and sisters:
We are always courageous,
    although we know that while we are at
        home in the body
    we are away from the Lord,
    for we walk by faith, not by sight.
Yet we are courageous,
    and we would rather leave the body and
        go home to the Lord.
Therefore, we aspire to please him,
    whether we are at home or away.
For we must all appear before the
        judgment seat of Christ,
    so that each may receive recompense,
    according to what he did in the body,
        whether good or evil.

## About Liturgy

*The oddness of Jesus:* Flannery O'Connor is often attributed with saying, "You shall know the truth, and the truth will make you odd." Mark's Jesus was certainly a bit odd with all his parables and strange sayings, which he refused to explain except to his own disciples. Yet, if we are to be his disciples today, we, too, need to be a bit weird ourselves. Really, who in their right mind believes that sacrifice, especially sacrificing one's own life even to death, is a good thing? What rational person embraces and forgives their enemies, sells all their possessions, and follows the way of life of a homeless preacher?

If we are to be Christians, we will certainly cause a few people to go, "huh?" Blessed Pope Paul VI said it more elegantly in his apostolic exhortation *Evangelii Nuntiandi*:

> Take a Christian or a handful of Christians who, in the midst of their own community, show their capacity for understanding and acceptance, their sharing of life and destiny with other people, their solidarity with the efforts of all for whatever is noble and good. Let us suppose that, in addition, they radiate in an altogether simple and unaffected way their faith in values that go beyond current values, and their hope in something that is not seen and that one would not dare to imagine. Through this wordless witness these Christians stir up irresistible questions in the hearts of those who see how they live: Why are they like this? Why do they live in this way? What or who is it that inspires them? Why are they in our midst? (21)

For those who do not yet have the eyes of faith, our words and actions might seem a bit strange. But this is the first step to planting a tiny seed that may grow without our knowing how. Our goal here with them is not to explain the mystery of our faith with catechisms, detailed exegesis, and theological arguments. First we plant the seed of faith by living a parabolic life that calls us to be courageous in being countercultural. Then, when they ask why, we say, come and see.

The liturgy, like the parables of Jesus, cannot be fully understood with rote answers and one-size-fits-all explanations. The Word and our sacraments are a lot more complex and interesting than that. Let us resist the temptation to overexplain our liturgies and simply strive to plant the seeds of faith, by celebrating the liturgy well and by living our faith boldly.

*Father's Day:* In the United States, this Sunday is Father's Day. Many parishes will want to recognize fathers at today's Mass. This is a good intention, but we also need to be careful. Fatherhood, like our symbols, has many meanings and layers. For some, this day will be joyful; for others, it will remind them of heartache, unfulfilled expectations, or past failures. Yes, recognize those who have nurtured us in many ways, and also acknowledge and support those who may find this day difficult to celebrate. If you decide to do a blessing of fathers during the Mass, chapter 56 in the *Book of Blessings* provides sample intercessions and a blessing that may be used at the end of Mass.

## About Liturgical Music

*Music suggestions:* Though Mark's Jesus does not give an explanation about the meaning of the two parables in today's gospel passage, the Alleluia verse sets us up to hear the reference to seeds as the word of God. In addition to a variety of settings of Psalm 19 ("Your words are spirit and life"), you might consider a hymn by Ricky Manalo, CSP, called "Many and Great" (OCP). The text uses much field and harvest imagery and connects it to our call to be sowers of the Word.

## SPIRITUALITY

**GOSPEL ACCLAMATION**
cf. Luke 1:76

℟. Alleluia, alleluia.
You, child, will be called prophet of the Most
  High,
for you will go before the Lord to prepare his
  way.
℟. Alleluia, alleluia.

### Gospel   Luke 1:57-66, 80; L587

When the time arrived for Elizabeth to
    have her child
  she gave birth to a son.
Her neighbors and relatives heard
  that the Lord had shown his
      great mercy toward her,
  and they rejoiced with her.
When they came on the eighth
      day to circumcise the child,
  they were going to call him
      Zechariah after his father,
  but his mother said in reply,
  "No. He will be called John."
But they answered her,
  "There is no one among your
      relatives who has this name."
So they made signs, asking his father
    what he wished him to be called.
He asked for a tablet and wrote, "John
    is his name,"
  and all were amazed.
Immediately his mouth was opened, his
    tongue freed,
  and he spoke blessing God.
Then fear came upon all their
    neighbors,
  and all these matters were discussed
    throughout the hill country of Judea.
All who heard these things took them
    to heart, saying,
  "What, then, will this child be?"
For surely the hand of the Lord was
    with him.

The child grew and became strong in
    spirit,
  and he was in the desert until the day
    of his manifestation to Israel.

### Reflecting on the Gospel

Families can be powerful indicators of paths we take in life. Children born into a family of those dedicated to public service often grow up to be public servants themselves. Those who teach for a living often have children in the teaching professions. And how many police officers and firefighters have come from families of the same. It's too simplistic to say we follow in our parents' footsteps, but it can also be challenging (but not impossible) for us to blaze new trails or to do something completely different. Our environment, especially our family environment, shapes who we are and who we become.

Luke is the sole voice in the New Testament telling us about the familial relationship between Elizabeth and Mary, making Jesus and John the Baptist cousins. Should we be surprised that each child was a charismatic preacher, attracting crowds, challenging religious and political leaders, and paying the ultimate price for their actions? What kind of relationship did Mary and Elizabeth have? What were their conversations to have resulted in the raising of two such sons? How did they act with one another and with their children? Perhaps surprisingly, we don't hear much about either Zechariah or Joseph. Luke tells us more about the women, and this might be a nod to the influence mothers have in our lives, and therefore in the lives of Jesus and John.

As Luke tells the story, Elizabeth was three months pregnant when Mary received the news that she would bear a son. Liturgically speaking, this feast is thus three months later than the annunciation (March 25) or six months prior to Christmas. The newborn John is a herald of the Messiah, even by his very birth. Like the marvelous conception and birth of Jesus, John too has something marvelous surrounding his conception and birth. Like the forebears in faith, Zechariah and Elizabeth are too old to have children. But God has other plans.

Today we consider the role of family in our own upbringing and that of John and his cousin Jesus. It has been said that the family is the domestic church. It is there that children first learn the faith, first learn what is important, what is a priority. And actions certainly speak more loudly than words. How our family acts indicates its priorities. A nourishing faith life, which is so important for so many in finding meaning in daily life, is often nurtured first in the family. May our families be places of safety, nourishment, love, care, and faith.

### Living the Paschal Mystery

The natural cycle of life involves both birth and death. Moments of joy, love, hope, and sheer happiness accompany the birth of a child. We wonder what she will do, what choices she will make, what her personality will be, etc. This entire future life is pure potential and opportunity in a newborn. And at the conclusion of one's life, we reflect back on what this person has become, the relationships and choices that made him who he was. We often look to the children and grandchildren, if the person was so blessed, and are in some ways comforted to know that something of the deceased lives on in his posterity.

Churches are often the points at which these significant life moments are ritualized, like baptism, marriage, or a funeral. Our faith can be nourished by such events, but also by the daily activities of life.

For Elizabeth and Mary, too, their faith was nourished by the joys of a newborn with all the hope and promise that brought. On this day we recognize how fundamentally human our relationship with God is. Through the sacred event of a birth, which we know ultimately leads to death, hope springs eternal and we live again the paschal mystery.

## Focusing the Gospel

*Luke 1:57-66, 80*

When their son is born, Zechariah is asked what he wishes to name his newborn. Zechariah writes on a tablet, "John is his name." Zechariah now understands what God has asked him and Elizabeth to do and resolves to accept that role. Zechariah's speech returns and his first words are a beautiful canticle praising God's goodness and prophesying the wonderful things that his son John would accomplish (the *Benedictus* hymn, which is omitted from today's reading).

Throughout Luke's gospel, the Holy Spirit is the agent of transformation and change—God is both the story and the storyteller. Through the grace of the Spirit, John goes on to realize his role in the story: to prepare a "highway" for the Lord's coming and to point out his presence in our midst.

## Focusing the First Reading

*Isa 49:1-6*

This is the second of the four "servant oracles" in Isaiah. It is not clear whether the prophet is speaking about the Emmanuel figure he envisions or the prophet himself. Many of the images in this reading mirror the gospel accounts of John and his preaching and baptizing at the Jordan.

## Focusing the Responsorial Psalm

*Ps 139:1-3, 13-14, 14-15 (14a)*

The verses of this iconic psalm celebrate the delicate care with which God creates the human body and profound and intimate relationship between God and his faithful, from the moment of an individual's conception through his or her journey through time. This image of God's "knowing" us "in [our] mother's womb" is a central theme in the readings for this solemnity of the birth of John the Baptist.

## Focusing the Second Reading

*Acts 13:22-26*

Today's second reading is Paul's first address to the people of Antioch, as recorded in the Acts of the Apostles. Paul begins his discourse on Jesus with John the Baptist, who heralded Jesus' coming with his preaching of a "baptism of repentance."

**PROMPTS FOR HOMILISTS, CATECHISTS, AND RCIA TEAMS**

When have you discovered God at work in your life, despite your initial doubts?

When has some unexpected joy left you without words to express gratitude, or when has a moment of sadness or grief left you speechless? In hindsight, what would you have liked to say?

What do you hear God saying to you in the depths of your heart that you try to suppress or ignore?

When was the last time you reacted to a set of circumstances in your life with the doubt of Zechariah, but were eventually able to cope with the situation with the optimism of Elizabeth?

## Model Penitential Act

*Presider:* Today, six months before we celebrate the birth of Jesus, we remember John the Baptist, the last of the prophets, who heralded the coming of the Messiah into our broken world. As we prepare to celebrate the Eucharist, let us call to mind our failure to recognize Christ's presence in our midst and ask the forgiveness of our loving Father. *[pause]*

> Father and Creator of all, who formed each of us in the womb: Lord, have mercy.
> Savior and Redeemer, who calls us to be prophets of your mercy: Christ, have mercy.
> Spirit of grace, who illuminates our hearts, making us a light to the nations: Lord, have mercy.

## Homily Points

• Today the church celebrates the birth of John the Baptist, the last great prophet who bridges the Old Testament and the New. John gives his life, as the Fourth Gospel says, to "testify to the light" of God's Christ. Many others throughout history—including our own time—have paid, as did John, the prophet's price to "testify to the light" of God's mercy and justice in their challenging of what was immoral and evil and their advocacy on behalf of the innocent victims of that evil. In our own baptisms, we accept God's call to be heralds of Christ the light of God and prophets of God's word of justice, compassion, and peace. Despite the "deserts" we wander through, despite the ridicule we must endure, God sends each one of us forth to be his prophets.

• After much internal struggle, Zechariah is finally able to embrace the promise of God. Like Zechariah, we would like to believe, despite ourselves. We would like to think that God is working marvels in our own time and place; we desperately want to believe that justice and peace, reconciliation and compassion, are possible. Faith does not demand that we put our doubts aside. Faith offers us a lens through which to see the small, hidden ways God acts in our midst and how God often works through us, despite our doubts and inability to readily see and understand. We understand poor Zechariah's inability to respond to such grace—we have been left speechless ourselves. But the promise of Emmanuel challenges us to grasp the reality of God's compassion bringing forth life from the seemingly dead, to embrace the idea that our God is a God of limitless and unconditional love that makes even the desert blossom.

## Model Universal Prayer (Prayer of the Faithful)

*Presider:* Christ, the light of God, has dawned. In joyful hope, let us pray.

*Response:* Lord, hear our prayer.

That our church may be a light of God's love and compassion for the human family . . .

That the "coastlands" and "distant peoples" of the world may one day be gathered in justice and peace before God . . .

That the poor, sick, troubled, and oppressed may be restored to health and wholeness through the love of Christ . . .

That students and young adults may hear God's call to live his Word of justice and compassion in their generous service to others . . .

*Presider:* Hear our prayers, O gracious God. Inspired by the prophetic ministry of John the Baptist, may we prepare our homes and hearts to welcome into our world the dawning of your Light, Christ Jesus, in whose name we make these prayers. **Amen.**

### COLLECT

Let us pray.

*Pause for silent prayer*

O God, who raised up Saint John the Baptist
to make ready a nation fit for Christ the Lord,
give your people, we pray,
the grace of spiritual joys
and direct the hearts of all the faithful
into the way of salvation and peace.
Through our Lord Jesus Christ, your Son,
who lives and reigns with you in the unity of the Holy Spirit,
one God, for ever and ever. **Amen.**

### FIRST READING

Isa 49:1-6

Hear me, O coastlands,
    listen, O distant peoples.
The LORD called me from birth,
    from my mother's womb he gave me my name.
He made of me a sharp-edged sword
    and concealed me in the shadow of his arm.
He made me a polished arrow,
    in his quiver he hid me.
You are my servant, he said to me,
    Israel, through whom I show my glory.

Though I thought I had toiled in vain,
    and for nothing, uselessly, spent my strength,
yet my reward is with the LORD,
    my recompense is with my God.
For now the LORD has spoken
    who formed me as his servant from the womb,
that Jacob may be brought back to him
    and Israel gathered to him;
and I am made glorious in the sight of the LORD,
    and my God is now my strength!
It is too little, he says, for you to be my servant,
    to raise up the tribes of Jacob,
    and restore the survivors of Israel;
I will make you a light to the nations,
    that my salvation may reach to the ends of the earth.

**RESPONSORIAL PSALM**
Ps 139:1b-3, 13-14ab, 14c-15

R̸. (14a) I praise you, for I am wonderfully
  made.

O LORD, you have probed me, you know
    me;
  you know when I sit and when I stand;
  you understand my thoughts from afar.
My journeys and my rest you scrutinize,
  with all my ways you are familiar.

R̸. I praise you, for I am wonderfully
  made.

Truly you have formed my inmost being;
  you knit me in my mother's womb.
I give you thanks that I am fearfully,
    wonderfully made;
  wonderful are your works.

R̸. I praise you, for I am wonderfully
  made.

My soul also you knew full well;
  nor was my frame unknown to you
When I was made in secret,
  when I was fashioned in the depths of
    the earth.

R̸. I praise you, for I am wonderfully
  made.

**SECOND READING**
Acts 13:22-26

In those days, Paul said:
"God raised up David as their king;
  of him God testified,
  *I have found David, son of Jesse, a man
    after my own heart;*
  *he will carry out my every wish.*
From this man's descendants God,
  according to his promise,
  has brought to Israel a savior, Jesus.
John heralded his coming by proclaiming
  a baptism of repentance
  to all the people of Israel;
and as John was completing his course,
  he would say,
  'What do you suppose that I am? I am
    not he.
Behold, one is coming after me;
  I am not worthy to unfasten the sandals
    of his feet.'

"My brothers, sons of the family of
    Abraham,
  and those others among you who are
    God-fearing,
  to us this word of salvation has been
    sent."

### About Liturgy

**Benedictus:** Every year, around the summer solstice, when, in the Northern Hemisphere, the time for daylight begins to shorten, the church marks the birth of John the Baptist. Like Christmas, this is a fixed feast, meaning its observance is always on the same date each year. Therefore, what a blessing to have the birth of John the Baptist fall on a Sunday this year so all can praise God for this other holy family!

In a way, however, the church recalls this "forerunner of Jesus" at the beginning of every day when it prays the Liturgy of the Hours. In Morning Prayer, the gospel canticle, which is the climax of this liturgy, comes from the song Zechariah sings the very moment his mouth is opened at the naming of his son, John. The opening words of that canticle are the source of its Latin title, the *Benedictus*: "Blessed be the Lord, the God of Israel, / for he has visited and brought redemption to his people" (Luke 1:68). That canticle ends with Zechariah addressing his newborn child: "And you, child, will be called prophet of the Most High, / for you will go before the Lord to prepare his ways, / to give his people knowledge of salvation / through the forgiveness of their sins, / because of the tender mercy of our God / by which the daybreak from on high will visit us / to shine on those who sit in darkness and death's shadow, / to guide our feet into the path of peace" (Luke 1:76-79, NABRE).

What does it mean for Christians that we sing this song about John the Baptist at the start of each new day? After having been silenced by sleep throughout the night, God opens our mouths, and one of the first things Christians do is sing this blessing of God whose dawn will break forth to shine on us and guide our way to peace. As the response to our silence being broken, we learn that singing holds a pride of place when it comes to giving praise to God. In the *Benedictus*, we join ourselves to the mission of John the Baptist, who came to prepare a way for the Lord by being a witness of God's salvation, living a simple and penitential life, and calling others to do the same. Our work each day, then, is to use our voice—like Zechariah and his son—and the witness of our lives to make God's presence known wherever we go.

**Vigil:** Note that this solemnity has a proper vigil. That means there is a different set of assigned readings and prayers for the Mass that is celebrated on the evening of June 23. Since that date is a Saturday this year, you might consider preparing your liturgical ministers to use the proper readings and prayers for the Vigil Mass that Saturday night and reserve the readings and prayers assigned for the Mass during the Day to June 24. The focus of the texts is very similar, so homilists and music ministers need not prepare different homilies or musical repertoire, except for the responsorial psalm.

### About Liturgical Music

**Music suggestions:** Although the gospel readings for both the Vigil and the Mass during the Day omit the text of Zechariah's canticle, it would be very appropriate to include a setting of the *Benedictus* in this weekend's Masses. Unless your assemblies are used to participating in the Liturgy of the Hours, they will likely be unfamiliar with the many settings of this canticle. However a simple way to introduce this text is to use one that is set to an already-familiar hymn. Here are several suggestions: "Benedictus: O Chosen Children" with beautiful text by Alan Hommerding is set to ELLACOMBE (WLP). FOREST GREEN is a very popular tune for the *Benedictus* paired with text by James Quinn ("Canticle of Zechariah," OCP), Ruth Duck ("Canticle of Zachary," GIA), and Carl Daw ("Benedictus," Hope Publishing). Any of these hymns can easily be used as the entrance procession for this weekend's Masses.

**JUNE 24, 2018**
## THE NATIVITY OF
## SAINT JOHN THE BAPTIST

**GOSPEL ACCLAMATION**
Matt 16:18

R⁊. Alleluia, alleluia.
You are Peter and upon this rock I will build my
    Church,
and the gates of the netherworld shall not
    prevail against it.
R⁊. Alleluia, alleluia.

## Gospel

Matt 16:13-19; L591

When Jesus went into the region of
    Caesarea Philippi
  he asked his disciples,
    "Who do people say that the Son
      of Man is?"
They replied, "Some say John the
    Baptist, others Elijah,
  still others Jeremiah or one
    of the prophets."
He said to them, "But who do
    you say that I am?"
Simon Peter said in reply,
    "You are the Christ,
      the Son of the
        living God."
Jesus said to him in reply,
    "Blessed are you, Simon
      son of Jonah.
For flesh and blood has not revealed
    this to you, but my heavenly
    Father.
And so I say to you, you are Peter,
    and upon this rock I will build my
      Church,
    and the gates of the netherworld
      shall not prevail against it.
I will give you the keys to the Kingdom
    of heaven.
Whatever you bind on earth shall be
    bound in heaven;
  and whatever you loose on earth
    shall be loosed in heaven."

*See Appendix A, p. 298, for the other readings.*

## Reflecting on the Gospel

Poor Paul! He came late to the Jesus movement. He never knew the historical Jesus or even witnessed Jesus' earthly ministry. So of course there is nothing in any of the four gospels about Paul. He first arrives on the scene in Acts of the Apostles, where he is present during Stephen's stoning. Paul then persecutes Jesus' followers. By the time he was finally baptized, his reputation among the disciples was so awful that they would not believe he had become a follower of Jesus. Though Paul eventually reached a mutual understanding with the leaders of the Jesus movement in Jerusalem, it appears to have been a misunderstanding as the battle of words between Peter and Paul in Antioch would reveal (Gal 2:1-14).

These two pillars of the church, Peter and Paul, did not quite see eye to eye on all issues. According to Acts, it's possible that they spent no more than a few weeks together throughout their entire lives. But they are eternally united as "founders" of the church in Rome, even though there was a thriving Christian community there before either set foot in the city. Their shared title of "founder" comes from the legends that each was martyred there; Paul was beheaded and Peter was crucified upside down.

The gospel for today gives us a seminal episode in Peter's life. In fact, according to Matthew's gospel, it was this episode whereby Jesus named Simon son of Jonah, "Peter," which means rock, as he and his confession would be the rock on which the church was built. Peter's confession of Jesus as "the Christ, the Son of the living God" is a hallmark of the New Testament. Matthew expands the story from what he found in Mark, giving more authority to Peter. Matthew mentions the terms "rock" and "church," which are not found in the Markan story. The Matthean story, even more than the Markan story, elevates the importance of Peter and sets the stage for later theological developments concerning the primacy of Peter, and therefore the primacy of the pope.

But today's solemnity is not for Peter only. It is for Peter and Paul. And thirteen letters, or about 25 percent of the New Testament, are attributed to Paul, a self-described apostle who did not witness the historical Jesus, and who seems to have been at odds on some issues with Peter. All of this is to say that no one person, not even Peter or Paul, has a complete lock on what it means to be a follower of Jesus. There is more than one way to live as a disciple. Moreover, being a disciple means not that there will be complete unanimity of opinion on all issues. Instead, being a disciple means simply being a follower of Jesus. These two disciples, apostles even, are our examples for today, each in his own way.

## Living the Paschal Mystery

Both Peter and Paul followed Jesus. Peter was one of the first disciples Jesus called, but Paul followed in a different way. He was called by the risen Lord and never referred to himself as a disciple, but as an apostle. Each of these apostles face a violent end reminiscent of Jesus' own death. Paul, by virtue of being a Roman citizen, is said to have been spared crucifixion and was beheaded. Peter, claiming that he was not worthy to die in the same manner as his Lord, was crucified upside down. These apostles were sent into the world, and each made mistakes. Peter denied Jesus and Paul persecuted Jesus' followers. But Peter and

Paul were ultimately true to their respective mission, despite heated arguments between them.

Our own call to discipleship, one of following Jesus, or perhaps even apostleship, being sent into the world, might too be punctuated with setbacks, difficulties, or even disagreements with other fellow disciples. We might not face a violent end like Peter or Paul, but we are called to face the paschal mystery of dying to self daily so that we might rise as disciples renewed in spirit.

### Focusing the Gospel

Peter's confession of faith is a turning point in the ministry of Jesus. Caesarea Philippi was the site of various temples and shrines dedicated to pagan gods, ranging from the Syrian god Baal to Pan, the Greek god of nature; in the middle of the city was a great white temple built by Herod and dedicated to the "divinity" of Caesar (hence the city's name). In this marketplace of gods and temples, Jesus asks his disciples what people are saying about him. They reply that many believe Jesus is the reincarnation of John the Baptist or the long-awaited return of the prophet Elijah or Jeremiah (Mal 4:5-6), whose return would signal the restoration of Israel. Before any can answer, Simon Peter declares, "You are the Christ, the Son of the living God." Jesus blesses the fisherman's faith and bestows on Simon a new name: "rock." Peter's faith is the "rock" that will be the foundation of Jesus' church. Peter is entrusted with the keys of the kingdom of heaven and the mission to proclaim the mercy and forgiveness of God.

### Model Penitential Act

*Presider:* Coming together to celebrate God's love in Word and sacrament, let us begin by seeking God's pardon for our failings and sins. *[pause]*

Father of reconciliation and peace: Lord, have mercy.
Lord Jesus, Word of God dwelling in our midst: Christ, have mercy.
Holy Spirit, God's love that heals and recreates: Lord, have mercy.

### Model Universal Prayer (Prayer of the Faithful)

*Presider:* Through Peter and Paul and the apostles we have heard the Good News. With hope, then, let us lift our voices in prayer to God, the Father of the risen Jesus.

*Response:* Lord, hear our prayer.

For the church's pastors and teachers, that they may be ministers of reconciliation and agents of God's forgiveness . . .

For all peoples of the world, that they may hear the Good News of the gospel . . .

For those who, like Paul, are persecuted for their faith or oppressed for their beliefs, that their witness to the truth will one day be exalted . . .

For our parish, that every prayer and work of ours may proclaim that Jesus is the Messiah . . .

*Presider:* Hear the prayers we raise to you, O God, for all your holy people. Grant us the constant faith of Peter, that we may proclaim your presence among us always; reassure us with the unwavering hope of Paul, that we may persevere in joy in this life as we await the life of the world to come. We ask these things in the name of your Son, Jesus Christ, the Messiah and Holy One. **Amen.**

### COLLECT

Let us pray.

*Pause for silent prayer*

O God, who on the Solemnity of the Apostles Peter and Paul
give us the noble and holy joy of this day,
grant, we pray, that your Church
may in all things follow the teaching
of those through whom she received
the beginnings of right religion.
Through our Lord Jesus Christ, your Son,
who lives and reigns with you in the unity of the Holy Spirit,
one God, for ever and ever. **Amen.**

### FOR REFLECTION

• Have you ever found yourself possessing the "keys to the kingdom" that "unlocked" God's grace to someone, or has someone "unlocked" such grace for you?

• When have you had an exchange like the one between Jesus and Peter (the gospel for today's Vigil Mass) in which a rift was healed, a chasm was crossed, a relationship was restarted?

### Homily Points

• The question Jesus asks Peter and his disciples is asked of us every day. Every decision we make is ultimately a response to the question, Who do you say I am? Our love for family and friends, our dedication to justice, our commitment to high moral standards, our effort toward reconciliation and forgiveness, our acts of kindness and charity declare most effectively our belief in Jesus as the Messiah and Redeemer.

• Christ entrusts to Peter and his fledgling church the "keys to the kingdom": his Gospel of compassion, justice, and hope to all. That Gospel was handed on by that first generation of disciples to the next generation and to the next and to the next . . . and now to us. By our simple expressions of compassion and love for others, we reveal God's kingdom in our midst; by our everyday efforts to heal divisions and lift up the broken and abused, we "loose" the hope of God's mercy and forgiveness in this time and place.

## ✝ SPIRITUALITY

**GOSPEL ACCLAMATION**
cf. 2 Tim 1:10

℟. Alleluia, alleluia.
Our Savior Jesus Christ destroyed death
and brought life to light through the Gospel.
℟. Alleluia, alleluia.

### Gospel  Mark 5:21-43; L98B

When Jesus had crossed again in the
    boat
  to the other side,
  a large crowd gathered around him,
      and he stayed close to the sea.
One of the synagogue officials, named
    Jairus, came forward.
Seeing him he fell at his feet and
    pleaded earnestly with him,
    saying,
  "My daughter is at the point of
    death.
Please, come lay your hands on her
  that she may get well and live."
He went off with him,
  and a large crowd followed him and
      pressed upon him.

There was a woman afflicted with
    hemorrhages for twelve years.
She had suffered greatly at the hands
    of many doctors
  and had spent all that she had.
Yet she was not helped but only grew
    worse.
She had heard about Jesus and came
    up behind him in the crowd
  and touched his cloak.
She said, "If I but touch his clothes, I
    shall be cured."
Immediately her flow of blood dried up.
She felt in her body that she was
    healed of her affliction.
Jesus, aware at once that power had
    gone out from him,
  turned around in the crowd and
      asked, "Who has touched my
      clothes?"

*Continued in Appendix A, p. 299, or*
Mark 5:21-24, 35b-43 *in Appendix A, p. 299.*

### Reflecting on the Gospel

Another Markan sandwich greets us today, a story wrapped in another story. The story of the woman touching Jesus' garment is sandwiched between the story of Jairus's daughter being raised from the dead. Mark tells the stories with such detail and verbosity that when Matthew has a chance to include them in his gospel he condenses the entire episode to fewer than ten verses! (See Matt 9:18-26.)

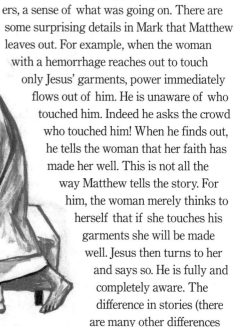

But for Mark, these details provide a color commentary and give us, the readers, a sense of what was going on. There are some surprising details in Mark that Matthew leaves out. For example, when the woman with a hemorrhage reaches out to touch only Jesus' garments, power immediately flows out of him. He is unaware of who touched him. Indeed he asks the crowd who touched him! When he finds out, he tells the woman that her faith has made her well. This is not all the way Matthew tells the story. For him, the woman merely thinks to herself that if she touches his garments she will be made well. Jesus then turns to her and says so. He is fully and completely aware. The difference in stories (there are many other differences as well) is part of the reason scholars believe Mark was written prior to Matthew. The earlier, Markan story was made "better" by Matthew. Yet, the Markan story preserves for us something that might approximate the historical Jesus more closely.

The story that forms a bookend around the woman with a hemorrhage is the raising of Jairus's daughter. Here Jesus continues his confrontation with evil, this time death. And he is victorious. Before he even arrives at the home, the twelve-year-old girl is pronounced dead. Jesus replies that she is only asleep, for which he is ridiculed and laughed at. But in the end, he raises the girl and admonishes the three disciples who were with him not to say anything.

Jesus' power is on clear display. Merely touching his garment with an act of faith is enough to heal somebody. Jesus himself raises the dead to new life. His identity is coming into sharper focus as we journey with him through this gospel.

### Living the Paschal Mystery

Medical professionals were rare in the ancient world. We almost take them for granted today. But for those in antiquity who suffered from one ailment or another, their lives were often destined for suffering and to be on the margins. We are not surprised to know that life spans were much shorter in the ancient world without access to medicine, proper care, or in some cases sanitary conditions. Despite all of our advances in medicine, human beings are still subject to death. We have not conquered that, but only delayed it.

Jesus' own power is expressed by stories of curing the woman with the hemorrhage and raising the dead. Jesus restores human beings to a full, active, and healthy life in one story. He literally raises the dead to life again in another. If he and his power can do these things, we should be paying attention.

We will find later in the gospel that there is more to his ministry than grand displays of power. There will be the necessary suffering and death. Once that aspect of his ministry is revealed, many if not most of his followers will fall away. It might not be too difficult to imagine following someone who raises the dead. It's quite another to see that same one put to death.

When we encounter moments of pain, suffering, and even the death of loved ones, it is good to remember that we follow one who seeks to restore, who seeks to raise the dead to life again. That is our common Christian hope.

### Focusing the Gospel

*Mark 5:21-43 (shorter form: Mark 5:21-24, 35b-43)*

Mark holds up both Jairus and the unnamed woman in today's gospel as models of faith. The message of the two healings is clear: "Do not be afraid; just have faith." The chronically ill woman is so convinced that Jesus not only can help her but *will* help her that she fights her way through the pushing and shoving crowds just to touch the cloak of Jesus. She realizes not only the power of Jesus to heal her but the depth of his love and compassion to *want* to heal her. Her faith is rewarded.

Jairus was a man of considerable authority and stature in the Jewish community. Yet, for the sake of his daughter, he puts aside his pride and his instinctive distrust of this itinerant rabbi to become a "beggar" for her before Jesus. Despite the ridicule of the mourners and the depth of his despair, Jesus is Jairus's hope.

In Mark's narrative, the raising of Jairus's daughter anticipates Jesus' resurrection. The love and mercy of God transcend death to reach into our own time and place.

### Focusing the First Reading

*Wis 1:13-15; 2:23-24*

Today's first reading from the book of Wisdom is a beautiful meditation on God the Creator and Sustainer of life, who made humankind in his "own nature" to be "imperishable." Death is the very antithesis of God whose "justice is undying."

### Focusing the Responsorial Psalm

*Ps 30:2, 4, 5-6, 11, 12, 13 (2a)*

Psalm 30 is a prayer of thanksgiving offered by a sufferer who, by God's mercy, has survived a near fatal disease. The newly healed gives thanks to God by sharing his or her story of salvation with the assembly of the faithful.

### Focusing the Second Reading

*2 Cor 8:7, 9, 13-15*

Paul is about to ask the Christian community for money to help the church in Jerusalem (an appeal that the churches in Macedonia have responded to with generosity and humility). Paul begins his "pitch" by urging the Corinthians to learn charity and generosity (in Greek: *charis*) from the example of Christ Jesus, the compassionate and humble healer.

---

**PROMPTS FOR HOMILISTS, CATECHISTS, AND RCIA TEAMS**

Have you known a parent whose love for his or her child truly reflected the love of God, the Father of all?

Have you ever feared someone or something only to discover that fear to be totally unfounded?

Who are the "afterthought" people in your community?

## Model Penitential Act

*Presider:* As we gather to celebrate these sacred mysteries, let us begin by seeking God's forgiveness and mercy. *[pause]*

God who fashioned all things into being: Lord, have mercy.

God in whose very image we are made: Christ, have mercy.

God who changes our mourning into dancing: Lord, have mercy.

## Homily Points

• In his gospel, Mark describes Jairus as "an official of the synagogue," a man of considerable authority in the Jewish community—an "establishment" figure, to be sure. But Jairus's love for his daughter enables him to risk his standing in the community and the reproach of his neighbors to ask this "antiestablishment" rabbi to save his daughter's life. Not only is the daughter restored to health, but Jairus and his family are transformed as well. Through such unconditional compassion—like the love of God the Father for us, his children—we not only bring healing to the suffering but find healing for our own brokenness; we not only restore life to the dying but restore a sense of hope to our own lives.

• *Do not fear. Trust.* Like the wailing mourners at the little girl's bedside, we sometimes resign ourselves to defeat as the regular order of things, to death as the only and final conclusion; we hesitate to offer our assistance to others, fearing how we might be perceived, wanting to guard our time and security, doubting our ability to provide any meaningful help. In healing the little girl and the hemorrhaging woman, however, Jesus shows us that the life and hope we bring into the world is through the providence of God and the goodness possessed by everyone as a son or daughter of God.

• Jesus does not hesitate to wade into the messiness of life in order to transform such turmoil into healing and restoration. He ignores custom and taboo in a way that modern readers may miss: in taking the dead girl by the hand, in allowing the sick woman to touch him, Jesus became unclean and unable to enter the synagogue. But to respond compassionately to the plight of these souls becomes more important, more sacred, than the "safety" of convention and tradition. Christ calls us to embrace such "fearless" compassion, risking our own sense of safety and satisfaction in order to bring that love into the lives of others.

## Model Universal Prayer (Prayer of the Faithful)

*Presider:* To the God who seeks not destruction but the life of his faithful, let us pray.

*Response:* Lord, hear our prayer.

For Pope N., for our bishops, priests, and deacons, for those who serve our church as teachers, counselors, and volunteers, that their ministries may touch the people they serve with compassion and understanding . . .

For our nation as we celebrate our Independence Day, that the Spirit of God may guide us in building our nation on the principles of liberty, equality, and justice for all . . .

For the sick and dying, for those who mourn and grieve, for struggling families and households, for those consumed by despair and fear, that the love of God will transform their "mourning into dancing" . . .

For our parish, that we may embrace the selfless poverty of Jesus in order to grow rich in God's mercy and peace . . .

*Presider:* O God, you know our needs before we realize them ourselves. Hear these prayers we offer to you for all your people, that you will bless all our brothers and sisters with your healing peace and reconciling love. We ask this in the name of Jesus, the healer and teacher. **Amen.**

### COLLECT

Let us pray.

*Pause for silent prayer*

O God, who through the grace of adoption
chose us to be children of light,
grant, we pray,
that we may not be wrapped in the
    darkness of error
but always be seen to stand in the bright
    light of truth.
Through our Lord Jesus Christ, your Son,
who lives and reigns with you in the unity
    of the Holy Spirit,
one God, for ever and ever. **Amen.**

### FIRST READING

Wis 1:13-15; 2:23-24

God did not make death,
    nor does he rejoice in the destruction of
        the living.
For he fashioned all things that they might
    have being;
    and the creatures of the world are
        wholesome,
and there is not a destructive drug among
    them
    nor any domain of the netherworld on
        earth,
    for justice is undying.
For God formed man to be imperishable;
    the image of his own nature he made
        him.
But by the envy of the devil, death entered
    the world,
    and they who belong to his company
        experience it.

# ✛ CATECHESIS

## RESPONSORIAL PSALM
Ps 30:2, 4, 5-6, 11, 12, 13

℟. (2a) I will praise you, Lord, for you
  have rescued me.

I will extol you, O LORD, for you drew me
    clear
  and did not let my enemies rejoice over
    me.
O LORD, you brought me up from the
    netherworld;
  you preserved me from among those
    going down into the pit.

℟. I will praise you, Lord, for you have
  rescued me.

Sing praise to the LORD, you his faithful
    ones,
  and give thanks to his holy name.
For his anger lasts but a moment;
  a lifetime, his good will.
At nightfall, weeping enters in,
  but with the dawn, rejoicing.

℟. I will praise you, Lord, for you have
  rescued me.

Hear, O LORD, and have pity on me;
  O LORD, be my helper.
You changed my mourning into dancing;
  O LORD, my God, forever will I give you
    thanks.

℟. I will praise you, Lord, for you have
  rescued me.

## SECOND READING
2 Cor 8:7, 9, 13-15

Brothers and sisters:
As you excel in every respect, in faith,
    discourse,
  knowledge, all earnestness, and in the
    love we have for you,
  may you excel in this gracious act also.

For you know the gracious act of our Lord
    Jesus Christ,
  that though he was rich, for your sake
    he became poor,
  so that by his poverty you might
    become rich.
Not that others should have relief while
    you are burdened,
  but that as a matter of equality
  your abundance at the present time
    should supply their needs,
  so that their abundance may also
    supply your needs,
  that there may be equality.
As it is written:
  *Whoever had much did not have more,*
    *and whoever had little did not have*
    *less.*

## About Liturgy

*The power of touch:* How often in the liturgy do we use our sense of touch? In both formal and informal gestures, we use our hands to hold, carry, sign, bless, offer, pray, reconcile, welcome, and send. In many ways, we need touch in order to be *in touch* with God who is right in our midst.

Yet, we often take for granted the gift of touch—a gift we receive and offer. Notice how quickly we tend to make the sign of the cross over ourselves or how casually we take a person's hand during the sign of peace with hardly a glance into their eyes or a moment of genuine human connection. Many are careful to attend to the touch they show the Body of Christ as they share in Communion. However the Body of Christ is also found in those around us, among the crowd of people that surrounds us every day. Most especially, the Body of Christ is found in those who have been discarded by society, pushed to the fringes, or made invisible by stigma, prejudice, or shame.

In liturgy, let us pay attention to how we reverence God in sacred gifts and in sacred people through the act of sacred touch. In doing this, we are training ourselves to find the one within the crowd of people we encounter each day who is most in need of God's healing, given in simple human touch and offered with true reverence and care.

## About Initiation

*The signing of the senses:* One of the most powerful moments among all the rites of the catechumenate is the signing of the senses during the Rite of Acceptance into the Order of Catechumens. In this ritual action, which is the "first consecration by the Church" (RCIA 41) of an adult who desires to be baptized, the cross is traced first by a priest or deacon on the person's forehead and then by the sponsor on other parts of the body.

Celebrants and sponsors need to do this gesture in such a way that communicates its intention: This person now belongs to Christ and is consecrated by the cross of Christ. This person, like St. Paul, now bears the brand marks of Christ on his or her body. Catechumens should remember long afterward the feeling of your hand gently yet firmly impressing the cross into their bodies. Therefore, more is needed than "air crosses" or a holy thumb. Use your entire hand to make the sign of the cross on them. Don't be afraid to keep a constant connection to them by placing your other hand on their arm as you sign their forehead, ears, eyes, lips, heart, and shoulders. Cradle their open hands in yours as you make the sign of the cross on their palms; and show your own need for their touch by taking their hand as you kneel down to make the sign of the cross on their feet.

## About Liturgical Music

*Patriotism in the liturgy:* The Sunday closest to the Fourth of July is always a balancing act between two "constitutions," that of our nation and that of the liturgy. At Sunday Eucharist, our focus is rightly on Christ who has broken down the barriers that divide us. However, no one will be converted to greater love for the liturgy or deeper love for Christ by beating them over the head with liturgical rubrics and principles.

If you decide to incorporate patriotic songs, choose your songs and when you will use them prudently. Some songs are more appropriate than others, even if they include the words "God" or "Hallelujah." One recommendation is "This Is My Song" written by Lloyd Stone and set to the tune "Finlandia," which provides a Christian context for belonging to a nation and works well at the preparation of gifts. Other appropriate times for patriotic songs are at prelude, postlude, and the recessional.

### JULY 1, 2018
# THIRTEENTH SUNDAY
# IN ORDINARY TIME

## ✝ SPIRITUALITY

### GOSPEL ACCLAMATION
cf. Luke 4:18

R/. Alleluia, alleluia.
The Spirit of the Lord is upon me,
for he sent me to bring glad tidings to the poor.
R/. Alleluia, alleluia.

### Gospel

Mark 6:1-6a; L101B

Jesus departed from there and came to
    his native place, accompanied
    by his disciples.
When the sabbath came he began
    to teach in the synagogue,
    and many who heard him were
    astonished.
They said, "Where did this man
    get all this?
What kind of wisdom has been
    given him?
What mighty deeds are wrought by
    his hands!
Is he not the carpenter, the son of
    Mary,
    and the brother of James and Joses
    and Judas and Simon?
And are not his sisters here with us?"
And they took offense at him.
Jesus said to them,
    "A prophet is not without honor
        except in his native place
    and among his own kin and in his
        own house."
So he was not able to perform any
    mighty deed there,
    apart from curing a few sick people
        by laying his hands on them.
He was amazed at their lack of faith.

### Reflecting on the Gospel

Have you ever been so familiar with someone that you knew what he would say in a given situation? Or have you ever known someone so well that you could predict her behavior? That's how well Jesus' townspeople and family thought they knew him. So, after Jesus had been away for some time performing his ministry, he returned to his hometown and faced the shock and surprise of those who thought they knew him.

The townspeople knew him from the time he was a little boy, but Jesus had grown up and become his own person. Those from his hometown had pegged him, put him in a box. He was the "carpenter," the son of Mary. They knew him and knew his family. Who was he to teach them?

In response, Jesus refers to himself as a prophet without honor in his own country, town, and even in his own house. Here too, like earlier stories in Mark, we have an indication of the situation in the Markan community. Jesus is without honor in his own house as many of the early Christians were likely without honor in their own house. As Jesus was rejected by those who knew him, many of the early Christians were likely rejected by those who knew them.

We are reminded of the adage, "familiarity breeds contempt." Those who were closest to Jesus for most of his life did not see him for who he was but for who they determined him to be.

As a result, he could do no mighty work there except a few minor healings! The Markan Jesus is in some ways dependent upon a faith response to perform mighty works. This is a reciprocal relationship with the believer. Of course, later gospels will, for the most part, modify that understanding so that Jesus' power is dependent upon nothing but his own will and that of God. But in this early gospel we hear something of the resistance Jesus faced and the resulting limitation in his ability to perform mighty works. Jesus was amazed at their unbelief. Their own limited understanding and their inability to perceive who he was limited the works he was able to perform.

### Living the Paschal Mystery

Today most of us are not in danger of being too familiar with Jesus the way those from his hometown were. We are not dismissive of the carpenter who was the son of Mary. But we can be effectively blind to the presence of Jesus in our midst in the modern world. We can be dismissive of those we confine to the margins of society. Who is that? A homeless person? A beggar? An immigrant? Or an undocumented person? What does that person know that we don't already know? What wisdom could that person have that we don't already possess?

There is a temptation in the religious realm and even societal realm to believe we have what we need to be complete and whole. There is little another person, especially one on the margins, could teach us about how to act, how to behave, or anything about God. That is precisely how the Nazarenes behaved with respect to Jesus. They thought they understood who he was. They knew his family, his backstory. What more did they need to know? In their minds, this upstart was too big for his britches. They took offense at him. Yet, God was effectively in their midst.

May we be open to finding the new, the unexpected, in familiarity. Let us not grow too familiar that we fail to see the presence of God in our midst.

## Focusing the Gospel
*Mark 6:1-6*
Mark begins a new theme in his gospel with today's reading that will be central to his story of Jesus: the obtuseness of people to the power and authority of Jesus. The people of Jesus' own hometown reject his message. They consider Jesus too much "one of them" to be taken seriously. They are too obsessed with superficialities—occupation, ancestry, origins—to realize the presence of God in their midst and to allow themselves to be affected by that presence.

Jesus redefines the meaning of authority as understood by his kinfolk: Jesus' authority is not derived from his ability to manipulate the fears, suspicions, apathy, or ignorance of those around him but from the spirit of mercy, justice, and compassion that he is able to call forth from them. The authority his hearers see in Jesus is rooted in wisdom that comes from experience and a lived commitment to act justly and selflessly.

## Focusing the First Reading
*Ezek 2:2-5*
Ezekiel is called by God to speak his word to his own people: Judean Jews who have been repatriated from their beloved Jerusalem to Babylon. God warns the prophet that his work will be very difficult: God is sending him to speak to a defeated, distrusted people who feel abandoned by God and will be immediately hostile to anyone who claims to speak for the God they have "rebelled against."

## Focusing the Responsorial Psalm
*Ps 123:1-2, 2, 3-4 (2cd)*
The master-slave relationship is the central image of Psalm 123. In ancient Near Eastern cultures, a master was responsible for providing for the slave; in return, the slave could be trusted for managing the property of the master. The psalmist seeks God (the master) to act on behalf of his servants (the slaves) who have been exiled and impoverished by their Babylonian captors.

## Focusing the Second Reading
*2 Cor 12:7-10*
The Corinthian church had been divided by members allying themselves with other "apostles." The splintering of the community at Corinth has been a source of great sorrow for Paul, who had reminded them that unity is to be had in Christ. In the final section of this series of Sunday readings from his two letters to the Corinthians, Paul reflects on some of his most difficult challenges: not to grow conceited, to discover strength in weakness, and to experience God's grace in times of hardship.

**PROMPTS FOR HOMILISTS, CATECHISTS, AND RCIA TEAMS**

Who are the "authorities" in your life whom you look up to and pay attention to?

Have you ever known someone who possessed the courageous, unwavering faith of a "prophet"?

When have you been "offended" by someone who spoke about a moral or ethical issue?

In what situations or set of circumstances has it been most difficult for you to live your faith?

## Model Penitential Act

*Presider:* Let us begin our celebration of the Eucharist by humbly placing our hearts before God, confident of his forgiveness for our sins and failings. *[pause]*

You heal the brokenhearted: Lord, have mercy.

You seek out and bring back the lost: Christ, have mercy.

You grasp the stumbling and lift up the fallen: Lord, have mercy.

## Homily Points

• In baptism, we are all called to the role of prophet—"one who proclaims" the presence of God in our midst. But such "prophecy" can be risky, terrifying, misinterpreted, threatening to others; to act and speak as a prophet can result in our being ostracized, ridiculed, rejected, and isolated. But faith of a true prophet never falters in the conviction that the justice of God will triumph over injustice, that God's mercy will triumph over hatred, that God's light will triumph over the darkness of sin and death.

• Authority is much more than rhetoric; it is the lived commitment of one's beliefs. Authentic authority is not invested by virtue of office or title or economic power, but in the wisdom that comes from experience and a commitment to do what is right and just that transcends expectations. True authority does not evoke fear; it enables growth, inspires beauty, makes hopes and dreams possible. Such is the authority of the rabbi Jesus of the gospels. The source of Jesus' authority is not the ability to manipulate his hearer's suspicions, apathy, or ignorance but to call forth from them a commitment to mercy, justice, and compassion. Those who speak not to our emotions and wants but to our consciences, who speak not in catchy slogans and buzzwords but in the convictions of their experience, who share with us from the wealth of their own hard work possess the authority that is of God, an authority that is worthy of our respect and attentiveness.

• Like the people of Jesus' hometown, we often fail to realize the presence of God in our very midst. When Jesus' prophetic words become difficult to comprehend, when his Gospel threatens our own safe, insulated world, when Jesus challenges our own incomplete and myopic view of God, we walk away from him or reject him outright, as the people of Nazareth did. Jesus calls us—dares us—to change our perspective, our belief systems, and ourselves to bring God's kingdom of peace and compassion to reality for all his sons and daughters. God dwells in our midst in the simplest acts of kindness, in the humblest efforts of compassion for others, in the singular attempts to secure the justice and peace of God in hidden and forgotten places.

## Model Universal Prayer (Prayer of the Faithful)

*Presider:* Let us lift up our eyes and hands to the Lord in prayer.

*Response:* Lord, hear our prayer.

That the Spirit of God may "enter" the hearts of all who serve the church as pastors, teachers, counselors, and ministers, enabling them to proclaim God's love for all his people . . .

That our president and the leaders of all nations, states, and cities may lead and govern with the authority born of wisdom and selflessness . . .

That the sick, the suffering, the addicted, and the dying may experience God's grace in our compassion and care . . .

That we, as a church and parish community, may be prophets of the justice and mercy of God . . .

*Presider:* We come to you in hope, O Lord, knowing that you will hear the prayers we ask in faith. May your Spirit of wisdom and truth rest upon us always, so that we may be prophets of your great love. In Jesus' name, we pray. **Amen.**

---

**COLLECT**

Let us pray.

*Pause for silent prayer*

O God, who in the abasement of your Son
have raised up a fallen world,
fill your faithful with holy joy,
for on those you have rescued from slavery
    to sin
you bestow eternal gladness.
Through our Lord Jesus Christ, your Son,
who lives and reigns with you in the unity
    of the Holy Spirit,
one God, for ever and ever. **Amen.**

**FIRST READING**

Ezek 2:2-5

As the LORD spoke to me, the spirit entered
    into me
    and set me on my feet,
    and I heard the one who was speaking
      say to me:
    Son of man, I am sending you to the
      Israelites,
    rebels who have rebelled against me;
    they and their ancestors have revolted
      against me to this very day.
Hard of face and obstinate of heart
    are they to whom I am sending you.
But you shall say to them: Thus says the
    Lord GOD!
And whether they heed or resist—for they
    are a rebellious house—
    they shall know that a prophet has been
      among them.

## RESPONSORIAL PSALM

Ps 123:1-2, 2, 3-4

R. (2cd) Our eyes are fixed on the Lord,
    pleading for his mercy.

To you I lift up my eyes
    who are enthroned in heaven—
as the eyes of servants
    are on the hands of their masters.

R. Our eyes are fixed on the Lord,
    pleading for his mercy.

As the eyes of a maid
    are on the hands of her mistress,
so are our eyes on the LORD, our God,
    till he have pity on us.

R. Our eyes are fixed on the Lord,
    pleading for his mercy.

Have pity on us, O LORD, have pity on us,
    for we are more than sated with
        contempt;
our souls are more than sated
    with the mockery of the arrogant,
    with the contempt of the proud.

R. Our eyes are fixed on the Lord,
    pleading for his mercy.

## SECOND READING

2 Cor 12:7-10

Brothers and sisters:
That I, Paul, might not become too elated,
    because of the abundance of the
        revelations,
    a thorn in the flesh was given to me, an
        angel of Satan,
    to beat me, to keep me from being too
        elated.
Three times I begged the Lord about this,
    that it might leave me,
    but he said to me, "My grace is
        sufficient for you,
    for power is made perfect in weakness."
I will rather boast most gladly of my
        weaknesses,
    in order that the power of Christ may
        dwell with me.
Therefore, I am content with weaknesses,
        insults,
    hardships, persecutions, and
        constraints,
    for the sake of Christ;
    for when I am weak, then I am strong.

### About Liturgy

***The view from the pew:*** A pastor sent out a survey to all his parish staff members to find out their perception of the quality of its liturgies. In general, most of the leaders—other priests, deacons, pastoral associates, and directors—ranked their liturgies fairly high. They saw their music as excellent in encouraging assembly participation. The preaching was above average and usually connected in a significant way to the lives of the parishioners. Their assemblies were welcoming communities where people felt like they mattered and they knew one another. The same survey was later sent to the parish leaders who served as volunteers for the many liturgical, catechetical, and pastoral ministries. These were the people you could count on every Sunday to sit in the front pews, be engaged in the Mass, and stay afterward to connect with friends and do other parish activities. They, too, like the staff members, tended to rank their parish's Sunday liturgies, in general, good to excellent in all areas.

Finally, the survey was sent to anyone and everyone in the pews over the course of several Sundays, so you had a wide range of responses from longtime parishioners, newcomers, one-time visitors, and back-row Catholics. The results were markedly different. People said the music, in general, was good, but most of the time they just listened because they didn't really know the songs or feel encouraged to sing. Most people couldn't say how the homily connected to their lives, but they really enjoyed Father's jokes. Lastly, many people said in general they felt welcomed, but other than their family or the friends they came with, no one else had a conversation with them that day at the parish or personally invited them to do something more beyond Mass.

Our point of view in the liturgy matters. If we're regularly up in front, at a mic, or in a position of authority in the parish, we will see a whole different view of the Sunday Mass than the person who sits in the back row, who comes in late, leaves early, or is there only because of culture, obligation, or habit. Neither perspective is a complete or accurate assessment of the parish or of what the parish does on Sunday. But our responsibility as liturgical leaders is to try to break out of our familiarity and bias with our experience and to see our parish liturgy from the perspective of those who are most often left out in the decision-making and whose voices are never heard or solicited—the outsider, the visitor, the seeker, the immigrant, and the ones we label as uninterested or uncommitted.

### About Liturgical Music

***Seeing the assembly as the choir:*** A 1982 United States bishops' document on liturgical music said, "The entire worshiping assembly exercises a ministry of music" (Liturgical Music Today, 63). Later in a 2007 document, the US bishops said, "The choir must not minimize the musical participation of the faithful. The congregation commonly sings unison melodies, which are more suitable for generally unrehearsed community singing. This is the primary song of the Liturgy" (Sing to the Lord, 28).

The assembly is the primary music minister, and their song is the primary song of the liturgy. The choir and other music ministers serve to support and enhance the song of the primary music makers.

One way choir members and music leaders can get a new perspective on how well they are doing in supporting the assembly's song is simply by sitting among the assembly every so often. Summer is the perfect time to do so. Have choir members sit in the pews throughout the church instead of in the choir area, and have them listen for, support, and appreciate even more the sound of the assembly.

**JULY 8, 2018**

# FOURTEENTH SUNDAY IN ORDINARY TIME

## ✚ SPIRITUALITY

**GOSPEL ACCLAMATION**
cf. Eph 1:17-18

℟. Alleluia, alleluia.
May the Father of our Lord Jesus Christ
enlighten the eyes of our hearts,
that we may know what is the hope that
belongs to our call.
℟. Alleluia, alleluia.

## Gospel

Mark 6:7-13; L104B

Jesus summoned the Twelve and
  began to send them out two
  by two
  and gave them authority over
    unclean spirits.
He instructed them to take nothing
  for the journey
  but a walking stick—
  no food, no sack, no money in
    their belts.
They were, however, to wear sandals
  but not a second tunic.
He said to them,
  "Wherever you enter a house, stay
    there until you leave.
Whatever place does not welcome you
  or listen to you,
  leave there and shake the dust off
    your feet
  in testimony against them."
So they went off and preached
  repentance.
The Twelve drove out many demons,
  and they anointed with oil many who
    were sick and cured them.

### Reflecting on the Gospel

"Discipleship" is a word tossed out quite often in Christian circles. The word "disciple" connotes follower, and being a follower is not something that is praised in our modern culture, which puts a premium on leadership, executives, and "alpha" types. For a Christian there is only one "alpha," who is Jesus. No disciple of Jesus ever takes the place of the master. The disciples are always just that, disciples, followers.

Even though the disciples will never achieve the rank of master, in the Gospel of Mark today Jesus gives the Twelve authority. He sends them on mission in six groups of two. The very word mission means to be sent. This will be the model for Christian evangelization. They travel light, without bread, bag, or money. They rely solely upon the kindness and generosity of those they meet. They are to remain in one house until they leave, not "trading up" as it were the longer they stayed. Their preaching is basically that of John the Baptist and the early days of Jesus himself, "Repent."

In their preaching the disciples also exercised their authority over evil, over the demons, over sickness, and over the unclean spirits. The authority that Jesus shared with his disciples for this mission meant that they too, like him, were agents of inclusion. They brought those from the margins into a relationship of wholeness. Like him, their deeds were coupled with preaching. The demand for repentance was paramount; and we can surmise that the demand was not received well by all, as Jesus' instructions for "shak[ing] the dust off your feet" indicate.

Not all disciples were chosen for this mission, but only the Twelve. The mission is to go out preaching and performing works of mercy. This probably doesn't sound much like parish plans today for the "new evangelization." But this is the "mission of the Twelve" and we might find something worthy of emulation here.

### Living the Paschal Mystery

How important is it for us to have a friend, a life partner, a spouse? A friend can be there to urge us on when the going is tough, to celebrate our victories and accomplishments with us. A friend is someone in whom we can take joy by celebrating their well-being. And when a friend suffers, we too suffer. A friendship is a gift of God.

Jesus too recognizes how important it is to have a partner. He sends the Twelve out two-by-two. These disciples are not lone wolves; they are not renegade rangers. They travel with one another for mutual support, which will likely form a bond of friendship if it were not there already.

Being called to be in a relationship with Jesus is to be also in a relationship with other disciples. None of us is on this path alone, and thank God for that.

The Christian life can never be a "Jesus and me" relationship. It always, and by necessity, involves other Christians, if not other people altogether.

Even the Twelve, chosen by name to be with Jesus in a more intimate relationship with him and one another, are not sole actors. They travel together two-by-two.

Who are my partners? Who travels with me two-by-two? This might be a good day to thank God and thank my partner.

### Focusing the Gospel
*Mark 6:7-13*
In today's gospel, the Twelve are sent out by Jesus to preach repentance and minister to the sick and those possessed by demons. These unlikely candidates for such a task are carefully prepared and taught by Jesus for this moment. They undertake their first preaching and healing tour, depending only on God for their inspiration and on the charity of others for their needs (remember that hospitality was considered a sacred responsibility in the East: it was not up to the stranger to seek hospitality but up to the prospective host to offer it). Jesus warns them to be prepared for the same rejection he has experienced from those they seek to serve.

### Focusing the First Reading
*Amos 7:12-15*
Today's first reading recounts the call of another unlikely prophet, Amos, a simple "shepherd and a dresser of sycamores." Despite his doubts about his abilities to do what God has called him to take on, Amos, the wise and earthy farmer, leaves his flocks and sycamores to proclaim the justice of God to the northern kingdom of Israel.

### Focusing the Responsorial Psalm
*Ps 85:9-10, 11-12, 13-14 (8)*
Psalm 85 was probably written a short time after the exiles returned to Jerusalem from Babylon. The city is in shambles and the once productive land is devastated; many believe that God has abandoned them. The psalmist offers this prayer not just for the rebuilding of their city and nation but for the restoration of their covenant of justice on which their nation was founded.

### Focusing the Second Reading
*Eph 1:3-14 (shorter form: 1:3-10)*
Today begins a series of passages from Paul's letter to the Ephesians, one of Paul's captivity epistles (though it is uncertain whether this letter was written by Paul himself or by someone writing on his behalf). The apostle spent two years with the Christian community at Ephesus, a port city on the Aegean coast in what is now western Turkey, but many scholars believe that this letter, given its strong theological bent and rather impersonal tone, was addressed to the larger church. Today's reading is the introduction to the letter, an opening that is both a prayer of blessing and a theological discourse on Christ as the revelation of God's love and wisdom and the church as the reflection of that revelation, themes the writer will develop throughout the course of the letter.

---

**PROMPTS FOR HOMILISTS, CATECHISTS, AND RCIA TEAMS**

Have you known prophets whose lives proclaimed the love of God, who followed Christ in their simple generosity and compassion for others?

Can you identify with Amos's lack of confidence in his call to be a prophet, with the Twelve's reluctance to set off on their first mission?

When have you experienced true repentance—when you found the grace and courage to change course in your life?

### *Model Penitential Act*

*Presider:* Let us begin our celebration of these sacred mysteries by calling to mind our sins. *[pause]*

Lord Jesus, in your love we become children of God: Lord, have mercy.

Lord Jesus, by your blood we experience God's grace and forgiveness: Christ, have mercy.

Lord Jesus, in the light of your wisdom we are sealed in the Holy Spirit: Lord, have mercy.

### Homily Points

• In Scripture, repentance is understood as more than feeling badly about what we have done (or not done); repentance is not just guilt or remorse. Repentance, in the gospel sense, is to acknowledge our failings with the resolve to move beyond them to a whole, more God-centered life. Repentance is a determined, focused action: to start over, to turn around, to change direction, to rethink one's attitude and perspective. In the gospel scheme of things, repentance is the beginning of realizing the kingdom of God in our lives, the re-creation of our loves in God's grace.

• In sending the Twelve on their first mission, Jesus instructs them to "travel light"—to focus on the journey and the ministry with which they have been entrusted, not on accumulating wealth, status, and power along the way. Clearing out the clutter of our lives in order to make room in our consciences for the more important values of God is a constant struggle for people of faith. But we have been called by Jesus to focus our lives on the treasures given us by God—love, reconciliation, forgiveness, compassion, generosity, mercy—that are found within our hearts and nurtured in a commitment to humble service to others.

• Like the journey of the Twelve through the region of Galilee and Amos's journey to Judah, our lives are journeys to the dwelling place of God. In breathing his life into us, God sets us on our journey of becoming the people God has called us to be. As we journey through this life, we can bring the hope and healing of "heaven" to others or we can be a source of the anger and despair that is sheer "hell"; we can expel the "demons" that destroy community and happiness or serve the "demons" of intolerance and selfishness. We are all called by God to the vocation of prophet (one who proclaims) and disciple (one who follows). It is a call to proclaim, in our places of work, study, and play, the good news of Christ, to follow him in his vision of justice, peace, and reconciliation.

### *Model Universal Prayer (Prayer of the Faithful)*

*Presider:* Let us now join our hearts and voices in prayer for all who journey with us to the kingdom of God.

*Response:* Lord, hear our prayer.

That all who serve our church as pastors, teachers, and counselors may be prophets of God's mercy and justice . . .

That all peoples, nations, and communities may safeguard the dignity due all men, women, and children as sons and daughters of God . . .

That the sick, the suffering, the addicted, and the dying may know the healing presence of Christ in our compassion and care . . .

That our parish's prayer and work may bring peace and healing to our community . . .

*Presider:* O God, you reveal your limitless love to us in the compassion and forgiveness we give and receive. Hear these prayers and instill in us your grace so that we may be the means for realizing these prayers. In Jesus' name, we pray. **Amen.**

**COLLECT**

Let us pray.

*Pause for silent prayer*

O God, who show the light of your truth
to those who go astray,
so that they may return to the right path,
give all who for the faith they profess
are accounted Christians
the grace to reject whatever is contrary to
the name of Christ
and to strive after all that does it honor.
Through our Lord Jesus Christ, your Son,
who lives and reigns with you in the unity
of the Holy Spirit,
one God, for ever and ever. **Amen.**

**FIRST READING**
Amos 7:12-15

Amaziah, priest of Bethel, said to Amos,
"Off with you, visionary, flee to the land
of Judah!
There earn your bread by prophesying,
but never again prophesy in Bethel;
for it is the king's sanctuary and a royal
temple."
Amos answered Amaziah, "I was no
prophet,
nor have I belonged to a company of
prophets;
I was a shepherd and a dresser of
sycamores.
The LORD took me from following the
flock, and said to me,
Go, prophesy to my people Israel."

**RESPONSORIAL PSALM**
Ps 85:9-10, 11-12, 13-14

R̲ʔ. (8) Lord, let us see your kindness, and
grant us your salvation.

I will hear what God proclaims;
the LORD—for he proclaims peace.
Near indeed is his salvation to those who
fear him,
glory dwelling in our land.

R̲ʔ. Lord, let us see your kindness, and
grant us your salvation.

Kindness and truth shall meet;
justice and peace shall kiss.
Truth shall spring out of the earth,
and justice shall look down from
heaven.

R̲ʔ. Lord, let us see your kindness, and
grant us your salvation.

The LORD himself will give his benefits;
   our land shall yield its increase.
Justice shall walk before him,
   and prepare the way of his steps.

℟. Lord, let us see your kindness, and
   grant us your salvation.

**SECOND READING**
Eph 1:3-14

Blessed be the God and Father of our Lord
      Jesus Christ,
   who has blessed us in Christ
   with every spiritual blessing in the
      heavens,
   as he chose us in him, before the
      foundation of the world,
   to be holy and without blemish before
      him.
In love he destined us for adoption to
      himself through Jesus Christ,
   in accord with the favor of his will,
   for the praise of the glory of his grace
   that he granted us in the beloved.

In him we have redemption by his blood,
   the forgiveness of transgressions,
   in accord with the riches of his grace
      that he lavished upon us.
In all wisdom and insight, he has made
      known to us
   the mystery of his will in accord with
      his favor
   that he set forth in him as a plan for the
      fullness of times,
   to sum up all things in Christ, in heaven
      and on earth.

In him we were also chosen,
   destined in accord with the purpose of
      the One
   who accomplishes all things according
      to the intention of his will,
   so that we might exist for the praise of
      his glory,
   we who first hoped in Christ.
In him you also, who have heard the word
      of truth,
   the gospel of your salvation, and have
      believed in him,
   were sealed with the promised Holy
      Spirit,
   which is the first installment of our
      inheritance
   toward redemption as God's possession,
      to the praise of his glory.

*or* Eph 1:3-10

*See Appendix A, p. 300.*

## About Liturgy

***Sent out on mission:*** We get the word "Mass" from the concluding words of the Mass in Latin: "Ite, missa est," literally translated as "Go, it is the dismissal." In this context, it makes more sense to say we *go from* Mass rather than we *go to* Mass, since Mass is essentially one giant sending forth on mission!

In fact, some liturgical theologians would say that the most important part of the Mass and its most important mandate is the dismissal and all its various forms: "Go forth, the Mass is ended"; "Go and announce the Gospel of the Lord"; "Go in peace, glorifying the Lord by your life"; "Go in peace." If, having heard God's word and shared in the Body and Blood of Christ, we do not live the Gospel and preach it in peace to the world by our words and actions, then we are merely doing ritualism, busywork meaning nothing. Saint John Paul II said it this way in his apostolic letter on the Eucharist: "We cannot delude ourselves: by our mutual love and, in particular, by our concern for those in need we will be recognized as true followers of Christ. This will be the criterion by which the authenticity of our Eucharistic celebrations is judged" (*Mane Nobiscum Domine* 28). For our Eucharist, for Mass, to be authentic, we must go out to the edges of society, what Pope Francis calls the "existential peripheries," and preach the good news, heal the sick, reconnect those who have been tossed aside by society, and rely only on the authority of Christ and the goodness of those with whom we break bread, our companions along the way.

## About Initiation

***The dismissal of catechumens:*** Once an unbaptized person becomes a catechumen, they are to be "kindly dismissed before the liturgy of the Eucharist begins" (RCIA 75.3). The meaning of this dismissal is similar to the dismissal given to the baptized at the very end of the Mass. Here, the catechumens are to go and announce the Gospel of the Lord. They do this by sharing their joy and spiritual experiences with one another (RCIA 67) and by spreading the Gospel and building up the church "by the witness of their lives and by professing their faith" (RCIA 75.4). Catechumens are dismissed not simply because they cannot yet pray the prayers of the faithful (the Creed, the universal prayer, the eucharistic prayer) or share in Communion; they are dismissed, like us, to glorify God by their lives so that when they eventually come to the eucharistic banquet, their Eucharist will be authentic because of their love and concern for those in need.

## About Liturgical Music

***Two-by-two:*** Normatively, the psalmist, like the lector, exercises this role alone. That is, usually only one person leads the responsorial psalm in dialogue with the assembly. However, a good way to help train new cantors in leading the psalm, especially those who may be younger or need a bit more direct support, is to schedule two people to lead the psalm together from the ambo. Both might intone the refrain and, if needed, use their arms (one with the left; the other with the right) to lead the assembly into each refrain. They also might sing the verses together, or alternate verses with one another. It would be best if they did not move back and forth between the microphone so as to avoid any visual distraction. Have them practice standing together in such a way that they can both access the microphone adequately without additional movement.

The goal is to build up the confidence and skills of new cantors. Therefore, once they are ready, they should be encouraged to lead the psalm on their own.

## ✝ SPIRITUALITY

### GOSPEL ACCLAMATION
John 10:27

℟. Alleluia, alleluia.
My sheep hear my voice, says the Lord;
I know them, and they follow me.
℟. Alleluia, alleluia.

### Gospel

Mark 6:30-34; L107B

The apostles gathered to-
gether with Jesus
and reported all they had
done and taught.
He said to them,
"Come away by yourselves
to a deserted place and
rest a while."
People were coming and going
in great numbers,
and they had no opportunity
even to eat.
So they went off in the boat by
themselves to a deserted
place.
People saw them leaving and many
came to know about it.
They hastened there on foot from all
the towns
and arrived at the place before them.

When he disembarked and saw the vast
crowd,
his heart was moved with pity for
them,
for they were like sheep without a
shepherd;
and he began to teach them many
things.

### Reflecting on the Gospel

The feeding of the multitudes is one of the few stories that are told in all four gospels. It must have made an impact on the early disciples, and it continues to impact us. The story is about how Jesus fulfills humanity's need for food, but at a much deeper level it's also about Jesus fulfilling humanity's most fundamental needs beyond food.

By this time in the gospel narrative Jesus has attracted such attention he can get no "down time." Even when he and his disciples try to get away, the crowd flocks to them, like the ancient paparazzi! Jesus meets them, has compassion on them, and teaches them. All of this is a prelude to the multiplication of the loaves in Mark's gospel (6:35-44), but next week we will hear John's version instead.

But in Mark's gospel, by the end of the day, the disciples display an attitude familiar to us: These people will want something to eat. Is that our problem? Let's get this crowd on the road so they can fend for themselves. The disciples seem indignant at Jesus' command to feed the crowd. In response, Jesus takes the loaves and fishes and feeds the crowd in language that can certainly be described as eucharistic. There are four hallmark verbs used in this story that are also used in our eucharistic prayer: *took* loaves (bread), *blessed* and *broke* them, and *gave* them to the disciples. Jesus satisfies the deepest longings of the human spirit. In providing them food, they ate and were satisfied. And there were leftovers! Jesus is an abundant giver. The cup runneth over.

This story echoes the prophet Elisha from 2 Kings 4:42-44, where Elisha commanded another man to give his twenty loaves and some grain to a hundred men. Not unlike the disciples, this man was incredulous that the few loaves would feed so many. But, in fact, all were fed and there was more left over. The gospel writers certainly had Elisha in mind when telling the story about Jesus. Some scholars believe Jesus himself had Elisha in mind when feeding the crowd. Perhaps for this reason Jesus was called a prophet by some of his contemporaries, for he acted as the prophets such as Elisha. Also, it is significant that in the story Jesus sees that the crowd was "like sheep without a shepherd"—this line is used frequently in the Old Testament (Num 27:17; 1 Kgs 22:17; 2 Chr 18:16; Isa 13:14). The image invokes pastoral imagery rooted in Sacred Scripture. Jesus takes the role of shepherd of this flock, giving them sustenance by his teaching and the multiplication of loaves and fishes.

Often it is heard that the miracle presented here is really one where the five thousand shared the food they had already brought to the place. However, such an interpretation misses both the clear allusion to the prophet Elisha story and the plain sense of the gospel story. Jesus provides more than enough to satisfy humanity's deepest needs both physical and spiritual.

### Living the Paschal Mystery

When we are in a relationship with Jesus, we will always have more than enough. Despite any claims to the contrary, Jesus himself will provide an abundance. Our needs will be met and we will be satisfied. When facing other people's dire circumstances, it can be a challenge not to respond as the disciples did in this gospel story: Why is this my problem? Let them fend for themselves. But we hear Jesus' command to the disciples as a command to us: "Give them some food yourselves" (Mark 6:37, NABRE). Even though the conditions may seem overwhelming, as Christians we are to do something. Once we start, God provides more than enough to accomplish the task. Giving in to hopelessness or callousness is not the response expected of a disciple of Christ.

### Focusing the Gospel

*Mark 6:30-34*

The Twelve return from their first mission of preaching and healing and report to Jesus. He gathers them in a "deserted" place to rest and regroup, but the people find them and keep coming. Even their attempt to escape by boat to the other side of the lake is foiled once word gets out.

This incident recorded by Mark in today's gospel (which precedes his account of the feeding of the multitude) offers two important insights into our church's ministry: The mission of the church does not spring from mass marketing techniques or publicity strategies but from the Gospel of compassion we seek to live and share, from the authority of our commitment to forgiveness and reconciliation. Leadership, inspired by the wisdom of God, means not dictating and ruling over others but inspiring, providing for, and selflessly caring for those whom we are called to lead.

### Focusing the First Reading

*Jer 23:1-6*

In his compassion for the crowd, Jesus becomes the wise and just "shepherd" envisioned by Jeremiah in today's first reading. Jeremiah sternly rebukes Israel's "shepherds," whose self-serving and ineffective leadership have deeply divided the nation. Jeremiah prophesies a new ruler for Israel, "a righteous shoot to David," who will "reign and govern wisely" and justly. That vision is realized in Jesus' compassion for the crowd in today's gospel.

### Focusing the Responsorial Psalm

*Ps 23:1-3, 3-4, 5, 6 (1)*

In the images of the compassionate shepherd who leads the people entrusted to him and the generous host of a great banquet welcoming all, the psalmist sings of his unfailing trust in the constant providence of God.

### Focusing the Second Reading

*Eph 2:13-18*

In today's reading from Ephesians, the apostle praises Christ as "our peace" who reconciles us to God and to one another. In him, we are able to break down the walls that divide Jew and Gentile, a reconciliation to which Paul was especially dedicated.

---

**PROMPTS FOR HOMILISTS, CATECHISTS, AND RCIA TEAMS**

Who are the "shepherds" in our culture who lead us away from God? What voices should we listen to in our search for God?

What attitudes, gifts, and skills make for a good leader?

Do you have a "deserted place" in your life?

What should we expect and seek from our belonging to a church community?

### Model Penitential Act

*Presider:* With humility and hope, let us ask God's forgiveness and peace for our sins and failings. *[pause]*

Lord, you are our Shepherd and guide: Lord, have mercy.

Lord, you walk with us in times of darkness: Christ, have mercy.

Lord, you spread your table of blessing before us: Lord, have mercy.

### Homily Points

• The "deserted place" can be a physical place of solitude; or it can be time we set aside to realize God's presence and feel grateful for God's grace. Our spirits need quiet deserts and sacred time to escape the demands of our calendars and "to-do" lists to experience God's peace, listen to God's voice in the quiet of our hearts, and realize God's presence in our lives in the love of family and friends. Jesus invites us to find spaces of prayer and make quiet time in our days to re-center our lives in the grace of God, to hear again the voice of Christ the Shepherd calling us to lives of joyful gratitude and fulfilling service.

• In our heeding those "shepherds" in our society who affirm and rationalize our fears, who give us "enemies" to direct our fears and promise to vanquish them for us, who reduce the complexities of life to simple rules and absolutes, we are the "shepherdless" for whom Jesus' heart breaks. In his Christ, God has raised up for us a Shepherd who leads us in our search, not for the empty riches of consumerism, but for the priceless treasures of compassion and reconciliation; a Shepherd who guides us in negotiating life's rough crags and dangerous drop-offs to make our way to God's eternal pasture of peace; a Shepherd who journeys with us to clear the obstacles of fear and self-interest in order to live lives centered in what is right and just.

• In the midst of recessions and terror, estrangements and despair, the voice of Christ the "Shepherd" calls us to see beyond our own disappointments and hurts to realize all we have to be grateful for and the many opportunities we have to be God's agents of grace bringing hope and healing into the lives of others. In turn, we become "shepherds," entrusted by God to care for one another as he cares for us, to be the means for others to experience God's grace in their lives.

### Model Universal Prayer (Prayer of the Faithful)

*Presider:* In the name of Christ Jesus, who is our peace, let us offer our prayers to our Father in heaven.

That our church may be a gathering place for the "remnant" from all lands and peoples . . .

That our president and all leaders may govern wisely and unite their nations and peoples in God's justice and peace . . .

That the anguish of the poor, oppressed, and imprisoned may be transformed into hope through our compassionate help . . .

That our deceased relatives and friends *[especially . . .]* may dwell forever in the house of God . . .

*Presider:* Hear these prayers we offer, O God, and gather us together in your peace to be about the work of reconciliation and mercy. We ask these things in the name of your Son, Jesus Christ, our Shepherd and peace. **Amen.**

Let us pray.

*Pause for silent prayer*

Show favor, O Lord, to your servants
and mercifully increase the gifts of your
    grace,
that, made fervent in hope, faith and
    charity,
they may be ever watchful in keeping your
    commands.
Through our Lord Jesus Christ, your Son,
who lives and reigns with you in the unity
    of the Holy Spirit,
one God, for ever and ever. **Amen.**

**FIRST READING**
Jer 23:1-6

Woe to the shepherds
    who mislead and scatter the flock of my
        pasture,
    says the Lord.
Therefore, thus says the Lord, the God of
    Israel,
    against the shepherds who shepherd
        my people:
    You have scattered my sheep and driven
        them away.
You have not cared for them,
    but I will take care to punish your evil
        deeds.
I myself will gather the remnant of my
    flock
    from all the lands to which I have driven
        them
    and bring them back to their meadow;
    there they shall increase and multiply.
I will appoint shepherds for them who will
    shepherd them
    so that they need no longer fear and
        tremble;
    and none shall be missing, says the
        Lord.

Behold, the days are coming, says the
    Lord,
    when I will raise up a righteous shoot
        to David;
    as king he shall reign and govern
        wisely,
    he shall do what is just and right in
        the land.
In his days Judah shall be saved,
    Israel shall dwell in security.
    This is the name they give him:
        "The Lord our justice."

## RESPONSORIAL PSALM

Ps 23:1-3, 3-4, 5, 6

R̸. (1) The Lord is my shepherd; there is
    nothing I shall want.

The LORD is my shepherd; I shall not want.
    In verdant pastures he gives me repose;
beside restful waters he leads me;
    he refreshes my soul.

R̸. The Lord is my shepherd; there is
    nothing I shall want.

He guides me in right paths
    for his name's sake.
Even though I walk in the dark valley
    I fear no evil; for you are at my side
with your rod and your staff
    that give me courage.

R̸. The Lord is my shepherd; there is
    nothing I shall want.

You spread the table before me
    in the sight of my foes;
you anoint my head with oil;
    my cup overflows.

R̸. The Lord is my shepherd; there is
    nothing I shall want.

Only goodness and kindness follow me
    all the days of my life;
and I shall dwell in the house of the LORD
    for years to come.

R̸. The Lord is my shepherd; there is
    nothing I shall want.

## SECOND READING

Eph 2:13-18

Brothers and sisters:
In Christ Jesus you who once were far off
    have become near by the blood of
        Christ.

For he is our peace, he who made both one
    and broke down the dividing wall of
        enmity, through his flesh,
    abolishing the law with its
        commandments and legal claims,
    that he might create in himself one new
        person in place of the two,
    thus establishing peace,
    and might reconcile both with God,
    in one body, through the cross,
    putting that enmity to death by it.
He came and preached peace to you who
        were far off
    and peace to those who were near,
    for through him we both have access in
        one Spirit to the Father.

## About Liturgy

**Come away and rest:** If you are in charge of the liturgy at your parish or have any kind of significant leadership role in the Mass, you know that Sundays are not always a day of rest. There's a reason the Greek term for liturgy, *leitourgia*, means "work" or "service" for the people. Preparing liturgy is a lot of work!

We who put ourselves at the service of the church by serving the liturgy need to remember, however, that we are not Christ. We must come away with Christ to rest a while so that our work can be fruitful for our communities, our families, and ourselves. We can do this best by taking time each day in private prayer on our own where we are not preparing a script, rearranging environment, or coordinating volunteers. We simply attend to God's abiding presence and listen, which is the first act of prayer. If you do not already have a daily practice of prayer, consider doing prayerful reading of Scripture, praying the Liturgy of the Hours, practicing *lectio divina*, or doing some other form of contemplation that allows you to simply listen for God's voice.

Second, we need to care for and tend to the needs of our bodies. In fact, as liturgists, we should be the first to insist that care for our bodies parallels our care for the Body of Christ in the Eucharist. So we must eat healthy foods and not skip meals—eating should be a sacred act both within the liturgy and outside of it. We need to exercise and get enough sleep. We also need to take time for rest, recreation, and vacation. These are not just good ideas; they are our visible and public witness that God is God and we are not.

Finally, the Day of the Lord is a day of rest because it is a day set aside for rendering worship of God, being joyful as is proper to the Lord's Day, and experiencing relaxation of body and mind (Code of Canon Law, 1247). Participating in the Sunday liturgy is not a retreat from the world, as if it is the only time we have with God. Having this kind of attitude toward Sunday Mass makes it a very individualistic endeavor we need to protect instead of the ritual prayer joyfully shared in community that it is intended to be. Rather, entering deeply into the holiness of Sunday—with all its divine work given for God and others—is how God reorients our days to the way the world is meant to be seen, that is, abundantly filled with blessings and always in union with its Creator.

## About Liturgical Music

**Music suggestions:** This Sunday gives us an opportunity over the summer months to reflect on the image of Jesus as shepherd. We have many well-known settings of Psalm 23, which can be used for today's psalm response. Also, consider exploring other lesser-known settings of this text and imagery for use as hymns during other parts of the Mass. For example, Curtis Stephan's "Pastures of the Lord" (Spirit and Song, OCP) is a gentle, contemporary hymn that combines many images from Psalm 23 with a bit of text from the Canticle of Simeon (*Nunc Dimittis*), which is the gospel canticle at Night Prayer, or Compline. You might consider using this as a song for the preparation of gifts. Christopher Walker's "Because the Lord Is My Shepherd" (OCP) is a more poetic and personal rendering of the psalm. The simplicity of the refrain coupled with the lilting melody and complex meters of the verses makes this a good choice for intergenerational, "family" choirs that include both children and adults.

**JULY 22, 2018**
# SIXTEENTH SUNDAY
# IN ORDINARY TIME

## ✠ SPIRITUALITY

**GOSPEL ACCLAMATION**
Luke 7:16

℞. Alleluia, alleluia.
A great prophet has risen in our midst.
God has visited his people.
℞. Alleluia, alleluia.

### Gospel

John 6:1-15; L110B

**Jesus went across the Sea of Galilee.
A large crowd followed him,
   because they saw the signs he was
      performing on the sick.
Jesus went up on the mountain,
   and there he sat down with his
      disciples.
The Jewish feast of Passover was
   near.
When Jesus raised his eyes
   and saw that a large crowd was
      coming to him,
   he said to Philip,
"Where can we buy enough food for
      them to eat?"
He said this to test him,
   because he himself knew what he was
      going to do.
Philip answered him,
"Two hundred days' wages worth of
      food would not be enough
for each of them to have a little."
One of his disciples,
   Andrew, the brother of Simon Peter,
      said to him,
"There is a boy here who has five
      barley loaves and two fish;
but what good are these for so many?"
Jesus said, "Have the people recline."
Now there was a great deal of grass in
   that place.
So the men reclined, about five thousand
   in number.**

*Continued in Appendix A, p. 300.*

### Reflecting on the Gospel

Beginning today, the church gives us five weeks of Sunday gospel readings from John. It's as though we are taking a break from Mark to hear from another evangelist. Throughout these five weeks we will be reading from John chapter 6, wherein we have the multiplication of the loaves followed by Jesus' walking on water, and the bread of life discourse. The theology and symbolism in John 6 is profound and has inspired centuries of contemplation and rich exegesis. We remember that the story of the multiplication of loaves is told in each of the four gospels, the only "miracle story" shared by each.

Last week we heard Mark's setup to the feeding of the five thousand, but this week we hear John's version rather than Mark's. The two stories have many similarities: two hundred denarii, five loaves and two fish, the crowd numbering five thousand men, and twelve baskets of leftovers, to name a few. But there are some differences to the stories as well.

John's theology is ultimately Christology. John has an intense focus on Jesus. In Mark's version of the multiplication of the loaves, the disciples come to Jesus with their concern about moving the people along before they have to feed them. In John, Jesus takes the initiative in asking Philip about feeding the people. And there is something equivalent to an editorial note saying that Jesus asked this question only to test him. Again, John's gospel shows Jesus clearly in charge, clearly taking the lead, clearly in the driver's seat. Even when he asks a question it is merely to test someone.

The eucharistic overtones so prominent in Mark are also present in John but in a different way. Rather than for four key verbs used by Mark, John uses a Greek term for the "fragments" (*klasmata*) that were collected and gathered into the baskets. This Greek term is used by the *Didache* (an early church book written in the first century, parts of which are akin to a catechism) to speak of Eucharist.

Finally, upon witnessing this sign (the multiplication of the loaves) the crowd explicitly recognizes Jesus as a prophet. No doubt the story of the prophet Elisha and the multiplication of the loaves from 2 Kings 4:42-44 was in mind. Jesus realized the crowd wanted to make him a king, so he makes a speedy solo exit.

The multiplication of the loaves, with its eucharistic overtones, its prominence on Jesus and his fulfilling human needs, and the growing recognition by the crowds that he must be a prophet demonstrate how pivotal this episode was and continues to be.

### Living the Paschal Mystery

Jesus satisfies human needs. The story tells us that the crowds followed Jesus because they saw the signs he did on those who were diseased. After witnessing another sign they will recognize him as a prophet. The recognition on the part of the crowds is based on Jesus satisfying human needs.

We can be reminded of family life and dealing with children. Often as long as all needs (and wants) are met things can seem to be going along well. The children are satisfied. We will see later in this same chapter of John that Jesus asks something of the crowds and most abandon him. It's easy to follow Jesus when we are on the receiving end of his bounty and goodness. It's easy for children to be happy when they are on the receiving end of parents' bounty and goodness. But what happens when the crowds are asked to make a commitment? What happens when family members are asked to step up and take some responsibility?

Growing into adult discipleship means that there will come a time (if it hasn't come already) when we will no longer be simply on the receiving end of the relationship. We will be called to enter further into a relationship with Jesus that is more mutually reciprocal, though Jesus will always be the teacher and we will always be in the position of disciples. Jesus will call the crowds closer to the circle with him. It's easy to be a follower, or a member of the crowd receiving goodies. Soon, those crowds will be invited to go deeper.

## Focusing the Gospel
*John 6:1-15*
Today the Lectionary interrupts the semi-continuous readings from Mark's gospel. Over the next five Sundays, the gospel readings will be taken from chapter 6 from the Gospel of John, the bread of life discourse of Jesus. Several scholars have suggested that chapter 6 of John's gospel may have originally been the text of a homily or treatise by an early Christian teacher on the developing sacrament of the Eucharist.

Jesus' feeding of the multitude with scraps of bread and fish is the only miracle recorded in all four gospels. This story was cherished by the first Christians for whom the Eucharist was becoming the center of their life together. Jesus' actions are indeed "eucharistic": bread (and fish) is collected, Jesus gives thanks (the word used in the Greek text of Mark's gospel is *eucharisteo*) and breaks the bread, and the community feasts.

The gospel readings over the next few Sundays will invite us to consider the deeper meanings of Eucharist: Christ, the Bread of Life, present to us in this sacrament that is given to us in order that we might become sacrament for one another.

## Focusing the First Reading
*2 Kgs 4:42-44*
The first reading recounts the prophet Elisha's feeding of a hundred people (the number symbolic of totality) with only twenty barley loaves (and there is some left over). The faithful Elisha is convinced that God will provide for his people in the midst of famine and depravation.

## Focusing the Responsorial Psalm
*Ps 145:10-11, 15-16, 17-18 (see 16)*
In the last verses of Psalm 145, every element of creation gives praise to God its Maker, whose very holiness is contained in every living thing.

## Focusing the Second Reading
*Eph 4:1-6*
Jesus' transforming the hungry crowd into a eucharistic community in today's gospel mirrors Paul's exhortation to the church at Ephesus to "live in a manner worthy of the call you have received," to be one in God's spirit of love, humility, and peace.

**PROMPTS FOR HOMILISTS, CATECHISTS, AND RCIA TEAMS**

We are part of many communities in our lives: families, parishes, classes, sports teams, businesses, etc. What have been some of your most joyful and enriching experiences of community and what made them so?

What "small gifts" have you received that have made a big difference in your life?

How can your community take this Eucharist beyond the walls of your church? How can the Eucharist be experienced in places other than this church, in ways other than this liturgy?

## Model Penitential Act

*Presider:* As we gather at the Lord's table to celebrate this Eucharist, let us begin by acknowledging our sins and failings assured of God's reconciling love. *[pause]*

O God, you are near to all who call upon you: Lord, have mercy.

O God, you are holy in all your works: Christ, have mercy.

O God, you satisfy the needs of every living thing: Lord, have mercy.

## Homily Points

• With the miracle of the loaves and fish, Jesus transforms a crowd of all ages, abilities, and backgrounds into a community of generosity. That vision of being a eucharistic community is recreated each time we gather here. That is the challenge of the gospel and the mandate of the Eucharist that is foreshadowed in this miracle story: to take up the hard work of reconciliation and compassion begun by God, who dwells here on our own grassy plain; to humbly bring the peace of God's dwelling place into our own homes; to become the Body and Blood of Jesus that we receive at his table where all—saints and sinners—are welcomed.

• After feeding the crowds with the scraps of bread and fish, Jesus asks his disciples to gather up the leftovers. As the twelve wicker baskets of leftovers attested to the sign Jesus had worked, our own baskets of "fragments" are signs of the many blessings we have received in our lives. Today's gospel also challenges us to realize the many things we waste in our lives that can be the difference between life and death for our brothers and sisters: our stored "wicker baskets" of clothing, food, household goods, toys and, yes, money can become signs of God's loving providence for all his sons and daughters.

• The multiplication of the loaves and fish did not start with nothing: Jesus was able to feed the crowds because one boy was willing to share what little he had; from his gift, small though it was, Jesus worked a wonder. Eucharist is possible when self defers to community, when serving others is exalted over being served, when superficial differences dissolve and the common and shared are honored above all else. In the Eucharist of Christ, the humble Servant-Redeemer, we seek to become what we receive: one bread, one cup, one body, one family. We are called by Christ to become the Eucharist we receive at this altar: giving thanks for what we have received by sharing those gifts—our talents, our riches, ourselves—to work our own miracles of creating communities of joyful faith.

## Model Universal Prayer (Prayer of the Faithful)

*Presider:* To God, the Father of all, let us pray.

*Response:* Lord, hear our prayer.

That Christian churches and communities may celebrate their common identity in "one Lord, one faith, [and] one baptism" . . .

That all peoples of this planet may work together to protect the earth, providing for the poor, needy, and displaced . . .

That the sick, the suffering, and the dying may know, in our care and compassion, the healing presence of the risen Jesus . . .

That all children and young people may possess the generosity of the young boy who gives his bread and fish to Jesus . . .

*Presider:* One in spirit through the bond of peace, we join our hearts and voices in these prayers, O God. Grant them a favorable hearing and, by your grace, may we work together to make them a reality. In Jesus' name, we pray. **Amen.**

## COLLECT

Let us pray.

*Pause for silent prayer*

O God, protector of those who hope in you,
without whom nothing has firm foundation, nothing is holy,
bestow in abundance your mercy upon us
and grant that, with you as our ruler and guide,
we may use the good things that pass
in such a way as to hold fast even now
to those that ever endure.
Through our Lord Jesus Christ, your Son,
who lives and reigns with you in the unity of the Holy Spirit,
one God, for ever and ever. **Amen.**

## FIRST READING

2 Kgs 4:42-44

A man came from Baal-shalishah bringing to Elisha, the man of God,
twenty barley loaves made from the firstfruits,
and fresh grain in the ear.
Elisha said, "Give it to the people to eat."
But his servant objected,
"How can I set this before a hundred people?"
Elisha insisted, "Give it to the people to eat.
For thus says the LORD,
'They shall eat and there shall be some left over.'"
And when they had eaten, there was some left over,
as the LORD had said.

## RESPONSORIAL PSALM
Ps 145:10-11, 15-16, 17-18

R℣. (cf. 16) The hand of the Lord feeds us;
   he answers all our needs.

Let all your works give you thanks, O
   LORD,
   and let your faithful ones bless you.
Let them discourse of the glory of your
   kingdom
   and speak of your might.

R℣. The hand of the Lord feeds us; he
   answers all our needs.

The eyes of all look hopefully to you,
   and you give them their food in due
   season;
you open your hand
   and satisfy the desire of every living
   thing.

R℣. The hand of the Lord feeds us; he
   answers all our needs.

The LORD is just in all his ways
   and holy in all his works.
The LORD is near to all who call upon him,
   to all who call upon him in truth.

R℣. The hand of the Lord feeds us; he
   answers all our needs.

## SECOND READING
Eph 4:1-6

Brothers and sisters:
I, a prisoner for the Lord,
   urge you to live in a manner worthy of
      the call you have received,
   with all humility and gentleness, with
      patience,
   bearing with one another through love,
   striving to preserve the unity of the
      spirit through the bond of peace:
one body and one Spirit,
   as you were also called to the one hope
      of your call;
one Lord, one faith, one baptism;
one God and Father of all,
   who is over all and through all and in
      all.

## About Liturgy

**Bread of Life discourse:** This Sunday begins five Sundays in which the church reflects on Jesus, the Bread of Life, as found in John's gospel. This set of five Sundays gives us, especially homilists, lectors, music ministers, and catechists, an opportunity for intense and sustained focus on the Eucharist and what it means to be fed by Jesus, the Bread of Life. To make the most of these coming Sundays, be sure to meet together as a liturgical team to set a course for coordinated contemplation on the eucharistic mystery and the various aspects of our understanding of Eucharist. For example, all the homilists could work together to integrate their homilies over the next five weeks, building one upon the other. Lectors could support one another by spending time together in faith sharing and meal sharing so that the Word becomes true food for their ministry. Music directors could select a "seasonal" Communion song or some other seasonal hymn that unifies all these Sundays together. Catechists could work with bulletin editors to provide additional resources to take home over these Sundays for households to connect the eucharistic table to their dinner table.

**How many Communion ministers is enough?:** In Norms for the Distribution and Reception of Holy Communion under Both Kinds in the Dioceses of the United States of America, the US bishops state that "a suitable number of ministers of Holy Communion are provided at each Mass" (30). What determines the suitable number is the size of the assembly that will participate in Communion. A standard rule of thumb is to have one minister of the Body of Christ for every one hundred communicants. The Norms go on to recommend that there be "two ministers of the Precious Blood for each minister of the Body of Christ, lest the liturgical celebration be unduly prolonged" (30).

## About Liturgical Music

**When does the Communion song begin?:** Have you noticed a moment of silence (sometimes a very long moment of silence) after the priest's invitation to Communion and the response by the assembly, "Lord, I am not worthy . . . " before the Communion song begins? The reason most music ministers give for this pause is that they (or the priest) feel it is irreverent for them to begin singing while the priest is taking Communion for himself. Therefore, they wait until after the priest has received or even until after all the Communion ministers are in place for distributing Communion to the assembly. Some even use this as the time to send the choir to Communion, thereby prolonging the beginning of the Communion song even further!

All this, however, goes against what is called for in the *General Instruction of the Roman Missal*: "While the Priest is receiving the Sacrament, the Communion Chant is begun . . . " (86). The Communion song begins *while the priest is receiving*, not after he has received. Synchronizing the start of the song with the reception of Communion by the priest teaches us that there is *one* Communion, not a separate one for "Father" and a separate one for everyone else. There is one bread, one Body, "one Lord, one faith, one baptism; / one God and Father of all, / who is over all and through all and in all" (Eph 4:5-6).

## ✠ SPIRITUALITY

**GOSPEL ACCLAMATION**
Matt 4:4b

℟. Alleluia, alleluia.
One does not live on bread alone, but by every
word that comes forth from the mouth of God.
℟. Alleluia, alleluia.

### Gospel

John 6:24-35; L113B

When the crowd saw that neither
    Jesus nor his disciples were
    there,
they themselves got into boats
and came to Capernaum looking
    for Jesus.
And when they found him across
    the sea they said to him,
    "Rabbi, when did you get here?"
Jesus answered them and said,
    "Amen, amen, I say to you,
    you are looking for me not because
        you saw signs
    but because you ate the loaves and
        were filled.
Do not work for food that perishes
    but for the food that endures for
        eternal life,
    which the Son of Man will give you.
For on him the Father, God, has set his
    seal."
So they said to him,
    "What can we do to accomplish the
        works of God?"
Jesus answered and said to them,
    "This is the work of God, that you
        believe in the one he sent."
So they said to him,
    "What sign can you do, that we may
        see and believe in you?
What can you do?
Our ancestors ate manna in the desert,
    as it is written:
    *He gave them bread from heaven to
        eat.*"

*Continued in Appendix A, p. 300.*

### Reflecting on the Gospel

Sourdough, pumpernickel, rye, whole wheat, ancient grain, pita, white, and many more are the breads from which we can choose in our modern, convenient grocery stores. Variety and selection are the hallmarks of our society. It's sometimes easy to forget how basic bread was to an ancient culture. It certainly wasn't a specialty item that afforded choice and distinction. Bread was the staple of life, consumed daily as an essential source of nutrition.

The day after the "multiplication of the loaves" the people were still seeking Jesus and found him in Capernaum. He admonishes them to seek not perishable food but the food of everlasting life. They only need to believe in him. The people, having just witnessed the sign of the multiplication of loaves the day before, wonder what further sign Jesus might give them. Irony, which is a hallmark of John's gospel, should not be lost.

The people demand a sign similar to Moses providing manna in the desert. At that time the Hebrew people had left Egypt and were wandering in the desert. They were fed by bread from heaven that appeared each morning. Jesus in turn reminds them that it was not Moses, but the Father who gives "true bread from heaven." Jesus' addition of the word "true" is significant. In a double entendre, Jesus says that the true bread "comes down from heaven and gives life to the world." This sets the stage for his claim at the conclusion of the reading, that Jesus himself is the Bread of Life.

Throughout the Gospel of John, Jesus is portrayed as the one who comes down from heaven. He is the one who gives life. This is a remarkable teaching, for Jesus refers to himself as having come down from heaven. Essentially, this is a teaching reflecting the prologue of John's gospel, "In the beginning was the Word, / and the Word was with God" (1:1, NABRE) and "the Word became flesh" (1:14, NABRE). No other gospel makes such a claim. Johannine theology is Christology. The true bread from heaven that gives eternal life is none other than Jesus himself, the Word of God made flesh.

### Living the Paschal Mystery

In the midst of such rich theological and christological statements that we find in the gospel reading today, what are we to do? The response that Jesus demands of us in this gospel is what was demanded of those who heard the discourse: Believe in the one whom the Father has sent. That, of course, is Jesus. We are called to recognize and believe that God the Father sent him into the world. Once we believe that, our lives will never be the same.

In this story we have no ethical demands, no commandments, no imperatives other than "believe." It's as though once we do accept and believe this fundamental reality, the morals and ethics will naturally flow from that. So we reflect on the mystery of the incarnation, the coming down from heaven to live among us, the bread of everlasting life. How are our lives different because of this belief?

## Focusing the Gospel

*John 6:24-35*

Jesus is speaking to two groups here: those who witnessed the miracle of the loaves (last Sunday's gospel) and those who did not see the miracle but have heard about it and want to see a similar sign. To the first group, Jesus tells them that there is something much deeper in this event than "food that perishes" being multiplied; the real "food" is the word of God proclaimed, its power and authority manifested in the miracles of the loaves.

To those who seek a sign as the Israelites sought a sign from Moses, Jesus reminds them that it was not Moses himself but God who provided their "grumbling" exodus ancestors with bread in the desert (recalled in today's first reading from Exodus). In Jesus, the Bread of Life, God gives his people true bread, which leads to everlasting life.

## Focusing the First Reading

*Exod 16:2-4, 12-15*

As noted above, today's first reading is the story of God's "raining down" manna in the desert for the starving Israelites as they begin their wilderness journey to the land promised them by God. Manna (in Hebrew the word means "what is it?") was actually the sweet-tasting honeydew secreted by insects that fed on the sap of tamarisk trees. In the dry desert air each morning, most of the moisture of the secreted substance would evaporate, leaving sticky droplets on the ground and plants that the Israelites would collect each morning. In this way the Israelites saw that God provided "bread from heaven" for them during their sojourn in the wilderness.

## Focusing the Responsorial Psalm

*Ps 78:3-4, 23-24, 25, 54 (24b)*

Psalm 78 is unique among the psalms in that it is more a teaching narrative than a song of praise. The psalm is a retelling of the story of the exodus, God's leading the Israelites from slavery in Egypt to freedom in their own country; the psalm memorializes for future generations the history of God's leading their ancestors and establishing the nation that is now their homeland. The verses selected for today's responsorial recount God's sustaining the Israelites with manna in the desert.

## Focusing the Second Reading

*Eph 4:17, 20-24*

Today's reading from Paul's letter to the Ephesians has a clear baptismal dimension. Former "Gentile" ways of life and attitudes must be put aside if one is to "put on the new self" that is the justice and peace of God in the risen Christ.

---

**PROMPTS FOR HOMILISTS, CATECHISTS, AND RCIA TEAMS**

Have you ever placed your trust in what you thought was "imperishable," but in the end proved to be very "perishable"?

What difference does the Eucharist make in your life that could not be fulfilled by other forms of prayer?

What forms of "manna" have "rained down" in your life?

In what real ways do we "become" the Body and Blood of Christ for others?

## Model Penitential Act

*Presider:* Trusting in the mercy of God, let us begin our celebration of the Eucharist by acknowledging our sins and failings. *[pause]*

Lord Jesus, the Bread of Life: Lord, have mercy.

Lord Jesus, Light of God's wisdom: Christ, have mercy.

Lord Jesus, Word of the Father's love: Lord, have mercy.

## Homily Points

• In today's gospel, Jesus' hearers want more "signs"—more of the "bread" that will fill their day-to-day hunger. But Jesus challenges them to go deeper than the loaves themselves: to realize the compassion of God in the miracle and the possibilities each one of them has to be that same "bread" of hope and generosity for one another. A life of true joy and meaning is driven not by "perishable" material things and fleeting experiences but by the "nonperishable" values of God.

• Perhaps the most difficult challenge of our time is to accomplish the "work" of God while "working" to establish and succeed in our careers, to make a place in our homes and hearts for the "bread" that is Christ amid the "fast food" being shoved in our faces from every direction. Jesus calls us to move beyond our desire for instant gratification and quick fixes and discover the word of God creating and animating our lives and our world. This is the "bread of heaven" that Jesus speaks of in today's gospel: selfless compassion, grace, and gratitude—the food that will not perish, the food that nurtures all that is good, the food that sustains us on our journey to meaning and purpose.

• The Eucharist demands more than the opening of our hands to take and our mouths to consume—the Eucharist demands that we open our hearts and spirits, as well, so that we may become what we receive. To receive the Eucharist worthily, we must not only consume the sacrament but allow ourselves to be consumed by the sacrament. In the profound simplicity of the bread and wine of the Eucharist, we are called to become the Christ we receive: Christ the servant, Christ the reconciler, Christ the wisdom and life of God.

## Model Universal Prayer (Prayer of the Faithful)

*Presider:* To our loving Father who calls us to this holy meal, let us pray.

*Response:* Lord, hear our prayer.

For Pope N., Bishop N., and all who serve and minister to our church, that they may model "righteousness and holiness of truth" . . .

That all nations, peoples, and races may find unity, understanding, and trust in the God and Father of all who is over all and is in all . . .

For those whose lives are in transition, for those who are coping with loss or hardship, that God will be bread for them on their journeys . . .

For our parish, that we may be a living sign of God's love in our community and world . . .

*Presider:* You have done great things for us, O Lord; rejoicing in the many blessings you have given us, we come to you with these prayers, confident, in faith, that you will hear them. In Jesus' name, we pray. **Amen.**

## COLLECT

Let us pray.

*Pause for silent prayer*

Draw near to your servants, O Lord,
and answer their prayers with unceasing kindness,
that, for those who glory in you as their Creator and guide,
you may restore what you have created
and keep safe what you have restored.
Through our Lord Jesus Christ, your Son,
who lives and reigns with you in the unity of the Holy Spirit,
one God, for ever and ever. **Amen.**

## FIRST READING

Exod 16:2-4, 12-15

The whole Israelite community grumbled against Moses and Aaron.
The Israelites said to them,
"Would that we had died at the Lord's hand in the land of Egypt,
as we sat by our fleshpots and ate our fill of bread!
But you had to lead us into this desert
to make the whole community die of famine!"

Then the Lord said to Moses,
"I will now rain down bread from heaven for you.
Each day the people are to go out and gather their daily portion;
thus will I test them,
to see whether they follow my instructions or not.

"I have heard the grumbling of the Israelites.
Tell them: In the evening twilight you shall eat flesh,
and in the morning you shall have your fill of bread,
so that you may know that I, the Lord, am your God."

In the evening quail came up and covered the camp.
In the morning a dew lay all about the camp,
and when the dew evaporated, there on the surface of the desert
were fine flakes like hoarfrost on the ground.
On seeing it, the Israelites asked one another, "What is this?"
for they did not know what it was.
But Moses told them,
"This is the bread that the Lord has given you to eat."

# CATECHESIS

## RESPONSORIAL PSALM

Ps 78:3-4, 23-24, 25, 54

℟. (24b) The Lord gave them bread from heaven.

What we have heard and know,
    and what our fathers have declared to us,
we will declare to the generation to come
    the glorious deeds of the LORD and his strength
    and the wonders that he wrought.

℟. The Lord gave them bread from heaven.

He commanded the skies above
    and opened the doors of heaven;
he rained manna upon them for food
    and gave them heavenly bread.

℟. The Lord gave them bread from heaven.

Man ate the bread of angels,
    food he sent them in abundance.
And he brought them to his holy land,
    to the mountains his right hand had won.

℟. The Lord gave them bread from heaven.

## SECOND READING

Eph 4:17, 20-24

Brothers and sisters:
I declare and testify in the Lord
    that you must no longer live as the Gentiles do,
    in the futility of their minds;
    that is not how you learned Christ,
    assuming that you have heard of him
        and were taught in him,
    as truth is in Jesus,
    that you should put away the old self of
        your former way of life,
    corrupted through deceitful desires,
    and be renewed in the spirit of your minds,
    and put on the new self,
    created in God's way in righteousness
        and holiness of truth.

## About Liturgy

***Communion and the tabernacle:*** There is a practice that continues to be common even though it has never been approved. That is the practice of getting and then distributing hosts from the tabernacle during the celebration of Mass. This practice weakens our understanding of both the Eucharist and the participation of the assembly and it should cease immediately. Here are the basic points we need to help our liturgical ministers understand in order to stop this practice.

First, the purpose of the tabernacle is this: "The reason for which the Church reserves the eucharist outside Mass is, primarily, the administration of viaticum to the dying and, secondarily, communion of the sick, communion outside Mass, and adoration of Christ present in the sacrament" (USCCB referring to Holy Communion and Worship of the Eucharist outside Mass, 5; http://www.usccb.org/prayer-and-worship/the-mass/order-of-mass/liturgy-of-the-eucharist/holy-communion-from-the-tabernacle.cfm). Therefore, the hosts in the tabernacle are set aside primarily for the dying who cannot be present at the community's Mass.

Second, in a liturgy in which Communion is distributed outside of Mass, such as a Communion service, the hosts are rightfully taken from the tabernacle. However, Mass is different from a Communion service, not because of who leads the liturgy or where the hosts come from but because of what is omitted in a Communion service, namely, the eucharistic prayer. This prayer, led by a priest on behalf of the gathered faithful, is the heart of the Mass. It is the great prayer of thanksgiving that recalls the Father's blessings through Christ and asks the Father to send the Holy Spirit to change the bread and wine into the Body and Blood of Christ, thus changing us who share in that Body and Blood. The hosts in the tabernacle are indeed the Body of Christ, but distributing them to the faithful at Mass dismisses their participation in the eucharistic prayer and severs the connection between offering Christ's sacrifice of praise and sharing in that same sacrifice in Communion. This is why the *General Instruction of the Roman Missal* says, "It is most desirable that the faithful, just as the priest himself is bound to do, receive the Lord's Body from hosts consecrated at the same Mass . . . so that even by means of the signs Communion will stand out more clearly as a participation in the sacrifice actually being celebrated" (85).

## About Liturgical Music

***The Communion song:*** What makes a good Communion song? The United States bishops' document, Sing to the Lord: Music in Divine Worship gives some good guidelines:

It should be a song people know since "the singing of the people should be preeminent" (189).

It can be a song that uses the proper antiphon for the day, a season antiphon, an antiphon and psalm from an approved collection, or another appropriate liturgical song (190).

Textual themes might include joy, wonder, gratitude, praise, themes from the gospel of the day, or references to eating and drinking the Body and Blood of Christ (191).

A responsorial psalm style of singing is recommended so the people can participate fully as they process to the altar; this may require a smaller repertoire of music so that people can become familiar with them (192).

If there is a large number of people to receive Communion, making the procession lengthy, more than one song might be chosen; a second song might be one sung by the choir alone or an instrumental (193).

It should fit with the spirit of the liturgical season (194).

**AUGUST 5, 2018**

# EIGHTEENTH SUNDAY IN ORDINARY TIME

## ✠ SPIRITUALITY

**GOSPEL ACCLAMATION**
John 6:51

℟. Alleluia, alleluia.
I am the living bread that came down from
    heaven, says the Lord;
whoever eats this bread will live forever.
℟. Alleluia, alleluia.

## Gospel

John 6:41-51; L116B

The Jews murmured about Jesus
    because he said,
    "I am the bread that came down
        from heaven,"
and they said,
    "Is this not Jesus, the son of Joseph?
Do we not know his father and mother?
Then how can he say,
    'I have come down from heaven'?"
Jesus answered and said to them,
    "Stop murmuring among yourselves.
No one can come to me unless the
    Father who sent me draw him,
    and I will raise him on the last
        day.
It is written in the prophets:
    *They shall all be taught by God.*
Everyone who listens to my Father and
    learns from him comes to me.
Not that anyone has seen the Father
    except the one who is from God;
    he has seen the Father.
Amen, amen, I say to you,
    whoever believes has eternal life.
I am the bread of life.
Your ancestors ate the manna in the
    desert, but they died;
    this is the bread that comes down
        from heaven
    so that one may eat it and not die.
I am the living bread that came down
    from heaven;
    whoever eats this bread will live
        forever;
    and the bread that I will give is my
        flesh for the life of the world."

## Reflecting on the Gospel

"Ratchet up the tension" is a phrase we hear when discussions are getting heated, when one side or the other refuses to back down, or when someone drives home the argument relentlessly. Often we can shy away from ratcheting up the tension as it can make people uncomfortable. And those who do not shy away from this can be seen as boorish, overzealous, or simply hotheaded. But in this story, Jesus is not afraid to ratchet up the tension. He is not afraid to deal with any ramifications thereof.

In the gospel reading from last week the people wanted Jesus to give them a sign like the manna in the desert. In response Jesus claimed that he was the Bread of Life come down from heaven. This week he goes even further. Not surprisingly the crowds are hesitant to believe such a claim. They know his family of origin. Jesus' father was Joseph. How could Jesus claim to have come down from heaven? Jesus does not back down. He does not say, "Oh, you misunderstood. I was speaking metaphorically." Instead, he takes it to the next level, as it were. He quotes Isaiah: "They shall all be taught by God." Both he and the crowds understood the meaning. He was placing himself on par with God or, rather, even equating himself with God. This was becoming too much. Jesus, whose father Joseph they knew, could not with a straight face imply that he had come down from heaven, teaching the people, in effect claiming to fulfill the passage from Isaiah saying they would be taught by God!

Rather than back down, Jesus goes another step further. He states flatly and perhaps boorishly that their ancestors ate manna and *died*. The people wanted Jesus to perform some sign akin to the manna, but in fact those who ate the manna died in any case. What Jesus provides gives eternal life. He himself is the Bread of Life, come down from heaven. And as a final trump card, he plays the line that ratchets it up once again. The bread he gives is his very flesh.

With Jesus' willingness to go one step further followed by another and yet another, we will not be surprised to learn that many of his followers will abandon him. What he was teaching and preaching was beyond credibility. This upstart preacher from Galilee, whose father was somebody known in the community, was delusional if he claimed he came down from heaven as true bread, which is his very flesh. Somebody preaching that today would likely be ridiculed and summarily dismissed, which is what will ultimately happen to Jesus.

## Living the Paschal Mystery

The eucharistic theology of the Gospel of John that emerges in this reading will reach a pinnacle next week.

Eucharist, the consumption of the Bread of Life, is the way we appropriate for ourselves the Word of God made flesh. The incarnational spirituality of this gospel comes full circle for the believer, who is invited to consume the Word of God, the Bread of Life.

When we receive Eucharist we can meditate on the foreshadowing of this spiritual gift by the manna in the desert. That is, the manna that was given to our ancestors in faith prefigured the Bread of Life come down from heaven, which is the Word made flesh. Rather than an esoteric idea divorced from our lived experience, the bread that Jesus gives is his very flesh. Communion with Jesus is not simply a mind-trip, but it is a partaking of his flesh.

This eucharistic theology is uniquely Johannine and it is delivered not at the Last Supper but, rather, on the day following the multiplication of the loaves. Jesus satisfies not merely our physical needs but, more importantly, our spiritual needs. Unlike those who consumed manna and died, when we consume the bread that he gives we will inherit eternal life.

## Focusing the Gospel
*John 6:41-51*
From time immemorial, bread has been the staff of life, the basic and central food in many diets. To the "murmuring" Jews ("murmuring" as their ancestors did in the desert), Jesus tries to help them see the deeper meaning of his claim to be "the bread that came down from heaven." Christ is the bread of heaven that transcends this experience of life to the life of God.

The critical verb in today's gospel is "believe." We need to trust that God provides for and sustains our faith in his gift of Jesus, the Bread of Life, in the same way that Old Testament wisdom nourished the discerning seeker of God.

## Focusing the First Reading
*1 Kgs 19:4-8*
God as Provider and Sustainer is also revealed in today's first reading, from the First Book of Kings. Elijah has defeated the prophets and priests of Baal, angering Queen Jezebel. The prophet is now a marked man and is forced to flee to the desert. The discouraged Elijah pleads with God to take his life; instead, God restores Elijah's hope and strength with bread and water provided by the angel. God does not demand Elijah—or us—to undertake the journey to his holy mountain without providing us with "food" for the journey.

## Focusing the Responsorial Psalm
*Ps 34:2-3, 4-5, 6-7, 8-9 (9a)*
The singer of Psalm 34 has been saved from some crisis or danger by God, learning true wisdom by his suffering. With gratitude to God, the psalmist now teaches what he has learned to the poor and lowly of his tribe and nation, urging them to seek refuge in the Lord's mercy as he has.

## Focusing the Second Reading
*Eph 4:30–5:2*
Paul articulates a vision of the church as "imitators of God," a community that is united in the love of God they have experienced and in their commitment to God's work of compassion and forgiveness.

---

**PROMPTS FOR HOMILISTS, CATECHISTS, AND RCIA TEAMS**

When have you been nourished by the "bread" of kindness, of forgiveness, of wisdom that another offered you?

How are we a "eucharistic" church?

In what ways can we give "life" to a "lifeless" situation?

How can a perspective of gratitude change the way we approach problems and difficult relationships?

## Model Penitential Act

*Presider:* To prepare ourselves to celebrate this sacrament of the Bread of Life, let us ask God's forgiveness for our sins and failings. *[pause]*

You who are bread for our life's journey: Lord, have mercy.

You who were handed over for our sakes: Christ, have mercy.

You who will raise us up to everlasting life with you: Lord, have mercy.

## Homily Points

• Jesus' friends and neighbors have a hard time connecting the carpenter's son they know with his claim to be true bread from heaven. But no matter what our circumstances, we can be "bread" for those suffering the hunger of poverty or alienation, we can be the face of God for those who struggle to find God, life for those entombed by fear and despair. As Jesus, the "bread of life," gave life to the world through his selfless compassion and humble servanthood to others, we too can participate in that same giving spirit of Jesus: looking beyond our own needs to the good of others, giving not from our treasure but from our poverty, nourishing one another in the compassion and selflessness of the Gospel.

• Today's gospel confronts us with the common "bread" we stuff ourselves with that offers little nourishment. We may "feed" on anger, pride, wealth—and still be unsatisfied. Jesus invites us to eat the "living bread" of compassion, reconciliation, justice that nourishes and inspires us to become "bread" for others, the bread that is not only *from* Jesus but *is* Jesus. A eucharistic perspective of gratitude can have a transforming effect in our lives: we see life as a gift, not an entitlement; we focus attention on our blessings, not our disappointments; we discover God in the love of others, not in ourselves. The one bread makes us one Body in Christ, bound to each other in the love of Christ, the Giver of the feast. As Christ is bread for us, we are bread for one another in our love of others; in our hunger for meaning in our lives, Christ's presence in the Eucharist is a source of hope.

• To possess the life of God is to be open to and make possible moments of grace—moments when the great love of God is especially real to us and we can make God's love real for others. God's grace is manifested in so many ways: in prayer and sacrament, especially the Eucharist; in the many gifts of creation, from the food that sustains us to the light of the sun that warms us; in the kindness and love of those who are consumed by God's unexplainable love; in acts of justice, compassion, and reconciliation, however small and unheralded, that transform us in God's peace and joy.

## Model Universal Prayer (Prayer of the Faithful)

*Presider:* To the Lord who hears the cry of the poor, let us pray.

*Response:* Lord, hear our prayer.

That all those who serve the church may lead us in the gospel way of love . . .

That all peoples of the world may honor one another as beloved children of God . . .

That God will bless the work of those who provide food and shelter to the poor, the needy, the lost, and the desperate . . .

That our gathering to celebrate Jesus, the Bread of Life, may make our parish a community of compassion, forgiveness, and peace . . .

*Presider:* Father of mercy, we place these prayers before you. As you have become bread for us, make us bread for one another; as your Spirit instills in us your love and peace, let us mirror that love and peace to one another. We offer these prayers in the name of Jesus, the Bread of Life. **Amen.**

## COLLECT

Let us pray.

*Pause for silent prayer*

Almighty ever-living God,
whom, taught by the Holy Spirit,
we dare to call our Father,
bring, we pray, to perfection in our hearts
the spirit of adoption as your sons and
 daughters,
that we may merit to enter into the
 inheritance
which you have promised.
Through our Lord Jesus Christ, your Son,
who lives and reigns with you in the unity
 of the Holy Spirit,
one God, for ever and ever. **Amen.**

## FIRST READING

1 Kgs 19:4-8

Elijah went a day's journey into the desert,
 until he came to a broom tree and sat
 beneath it.
He prayed for death, saying:
 "This is enough, O LORD!
Take my life, for I am no better than my
 fathers."
He lay down and fell asleep under the
 broom tree,
 but then an angel touched him and
 ordered him to get up and eat.
Elijah looked and there at his head was a
 hearth cake
 and a jug of water.
After he ate and drank, he lay down again,
 but the angel of the LORD came back a
 second time,
 touched him, and ordered,
 "Get up and eat, else the journey will be
 too long for you!"
He got up, ate, and drank;
 then strengthened by that food,
 he walked forty days and forty nights
 to the mountain of God, Horeb.

## RESPONSORIAL PSALM

Ps 34:2-3, 4-5, 6-7, 8-9

℟. (9a) Taste and see the goodness of the Lord.

I will bless the LORD at all times;
   his praise shall be ever in my mouth.
Let my soul glory in the LORD;
   the lowly will hear me and be glad.

℟. Taste and see the goodness of the Lord.

Glorify the LORD with me,
   let us together extol his name.
I sought the LORD, and he answered me
   and delivered me from all my fears.

℟. Taste and see the goodness of the Lord.

Look to him that you may be radiant with joy,
   and your faces may not blush with shame.
When the afflicted man called out, the LORD heard,
   and from all his distress he saved him.

℟. Taste and see the goodness of the Lord.

The angel of the LORD encamps
   around those who fear him and delivers them.
Taste and see how good the LORD is;
   blessed the man who takes refuge in him.

℟. Taste and see the goodness of the Lord.

## SECOND READING

Eph 4:30–5:2

Brothers and sisters:
Do not grieve the Holy Spirit of God,
   with which you were sealed for the day of redemption.
All bitterness, fury, anger, shouting, and reviling
   must be removed from you, along with all malice.
And be kind to one another,
   compassionate,
   forgiving one another as God has forgiven you in Christ.

So be imitators of God, as beloved children, and live in love,
   as Christ loved us and handed himself over for us
   as a sacrificial offering to God for a fragrant aroma.

### About Liturgy

***Sending Communion ministers to the sick and homebound:*** The US bishops' document, Introduction to the Order of Mass: A Pastoral Resource of the Bishops' Committee on the Liturgy discusses the sending of Communion ministers to the sick from the Sunday Mass (21). However, there is no official ritual text for doing this. Therefore, how this happens varies greatly and can be a good opportunity to reflect more deeply on this important ministry of the assembly to those unable to be present at the Sunday gathering.

It may be most efficient to give hosts from the tabernacle to Communion ministers to the sick after Mass is over. Yet, visiting the sick is an important work of mercy. Therefore, help the assembly show its care for absent members by visibly connecting how we nourish the sick through the Sunday assembly's sharing at the altar. The Introduction to the Order of Mass gives two suggestions for how this might happen: (1) After Communion distribution has ended, the ministers to the sick receive from the priest pyxes filled with consecrated hosts from Mass. The ministers then may leave immediately or wait until the end of Mass to join in the concluding procession. (2) As the ministers to the sick come forward to receive Communion themselves, they have their pyxes filled by the Communion minister they go to. Then they share in Communion. They either leave immediately afterward or wait until the end of Mass.

Either option is fine, but the first option is more of a ritual moment you can use to form the assembly. At an appropriate point during the altar preparation or the Communion rite, the priest, deacon, or another minister fills the pyxes that have been placed on the altar or a credence table. Then, once the entire assembly has shared in Communion and a moment of silent prayer, all stand as the priest invites the Communion ministers to the sick forward to receive their pyxes. If the assembly is small and it seems appropriate, he might ask each minister the names of those they will be visiting. Then, in a similar way that catechumens are dismissed, the priest says words of instruction and dismissal, such as: "Take the Word of God, the Bread of Life, and the prayers of this assembly to our sisters and brothers who are ill. For we who are many are one body, for we all share in the one bread and the one cup, the Body and Blood of Christ. Go in peace." The ministers to the sick immediately leave the assembly, during which a short acclamation might be sung, or they might remain until the concluding procession.

### About Liturgical Music

***Music ministers and Communion:*** How and when your music ministers go to Communion says a lot about the role of music and the choir in the liturgy. The purpose of the Communion song is "to express the spiritual union of the communicants by means of the unity of their voices, to show gladness of heart, and to bring out more clearly the 'communitarian' character of the procession to receive the Eucharist" (*General Instruction of the Roman Missal*, 86). When it refers to the "communicants" it means the entire assembly. Therefore, the entire assembly uses its voice to show gladness and unity.

In some places, the choir receives Communion first before they begin the song; or they receive last after they have stopped singing. Either way leaves a long period of silence while the choir shares in Communion. Yet, if the entire assembly is meant to use its voice in song during Communion, why then would there not be any singing while the music ministers receive Communion themselves? Send choir members to receive Communion *during* the Communion song. Be sure they continue singing as they process to the altar. Use music the assembly knows well so it can sing strongly even as the choir and musicians go to Communion.

## GOSPEL ACCLAMATION

R℣. Alleluia, alleluia.
Mary is taken up to heaven;
a chorus of angels exults.
R℣. Alleluia, alleluia.

## Gospel

Luke 1:39-56; L622

Mary set out
and traveled to the hill country in haste
to a town of Judah,
where she entered the house of
Zechariah
and greeted Elizabeth.
When Elizabeth heard Mary's greeting,
the infant leaped in her womb,
and Elizabeth, filled with the Holy
Spirit,
cried out in a loud voice and said,
"Blessed are you among women,
and blessed is the fruit of your
womb.
And how does this happen to me,
that the mother of my Lord should
come to me?
For at the moment the sound of
your greeting reached my
ears,
the infant in my womb leaped for joy.
Blessed are you who believed
that what was spoken to you by the
Lord
would be fulfilled."

And Mary said:

"My soul proclaims the greatness of
the Lord;
my spirit rejoices in God my Savior
for he has looked with favor on his
lowly servant.
From this day all generations will call
me blessed:
the Almighty has done great things
for me,
and holy is his Name.
He has mercy on those who fear him
in every generation.
He has shown the strength of his arm,
and has scattered the proud in their
conceit.

*Continued in Appendix A, p. 301.*

*See Appendix A, p. 301, for the other readings.*

### Reflecting on the Gospel

In a musical, the dialogue and action is punctuated with songs and dancing. The singing carries the story forward, and often the lyrics offer resolution to a story line, or emphasize the meaning of a particular action. For example, in *Guys and Dolls*, the gambler sings, "Luck Be a Lady" in the midst of a craps game. Or in *Hello, Dolly!*, the waiters sing the title song, welcoming Dolly back to the elegant Harmonia Gardens. "Getting to Know You" in *The King and I* is a song that Anna sings to the children as they truly get to know one another.

Though the Gospel of Luke is not a musical or a show tune, Luke does punctuate his gospel and his Acts of the Apostles with something akin to a song, or perhaps an aria, meant to emphasize a point in the story. We even refer to these parts of the gospel narrative as *canticles* (Mary's canticle in Luke 1:46-55 and Zechariah's canticle in Luke 1:68-79). But even Simeon's prophecy (Luke 2:25-35) and Stephen's temple speech (Acts 7) are examples of Luke punctuating his work with this narrative device.

The canticle we hear in today's gospel reading is from Mary. It is also referred to as the *Magnificat* ("magnifies"), which is the first word in the Latin translation. She utters this upon hearing her cousin Elizabeth state that the infant in her womb (John) "leapt for joy." Mary proclaims a profound reversal of fortune. The rulers are thrown down from their thrones and the lowly are lifted up. The rich are sent away empty while the hungry receive their fill. Mary sounds like she was quite a preacher! Is there any wonder where Jesus received his own sense of justice and identification with those who were on the bottom rungs of society? These messages were imbibed by the young Jesus and we hear their echo in his own preaching as an adult.

The worldly standards do not apply with God. An upheaval is about to take place. For to God, the lowly will be raised and the hungry will be filled. Not only that, but the rulers and the rich will be cast down. Simply raising the downtrodden is not enough. Those with power will be reduced. With such a message, it's no wonder Jesus was executed. Once we start talking about money and privilege, those with a vested interest in the status quo will do anything to maintain it.

These words of Mary's canticle are a far cry from a show tune. For those at the top of society they are a warning shot across the bow. For those heretofore shut out of privilege, these words are hope that God has heard their cry. This message sets the stage for Jesus' own ministry, and ultimately ours.

### Living the Paschal Mystery

It can be difficult for those of us in "developed" countries to hear the canticle of Mary with its emphasis on overturning the privileged order. Many, if not most, of us benefit from the systems that give us in developed countries the best of the world's goods and services. On a global scale, we are counted among the rich. In fact, we may have more in common with the ancient Romans, who were also the beneficiaries of the economic order they established, than with the early Christian disciples.

Mary's words are a powerful reminder to us that those who enjoy the riches of the earth, who sit in positions of power, will be overthrown. The riches are not "ours" and power is not "for us." Instead, all is God's and will be shared with all. Gaming the system, hoarding, taking, controlling will all be disrupted. This is the good news, and this is what Mary, the first disciple, proclaimed. Perhaps for this reason she is honored above others and was assumed into heaven. May our worldview be like hers in recognizing that God's priorities are not the world's.

## Focusing the Gospel

The gospel reading is Mary's *Magnificat*, her song of hope and joy in the Christ she will bear. Upon arriving at the house of her cousin Elizabeth, Mary is embraced by Elizabeth, who greets her as "the mother of my Lord." Mary is immediately caught up in Elizabeth's joy and responds with the hymn that has become known as the *Magnificat*, from the first word in the Latin translation of Mary's canticle, "My soul magnifies the Lord . . ." (Mary's words here are similar to the song of thanksgiving sung by Hannah in the Old Testament book of Samuel, after her son Samuel is accepted by the priest Eli into the Lord's service.)

The words of the *Magnificat* should dispel any notion we might hold of Mary as a reserved, diffident figure. Mary's canticle is nothing less than a prophetic, cutting-edge declaration of faith in the living, creating love of God. Her song celebrates God's saving work of the past and anticipates the saving work of the child in her womb. The *Magnificat* is the first proclamation of the Gospel of the Christ: Mary is the "lowly servant" on whom God looks with favor. She mirrors the Good News her Son will proclaim: the Gospel of forgiveness, humble service to one another, justice, and, ultimately, resurrection.

## Model Penitential Act

*Presider:* With the faith and trust of Mary, let us place our hearts before God, confident of his mercy and forgiveness. *[pause]*

Lord God, you show your favor to the poor and lowly: Lord, have mercy.

Lord God, you feed the hungry with good things: Christ, have mercy.

Lord God, you remember your promise of mercy to your servants: Lord, have mercy.

## Model Universal Prayer (Prayer of the Faithful)

*Presider:* With confident faith in God, the Lord who has done great things for us, let us pray.

*Response:* Lord, hear our prayer.

That the peace and mercy of God may dwell within the "tent" of our church . . .

That all nations and peoples may seek to raise up the dignity of every person as a child of God . . .

That our generous sharing of this year's harvest with the poor and hungry may be our song of thanks to God our Savior . . .

That parents and guardians may see in Mary and Elizabeth models of loving patience and selfless devotion . . .

*Presider:* O God, hear the prayers we offer. May Mary's prayer, the gift of a mother's love, be our joy; may her faith, the humble response of her generous heart, inspire us to live lives worthy of your promise. We ask these things in the name of your Son, Mary's child, Jesus Christ. **Amen.**

---

**COLLECT**

Let us pray.

*Pause for silent prayer*

Almighty ever-living God,
who assumed the Immaculate Virgin Mary,
    the Mother of your Son,
body and soul into heavenly glory,
grant, we pray,
that, always attentive to the things that are above,
we may merit to be sharers of her glory.
Through our Lord Jesus Christ, your Son,
who lives and reigns with you in the unity of
    the Holy Spirit,
one God, for ever and ever. **Amen.**

---

**FOR REFLECTION**

• What single image of Mary's *Magnificat* most resonates with you?

• In what "arks" have you experienced the presence of God in your midst?

• What aspect or event in your life would you put forward as your witness to the resurrection?

---

## Homily Points

• Mary knows that in the promise she has received from God, history will be turned upside down. She is the lowly servant on whom God has looked with favor. Mary's song is the first proclamation of the Gospel of the Christ who comes to reveal God's reign: the blessedness of the humble servant over the conceited; God's raising the poor and casting down the mighty; joy in the God who is filled with mercy and not condemnation; hope in the promise of good things for the hungry and poor.

• In the song she "sings" in response to Elizabeth's greeting, Mary has grasped the reign of God her child will proclaim. The simplicity and poverty into which her child is to be born are part of God's re-creation of humanity. Her child—God's Christ—comes to call us to his Father's banquet of "good things" where the hungry, the lowly, and the poor will be guests of honor. Mary understands and rejoices in what is to come. Her song hopefully anticipates the amazing things that began with her yes to God.

## ✝ SPIRITUALITY

**GOSPEL ACCLAMATION**
John 6:56

R̸. Alleluia, alleluia.
Whoever eats my flesh and drinks my blood
remains in me and I in him, says the Lord.
R̸. Alleluia, alleluia.

## Gospel

John 6:51-58; L119B

Jesus said to the crowds:
  "I am the living bread that came
      down from heaven;
  whoever eats this bread will
      live forever;
  and the bread that I will give
  is my flesh for the life of the world."

The Jews quarreled among themselves,
      saying,
  "How can this man give us his flesh
      to eat?"
Jesus said to them,
  "Amen, amen, I say to you,
  unless you eat the flesh of the Son of
      Man and drink his blood,
  you do not have life within you.
Whoever eats my flesh and drinks my
      blood
      has eternal life,
  and I will raise him on the last day.
For my flesh is true food,
  and my blood is true drink.
Whoever eats my flesh and drinks my
      blood
      remains in me and I in him.
Just as the living Father sent me
  and I have life because of the Father,
  so also the one who feeds on me
  will have life because of me.
This is the bread that came down from
      heaven.
Unlike your ancestors who ate and still
      died,
  whoever eats this bread will live
      forever."

### Reflecting on the Gospel

"Repetition is the mother of learning" (*Repetitio mater studiorum est*). This Latin phrase demonstrates the value that the ancients found in repetition. While we might not want to attend the kinds of schools they did, writing lessons again and again on their slates with a stylus, there was some wisdom in their saying.

Today's gospel begins with the same verse that formed the conclusion of last week's gospel: "I am the living bread that came down from heaven; / whoever eats this bread will live forever; / and the bread that I will give / is my flesh for the life of the world." In case we didn't get it last week, these are important words worthy of repetition.

That line last week was the pinnacle of a series of "ratcheting it up" on Jesus' behalf. This week, that line merely sets the stage for Jesus' going even further. If we thought he was ratcheting it up last week, we are in for more. His opponents immediately questioned Jesus' meaning about his flesh being true food. In reply Jesus does not apologize for an apparent misunderstanding. He does not say that his image was only a metaphor, not meant to be taken literally. Instead, he adds the term "blood" to flesh and continues with his preaching to mean that unless someone consumes his flesh *and blood* there is no life in that person. And so that there is no room for misunderstanding, he claims his flesh is true food and his blood true drink.

Jesus then spells out the relationship between the Father, himself, and his believers: Jesus has life because of the Father, and those who "feed on" Jesus have life because of him. They abide in him and he in them. The Greek term translated here as "feed on" can mean "gnaw, munch, or crunch." The term is graphic indeed, and its use is purposeful.

We will not be surprised to see the puzzlement and anger on the part of his opponents grow. Jesus is not backing down; he is not backing away. He continues to raise the stakes and make claims that sound more and more baffling to the crowds and to many others. Only with eyes of faith can we, like his disciples, accept this teaching. Many more are those who will walk away bewildered.

### Living the Paschal Mystery

Scripturally speaking, our eucharistic theology is rooted not only in the Synoptic accounts of the Last Supper and in Paul's account of the Lord's Supper but also in the bread of life discourse from the Gospel of John. This Johannine eucharistic theology is packed into this discourse because there is no "institution narrative" of the Eucharist at the Last Supper in the Gospel of John. For this evangelist, the Last Supper is the occasion of the washing of feet. Yet, John's theology of Eucharist might be said to be the most profound, reflective, and deep in the entire New Testament.

The Word of God made flesh comes to his believers as flesh. The Bread of Life come down from heaven is literally (not merely figuratively) consumed by the believers who abide in him and thus attain eternal life. The life that is enjoyed by the Word of God because of the Father is given to those who in turn gnaw on that same word.

The bread of life discourse is not merely a lesson for ancient Christians. But in our eucharistic liturgies this discourse finds its true expression, for it is there that this reading is fulfilled each and every time. We believers are united to the Word when we feed on the bread, the Word of God made flesh. The incarnational reality of the Son of God finds expression in the incarnational sacramentality of the Eucharist. This is truly a lesson worth repeating at least every week, for "repetition is the mother of learning."

## Focusing the Gospel

*John 6:51-58*

Two dimensions of Jewish worship provide the context of today's gospel, the fourth part of the bread of life discourse in John 6.

In Jewish thought, blood was considered to be life (Deut 12:23): as blood drained away from a living being so did life itself. The Jews, therefore, considered blood sacred, as belonging to God alone (Leviticus 17:10-14 includes a clear prohibition against consuming any form of blood). In animal sacrifices, blood was ritually drained from the carcass as belonging to God, the author of life. With this as a background, then, John's theology of the Eucharist includes Jesus' exhortation to drink his blood, that is, to share in his life. To "feast" on Jesus is to feast on the very life of God: to consume the bread of the Eucharist is to assimilate Jesus' life-giving presence in the very fiber of our being.

The graphic imagery that likely turned off so many of Jesus' own followers can be a turnoff even today. Jesus doesn't couch his words by claiming he speaks metaphorically. He doubles down on the "flesh and blood" language as he himself is the incarnation of the Word. When we consume the Eucharist, the Body and Blood, we consume Jesus himself.

## Focusing the First Reading

*Prov 9:1-6*

Today's first reading imagines God's Wisdom as a hostess giving a grand banquet to which she invites all who would forsake the conventions and ways of the world in order to discern the peace and justice of the Holy One, the Light of true wisdom.

## Focusing the Responsorial Psalm

*Ps 34:2-3, 4-5, 6-7 (9a)*

Last Sunday's responsorial Psalm 34 is sung again today (minus verses 8-9). The psalm is a poor man's humble song of thanksgiving to the God of mercy who has saved him from catastrophe or illness.

## Focusing the Second Reading

*Eph 5:15-20*

A far less eloquent image of food and drink is the focus of today's second reading. Paul admonishes the Ephesians to avoid "get[ting] drunk on wine, in which lies debauchery." These "evil" days are coming to an end, Paul warns; the time has come "to understand what is the will of the Lord" in all things and live accordingly.

---

**PROMPTS FOR HOMILISTS, CATECHISTS, AND RCIA TEAMS**

Today's readings contain several images of preparing and sharing meals. How do these images help us understand what it means to become a eucharistic community?

Have you ever participated in some sharing of food or drink that you found to be a meaningful experience of "communion"?

How would you define wisdom? What are the defining characteristics of a "wise" man or woman? Who is or was the wisest person you have known?

## Model Penitential Act

*Presider:* Trusting in the constant forgiveness of God, let us call to mind our sins and failings. *[pause]*

You are the light of wisdom and grace: Lord, have mercy.

You feed us with bread from heaven: Christ, have mercy.

You remain in us and we in you in your Son's Body and Blood: Lord, have mercy.

## Homily Points

• Jesus calls himself the "bread of life" and, in rather unsettling images, invites his hearers to eat his flesh and drink his blood. While the idea was repulsive to the Jews, Jesus' words evoked for the first Christian community the eucharistic supper they gathered together to share on Sunday. But in calling himself "bread," in inviting us to feast on his own Body and Blood, Jesus reminds us that his spirit of compassion, reflection of the Father's love, and Gospel of peace should nourish us and focus our consciousness on seeking God. In Jesus, God is both provider and provision, both the preparer of the feast and the feast itself, both the giver and the gift. The love of God that is Jesus the Bread of Life is real food for our hungry selves, real drink that is the very life of God flowing through us.

• In inviting us to feed on his flesh and drink of his blood, Jesus invites us to embrace the life of his Father: the life in which we come to realize our ability to love and understand that love in our lives; the life that readily offers forgiveness and seeks reconciliation with all; the life that finds liberating joy in humbly serving and giving to others. In the bread he gives us to eat, we become the Body of Christ with and for one another; in his blood he gives us to drink, his life of compassion, justice, and selflessness flows within us, and we become what we have received: a sacrament of unity, peace, and reconciliation.

• We are sustained by many kinds of "food": our engines and machines are propelled by different fuels; the many facets of our careers are financed by all forms of capital. But Jesus' words about his flesh and blood as "real food" challenge us to consider what sustains us as human beings, as loving parents and children, as brothers and sisters of all with whom we share this good earth. In the "bread" he gives us to eat, Christ distinguishes the values of God from the values of the marketplace; he instructs us on how to respond to the world's challenges with a sense of justice and a spirit of generosity; he teaches us how to overcome our fears to become the people of compassion, reconciliation, and justice God created us to be.

## Model Universal Prayer (Prayer of the Faithful)

*Presider:* In word and sacrament, God is present to us. And so, let us pray.

*Response:* Lord, hear our prayer.

That, in this sacrament of the Bread of Life, we become the Body of Christ . . .

That the wisdom of God may guide Pope N. and the ministers of our church and President N. and the leaders of our nation . . .

That we make places at our tables for the poor, the homeless, and the forgotten . . .

That the faithful who have died *[especially . . . ]* may be raised up by Christ on the last day . . .

*Presider:* With gratitude and hope, we offer these prayers to you, Father of grace, trusting in your loving mercy and providence. We offer these prayers to you in the name of Jesus, the Bread of Life. **Amen**.

Let us pray.

*Pause for silent prayer*

O God, who have prepared for those who love you
good things which no eye can see,
fill our hearts, we pray, with the warmth of your love,
so that, loving you in all things and above all things,
we may attain your promises,
which surpass every human desire.
Through our Lord Jesus Christ, your Son,
who lives and reigns with you in the unity of the Holy Spirit,
one God, for ever and ever. **Amen.**

**FIRST READING**
Prov 9:1-6

Wisdom has built her house,
    she has set up her seven columns;
she has dressed her meat, mixed her wine,
    yes, she has spread her table.
She has sent out her maidens; she calls
    from the heights out over the city:
"Let whoever is simple turn in here;
    To the one who lacks understanding,
        she says,
Come, eat of my food,
    and drink of the wine I have mixed!
Forsake foolishness that you may live;
    advance in the way of understanding."

## RESPONSORIAL PSALM

Ps 34:2-3, 4-5, 6-7

R℣. (9a) Taste and see the goodness of the Lord.

I will bless the LORD at all times;
    his praise shall be ever in my mouth.
Let my soul glory in the LORD;
    the lowly will hear me and be glad.

R℣. Taste and see the goodness of the Lord.

Glorify the LORD with me,
    let us together extol his name.
I sought the LORD, and he answered me
    and delivered me from all my fears.

R℣. Taste and see the goodness of the Lord.

Look to him that you may be radiant with joy,
    and your faces may not blush with shame.
When the poor one called out, the LORD heard,
    and from all his distress he saved him.

R℣. Taste and see the goodness of the Lord.

## SECOND READING

Eph 5:15-20

Brothers and sisters:
Watch carefully how you live,
    not as foolish persons but as wise,
    making the most of the opportunity,
    because the days are evil.
Therefore, do not continue in ignorance,
    but try to understand what is the will of the Lord.
And do not get drunk on wine, in which lies debauchery,
    but be filled with the Spirit,
    addressing one another in psalms and hymns and spiritual songs,
    singing and playing to the Lord in your hearts,
    giving thanks always and for everything
    in the name of our Lord Jesus Christ to God the Father.

## About Liturgy

*Communion from the cup:* One criticism you may still hear about the post–Vatican II Eucharist is that there's too much emphasis on Communion as "banquet" and not enough on Communion as "sacrifice." Well, when a significant number of people who come to Communion avoid drinking the Blood of Christ, or when not having the Communion cup available to the assembly is "normal," then our celebrations of the Eucharist are neither banquet nor sacrifice.

The *General Instruction of the Roman Missal*, 281, puts the two images together: "Holy Communion has a fuller form as a sign when it is distributed under both kinds. For in this form the sign of the Eucharistic banquet is more clearly evident and clear expression is given to the divine will by which the new and eternal Covenant is ratified in the Blood of the Lord." However, since the Council of Trent, the church has also taught that Christ, whole and entire, is present in the consecrated bread. If we receive only the Body of Christ, we receive the full grace of the sacrament. So why bother receiving from the cup?

In today's first reading, Wisdom invites us, "Come, eat of my food, / and drink of the wine I have mixed!" and at every Eucharist, we hear Jesus' command, "Take this, all of you, and drink from it . . ." Drinking from the eucharistic cup is essential to understanding the meaning of Communion and Jesus' sacrifice—a sacrifice in which we participate. Rev. Edward Foley, OFMCap, said that eating the Body of Christ shows us *who* we are to become. But drinking the Blood of Christ shows us *how* to do that, and to do that on Christ's terms, not ours.

Drinking the Blood of Christ makes us accountable to the "amen" we gave in assenting to becoming what we have eaten, the Body of Christ. "Will you drink this cup?" In other words, will you pour yourself out for the sake of others as Jesus did for us? In these days of hand sanitizers, drinking from a common cup may be unusual. Yet it is essential if we are to *be* the Body of Christ for others.

## About Liturgical Music

*Why we sing after Communion:* If you've been doing liturgical music for a while, you might have grown up with the four-song "plug and play" approach to liturgical music: look at the readings, choose four songs that go with them, and add a few acclamations in between. But we all know that music for Mass is much more of an art form than a science. First we need to know the "why" behind the song. Every part of the Mass has a particular purpose, and that purpose may require the accompaniment of sung music. It might even be fulfilled only by the singing of a song, as in the Gloria, the purpose of which is simply to praise the triune God in song. One area where we often misunderstand the "why" of the song is after the distribution of Communion. The *General Instruction of the Roman Missal* is quite clear about what happens after Communion: "When the distribution of Communion is over, if appropriate, the Priest and faithful pray quietly for some time. If desired, a Psalm or other canticle of praise or a hymn may also be sung by the whole congregation" (88). If you choose the psalm, canticle of praise, or hymn option, you also need to remember the last part of that sentence, which is key to knowing the song's purpose: "sung by the whole congregation." The purpose of the optional song sung after Communion is not to give the people a chance to meditate; nor is it time for the music ministers to sing a song on their own. The purpose is to give praise to God together as one Body of Christ having shared in the one bread and the one cup.

**AUGUST 19, 2018**
## TWENTIETH SUNDAY IN ORDINARY TIME

## ✦ SPIRITUALITY

### Gospel

John 6:60-69; L122B

Many of Jesus' disciples who were listening said,
  "This saying is hard; who can accept it?"
Since Jesus knew that his disciples were murmuring about this,
  he said to them, "Does this shock you?
What if you were to see the Son of Man ascending
  to where he was before?
It is the spirit that gives life,
  while the flesh is of no avail.
The words I have spoken to you are Spirit and life.
But there are some of you who do not believe."
Jesus knew from the beginning the ones who would not believe
  and the one who would betray him.
And he said,
  "For this reason I have told you that no one can come to me
  unless it is granted him by my Father."

As a result of this,
  many of his disciples returned to their former way of life
  and no longer accompanied him.
Jesus then said to the Twelve, "Do you also want to leave?"
Simon Peter answered him, "Master, to whom shall we go?
You have the words of eternal life.
We have come to believe
  and are convinced that you are the Holy One of God."

### Reflecting on the Gospel

Today is the fifth and final Sunday of our reading from John 6, the second longest chapter in the New Testament (Luke 1 is the longest). Even so, we do not read the entire sixth chapter of John. We skipped Jesus' walking on water (John 6:16-21)! The church gives us five Sundays with this chapter precisely because of its profound eucharistic theology. What began with the multiplication of the loaves ends the following day with nearly all of his disciples abandoning him and returning to their former way of life precisely because of this "hard" saying, the consumption of Jesus' very flesh and blood.

Jesus then asks the Twelve if they too will leave. We have the impression that if they had chosen to leave, Jesus would simply have started anew. He was not going to change his teaching to attract the crowds. Instead, he would teach what he knew to be true, for his words were Spirit and life. Jesus knows that nobody can come to him, can believe in him, unless it is granted by the Father. In our words, we say faith is a gift. We cannot come to Jesus unless we are given the gift of faith. Only if that special gift is granted by the Father will one believe. All the arguments, discussions, proofs, demonstrations, blog posts, and talks cannot guarantee faith. It is a gift given not by us, but by God the Father.

How do the Twelve respond when Jesus asks whether they too might leave? Simon Peter answers with a question of his own: "to whom shall we go? / You have the words of eternal life . . . you are the Holy One of God." Thus we have in John's gospel Peter's "confession" that comes as the culmination of this profound chapter in which we have the multiplication of the loaves, Jesus' walking on water, and the bread of life discourse. After witnessing such deeds and speech Simon Peter speaks for all disciples, "to whom shall we go?" Jesus' words are everlasting life. To leave Jesus is in many senses to leave life itself. For Simon Peter, then, there is no other place or person to whom he might go. He is not returning to his former way of life. He has been introduced to something more, eternal life from the Word of God come down from heaven. For the one who has faith, in the face of such a revelation there is no other choice.

### Living the Paschal Mystery

Peter's response can be our own when faced with the overwhelming mystery of the gift of faith in the one sent from God. Yet, we should be humble with respect to this mystery, for the gift is not given to all, but only to those whom the Father grants it. In light of this it is good to be patient with those who do not share our faith. And when another does come to faith we can be assured that it is not because of our wondrous evangelization, our dedication to a particular program, or our having memorized specific Scripture verses. God grants faith to those to whom he will.

Even Jesus himself allowed many of his disciples (not merely the crowds) to return to their former way of life when his teaching seemed too hard. Our faith is not subject to scientific scrutiny after which a demonstrable proof will be accepted by a rational mind. Instead, faith is a gift.

We can be thankful for this gift of faith that leads to eternal life. We can share it with others. But ultimately it is God the Father who is the giver. Once granted this gift, we, like the disciples, have nowhere to turn but to Jesus. In light of his challenging teachings, the response of Peter is our own. "Master, to whom shall we go? / You have the words of eternal life."

## Focusing the Gospel

*John 6:60-69*

Today's concluding section of the bread of life discourse from John's gospel is a turning point for Jesus' disciples. Will they join the ranks of the skeptics, who cannot fathom Jesus and his talk of "eating his flesh," or will they commit themselves to Jesus—and the shadows of the cross that are beginning to fall? Jesus' question is direct and to the point: "Do you also want to leave?" Peter's simple, plaintive answer is the confession of faith voiced by disciples of every age who have come to taste the Word of God made flesh. They have come to believe that he has the words of eternal life.

## Focusing the First Reading

*Josh 24:1-2a, 15-17, 18b*

Joshua, the commander of Israel's military forces, succeeded Moses as leader of the Israelites. In the conclusion to the book bearing his name, Joshua and the tribes of Israel are at a turning point in their relationship with Yahweh. Their long exodus journey has been completed; the Israelites have fought for and arrived at the land God has given them. At Shechem, Joshua challenges the Israelites to either embrace the gods of the land in which they now dwell or reaffirm their covenant with the God who brought them out of Egyptian captivity to freedom in this new place. The people elect to renew their covenant with God. Like Peter and the disciples in today's gospel, Joshua and the new nation of Israel are called to embrace the word of the God of justice and redemption.

## Focusing the Responsorial Psalm

*Ps 34:2-3, 16-17, 18-19, 20-21 (9a)*

On this Sunday that concludes our reading of Jesus' bread of life discourse in chapter 6 of John's gospel, the final verses of Psalm 34 are sung, a hymn of thanksgiving to the God of mercy who protects the poor and brokenhearted.

## Focusing the Second Reading

*Eph 5:21-32*

Throughout Scripture, prophets and sages often employ the images of marriage and betrothal to portray God's loving relationship with his people. Paul writes in that tradition in today's reading from Ephesians. Though Paul's language may sound dated and sexist to contemporary ears, if read in the context of Paul's time two thousand years ago, the apostle beautifully equates the relationship between husband and wife as it was understood in antiquity to that of Christ and his church. In modernity we would say that obedience and subordination are required of both husband and wife: spouses give to each other completely, willingly, and unreservedly, just as Jesus the crucified gave himself completely, willingly, and unreservedly for humankind. The love of God is what distinguishes the church from the rest of society; ancient Christian marriage is a model of the sacrificial love of Christ for his church.

---

**PROMPTS FOR HOMILISTS, CATECHISTS, AND RCIA TEAMS**

What "sayings" of Jesus do you find especially hard to accept?

When have you experienced "spirit and life" in your struggle to live the Gospel?

In what ordinary and simple ways do families "serve the Lord" in the spirit of Joshua?

In light of Paul's words to husbands and wives in today's second reading, how does married life mirror the relationship of Christ and the church?

## Model Penitential Act

*Presider:* To prepare ourselves to celebrate these sacred mysteries, let us confess our sins and faults, humbly seeking the mercy of God. *[pause]*

You bring us to the freedom of your grace: Lord, have mercy.

You took on our humanity in order to restore us to life: Christ, have mercy.

You alone have the words of eternal life: Lord, have mercy.

## Homily Points

• Those who cannot endure Jesus' talk about giving his "flesh to eat" leave him, cynical and disappointed. Such hopelessness can eventually destroy us; the sense that God has abandoned us can cripple us emotionally and spiritually. Peter responds (on behalf of the Twelve?) with a simple but profound confession of faith in Jesus. This faith is a gift from the Father and leads to a greater friendship with Jesus so that Jesus himself will later call them "friends." We who have also been given that great gift of faith in Jesus are also called to greater friendship with him.

• Peter's conviction resonates with all of us who have experienced, in times of crisis, God's love in the support of family and friends. Jesus' "words of eternal life" are the light that illuminates our everyday journeys; they are the wisdom that guides us along the sometimes lonely and dangerous road to the dwelling place of God. Jesus' Gospel is not a warm fluffy blanket to wrap up in nor is it a protective coating designed to ward off sin and evil. The Gospel demands putting aside our own needs and wants to find joy in imitating Jesus' attitude of service to others. Despite our own doubts and fears, we know that, in the end, Jesus himself will triumph, for that is the gospel story.

• While we know that Jesus' words are eternal life, and that he has come down from heaven as the Bread of Life, they can also be too difficult for many to hear. The image of gnawing on his flesh is comprehensible only when we recognize that he is the Word made flesh. Merely listening to the word is not complete. We consume the flesh, the Bread of Life. This is an early indication of the incarnational theology and ultimate sacramentality present in John's gospel. The incarnation is celebrated in the Eucharist today. We listen to the word (Liturgy of the Word) and consume the Word made flesh (Liturgy of the Eucharist)—real food that leads to eternal life. This saying is hard, but to whom else shall we go? These are the words of eternal life.

## Model Universal Prayer (Prayer of the Faithful)

*Presider:* "Master, to whom shall we go? / You have the words of eternal life." With Peter's simple expression of faith echoing in our hearts, let us pray.

*Response:* Lord, hear our prayer.

That our church may take on the hard demands of Jesus' Gospel of justice . . .

That all nations, peoples, and races may find unity, understanding, and trust in the God and Father of all who is over all and is in all . . .

That the sick, suffering, and dying find peace in God, who heals the brokenhearted . . .

That all families in our community, like Joshua's household, serve the Lord in their love and support of one another and their contributions to our neighborhoods . . .

*Presider:* Gracious God, hear our prayers. Instill in us your Spirit so that we may carry on in the certainty of your Son's words of spirit and life. In his name, we pray. **Amen.**

### COLLECT

Let us pray.

*Pause for silent prayer*

O God, who cause the minds of the faithful to unite in a single purpose,
grant your people to love what you command
and to desire what you promise,
that, amid the uncertainties of this world,
our hearts may be fixed on that place where true gladness is found.
Through our Lord Jesus Christ, your Son,
who lives and reigns with you in the unity of the Holy Spirit,
one God, for ever and ever. **Amen.**

### FIRST READING

Josh 24:1-2a, 15-17, 18b

Joshua gathered together all the tribes of Israel at Shechem,
summoning their elders, their leaders, their judges, and their officers.
When they stood in ranks before God,
Joshua addressed all the people:
"If it does not please you to serve the LORD,
decide today whom you will serve,
the gods your fathers served beyond the River
or the gods of the Amorites in whose country you are now dwelling.
As for me and my household, we will serve the LORD."

But the people answered,
"Far be it from us to forsake the LORD for the service of other gods.
For it was the LORD, our God,
who brought us and our fathers up out of the land of Egypt,
out of a state of slavery.
He performed those great miracles before our very eyes
and protected us along our entire journey
and among the peoples through whom we passed.
Therefore we also will serve the LORD, for he is our God."

### RESPONSORIAL PSALM

Ps 34:2-3, 16-17, 18-19, 20-21

℟. (9a) Taste and see the goodness of the Lord.

I will bless the LORD at all times;
his praise shall be ever in my mouth.
Let my soul glory in the LORD;
the lowly will hear me and be glad.

℟. Taste and see the goodness of the Lord.

The LORD has eyes for the just,
  and ears for their cry.
The LORD confronts the evildoers,
  to destroy remembrance of them from
    the earth.

R̸. Taste and see the goodness of the Lord.

When the just cry out, the LORD hears them,
  and from all their distress he rescues
    them.
The LORD is close to the brokenhearted;
  and those who are crushed in spirit he
    saves.

R̸. Taste and see the goodness of the Lord.

Many are the troubles of the just one,
  but out of them all the LORD delivers him;
he watches over all his bones;
  not one of them shall be broken.

R̸. Taste and see the goodness of the Lord.

**SECOND READING**
Eph 5:21-32

Brothers and sisters:
Be subordinate to one another out of
    reverence for Christ.
Wives should be subordinate to their
    husbands as to the Lord.
For the husband is head of his wife
    just as Christ is head of the church,
    he himself the savior of the body.
As the church is subordinate to Christ,
    so wives should be subordinate to their
        husbands in everything.
Husbands, love your wives,
    even as Christ loved the church
    and handed himself over for her to
        sanctify her,
    cleansing her by the bath of water with
        the word,
    that he might present to himself the
        church in splendor,
    without spot or wrinkle or any such thing,
    that she might be holy and without
        blemish.
So also husbands should love their wives
    as their own bodies.
He who loves his wife loves himself.
For no one hates his own flesh
    but rather nourishes and cherishes it,
    even as Christ does the church,
    because we are members of his body.
*For this reason a man shall leave his father*
    *and his mother*
    *and be joined to his wife,*
    *and the two shall become one flesh.*
This is a great mystery,
    but I speak in reference to Christ and
        the church.

*or Eph 5:2a, 25-32 in Appendix A, p. 302.*

## About Liturgy

***Ministers of Communion:*** As we come to the final weeks of Summer Ordinary Time and enter into another season of fall liturgies, this is a good time to search for new liturgical ministers and to offer ongoing formation for current ministers. Let's examine two basic training points for Communion ministers that might get overlooked in all the details of doing this ministry.

*Focus on the right things*: The focus of the Communion minister is always on the following two aspects of the presence of Christ: First, Christ is present in the consecrated elements of bread and wine, the Body and Blood of Christ. The way the minister carries, holds, and moves with these should convey their preciousness and centrality to the community's gathering. Second, Christ is present in the people of God, within every individual who stands before them, no matter how short that time is. Every gesture and movement in their interactions with the assembly should also convey reverence for the precious gift of Christ present in each person we meet.

*Take enough time:* Communion ministers have about four seconds to *minister* to the person before them. That's not a lot of time to convey everything that Communion means. There can also be pressure to move the Communion line quickly because the Mass went long and the next group is already starting to come in! Yet four seconds is certainly enough time to be present *as* the Body of Christ for the person before us. Therefore let us not dismiss being a *minister* in order to *administer* the Body and Blood of Christ efficiently. With each person, we must take the time to smile and look at them lovingly in their eyes; to speak clearly and confidently, proclaiming joyfully, "The Body/Blood of Christ." If there are a large number of communicants or not enough time to do this well, the solution is not to speed up the pace but to assign more Communion ministers to this important work the assembly does for one another through Christ.

## About Liturgical Music

***Connecting the gospel to Communion:*** In today's gospel, we hear Simon Peter say, "Master, to whom shall we go? / You have the words of eternal life" (John 6:68). This is a fitting concluding statement to the Johannine readings we've heard over the last five weeks focusing on Jesus, the living Bread. John's gospel began with Jesus the Logos, the Word, and here, that Word becomes the words of eternal life with which we are fed, in which we find our only refuge.

The US bishops' document on music in the liturgy, Sing to the Lord, says, "Following ancient Roman liturgical tradition, the Communion song might reflect themes of the Gospel reading of the day" (191). We often look for Communion songs with texts that speak of the act of eating and drinking the Body and Blood of Christ. Yet making an intentional connection between the nourishment we receive at the altar of the Eucharist and that which we had received at the altar of the Word unites two aspects of the presence of Christ we encounter at Mass: Christ in Word and in sacrament.

***Music suggestions:*** Bob Hurd has written three collections of music for Communion with Oregon Catholic Press that echo the Scriptures of the day and connect them to the action of sharing in the Eucharist. Two of these are called *A Lenten Journey* and *One with the Risen Lord*, which focus on the seasons of Lent and Easter respectively. The third collection, *Dining in the Kingdom*, focuses on the Communion rite and connects it with images from Ordinary Time Scripture texts. One piece, "To Whom Else Shall We Go," fits perfectly with today's gospel. The gentle pulse of music nicely accompanies us in procession to the altar.

**AUGUST 26, 2018**
## TWENTY-FIRST SUNDAY
## IN ORDINARY TIME

## SPIRITUALITY

**GOSPEL ACCLAMATION**
James 1:18

R̸. Alleluia, alleluia.
The Father willed to give us birth by the word
    of truth
that we may be a kind of firstfruits of his
    creatures.
R̸. Alleluia, alleluia.

## Gospel    Mark 7:1-8, 14-15, 21-23;
L125B

When the Pharisees with some
    scribes who had come from
    Jerusalem
    gathered around Jesus,
    they observed that some of his
        disciples ate their meals
    with unclean, that is, unwashed,
        hands.
—For the Pharisees and, in fact, all
    Jews,
    do not eat without carefully wash-
        ing their hands,
    keeping the tradition of the elders.
And on coming from the marketplace
    they do not eat without purifying
        themselves.
And there are many other things that
    they have traditionally observed,
    the purification of cups and jugs and
        kettles and beds.—
So the Pharisees and scribes questioned
    him,
    "Why do your disciples not follow the
        tradition of the elders
    but instead eat a meal with unclean
        hands?"
He responded,
    "Well did Isaiah prophesy about you
        hypocrites, as it is written:
    *This people honors me with their
        lips,*
        *but their hearts are far from me;*
    *in vain do they worship me,*
        *teaching as doctrines human
            precepts.*
    You disregard God's commandment but
        cling to human tradition."

*Continued in Appendix A, p. 302.*

### Reflecting on the Gospel

Today we return to the Gospel of Mark after a five-week trip through John 6. In some ways Mark may seem to be familiar territory after the theological digression through the bread of life discourse and its antecedents. There are some explanatory notes in the gospel today that seem intended for a non-Jewish audience. Mark tells us about some Jewish practices of the time that would have been unfamiliar to the readers of his gospel. For this reason among others the audience would have been sizably, if not majority, Gentile. So quickly (a few decades) after Jesus' death and resurrection the gospel message moved beyond the Jewish soil where it first took root, and grew among Gentiles. It's almost like a cultivated ivy that leaped over a natural boundary to take root beyond the garden.

With this gospel reading it is as though we are listening in to one side of a family feud. We hear the early Christians' take on their elder sibling's faith. Not surprisingly, the Christians were critical of Jewish practices, claiming they missed the point. But it would be a misreading to see this only as a history lesson. The practices criticized in this gospel are perilously close to those of any religious person. There is a strong temptation to believe that we, by our actions and good deeds, make ourselves worthy of God. It can be easy to focus on the externals of religious practice and miss the point of religion. It can be easy to focus on ritual washing, or any ritual, and miss the deeper, more meaningful action that the ritual points to.

We can imagine attending a birthday party with the focus on what kind and flavor of cake and ice cream, when the "Happy Birthday" song is sung, how it is sung, who sings it, whether there is a birthday wish, whether the wish was "voiced" thereby nullifying it, or kept to the wisher thereby guaranteeing its fruition, and many other details of the event. All of the focus on the external ritual of the birthday can cause us to forget that this is a celebration of life for the one whose birthday it is. The party with its attendant rituals should not pull us away from the celebration of the individual.

The early Christians (like Isaiah who is quoted) criticized those who would misplace the emphasis on the externals. Their admonition is not for their theological opponents only. It's also for us.

### Living the Paschal Mystery

Why is it so easy to think that if we "do it right" all will be well? In fact we all have had experience with so much time and energy going into presentation, preparation, details, etc. that we are left missing the mark. We have probably seen this happen at holiday gatherings, birthday parties, and more. But it can also happen in one's day-to-day routine. Things need to be fixed, addressed, or made better. Our attention on these details, important as they may seem, can pull us away from real human beings seeking relationship. Being present, without distraction, to those around us is often a more profound gift than any other external.

When a child seeks our attention, a parent calls to check in, or a friend asks how we are doing, each of these is a moment of grace. Being available to another without critique or commentary is a tremendous gift. Rather than focus on externals, this gospel reminds us to take a few moments to examine what really matters. Once we do that, we can place our focus there. This may cause us to reprioritize our thoughts and actions, but that is precisely the point.

### Focusing the Gospel

*Mark 7:1-8, 14-15, 21-23*

Today we return to Mark's gospel with a confrontation that Mark's Christian readers knew all too well. A contentious debate raged in the early church as to whether or not Christians should continue to observe the ritual practices of Judaism. Jesus challenges the scribes' insistence that faithfulness to ceremonial washings and other rituals constitutes complete faithfulness to the will of God. He scandalizes his hearers by proclaiming, "Nothing that enters one from outside can defile that person; / but the things that come out from within are what defile." It is the good that one does, motivated by the spirit of God within a believer's heart, that is important in the eyes of God, not how scrupulously he or she keeps the laws and rituals mandated by tradition.

### Focusing the First Reading

*Deut 4:1-2, 6-8*

Over the course of the centuries, the scribes of Judaism constructed a rigid order of definitions, admonitions, principles, and laws based on the Pentateuch, summarized in Moses' eloquent words to the nation of Israel in today's first reading. As a result, the ethical and moral foundation of the law was often buried under a mountain of rules and taboos. Jesus' teachings (such as today's encounter with the Pharisees over the rituals of washing) refocus the canons of Israel on discerning the word of God in the sanctuary of the human heart and living one's life on that discernment. Jesus' continuing challenges to the accepted order of the law and tradition further widen the gulf between Jesus and the Jewish establishment.

### Focusing the Responsorial Psalm

*Ps 15:2-3, 3-4, 4-5 (1a)*

Psalm 15 was probably sung as an entrance song at temple worship. It begins with a question that is omitted from today's responsorial: "Lord, who may abide in your tent?" (NABRE). The rest of the psalm answers the question. The verses selected for today's responsorial emphasize God's call to justice and kindness as centered in the human heart.

### Focusing the Second Reading

*Jas 1:17-18, 21b-22, 27*

The second reading over the next five Sundays is taken from the letter traditionally attributed to James, "the brother of the Lord" and leader of the Jerusalem community. This brief epistle is a series of guidelines on the role of Christian morals in everyday life. Many scholars believe the letter of James was originally a sermon or series of homilies that were recorded in writing by a scribe. Today's passage from James exhorts us to be constantly open to the "gift" of God's word that has been "planted" within us and act upon that word by works of generosity and compassion ("Be doers of the word and not hearers only").

**PROMPTS FOR HOMILISTS, CATECHISTS, AND RCIA TEAMS**

Recall experiences in your life when your "heart" required you to act contrary to your "head."

Why do people become disaffected by religion that has become "institutionalized"? How can a parish community respond to such disaffection?

What practice or ritual of your faith do you find most meaningful to you, that inspires you in living your faith, that makes you most aware and appreciative of God's presence in your life?

What's the difference between one's *faith* and one's *religion*?

## Model Penitential Act

*Presider:* Confident of God's constant mercy and forgiveness, let us call to mind our sins and failings. *[pause]*

Father of compassion and peace: Lord, have mercy.

Word of God made human for us: Christ, have mercy.

Spirit of wisdom and grace: Lord, have mercy.

## Homily Points

• As Jesus makes clear in today's gospel, who we are, what we believe, how we respond to life's challenges begin within our hearts, the place where God dwells inside every one of us. Conversely, the evil we are capable of, the hurt we inflict on others, the degrading of the world that God created also begin within our hearts—when God is displaced by selfishness, anger, greed, hatred. Today's gospel challenges us to look into the depths of our hearts to realize exactly what we feel passionate about, what we truly believe, what we are called to do with this life God has given us. The meaning of faith is centered in our hearts, in that most personal of spaces where God dwells inside of us.

• In the hurts, indignities, and injustices perpetrated against us, what is often worse than the act itself is what the act does to us as persons: we respond with suspicion, cynicism, self-absorption, anger, vengeance. To be a disciple of Jesus is not to let those things "outside" us displace the grace of God "inside" us, but to let God's presence transform into compassion and reconciliation the evil that we have encountered "outside" us.

• Sometimes we become so absorbed with the formality of the rituals and texts we pray that we lose sight of the meaning of the words or what the rite is designed to express. Like the Pharisees who are obsessed with the details of ritual hand washing, we may disconnect going to church from being church, the ritual of baptism from the life of baptism, the Communion wafer from eucharistic life. Christ calls us, in today's gospel, to worship God with the integrity of our hearts, to live the words of the prayers that have become rote in our lives, to embrace the true gospel "traditions" of compassion, mercy, and forgiveness. Words and rituals help us express our faith—but faith begins within ourselves, in our beliefs and perspective of the world and our attitudes toward others.

## Model Universal Prayer (Prayer of the Faithful)

*Presider:* To our Father in heaven, who hears the yearnings of every human heart, let us pray.

*Response:* Lord, hear our prayer.

That the pastors and ministers of our church may inspire human hearts to embrace God's mercy and love in their lives . . .

That all businesses and financial institutions may put justice and the common good of their workers, clients, and customers before corporate interests and profit . . .

That the generosity we extend to the poor, the hungry, and the homeless may be an offering of thanksgiving for God's many blessings to us . . .

That the word of God planted in all of us may be revealed in our parish's worship and work together . . .

*Presider:* May your word of life and love "take root" in our hearts, O God, so that these prayers we offer may become a harvest of justice and peace for all our brothers and sisters. In Jesus' name, we pray. **Amen.**

**COLLECT**

Let us pray.

*Pause for silent prayer*

God of might, giver of every good gift,
put into our hearts the love of your name,
so that, by deepening our sense of
     reverence,
you may nurture in us what is good
and, by your watchful care,
keep safe what you have nurtured.
Through our Lord Jesus Christ, your Son,
who lives and reigns with you in the unity
     of the Holy Spirit,
one God, for ever and ever. **Amen.**

**FIRST READING**

Deut 4:1-2, 6-8

Moses said to the people:
     "Now, Israel, hear the statutes and
          decrees
     which I am teaching you to observe,
     that you may live, and may enter in and
          take possession of the land
     which the LORD, the God of your
          fathers, is giving you.
In your observance of the commandments
     of the LORD, your God,
     which I enjoin upon you,
     you shall not add to what I command
          you nor subtract from it.
Observe them carefully,
     for thus will you give evidence
     of your wisdom and intelligence to the
          nations,
     who will hear of all these statutes and
          say,
     'This great nation is truly a wise and
          intelligent people.'
For what great nation is there
     that has gods so close to it as the LORD,
          our God, is to us
     whenever we call upon him?
Or what great nation has statutes and
          decrees
     that are as just as this whole law
     which I am setting before you today?"

**RESPONSORIAL PSALM**

Ps 15:2-3, 3-4, 4-5

R꜄. (1a) The one who does justice will live in the presence of the Lord.

Whoever walks blamelessly and does justice;
  who thinks the truth in his heart
  and slanders not with his tongue.

R꜄. The one who does justice will live in the presence of the Lord.

Who harms not his fellow man,
  nor takes up a reproach against his neighbor;
by whom the reprobate is despised,
  while he honors those who fear the LORD.

R꜄. The one who does justice will live in the presence of the Lord.

Who lends not his money at usury
  and accepts no bribe against the innocent.
Whoever does these things
  shall never be disturbed.

R꜄. The one who does justice will live in the presence of the Lord.

**SECOND READING**

Jas 1:17-18, 21b-22, 27

Dearest brothers and sisters:
All good giving and every perfect gift is from above,
  coming down from the Father of lights,
  with whom there is no alteration or shadow caused by change.
He willed to give us birth by the word of truth
  that we may be a kind of firstfruits of his creatures.

Humbly welcome the word that has been planted in you
  and is able to save your souls.

Be doers of the word and not hearers only, deluding yourselves.

Religion that is pure and undefiled before God and the Father is this:
  to care for orphans and widows in their affliction
  and to keep oneself unstained by the world.

## About Liturgy

***Loving the people who do the liturgy:*** In this week's return to Mark, liturgists might get a bit nervous with today's gospel reading. Aren't disciplines and observing the rules important? Isn't following tradition a good thing? If we just tossed out all the guidelines, wouldn't liturgy become a free-for-all, with everyone doing their own thing and following their own preferences?

As one who has studied liturgy and all the liturgical books and at some point in my life debated the value of one shade of violet over another shade of purple for Advent . . . and had the same heated discussion all over again at Lent . . . I know exactly the sin of pedantry. And if it's not a sin, it should be.

There's a reason so many of us can get so caught up in the rules and rubrics of communal prayer. I want to believe that it's because liturgy touches each of us so deeply, especially when it's done well. Great liturgy moves us at a core place that we can't explain very rationally. So we go to the books and laws and the rational things we can control, and we put our heart and soul into "protecting" those in order to protect that which we love—the liturgy itself. Then come the blog posts and the rantings and the mean-spirited comments. Then come all the evil thoughts from within that defile and indeed make us what Jesus says today, hypocrites.

Our job as liturgists is certainly to love the liturgy. But our mission as disciples is to love even more the people who do the liturgy. All members of the household of God, like us, have their foibles, their weaknesses, their personal likes and dislikes, and we are called to love them even at the expense of "correct" liturgy. For there can never be "correct" liturgy without true love for one another.

## About Liturgical Music

***What motivates us?:*** In 1982, the United States bishops issued guidelines for liturgical musicians, called Liturgical Music Today. It was the companion to the statement issued ten years earlier, called Music in Catholic Worship. Today those two documents have been succeeded by a new document called Sing to the Lord: Music in Divine Worship, issued in 2007. Although the latest document is inspired by and contains many references to its predecessors, there are some parts from the older documents that deserve to be remembered.

In light of today's gospel reading, this passage from Liturgical Music Today encapsulates everything that liturgical musicians should strive to be in order to honor God with both their lips and their hearts in true worship and obedience to God's commands:

> What motivates the pastoral musician? Why does he or she give so much time and effort to the service of the church at prayer? The only answer can be that the church musician is first a disciple and then a minister. The musician belongs first of all to the assembly; he or she is a worshipper above all. Like any member of the assembly, the pastoral musician needs to be a believer, needs to experience conversion, needs to hear the Gospel and so proclaim the praise of God. Thus, the pastoral musician is not merely an employee or volunteer. He or she is a minister, someone who shares faith, serves the community, and expresses the love of God and neighbor through music. (64)

## SPIRITUALITY

**GOSPEL ACCLAMATION**
cf. Matt 4:23

R✘. Alleluia, alleluia.
Jesus proclaimed the Gospel of the kingdom
and cured every disease among
    the people.
R✘. Alleluia, alleluia.

### Gospel

Mark 7:31-37; L128B

Again Jesus left the
    district of Tyre
and went by way
    of Sidon to the
    Sea of Galilee,
into the district of the
    Decapolis.
And people brought to him a
    deaf man who had a speech
    impediment
and begged him to lay his hand on
    him.
He took him off by himself away from
    the crowd.
He put his finger into the man's ears
    and, spitting, touched his tongue;
    then he looked up to heaven and
        groaned, and said to him,
    *"Ephphatha!"*—that is, "Be
        opened!"—
And immediately the man's ears were
    opened,
    his speech impediment was removed,
    and he spoke plainly.
He ordered them not to tell anyone.
But the more he ordered them not to,
    the more they proclaimed it.
They were exceedingly astonished and
    they said,
    "He has done all things well.
He makes the deaf hear and the mute
    speak."

### Reflecting on the Gospel

Have you ever seen odd behavior from someone you knew, or rather, thought you knew?! People, even close friends, can surprise us sometimes with their actions. Today we hear about a frankly odd miracle story that occurs only in the Gospel of Mark. Matthew and Luke, who used Mark as a source, apparently thought they had other miracle stories they could tell that would make the same point without repeating this one. And the Gospel of John tells us only seven "signs" that Jesus performed, and this is not one.

Upon reading this unique Markan story, I often imagine the episode and how it might be portrayed in artwork. Can we imagine Jesus putting his finger in another person's ear? Or Jesus spitting and touching the person's tongue, groaning in a foreign language? Even so, that's precisely what the gospel tells us happened. And the Aramaic term preserved in the Greek New Testament, *Ephphatha* is in the imperative singular form and clearly means, "Be opened."

Perhaps we are not surprised to hear that in the early centuries after Jesus' death and resurrection many thought of him as a magician. Even in the Acts of the Apostles, when the disciples heal in Jesus' name, Simon Magus offers them money so he can do the same. On some early Christian sarcophagi (burial chambers) Jesus is at times portrayed with a magic wand. We might excuse some of the crowds for thinking that Jesus had magic powers as it seems some later Christians did too!

But Jesus was not a magician. His mighty deeds were ushering in the kingdom of God. His actions were being done "by the finger of God" rather than by a magic wand. Jesus was more than a wonder-worker, though he definitely worked wonders.

The mighty deeds of Jesus were about restoration, healing, and wholeness. Those on the margins, those outcast, and those who were relegated to a kind of second-class citizenship on account of physical ailments were healed, made whole, and thereby restored to the community.

And as so often happens in the Gospel of Mark, Jesus orders those he heals not to tell anyone about it, but to no avail. Something so astonishing could not be kept under wraps. Almost like children, the more he told them not to, the more they proclaimed it. That is true evangelical zeal!

### Living the Paschal Mystery

We might not witness such dramatic deeds as the deaf hearing, or the mute speaking, but we witness God's activity in the world on a daily basis. We can participate in the activity of Jesus by bringing in the excluded, reaching out to those on the margins, and empathizing with those who have less. Each time we go outside of ourselves to deal with the needs of another person, we are acting as an "other Christ" or an *alter Christus*. By virtue of our baptism that is our vocation, to be another Christ on earth, ministering to those in need wherever and whenever we find them. Figuratively, and even literally, we can help to give voice to the voiceless, and assist those who cannot hear to hear. The voiceless might not be a mute, but instead the marginalized without access to the microphone of public debate. Those who cannot hear might not be the deaf, but those who are figuratively deaf to the injustice in our world. As another Christ, it is our duty as baptized Christians to enact God's kingdom on earth. Today we are given a model for doing that. When we do so, our behavior might be thought of as odd, but it is nevertheless our calling and our vocation.

## Focusing the Gospel

*Mark 7:31-37*

*Ephphatha*—"Be opened!" The exhortation *Ephphatha* is not only addressed to the man born deaf but also to his disciples both then and now who fail to hear and see and speak the presence of God in their very midst.

The Aramaic term *Ephphatha* literally means "be opened": Jesus "opens" not only the man's ears but also a life of community, shutting the door on exclusion from the people of God. Jesus' curing of the deaf man with spittle is an act of re-creation. God has entered human history in the extraordinary ministry of Jesus.

Mark includes several interesting details in his story of Jesus' curing of the deaf man. When presented with the deaf man, Jesus stops, makes time for the man, and takes him away from the crowd to a quiet, safe place. Jesus then "put his finger into the man's ears / and, spitting, touched his tongue." Jesus cures the man with only a fleeting word and, by his touch, he enters into the man's struggle and pain—in doing so, Jesus brings hope and healing to his life.

Throughout Mark's gospel, Jesus insists that his healings be kept quiet in order that his full identity be revealed and understood only in the light of his cross and resurrection. But this man, like so many others, cannot keep the Good News to himself. He is compelled to proclaim it despite an injunction from Jesus himself.

## Focusing the First Reading

*Isa 35:4-7a*

Isaiah's vision of a Messiah who would come with hope and healing is realized in the Jesus of the gospels: the deaf hear, the blind see, the silent are given voice, and the lame "leap like a stag."

## Focusing the Responsorial Psalm

*Ps 146:7, 8-9, 9-10 (1b)*

The Lord as healer of the sick, restorer of the broken, and protector of the fallen is praised by the psalmist in the second half of Psalm 146. True wisdom, the psalmist proclaims, is to trust in the God of creation, the Lord who is the source of all that is good.

## Focusing the Second Reading

*Jas 2:1-5*

Today's homily from the writer of James admonishes the community not to show favoritism to those who impress with their wealth or celebrity. The gospel calls us to see all men and women as equal sons and daughters of God—with a clear preference given to "those who are poor in the world" whom God has made "rich in faith and heirs of the kingdom."

**PROMPTS FOR HOMILISTS, CATECHISTS, AND RCIA TEAMS**

In what ways can we be "deaf" to the love of God?

When have you been especially blessed by another person's gift of simple listening?

What attitudes, situations, troubles, etc., in your life would you ask Jesus to "release" you from?

Who are among the most difficult to welcome into our lives? Who are those among us most often forgotten or ignored, if not out-and-out rejected? How can we create a place of welcome to them within our parish community?

## Model Penitential Act

*Presider:* Let us begin our celebration of the Eucharist by asking the God of mercy and healing to forgive us our sins and restore us to hope. *[pause]*

You heal the sick and infirm: Lord, have mercy.

You heal the broken and bring back the lost: Christ, have mercy.

You lift up the poor and the oppressed: Lord, have mercy.

## Homily Points

• Throughout the gospel, Jesus calls us to be open—*Ephphatha!*—to the possibilities for transformation through selfless love, for re-creation that is enabled by humble generosity, for restoration that can be brought about by perseverance and courage in the face of destruction. In times of grief, fear, and despair, we can be "deaf" to the presence of God, isolating ourselves from God's compassion and hope in the midst of such pain. But the spirit of *Ephphatha* is to recognize the possibilities for transforming our lives and the lives of the broken and isolated in the completeness and hope of God's loving presence in our midst. Discipleship is centered in Jesus' spirit of *Ephphatha*: to be "open" to the presence of God in times of joy and sorrow, to allow ourselves to be the means of God's healing and life for those unable to sense it.

• Jesus restores the deaf man's hearing with actions and the word *Ephphatha*—"Be opened!" In the midst of all the noise in our lives, we can be "deaf" to the presence of God. Fear and ignorance often distort our ability not only to hear but to see the good in the midst of bad, to recognize the reasons to hope in the midst of despair, to realize the possibilities for building community despite alienation. Jesus' word of *Ephphatha* is spoken to us, as well: that our hearts and spirits "be opened" to accepting God's love from those who are different and "uncool," to realizing God's presence in times and places that make us squirm, to seeking God's grace despite our difficulty to trust, to accept, to understand.

• The Aramaic phrase *Ephphatha* literally means "be opened": Jesus "opens" not only the man's ears but also his entire person to life in the community. *Ephphatha* is the prayer of every disciple: that we may be "opened" from our fears, our arrogance, our self-centeredness that make us "deaf" to God speaking in our midst and "mute" in responding to the cries of our brothers and sisters in our midst.

## Model Universal Prayer (Prayer of the Faithful)

*Presider: Ephphatha!*—"Be opened!" With hearts and spirits opened to God's healing presence, let us pray.

*Response:* Lord, hear our prayer.

For our church and parish community, that our work and worship together may bring healing and hope to our world . . .

For the ministers of our church and the leaders of nations, that they may proclaim the justice and peace of God without fear or compromise . . .

For the poor, the homeless, and all those in need, that they may find places of honor and welcome in our homes, parish, and community . . .

For local families in crisis, that God may be present to them in their love for one another and the care and support of family and friends . . .

*Presider:* Open our eyes and ears and hearts to your Spirit, O God, that everything we do and every moment you give us may speak of your loving presence in our world and bring to joyful completion these prayers we offer to you in the name of your Son, Jesus the compassionate healer. **Amen.**

## COLLECT

Let us pray.

*Pause for silent prayer*

O God, by whom we are redeemed and
receive adoption,
look graciously upon your beloved sons
and daughters,
that those who believe in Christ
may receive true freedom
and an everlasting inheritance.
Through our Lord Jesus Christ, your Son,
who lives and reigns with you in the unity
of the Holy Spirit,
one God, for ever and ever. **Amen.**

## FIRST READING

Isa 35:4-7a

Thus says the LORD:
Say to those whose hearts are
frightened:
Be strong, fear not!
Here is your God,
he comes with vindication;
with divine recompense
he comes to save you.
Then will the eyes of the blind be
opened,
the ears of the deaf be cleared;
then will the lame leap like a stag,
then the tongue of the mute will sing.
Streams will burst forth in the desert,
and rivers in the steppe.
The burning sands will become pools,
and the thirsty ground, springs of
water.

# CATECHESIS

## RESPONSORIAL PSALM

Ps 146:6-7, 8-9, 9-10

R̸. (1b) Praise the Lord, my soul!
*or:*
R̸. Alleluia.

The God of Jacob keeps faith forever,
    secures justice for the oppressed,
    gives food to the hungry.
The Lᴏʀᴅ sets captives free.

R̸. Praise the Lord, my soul!
*or:*
R̸. Alleluia.

The Lᴏʀᴅ gives sight to the blind;
    the Lᴏʀᴅ raises up those who were
        bowed down.
The Lᴏʀᴅ loves the just;
    the Lᴏʀᴅ protects strangers.

R̸. Praise the Lord, my soul!
*or:*
R̸. Alleluia.

The fatherless and the widow the Lᴏʀᴅ
    sustains,
    but the way of the wicked he thwarts.
The Lᴏʀᴅ shall reign forever;
    your God, O Zion, through all
        generations.
Alleluia.

R̸. Praise the Lord, my soul!
*or:*
R̸. Alleluia.

## SECOND READING

Jas 2:1-5

My brothers and sisters, show no
    partiality
as you adhere to the faith in our
    glorious Lord Jesus Christ.
For if a man with gold rings and fine
    clothes
comes into your assembly,
and a poor person in shabby clothes
    also comes in,
and you pay attention to the one
    wearing the fine clothes
and say, "Sit here, please,"
while you say to the poor one, "Stand
    there," or "Sit at my feet,"
have you not made distinctions among
    yourselves
and become judges with evil designs?

Listen, my beloved brothers and sisters.
Did not God choose those who are poor in
    the world
    to be rich in faith and heirs of the
        kingdom
    that he promised to those who love him?

## About Liturgy

*Hierarchy in the liturgy:* This week's second reading from James helps us reflect on distinctions and hierarchy in the liturgy. Paragraph 28 of the Constitution on the Sacred Liturgy reminds us, "All taking part in liturgical celebrations, whether ministers or members of the congregation, should do all that pertains to them, and no more, taking into account the rite and the liturgical norms."

Whenever the church gathers, it gathers as one body. Yet it is a body, as St. Paul says, made up of many parts. Each part, like the parts of the body, has a specific role to play in order to help the body function at its fullest and most effective capacity. If the foot tried to do what the hand does, it might succeed, but it couldn't be as effective as the hand in doing those things. In addition, the functions that only the foot could do would be neglected as it tried to be a hand.

Likewise in the liturgy, each minister has a specific part to play. If we tried to do multiple parts, for example, serve as a lector and a Communion minister in the same Mass, whether by choice or by necessity, the liturgy would not be as effective in reflecting the integral relationship of the members of the Body of Christ. This is what is meant by "hierarchy." It is not meant as a term that pits one member against another and measures their relative value. Rather, hierarchy reflects each part's inherent worth and our essential need, as the Body of Christ, for one another. No one and no part in the body is dispensable. This relational equality of roles is emphasized in paragraph 32 of the same document: "In the liturgy, apart from the distinctions arising from liturgical function or sacred Orders and apart from the honors due to civil authorities in accordance with liturgical law, no special preference is to be accorded any private persons or classes of persons, whether in the ceremonies or by external display."

Liturgy is never an event for the privileged. It is a public act for all who desire to play their part in the Body of Christ.

## About Liturgical Music

*The role of the responsorial psalm:* In order to select the most appropriate songs for a liturgy, often liturgical musicians try to discern a particular Sunday's "theme" or focus. This is at once a good yet futile endeavor. Futile because every liturgy's "theme" is always the same: the paschal mystery of Christ. When we gather in the name of the Trinity, we are always gathered by the action of Christ. We recall the love of God the Father through the life, death, and resurrection of Christ. We hope in the promise of eternal life in Christ that transforms our present time even now. This is the constant theme of every liturgy.

However, we can explore various facets of that theme, as a diamond might reflect a particular color if the light catches it at the right spot. To help us discern what that facet of the paschal mystery might be for any Sunday, we can turn to the responsorial psalm. This sung response gives us a musical summary of that day's focus in that it frames how we might understand the first reading of that day. In turn, the first reading is always connected in imagery or focus to the gospel reading, which serves as the "lens" for clarifying that day's focus.

If you need some help discerning a liturgy's theme, read the gospel reading and then the first reading. Finally, reflect on the psalm as a summary of the connective theme between those two passages.

**SEPTEMBER 9, 2018**
# TWENTY-THIRD SUNDAY
# IN ORDINARY TIME

## SPIRITUALITY

### GOSPEL ACCLAMATION
Gal 6:14

℟. Alleluia, alleluia.
May I never boast except in the cross of our Lord
through which the world has been crucified to me and I to the world.
℟. Alleluia, alleluia.

### Gospel

Mark 8:27-35; L131B

Jesus and his disciples set out
    for the villages of Caesarea Philippi.
Along the way he asked his disciples,
    "Who do people say that I am?"
They said in reply,
    "John the Baptist, others Elijah,
    still others one of the prophets."
And he asked them,
    "But who do you say that I am?"
Peter said to him in reply,
    "You are the Christ."
Then he warned them not to tell anyone
    about him.

He began to teach them
    that the Son of Man must suffer greatly
    and be rejected by the elders, the chief
        priests, and the scribes,
    and be killed, and rise after three days.
He spoke this openly.
Then Peter took him aside and began to
    rebuke him.
At this he turned around and, looking at
    his disciples,
    rebuked Peter and said, "Get behind
        me, Satan.
You are thinking not as God does, but as
    human beings do."

He summoned the crowd with his
    disciples and said to them,
    "Whoever wishes to come after me
        must deny himself,
    take up his cross, and follow me.
For whoever wishes to save his life will
    lose it,
    but whoever loses his life for my sake
    and that of the gospel will save it."

### Reflecting on the Gospel

There is a story of the US civil rights era where one person told another how much he admired Martin Luther King Jr. The second person responded that there was a group who was going to march with Dr. King. If he was an admirer, would he like to join them in the march? "No," the first person said. "I could get hurt doing that. I'm an admirer, not a follower."

Jesus tells the crowds and his disciples that to be one of his followers one must be ready to "take up his cross, and follow me." Jesus does not need admirers. But he does want followers. And those followers might get hurt. In fact, they are told to take up their cross. The Christian life is not likened to a recliner, but a cross. As founder and leader of this movement, Jesus foretells his own suffering and death. This is met with incredulity on Peter's part so much so that he rebukes Jesus! True to form, Peter's rebuking of Jesus comes on the heels of his confession that Jesus is the Christ. It seems Peter misunderstood the implication of his own confession. This should be a warning for us too who confess Jesus as Christ, Lord, or any other title we choose. Our own understanding of who Jesus is, and what he is to do, may not conform to the reality of who Jesus is, and what he is to do. Though Peter had been one of the first disciples called by Jesus, and had witnessed his ministry up to this point, he still misunderstood.

This story of "Peter's confession" forms the centerpiece of the Gospel of Mark. Not only is it in the literal center of the gospel (chapter 8 of 16 chapters) but it is the narrative center as well. We the readers learned in Mark 1:1 that this is the gospel of Jesus *Christ*, the Son of God. Now in chapter 8, for the first time in the gospel, a human being (Peter) recognizes Jesus for who he is, the Christ. Not until the death of Jesus will another human being (the centurion) recognize Jesus as Son of God, the second title of Jesus from Mark 1:1. This becomes a literary way of expressing Jesus' identity. He is Christ, and he will suffer and die. Only after doing so can he be fully understood as Son of God.

Nowhere in the Hebrew Scriptures, what we call the Old Testament, does it say that the Messiah would die, much less even suffer. This is likely why Peter rebukes Jesus after Jesus says he will suffer and die. Peter thinks Jesus has it all wrong: the Christ is not going to suffer, but will rule triumphantly. Jesus, however, knows otherwise. Jesus can only be the Christ, the Son of God, by suffering and dying on the cross. His disciples are called not to be mere admirers, but to take up their crosses and follow him.

### Living the Paschal Mystery

It's so much more convenient and easy to be an admirer of Jesus rather than a follower. But Jesus is not calling admirers. He wants those who will take up their own cross in following him. Our crosses will be those burdens we carry by doing justice, as Jesus did. We will bear our crosses when we tend to the sick, shelter the homeless, feed the hungry, clothe the naked, give drink to the thirsty, and more. In classical Catholic terms, we refer to these as the corporal works of mercy. Performing these acts of mercy takes us outside of ourselves. It places others' needs ahead of our own. We die to self so that others might live.

Following Jesus is not about convenience, easy living, or mere admiration. We only need to see the image of the cross to be reminded of that. As Jesus had his cross, we have ours. To be his disciples, we are to take it up and carry it.

## Focusing the Gospel

*Mark 8:27-35*

In today's gospel, Peter is a model of vacillating faith—a model that typifies our own reaction to the call to discipleship.

Caesarea Philippi was a bazaar of worship places and temples, with altars erected to every concept of divinity from the gods of Greece to the godhead of Caesar. Amid this marketplace of gods, Jesus asks the Twelve, "Who do people say that I am? . . . who do *you* say that I am?" This is a turning point in Mark's gospel: Peter responds, on behalf of the Twelve (?), by saying that Jesus is the Messiah. Now for the first time in Mark's gospel, Jesus speaks about dark things ahead of him: rejection, suffering, death, and ultimate resurrection (concepts that the disciples are unable to grasp).

To the question Jesus poses (a moment recorded in all three Synoptics), Peter immediately confesses his faith in Jesus as the Messiah, the long-awaited Anointed One of God. But when Jesus begins to speak as one who will suffer rejection and death, Peter immediately objects. Peter's reaction is in keeping with what was the accepted notion of the time of a messiah who would restore the ancient Davidic kingdom's political and economic fortunes. Jesus' rebuke of Peter challenges that image of the Christ as a human construct, not that of God.

## Focusing the First Reading

*Isa 50:4c-9a*

Today's first reading is taken from the third Servant Song of the prophet Isaiah (a portion of this passage is read every year on Palm Sunday). Isaiah portrays God's servant as one who will be insulted, abused, and rejected for the word God has called him to proclaim. The prophet himself seems to have seen this figure as Israel personified (Isa 49:3); Christians see this as a prophecy that is ultimately fulfilled in Jesus.

## Focusing the Responsorial Psalm

*Ps 116:1-2, 3-4, 5-6, 8-9 (9)*

When a faithful Jew was saved from illness or catastrophe, he would come to the temple to offer a sacrifice of thanksgiving to the Lord for his deliverance. The first half of Psalm 116 is the song of such thanksgiving. In the Old Testament, the Hebrew term translated here as *gracious* is used only for the Lord, describing God's constant and limitless protection and help to the humble and just.

## Focusing the Second Reading

*Jas 2:14-18*

Today's reading from James's letter is the heart of the epistle: the relationship of faith to good works. Faith that is alive naturally manifests itself in action. Dead faith produces no good works, inspires no loving response to the Word we have heard, and possesses no power to save. It is not faith at all. It is dead. Living faith, however, rejoices in God's word and celebrates that presence in acts of compassion and reconciliation.

---

### PROMPTS FOR HOMILISTS, CATECHISTS, AND RCIA TEAMS

In what ways can we "crucify" our own interests for the sake of others?

How do our actions sometimes give conflicting answers to Jesus' question in today's gospel: "Who do you say that I am?"

In whom have you seen the face of the crucified Christ?

What is the most difficult and challenging cross that you carry? Has it ever been a means of resurrection in your life?

Has "knowing" Jesus ever posed a serious challenge to you?

## Model Penitential Act

*Presider:* As we prepare to celebrate these sacred mysteries, let us call to mind our sins and failings. *[pause]*

Christ Jesus, you call us out of darkness into light: Lord, have mercy.

Christ Jesus, you lead us from death to God's dwelling place: Christ, have mercy.

Christ Jesus, you transform our crosses into the life of your resurrection: Lord, have mercy.

## Homily Points

• The question Jesus poses to his disciples he also poses to us: Who do you say I am? Every decision we make, every action we take proclaims who we believe Jesus is and what his Gospel means to us. Sometimes answering that question demands that we put aside our fears and self-importance to say to ourselves and our community, "You are the Christ whom God has sent to teach us his way of humble gratitude, joyful service, and just peace." Our love for family and friends, our commitment to the highest moral standards, our willingness to take the first step toward reconciliation and forgiveness is our confession of faith in Jesus as the Love and Word of God incarnate.

• Taking up our crosses—however heavy the wood, whatever Calvary that cross takes us—sometimes demands a difficult change in our lives. But in "dying" to ourselves we can "rise" to the life of God. In some of the hardest words he speaks in the gospel, Jesus reminds us that real discipleship means to "crucify" our own needs and comfort for that of others; to take on with humility the demanding role of servant to those in need; to intentionally seek the happiness of those we love regardless of the cost to ourselves. Christ calls us to be his disciples exactly where we are. He asks us to take up our crosses in the everyday joys and sorrows we live in our homes and communities.

• Peter's urging Jesus not to talk about the passion that is before them and keep it "upbeat" is an attempt to deny the reality of suffering. Peter's reaction is much like our own: we readily embrace the reassuring, optimistic Jesus of Easter glory—but back away from the suffering, humiliated, crucified Jesus. For Jesus, the challenge of the pain and disappointment we confront is not to sink into self-pity or deny our anger or passively accept the role of victim. To follow Jesus is to accept the reality of our suffering and transform such experiences of the cross into moments of resurrection in which generous compassion, humble growth, and selfless consolation are brought to life.

## Model Universal Prayer (Prayer of the Faithful)

*Presider:* Let us offer our prayers to our gracious and merciful Father in heaven.

*Response:* Lord, hear our prayer.

That all who serve our church may proclaim the Gospel with courage and integrity . . .

That the laws of the world's governments may honor the dignity of the poor . . .

That the victory of the crucified Christ will be the strength of those believers and churches who are persecuted for their faith and beliefs . . .

That every ministry of our parish may proclaim the Messiah's presence among us . . .

*Presider:* Gracious God, hear the prayers we lift up to you. By your grace, may we follow your Son by "crucifying" our self-interests and wants and take up our crosses to bring the life of his resurrection into our world. We offer these prayers in the name of Jesus, the Messiah and Redeemer. **Amen.**

COLLECT

Let us pray.

*Pause for silent prayer*

Look upon us, O God,
Creator and ruler of all things,
and, that we may feel the working of your mercy,
grant that we may serve you with all our heart.
Through our Lord Jesus Christ, your Son,
who lives and reigns with you in the unity of the Holy Spirit,
one God, for ever and ever. **Amen.**

### FIRST READING
Isa 50:4c-9a

The Lord GOD opens my ear that I may hear;
and I have not rebelled,
have not turned back.
I gave my back to those who beat me,
my cheeks to those who plucked my beard;
my face I did not shield
from buffets and spitting.

The Lord GOD is my help,
therefore I am not disgraced;
I have set my face like flint,
knowing that I shall not be put to shame.
He is near who upholds my right;
if anyone wishes to oppose me,
let us appear together.
Who disputes my right?
Let that man confront me.
See, the Lord GOD is my help;
who will prove me wrong?

### RESPONSORIAL PSALM
Ps 116:1-2, 3-4, 5-6, 8-9

R̸. (9) I will walk before the Lord, in the land of the living.
*or:*
R̸. Alleluia.

I love the LORD because he has heard
my voice in supplication,
because he has inclined his ear to me
the day I called.

R̸. I will walk before the Lord, in the land of the living.
*or:*
R̸. Alleluia.

The cords of death encompassed me;
 the snares of the netherworld seized
  upon me;
 I fell into distress and sorrow,
and I called upon the name of the LORD,
 "O LORD, save my life!"

R̸. I will walk before the Lord, in the land
 of the living.
 *or:*
R̸. Alleluia.

Gracious is the LORD and just;
 yes, our God is merciful.
The LORD keeps the little ones;
 I was brought low, and he saved me.

R̸. I will walk before the Lord, in the land
 of the living.
 *or:*
R̸. Alleluia.

For he has freed my soul from death,
 my eyes from tears, my feet from
  stumbling.
I shall walk before the LORD
 in the land of the living.

R̸. I will walk before the Lord, in the land
 of the living.
 *or:*
R̸. Alleluia.

### SECOND READING
Jas 2:14-18

What good is it, my brothers and sisters,
 if someone says he has faith but does
  not have works?
Can that faith save him?
If a brother or sister has nothing to wear
 and has no food for the day,
 and one of you says to them,
 "Go in peace, keep warm, and eat well,"
 but you do not give them the necessities
  of the body,
 what good is it?
So also faith of itself,
 if it does not have works, is dead.

Indeed someone might say,
 "You have faith and I have works."
Demonstrate your faith to me without
 works,
 and I will demonstrate my faith to you
  from my works.

## About Liturgy

***Liturgy and social justice:*** Sometimes there is a debate among people of goodwill about which is more important, liturgy or doing works of justice. We hear this dichotomy in phrases like, "As long as I love others, I don't really have to go to Mass"; or its opposite, "As long as I go to Mass, I'll be a good Catholic."

The truth, however, is that both worship and social justice are necessary because both are really one and the same action. One cannot love others as Christ loved us without giving praise to God in the gathering of the assembly. This is because the very command of Jesus, if we wanted to remember him, was to "do this," that is, eat and drink of his Body and Blood. Furthermore, one cannot give true worship to the Father without living as Jesus lived. This is because the very command of Jesus, if we wanted to gain the life he promised, was to "take up [your] cross, and follow me," that is, love the outcast, dine with the sinner, reconcile with the enemy, and put aside your needs and lose your life in order to save it.

What we do on Sunday in the Eucharist is the mirror reflection of how we live our lives in service to those in need throughout the week. How we serve others wherever we go in our daily lives reflects the authenticity of our prayer on Sunday. For Christians, proclaiming the Word, sharing the Eucharist, serving those in need, and carrying our cross with joy in the world is one continuous act of worship and discipleship.

Saint John Paul II said it most eloquently this way in his apostolic letter on the Eucharist: "We cannot delude ourselves: by our mutual love and, in particular, by our concern for those in need we will be recognized as true followers of Christ. This will be the criterion by which the authenticity of our Eucharistic celebrations is judged" (*Mane nobiscum Domine* 28).

## About Liturgical Music

***A bit of Lent in September:*** When it comes time for Lent and the Sacred Triduum, liturgical musicians might wonder how to help their assemblies learn so much music for those sacred days in such a way that it is music the assembly will already know and sing "by heart" when these paschal celebrations come around in the liturgical year.

One way we can train our assemblies to learn the music of our most important celebrations of the year is to find opportunities throughout the entire liturgical year to incorporate some of our Lenten and Triduum songs. Today's readings give us a good opportunity to focus on some hymns around the cross, sacrifice, and discipleship.

***Song suggestions:*** Some songs that may work for both this Sunday and Lent and the Triduum include hymns that reflect on the cross and our call to follow Jesus ever to Jerusalem. "Take Up Your Cross" with text by Charles Everest (public domain) and set to a familiar hymn tune adapted by J. S. Bach works well. A contemporary reflection on "O Sacred Head" is a song of the same name by Bob Hurd (OCP) that connects the Suffering Servant of the first reading to those who suffer injustice today. Though the text is certainly related to Good Friday, it could serve as a good reminder that every day is a call to share in the cross of Christ by our own daily sacrifice for the other, especially those most in need. Another appropriate hymn is "In the Cross of Christ" by Marty Haugen (GIA). Choose the verses well—perhaps verses 1, 4, and 5—to help the assembly recognize how we all bear the one cross of Christ in our daily lives.

## ✝ SPIRITUALITY

**GOSPEL ACCLAMATION**
cf. 2 Thess 2:14

R̸. Alleluia, alleluia.
God has called us through the Gospel
to possess the glory of our Lord Jesus Christ.
R̸. Alleluia, alleluia.

### Gospel

Mark 9:30-37; L134B

Jesus and his disciples left
    from there and began a
    journey through Galilee,
but he did not wish anyone
    to know about it.
He was teaching his disciples
    and telling them,
    "The Son of Man is to be
        handed over to men
    and they will kill him,
    and three days after his
        death the Son of Man
        will rise."
But they did not understand
    the saying,
    and they were afraid to question him.

They came to Capernaum and, once
    inside the house,
    he began to ask them,
    "What were you arguing about on the
        way?"
But they remained silent.
They had been discussing among
    themselves on the way
    who was the greatest.
Then he sat down, called the Twelve,
    and said to them,
    "If anyone wishes to be first,
    he shall be the last of all and the
        servant of all."
Taking a child, he placed it in their midst,
    and putting his arms around it, he
        said to them,
    "Whoever receives one child such as
        this in my name, receives me;
    and whoever receives me,
    receives not me but the One who sent
        me."

### Reflecting on the Gospel

The disciples are examples for us in so many ways, but today their example might not be what we expect. Here not only do they misunderstand Jesus (again) but they are afraid to ask him any questions. They are arguing amongst themselves. So Jesus turns the table and questions them. He wants them to tell him what they were arguing about. This almost sounds like a family squabble among the children where the parent has to step in and put a foot down. Perhaps like petulant children called on the carpet, the disciples remain silent. They do not have an answer for Jesus.

Is this the way the disciples really acted? Are these the saints we revere? Are their actions worthy of emulation? The disciples serve as an example for us in that despite their misunderstanding, their arguments, even their petty jealousies about who would be the greatest, they continued to follow Jesus. Jesus does not expect perfection. The disciples clearly show that! Jesus accepts people for who they are and where they are. He asks that they follow him.

Jesus then teaches the Twelve about leadership and being counted as the first. The leader is to be the servant. This upends ancient ideas and certainly modern thinking about being "number one." Power, riches, and authority, both in antiquity and now, are often used to amass more. But for the Christian it is to be different. For those who desire to be first, the greatest, the best, they are to be the last, the least, the servant of all.

Jesus places a child, one who has virtually no power or authority, in their midst. A child cannot return in like manner the kindness shown to it. The relationship with a child is one where we provide for and care for the child without expectation of return. What parent says to a child, "You'll need to pay me back for everything I spent on you while you were growing up in our home"? We pour our hearts (and our wallets) out for our children. Christian discipleship is likened to that relationship. Rather than doing political favors for those who can (and do) repay in kind, we are invited to accept the child and all the self-giving on our part that entails. This, rather than clawing one's way to the top, is the true marker of Christian love and service.

### Living the Paschal Mystery

Discipleship turns our modern value system on its head. Yet we, like the disciples, have difficulty seeing that. We continue to debate popularity, count Twitter followers and Facebook friends, and admire those with power and authority. But in today's gospel we are reminded to consider those who have little standing in the world.

The parent's love for a child is a true reflection of Christian love and service. The parent does not count the cost of late nights, extra food on the table, additional expenses, or the anxiety that can naturally come with a child. Instead, motivated by love, the parent moves beyond oneself to care for another. We are called by Jesus to behave in like manner to others. We do not treat them as children, but we are to serve without counting the cost, to give without expecting anything in return.

Often both in antiquity and in the modern world relationships are governed by a mutual beneficence or, more crassly, favor trading. Laws have been established to prevent the most egregious forms of this behavior, but it happens nonetheless at multiple levels. Though we are in the midst of the world, Christians are to have a different standard. Christians are to be of service. This kind of action may seem out of place. The maxim "Nice guys finish last" has more than a ring of truth to it. But Jesus reminds us today, "If anyone wishes to be first, / he shall be the last of all and the servant of all." This message is difficult to hear and more difficult to follow. For most of us these are not the values we see lived every day. But by enacting them we bring about the kingdom of God on earth.

## Focusing the Gospel
*Mark 9:30-37*
Conflicting hopes and expectations of the long-awaited "age of the messiah" collide in today's gospel.

A somber Jesus speaks cryptically of the death and resurrection awaiting him in Jerusalem, while those closest to him argue about their own greatness and status in the Messiah's reign (that must have been quite a conversation among the disciples to elicit such a strong reaction from Jesus!). Many of the Jews of Jesus' time dreamed of a messiah who would restore their nation's political zenith as it was under David—but Jesus explains to them (yet again) that the Messiah's reign will be a kingdom of spirit and conversion in which humble service, not wealth and influence, will be exalted. Jesus makes clear the great paradox of discipleship: Do you wish to be first? Then become last. Do you seek to attain greatness? Then become small. Do you want to be masters? Then become the servants of those you wish to rule.

To emphasize the point, Jesus picks up and places a little child in the midst of these would-be masters. A child has no influence in the affairs of society. Just the opposite is true: a child needs everything. To be "great" in the reign of God, Jesus says, one must receive the "child," and become self-giving.

## Focusing the First Reading
*Wis 2:12, 17-20*
Those who stand up for what is right, who speak out against injustice, who advocate for the powerless face the ridicule, revilement, and torture of the powerful and greedy "wicked" who perceive such "just one[s]" as a threat. This was the fate of many of the prophets of the Old Testament—and of Jesus in the gospels. Today's first reading from the book of Wisdom portrays the evil machinations that suppress and eliminate those who dare to speak God's word of justice.

## Focusing the Responsorial Psalm
*Ps 54:3-4, 5, 6-8 (6b)*
Today's responsorial psalm is the lament of someone who has endured great hardship at the hands of the wicked (as the "just one" faces in today's first reading), but the psalmist refuses to despair and remains confident in the justice of God.

## Focusing the Second Reading
*Jas 3:16–4:3*
In today's passage from the letter of James, the writer speaks to the theme of service by exhorting the Christian community to put one's own individual "passions" last for the good of all. War and conflict are futile, James writes; God calls the church community to "cultivate peace."

## Model Penitential Act

*Presider:* Let us place our hearts and spirits in the presence of God, seeking his forgiveness for our sins. *[pause]*

O God, you save the faithful who call to you in hope: Lord, have mercy.

O God, you uphold the innocent and defenseless: Christ, have mercy.

O God, you raise up the dead to life: Lord, have mercy.

## Homily Points

• We are often willing to sacrifice the common good for our self-interest; we measure the severity of a problem by its impact on us; we may manipulate the misfortune of others to our advantage. In today's gospel, Jesus challenges us to instead seek the "greatness" of being last, the "authority" of being the servant to others, the power of advocating for justice for the poor and victimized. In practicing such service, we learn compassion, become responsible adults and contributing members of society, and find meaning in our lives. Jesus challenges us to put another's hopes and dreams ahead of our own, to affirm the gifts of others for no other reason than the common good, to seek reconciliation and community at all costs.

• For the disciple of Jesus, the child represents the vulnerabilities that every one of us experiences in our lives—and the child reminds us of Jesus' call to take up his work of reaching out to those overwhelmed by such anxiety and despair. The poorest and neediest, the forgotten and rejected, the "least" and the "lowly" are living signs of God's grace in our midst. In the service and respect we give to all as sons and daughters of God, Jesus says, we welcome into our midst the very presence of God. Only in putting ourselves in the humble service of the lowly child can we hope to claim a place in the kingdom of God.

• The faith of a child is anything but "childish." In their simple joy and wonder of the world they are constantly discovering, in their ready acceptance of our love, in their total dependence on us for nurturing, children are the ideal teachers of humble servanthood and constant thanksgiving that Jesus asks of us. Children possess an honesty and a generosity that, sadly, many adults somehow outgrow. Christ calls us to embrace the uncomplicated but genuine faith of a child: to love God and others without condition. Childlike faith is never discouraged, never becomes cynical or jaded, never ceases to be amazed and grateful for the many ways God reveals his presence in our lives.

## Model Universal Prayer (Prayer of the Faithful)

*Presider:* To our merciful and loving God, let us pray:

*Response:* Lord, hear our prayer.

That our church may seek to become a community of reconciliation and forgiveness . . .

That all nations may seek to "cultivate peace" through a commitment to justice and respect for the world's peoples . . .

That we may imitate the compassion of Jesus the servant in our care for the sick, the suffering, the addicted, and the dying . . .

That our parish's religious education teachers and catechists may guide and inspire our children, teenagers, and adults in the wonders and wisdom of God . . .

*Presider:* Hear our prayers, O God. May we possess the spirit of humility and generosity of your Son that enables us to be the means for making possible what we have asked of you. In Jesus' name, we pray. **Amen.**

**COLLECT**

Let us pray.

*Pause for silent prayer*

O God, who founded all the commands of
your sacred Law
upon love of you and of our neighbor,
grant that, by keeping your precepts,
we may merit to attain eternal life.
Through our Lord Jesus Christ, your Son,
who lives and reigns with you in the unity
of the Holy Spirit,
one God, for ever and ever. **Amen.**

**FIRST READING**
Wis 2:12, 17-20

The wicked say:
Let us beset the just one, because he is
obnoxious to us;
he sets himself against our doings,
reproaches us for transgressions of the
law
and charges us with violations of our
training.
Let us see whether his words be true;
let us find out what will happen to
him.
For if the just one be the son of God,
God will defend him
and deliver him from the hand of his
foes.
With revilement and torture let us put
the just one to the test
that we may have proof of his
gentleness
and try his patience.
Let us condemn him to a shameful
death;
for according to his own words, God
will take care of him.

# CATECHESIS

## RESPONSORIAL PSALM

Ps 54:3-4, 5, 6-8

Ry. (6b) The Lord upholds my life.

O God, by your name save me,
   and by your might defend my cause.
O God, hear my prayer;
   hearken to the words of my mouth.

Ry. The Lord upholds my life.

For the haughty have risen up against me,
   the ruthless seek my life;
   they set not God before their eyes.

Ry. The Lord upholds my life.

Behold, God is my helper;
   the Lord sustains my life.
Freely will I offer you sacrifice;
   I will praise your name, O Lord, for its
      goodness.

Ry. The Lord upholds my life.

## SECOND READING

Jas 3:16–4:3

Beloved:
Where jealousy and selfish ambition exist,
   there is disorder and every foul practice.
But the wisdom from above is first of all
      pure,
   then peaceable, gentle, compliant,
   full of mercy and good fruits,
   without inconstancy or insincerity.
And the fruit of righteousness is sown in
      peace
   for those who cultivate peace.

Where do the wars
   and where do the conflicts among you
      come from?
Is it not from your passions
   that make war within your members?
You covet but do not possess.
You kill and envy but you cannot obtain;
   you fight and wage war.
You do not possess because you do not
      ask.
You ask but do not receive,
   because you ask wrongly, to spend it on
      your passions.

## About Liturgy

**Serving without counting the cost:** In many ways, liturgists and music coordinators really do follow Jesus' call from today's gospel: "If anyone wishes to be first, / he shall be the last of all and the servant of all" (Mark 9:35). There is so much that we do and not for any gain or praise. Much of what we do to prepare an assembly for liturgy is never seen: hours of rehearsing; long nights spent at the computer and the photocopier creating and preparing worship aids; the endless phone calls and emails to volunteers, committee members, and staff persons so that everyone can be on the same page. And, in an ironic twist to this Scripture passage, we are often the first *and* the last to be at the church, just so the assembly can focus simply on praying well.

Absolutely, we must serve without counting the cost. Yet that does not mean we should not want, as well as give, recognition. One of the most important skills we need to practice as liturgical leaders is the art of saying thank you, especially to those who assist and work with us to prepare the liturgy well. A simple, handwritten note or a "shout-out" in the weekly bulletin or email blast goes a long way to giving people the encouragement they need to know that they are not alone in this work we share. And when we long for a bit of recognition ourselves for the role we play in the community's liturgy, let us seek out the best kinds of compliments—those that shine the light not on what we have accomplished but on what God has done through the work of the people of God acting together, that is, giving worthy praise and honor to God that strengthens us to glorify God by our lives.

## About Liturgical Music

**Loving the sound of the singing assembly:** "The most beautiful sound any liturgical musician longs to hear is the sound of a singing assembly." Though the statement's source is unknown, its message is true. We long, more than anything, to hear the assembly singing with everything they've got. There is nothing like it once you've heard it.

The trick, however, is to *hear* it. Today's gospel reading reminds us that we who serve must put others first. That can be difficult when much of our ministry requires skilled, artistic performance. Sometimes, we can get so caught up with listening for how *we* sound on our instrument or in the microphone, or we're worried about how the choir sounds and if they're in tune or are balanced. These are certainly important sounds for us to attend to, but we cannot do so at the expense of the sound of the singing assembly. If you cannot hear the assembly sing, there are several possible reasons: they don't know the song or can't sing the song because it's too high, too low, too fast or slow, or some other musical reason; they don't like the song or don't connect with the song because it doesn't reflect the experience of what we believe, or it doesn't challenge them enough to inspire them to give their voices to it; or the way the song has been taught or presented in its performance or the way the choir or cantor leads it discourages the assembly from singing or communicates to them that their participation is optional.

Next time you minister as a liturgical musician, listen more intently for the sound of the assembly, because the more you listen for it, the more you'll notice when it's not there, and when it is, the more you will love it and foster it. When we do this, the more the assembly will find their voice and love it, too.

**SEPTEMBER 23, 2018**
# TWENTY-FIFTH SUNDAY
# IN ORDINARY TIME

## ✠ SPIRITUALITY

**GOSPEL ACCLAMATION**
cf. John 17:17b, 17a

℟. Alleluia, alleluia.
Your word, O Lord, is truth;
consecrate us in the truth.
℟. Alleluia, alleluia.

## Gospel

Mark 9:38-43, 45, 47-48; L137B

At that time, John said to Jesus,
    "Teacher, we saw someone driving
        out demons in your name,
    and we tried to prevent him because
        he does not follow us."
Jesus replied, "Do not prevent him.
    There is no one who performs a
        mighty deed in my name
    who can at the same time speak ill
        of me.
For whoever is not against us is for
    us.
Anyone who gives you a cup of water
    to drink
    because you belong to Christ,
    amen, I say to you, will surely not lose
        his reward.

"Whoever causes one of these little ones
    who believe in me to sin,
    it would be better for him if a great
        millstone
    were put around his neck
    and he were thrown into the sea.
If your hand causes you to sin, cut it off.
It is better for you to enter into life maimed
    than with two hands to go into Gehenna,
    into the unquenchable fire.
And if your foot causes you to sin, cut it off.
It is better for you to enter into life crippled
    than with two feet to be thrown into
        Gehenna.
And if your eye causes you to sin, pluck it
    out.
Better for you to enter into the kingdom of
    God with one eye
    than with two eyes to be thrown into
        Gehenna,
    where 'their worm does not die, and the
        fire is not quenched.'"

### Reflecting on the Gospel

In grade school most of us learned about "tattletales," those fellow grade-schoolers who were so eager to impress the teacher or another adult that they "tattled" on their fellow students. "Joey didn't do what you asked him to do!" "Mirta called me a name!" "Jorge is eating the cookies!" But too often the tattletales did not receive the response they expected. Often it was, "Nobody likes a tattletale."

Today the disciples, in their continuing streak of misunderstanding, come to Jesus with some news. It's as though they are tattling, "We saw someone doing something in your name, but he's not in our group so we stopped him." Jesus responds with the equivalent of, "No one likes a tattletale." He then makes a claim that can be described as "big tent" Christianity, in saying that "whoever is not against us is for us." The double negative "not against" is significant, and seems to be a rather low bar. If simply not being against is the equivalent of being "for" there seems to be hope!

Yet, this rather low-bar admonition is followed immediately by a stern and disturbing warning: Causing a little one to sin is worthy of death. What then follows are a series of prophetic hyperbole intended to make the point that the kingdom of God is worth any price. Lopping off a body part that causes one to sin is better than losing eternal life. The early church recognized these commands concerning self-maiming as hyperbole and did not take them literally. These are warnings to sever any relationship that causes sin. The kingdom of God is the ultimate prize worth any price.

### Living the Paschal Mystery

We can be so eager to define who is in and who is outside of the group. There seems to be something in our DNA or evolution that wants to create and protect the tribe, the clan, the group. We have heard it said, "If you're not with us, you're against us." This clear demarcation is intended, among other things, to rally the group, and to warn others against harming the group. But Jesus does not draw the lines so starkly. For him, "whoever is not against us is for us." That leaves a rather large group!

For Jesus, the group is expansive, and we should be too. In the United States, not many people are actively against Christians. To be sure, there are parts of the world where being Christian can be a death sentence. But that happens only rarely, if ever, in developed parts of the world.

Rather than look for enemies, and seek to find those who are against us, Jesus tells his disciples essentially that by their actions you shall know them. If someone is not part of the group but is still performing the actions of the members of the group, that person is with us. The disciples' continuing streak of misunderstanding is met with Jesus' teaching them values contrary to their expectations once again.

## Focusing the Gospel

*Mark 9:38-43, 45, 47-48*

As we have seen throughout Mark's gospel, the people of Jesus' time held great stock in the existence of demons: whatever mental illness or physical infirmity they could not understand or explain was considered the presence of some "demon." It was also believed that a demon could be exorcised if one could invoke the name of a still more powerful spirit.

The apostle John has tried to stop someone who seemed to be invoking Jesus' name to cast out a demon. John's concern, at first reading, appears to have some merit—but recall the ongoing battle among the disciples as to who is the greatest among them. Jesus responds, therefore, by condemning the disciples' jealousy and intolerance, warning against an elitist view of discipleship that diminishes or even seeks to eliminate the good done by "outsiders."

Today's gospel includes Jesus' exhortation that it is better to lose one's limb if it leads one to sin. Two notes about these final verses: The "millstone" Jesus speaks of was a large piece of stone that was turned by a pack animal to grind grain. Drowning a criminal by tying him to one of these stones was a method of execution in Rome and Palestine. Gehenna holds a grisly place in Jewish history. The young King Ahaz (2 Chr 38:3) practiced child immolation to the "fire god" at Gehenna. In Jesus' time, Gehenna, a ravine outside Jerusalem, served as the city's refuse site. For Jews of the time, Gehenna was synonymous with our concept of hell.

## Focusing the First Reading

*Num 11:25-29*

Today's first reading recalls a story from the exodus that parallels today's gospel. Moses' young assistant, Joshua, expresses his concern that Eldad and Medad, who were called to be elders but were not formally confirmed as such by Moses, were nonetheless "prophesying" among the Israelites. Moses realizes that God's spirit cannot be constricted by human limitations or expectations; he does not seek to control that spirit nor is he protective of his own prophetic gift. Rather than stop the two "unauthorized" prophets, Moses offers thanks to God for the gift he has bestowed on Israel through the two and the hope that all God's people might become "prophets" of justice and mercy.

## Focusing the Responsorial Psalm

*Ps 19:8, 10, 12-13, 14 (9a)*

Today's responsorial psalm is the second section of Psalm 19, a poem in praise of the "law" of the covenant. For the psalmist, the law is not a restriction but the source of wisdom. In the keeping of the law, the faithful realize the goodness of God's creation and the enduring love of God for his people.

## Focusing the Second Reading

*Jas 5:1-6*

Today's second reading, the final in this series of readings from the letter of James, is a harsh indictment of the self-absorbed rich who have defrauded workers of their just wage, who have lived lives of luxury at the expense of the poor, and who have subjected the innocent to trial for their own gains. The writer of James echoes many prophets of old in warning that wealth of the rich will one day decay into nothing and that God will exact a heavy price from them for their exploitation of the poor.

**PROMPTS FOR HOMILISTS, CATECHISTS, AND RCIA TEAMS**

When have you given or received the Gospel "cup of water to drink" in Christ's name?

How does faith become "elitist"?

Consider ways in which something that is essentially good can also be used destructively.

How do "non-teachers" lead others to God?

When have you experienced the Spirit of God at an unexpected time, from an unexpected source?

## Model Penitential Act

*Presider:* The Lord of mercy has gathered us together at his table. Let us begin by acknowledging our sins and failings and, through his mercy, celebrate these sacred mysteries in his peace. *[pause]*

> Father of compassion: Lord, have mercy.
> Redeemer of peace: Christ, have mercy.
> Spirit of grace: Lord, have mercy.

## Homily Points

• Jesus does not ask us to initiate great programs of reform or embark on high-profile exploits for the kingdom of God. He asks us to be his disciples by taking on the small kindnesses that mirror the love of God. He calls us to be God's prophets by living unheralded lives of integrity and honesty that reflect the justice and peace of God. Jesus promises us that even the simplest act of compassion—the Gospel "cup of water to drink"—will one day be honored by God in his kingdom. All those in need have a claim on our charity because they belong to Christ.

• Some sins are so complex or ingrained in our lives that we feel we must accommodate such evil to make the rest of life work. But Jesus makes clear that no sin is too "big" to dissuade us in our search for God. Christ calls us not to allow prestige, wealth, or instant gratification to desensitize us to God's presence in our lives or diminish God's love we cherish in family and friends. Faith demands that we "let go" of whatever makes us less than what God has created us to be—and that includes not only "cutting off" the sinful hand or "tearing out" the evil eye, but also letting go of our self-centeredness, prejudices, and vengeance that destroy our families and relationships.

• In today's gospel, Jesus exalts the work of those who teach, by the example of their lives, his Gospel of justice, reconciliation, and compassion. To show our children the meaning that our faith gives to our days, to help those alienated from God reconnect with the sacred in their lives, to reveal the love and mercy of God to those who do not know God are both the great joy and the great responsibility of our baptisms. To "teach" with conviction without judgment, by example rather than by dogma, is to transform our world one generation at a time, to establish the reign of God one stone upon another.

## Model Universal Prayer (Prayer of the Faithful)

*Presider:* Let us join our hearts and voices in prayer for all God's sons and daughters.

*Response:* Lord, hear our prayer.

That the Spirit of God may enable our church to speak God's prophetic word of compassion and justice in our ministries of prayer and service . . .

That the wisdom of God will guide lawyers, judges, and legislators in the holy work of securing justice for the poor and the powerless . . .

That we may readily offer the "cup of water" of compassion and care to the sick, the suffering, the recovering, the dying, and all who belong to Christ . . .

That the faithful who have died *[especially . . .]* may be welcomed by Christ into the dwelling place of his Father . . .

*Presider:* May our offering of these prayers, O God, inspire us to be about the work of reconciliation and justice, of mercy and peace, entrusted to us by your Son, Christ Jesus, in whose name we pray. **Amen.**

### COLLECT
Let us pray.

*Pause for silent prayer*

O God, who manifest your almighty power
above all by pardoning and showing
    mercy,
bestow, we pray, your grace abundantly
    upon us
and make those hastening to attain your
    promises
heirs to the treasures of heaven.
Through our Lord Jesus Christ, your Son,
who lives and reigns with you in the unity
    of the Holy Spirit,
one God, for ever and ever. **Amen.**

### FIRST READING
Num 11:25-29

The LORD came down in the cloud and
    spoke to Moses.
Taking some of the spirit that was on
    Moses,
    the LORD bestowed it on the seventy
        elders;
    and as the spirit came to rest on them,
        they prophesied.

Now two men, one named Eldad and the
    other Medad,
    were not in the gathering but had been
        left in the camp.
They too had been on the list, but had not
    gone out to the tent;
    yet the spirit came to rest on them also,
    and they prophesied in the camp.
So, when a young man quickly told Moses,
    "Eldad and Medad are prophesying in
        the camp,"
    Joshua, son of Nun, who from his youth
        had been Moses' aide, said,
    "Moses, my lord, stop them."
But Moses answered him,
    "Are you jealous for my sake?
Would that all the people of the LORD were
    prophets!
Would that the LORD might bestow his
    spirit on them all!"

### RESPONSORIAL PSALM
Ps 19:8, 10, 12-13, 14

R̸. (9a) The precepts of the Lord give joy
    to the heart.

The law of the LORD is perfect,
    refreshing the soul;
the decree of the LORD is trustworthy,
    giving wisdom to the simple.

R̸. The precepts of the Lord give joy to
    the heart.

The fear of the LORD is pure,
   enduring forever;
the ordinances of the LORD are true,
   all of them just.

R̞. The precepts of the Lord give joy to
   the heart.

Though your servant is careful of them,
   very diligent in keeping them,
yet who can detect failings?
   Cleanse me from my unknown faults!

R̞. The precepts of the Lord give joy to
   the heart.

From wanton sin especially, restrain your
   servant;
   let it not rule over me.
Then shall I be blameless and innocent
   of serious sin.

R̞. The precepts of the Lord give joy to
   the heart.

### SECOND READING
Jas 5:1-6

Come now, you rich, weep and wail over
   your impending miseries.
Your wealth has rotted away, your clothes
   have become moth-eaten,
   your gold and silver have corroded,
   and that corrosion will be a testimony
      against you;
   it will devour your flesh like a fire.
You have stored up treasure for the last
   days.
Behold, the wages you withheld from the
   workers
   who harvested your fields are crying
      aloud;
   and the cries of the harvesters
   have reached the ears of the Lord of
      hosts.
You have lived on earth in luxury and
   pleasure;
   you have fattened your hearts for the
      day of slaughter.
You have condemned;
   you have murdered the righteous one;
   he offers you no resistance.

## About Liturgy

*Discipleship, not membership:* In today's gospel, Jesus seems to encourage a "big tent" approach to religion. But his teaching in this passage may be much more nuanced. Jesus does not dwell on membership alone but on the purpose of discipleship, that is, to do good. Pope Francis picked up on this theme in one of his morning homilies on this same gospel passage: "Jesus reprimands them. 'Do not prevent him, let him do good.' The disciples, without thinking, were fixed on an idea: we alone can do good, because we alone possess the truth. And none of those who do not possess the truth can do good" (Domus Sanctae Marthae, May 22, 2013).

As liturgical leaders, we, too, can get pretty fixed on the idea that we alone know what's best. We've got our training, certificates, and degrees. We've read the books and know the rituals and rubrics. So we won't be including anyone's unusual requests for their wedding, or the First Communion Mass, or the youth Mass. We won't let just anyone come in and do a liturgical ministry without the same level of training we did. We are the experts, so just leave the liturgy to us.

In all these big and small ways, we put the focus on who has the qualifications to be members of our specialized group. Instead, we should be asking ourselves who is willing to commit to the reason for all this training, that is, to lead others to Christ. No one will fall more deeply in love with Christ because we rigidly followed the rubrics. No one will be drawn to the beauty of the liturgy because we insisted on doing things the way we've always done it, and that is our way!

Pope Francis continued in his homily, "The disciples were somewhat intolerant," but "Jesus broadened their horizons and we may imagine that he said: 'If this person can do good, we can all do good. So can anyone who is not one of us.'" The Spirit is at work in ways and people we might never expect. Our job is to broaden our horizons, let the Spirit work, and get out of the way.

## About Liturgical Music

*Singing in a different key:* In the liturgy wars, music is often at the center of the battle. Each of us has our preference for style of music. Some couldn't imagine liturgy without drums and a band; others wouldn't ever set foot in a church without an organ. We all have our likes and dislikes. Some of us have a running list of hymns we love and those we'd pay someone to never play again. Beyond musical style and repertoire, we can also get into a kind of territorialism so that we might say, "This is the adult choir. We don't sing that praise and worship stuff." Or, "Our choir has always been the choir for Holy Thursday! What do you mean we're going to gather all the choirs, including the Spanish choir, and all sing that day?" When we start to hear these kinds of comments, we see how much this gospel reading also applies to us.

In liturgical music, there is really only one choir. That is the choir of the singing assembly, and they sing in many different keys in a variety of styles and languages, all for the purpose of glorifying God by the offering of their voices. We who gather each week to rehearse and prepare liturgical music do so in order to support them, the community's one choir. Let us unite our voices to theirs in a spirit of sacrifice, encouragement, patience, and love for the mission we all share.

## ✝ SPIRITUALITY

**GOSPEL ACCLAMATION**
1 John 4:12

R̸. Alleluia, alleluia.
If we love one another, God remains
    in us
and his love is brought
    to perfection
    in us.
R̸. Alleluia,
    alleluia.

### Gospel

Mark 10:2-16;
L140B

The Pharisees
    approached
    Jesus and asked,
"Is it lawful for a husband
    to divorce his wife?"
They were testing him.
He said to them in
    reply, "What
    did Moses
    command
    you?"
They replied,
    "Moses permitted a husband to write a
        bill of divorce
    and dismiss her."
But Jesus told them,
    "Because of the hardness of your hearts
    he wrote you this commandment.
But from the beginning of creation, *God
    made them male and female.*
*For this reason a man shall leave his father
    and mother*
    *and be joined to his wife,*
    *and the two shall become one flesh.*
So they are no longer two but one flesh.
Therefore what God has joined together,
    no human being must separate."
In the house the disciples again questioned
    Jesus about this.

*Continued in Appendix A, p. 302, or*
Mark 10:2-12 *in Appendix A, p. 302.*

### Reflecting on the Gospel

Jesus' sayings are hard. Sometimes there are few ways we can explain away the plain meaning of the text. We tend to be familiar with the stories of Jesus that remind us that the law was made for humans, not humans for the law. To illustrate this point we have stories such as Jesus healing on the Sabbath.

But in today's gospel, rather than offer a flexible interpretation of the Mosaic law concerning divorce, Jesus doubles down. He tells the audience that the only reason Moses even permitted divorce was because of human stubbornness. In actuality, Jesus says, in quoting Genesis, "what God has joined together, / no human being must separate." He goes even further (thus the doubling down) and makes a startling statement that the man who divorces his wife and marries another commits adultery. And for parity's sake, he says that the woman who divorces her husband and marries another commits adultery. In fact, many scholars see in the prohibition against women as well as men that the audience was likely Roman. Roman women, unlike Jewish women, had the right to divorce their husbands.

In any case, this prohibition was, and remains, extreme. We can see evidence that the early church considered this extreme because Matthew's gospel (which uses Mark as a source) already amends the prohibition and makes an exception for divorce in cases of unlawful marriage, sometimes erroneously translated as "sexual immorality" (see Matt 19:9).

But Matthew was not the only New Testament text to relax Jesus' absolute prohibition on divorce. Paul too, writing before any gospel was composed, was aware of Jesus' radical teaching on divorce. He even quotes it before offering an exception (1 Cor 7:10-16)! Paul basically says that if a Christian has an unbelieving spouse who separates, the Christian person is not bound. Today the church refers to this as the "Pauline privilege" and it applies in RCIA and other cases.

But back to the gospel. This passage seems to be of the kind that we have seen before in the Gospel of Mark, where Jesus might say, if your right hand causes you to sin, cut it off! Or if your eye causes you to sin, pluck it out! The idea that there would be no divorce is a great ideal, but unfortunately it does not match lived experience. The fact that two New Testament authors already created exceptions is clear evidence of that. The early church understood that some of Jesus' sayings were not to be taken so literally, as difficult as that might seem to us.

As adults, we need to approach faith with a certain maturity. Rather than accept at face value each and every saying in the Bible, or even each and every saying of Jesus (!), we discern the meaning of the text in a community of faith.

### Living the Paschal Mystery

In 1980 the US bishops published a document titled Called and Gifted: The American Catholic Laity. It was short and was often published as a brochure, but it was nonetheless an important text commemorating the fifteenth anniversary of the *Decree on the Apostolate of the Laity.* The bishops spoke of the four calls of laity: adulthood, holiness, ministry, and community. Today's gospel definitely calls us to adulthood, to a mature reading of the text.

The US bishops wrote in 1980, "Adulthood implies knowledge, experience and awareness, freedom and responsibility, and mutuality in relationships. It is true, however, that the experience of lay persons 'as church members' has not always reflected this understanding of adulthood." What a remarkable statement from the bishops! So, we read today's gospel in light of our knowledge and experience of human relationships. We grapple with its meaning, recognizing that Jesus' sayings are hard. But we never stop following. We never stop being a disciple. We are adults in his church, with freedom, responsibility, and mutuality in relationships.

## Focusing the Gospel

*Mark 10:2-16 (shorter form: Mark 10:2-12)*

The question of divorce was among the most divisive issues in Jewish society. The book of Deuteronomy stipulated that a husband could divorce his wife for "something indecent" (24:1, NABRE). Interpretations of exactly what constituted "something indecent" varied greatly, ranging from adultery to accidentally burning the evening meal. Further, the wife was regarded under the law as the husband's chattel, with neither a legal right to protection nor recourse to seeking a divorce on her own. In biblical times, marriages were arranged rather than the product of romantic love. Marriages were often arranged in the husband's favor: the husband could divorce his wife for almost any reason, and the woman was treated (according to the law) as little better than property. Divorce, then, was easy to obtain among the male Jews of Jesus' time.

In today's gospel, Jesus cites the Genesis account of the creation of man and woman (the first reading) to emphasize that husband and wife are equal partners in the covenant of marriage ("the two shall become one flesh"). The language of Genesis indicates that the Creator intends for the marriage union to possess the same special covenantal nature as God's covenant with Israel. As authoritative teacher of Torah (Law), Jesus cites Genesis in making an absolute prohibition of divorce, something allowed by the law (in Deuteronomy). This kind of appeal to his own personal authority in matters of Mosaic law would have been frustrating to Jewish authorities. It is likely this kind of perceived arrogance led these same authorities to seek an end to this Galilean upstart.

Today's longer gospel reading also includes Mark's story of Jesus' welcoming the little children. Again, Jesus holds up the model of a child's simplicity and humility as the model for the servant-disciple.

## Focusing the First Reading

*Gen 2:18-24*

The first reading is the Genesis account of the creation of man and woman, cited by Jesus in today's gospel. The story reveals the divine origins of marriage and God's entrusting to faithful spouses the work of continuing his creation.

## Focusing the Responsorial Psalm

*Ps 128:1-2, 3, 4-5, 6 (cf. 5)*

This short psalm is a prayer of blessing upon the father (considered the head of the family in this patriarchal society) and his family. The stability and peace of Israel as a nation and society is centered in the blessing of its families.

## Focusing the Second Reading

*Heb 2:9-11*

Today begins a series of seven short readings from the "letter" to the Hebrews. Scripture scholars, both modern and ancient, overwhelmingly agree that the apostle Paul did not write Hebrews, which is more of a sermon or theological treatise than a letter. Note that the Lectionary does not even use Paul's name in introducing the "letter," which might have been addressed to a community of Jews longing for the temple liturgy after having embraced the new Christian faith. A central image of Hebrews—Jesus the eternal High Priest, whose sacrifice of his own life reconciles humanity to God—would resonate with such a community.

In today's reading, the writer of Hebrews praises the humility of Christ, who took on our humanity in order to "taste death" so as to liberate us from death and the slavery of sin. In taking on our humanity so fully, Christ becomes our "brother."

**PROMPTS FOR HOMILISTS, CATECHISTS, AND RCIA TEAMS**

In what ways do wives and husbands "live" the sacrament of marriage?

How does a covenant relationship differ from a contract arrangement?

Have you ever come to realize a time when you acted out of the "hardness" of your own heart?

What wisdom have you learned from a child?

## Model Penitential Act

*Presider:* As we prepare to celebrate these sacred mysteries, let us seek the forgiveness of God for our sins and failings. *[pause]*

Lord, Creator and Sustainer of all life: Lord, have mercy.

Lord, Redeemer and Restorer of our fallen humanity: Christ, have mercy.

Lord, Source of all love and reconciliation: Lord, have mercy.

## Homily Points

• "Two shall become one"—one in heart, one in hope, one in love, one in God. In marriage that is of Christ, husband and wife are bound as one in such love: love that happily gives rather than takes, lets go rather than clings, liberates rather than imprisons. A couple's life together—a life centered in trust, forgiveness, and humility—and their generous response to the vocation of parenthood model the unfathomable and profound love of God. Marriage is more than a legal contract between two "parties" but a *sacrament*: a living sign of God's presence and grace in our midst, the manifestation of God's love that knows neither condition nor limit in its ability to give and forgive.

• Children possess an uncomplicated but genuine, straight-to-the-heart understanding of the things of God that for some reason we adults sadly outgrow. Childlike faith is never discouraged, cynical, or jaded; never ceases to be amazed and grateful for the many ways God reveals his presence in our lives. The faith of a child is anything but "childish." It is this childlike quality of faith Jesus asks his followers to embrace: faith that does not separate words and actions, that is centered in loving God and others without condition or expectation. The power of such simple childlike faith is its ability to overcome every rationalization, fear, complication, and agenda in order to mirror the selfless generosity of Christ Jesus. Only in embracing childlike kindness, compassion, and forgiveness can we realize the kingdom of God.

## Model Universal Prayer (Prayer of the Faithful)

*Presider:* Let us now lift our hearts and voices in prayer to God for all the human family.

*Response:* Lord, hear our prayer.

For Pope N. and our bishops, priests, and deacons, for our ministers, catechists, and counselors, that their work and ministries may be sources of reconciliation and justice for all men and women of goodwill . . .

For the world's nations, peoples, and societies, that they may realize their shared humanity in their work to protect and share the gifts of God's blessed earth . . .

For the sick, the suffering, the recovering, and the dying, that the God of compassion may restore them to health and hope . . .

For married couples in our community, that, in their life together, they may mirror for all of us the love of God . . .

*Presider:* To you who are the Father of creation, the Source of love and peace, and the Protector of the poor and lost, we offer these prayers for all our brothers and sisters. Hear and grant these prayers we offer, O God, in the name of your Son, Jesus the Christ. **Amen.**

**COLLECT**

Let us pray.

*Pause for silent prayer*

Almighty ever-living God,
who in the abundance of your kindness
surpass the merits and the desires of
those who entreat you,
pour out your mercy upon us
to pardon what conscience dreads
and to give what prayer does not dare to
ask.
Through our Lord Jesus Christ, your Son,
who lives and reigns with you in the unity
of the Holy Spirit,
one God, for ever and ever. **Amen.**

**FIRST READING**

Gen 2:18-24

The LORD God said: "It is not good for the
man to be alone.
I will make a suitable partner for him."
So the LORD God formed out of the ground
various wild animals and various birds
of the air,
and he brought them to the man to see
what he would call them;
whatever the man called each of them
would be its name.
The man gave names to all the cattle,
all the birds of the air, and all wild
animals;
but none proved to be the suitable
partner for the man.

So the LORD God cast a deep sleep on the
man,
and while he was asleep,
he took out one of his ribs and closed
up its place with flesh.
The LORD God then built up into a woman
the rib
that he had taken from the man.
When he brought her to the man, the man
said:
"This one, at last, is bone of my bones
and flesh of my flesh;
this one shall be called 'woman,' for
out of 'her man' this one has been
taken."
That is why a man leaves his father and
mother
and clings to his wife,
and the two of them become one flesh.

# CATECHESIS

**RESPONSORIAL PSALM**
Ps 128:1-2, 3, 4-5, 6

R℣. (cf. 5) May the Lord bless us all the
days of our lives.

Blessed are you who fear the LORD,
who walk in his ways!
For you shall eat the fruit of your
handiwork;
blessed shall you be, and favored.

R℣. May the Lord bless us all the days of
our lives.

Your wife shall be like a fruitful vine
in the recesses of your home;
your children like olive plants
around your table.

R℣. May the Lord bless us all the days of
our lives.

Behold, thus is the man blessed
who fears the LORD.
The LORD bless you from Zion:
may you see the prosperity of
Jerusalem
all the days of your life.

R℣. May the Lord bless us all the days of
our lives.

May you see your children's children.
Peace be upon Israel!

R℣. May the Lord bless us all the days of
our lives.

**SECOND READING**
Heb 2:9-11

Brothers and sisters:
He "for a little while" was made "lower
than the angels,"
that by the grace of God he might taste
death for everyone.

For it was fitting that he,
for whom and through whom all things
exist,
in bringing many children to glory,
should make the leader to their
salvation perfect through suffering.
He who consecrates and those who are
being consecrated
all have one origin.
Therefore, he is not ashamed to call them
"brothers."

## About Liturgy

**The spirit of the law:** The liturgy has many laws and directives established to regulate and guide our common worship. These guidelines help to ensure a deep unity among all our communities while enabling a great flexibility so that the liturgy can be inculturated into the many ways these communities pray. Our challenge as liturgical coordinators is to be solidly rooted in the laws of liturgy while being able to understand the spirit behind those laws so that we can let the liturgy flourish in creative ways within a specific community and assembly. We can do this by practicing three disciplines:

1. Know the teaching: We do not "create" liturgy. Rather, we practice the tradition as it has been handed down to us from a community larger than our own, that is, from the generations before us that have celebrated that liturgy and from the wisdom of the universal church today. Be sure to read and study the foundational liturgical document from Vatican II, the Constitution on the Sacred Liturgy, and other principle documents. These include the *General Instruction of the Roman Missal*; Sing to the Lord: Music in Divine Worship; and Built of Living Stones: Art, Architecture, and Worship.

2. Understand the skill of prudent and intelligent adaptation: Jazz musicians cannot improvise until they know in their bones the deep structure of a melody and its chord progression. It's the same with liturgy. You must know the ritual structure and the purpose of each ritual action. You also need to be able to identify the climax or turning point of each liturgy and how each part builds upon and flows from that climax. Only then will you be able to shape authentic liturgy for the specific needs of your community.

3. Finally, nurture an attitude of humility: No one person "owns" the liturgy or has the full vision of what liturgy should look like for a community. This is because the liturgy belongs to the people who praise God through it and are sanctified by it. We need to approach both the requirements of the law and the needs of the people with reverence. Understand that the liturgy works gradually to shape us. We are not called to prepare perfect liturgy but to be as faithful as we can be at that moment to the needs of both the liturgy and the people who pray it.

## About Initiation

**Annulments:** One of the most painful things to deal with in the RCIA is marriage issues and annulments. It can be difficult to explain to inquirers, catechumens, candidates, and their loved ones the reasons for annulments and the laws surrounding Christian marriage. Whatever the issue you are dealing with, recall that your responsibility is to present the beauty of the teaching of the church with great mercy and compassion. The RCIA is not the place to air your own grievances about the church's teachings or to make any promises about the outcome of a person's annulment process, even if you have gone through a similar experience. There may be situations that can never be resolved within the scope of our current laws. For these, we commit to continued prayer and hope that the Spirit will find a way for reconciliation as we strive to give the best of our care to those in pain.

## About Liturgical Music

**Wedding choirs:** Music for weddings is first and foremost liturgical music. Therefore the guidelines in place for music at Sunday Mass also apply to weddings. To help put this practice in place and to show our care for those entering the vocation of spouses, consider making weddings part of the Sunday Mass choir's ministry. Just as we may have a "resurrection" choir made up of parish music ministers who serve at funerals, let us be ministers for the couples who choose to celebrate the beginning of their marriage in our parish.

**OCTOBER 7, 2018**
## TWENTY-SEVENTH SUNDAY IN ORDINARY TIME

## ✚ SPIRITUALITY

### Gospel

Mark 10:17-30; L143B

As Jesus was setting out on a
　　journey, a man ran up,
　　knelt down before him, and asked
　　him,
　　"Good teacher, what must I do to
　　　　inherit eternal life?"
Jesus answered him, "Why do you
　　call me good?
No one is good but God alone.
You know the commandments: *You
　　shall not kill;
　　you shall not commit adultery;
　　you shall not steal;
　　you shall not bear false witness;
　　you shall not defraud;
　　honor your father and your mother.*"
He replied and said to him,
　　"Teacher, all of these I have observed
　　　　from my youth."
Jesus, looking at him, loved him and said
　　to him,
　　"You are lacking in one thing.
Go, sell what you have, and give to the
　　poor
　　and you will have treasure in heaven;
　　then come, follow me."
At that statement his face fell,
　　and he went away sad, for he had many
　　possessions.

Jesus looked around and said to his
　　disciples,
　　"How hard it is for those who have
　　　　wealth
　　to enter the kingdom of God!"
The disciples were amazed at his words.

*Continued in Appendix A, p. 303, or
Mark 10:17-27 in Appendix A, p. 303.*

### Reflecting on the Gospel

How many of us have wished to meet Jesus? Or to have been one of his followers? Or perhaps, like today's gospel, simply to have been able to ask Jesus a question? The man who does receives a loving look from Jesus. It even sounds like Jesus admired the goodwill of this person, who desired eternal life. The questioner has followed all of the commandments. He is in right standing with the law. But he feels there is more. Jesus, in turn, gives him a challenge that he gave to no other person. Namely, Jesus tells him to sell his many possessions, give the proceeds to the poor, and then follow him.

Now the burden falls back to the man, for he has many possessions. Will he choose to let go of the possessions and follow Jesus? We know that he did not. Instead, he clung to his possessions. He loved them more than he wanted to follow Jesus. And this is a warning shot to all who would follow Jesus. Whom or what do we love more? Possessions? Jesus?

Upon hearing Jesus' command, our face might fall, like the man with many possessions. Somehow it might be easier to simply follow a set of rules, to carry out the dictates of the law. For us, it might be easier to attend Mass each week, including holy days. But Jesus demands more than that. He wants a complete and total commitment of the individual. And with this man, Jesus seems to know that for him, the one thing holding him back is his wealth. So Jesus invites him to discard it.

As mentioned above, it is critical to keep in mind that this is the only person to whom Jesus gives this invitation. And it seems the invite is directed to him precisely because he has so much wealth. Jesus goes for the jugular, as it were. He finds and knows the one thing keeping the man from following him, and zeroes in on it. Can the man discard his possessions? What does Jesus invite us to discard?

### Living the Paschal Mystery

Each of us likely has something or another holding us back from a complete and wholehearted commitment to following Jesus. For some it might be a sense of pride and social standing we receive from our position at work. What happens when that is gone? What happens when the job is lost?

Of course, in the end, at our death, we take no earthly possessions with us. What matters more is love, relationships, care, and concern we have shown to others. A desperate clinging to that which is merely passing makes one unfit to be a follower of Jesus. This week we are reminded that no earthly possession, no job title or position, and no status is anything compared to the relationship we have with Jesus as one of his followers.

## Focusing the Gospel

*Mark 10:17-30 (shorter form: Mark 10:17-27)*

The young rich man is one of the most pitiable characters in the gospels. Clearly, Jesus' teachings and healings have touched something in him, but his enthusiasm outdistances his commitment. Assuring Jesus that he has kept the "you shall *nots*" of the law, Jesus confronts the rich young man with the "you *shalls*" of the reign of God: "Go, sell what you have, and give to the poor."

And, as Mark describes it, the man's face fell and "he went away sad." He can't bring himself to do it. His faith is not strong enough to give up the wealth he possesses for the "treasure in heaven." The young man walks away, certainly sad and perhaps feeling even somewhat disillusioned that his hero Jesus is not what he thought and hoped he would be.

Jesus then takes the moment to turn another Jewish belief upside down. Popular Jewish morality was simple: prosperity was a sign that one had found favor with God. There was a definite "respectability" to being perceived as wealthy and rich (how little things have changed). But great wealth, Jesus points out, is actually a hindrance to heaven: the rich may tend to look at things in terms of price, value, and the "bottom line." Jesus preaches *detachment* from things in order to become completely *attached* to the life and love of God.

Throughout the gospel, Jesus points to the inadequacy of viewing religion as a series of codes and laws. The young man was no different than his contemporaries in seeing one's relationship with God as based on a series of rules. But discipleship is much more than following rules. It is a call to do, to act, to reach out in the love of God. Jesus calls us not to follow a code of conduct but, rather, to embrace the Spirit that gives meaning and purpose to the law. Jesus readily acknowledges that such detachment from the things of the world is difficult; it can only be accomplished through the grace of God.

## Focusing the First Reading

*Wis 7:7-11*

The sage of the book of Wisdom praises wisdom as the search for God in all things. Such wisdom is more valuable than any of the riches and treasures of the world—an idea that the rich young man in today's gospel cannot grasp.

## Focusing the Responsorial Psalm

*Ps 90:12-13, 14-15, 16-17 (14)*

Psalm 90 is the prayer offered by a nation or tribe seeking God's protection in a time of crisis or distress. The verses that make up today's responsorial, however, are a prayer for wisdom: to recognize God's goodness and providence in the love of family and the productivity of their work.

## Focusing the Second Reading

*Heb 4:12-13*

The word of God is much more than the words on the page or stories from a time long ago. For the writer of Hebrews, the word of God is a living entity and power, "sharper than any two-edged sword," judging every human heart and spirit, holding us accountable before God. In the final verse, the subject changes from the word of God to God himself ("him"), the omniscient God who sees what is hidden and will call all of us to account for our lives.

**PROMPTS FOR HOMILISTS, CATECHISTS, AND RCIA TEAMS**

Has your possession of something of value ever turned out to be an unhappy, unsatisfying experience for you?

Have you ever known anyone like the rich young man in today's gospel?

How have our consumer-oriented culture and society's emphasis on winning at all costs diminished the human spirit?

## Model Penitential Act

*Presider:* As we prepare to celebrate these sacred mysteries, let us acknowledge our sins, seeking the mercy of God and the forgiveness of one another. *[pause]*

Lord God, you are the source of all that is good: Lord, have mercy.

Lord God, your Word is light and life: Christ, have mercy.

Lord God, you enable us to realize your kingdom of peace: Lord, have mercy.

## Homily Points

• Jesus asks the rich young man to not only help the poor but *become* poor, to find the treasure of heaven by giving up the treasure of earth. Jesus asks us to put aside what is keeping us from God in order to fully engage with those in need. Wealth should enable us to live life to the fullest, but often what we possess can weigh us down. The prosperity that should enable us to complete our life's journey becomes more important than the journey itself. Jesus asks everything of us as the cost of being his disciples, but Jesus asks only for what we have, not what we don't have. We all possess talents given by God for the work of making God's kingdom a reality in the here and now.

• Wealth is seductive: what we consume can consume us. Whatever we possess that inhibits us from embracing God's love is a curse, not a blessing. The question is not whether money is good or bad; the Gospel challenge is what we do with our wealth and responsibility for the blessings God has given us for the benefit of all. The rich young man can't embrace Jesus' call to let go of what is so central to his person. While our livelihood is important, sometimes we let money rule not only our budgets but our hearts and spirits as well. Jesus warns his followers that the mindless pursuit of money can blind us to the love of others and devalue the compassion, forgiveness, and joy that are the treasures of God's kingdom.

• In some strange sense, we are more whole when we are incomplete. The individual who has everything is in some ways a poor man; the "rich" will never know what it feels like to yearn, to hope, to nourish the soul with the dream of something better, to receive with gratitude something they already possess. As the rich young man in today's gospel cannot understand, there is a wholeness to those who can give their time, money, and strength to others and not feel diminished in doing so. There is a wholeness to those who can accept their limitations, who learn that they are strong enough to go through a tragedy and survive, who can lose something or someone and still feel complete.

## Model Universal Prayer (Prayer of the Faithful)

*Presider:* "All things are possible for God." With faith in Jesus' promise, then, let us pray.

*Response:* Lord, hear our prayer.

That our church leaders may humbly proclaim the "living and effective" word of God . . .

That the world's governments may work together to provide all peoples with their just share of the earth's harvest . . .

That we may embrace the Gospel spirit of poverty for the sake of the poor, homeless, and hungry . . .

That our parish community may seek to follow Christ in every dimension of our life together . . .

*Presider:* Hear these prayers we offer to you, O God. Open our hearts to embrace the spirit of your Son's Gospel, that we may bring to fulfillment your kingdom in this time and place of ours. In Jesus' name, we pray. **Amen.**

## COLLECT

Let us pray.

*Pause for silent prayer*

May your grace, O Lord, we pray,
at all times go before us and follow after
and make us always determined
to carry out good works.
Through our Lord Jesus Christ, your Son,
who lives and reigns with you in the unity
of the Holy Spirit,
one God, for ever and ever. **Amen.**

## FIRST READING

Wis 7:7-11

I prayed, and prudence was given me;
I pleaded, and the spirit of wisdom
came to me.
I preferred her to scepter and throne,
and deemed riches nothing in comparison
with her,
nor did I liken any priceless gem to her;
because all gold, in view of her, is a little
sand,
and before her, silver is to be accounted
mire.
Beyond health and comeliness I loved her,
and I chose to have her rather than the
light,
because the splendor of her never yields
to sleep.
Yet all good things together came to me in
her company,
and countless riches at her hands.

## RESPONSORIAL PSALM
Ps 90:12-13, 14-15, 16-17

R︎. (14) Fill us with your love, O Lord, and we will sing for joy!

Teach us to number our days aright,
  that we may gain wisdom of heart.
Return, O Lᴏʀᴅ! How long?
  Have pity on your servants!

R︎. Fill us with your love, O Lord, and we will sing for joy!

Fill us at daybreak with your kindness,
  that we may shout for joy and gladness
    all our days.
Make us glad, for the days when you afflicted us,
  for the years when we saw evil.

R︎. Fill us with your love, O Lord, and we will sing for joy!

Let your work be seen by your servants
  and your glory by their children;
and may the gracious care of the Lord our
    God be ours;
  prosper the work of our hands for us!
  Prosper the work of our hands!

R︎. Fill us with your love, O Lord, and we will sing for joy!

## SECOND READING
Heb 4:12-13

Brothers and sisters:
Indeed the word of God is living and
    effective,
  sharper than any two-edged sword,
  penetrating even between soul and
      spirit, joints and marrow,
  and able to discern reflections and
      thoughts of the heart.
No creature is concealed from him,
  but everything is naked and exposed to
      the eyes of him
  to whom we must render an account.

## About Liturgy

**Lector best practices:** Today's second reading reminds us that the word of God is "living and effective." Yet ministers still have the responsibility to bring that Word to life by their careful preparation and proclamation. Here are some best practices to help lectors, deacons, and priests be more effective in this important ministry:

If you are the first reader, do not be afraid to wait until the assembly is ready to be attentive. Wait until they have sat down, then wait a few more moments until they have settled in to listen before you begin.

Memorize the opening declaration that states where the reading is from so that you can look at the assembly as you say this. Then memorize the first sentence or phrase of the reading so that you do not break eye contact with the assembly at the beginning of the reading.

Spend some time each day during the week before you are scheduled to read to practice your reading out loud; get help with the pronunciation and meaning of any unusual words.

If you have the first reading, read it in conjunction with the gospel reading for that day because the gospel reading gives the thematic context for the first reading.

As you practice your reading, look for one sentence or phrase that seems to be the heart or main point of the reading. Practice and memorize that sentence or phrase so that you can look up from the book and make eye contact with the assembly as you proclaim that part of the reading.

Say the final statement, "The word of the Lord" or "The gospel of the Lord," as a declaration. If you proclaim this statement strongly and with confidence, the assembly will likely respond in the same way.

If possible, gather with other lectors and liturgical ministers assigned for your Sunday and with the homilist who will preach on those readings to do some faith sharing and breaking open of the word together in preparation for serving at the Mass.

Remember that you communicate as much with your body language and facial expression as you do with your voice. Practice in front of a mirror or take a video recording of yourself to make sure your body communicates your intended message.

Connect with your reading by praying with it and letting it penetrate your own spirit and discern the thoughts of your heart. Reflect on how it affirms or challenges how you live as a disciple.

## About Liturgical Music

**Seasonal psalms and common responses:** The responsorial psalm is sung by the entire assembly in dialogue with the psalmist who leads the singing, and normally the text of the psalm is taken from the assigned psalm in the Lectionary for that liturgical day. However, the *General Instruction of the Roman Missal*, 61, allows for the use of a seasonal psalm or a common psalm response that is more familiar to the assembly in order to facilitate better communal singing. These are listed by liturgical season so that you can select an antiphon or an alternative psalm that is appropriate for that day.

Common psalm responses for Ordinary Time are listed according to their genre. They are either a psalm of praise ("Praise the Lord for he is good"; "We praise you, O Lord, for all your works are wonderful"; or "Sing to the Lord a new song"), or a psalm of petition ("The Lord is near to all who call on him"; "Hear us, Lord, and save us"; or "The Lord is kind and merciful"). Use these antiphons in place of the one assigned for the day while keeping the day's proper verses. Seasonal responsorial psalms are alternative psalms that can replace the entire proper psalm. You can find all these common responses and seasonal psalms listed in its own section in the Lectionary.

**OCTOBER 14, 2018**
# TWENTY-EIGHTH SUNDAY IN ORDINARY TIME

## ✛ SPIRITUALITY

**GOSPEL ACCLAMATION**
Mark 10:45

R⁊. Alleluia, alleluia.
The Son of Man came to serve
and to give his life as a ransom for many.
R⁊. Alleluia, alleluia.

### Gospel    Mark 10:35-45; L146B

James and John, the sons of Zebedee, came
    to Jesus and said to him,
    "Teacher, we want you to do for us
        whatever we ask of you."
He replied, "What do you wish me to do
    for you?"
They answered him, "Grant that in your
    glory
    we may sit one at your right and the
        other at your left."
Jesus said to them, "You do not know
    what you are asking.
Can you drink the cup that I drink
    or be baptized with the baptism
        with which I am baptized?"
They said to him, "We can."
Jesus said to them, "The cup that I
    drink, you will drink,
    and with the baptism with which I am
        baptized, you will be baptized;
    but to sit at my right or at my left is not
        mine to give
    but is for those for whom it has been
        prepared."
When the ten heard this, they became
    indignant at James and John.
Jesus summoned them and said to them,
    "You know that those who are recognized
        as rulers over the Gentiles
    lord it over them,
    and their great ones make their authority
        over them felt.
But it shall not be so among you.
Rather, whoever wishes to be great among
    you will be your servant;
    whoever wishes to be first among you will
        be the slave of all.
For the Son of Man did not come to be
    served
    but to serve and to give his life as a
        ransom for many."

*or* Mark 10:42-45 *in Appendix A, p. 303.*

### Reflecting on the Gospel

Two men in cahoots together, scheming to get special treatment. This kind of setup is familiar in movies, the news, politics, and even (unfortunately) in daily life. And today we hear about it in the gospel. Human nature being what it is, two men, brothers in this case, are angling to get a better deal. They speak with Jesus on their own, in private. Their rather bold statement, "we want you to do for us whatever we ask of you" is met with open receptivity on Jesus' part. The way this story begins is reminiscent of children asking something of their parents. As a patient, listening parent, Jesus asks the brothers, "What do you wish me to do for you?" What would be our own reply to Jesus at that moment? His question is wide open. What do we want from Jesus? This question can be the source of fruitful meditation and prayer throughout the week.

For the brothers, they want glory, to sit at Jesus' side in his kingdom. They still imagine that Jesus will be a powerful earthly King, ruling over an independent and free Jewish people. But as Jesus did with Peter after Peter proclaimed him the Messiah, Jesus corrects James and John's misconception. Jesus told Peter that the Son of Man would suffer and ultimately die. He will invite the sons of Zebedee to do the same by asking if they can drink the cup that he drinks. This is a cup of suffering, an image reminiscent of the one spoken of by the prophet Jeremiah and in the Psalms. Before glory there must be suffering and even death. When the brothers seek glory, and a seat at either side of Jesus, they do not realize that they are thereby accepting suffering.

James and John's desire for glory provides Jesus the chance to expound once again on Christian discipleship, which is not the way of the world. For the disciples, greatness comes in service. The servant is the master. Jesus, the true Master and teacher, did not come to be served, but to serve. Even today, the gospel message of service flies in the face of cultural mores. How many powerful people with authority have underlings to do their bidding? In the power structures we find at work, in family, and in the marketplace, those at the top set the agenda and have their wishes carried out. Those who surround the powerful carry out the wishes and commands of the top. With Jesus, this structure is inverted. The greatest is truly the one who serves. The mark of greatness is humility.

### Living the Paschal Mystery

Gospel values should cause us to rethink how we are living our lives. We are never "there," having arrived at Christian perfection, with nothing more to do. Instead, the message of Jesus consistently calls us to go deeper, question more, and change our behavior to more closely match the Master. For what purpose do we do what we do? Are we seeking the golden ring? The life of retirement and leisure? Do we want to be the most important or admired person in the room? Is personal glory the goal? Rather, the Christian life is about self-emptying service. The Christian life does not put the self in the center, but puts the other, with his or her needs, in the center. Today we might ask ourselves, whose needs will I put before my own?

## Focusing the Gospel

*Mark 10:35-45 (shorter form: Mark 10:42-45)*

In the gospel reading a few weeks ago (but just a chapter ago in Mark's gospel), Jesus admonished his disciples for their pointless argument among themselves as to who was the most important. James and John apparently did not get the message. In today's gospel account, the two sons of Zebedee—who, with Peter, make up Jesus' inner circle—ask for places of honor and influence when Jesus begins his reign. James and John proclaim their willingness to "drink the cup" of suffering and share in the "bath" or "baptism" of suffering Jesus will experience (the Greek word used here is *baptizein*, meaning "to immerse" oneself in an event or situation).

Most readers share the other disciples' indignation at the incredible nerve of James and John to make such a request. (Matthew, in his gospel, casts the two brothers in a better light by having their mother make the request [Matt 20:20].) Jesus calls the disciples together to try again to make them understand that he calls them to greatness through service. Jesus' admonition to them is almost a pleading: If you really understand me and what I am about, if you really want to be my disciple, if you really seek to be worthy of my name, then you must see the world differently and respond to its challenges with a very different set of values. The world may try to justify vengeance rather than forgiveness, to glorify self-preservation over selflessness, to insist on preserving the system and convention for the sake of compassion and justice—*but it cannot be that way with you.*

## Focusing the First Reading

*Isa 53:10-11*

In his fourth and last song of the "servant," the prophet Isaiah exalts the one whose suffering will reconcile the people with God. This text especially resonated with the first generation of Christians after the resurrection who struggled to make sense of the suffering and death of Jesus. For Isaiah, the suffering of the "servant" is the means to God's re-creation of humanity: from the dark injustice of his death, the light of God's justice dawns; from the apparent hopelessness of his destruction, a life centered in God is made possible for humankind. (These two verses from Isaiah 53 are the conclusion to the first reading on Good Friday.)

## Focusing the Responsorial Psalm

*Ps 33:4-5, 18-19, 20, 22 (22)*

The psalmist invites the just to join in this song of praise to the God of mercy. The images of these latter verses of Psalm 33 exalt the virtues of humility, perseverance, and gratitude.

## Focusing the Second Reading

*Heb 4:14-16*

The writer of the letter to the Hebrews praises Jesus as the "great high priest" who, in his death and resurrection, reveals a God of great mercy and compassion. (These verses are also read as part of the second reading on Good Friday.)

**PROMPTS FOR HOMILISTS, CATECHISTS, AND RCIA TEAMS**

Who is or was the most "humble" person you have known—and what did his or her humility teach you?

Have you ever worked or served with someone who led by the "power" of service and the example of commitment?

When have you found it most difficult to heed the words of Jesus, "it shall not be so among you"?

Have you ever had to confront another's ambition or arrogance, similar to the attitude of James and John in today's gospel?

### Model Penitential Act

**Presider:** Let us begin our celebration of the Eucharist by placing our hearts before God, asking for his mercy for our sins and failings. *[pause]*

Jesus, you offered your life for our redemption: Lord, have mercy.

Jesus, you call us to seek the greatness of humble service: Christ, have mercy.

Jesus, you sit at the Father's right hand to intercede for us: Lord, have mercy.

### Homily Points

• Jesus challenges us: Can you drink the cup I will drink and immerse yourself in my baptism? Our first inclination is to say, No, Lord, we can't; it's more than we can do. What Jesus asks of us is not easy: his life of humble service, his emptying himself for the sake of others. But if we try to imitate Jesus, then the grace of God's wisdom and strength is ours, the Spirit of God's compassion and mercy is upon us. We find that we *can* drink Jesus' cup of humble compassion, we *can* live his baptism of generosity, we *can* bring good out of evil. It won't always be pretty or go smoothly—but we *can*.

• The distinguishing mark of discipleship is the attitude of humble, joyful service to others that Jesus lifts up in today's gospel. It is a perspective that flies in the face of the what's-in-it-for-me, take-no-prisoners approach we often assume in our dealings with others. Jesus' admonition—"it shall not be so among you"—is perhaps the greatest challenge of the gospel, calling us not to accept "business as usual," not to accept injustice as "the way things are," not to justify our flexible morals with the mantra "everybody does it." Only in imitating the servanthood of Christ do we experience the true depth of our faith; only in embracing his compassion and humility in our lives do we enable the Spirit to transform our world in God's life and love.

• The word *humility* comes from the same root as the word *humus*, "(from the) ground." Humility recognizes that we are all "lowly" or "(from the) ground" and equal before God. Humility is the grace to let go of our pride and ego in order to realize the common good we share with others as given to all of us by God. Authentic faith is centered in humility that begins with valuing life as a gift from God, a gift we have received only through God's mysterious love, not through anything we have done to deserve it. To be an authentic disciple of Jesus means to put ourselves in the humble role of servant to others, to intentionally seek the happiness of those we love regardless of the cost to ourselves.

### Model Universal Prayer (Prayer of the Faithful)

**Presider:** To the Lord of kindness and mercy, let us pray.

**Response:** Lord, hear our prayer.

That, as a church, we may seek the greatness of service to all who come to this table . . .

That the leaders of nations may possess the authority that is reflected in dedicated and selfless service to all . . .

That those who are forced to "drink the cup" of suffering may persevere in faith in order to experience the victory of Christ's resurrection . . .

That Jesus our great High Priest may bring to the Father's "throne of grace" the souls of those who have died *[especially . . . ]* . . .

**Presider:** Hear these prayers, O God. By your mercy and grace, may we create your kingdom here and now by embracing your Son's attitude of humble and selfless service to all. In Jesus' name, we pray. **Amen**.

### COLLECT

Let us pray.

*Pause for silent prayer*

Almighty ever-living God,
grant that we may always conform our
    will to yours
and serve your majesty in sincerity of
    heart.
Through our Lord Jesus Christ, your Son,
who lives and reigns with you in the unity
    of the Holy Spirit,
one God, for ever and ever. **Amen.**

### FIRST READING

Isa 53:10-11

The LORD was pleased
    to crush him in infirmity.

If he gives his life as an offering for sin,
    he shall see his descendants in a long
        life,
    and the will of the LORD shall be
        accomplished through him.

Because of his affliction
    he shall see the light in fullness of days;
through his suffering, my servant shall
        justify many,
    and their guilt he shall bear.

## RESPONSORIAL PSALM
Ps 33:4-5, 18-19, 20, 22

℟. (22) Lord, let your mercy be on us, as
we place our trust in you.

Upright is the word of the LORD,
and all his works are trustworthy.
He loves justice and right;
of the kindness of the LORD the earth
is full.

℟. Lord, let your mercy be on us, as we
place our trust in you.

See, the eyes of the LORD are upon those
who fear him,
upon those who hope for his kindness,
to deliver them from death
and preserve them in spite of famine.

℟. Lord, let your mercy be on us, as we
place our trust in you.

Our soul waits for the LORD,
who is our help and our shield.
May your kindness, O LORD, be upon us
who have put our hope in you.

℟. Lord, let your mercy be on us, as we
place our trust in you.

## SECOND READING
Heb 4:14-16

Brothers and sisters:
Since we have a great high priest who has
passed through the heavens,
Jesus, the Son of God,
let us hold fast to our confession.
For we do not have a high priest
who is unable to sympathize with our
weaknesses,
but one who has similarly been tested in
every way,
yet without sin.
So let us confidently approach the throne
of grace
to receive mercy and to find grace for
timely help.

### About Liturgy

*Why go to Mass?* If you asked a group of Catholics why they go to Mass, you might get a mix of responses. Many will say Sunday Mass is the center of their week and the heart of their faith. Others might say it's their time to refocus on God and give thanks. Still others are there because it's where they can gather with close friends and family in prayer. And perhaps a few will say that it's an obligation or simply that it's what good Catholics are supposed to do.

In the late nineteenth and early twentieth centuries, some of those who helped bring about a renewal in the liturgy that led to the principles we find in Vatican II saw a profound purpose for going to Mass that focused on what happened outside of Mass. The Benedictine monks of Saint John's Abbey in Collegeville, Minnesota, led by the vision of Fr. Virgil Michel, OSB, saw that liturgy was an act of social justice. If the liturgy could be prepared beautifully with the best that human art and creativity could provide, and if the assembly could understand and engage fully in that liturgy, then ordinary Catholics would be filled with the hope and joy of Christ. Those who understood the meaning of the Mass would no longer be confined to just the ordained or those who had special knowledge or degrees. The purpose would be clear for all who participated in it. That weekly encounter with the living Christ in a way that was meaningful and transcendent would lead them to transform their homes, neighborhoods, and workplaces with that same hope and joy. For these monks, good liturgy was transformative not only of bread and wine but of the people who participated in that sacrifice. Coming to Mass always had to connect with what happened before and after it so that, truly, "the liturgy is the summit toward which the activity of the church is directed; it is also the source from which all its power flows" (Constitution on the Sacred Liturgy, 10). When the faithful are able to participate fully in this source and summit of their lives, they learn what it means to live as Christians in their daily lives, for the liturgy "is the primary [and] indispensable source from which the faithful are to derive the true Christian spirit" (ibid., 14).

Why go to Mass? Because it changes the world.

### About Liturgical Music

*Song suggestions:* Today's readings give us another foreshadowing of Jerusalem and Jesus' humiliation on the cross. Yet that crucifixion is merely the culmination of a life of humility that began with the incarnation. A beautiful contemporary hymn that is easily accessible by choir and assembly is Rory Cooney's "To You Who Bow" (GIA Publications). The text is a song of praise to the God who bows—in Johannine Christology, the God who lowered himself to be one with humanity—that we might be raised up through our participation in Christ's humility. The text beautifully intertwines the imagery from Isaiah's Suffering Servant with the Philippian's canticle of Jesus who did not cling to his divinity but embraced the lowliness of humanity. This piece would be good for both this Sunday and the Sundays leading up to the solemnity of Christ the King, as well as the final weeks of Lent and Good Friday.

## ✠ SPIRITUALITY

**GOSPEL ACCLAMATION**
cf. 2 Tim 1:10

℟. Alleluia, alleluia.
Our Savior Jesus Christ destroyed death
and brought life to light through the Gospel.
℟. Alleluia, alleluia.

### Gospel

Mark 10:46-52; L149B

As Jesus was leaving Jericho with
his disciples and a sizable
crowd,
Bartimaeus, a blind man, the
son of Timaeus,
sat by the roadside begging.
On hearing that it was Jesus of
Nazareth,
he began to cry out and say,
"Jesus, son of David, have pity
on me."
And many rebuked him, telling him to
be silent.
But he kept calling out all the more,
"Son of David, have pity on me."
Jesus stopped and said, "Call him."
So they called the blind man, saying to
him,
"Take courage; get up, Jesus is
calling you."
He threw aside his cloak, sprang up,
and came to Jesus.
Jesus said to him in reply, "What do
you want me to do for you?"
The blind man replied to him, "Master,
I want to see."
Jesus told him, "Go your way; your
faith has saved you."
Immediately he received his sight
and followed him on the way.

### Reflecting on the Gospel

The Gospel of Mark introduces us to a variety of characters not seen elsewhere or even mentioned again in the New Testament. Bartimaeus, the blind man, is one such example. We have not been told of him in any story prior to this in the Gospel of Mark. And after this brief episode we will never hear of him again. Matthew and Luke will tell different versions of the story, but each is built on Mark. It's as though the reader or the early community would have known Bartimaeus as the blind man who sat begging on the road to Jericho.

From the way the story is told, Bartimaeus certainly had heard of Jesus, for upon learning that he was on the road, Bartimaeus immediately cries out. His behavior is judged to be uncouth and undignified, not worthy of Jesus or his followers. The response Bartimaeus receives is one that we might expect in "polite society." He is shut down. We can imagine the rebukes: Nobody wants to hear a shrieking blind man calling out for Jesus. Let Jesus and his followers pass in peace. Don't make a scene. Bartimaeus will have none of it and cries out all the more. It's as though nothing else matters but Jesus and the power he has.

In an exchange reminiscent of Jesus' interaction with James and John last week, Jesus asks him point-blank, "What do you want me to do for you?" Here again we might ask ourselves, how would we respond to Jesus' query? Face-to-face with Jesus and his direct question, "What do you want?" How are we to answer? We recall how James and John answered. They wanted glory. They wanted to sit at either side of Jesus in the kingdom. But Bartimaeus responds differently. He simply wants to see. For him, not one of the Twelve, not one of the chosen from the beginning, there is no grasping for power, glory, or authority. Bartimaeus merely wants to be made whole.

Jesus' response and Bartimaeus's healing is immediate and simultaneous. His sight is restored and he follows Jesus. Perhaps surprisingly, we never hear of Bartimaeus again. He is now a true disciple, a follower of Jesus. And his faith response to Jesus is a model for us, perhaps even a better model than the brothers James and John.

### Living the Paschal Mystery

At times we can think of the disciples as something of superheroes. The stories told about them in catechetical classes or homilies can make them seem like exemplars of faith. Today we hear about another disciple, not one of the Twelve, but a follower of Jesus nevertheless. It's not an accident that the story of Bartimaeus follows immediately upon the story of James and John. In each story Jesus asks, "What do you want me to do for you?" That question is asked of us too. Will our answer be like the brothers who want to game the system for their own glory? Or will our answer be like the blind Bartimaeus who seeks merely to see? Though the brothers James and John were called by Jesus from the beginning, it seems that Bartimaeus has a better self-understanding. He is more humble and less grandiose than the "real" disciples. Bartimaeus, about whom we know very little, serves as a prime example of discipleship. What do we seek of Jesus? What do we want Jesus to do for us?

## Focusing the Gospel

*Mark 10:46-52*

Mark's story of the blind Bartimaeus, which takes place just before Jesus' Palm Sunday entry into Jerusalem in Mark's gospel, is as much a "call" story as a healing story. For Mark, Bartimaeus is a model of faith. The blind beggar calls out to Jesus using the messianic title "Son of David." He first asks, not for his sight, but for compassion: he understands that this Jesus, unlike other preachers and healers, operates out of a spirit of love and compassion for humanity, and so Bartimaeus places his faith in that spirit. Ironically, the blind Bartimaeus "sees" in Jesus the spirit of compassionate service that, until now, his "seeing" disciples have so far been unable to comprehend.

## Focusing the First Reading

*Jer 31:7-9*

Bartimaeus is one of Jeremiah's "remnant" of the humble and faithful poor—including the blind, the lame, the sick, mothers and their children—whom the Lord will gather from exile and restore as a nation.

## Focusing the Responsorial Psalm

*Ps 126:1-2, 2-3, 4-5, 6 (3)*

The exiled Jews have returned to their homeland from Babylon. Grateful for their deliverance, they realize a great deal of work is ahead of them in rebuilding the city and recultivating the scorched earth. Psalm 126 is both the returning Jews' song of thanks to God for their deliverance and their plea to God for help in restoring their country.

## Focusing the Second Reading

*Heb 5:1-6*

Today's reading from the letter to the Hebrews exalts the great reconciling love of God to raise up Jesus Christ as our eternal High Priest, the perfect mediator between God and humankind. Priesthood is not a call that one assumes on one's own, for one's own glory or satisfaction; the call to priesthood comes from God to an individual for the blessing and service of his people.

---

**PROMPTS FOR HOMILISTS, CATECHISTS, AND RCIA TEAMS**

Have you ever experienced blindness of any kind—physical, emotional, intellectual? How were your eyes or consciousness finally opened to what you did not see or understand?

Did you ever fail to recognize the goodness of God in your midst during a difficult time in your life?

Who do you know who are among the faithful "remnant" like Bartimaeus: individuals who, despite the poverty and challenges they face, show us the light and riches of God?

235

## Model Penitential Act

*Presider:* Let us begin our celebration of these sacred mysteries by humbly asking God's healing mercy for our sins and failings. *[pause]*

You gather us together in your love: Lord, have mercy.

You open our eyes to see your goodness in our midst: Christ, have mercy.

You restore us to hope by your forgiveness and peace: Lord, have mercy.

## Homily Points

• In today's gospel, a blind man asks to see. Jesus responds, *Look with the eyes of the faith you already possess.* The man does receive his physical sight, but more importantly, Jesus affirms Bartimaeus's ability to "see" God's compassion in his midst, to "see" the possibilities for transforming hope and recreating love to heal the brokenness in his life, to "see" his ability to be the means for God's justice and reconciliation. Jesus opens the eyes of our hearts as well, enabling us to realize the opportunities we have to bring light, peace, and mercy along our way to the dwelling place of God.

• In today's gospel, the blind Bartimaeus cries out to Jesus, not asking for physical sight, but for compassion: Bartimaeus recognizes that his need for God's grace is far more important than the ability to see. Ironically, this blind man "sees" the compassion of Jesus that many of Jesus' "seeing" disciples do not recognize. Jesus responds to him out of deep compassion for every human being. In our busy lives, we may become blind to the people and things that bring real joy and meaning; in the many demands on us, we may no longer see possibilities for doing good things. We recast a situation to justify our self-absorption, lack of compassion, avoidance of anyone unpleasant, refusal to accept responsibility for our actions (or inactions). The blind Bartimaeus's cry is our prayer: "Master, I want to see"—to "see" with the human heart, to perceive in the spirit, to comprehend in God's wisdom.

• In the reign of God, no one is worthless, no one is marginal, no one is an outcast. As Jesus is about to enter Jerusalem to complete his mission as Messiah, he meets one of the marginalized of his society: a blind man not even accorded a name of his own (he is simply known as "Bartimaeus," "son of Timaeus"). Today's gospel challenges us to see all human beings with eyes of faith, realizing that we are all part of the "remnant" of Jeremiah's prophecy, that all of us are sons and daughters of our compassionate Father in heaven.

## Model Universal Prayer (Prayer of the Faithful)

*Presider:* "The Lord has done great things for us." Let us pray with confidence.

*Response:* Lord, hear our prayer.

That all church leaders and ministers may realize that their call has come from God for the service of his beloved people . . .

That all who serve us in government may protect the sacred dignity of every person . . .

That the suffering, the troubled, and the ill may know the love and hope of God . . .

That our parish family may be a community of Christ's compassion and reconciliation . . .

*Presider:* Lord of light, open our eyes to the light of your love so that we may bring to reality the prayers and hopes that you alone see in the depths of our hearts. We make these prayers to you in the name of Jesus, the healing Christ. **Amen.**

**COLLECT**

Let us pray.

*Pause for silent prayer*

Almighty ever-living God,
increase our faith, hope and charity,
and make us love what you command,
so that we may merit what you promise.
Through our Lord Jesus Christ, your Son,
who lives and reigns with you in the unity
    of the Holy Spirit,
one God, for ever and ever. **Amen.**

**FIRST READING**

Jer 31:7-9

Thus says the LORD:
Shout with joy for Jacob,
    exult at the head of the nations;
    proclaim your praise and say:
The LORD has delivered his people,
    the remnant of Israel.
Behold, I will bring them back
    from the land of the north;
I will gather them from the ends of the
      world,
    with the blind and the lame in their
       midst,
the mothers and those with child;
    they shall return as an immense throng.
They departed in tears,
    but I will console them and guide them;
I will lead them to brooks of water,
    on a level road, so that none shall
       stumble.
For I am a father to Israel,
    Ephraim is my firstborn.

## RESPONSORIAL PSALM

Ps 126:1-2, 2-3, 4-5, 6

R℣. (3) The Lord has done great things for
us; we are filled with joy.

When the LORD brought back the captives
of Zion,
we were like men dreaming.
Then our mouth was filled with laughter,
and our tongue with rejoicing.

R℣. The Lord has done great things for us;
we are filled with joy.

Then they said among the nations,
"The LORD has done great things for
them."
The LORD has done great things for us;
we are glad indeed.

R℣. The Lord has done great things for us;
we are filled with joy.

Restore our fortunes, O LORD,
like the torrents in the southern desert.
Those that sow in tears
shall reap rejoicing.

R℣. The Lord has done great things for us;
we are filled with joy.

Although they go forth weeping,
carrying the seed to be sown,
they shall come back rejoicing,
carrying their sheaves.

R℣. The Lord has done great things for us;
we are filled with joy.

## SECOND READING

Heb 5:1-6

Brothers and sisters:
Every high priest is taken from among
men
and made their representative before
God,
to offer gifts and sacrifices for sins.
He is able to deal patiently with the
ignorant and erring,
for he himself is beset by weakness
and so, for this reason, must make sin
offerings for himself
as well as for the people.
No one takes this honor upon himself
but only when called by God,
just as Aaron was.
In the same way,
it was not Christ who glorified himself
in becoming high priest,
but rather the one who said to him:
*You are my son: this day I have
begotten you;*
just as he says in another place:
*You are a priest forever according to
the order of Melchizedek.*

## About Liturgy

**The penitential act:** The penitential act in the Mass, formerly known as the penitential rite, is very familiar to those who prepare the liturgy. But there are a couple things that you might not be aware of in this brief rite.

First, the penitential act may take three different forms. Many already know form A, the *Confiteor*, and form C, the triple invocation of Christ with the response, "Lord, have mercy" or "Christ, have mercy." Form B is less well-known. It is a short dialogue between priest and people:

Priest: Have mercy on us, O Lord.
People: For we have sinned against you.
Priest: Show us, O Lord, your mercy.
People: And grant us your salvation.

This concludes with the absolution and the singing of the *Kyrie*. These Sundays of fall Ordinary Time, especially in connection with today's gospel reading, may be a good time to introduce this option if it is not already normally used in your parish.

Second, the invocations for form C have a specific purpose. They are invocations of praise for Christ who shows us mercy. However, sometimes when presiders, deacons, or coordinators write their own invocations, which is an option, this purpose becomes lost in a litany of our own sins. For example, you might hear, "When we have turned away from you, Lord have mercy . . . When we fail to do your will, Christ have mercy . . ." Although it is good for us to recall our own sinfulness, the purpose of this litany is to focus on and give praise for the power and goodness of Christ who is rich in mercy. In fact, the time for recalling our own sinfulness is *during the silence* that follows the priest's invitation to "acknowledge our sins, / and so prepare ourselves to celebrate the sacred mysteries" (Roman Missal). Therefore, be sure to make this a substantial period of silence.

Take a look at the sample invocations provided in Appendix VI of the Roman Missal, and you will see that every single invocation has Christ as the subject and proclaims what Christ has done to save us. If you choose to prepare your own invocations, be sure to make Christ the subject of each sentence, and focus on what Christ has done to save his people.

## About Liturgical Music

**Singing the Lamb of God:** During the fraction of the bread, the choir or cantor, in dialogue with the assembly, sings the Lamb of God. This litany, like the penitential act, is a litany of praise for Christ who has mercy on us and saves us. Unlike the penitential act, this invocation accompanies an action, that of breaking the eucharistic bread that will be given to the assembly. Because the Lamb of God is meant to accompany this ritual action, it should begin and end with the action. Therefore, be sure to be ready to begin singing the first "Lamb of God" as the priest begins to break the consecrated bread. In addition, repeat the invocation as many times as needed (not just three times), always ending with "grant us peace," until the breaking of the bread has concluded. If it seems appropriate, the accompaniment might continue instrumentally until the presider is ready to begin the following dialogue, "Behold the Lamb of God . . ."

**GOSPEL ACCLAMATION**
Matt 11:28

R͞/. Alleluia, alleluia.
Come to me, all you who labor and are burdened,
and I will give you rest, says the Lord.
R͞/. Alleluia, alleluia.

## Gospel

Matt 5:1-12a; L667

When Jesus saw the crowds, he
    went up the mountain,
and after he had sat down, his
    disciples came to him.
He began to teach them, saying:

"Blessed are the poor in spirit,
    for theirs is the Kingdom of
        heaven.
Blessed are they who mourn,
    for they will be comforted.
Blessed are the meek,
    for they will inherit the land.
Blessed are they who hunger
        and thirst for righteousness,
    for they will be satisfied.
Blessed are the merciful,
    for they will be shown mercy.
Blessed are the clean of heart,
    for they will see God.
Blessed are the peacemakers,
    for they will be called children of
        God.
Blessed are they who are persecuted
        for the sake of righteousness,
    for theirs is the Kingdom of
        heaven.
Blessed are you when they insult you
        and persecute you
    and utter every kind of evil against
        you falsely because of me.
Rejoice and be glad,
    for your reward will be great in
        heaven."

*See Appendix A, p. 304, for the other readings.*

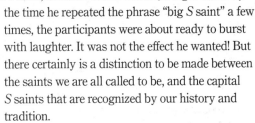

## Reflecting on the Gospel

In an RCIA class the relatively new team leader was covering the topic of "saints." He was making the point that all of us are called to be saints, with a lowercase *s*. He juxtaposed that to the capital *S* saints, like Francis of Assisi, Hildegard of Bingen, Augustine, or Thomas Aquinas. However, he distinguished the two not by lowercase or capital, but by little *s* and big *S*. He referred to his grandmother as a little *s* saint, not like Mother Teresa, a big *S* saint. By the time he repeated the phrase "big *S* saint" a few times, the participants were about ready to burst with laughter. It was not the effect he wanted! But there certainly is a distinction to be made between the saints we are all called to be, and the capital *S* saints that are recognized by our history and tradition.

Saint Paul called the recipients of his letters "saints," not in the sense that they were "holy rollers," but rather that they were called by God to be set apart in the world. They were dedicated to God.

And perhaps there can be no better gospel reading on a day that celebrates all the saints than the Beatitudes of Matthew. Some church fathers called the Beatitudes a self-portrait of Jesus. Jesus was poor in spirit. He mourned. He was meek; he hungered and thirsted for righteousness and was persecuted for its sake. Yet he remained merciful, clean of heart, and a peacemaker. In doing so, Jesus gave a model for what discipleship should look like, as a disciple follows Jesus. If we are to follow him, the Beatitudes should not only be a self-portrait of Jesus, but a portrait of us too. Of course, living the Beatitudes is a tall order. But in so doing we will find ourselves to be the lowercase *s* saints we are called to be. We will be worthy of the name Paul gives to his Christian communities, for we will be dedicated to God, set apart in the world.

## Living the Paschal Mystery

Sometimes the saints can appear as heroes or heroines, beyond the reach of our everyday experience. For example, who can live the life of Mother Teresa, abandoning everything to take care of the sick and dying on the streets? But there are other ways we care for the sick and dying in our own midst, and those ways should not be discounted. When we care for our children or our aging parents or family members, we are essentially doing something similar. The quotidian acts of self-sacrifice are those by which we live out our identity as saints with a lowercase *s*. We perform our ordinary, daily tasks in an extraordinary way, infused with love and care. We die to ourselves daily and put others' needs ahead of our own wants and desires. Living the Beatitudes, living our call to be set apart for God's service, means there is very little chance we will ever be venerated by millions of faithful as a capital *S* saint, but that is not our goal. Instead, we serve the needs and the needy of those before us. There is no requirement to go far. Family life and lives of friends give us many opportunities to live our call, die to self, and rise with Christ.

## Focusing the Gospel

Today's gospel is the beautiful "Beatitudes" reading from the Sermon on the Mount, Matthew's compilation of the sayings and teachings of Jesus. The word "blessed," as used by Jesus in these nine maxims, indicates a joy that is Godlike in its serenity and totality. For example, "the poor in spirit" are "blessed" as they are detached from material things and put their trust in God. "The meek" refers to true humility that banishes all pride; they are "blessed" who accept the necessity to learn and grow and realize their need to be forgiven. "They who hunger and thirst for righteousness" seek the things of God—justice, mercy, reconciliation—in every relationship and encounter. "The merciful" indicates the ability to see things from other people's perspectives, enabling us to consider things from their experiences and feel their joys and sorrows. "The clean of heart" are those who worship God with integrity and humility. "The peacemakers" are blessed because peace is everything that provides and makes for humanity's highest good (it should be noted, too, they are described as peace-makers and not simply peace-lovers). The final two Beatitudes are a warning of the suffering and abuse the follower of Jesus will encounter, but, in the struggle to live Jesus' Gospel, his vision of God's kingdom will be brought to completion.

## Model Penitential Act

**Presider:** With joy and thanksgiving we gather to celebrate the Supper of the Lamb of God, sacrificed for us. Let us begin our Eucharist on this All Saints' Day by seeking God's mercy for our sins and failings. *[pause]*

Lord Jesus, you are the Light and Word of God: Lord, have mercy.

Lord Jesus, you are the Lamb of God sacrificed for us so that we might live: Christ, have mercy.

Lord Jesus, you are the joy of all saints and hope of all sinners: Lord, have mercy.

## Model Universal Prayer (Prayer of the Faithful)

**Presider:** Let us join our prayers with those of the saints in asking God's blessings upon all his holy people.

**Response:** Lord, hear our prayer.

For all who serve the church, that their ministry among us may build bridges from this life to the eternal life of God . . .

For the nations and peoples of the world, that they may work together to establish God's holy city of peace . . .

For those who work for equality and justice, who are persecuted and suffer for their beliefs, that their prophetic witness may make the "new Jerusalem" a reality in this time and place . . .

For our parish family, that we may become a people of the Beatitudes, seeking God's presence and joy in all things . . .

**Presider:** Father, we join our prayers this day with the eternal praise of the blessed in heaven. May we possess your grace to realize your kingdom of compassion and in this world as we await its fulfillment in the next. We offer our prayer to you in the name of your Son, Jesus the Lord. **Amen.**

---

**COLLECT**

Let us pray.

*Pause for silent prayer*

Almighty ever-living God,
by whose gift we venerate in one celebration
the merits of all the Saints,
bestow on us, we pray,
through the prayers of so many intercessors,
an abundance of the reconciliation with you
for which we earnestly long.
Through our Lord Jesus Christ, your Son,
who lives and reigns with you in the unity of
    the Holy Spirit,
one God, for ever and ever. **Amen.**

---

**FOR REFLECTION**

• Who are the saints in your life that you remember today with gratitude?

• Which of the nine maxims of today's gospel do you find especially meaningful in your life? Have you known a "saint" who mirrored that particular Beatitude?

• What is the most intimidating or daunting challenge of becoming a "saint"?

## Homily Points

• Today we honor the holy men and women who have touched our lives: the loving parent, the loyal friend, the responsible farmer, the generous business owner, the dedicated teacher, the faithful pastor, the Christlike religious brother and sister. These saints have moved beyond their sins to realize the possibilities for forgiveness in their lives; possessed the openness of heart to embrace God's love; struggled to imitate the humility and compassion of the Gospel.

• Despite the saints' departure from our world for God's world, their "light" continues to illuminate the darkness of ignorance, confusion, doubt, and despair in our lives. The memories of what they taught us and inspired us to do remain as markers as we complete our own journeys to God. We give thanks to God for these saints who, in our memories of them, continue to bless and grace our lives with the light of God's compassion and peace.

**GOSPEL ACCLAMATION**
See John 6:40

This is the will of my Father, says the Lord,
that everyone who sees the Son and believes in
   him
may have eternal life.

## Gospel

John 6:37-40; L668

**Jesus said to the crowds:
"Everything that the Father gives
   me will come to me,
  and I will not reject anyone who
   comes to me,
  because I came down from
   heaven not to do my own
   will
  but the will of the one who sent
   me.
And this is the will of the one
   who sent me,
  that I should not lose anything
   of what he gave me,
  but that I should raise it on the last
   day.
For this is the will of my Father,
  that everyone who sees the Son and
   believes in him
  may have eternal life,
  and I shall raise him on the last day."**

*See Appendix A, p. 305, for the other readings.*

*or any other readings from L668 or any readings
from the Masses for the Dead (L1011–1016)*

### Reflecting on the Gospel

The word "soul" is polyvalent. It can mean almost anything to anyone, even in antiquity. For Plato, the soul was immortal, existing before the body and joined to it in the womb. For Aristotle, the soul was mortal, dying with the body. And of course there is no word in Hebrew, the language of the Old Testament, that fully captures or translates the Greek notion of "soul." Fast-forward to today and we hear the word "soul" bandied about quite often. If we wanted to have

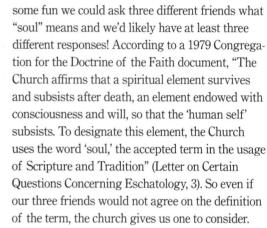

some fun we could ask three different friends what "soul" means and we'd likely have at least three different responses! According to a 1979 Congregation for the Doctrine of the Faith document, "The Church affirms that a spiritual element survives and subsists after death, an element endowed with consciousness and will, so that the 'human self' subsists. To designate this element, the Church uses the word 'soul,' the accepted term in the usage of Scripture and Tradition" (Letter on Certain Questions Concerning Eschatology, 3). So even if our three friends would not agree on the definition of the term, the church gives us one to consider.

And so today we commemorate All Souls' Day, or perhaps, in light of the church's definition of "soul," All Human Selves Day. So we are celebrating all those who have gone before us in faith. We commemorate "All the Faithful Departed."

How appropriate, then, that on this day we hear Jesus from John's gospel speaking about how his mission is not to lose anything the Father gave him. Jesus will raise them up. This promise is eternal and eschatological. It is eternal in that it was not meant for Jesus' generation only, but that the promise endures through the ages up to and including us. The promise is eschatological in that Jesus will raise those who have been given to him on the last day.

This hope of resurrection, of being raised on the last day, is central to our faith. This hope reminds us that this world is not all there is. Those who have died may seem gone from us, but as the book of Wisdom tells us, "The souls of the just are in the hand of God" (Wis 3:1). Saint Paul encourages us not to be like those who have no hope (in the afterlife). Instead, "we shall always be with the Lord" (1 Thess 4:17). Jesus himself looks after us as a prized possession. Our destiny is to be with him; and that is what we celebrate today: all those who have died with Christ and are with him now.

### Living the Paschal Mystery

Our days can seem so busy, so harried. But each day is a precious gift that can never be relived. We have all seen old photos from time gone by. What were those people doing the hour after the photo was taken (whatever photo it might be)? What were their worries? What were their priorities? What was so important to them that had to be done that very day? And how important or critical do those things seem now, decades later? Does anyone remember? Where are all those people in these old photos? Many, if not most or even all of them, have died, and with them all of their cares, concerns, and worries. Each of us too will someday depart this earth. We will die. What will happen to our cares and concerns then? What will we have done or accomplished with our busy, sometimes frenetic pace? We hope we have formed lasting relationships of love and care, not merely occupied our time with being busybodies. But as our Christian faith reminds us, our death is not the end. We will be raised by Jesus, who does not lose anything given to him by the Father. And this, our own death and subsequent rising, is our own personal paschal mystery. May we then live each day to the fullest, knowing we can never get it back. Let us invest our time, cares, and concerns with that which lasts: bonds of love.

### Focusing the Gospel

Since the mid sixth century, monastic communities have observed a day of prayer for the deceased monks of their monasteries. The monasteries of Cluny established the practice of praying the Mass and Office of the Dead on the day after All Saints' Day. November 2 was adapted as All Souls' Day by the universal church in the fourteenth century.

The theological underpinnings of today's feast is the acknowledgment of God's mercy despite our human frailty and of Christ as the hope of the living and the dead. While yesterday's solemnity celebrates the victory of the saints, today's somber and more austere commemoration focuses on the reality of death as the transition from this life to the life of God.

In John 6:37-40, Jesus concludes the bread of life discourse, reiterating that God seeks salvation and eternal life for every member of the human family and has raised up Jesus as his Christ to be the means to resurrection.

### Model Penitential Act

**Presider:** Let us begin our celebration of these sacred mysteries by seeking the mercy of God, who raises us up from our sin and despair to bring us into the light of his dwelling place. *[pause]*

Father of compassion and consolation: Lord, have mercy.
Risen Lord, joy of saints and hope of sinners: Christ, have mercy.
Spirit of love, illumination of God's dwelling place: Lord, have mercy.

### Model Universal Prayer (Prayer of the Faithful)

**Presider:** To God, the Father of mercy and the Lord of compassion, let us pray.

**Response:** Lord, hear our prayer.

That our church may be a community of hope in the promise of Jesus' resurrection . . .

That God will destroy the hate that divides the nations and peoples of the world and bring them together in his ways of justice and peace . . .

That Jesus' compassion may be present to all who bear the cross of serious illness and those who care for them . . .

That those who mourn the deaths of family and friends may find the strength to continue their own lives' journeys . . .

**Presider:** Hear, O Lord, our prayers this day for our relatives and friends who have gone before us, marked with the sign of faith. We give you thanks for the blessing of their presence in our lives. We commend them to you again, consoled that you have made a place for them in your dwelling place and looking forward to that day when we take our places with them at your table in heaven. We make these prayers in the name of Jesus, the risen One. **Amen.**

---

**COLLECT (from the first Mass)**
Let us pray.

*Pause for silent prayer*

Listen kindly to our prayers, O Lord,
and, as our faith in your Son,
raised from the dead, is deepened,
so may our hope of resurrection for your
      departed servants
also find new strength.
Through our Lord Jesus Christ, your Son,
who lives and reigns with you in the unity of
      the Holy Spirit,
one God, for ever and ever. **Amen.**

---

**FOR REFLECTION**

• What does the reality of death reveal to us about the nature of life?

• What do you most cherish in the memories of those you remember this day?

• In times of grief and mourning, how have you sustained your hope of Jesus' promise of the resurrection?

---

### Homily Points

• This life of ours is a gift from God. In death, we return this life to God, who transforms the existence we have known into a new life in his dwelling place. In both life and death we are God's. In life, God's Spirit illuminates us; in death, God takes us to himself. Our deceased loved ones remain with us, here and now, in the values and skills they taught us, the justice and generosity they inspire in us. They have made a worthy gift to God of the life God gave them.

• The trust that compels us to plant bulbs in the hard November ground enables us to see the hope of new life: our conviction in Easter's promise warms our winter hearts as we await new life in the eternal spring to come. Just as we have lived this life with Christ, we take our leave of this world with Christ; the baptism that made us part of his death now makes us part of his resurrection. We live always in the promise of Easter's empty tomb: every step in the warmth of this earth and through the winter night is guided by Christ's light.

## ✝ SPIRITUALITY

**GOSPEL ACCLAMATION**
John 14:23

℟. Alleluia, alleluia.
Whoever loves me will keep my word,
says the Lord; and my Father will love him
and we will come to him.
℟. Alleluia, alleluia.

### Gospel

Mark 12:28b-34; L152B

One of the scribes came to Jesus
and asked him,
"Which is the first of all the
commandments?"
Jesus replied, "The first is this:
*Hear, O Israel!*
*The Lord our God is Lord*
*alone!*
*You shall love the Lord your*
*God with all your heart,*
*with all your soul,*
*with all your mind,*
*and with all your strength.*
The second is this:
*You shall love your neighbor as*
*yourself.*
There is no other commandment
greater than these."
The scribe said to him, "Well said,
teacher.
You are right in saying,
'He is One and there is no other than
he.'
And 'to love him with all your heart,
with all your understanding,
with all your strength,
and to love your neighbor as
yourself'
is worth more than all burnt offerings
and sacrifices."
And when Jesus saw that he answered
with understanding,
he said to him,
"You are not far from the kingdom of
God."
And no one dared to ask him any more
questions.

### Reflecting on the Gospel

How is the Christian life, or life as a Roman Catholic, summed up? What Scripture passage, text from the Catechism, or saying from a saint or pope would you use to encapsulate Christianity? The question sounds like a bizarre parlor game at a gathering of theologians! Any answer can be found lacking. Focus on the sacraments and one might counter with liturgy. Affirm the Creed and someone might critique you for excluding Mass. Mention Mary and the saints and you could be accused of neglecting Jesus.

Something similar is the setting for the gospel today. One of the scribes, one of those learned in the law and all things Jewish, came to Jesus with a deceptively simple question. "Which is the first of all the commandments?" How Jesus answers will reveal much about his learning, his presuppositions, any of his biases, or, worst of all, his ignorance. Like a parlor game, this question is designed to show off the skill and knowledge of the questioner as much as the one questioned. Whatever answer Jesus offers can undoubtedly be critiqued. Will he respond with the first of the Ten Commandments? the first commandment issued in the book of Genesis? Or will Jesus somehow choose one commandment to be the first, in the sense of primary?

Jesus' answer cleverly combines two commandments (Deut 6:4; Lev 19:18) to be the greatest. "There is no other commandment greater than these." In fact, though each commandment is in the Torah, scholars know of no other prophet or teacher prior to Jesus who had ever combined these two commandments in this way. Thus, modern scholars believe this unique combination stems from the teaching of the historical Jesus. It was he who combined the commandment to love God with the commandment to love one's neighbor. In this, the law is summed up and is more meaningful than burnt offerings and sacrifices, that is, many of the other prescripts and commandments of the law.

There is nothing for the interlocutor to critique. He affirms and admiringly repeats Jesus' response, for which he is told, "You are not far from the kingdom of God." Jesus so embodies the law that no one else has the courage to ask him any questions. The theological parlor game is concluded for the day.

But for us Christians, how is the Christian life summed up? By going to Mass on Sundays and holy days? By making First Fridays? By observing Lent? Or are those acts more akin to the burnt offerings and sacrifices prescribed by the law? Might there be something more foundational to the Christian life than even doctrines, creeds, holy days, or Lent? Perhaps Jesus' words are meant for us too. If only we love God and love our neighbor as ourselves.

### Living the Paschal Mystery

There is a Texas saying, "boil the pot dry." It means when we get down to the gist of the matter, what's left? When we boil away any excess, what remains? Today, Jesus will "boil the pot dry" and let us know that the essence of the Torah is to love God and to love one's neighbor as oneself. The simplicity of this command is shocking to those of us who might prefer external observance demanded by prescripts and commandments. In many ways it would be easier to follow a set of dos and don'ts rather than to "love God" and "love your neighbor." When we love, there is no instructional booklet. There is no guide as to what to avoid or what precisely to do. In many ways, today's gospel can be summed up in the words of St. Augustine, who said, "Love God and do what you will."

## Focusing the Gospel

*Mark 12:28b-34*

In today's gospel, Jesus "synthesizes" his entire Mosaic law into the one "Great Commandment." The Jews knew these two commandments well. To this day, observant Jews twice daily pray the Shema: to love God "with all your heart, and with all your soul, and with all your strength." The word *shema* means "hear," from the first words of the prayer, "Hear, O Israel . . ." The text for the Shema, which is also inscribed in the mezuzah, the small container affixed to the door of every observant Jewish home, is found in Deuteronomy 6:4-6 (today's first reading). The book of Leviticus outlined in great detail a Jew's ethical and moral responsibility to "love" one's neighbor. But Jesus is the first to weave these two ideas into a single commandment: "There is no other commandment greater than these." The only way we can adequately express our love for God is in the love we extend to our neighbor; to do so is the beginning of the kingdom of God.

## Focusing the First Reading

*Deut 6:2-6*

Today's first reading, as noted above, is Moses' first articulation of the Shema prayer, a prayer that serves as a beautiful summary of the law of Israel's covenant with God.

## Focusing the Responsorial Psalm

*Ps 18:2-3, 3-4, 47, 51 (2)*

Psalm 18 is a royal song of thanksgiving for a military victory (the text appears almost in total in 2 Samuel 22, in which David gives thanks for Israel's defeat of the Philistine armies). In his humble expression of gratitude to God "my rock," the king invites his people to join in his hymn of thanksgiving.

## Focusing the Second Reading

*Heb 7:23-28*

In today's reading from Hebrews, the sinless Christ's sacrifice is portrayed as the perfect and complete offering, reconciling God and humanity for all time. Because he lives on in his resurrection, Christ continues as our High Priest, interceding for us before the Father.

---

**PROMPTS FOR HOMILISTS, CATECHISTS, AND RCIA TEAMS**

How is love an act of "creation"?

Have you ever been confronted with a situation in which love demanded more than you were ready to give?

In what ways is Jesus' vision of the kingdom of God a reality here and now?

What are the real-life implications of loving God with your whole "heart"? with your whole "soul"? with your whole "mind"? with your whole "strength"? Which of these do you find most challenging?

What is the most difficult personal need or want to put aside in order to "love your neighbor as yourself"?

## Model Penitential Act

*Presider:* As we gather to celebrate these sacred mysteries, let us seek the mercy of God for our sins and failings. *[pause]*

Father of all that is good: Lord, have mercy.

Lord, both the giver and the gift we offer in this Eucharist: Christ, have mercy.

Spirit of God, source of love in our homes and hearts: Lord, have mercy.

## Homily Points

• To love as God "commands" and Jesus teaches requires a spirit of humility that realizes that we are all sons and daughters of God who are called to use whatever gifts we possess—regardless of how small or insignificant they may seem—for the building of his kingdom. There is no greater sacrifice of praise we can make to God for his many blessings to us, no greater song of thanks we can offer than to honor God in those who have been created in God's image. To love as God loves demands every fiber of our being—our heart, our soul, our mind, our strength. The love of God forces us outside our comfort zone, to put our own feelings and wants on the line, to risk being hurt or misunderstood for the sake of the beloved.

• In creating us, God invites us to participate in the work of creation by embracing God's spirit of love. In today's gospel, Jesus lifts up such love as the center of the kingdom of God. Devotion to God is not genuine unless it includes love for neighbor; commitment to others is incomplete without recognition of God as the Source of all love. It is in the compassion and kindness extended to others that our humanity most resembles God; it is in the respect and honor in which we hold others that we most praise the God of love; it is in acts of charity and selflessness that we mirror the love of God in our midst. In the twofold "Great Commandment" we discover a purpose to our lives much greater and larger than ourselves and our own needs, interests, prejudices, and biases. In loving God in one another, we find the ultimate meaning and purpose of the gifts of faith and life.

## Model Universal Prayer (Prayer of the Faithful)

*Presider:* To God, the Father of compassion and Author of love, let us pray.

*Response:* Lord, hear our prayer.

That church leaders may seek to imitate the compassion and humility of Jesus Christ, the Eternal High Priest . . .

That God's commandment of love may be at the heart of the laws of all the world's governments . . .

That the sick, the suffering, and the dying may know, in our care and compassion, the healing presence of the risen Jesus . . .

That God will breathe his Spirit of love into every ministry of our parish community . . .

*[Election Day:]* That the wisdom of God may illuminate our minds and the Spirit of God enliven our hearts as we cast our votes this week for those who will lead our nation, state, and community . . .

*Presider:* Hear our prayer, O Lord, for all our brothers and sisters. Instill in us your Spirit of love to imitate the selfless humility of your Son so that we may realize your kingdom of compassion and peace in our own time and place. In Jesus' name, we pray. **Amen.**

## COLLECT

Let us pray.

*Pause for silent prayer*

Almighty and merciful God,
by whose gift your faithful offer you
right and praiseworthy service,
grant, we pray,
that we may hasten without stumbling
to receive the things you have promised.
Through our Lord Jesus Christ, your Son,
who lives and reigns with you in the unity
    of the Holy Spirit,
one God, for ever and ever. **Amen.**

## FIRST READING

Deut 6:2-6

Moses spoke to the people, saying:
"Fear the LORD, your God,
    and keep, throughout the days of your
        lives,
    all his statutes and commandments
        which I enjoin on you,
    and thus have long life.
Hear then, Israel, and be careful to observe
        them,
    that you may grow and prosper the
        more,
    in keeping with the promise of the
        LORD, the God of your fathers,
    to give you a land flowing with milk
        and honey.

"Hear, O Israel! The LORD is our God, the
        LORD alone!
Therefore, you shall love the LORD, your
        God,
    with all your heart,
    and with all your soul,
    and with all your strength.
Take to heart these words which I enjoin
    on you today."

## RESPONSORIAL PSALM

Ps 18:2-3, 3-4, 47, 51

℟. (2) I love you, Lord, my strength.

I love you, O Lord, my strength,
  O Lord, my rock, my fortress, my
    deliverer.

℟. I love you, Lord, my strength.

My God, my rock of refuge,
  my shield, the horn of my salvation, my
    stronghold!
Praised be the Lord, I exclaim,
  and I am safe from my enemies.

℟. I love you, Lord, my strength.

The Lord lives! And blessed be my rock!
  Extolled be God my savior,
you who gave great victories to your king
  and showed kindness to your anointed.

℟. I love you, Lord, my strength.

## SECOND READING

Heb 7:23-28

Brothers and sisters:
The levitical priests were many
  because they were prevented by death
    from remaining in office,
  but Jesus, because he remains forever,
  has a priesthood that does not pass
    away.
Therefore, he is always able to save those
    who approach God through him,
  since he lives forever to make
    intercession for them.

It was fitting that we should have such a
    high priest:
  holy, innocent, undefiled, separated
    from sinners,
  higher than the heavens.
He has no need, as did the high priests,
  to offer sacrifice day after day,
    first for his own sins and then for those
      of the people;
  he did that once for all when he offered
    himself.
For the law appoints men subject to
    weakness to be high priests,
  but the word of the oath, which was
    taken after the law,
  appoints a son,
  who has been made perfect forever.

## About Liturgy

**The Creed:** Today's gospel gives us an opportunity to reflect on the Creed, which we might often rush through. This long statement of what we believe came into general universal use in the Roman Rite relatively late in our liturgical history in the eleventh century. Before that, it was included in the Mass either as a definitive statement against any heretical teachings that may have been common in that part of the world or as part of the baptismal liturgy. The Creed is also called the profession of faith or the "symbol." This last term is especially baptismal in that it refers to the common heritage that symbolizes the unity of all Christians. Only those who knew it and were able to profess it were considered Christians. Even today, there is a specific ritual for "handing on" or presenting the Creed symbolically to those preparing for baptism. In fact, today's first reading is the assigned reading for that presentation of the Creed found in the Rite of Christian Initiation of Adults.

The connection between today's gospel reading and the first reading, summarized by the psalm, is love for God. When we state what we believe, we are doing more than simply listing the tenets of our faith as if faith were merely an intellectual assent to a set of doctrines. As Christians, when we say, "I believe," we are actually saying something more like, "I believe with all my heart." The readings today call us not merely to affirm God but to *love* God with everything we are. That is why love of God and love of neighbor, manifested by our visible behaviors, is the crux—the heart—of our faith in Christ. Today invite the assembly to speak the Creed slowly, taking time to pause at the end of each line to reflect on its meaning and how it calls us to open our hearts to God and to one another.

## About Initiation

**The presentation of the Creed:** In the catechumenate, the presentation of the Creed (RCIA 157–63) is normally celebrated during Lent. However, the RCIA gives the option to "anticipate" its celebration earlier in the liturgical year (see 104–5). The reason for this is that the Lenten season is relatively short and already filled with many other significant liturgies for those to be baptized. If you have catechumens who are already far along in their formation, today or at a weekday Mass during this coming week may be a good time to celebrate the presentation of the Creed with a gathering of the faithful. Note that the presentation is an *oral* presentation. (The word "catechesis" means literally, "oral instruction.") Nowhere in the rite does it imply giving a physical copy of the Creed as part of the ritual action. The handing on is done by the faithful prayerfully speaking the Creed to the catechumens who, in turn, prayerfully receive it by hearing the words and taking them to heart.

## About Liturgical Music

**Singing by heart:** Although the choir is usually not expected to memorize the songs they sing, there is nothing like being able to sing a song *by heart* with words you truly believe *in your heart*. If you find that you are always relying on your music for the words and notes, especially for acclamations and antiphons you already know by heart, practice a discipline of trust in yourself and in your fellow-singers (that is, the assembly) by putting your music away for these already-familiar responses and hymns and just singing *from your heart*. You might find that not only will you be able to pray the liturgy better and believe more fervently the words you sing but also you'll project your voice more because you won't be looking down into your music.

**NOVEMBER 4, 2018**
# THIRTY-FIRST SUNDAY IN ORDINARY TIME

## ✠ SPIRITUALITY

**GOSPEL ACCLAMATION**
Matt 5:3

℟. Alleluia, alleluia.
Blessed are the poor in spirit,
for theirs is the kingdom of heaven.
℟. Alleluia, alleluia.

### Gospel

Mark 12:38-44; L155B

In the course of his teaching Jesus said to the crowds,
  "Beware of the scribes, who like to go around in long robes
and accept greetings in the marketplaces,
  seats of honor in synagogues,
  and places of honor at banquets.
They devour the houses of widows and, as a pretext,
  recite lengthy prayers.
They will receive a very severe condemnation."

He sat down opposite the treasury and observed how the crowd put money into the treasury.
Many rich people put in large sums.
A poor widow also came and put in two small coins worth a few cents.
Calling his disciples to himself, he said to them,
  "Amen, I say to you, this poor widow put in more
  than all the other contributors to the treasury.
For they have all contributed from their surplus wealth,
  but she, from her poverty, has contributed all she had,
  her whole livelihood."

*or Mark 12:41-44 in Appendix A, p. 306.*

### Reflecting on the Gospel

Who are the four people you would like to have dinner with in heaven? Many of us might choose famous personalities from history. Others might choose long-lost relatives. Whomever we choose, these are people we really want to be with. We'd want to spend time with them and learn from their experiences. On the flip side, there are those who love going to dinner parties, being seen at dinner parties. They love to rub shoulders with the powerful, the movers, and the shakers. They like their tickets to the cultural events, the opera, the symphony, baseball and football games. This type of person who loves to be seen is a well-known character in literature. It seems even in Jesus' time these people were readily spotted. For Jesus, they become a target. Jesus is especially critical of this character type who also happens to be a religious leader (!) who "devour[s] the houses of widows." They pray for show, and enjoy the privileges that come with their office. Their condemnation will be severe. In many respects Jesus' critique of the religious authorities is echoed by Pope Francis's critique of religious authorities. Even though we may not be religious authorities, the critique certainly applies to us as well. Is our going to church for show? Is it more cultural and societal than religious and spiritual?

In the second vignette in today's gospel Jesus criticizes the rich, who give large sums to make a show, and to attract attention to their giving. Even though their gifts were large, and undoubtedly made a difference, these people gave from their excess. It was pocket change, not the milk money. The poor widow, she whose house is being devoured by the religious authorities, gives everything she has. In other words, they who had much gave little of what they had. She who had little gave everything she had. What kind of givers are we? Do we give of ourselves or from our excess? Jesus' message is to give everything we have, without holding anything back. It's too easy to game the system, to make a show out of giving, to have our names on plaques or printed in newsletters. Today many charitable organizations and parishes even have giving clubs with various levels. And, of course, there is an entire industry today that has been developed around giving and fundraising.

But Jesus is speaking of something more profound. Rather than the annual fundraising appeal that each of us participate in, or charitable contributions that are a hallmark of Christianity, we are summoned by Jesus to give our entire selves. Rather than write a check equivalent to a family dinner at a restaurant, Jesus wants us entirely, without reservation.

### Living the Paschal Mystery

Our lives can be saturated with requests for giving, to the parish, Boy Scout popcorn, Girl Scout cookies, band, sports teams, charitable causes, and more. These are all good deeds that are done from our sense of Christian charity. But there can be a temptation for some, especially religious leaders, to become enamored by the funds themselves and the kind of life they can provide. At that point hypocrisy can ensue, encouraging others to give without making a similar commitment ourselves. Christians in the early centuries of the church recognized this all too often and had a name for those who would use the name of Jesus to make a comfortable life for themselves: Christ-monger. We are probably familiar with the modern televangelist style Christ-monger. But rather than point the finger outward, it's a good opportunity to examine ourselves and ask why we give, whether we give for pure charitable motives, or whether there might be some other hidden motives.

In the end, Jesus doesn't want our money. He wants us. He wants a total personal commitment from each of us to be his follower. When that happens, we will not count the cost, which would be greater than any price we could pay, for we are his.

## Focusing the Gospel
*Mark 12:38-44 (shorter form: Mark 12:41-44)*
Preaching in the Jerusalem temple days before the Last Supper and his crucifixion, Jesus indicts the scribes for their lavish but empty show of faith. His indictment of them can just as easily apply today. Those who make a show of religious practice rather than live the essence of the message are worthy of indictment. They would enjoy the privilege that comes with religious authority and even use it to devour the estates of the widows, in other words, the powerless. Their faith is empty and, in the end, their judgment will be severe.

Throughout Scripture, widows were the epitome of destitution and powerlessness (today's first reading from 1 Kings is an example). Jesus again makes a considerable impact on his hearers, then, by lifting up an impoverished widow as the model of faithful generosity—as well as embodying the "Great Commandment" that Jesus spoke of in last Sunday's gospel. Only that which is given not from our abundance but from our own need and poverty—and given totally, completely, humbly, and joyfully—is a gift fitting for God.

## Focusing the First Reading
*1 Kgs 17:10-16*
Today's first reading recalls Elijah's encounter with a poor widow. Despite her desperate poverty, she agrees to share the little that she has with the prophet. Elijah tells her not to be afraid, promising that her jar of flour will not go empty and her oil jug will not run dry.

## Focusing the Responsorial Psalm
*Ps 146:7, 8-9, 9-10 (1b)*
This psalm (one of the "Hallelujah" psalms that conclude the Psalter) is the hymn of someone who has experienced the goodness of God in his or her own struggles and now invites the poor, the physically challenged, the oppressed, and the imprisoned to embrace the wisdom he or she has discovered in keeping faith in the Lord of justice and mercy.

## Focusing the Second Reading
*Heb 9:24-28*
The writer of Hebrews continues his teaching to Jewish converts about the eternal priesthood of Christ as the completion of the priesthood originating with Moses and Aaron. In the sacrifice of his life, Christ has won salvation for those who have died; he will return at the end of time to gather the surviving faithful to God's dwelling place.

**PROMPTS FOR HOMILISTS, CATECHISTS, AND RCIA TEAMS**

Have you ever met the "widow" of today's gospel?

What form has the "widow's penny" taken in your own giving? When have you given from your "poverty" rather than your surplus?

Have you ever been the recipient of someone's "reckless" giving?

Have you ever worked to obtain an honor or recognition that turned out to be less than satisfying?

## Model Penitential Act

*Presider:* Gathered by our Father in heaven to celebrate these sacred mysteries, let us seek his mercy and peace by calling to mind our sins. *[pause]*

O God, you give food to the hungry: Lord, have mercy.

O God, you secure justice for the oppressed: Christ, have mercy.

O God, free those held captive by sin, grief, and despair: Lord, have mercy.

## Homily Points

• In exalting the poor widow's gift, Jesus makes us realize that numbers are not the true value of giving in the "economy" of God. It is what we give from our want, not from our extra, that reveals what we truly value and what we want our lives and world to be. It is not the measure of the gift but the measure of the love that directs the gift that is great before God. It is not the knowledge we have attained nor the wealth we command but our willingness to put those things at the service of others that gives meaning to our faith. It is not the size of what we give or the impact of what we do but the love and sacrifice in which we give that makes our gift to another holy in God's eyes.

• God's kingdom is realized in our embracing Christ's spirit of servanthood that is centered in respect for all as sons and daughters of God; that finds fulfillment in the compassion and kindness we can extend to others; that enables us to place the common good and the needs of others less fortunate than ourselves above our own wants and interests. Jesus exhorts his listeners to look beyond titles, dress, and positions and consider the heart and soul of those who would lead others. He calls us to honor the dignity of the servant over the power of the rich, seek generous humility over cynical celebrity, and embrace the generosity of the widow rather than the empty gestures of the scribe.

• The widow's penny can take many forms: a warm coat given to the poor, an hour spent each week teaching religious education to children, a quilt made to raise money for a worthy cause, a pan of lasagna for a family going through a difficult time. The widow's penny accomplishes great things not because of the size of the gift but because of the love and compassion that compels her to give. The widow's "reckless" giving from her poverty challenges our concept of planned, tax deductible, and convenient giving. Jesus' concept of charity is centered in unconditional love that makes such sacrificial giving a joy.

## Model Universal Prayer (Prayer of the Faithful)

*Presider:* In the name of Christ Jesus, let us join our hearts and voices in prayer to God.

*Response:* Lord, hear our prayer.

That humble service and grateful sacrifice may be the center of our church's ministries . . .

That all nations and peoples may be dedicated to the work of peace and justice and the elimination of oppression and persecution from our world . . .

That, like the poor widow, we may respond to the plight of those in need, not from our surplus, but from our poverty . . .

That we may seek out and honor the insight and wisdom of senior members of our families and communities . . .

*Presider:* O God, you know our needs before we know them ourselves. With trust in your constant love and providence, we ask you to hear these prayers we offer for the people who await your salvation in your Son, Jesus Christ, in whose name we pray. **Amen**.

## COLLECT

Let us pray.

*Pause for silent prayer*

Almighty and merciful God,
graciously keep from us all adversity,
so that, unhindered in mind and body alike,
we may pursue in freedom of heart
the things that are yours.
Through our Lord Jesus Christ, your Son,
who lives and reigns with you in the unity of the Holy Spirit,
one God, for ever and ever. **Amen.**

## FIRST READING

1 Kgs 17:10-16

In those days, Elijah the prophet went to Zarephath.
As he arrived at the entrance of the city,
a widow was gathering sticks there; he called out to her,
"Please bring me a small cupful of water to drink."
She left to get it, and he called out after her,
"Please bring along a bit of bread."
She answered, "As the LORD, your God, lives,
I have nothing baked; there is only a handful of flour in my jar
and a little oil in my jug.
Just now I was collecting a couple of sticks,
to go in and prepare something for myself and my son;
when we have eaten it, we shall die."
Elijah said to her, "Do not be afraid.
Go and do as you propose.
But first make me a little cake and bring it to me.
Then you can prepare something for yourself and your son.
For the LORD, the God of Israel, says,
'The jar of flour shall not go empty,
nor the jug of oil run dry,
until the day when the LORD sends rain upon the earth.'"
She left and did as Elijah had said.
She was able to eat for a year, and he and her son as well;
the jar of flour did not go empty,
nor the jug of oil run dry,
as the LORD had foretold through Elijah.

## RESPONSORIAL PSALM
Ps 146:7, 8-9, 9-10

R℣. (1b) Praise the Lord, my soul!
*or:*
R℣. Alleluia.

The LORD keeps faith forever,
  secures justice for the oppressed,
  gives food to the hungry.
The LORD sets captives free.

R℣. Praise the Lord, my soul!
*or:*
R℣. Alleluia.

The LORD gives sight to the blind;
  the LORD raises up those who were
    bowed down.
The LORD loves the just;
  the LORD protects strangers.

R℣. Praise the Lord, my soul!
*or:*
R℣. Alleluia.

The fatherless and the widow he sustains,
  but the way of the wicked he thwarts.
The LORD shall reign forever;
  your God, O Zion, through all
    generations. Alleluia.

R℣. Praise the Lord, my soul!
*or:*
R℣. Alleluia.

## SECOND READING
Heb 9:24-28

Christ did not enter into a sanctuary made
    by hands,
  a copy of the true one, but heaven itself,
  that he might now appear before God
    on our behalf.
Not that he might offer himself repeatedly,
  as the high priest enters each year into
    the sanctuary
  with blood that is not his own;
  if that were so, he would have had to
    suffer repeatedly
  from the foundation of the world.
But now once for all he has appeared at
    the end of the ages
  to take away sin by his sacrifice.
Just as it is appointed that human beings
    die once,
  and after this the judgment, so also
    Christ,
  offered once to take away the sins of
    many,
  will appear a second time, not to take
    away sin
  but to bring salvation to those who
    eagerly await him.

## About Liturgy

**The preparation of the gifts:** From the beginnings of the church, bread and wine have always been brought forward by the community in the celebration of the Eucharist. In these home gatherings, members of the community simply placed bread and wine onto the table that served as the altar. As the church grew in number and the Eucharist came to be celebrated in public buildings, by the third century deacons assisted in gathering the gifts of the people, which included not only the bread and wine for the Mass but other goods such as food for the poor in the form of livestock, wheat, and grapes, as well as gifts to assist the work of the church, such as candles and other crafted goods. However during the Middle Ages, as the practice of sharing in Communion by the faithful declined, this lavish procession of gifts also began to disappear. In place of presenting homemade bread and wine, unleavened hosts began to be used, and only enough wine for the clergy was needed. Therefore, a full procession of gifts fell out of use in favor of the priest and deacons placing the hosts and wine onto the altar themselves. The faithful's participation in this minimal preparation of gifts was reduced to a collection of money to be given to the poor and to fund the work of the church.

Vatican II restored the simple but significant procession of bread and wine coming from the members of the faithful. The *General Instruction of the Roman Missal* speaks of this restoration: "It is a praiseworthy practice for the bread and wine to be presented by the faithful . . . Even though the faithful no longer bring from their own possessions the bread and wine intended for the liturgy as was once the case, nevertheless the rite of carrying up the offerings still keeps its spiritual efficacy and significance" (73).

Although it is secondary to the Liturgy of the Word that precedes it and the Liturgy of the Eucharist that follows it, take care with this procession of gifts. The meaning of this simple action is summarized in the words that accompany its reception by the priest at the altar. These are the "fruit of the earth" and the "fruit of the vine" that God had first given to us. Now, transformed by the "work of human hands," we give these earthly gifts back to God so that we might receive them again, transformed by the work of the Spirit into holy gifts for God's holy people. These gifts, along with the money that is collected, represent the sacrifice we have made and promise to make daily in our lives as a participation in the eternal sacrifice of Christ.

## About Liturgical Music

**Music during the preparation of the gifts:** There are many options for the music used during the preparation of the gifts. The *General Instruction of the Roman Missal* calls for the offertory chant to be sung during the procession, continuing at least until the gifts are placed on the altar. The US bishops' document on music, Sing to the Lord, further clarifies that this may be a time for the choir to sing alone (30), or for instrumental music (44 and 174), or for an antiphonal song between cantor and people (37).

The text for any song used during the procession is also very flexible. Therefore, this part of the Mass is a good time to present new songs for the assembly to learn or for a choral piece that complements the readings or liturgical feast. Whatever you choose, be sure that the music does not unduly prolong this relatively brief ritual action.

**NOVEMBER 11, 2018**
# THIRTY-SECOND SUNDAY IN ORDINARY TIME

## ✠ SPIRITUALITY

**GOSPEL ACCLAMATION**
Luke 21:36

℟. Alleluia, alleluia.
Be vigilant at all times
and pray that you have the strength to
    stand before the Son of Man.
℟. Alleluia, alleluia.

## Gospel

Mark 13:24-32; L158B

**Jesus said to his disciples:**
**"In those days after that**
        **tribulation**
    **the sun will be darkened,**
    **and the moon will not give its**
        **light,**
    **and the stars will be falling**
        **from the sky,**
    **and the powers in the heavens**
        **will be shaken.**

**"And then they will see 'the Son of**
        **Man coming in the clouds'**
    **with great power and glory,**
    **and then he will send out the angels**
    **and gather his elect from the four**
        **winds,**
    **from the end of the earth to the end**
        **of the sky.**

**"Learn a lesson from the fig tree.**
**When its branch becomes tender and**
        **sprouts leaves,**
    **you know that summer is near.**
**In the same way, when you see these**
        **things happening,**
    **know that he is near, at the gates.**
**Amen, I say to you,**
    **this generation will not pass away**
    **until all these things have taken**
        **place.**
**Heaven and earth will pass away,**
    **but my words will not pass away.**

**"But of that day or hour, no one knows,**
        **neither the angels in heaven, nor the**
        **Son, but only the Father."**

### Reflecting on the Gospel

"The end of the world is at hand!" says the placard carried by the devout believer on the side of the street. Each age has had its share of true believers who maintained that the world was doomed, ready to be destroyed by God who was waiting for only a few moments before bringing down his fiery wrath on the heathens. In Jesus' own day, and in the decades that followed, apocalyptic fever was high. Messianic expectation combined with a desire for God's judgment of the wicked were saturating the environment. And yet, the world continued, and Rome dominated for hundreds of years hence. At the turn of the first millennium monasteries and convents were filling up with those who understood that the thousand-year reign of the saints (understood as the church) was quite literally being fulfilled, after which the dragon who had been locked up for one thousand years would be released (Rev 20:2-6)! What other more definite sign would one need than the authority of Scripture to know that the end was near? Yet, the year 1,000 came and went, followed by 1,001, 1,002, and so on. The monasteries and convents gradually lost some of their devoted converts from only a few years earlier.

In our own day there are many prophecies and predictions about the end of the world, a "black pope" (the Jesuit pope, as Jesuits wear black?), and more oddball fanciful extrapolations of various sorts. Preaching about the end of the world with zany predictions about pending doom can certainly attract attention and might even bring in the parishioners and churchgoers, but is it accurate?

In today's gospel perhaps the most significant line is at the end, when Jesus says, "But of that day or hour, no one knows, / neither the angels in heaven, nor the Son, but only the Father." Despite that rather stark, plain sentence, we have all undoubtedly heard some say, "Jesus says nobody knows the day or hour, but he doesn't say anything about the month or the year!" And then the wild predictions start again. Such interpretations miss the mark wildly.

Rather than worry about when the world will end, it might be more productive to wonder about my own personal end. That is, when will I die? How have I prepared myself for that eventual end? How have I lived my days knowing that nothing I accumulate on earth will be taken with me when I pass from this life? We know that we are definitely going to experience our own personal end, our own death. We are less likely to be here for the end of the world.

### Living the Paschal Mystery

Our life on earth is part of the paschal mystery, the dying and rising of Christ. All of creation is wrapped up in this paschal mystery. The food I consume each day was once living, but is transformed into energy that nourishes me. There is a natural cycle of life and death. And I know that my life is but a small part of the grand story of the cosmos, the earth, evolution, and life itself. Creatures have been on this earth for hundreds of millions of years, and they will continue to live on this earth far beyond the time of my passing. My time here is a grace. It is a free gift. Nothing I did or will do earned my own existence, and nothing I do can guarantee my number of days. My time on this earth is limited. My life will come to an end; of that I can be sure. But the paschal mystery continues. The cycle of life, death, and new life will continue. Since our time here is limited, it seems best to make the most of it, to enjoy the life-giving relationships we share, to acknowledge and love those we care about, and to grow in deeper communion with our God, the source of all goodness and life.

## Focusing the Gospel
*Mark 13:24-32*

The early Christians expected Christ to return in their lifetimes. When their world began to collapse around them under the Roman onslaught of Jerusalem, they wondered in their anguish, When will Jesus return for us? Like the members of the early church, we live on the edge of eternity; with every experience of loss, with every sign of illness, with every hint of age creeping upon us, we become more and more aware of our mortality. Jesus neither denies the pain and anguish of the end (citing in today's gospel reading the graphic images of the prophet Daniel) nor that the earth will pass away. But the important thing is not when Jesus will come but our readiness to meet him. The blossoming fig tree is held up by Jesus as a symbol of our lifelong struggle to bring to fulfillment the kingdom of God. The growth and blossoming of the fig tree mirrors our own growth in wisdom and understanding as God's reign becomes more and more a reality in our lives.

## Focusing the First Reading
*Dan 12:1-3*

As we read today in Mark's gospel, Jesus uses several images from the prophet Daniel to describe the final days. Today's first reading is Daniel's vision of the archangel Michael, Israel's heavenly defender, raising up in a time of great "distress" the souls of the faithful whose names are "found written in the book" of life. This is one of the few images of a "resurrection" of the just found in the Jewish Scriptures.

## Focusing the Responsorial Psalm
*Ps 16:5, 8, 9-10, 11 (1)*

Psalm 16 was one of the first psalms the early Christian community interpreted as referring to Christ, seeing a clear resurrection theme in the verses that make up today's responsorial: The images of the cup and "portion" are symbols of God's providence. The psalm imagines this life as a journey (the "path to life" taught by the gospel Jesus) that leads to ultimate "fullness of joys in your presence."

## Focusing the Second Reading
*Heb 10:11-14, 18*

On this next-to-last Sunday of the liturgical year, the final reading in this series from the "letter" to the Hebrews praises Christ, our Eternal High Priest, whose sacrifice completes the Old Testament priesthood of those Jewish priests to whom this letter is addressed. Christ, the Eternal High Priest, who has offered the perfect sacrifice that has "consecrated" humankind, now sits at the right hand of God until the fulfillment of the kingdom of God.

---

**PROMPTS FOR HOMILISTS, CATECHISTS, AND RCIA TEAMS**

What "signs" around you remind you of the brevity of life and the preciousness of time?

What "heaven" and "earth" do you sense "passing away" in your life?

Have you known an "angel" in your life who has "gathered" you to God?

The month of November is the traditional month for remembering and praying for the dead. What does this month—the month of the grayness of the coming winter, the month of Thanksgiving, the month that leads to the beginning of Advent—teach us about death and resurrection?

251

### Model Penitential Act

*Presider:* With confidence and hope in God's mercy and peace, let us begin this celebration of the Eucharist by calling to mind our sins. *[pause]*

You raise us from dust to life: Lord, have mercy.

You gather your people from the ends of the earth in your peace: Christ, have mercy.

You welcome us into the eternity of your dwelling place: Lord, have mercy.

### Homily Points

• There are signs all around us, like the late autumn winds of November, that remind us we live in the shadow of eternity. In everyone's life, the "fig tree" grows and flowers, reaps its precious harvest, and then withers. Jesus urges us to recognize such signs with eyes and spirits of faith: to appreciate the precious gift of our limited time on earth; to realize that pain and triumph are opportunities for understanding God's transforming presence in one another; to understand that the "passing away" of our own "heaven and earth" is part of our journey to God's dwelling place. With every change in direction and new milestone, we journey closer to the promise of the Easter Christ.

• In today's gospel, Jesus prophesies that he will send out the angels to gather the "elect." No effort will be spared; the angels will scour "earth" and "sky" so no one is left behind; all will be embraced in the Father's love. But the angels' work to lift up the unacknowledged "saints" in our midst begins here and now. We can be the "angels" who exalt the humble servant, who give hope to the persevering, who pick up the stumbling, who heal those broken in body or spirit. In our own baptisms, Jesus empowers us to begin the work of building the Father's kingdom by "gathering" his elect into the immeasurable love of God through our own acts of compassion, reconciliation, and justice.

• Life is a journey of change—sometimes frightening, often traumatic, always difficult. But when our "heavens and earths" pass away, the promise of God's life and the gospel values remain constant. The unsettling images Jesus articulates in today's gospel confront us with the reality that the things we give our lives to—our careers, our portfolios, our bodies, our celebrity—will one day be no more and their loss will leave us bitter and disillusioned. Christ calls us to embrace not the things of the world but the things of God: the eternal treasures of love and mercy, the joy that comes from selfless giving, the satisfaction that comes from lifting up the hopes and dreams of others.

### Model Universal Prayer (Prayer of the Faithful)

*Presider:* To God, who is our life and our hope, let us pray.

*Response:* Lord, hear our prayer.

That all who serve the church may proclaim the Gospel of forgiveness and mercy . . .

That all peoples of the world may put aside mistrust, prejudice, and hatred and create God's kingdom of justice and reconciliation . . .

That those who are experiencing traumatic change in their lives due to separation, unemployment, illness, or abandonment may realize the hope of Christ who accompanies them on their journeys . . .

That those who fight and suffer for justice may shine like the "stars" of the "firmament," inspiring us to join them in their struggle . . .

*Presider:* O God, you are the beginning and end of all things and seasons. Hear these prayers we offer in the hope of your mercy, as we live in joyful expectation of your eternal reign of peace. In Jesus' name, we pray. **Amen.**

---

**COLLECT**

Let us pray.

*Pause for silent prayer*

Grant us, we pray, O Lord our God,
the constant gladness of being devoted
    to you,
for it is full and lasting happiness
to serve with constancy
the author of all that is good.
Through our Lord Jesus Christ, your Son,
who lives and reigns with you in the unity
    of the Holy Spirit,
one God, for ever and ever. **Amen.**

**FIRST READING**

Dan 12:1-3

In those days, I, Daniel,
    heard this word of the Lord:
"At that time there shall arise
    Michael, the great prince,
    guardian of your people;
it shall be a time unsurpassed in distress
    since nations began until that time.
At that time your people shall escape,
    everyone who is found written in the
    book.

"Many of those who sleep in the dust of
    the earth shall awake;
    some shall live forever,
others shall be an everlasting horror
    and disgrace.

"But the wise shall shine brightly
    like the splendor of the firmament,
and those who lead the many to justice
    shall be like the stars forever."

## RESPONSORIAL PSALM

Ps 16:5, 8, 9-10, 11

R7. (1) You are my inheritance, O Lord!

O LORD, my allotted portion and my cup,
    you it is who hold fast my lot.
I set the LORD ever before me;
    with him at my right hand I shall not be
        disturbed.

R7. You are my inheritance, O Lord!

Therefore my heart is glad and my soul
    rejoices,
    my body, too, abides in confidence;
because you will not abandon my soul to
    the netherworld,
    nor will you suffer your faithful one to
        undergo corruption.

R7. You are my inheritance, O Lord!

You will show me the path to life,
    fullness of joys in your presence,
    the delights at your right hand forever.

R7. You are my inheritance, O Lord!

## SECOND READING

Heb 10:11-14, 18

Brothers and sisters:
Every priest stands daily at his ministry,
    offering frequently those same sacrifices
        that can never take away sins.
But this one offered one sacrifice for sins,
    and took his seat forever at the right
        hand of God;
    now he waits until his enemies are made
        his footstool.
For by one offering
    he has made perfect forever those who
        are being consecrated.

Where there is forgiveness of these,
    there is no longer offering for sin.

## About Liturgy

**The end times:** With the recent celebration of All Saints and All Souls, and now the final days of this liturgical year, the church is fully focused on the "end time," also called the *eschaton*, the days of fulfillment of all that God has promised. Despite the doom and gloom message some may see in today's gospel, our Christian focus on the end time is one of joy and is a constant throughout the year because it is at the very heart of what we do at every Eucharist. At every Mass, we remember what the Father has done for us through Christ, his Son. This remembering of Christ's death and resurrection never keeps us looking backwards into the past. Rather, our *anamnesis*, our memorial, always propels us to the future promise, the *eschaton* in which Christ even now is gathering all creation to himself to present it as a final gift of sacrifice and praise to the Father.

In this context, the Christian approach to death and the end of what we know as the world around us is not a time for worry or anxiety. Rather, like the psalm that is prescribed as the common psalm for the final weeks of Ordinary Time, as we approach the nearing of our own end, we too can say with the psalmist, "Let us go rejoicing to the house of the Lord" (Ps 122).

As we continue this month of remembering the dead, you might plan for a celebration of Evening Prayer (Vespers) or Night Prayer (Compline) to conclude these last two Sundays of the liturgical year. These official liturgies of the church taken from the Liturgy of the Hours are great opportunities to invite the community to conclude the Lord's Day in common prayer. Their liturgical structure is also flexible enough when prayed within a parish community setting in these November days to include reflections by community members and a time for sharing of stories of loved ones who have died.

## About Liturgical Music

**Nunc Dimittis:** In the Liturgy of the Hours, the last liturgy for each day is Compline, or Night Prayer. It is structured a bit like Morning or Evening Prayer in that it is centered on the psalms, but it begins with an examination of conscience that invites the assembly to recall the day and to ask God for forgiveness and strength. Like the other main Hours, Compline culminates with a gospel canticle, this one taken from Luke's gospel and the words of Simeon at the temple: "Now, Master, you may let your servant go / in peace, according to your word, / for my eyes have seen your salvation, / which you prepared in sight of all the peoples, / a light for revelation to the Gentiles, / and glory for your people Israel" (Luke 2:29-32, NABRE).

In these last days of the liturgical year, you might consider including a setting of this canticle in the Sunday Mass. One beautiful setting is by Janèt Sullivan Whitaker called "Song of Simeon" (OCP). Her setting takes the form of a repeated short refrain, much in the style of Taizé. You might use this as a song of praise after Communion or even as a more meditative dismissal song at the end of Mass to distinguish these final weeks of the liturgical year. This canticle might also be used during any prayer service that remembers those who have died. In this context, it might be used as a sung response to a litany of names recalling our beloved dead.

**NOVEMBER 18, 2018**
# THIRTY-THIRD SUNDAY
# IN ORDINARY TIME

## GOSPEL ACCLAMATION
1 Thess 5:18

℟. Alleluia, alleluia.
In all circumstances, give thanks,
for this is the will of God for you in Christ Jesus.
℟. Alleluia, alleluia.

## Gospel

Luke 17:11-19; L947.6

**As Jesus continued his journey to Jerusalem,**
  **he traveled through Samaria and Galilee.**
**As he was entering a village, ten lepers met him.**
**They stood at a distance from him and raised their voices, saying,**
  **"Jesus, Master! Have pity on us!"**
**And when he saw them, he said,**
  **"Go show yourselves to the priests."**
**As they were going they were cleansed.**
**And one of them, realizing he had been healed,**
  **returned, glorifying God in a loud voice;**
  **and he fell at the feet of Jesus and thanked him.**
**He was a Samaritan.**
**Jesus said in reply,**
  **"Ten were cleansed, were they not?**
**Where are the other nine?**
**Has none but this foreigner returned to give thanks to God?"**
**Then he said to him, "Stand up and go; your faith has saved you."**

*See Appendix A, p. 306, for the other readings.*

*Additional reading choices may be found in the* Lectionary for Mass, *vol. IV, "In Thanksgiving to God," nos. 943–947.*

## Reflecting on the Gospel

Turkey, mashed potatoes, stuffing, cranberries, family, friends, and relatives are some of the words that might come to mind when we consider this day, a uniquely American holiday. We all recall that Abraham Lincoln was the US president who truly established this national holiday, in the midst of the great Civil War. Though party politics may seem rough-and-tumble today, things are much, much better than brother taking up arms against brother, and state fighting state, which characterized this tumultuous time in the nineteenth century. In the midst of that great strife more than 150 years ago Lincoln proclaimed a national holiday of Thanksgiving. Though nobody could have known it, they had nearly two years left before the war was finally concluded. If the divided nation could find a way to be thankful in the midst of such tumult, war, and chaos, we can certainly be thankful today.

We have so many gifts, resources, and blessings, that it would be shameful not to stop and offer gratitude. This is why the church gives us the reading from the Gospel of Luke today where Jesus heals ten lepers but only one expresses thanks. Perhaps there is something in the human condition that does not naturally say "thank you." But it's good to be reminded of polite manners. And yet, the expression of gratitude is much more than simply being polite. Jesus did not need gratitude; those who had been cured needed to express it. In other words, saying thank you is not as much for the one who gave as it is for the one who receives. Cultivating an "attitude of gratitude" makes our lives more appreciative. We become more giving and generous when we say and develop a habit of expressing "thank you."

Perhaps this is why Jesus remarked that only the foreigner, the Samaritan, said "thank you." The expression is less about Jesus than it is about the one who was healed. How appropriate, then, that on this day we take time to say "thank you" and in doing so we develop ourselves as more generous and more giving.

## Living the Paschal Mystery

When we neglect to say thank you it's often a simple oversight. Our busy lives get in the way of first writing, and then actually sending, that thank-you note, which can remain on the desk too long. We mean to say thank you, but it can be relegated to something superfluous rather than necessary. But our expression of gratitude does as much for us as it does for the one who gave the gift. Both the gift and the expressed gratitude communicate something of the relationship between both.

The paschal mystery calls us to enter into the relationship of dying to ourselves and our own agenda. When we do so we reprioritize the other. We recognize that all of life is a gift for which we can give thanks. Our families, relationships, bonds of love, care, and concern are true treasures that are eternal. And more than that, so many have material blessings for which we are to be thankful. But the eternal bonds of love and care are what will last.

## Focusing the Gospel

The grateful Samaritan leper is one of the great saints of Luke's gospel. In accordance with Mosaic law, lepers were cast out of the community, left to fend for themselves outside the gates of their cities. This group of lepers included both Jews (Galileans) and Samaritans: they are so desperate in their plight that the bitter animosity between Jew and Samaritan evaporates in their need to depend on one another. In sending the lepers off to those who can legally verify a cure rather than curing them outright, Jesus puts the lepers' faith to the test. Only one—one of those despised Samaritans—realizes not only that he has been made clean but that he has been touched by God. The Samaritan leper's returning to Jesus to give thanks reflects the healing that has taken place not only in his body but in his very being. Faith is the constant awareness of the great love and compassion of God, an awareness that moves us to praise and acts of thanksgiving.

## Model Penitential Act

*Presider:* We gather together today, as a nation and as a community of faith, to give thanks to God for his many blessings to us and our families. In a spirit of gratitude and humility, let us begin this celebration of the Eucharist by seeking God's mercy for our sins of ingratitude. *[pause]*

Father of compassion and Maker of all that is good: Lord, have mercy.
Light of reconciliation and Word of peace: Christ, have mercy.
Spirit of love and well-spring of every blessing: Lord, have mercy.

## Model Universal Prayer (Prayer of the Faithful)

*Presider:* Let us join our hearts and raise our voices in prayer to the Lord of the harvest.

*Response:* Lord, hear our prayer.

For our church, that we may be a people dedicated to thankfulness . . .

For the nations and peoples of the world, that God's justice and mercy may be the cornerstone of lasting peace . . .

For the sick and suffering, the grieving and troubled, the abused and addicted, that we may reach out to them with the compassion and healing of Christ . . .

For all of us citizens, that we may be faithful and generous and responsible stewards of God's creation . . .

*Presider:* We give you thanks, O God, for your many blessings to us. May a spirit of constant gratitude dwell in our hearts, enabling us to make thanksgiving a practice of generosity, reconciliation, and justice, in which we give thanks to you by sharing our blessings with all our brothers and sisters in your Christ, in whose name we offer these prayers. **Amen.**

---

**COLLECT**
Let us pray.

*Pause for silent prayer*

Father all-powerful,
your gifts of love are countless
and your goodness infinite;
as we come before you on Thanksgiving Day
with gratitude for your kindness,
open our hearts to have concern
for every man, woman, and child,
so that we may share your gifts in loving service.
Through our Lord Jesus Christ your Son,
who lives and reigns with you in the unity of
    the Holy Spirit,
One God, for ever and ever. **Amen.**

---

**FOR REFLECTION**

• Have you ever been grateful for something or someone you first found to be a burden?

• How can we "practice" thanksgiving? Why is it difficult to focus on what we have to be grateful for rather than be overwhelmed with our disappointments and hurts?

• What reasons can you imagine the lepers had for not returning to Jesus to thank him?

## Homily Points

• We all stand together before God as his sons and daughters. In such a spirit of humility, we see life as a gift, not an entitlement; we focus our attention on blessings rather than disappointments; we discover God in the love of others rather than in ourselves. Gratitude is the perspective of seeing every human being as worthy of respect as a child of God. Gratitude requires the humility both to give from our poverty and to receive despite our wealth and status.

• The practice of gratitude is grounded in the conviction that God has breathed his life into us for no other reason than love so deep we cannot begin to fathom it, and that the only fitting response to such unmerited love is to stand humbly before God in gratitude. To practice gratitude can transform cynicism and despair into optimism and hope and make whatever good we do an experience of grace.

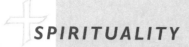

## SPIRITUALITY

**GOSPEL ACCLAMATION**
Mark 11:9, 10

℟. Alleluia, alleluia.
Blessed is he who comes in the name of the
    Lord!
Blessed is the kingdom of our father
    David that is to come!
℟. Alleluia, alleluia.

### Gospel

John 18:33b-37; L161B

Pilate said to Jesus,
    "Are you the King of the Jews?"
Jesus answered, "Do you say this
    on your own
    or have others told you about
        me?"
Pilate answered, "I am not a Jew,
    am I?
Your own nation and the chief
    priests handed you over to me.
What have you done?"
Jesus answered, "My kingdom does not
    belong to this world.
If my kingdom did belong to this world,
    my attendants would be fighting
    to keep me from being handed over
        to the Jews.
But as it is, my kingdom is not here."
So Pilate said to him, "Then you are a
    king?"
Jesus answered, "You say I am a king.
For this I was born and for this I came
    into the world,
    to testify to the truth.
Everyone who belongs to the truth
    listens to my voice."

### Reflecting on the Gospel

Stories of kings and queens are often relegated to fairy tales or medieval gallantry. Sometimes, of course, we see modern royalty in the media, and many might remember the wedding of Prince Charles and Princess Diana decades ago, and more recently their son Prince William's wedding to Kate Middleton. But modern royals tend to be figureheads rather than political heads of state. So it can seem a bit odd to celebrate Christ as King. He is certainly more than a figurehead.

Of course, the image of king is deeply rooted in the ancient world, and not limited to biblical texts. Oftentimes in antiquity the king, or supreme ruler, approached the status of the divine. For example, Julius Caesar's clan was named for Julius, the son of Aeneas (the prince of Troy), who was said to be the son of the goddess Venus. Julius Caesar received honors of divinity in his lifetime, and after he was assassinated the Roman Senate officially declared him divine. Centuries before, the kings of Judah and Israel were sometimes called divine, or sons of God.

The biblical authors also applied the title of King to God, as Yahweh was "the great God, / the great king over all gods" (Ps 95:3, NABRE). By the time Jesus was on the scene, the Roman occupation of Judea led the people to long for their own king, to establish the kingdom as independent once again. It's no surprise that the Romans, always on the lookout for those who might attempt insurrection, crucified Jesus as "King of the Jews." The mocking, derisive sign became something the early Christians did not shy away from, but proclaimed. In essence, the early Christians said, Jesus was in fact king, but he was king in a way unforeseen.

The gospel reading for today brings us into the scene between Jesus and Pilate. Of course, we know how it will end, ultimately with the crucifixion and the antagonizing sign proclaiming Jesus, "King." But here in the midst of the conversation we hear eternal questions that cause us to consider, "What is truth?" Jesus makes a straightforward claim, that he is a king, and he has been sent to testify to the truth. Pilate, vested with political authority, including the power to inflict capital punishment, is wrapped up in a semantic argument about the nature of truth. He doesn't see the incarnation of truth, the King of Kings, standing before his very eyes. And in Pilate's blindness, he will put to death Jesus as King of the Jews.

So the early Christians, and even us today, continue to proclaim Jesus as King. He is no mere figurehead. Instead, he shares the title with Yahweh, "great king over the gods." What Pilate said in mockery was utterly true. Jesus Christ is King.

### Living the Paschal Mystery

The mocking tone of the political authority in calling Jesus "King" seemed to squelch this minor upstart who might have led an insurrection. But Jesus' followers began to proudly proclaim that mocking title. Jesus was King. But his kingship was of an entirely different kind than that expected by the people. Rather than a military conquest of an occupying force that restored the independence of the Jewish people, Jesus' kingship involved suffering and death, which then led to resurrection and exaltation. The kingship of Jesus is not one of splendid pageantry. It is not even the sort of medieval gallantry. Instead, he is enthroned in heaven, with our great God who is king over all gods. As Jesus underwent death before his exaltation, so must we. Our own path to glory, exaltation, and ultimate resurrection comes through a dying to self.

## Focusing the Gospel

*John 18:33b-37*

We celebrate the kingship of Jesus with John's gospel account of what is perhaps Jesus' most humiliating moment: his appearance before Pilate. It is a strange exchange: Pilate, a government functionary with power to inflict punishment, is being encouraged ("you are not a Friend of Caesar" [John 19:12, NABRE]) by the religious authorities into executing Jesus—but it is the accused who dominates the meeting and takes on the role of inquisitor. In their exchange, Jesus refuses to accept Pilate's narrow understanding of power and truth, explaining to the procurator (to no avail) that Jesus "rules" a kingdom not of this world—power that Pilate does not comprehend.

## Focusing the First Reading

*Dan 7:13-14*

The prophet Daniel has a vision of the heavenly court in which "one . . . coming, / on the clouds" (that is, from God) unites all nations and peoples of the earth into an eternal dominion of peace. The "Son of man" (a title Jesus will use to describe himself) that Daniel envisions is the perfect mediator between God and his people to inaugurate God's reign on earth.

## Focusing the Responsorial Psalm

*Ps 93:1, 1-2, 5 (1a)*

These verses for Psalm 93 (one of the Psalter's "enthronement" psalms) celebrate the universal kingship of God, a reign that transcends all times and places.

## Focusing the Second Reading

*Rev 1:5-8*

The visionary John, in the opening to the book of Revelation, has a vision similar to Daniel's in the first reading, but identifies the one "coming amid the clouds" as Jesus, "the firstborn of the dead"—the first to experience the resurrection. Christ's sovereignty is centered in his love for us, his freeing us from sin, and his making us into a kingdom and priests of God.

---

**PROMPTS FOR HOMILISTS, CATECHISTS, AND RCIA TEAMS**

What is the essential "truth" revealed by Jesus in the gospels?

What are the characteristics and the values of the kingdom of God?

What does the title of "King" help us to understand about Jesus?

## Model Penitential Act

*Presider:* The risen Christ has called us to his table to celebrate the sacrament of his Body and Blood. Let us begin by seeking the forgiveness and peace of his kingdom by acknowledging our sins and failings. *[pause]*

> You are the firstborn of the dead and ruler of all nations and peoples: Lord, have mercy.
> You are our Redeemer who frees us from our sins: Christ, have mercy.
> You are "the one who is and who was and who is to come": Lord, have mercy.

## Homily Points

• The kingdom of Jesus is not found in the world's centers of power, as it is not of this world. It is built not by deals among the world's powerbrokers but by the calloused hands of faithful and generous souls. Christ's reign is influenced not by political or economic power but by compassion, humility, and justice. We who have been baptized into the life, death, and resurrection of Christ are called to keep our eyes on that otherworldly kingdom. The "kingship" of Jesus is partially realized in our embracing a vision of humankind as a family made in the image of God, a vision of one another as brothers and sisters in Christ, a vision of the world centered in the hope and compassion taught by Christ.

• On this last Sunday of the liturgical year, we celebrate the solemnity of Christ the King, the Anointed One of God who comes to reveal the truth of God's love for all of us. In the figure of the gospel Jesus, we realize the essential truth of life: that we are loved by the God who created us to a degree we cannot begin to fathom; that we are loved by a God who refuses to give up or reject or destroy his beloved creation, a creation that has hardly lived up to its promise; that we are loved by a God who humbles himself to become one of us in order to make us like him, to realize that we have been created in his image by his very breath blown into our hearts. It is that very "truth" that stands right before Pilate, and he is unable to fathom it. To be a faithful disciple of Christ is to be a servant to the truth that is the complete and unconditional love of God for humankind: love that liberates and renews, that gives and sustains life and hope, that illuminates our vision and understanding to enable us to see our world in the intended design of God.

## Model Universal Prayer (Prayer of the Faithful)

*Presider:* Seeking the fulfillment of Christ's reign, let us join our hearts and voices in prayer.

*Response:* Lord, hear our prayer.

That all church leaders may embrace Christ's priesthood of loving and humble service . . .

That all peoples, nations, and cultures may "serve" God's vision of peace, justice, and progress for all his sons and daughters . . .

That God will embrace in his love the victims of violence and war and bring all people of goodwill together to create his kingdom of justice and peace . . .

That, as a parish community, we may be faithful witnesses to the love and mercy of God . . .

*Presider:* Lord God, may these prayers we offer and our commitment to their fulfillment lead to the realization of your kingdom in our time and place, until the coming of our Redeemer and King, your Son, our Lord Jesus Christ, in whose name we offer these prayers. **Amen.**

## COLLECT

Let us pray.

*Pause for silent prayer*

Almighty ever-living God,
whose will is to restore all things
in your beloved Son, the King of the
    universe,
grant, we pray,
that the whole creation, set free from
    slavery,
may render your majesty service
and ceaselessly proclaim your praise.
Through our Lord Jesus Christ, your Son,
who lives and reigns with you in the unity
    of the Holy Spirit,
one God, for ever and ever. **Amen.**

## FIRST READING

Dan 7:13-14

As the visions during the night continued,
    I saw
    one like a Son of man coming,
        on the clouds of heaven;
    when he reached the Ancient One
        and was presented before him,
    the one like a Son of man received
        dominion, glory, and kingship;
    all peoples, nations, and languages
        serve him.
    His dominion is an everlasting dominion
        that shall not be taken away,
    his kingship shall not be destroyed.

## RESPONSORIAL PSALM
Ps 93:1, 1-2, 5

R̸. (1a) The Lord is king; he is robed in
  majesty.

The LORD is king, in splendor robed;
  robed is the LORD and girt about with
  strength.

R̸. The Lord is king; he is robed in
  majesty.

And he has made the world firm,
  not to be moved.
Your throne stands firm from of old;
  from everlasting you are, O LORD.

R̸. The Lord is king; he is robed in
  majesty.

Your decrees are worthy of trust indeed;
  holiness befits your house,
  O LORD, for length of days.

R̸. The Lord is king; he is robed in
  majesty.

## SECOND READING
Rev 1:5-8

Jesus Christ is the faithful witness,
  the firstborn of the dead and ruler of
  the kings of the earth.
To him who loves us and has freed us
  from our sins by his blood,
  who has made us into a kingdom,
  priests for his God and Father,
  to him be glory and power forever and
  ever. Amen.

Behold, he is coming amid the clouds,
  and every eye will see him,
  even those who pierced him.
All the peoples of the earth will lament
  him.
  Yes. Amen.

"I am the Alpha and the Omega," says the
  Lord God,
  "the one who is and who was and who
  is to come, the almighty."

## About Liturgy

*A paradoxical faith:* Today's solemnity titled "Our Lord Jesus Christ, King of the Universe" is filled with paradox. Rather than a superhuman figure ruling with power and might over the cosmos, the gospel reading draws us back to Jesus's passion with the backdrop of the cross as our King's throne and the crucifixion, his coronation. This juxtaposition gives liturgical coordinators, homilists, and musicians fair warning that this day is about a different kind of kingship. Therefore any semblance of triumphalism seems very much out of step with the message of this day. As we come to the close of the liturgical year with this last Sunday of Ordinary Time, we can certainly plan for a fitting and solemn celebration that praises Christ the King. Yet it needs to be tempered with the understanding that the title of "King" is more closely tied with the sense of "governance" that makes one responsible for the care and well-being of others. For us who have been baptized in Christ as "priest, prophet, and king," we recall that we have been given to one another, to be neighbor and kin to each other and good stewards of the earth. The observance of the Thanksgiving holiday this weekend with its themes of giving thanks, family, creation, and bounty can help us express this more humble sense of stewardship that is the primary role of those who have been crowned as children of God.

Because of the Thanksgiving holiday, you may have more visitors at your parish this weekend. Be sure to attend to your guests and to make this an opportunity for genuine welcome, evangelization, and invitation. It's also not too early to let people know about your Advent and Christmas liturgy schedule. And remember that children may be returning home from college for the holidays, so make sure to welcome them back and let them know that the community remembers them.

## About Initiation

*Welcoming visiting catechumens:* Catechumens have the right and duty to be nourished by the church's prayer, especially in the Liturgy of the Word at the Sunday gathering. This is true also for visitors and students home from college who are in town for the holidays. If you are celebrating the dismissal of catechumens, be sure to make an open invitation to any visiting catechumens to be part of your parish's dismissal that Sunday. Also, be sure to connect with any local Catholic colleges or universities with Catholic centers in case they have any catechumens who are in need of a worshiping community to attend while they are on school break. This is a great way to catechize both the catechumens and your community that when we become Christian, we belong to a worldwide family that goes beyond our own Sunday communities.

## About Liturgical Music

*Song suggestions:* Today is the last Sunday for singing the Gloria until the Christmas season, so it would be a great time to enhance your setting with additional instruments. Be sure to select a setting that the assembly knows well already.

In addition to the traditional hymns "To Jesus Christ, Our Sovereign King" and "Soon and Very Soon," consider other texts that highlight the kind of "kingship" we honor today. Roc O'Connor's well-known setting of the Philippians 2 canticle, "Jesus, the Lord" (OCP), would be very appropriate for the preparation of the gifts or as a song of praise after Communion. Jesse Manibusan explores the meaning of "kingship" in his beautiful song, "What Sort of King" (OCP). A wonderful choice for Communion is Steve Warner's setting of text from St. Cyril of Jerusalem called "Make of Our Hands a Throne" (WLP). Another traditional hymn that focuses on Christ's sacrifice as the reason we honor him as king is "Let All Mortal Flesh Keep Silence."

**NOVEMBER 25, 2018**
# OUR LORD JESUS CHRIST,
# KING OF THE UNIVERSE

Readings *(continued)*

## *The Immaculate Conception of the Blessed Virgin Mary,* December 8, 2017

### Gospel (cont.)
Luke 1:26-38; L689

He will be great and will be called Son of the Most High,
  and the Lord God will give him the throne of David his father,
  and he will rule over the house of Jacob forever,
  and of his Kingdom there will be no end."
But Mary said to the angel,
  "How can this be,
  since I have no relations with a man?"
And the angel said to her in reply,
  "The Holy Spirit will come upon you,
  and the power of the Most High will overshadow you.
Therefore the child to be born
  will be called holy, the Son of God.

And behold, Elizabeth, your relative,
  has also conceived a son in her old age,
  and this is the sixth month for her who was called barren;
  for nothing will be impossible for God."
Mary said, "Behold, I am the handmaid of the Lord.
May it be done to me according to your word."
Then the angel departed from her.

### FIRST READING
Gen 3:9-15, 20

After the man, Adam, had eaten of the tree,
  the Lord God called to the man and asked
    him, "Where are you?"
He answered, "I heard you in the garden;
  but I was afraid, because I was naked,
  so I hid myself."
Then he asked, "Who told you that you were
    naked?
You have eaten, then,
  from the tree of which I had forbidden you
    to eat!"
The man replied, "The woman whom you put
    here with me—
  she gave me fruit from the tree, and so I
    ate it."
The Lord God then asked the woman,
  "Why did you do such a thing?"
The woman answered, "The serpent tricked
    me into it, so I ate it."

Then the Lord God said to the serpent:
  "Because you have done this, you shall be
    banned
    from all the animals
    and from all the wild creatures;
  on your belly shall you crawl,
    and dirt shall you eat
    all the days of your life.
  I will put enmity between you and the
    woman,
    and between your offspring and hers;
  he will strike at your head,
    while you strike at his heel."

The man called his wife Eve,
  because she became the mother of all the
    living.

### RESPONSORIAL PSALM
Ps 98:1, 2-3ab, 3cd-4

R̸. (1a) Sing to the Lord a new song, for he has
  done marvelous deeds.

Sing to the Lord a new song,
  for he has done wondrous deeds;
His right hand has won victory for him,
  his holy arm.

R̸. Sing to the Lord a new song, for he has
  done marvelous deeds.

The Lord has made his salvation known:
  in the sight of the nations he has revealed
    his justice.
He has remembered his kindness and his
    faithfulness
  toward the house of Israel.

R̸. Sing to the Lord a new song, for he has
  done marvelous deeds.

All the ends of the earth have seen
  the salvation by our God.
Sing joyfully to the Lord, all you lands;
  break into song; sing praise.

R̸. Sing to the Lord a new song, for he has
  done marvelous deeds.

### SECOND READING
Eph 1:3-6, 11-12

Brothers and sisters:
Blessed be the God and Father of our Lord
    Jesus Christ,
  who has blessed us in Christ
  with every spiritual blessing in the heavens,
  as he chose us in him, before the foundation
    of the world,
  to be holy and without blemish before him.
In love he destined us for adoption to himself
    through Jesus Christ,
  in accord with the favor of his will,
  for the praise of the glory of his grace
  that he granted us in the beloved.

In him we were also chosen,
  destined in accord with the purpose of the
    One
  who accomplishes all things according to
    the intention of his will,
  so that we might exist for the praise of his
    glory,
  we who first hoped in Christ.

## Gospel (cont.)
Matt 1:1-25; L13ABC

Asaph became the father of Jehoshaphat,
  Jehoshaphat the father of Joram,
  Joram the father of Uzziah.
Uzziah became the father of Jotham,
  Jotham the father of Ahaz,
  Ahaz the father of Hezekiah.
Hezekiah became the father of Manasseh,
  Manasseh the father of Amos,
  Amos the father of Josiah.
Josiah became the father of Jechoniah and his brothers
  at the time of the Babylonian exile.

After the Babylonian exile,
  Jechoniah became the father of Shealtiel,
  Shealtiel the father of Zerubbabel,
  Zerubbabel the father of Abiud.
Abiud became the father of Eliakim,
  Eliakim the father of Azor,
  Azor the father of Zadok.
Zadok became the father of Achim,
  Achim the father of Eliud,
  Eliud the father of Eleazar.
Eleazar became the father of Matthan,
  Matthan the father of Jacob,
  Jacob the father of Joseph, the husband of Mary.
Of her was born Jesus who is called the Christ.

Thus the total number of generations
  from Abraham to David
  is fourteen generations;
  from David to the Babylonian exile,
  fourteen generations;
  from the Babylonian exile to the Christ,
  fourteen generations.

Now this is how the birth of Jesus Christ came about.
When his mother Mary was betrothed to Joseph,
  but before they lived together,
  she was found with child through the Holy Spirit.
Joseph her husband, since he was a righteous man,
  yet unwilling to expose her to shame,
  decided to divorce her quietly.
Such was his intention when, behold,
  the angel of the Lord appeared to him in a dream and said,
  "Joseph, son of David,
  do not be afraid to take Mary your wife into your home.
For it is through the Holy Spirit
  that this child has been conceived in her.
She will bear a son and you are to name him Jesus,
  because he will save his people from their sins."
All this took place to fulfill
  what the Lord had said through the prophet:
    *Behold, the virgin shall conceive and bear a son,*
      *and they shall name him Emmanuel,*
    which means "God is with us."
When Joseph awoke,
  he did as the angel of the Lord had commanded him
  and took his wife into his home.
He had no relations with her until she bore a son,
  and he named him Jesus.

*or* Matt 1:18-25

This is how the birth of Jesus Christ came about.
When his mother Mary was betrothed to Joseph,
  but before they lived together,
  she was found with child through the Holy Spirit.
Joseph her husband, since he was a righteous man,
  yet unwilling to expose her to shame,
  decided to divorce her quietly.
Such was his intention when, behold,
  the angel of the Lord appeared to him in a dream and said,
  "Joseph, son of David,
  do not be afraid to take Mary your wife into your home.
For it is through the Holy Spirit
  that this child has been conceived in her.
She will bear a son and you are to name him Jesus,
  because he will save his people from their sins."
All this took place to fulfill
  what the Lord had said through the prophet:
    *Behold, the virgin shall conceive and bear a son,*
      *and they shall name him Emmanuel,*
    which means "God is with us."
When Joseph awoke,
  he did as the angel of the Lord had commanded him
  and took his wife into his home.
He had no relations with her until she bore a son,
  and he named him Jesus.

## FIRST READING
Isa 62:1-5

For Zion's sake I will not be silent,
　　for Jerusalem's sake I will not be quiet,
until her vindication shines forth like the
　　　dawn
　　and her victory like a burning torch.

Nations shall behold your vindication,
　　and all the kings your glory;
you shall be called by a new name
　　pronounced by the mouth of the LORD.
You shall be a glorious crown in the hand of
　　　the LORD,
　　a royal diadem held by your God.
No more shall people call you "Forsaken,"
　　or your land "Desolate,"
but you shall be called "My Delight,"
　　and your land "Espoused."
For the LORD delights in you
　　and makes your land his spouse.
As a young man marries a virgin,
　　your Builder shall marry you;
and as a bridegroom rejoices in his bride
　　so shall your God rejoice in you.

## RESPONSORIAL PSALM
Ps 89:4-5, 16-17, 27, 29

R℣. (2a) For ever I will sing the goodness of
　　the Lord.

I have made a covenant with my chosen one,
　　I have sworn to David my servant:
forever will I confirm your posterity
　　and establish your throne for all
　　　generations.
R℣. For ever I will sing the goodness of the
　　Lord.

Blessed the people who know the joyful shout;
　　in the light of your countenance, O LORD,
　　　they walk.
At your name they rejoice all the day,
　　and through your justice they are exalted.
R℣. For ever I will sing the goodness of the
　　Lord.

He shall say of me, "You are my father,
　　my God, the rock, my savior."
Forever I will maintain my kindness toward
　　him,
　　and my covenant with him stands firm.
R℣. For ever I will sing the goodness of the
　　Lord.

## SECOND READING
Acts 13:16-17, 22-25

When Paul reached Antioch in Pisidia and
　　　entered the synagogue,
　　he stood up, motioned with his hand, and
　　　said,
　　"Fellow Israelites and you others who are
　　　God-fearing, listen.
The God of this people Israel chose our
　　ancestors
　　and exalted the people during their sojourn
　　　in the land of Egypt.
With uplifted arm he led them out of it.
Then he removed Saul and raised up David
　　as king;
　　of him he testified,
　　'I have found David, son of Jesse, a man
　　　after my own heart;
　　he will carry out my every wish.'
From this man's descendants God, according
　　to his promise,
　　has brought to Israel a savior, Jesus.
John heralded his coming by proclaiming a
　　baptism of repentance
　　to all the people of Israel;
　　and as John was completing his course, he
　　　would say,
　　'What do you suppose that I am? I am not
　　　he.
Behold, one is coming after me;
　　I am not worthy to unfasten the sandals of
　　　his feet.'"

---

**The Nativity of the Lord,** *December 25, 2017 (Mass at Midnight)*

## Gospel (cont.)
Luke 2:1-14; L14ABC

She wrapped him in swaddling clothes and laid him in a manger,
　　because there was no room for them in the inn.

Now there were shepherds in that region living in the fields
　　and keeping the night watch over their flock.
The angel of the Lord appeared to them
　　and the glory of the Lord shone around them,
　　and they were struck with great fear.
The angel said to them,
　　"Do not be afraid;
　　for behold, I proclaim to you good news of great joy
　　that will be for all the people.
For today in the city of David
　　a savior has been born for you who is Christ and Lord.
And this will be a sign for you:
　　you will find an infant wrapped in swaddling clothes
　　and lying in a manger."

And suddenly there was a multitude of the heavenly host with the
　　angel,
　　praising God and saying:
　　"Glory to God in the highest
　　　and on earth peace to those on whom his favor rests."

## The Nativity of the Lord, *December 25, 2017 (Mass at Midnight)*

### FIRST READING
Isa 9:1-6

The people who walked in darkness
   have seen a great light;
upon those who dwelt in the land of gloom
   a light has shone.
You have brought them abundant joy
   and great rejoicing,
as they rejoice before you as at the harvest,
   as people make merry when dividing spoils.
For the yoke that burdened them,
   the pole on their shoulder,
and the rod of their taskmaster
   you have smashed, as on the day of Midian.
For every boot that tramped in battle,
   every cloak rolled in blood,
   will be burned as fuel for flames.
For a child is born to us, a son is given us;
   upon his shoulder dominion rests.
They name him Wonder-Counselor, God-Hero,
   Father-Forever, Prince of Peace.
His dominion is vast
   and forever peaceful,
from David's throne, and over his kingdom,
   which he confirms and sustains
by judgment and justice,
   both now and forever.
The zeal of the LORD of hosts will do this!

### RESPONSORIAL PSALM
Ps 96:1-2, 2-3, 11-12, 13

R̲. (Luke 2:11) Today is born our Savior,
   Christ the Lord.

Sing to the LORD a new song;
   sing to the LORD, all you lands.
Sing to the LORD; bless his name.

R̲. Today is born our Savior, Christ the Lord.

Announce his salvation, day after day.
   Tell his glory among the nations;
   among all peoples, his wondrous deeds.

R̲. Today is born our Savior, Christ the Lord.

Let the heavens be glad and the earth rejoice;
   let the sea and what fills it resound;
   let the plains be joyful and all that is in
      them!
Then shall all the trees of the forest exult.

R̲. Today is born our Savior, Christ the Lord.

They shall exult before the LORD, for he
   comes;
   for he comes to rule the earth.
He shall rule the world with justice
   and the peoples with his constancy.

R̲. Today is born our Savior, Christ the Lord.

### SECOND READING
Titus 2:11-14

Beloved:
The grace of God has appeared, saving all
   and training us to reject godless ways and
      worldly desires
   and to live temperately, justly, and devoutly
      in this age,
   as we await the blessed hope,
   the appearance of the glory of our great
      God
   and savior Jesus Christ,
   who gave himself for us to deliver us from
      all lawlessness
   and to cleanse for himself a people as his
      own,
   eager to do what is good.

## The Nativity of the Lord, *December 25, 2017 (Mass at Dawn)*

### FIRST READING
Isa 62:11-12

See, the LORD proclaims
   to the ends of the earth:
say to daughter Zion,
   your savior comes!
Here is his reward with him,
   his recompense before him.
They shall be called the holy people,
   the redeemed of the LORD,
and you shall be called "Frequented,"
   a city that is not forsaken.

### RESPONSORIAL PSALM
Ps 97:1, 6, 11-12

R̲. A light will shine on us this day: the Lord
   is born for us.

The LORD is king; let the earth rejoice;
   let the many isles be glad.
The heavens proclaim his justice,
   and all peoples see his glory.

R̲. A light will shine on us this day: the Lord
   is born for us.

Light dawns for the just;
   and gladness, for the upright of heart.
Be glad in the LORD, you just,
   and give thanks to his holy name.

R̲. A light will shine on us this day: the Lord
   is born for us.

### SECOND READING
Titus 3:4-7

Beloved:
When the kindness and generous love
   of God our savior appeared,
not because of any righteous deeds we had
      done
   but because of his mercy,
he saved us through the bath of rebirth
   and renewal by the Holy Spirit,
whom he richly poured out on us
   through Jesus Christ our savior,
so that we might be justified by his grace
   and become heirs in hope of eternal life.

## Gospel (cont.)

John 1:1-18; L16ABC

And the Word became flesh
    and made his dwelling among us,
    and we saw his glory,
    the glory as of the Father's only Son,
    full of grace and truth.
John testified to him and cried out, saying,
    "This was he of whom I said,
    'The one who is coming after me ranks ahead of me
    because he existed before me.'"
From his fullness we have all received,
    grace in place of grace,
    because while the law was given through Moses,
    grace and truth came through Jesus Christ.
No one has ever seen God.
The only Son, God, who is at the Father's side,
    has revealed him.

*or* John 1:1-5, 9-14

In the beginning was the Word,
    and the Word was with God,
    and the Word was God.
He was in the beginning with God.

All things came to be through him,
    and without him nothing came to be.
What came to be through him was life,
    and this life was the light of the human race;
    the light shines in the darkness,
    and the darkness has not overcome it.
The true light, which enlightens everyone,
    was coming into the world.
He was in the world,
    and the world came to be through him,
    but the world did not know him.
He came to what was his own,
    but his own people did not accept him.

But to those who did accept him
    he gave power to become children of God,
    to those who believe in his name,
    who were born not by natural generation
    nor by human choice nor by a man's decision
    but of God.
And the Word became flesh
    and made his dwelling among us,
    and we saw his glory,
    the glory as of the Father's only Son,
    full of grace and truth.

## FIRST READING

Isa 52:7-10

How beautiful upon the mountains
    are the feet of him who brings glad tidings,
announcing peace, bearing good news,
    announcing salvation, and saying to Zion,
    "Your God is King!"

Hark! Your sentinels raise a cry,
    together they shout for joy,
for they see directly, before their eyes,
    the LORD restoring Zion.
Break out together in song,
    O ruins of Jerusalem!
For the LORD comforts his people,
    he redeems Jerusalem.
The LORD has bared his holy arm
    in the sight of all the nations;
all the ends of the earth will behold
    the salvation of our God.

## RESPONSORIAL PSALM

Ps 98:1, 2-3, 3-4, 5-6

℟. (3c) All the ends of the earth have seen the
    saving power of God.

Sing to the LORD a new song,
    for he has done wondrous deeds;
his right hand has won victory for him,
    his holy arm.

℟. All the ends of the earth have seen the
    saving power of God.

The LORD has made his salvation known:
    in the sight of the nations he has revealed
    his justice.
He has remembered his kindness and his
    faithfulness
    toward the house of Israel.

℟. All the ends of the earth have seen the
    saving power of God.

All the ends of the earth have seen
    the salvation by our God.
Sing joyfully to the LORD, all you lands;
    break into song; sing praise.

℟. All the ends of the earth have seen the
    saving power of God.

Sing praise to the LORD with the harp,
    with the harp and melodious song.
With trumpets and the sound of the horn
    sing joyfully before the King, the LORD.

℟. All the ends of the earth have seen the
    saving power of God.

## SECOND READING

Heb 1:1-6

Brothers and sisters:
In times past, God spoke in partial and
    various ways
    to our ancestors through the prophets;
in these last days, he has spoken to us
    through the Son,
    whom he made heir of all things
    and through whom he created the universe,
who is the refulgence of his glory,
    the very imprint of his being,
    and who sustains all things by his
    mighty word.
When he had accomplished purification
    from sins,
    he took his seat at the right hand of the
    Majesty on high,
    as far superior to the angels
    as the name he has inherited is more
    excellent than theirs.

For to which of the angels did God ever say:
    *You are my son; this day I have begotten*
      *you?*
Or again:
    *I will be a father to him, and he shall be a*
      *son to me?*
And again, when he leads the firstborn into
    the world, he says:
    *Let all the angels of God worship him.*

## Gospel (cont.)
Luke 2:22-40; L17B

for my eyes have seen your salvation,
which you prepared in sight of all the peoples,
a light for revelation to the Gentiles,
and glory for your people Israel."
The child's father and mother were amazed at what was said about
him;
and Simeon blessed them and said to Mary his mother,
"Behold, this child is destined
for the fall and rise of many in Israel,
and to be a sign that will be contradicted
—and you yourself a sword will pierce—
so that the thoughts of many hearts may be revealed."
There was also a prophetess, Anna,
the daughter of Phanuel, of the tribe of Asher.
She was advanced in years,
having lived seven years with her husband after her marriage,
and then as a widow until she was eighty-four.
She never left the temple,
but worshiped night and day with fasting and prayer.
And coming forward at that very time,
she gave thanks to God and spoke about the child
to all who were awaiting the redemption of Jerusalem.

When they had fulfilled all the prescriptions
of the law of the Lord,
they returned to Galilee,
to their own town of Nazareth.
The child grew and became strong, filled with wisdom;
and the favor of God was upon him.

*or* Luke 2:22, 39-40

When the days were completed for their purification
according to the law of Moses,
the parents of Jesus took him up to Jerusalem
to present him to the Lord.

When they had fulfilled all the prescriptions
of the law of the Lord,
they returned to Galilee,
to their own town of Nazareth.
The child grew and became strong, filled with wisdom;
and the favor of God was upon him.

### SECOND READING (cont.)
Heb 11:8, 11-12, 17-19

By faith Abraham, when put to the test, offered up Isaac,
and he who had received the promises was ready to offer
his only son,
of whom it was said,
"Through Isaac descendants shall bear your name."
He reasoned that God was able to raise even from the dead,
and he received Isaac back as a symbol.

### FIRST READING
Sir 3:2-6, 12-14

God sets a father in honor over his children;
a mother's authority he confirms over her
sons.
Whoever honors his father atones for sins,
and preserves himself from them.
When he prays, he is heard;
he stores up riches who reveres his mother.
Whoever honors his father is gladdened by
children,
and, when he prays, is heard.
Whoever reveres his father will live a long life;
he who obeys his father brings comfort to
his mother.

My son, take care of your father when he is
old;
grieve him not as long as he lives.
Even if his mind fail, be considerate of him;
revile him not all the days of his life;
kindness to a father will not be forgotten,
firmly planted against the debt of your sins
—a house raised in justice to you.

### RESPONSORIAL PSALM
Ps 128:1-2, 3, 4-5

℟. (cf. 1) Blessed are those who fear the Lord
and walk in his ways.

Blessed is everyone who fears the LORD,
who walks in his ways!
For you shall eat the fruit of your handiwork;
blessed shall you be, and favored.

℟. Blessed are those who fear the Lord and
walk in his ways.

Your wife shall be like a fruitful vine
in the recesses of your home;
your children like olive plants
around your table.

℟. Blessed are those who fear the Lord and
walk in his ways.

Behold, thus is the man blessed
who fears the LORD.
The LORD bless you from Zion:
may you see the prosperity of Jerusalem
all the days of your life.

℟. Blessed are those who fear the Lord and
walk in his ways.

## SECOND READING
Col 3:12-21

Brothers and sisters:
Put on, as God's chosen ones, holy and
    beloved,
    heartfelt compassion, kindness, humility,
        gentleness, and patience,
    bearing with one another and forgiving one
        another,
    if one has a grievance against another;
    as the Lord has forgiven you, so must you
        also do.
And over all these put on love,
    that is, the bond of perfection.
And let the peace of Christ control your
        hearts,
    the peace into which you were also called in
        one body.
And be thankful.
Let the word of Christ dwell in you richly,
    as in all wisdom you teach and admonish
        one another,
    singing psalms, hymns, and spiritual songs
    with gratitude in your hearts to God.

And whatever you do, in word or in deed,
    do everything in the name of the Lord
        Jesus,
    giving thanks to God the Father through
        him.

Wives, be subordinate to your husbands,
    as is proper in the Lord.
Husbands, love your wives,
    and avoid any bitterness toward them.
Children, obey your parents in everything,
    for this is pleasing to the Lord.
Fathers, do not provoke your children,
    so they may not become discouraged.

*or* Col 3:12-17

Brothers and sisters:
Put on, as God's chosen ones, holy and beloved,
    heartfelt compassion, kindness, humility,
        gentleness, and patience,
    bearing with one another and forgiving one
        another,
    if one has a grievance against another;
    as the Lord has forgiven you, so must you
        also do.

And over all these put on love,
    that is, the bond of perfection.
And let the peace of Christ control your
        hearts,
    the peace into which you were also called in
        one body.
And be thankful.
Let the word of Christ dwell in you richly,
    as in all wisdom you teach and admonish
        one another,
    singing psalms, hymns, and spiritual songs
    with gratitude in your hearts to God.
And whatever you do, in word or in deed,
    do everything in the name of the Lord
        Jesus,
    giving thanks to God the Father through
        him.

---

## *Solemnity of Mary, the Holy Mother of God,* January 1, 2018

### FIRST READING
Num 6:22-27

The LORD said to Moses:
    "Speak to Aaron and his sons and tell them:
    This is how you shall bless the Israelites.
Say to them:
    The LORD bless you and keep you!
    The LORD let his face shine upon
        you, and be gracious to you!
    The LORD look upon you kindly and
        give you peace!
So shall they invoke my name upon the
        Israelites,
    and I will bless them."

### RESPONSORIAL PSALM
Ps 67:2-3, 5, 6, 8

R∕. (2a) May God bless us in his mercy.

May God have pity on us and bless us;
    may he let his face shine upon us.
So may your way be known upon earth;
    among all nations, your salvation.

R∕. May God bless us in his mercy.

May the nations be glad and exult
    because you rule the peoples in equity;
    the nations on the earth you guide.

R∕. May God bless us in his mercy.

May the peoples praise you, O God;
    may all the peoples praise you!
May God bless us,
    and may all the ends of the earth fear him!

R∕. May God bless us in his mercy.

### SECOND READING
Gal 4:4-7

Brothers and sisters:
When the fullness of time had come, God sent
        his Son,
    born of a woman, born under the law,
    to ransom those under the law,
    so that we might receive adoption as sons.
As proof that you are sons,
    God sent the Spirit of his Son into our
        hearts,
    crying out, "Abba, Father!"
So you are no longer a slave but a son,
    and if a son then also an heir, through God.

## Gospel (cont.)

Matt 2:1-12; L20ABC

Then Herod called the magi secretly
  and ascertained from them the time of the star's appearance.
He sent them to Bethlehem and said,
  "Go and search diligently for the child.
When you have found him, bring me word,
  that I too may go and do him homage."
After their audience with the king they set out.
And behold, the star that they had seen at its rising preceded them,
  until it came and stopped over the place where the child was.

They were overjoyed at seeing the star,
  and on entering the house
  they saw the child with Mary his mother.
They prostrated themselves and did him homage.
Then they opened their treasures
  and offered him gifts of gold, frankincense, and myrrh.
And having been warned in a dream not to return to Herod,
  they departed for their country by another way.

## Ash Wednesday, *February 14, 2018*

### FIRST READING

Joel 2:12-18

Even now, says the LORD,
  return to me with your whole heart,
  with fasting, and weeping, and mourning;
Rend your hearts, not your garments,
  and return to the LORD, your God.
For gracious and merciful is he,
  slow to anger, rich in kindness,
  and relenting in punishment.
Perhaps he will again relent
  and leave behind him a blessing,
Offerings and libations
  for the LORD, your God.

Blow the trumpet in Zion!
  proclaim a fast,
  call an assembly;
Gather the people,
  notify the congregation;
Assemble the elders,
  gather the children
  and the infants at the breast;
Let the bridegroom quit his room
  and the bride her chamber.
Between the porch and the altar
  let the priests, the ministers of the LORD,
    weep,
And say, "Spare, O LORD, your people,
  and make not your heritage a reproach,
  with the nations ruling over them!
Why should they say among the peoples,
  'Where is their God?'"

Then the LORD was stirred to concern for his
    land
  and took pity on his people.

### RESPONSORIAL PSALM

Ps 51:3-4, 5-6ab, 12-13, 14, and 17

R̸. (see 3a) Be merciful, O Lord, for we have
    sinned.

Have mercy on me, O God, in your goodness;
  in the greatness of your compassion wipe
    out my offense.
Thoroughly wash me from my guilt
  and of my sin cleanse me.

R̸. Be merciful, O Lord, for we have sinned.

For I acknowledge my offense,
  and my sin is before me always:
"Against you only have I sinned,
  and done what is evil in your sight."

R̸. Be merciful, O Lord, for we have sinned.

A clean heart create for me, O God,
  and a steadfast spirit renew within me.
Cast me not out from your presence,
  and your Holy Spirit take not from me.

R̸. Be merciful, O Lord, for we have sinned.

Give me back the joy of your salvation,
  and a willing spirit sustain in me.
O Lord, open my lips,
  and my mouth shall proclaim your praise.

R̸. Be merciful, O Lord, for we have sinned.

### SECOND READING

2 Cor 5:20–6:2

Brothers and sisters:
We are ambassadors for Christ,
  as if God were appealing through us.
We implore you on behalf of Christ,
  be reconciled to God.
For our sake he made him to be sin who did
    not know sin,
  so that we might become the righteousness
    of God in him.

Working together, then,
  we appeal to you not to receive the grace of
    God in vain.
For he says:

*In an acceptable time I heard you,
  and on the day of salvation I helped you.*

Behold, now is a very acceptable time;
  behold, now is the day of salvation.

## Gospel (cont.)

John 2:13-25; L29B

But he was speaking about the temple of his body.
Therefore, when he was raised from the dead,
his disciples remembered that he had said this,
and they came to believe the Scripture
and the word Jesus had spoken.

While he was in Jerusalem for the feast of Passover,
many began to believe in his name

when they saw the signs he was doing.
But Jesus would not trust himself to them because he knew them all,
and did not need anyone to testify about human nature.
He himself understood it well.

## RESPONSORIAL PSALM

Ps 19:8, 9, 10, 11

R℣. (John 6:68c) Lord, you have the words of
everlasting life.

The law of the Lord is perfect,
refreshing the soul;
the decree of the Lord is trustworthy,
giving wisdom to the simple.

R℣. Lord, you have the words of everlasting life.

The precepts of the Lord are right,
rejoicing the heart;
the command of the Lord is clear,
enlightening the eye.

R℣. Lord, you have the words of everlasting life.

The fear of the Lord is pure,
enduring forever;
the ordinances of the Lord are true,
all of them just.

R℣. Lord, you have the words of everlasting life.

They are more precious than gold,
than a heap of purest gold;
sweeter also than syrup
or honey from the comb.

R℣. Lord, you have the words of everlasting life.

## SECOND READING

1 Cor 1:22-25

Brothers and sisters:
Jews demand signs and Greeks look for
wisdom,
but we proclaim Christ crucified,
a stumbling block to Jews and foolishness
to Gentiles,
but to those who are called, Jews and
Greeks alike,
Christ the power of God and the wisdom
of God.
For the foolishness of God is wiser than
human wisdom,
and the weakness of God is stronger than
human strength.

## FIRST READING

Exod 17:3-7

In those days, in their thirst for water,
the people grumbled against Moses,
saying, "Why did you ever make us leave
Egypt?
Was it just to have us die here of thirst
with our children and our livestock?"
So Moses cried out to the Lord,
"What shall I do with this people?
A little more and they will stone me!"
The Lord answered Moses,
"Go over there in front of the people,
along with some of the elders of Israel,
holding in your hand, as you go,
the staff with which you struck the river.
I will be standing there in front of you on the
rock in Horeb.
Strike the rock, and the water will flow from it
for the people to drink."
This Moses did, in the presence of the elders
of Israel.
The place was called Massah and Meribah,
because the Israelites quarreled there
and tested the Lord, saying,
"Is the Lord in our midst or not?"

## RESPONSORIAL PSALM

Ps 95:1-2, 6-7, 8-9

R℣. (8) If today you hear his voice, harden not
your hearts.

Come, let us sing joyfully to the Lord;
let us acclaim the Rock of our salvation.
Let us come into his presence with
thanksgiving;
let us joyfully sing psalms to him.

R℣. If today you hear his voice, harden not
your hearts.

Come, let us bow down in worship;
let us kneel before the Lord who made us.
For he is our God,
and we are the people he shepherds, the
flock he guides.

R℣. If today you hear his voice, harden not
your hearts.

Oh, that today you would hear his voice:
"Harden not your hearts as at Meribah,
as in the day of Massah in the desert,
Where your fathers tempted me;
they tested me though they had seen my
works."

R℣. If today you hear his voice, harden not
your hearts.

## SECOND READING

Rom 5:1-2, 5-8

Brothers and sisters:
Since we have been justified by faith,
we have peace with God through our Lord
Jesus Christ,
through whom we have gained access by
faith
to this grace in which we stand,
and we boast in hope of the glory of God.

And hope does not disappoint,
because the love of God has been poured
out into our hearts
through the Holy Spirit who has been given
to us.
For Christ, while we were still helpless,
died at the appointed time for the ungodly.
Indeed, only with difficulty does one die for a
just person,
though perhaps for a good person one
might even find courage to die.
But God proves his love for us
in that while we were still sinners Christ
died for us.

## *Gospel*
John 4:5-42; L28A

Jesus came to a town of Samaria called Sychar,
near the plot of land that Jacob had given to his son Joseph.
Jacob's well was there.
Jesus, tired from his journey, sat down there at the well.
It was about noon.

A woman of Samaria came to draw water.
Jesus said to her,
"Give me a drink."
His disciples had gone into the town to buy food.
The Samaritan woman said to him,
"How can you, a Jew, ask me, a Samaritan woman, for a drink?"
—For Jews use nothing in common with Samaritans.—
Jesus answered and said to her,
"If you knew the gift of God
and who is saying to you, 'Give me a drink,'
you would have asked him
and he would have given you living water."
The woman said to him,
"Sir, you do not even have a bucket and the cistern is deep;
where then can you get this living water?
Are you greater than our father Jacob,
who gave us this cistern and drank from it himself
with his children and his flocks?"
Jesus answered and said to her,
"Everyone who drinks this water will be thirsty again;
but whoever drinks the water I shall give will never thirst;
the water I shall give will become in him
a spring of water welling up to eternal life."
The woman said to him,
"Sir, give me this water, so that I may not be thirsty
or have to keep coming here to draw water."

Jesus said to her,
"Go call your husband and come back."
The woman answered and said to him,
"I do not have a husband."
Jesus answered her,
"You are right in saying, 'I do not have a husband.'
For you have had five husbands,
and the one you have now is not your husband.
What you have said is true."
The woman said to him,
"Sir, I can see that you are a prophet.
Our ancestors worshiped on this mountain;
but you people say that the place to worship is in Jerusalem."
Jesus said to her,
"Believe me, woman, the hour is coming
when you will worship the Father
neither on this mountain nor in Jerusalem.
You people worship what you do not understand;
we worship what we understand,
because salvation is from the Jews.
But the hour is coming, and is now here,
when true worshipers will worship the Father in Spirit and truth;
and indeed the Father seeks such people to worship him.
God is Spirit, and those who worship him
must worship in Spirit and truth."
The woman said to him,
"I know that the Messiah is coming, the one called the Christ;
when he comes, he will tell us everything."
Jesus said to her,
"I am he, the one speaking with you."

At that moment his disciples returned,
and were amazed that he was talking with a woman,
but still no one said, "What are you looking for?"
or "Why are you talking with her?"
The woman left her water jar
and went into the town and said to the people,
"Come see a man who told me everything I have done.
Could he possibly be the Christ?"
They went out of the town and came to him.
Meanwhile, the disciples urged him, "Rabbi, eat."
But he said to them,
"I have food to eat of which you do not know."
So the disciples said to one another,
"Could someone have brought him something to eat?"
Jesus said to them,
"My food is to do the will of the one who sent me
and to finish his work.
Do you not say, 'In four months the harvest will be here'?
I tell you, look up and see the fields ripe for the harvest.
The reaper is already receiving payment
and gathering crops for eternal life,
so that the sower and reaper can rejoice together.
For here the saying is verified that 'One sows and another reaps.'
I sent you to reap what you have not worked for;
others have done the work,
and you are sharing the fruits of their work."

Many of the Samaritans of that town began to believe in him
because of the word of the woman who testified,
"He told me everything I have done."
When the Samaritans came to him,
they invited him to stay with them;
and he stayed there two days.
Many more began to believe in him because of his word,
and they said to the woman,
"We no longer believe because of your word;
for we have heard for ourselves,
and we know that this is truly the savior of the world."

*or*
John 4:5-15, 19b-26, 39a, 40-42; L28A

Jesus came to a town of Samaria called Sychar,
near the plot of land that Jacob had given to his son Joseph.
Jacob's well was there.
Jesus, tired from his journey, sat down there at the well.
It was about noon.

A woman of Samaria came to draw water.
Jesus said to her,
"Give me a drink."
His disciples had gone into the town to buy food.
The Samaritan woman said to him,
"How can you, a Jew, ask me, a Samaritan woman, for a drink?"
—For Jews use nothing in common with Samaritans.—
Jesus answered and said to her,
"If you knew the gift of God

and who is saying to you, 'Give me a drink,'
  you would have asked him
  and he would have given you living water."
The woman said to him,
  "Sir, you do not even have a bucket and the cistern is deep;
  where then can you get this living water?
Are you greater than our father Jacob,
  who gave us this cistern and drank from it himself
  with his children and his flocks?"
Jesus answered and said to her,
  "Everyone who drinks this water will be thirsty again;
  but whoever drinks the water I shall give will never thirst;
  the water I shall give will become in him
  a spring of water welling up to eternal life."
The woman said to him,
  "Sir, give me this water, so that I may not be thirsty
  or have to keep coming here to draw water.

"I can see that you are a prophet.
Our ancestors worshiped on this mountain;
  but you people say that the place to worship is in Jerusalem."
Jesus said to her,
  "Believe me, woman, the hour is coming
  when you will worship the Father
  neither on this mountain nor in Jerusalem.

You people worship what you do not understand;
  we worship what we understand,
  because salvation is from the Jews.
But the hour is coming, and is now here,
  when true worshipers will worship the Father in Spirit and truth;
  and indeed the Father seeks such people to worship him.
God is Spirit, and those who worship him
  must worship in Spirit and truth."
The woman said to him,
  "I know that the Messiah is coming, the one called the Christ;
  when he comes, he will tell us everything."
Jesus said to her,
  "I am he, the one speaking with you."

Many of the Samaritans of that town began to believe in him.
When the Samaritans came to him,
  they invited him to stay with them;
  and he stayed there two days.
Many more began to believe in him because of his word,
  and they said to the woman,
  "We no longer believe because of your word;
  for we have heard for ourselves,
  and we know that this is truly the savior of the world."

**SECOND READING**
Eph 2:4-10

Brothers and sisters:
God, who is rich in mercy,
  because of the great love he had for us,
  even when we were dead in our
    transgressions,
  brought us to life with Christ—by grace
    you have been saved—,
  raised us up with him,
  and seated us with him in the heavens in
    Christ Jesus,
  that in the ages to come
  He might show the immeasurable riches of
    his grace
  in his kindness to us in Christ Jesus.
For by grace you have been saved through
    faith,
  and this is not from you; it is the gift of
    God;
  it is not from works, so no one may boast.
For we are his handiwork, created in Christ
    Jesus for the good works
  that God has prepared in advance,
  that we should live in them.

**FIRST READING**
1 Sam 16:1b, 6-7, 10-13a

The Lord said to Samuel:
  "Fill your horn with oil, and be on your
    way.
I am sending you to Jesse of Bethlehem,
  for I have chosen my king from among his
    sons."

As Jesse and his sons came to the sacrifice,
  Samuel looked at Eliab and thought,
  "Surely the Lord's anointed is here before
    him."
But the Lord said to Samuel:
  "Do not judge from his appearance or from
    his lofty stature,
  because I have rejected him.
Not as man sees does God see,
  because man sees the appearance
  but the Lord looks into the heart."
In the same way Jesse presented seven sons
    before Samuel,
  but Samuel said to Jesse,
  "The Lord has not chosen any one of
    these."

Then Samuel asked Jesse,
  "Are these all the sons you have?"
Jesse replied,
  "There is still the youngest, who is tending
    the sheep."
Samuel said to Jesse,
  "Send for him;
  we will not begin the sacrificial banquet
    until he arrives here."
Jesse sent and had the young man brought to
    them.
He was ruddy, a youth handsome to behold
  and making a splendid appearance.
The Lord said,
  "There—anoint him, for this is the one!"
Then Samuel, with the horn of oil in hand,
  anointed David in the presence of his
    brothers;
  and from that day on, the spirit of the Lord
    rushed upon David.

## RESPONSORIAL PSALM
Ps 23:1-3a, 3b-4, 5, 6

R℣. (1) The Lord is my shepherd; there is
    nothing I shall want.

The Lᴏʀᴅ is my shepherd; I shall not want.
    In verdant pastures he gives me repose;
beside restful waters he leads me;
    he refreshes my soul.

R℣. The Lord is my shepherd; there is nothing
    I shall want.

He guides me in right paths
    for his name's sake.
Even though I walk in the dark valley
    I fear no evil; for you are at my side
with your rod and your staff
    that give me courage.

R℣. The Lord is my shepherd; there is nothing
    I shall want.

You spread the table before me
    in the sight of my foes;
you anoint my head with oil;
    my cup overflows.

R℣. The Lord is my shepherd; there is nothing
    I shall want.

Only goodness and kindness follow me
    all the days of my life;
and I shall dwell in the house of the Lᴏʀᴅ
    for years to come.

R℣. The Lord is my shepherd; there is nothing
    I shall want.

## SECOND READING
Eph 5:8-14

Brothers and sisters:
You were once darkness,
    but now you are light in the Lord.
Live as children of light,
    for light produces every kind of goodness
    and righteousness and truth.
Try to learn what is pleasing to the Lord.
Take no part in the fruitless works of
    darkness;
    rather expose them, for it is shameful even
      to mention
    the things done by them in secret;
    but everything exposed by the light
      becomes visible,
for everything that becomes visible is light.
Therefore, it says:
    "Awake, O sleeper,
    and arise from the dead,
    and Christ will give you light."

## Gospel
John 9:1-41; L31A

As Jesus passed by he saw a man blind from birth.
His disciples asked him,
    "Rabbi, who sinned, this man or his parents,
    that he was born blind?"
Jesus answered,
    "Neither he nor his parents sinned;
    it is so that the works of God might be made visible through him.
We have to do the works of the one who sent me while it is day.
Night is coming when no one can work.
While I am in the world, I am the light of the world."
When he had said this, he spat on the ground
    and made clay with the saliva,
    and smeared the clay on his eyes, and said to him,
    "Go wash in the Pool of Siloam"—which means Sent—.
So he went and washed, and came back able to see.

His neighbors and those who had seen him earlier as a beggar said,
    "Isn't this the one who used to sit and beg?"
Some said, "It is,"
    but others said, "No, he just looks like him."
He said, "I am."
So they said to him, "How were your eyes opened?"
He replied,
    "The man called Jesus made clay and anointed my eyes
    and told me, 'Go to Siloam and wash.'
So I went there and washed and was able to see."
And they said to him, "Where is he?"
He said, "I don't know."

They brought the one who was once blind to the Pharisees.
Now Jesus had made clay and opened his eyes on a sabbath.
So then the Pharisees also asked him how he was able to see.
He said to them,
    "He put clay on my eyes, and I washed, and now I can see."
So some of the Pharisees said,

"This man is not from God,
    because he does not keep the sabbath."
But others said,
    "How can a sinful man do such signs?"
And there was a division among them.
So they said to the blind man again,
    "What do you have to say about him,
    since he opened your eyes?"
He said, "He is a prophet."

Now the Jews did not believe
    that he had been blind and gained his sight
    until they summoned the parents of the one who had gained his
      sight.
They asked them,
    "Is this your son, who you say was born blind?
How does he now see?"
His parents answered and said,
    "We know that this is our son and that he was born blind.
We do not know how he sees now,
    nor do we know who opened his eyes.
Ask him, he is of age;
    he can speak for himself."
His parents said this because they were afraid
    of the Jews, for the Jews had already agreed
    that if anyone acknowledged him as the Christ,
    he would be expelled from the synagogue.
For this reason his parents said,
    "He is of age; question him."

So a second time they called the man who had been blind
    and said to him, "Give God the praise!
We know that this man is a sinner."
He replied,
    "If he is a sinner, I do not know.

## Gospel (cont.)
John 9:1-41; L31A

One thing I do know is that I was blind and now I see."
So they said to him,
"What did he do to you?
How did he open your eyes?"
He answered them,
"I told you already and you did not listen.
Why do you want to hear it again?
Do you want to become his disciples, too?"
They ridiculed him and said,
"You are that man's disciple;
we are disciples of Moses!
We know that God spoke to Moses,
but we do not know where this one is from."
The man answered and said to them,
"This is what is so amazing,
that you do not know where he is from, yet he opened my eyes.
We know that God does not listen to sinners,
but if one is devout and does his will, he listens to him.
It is unheard of that anyone ever opened the eyes of a person born
blind.
If this man were not from God,
he would not be able to do anything."
They answered and said to him,
"You were born totally in sin,
and are you trying to teach us?"
Then they threw him out.

When Jesus heard that they had thrown him out,
he found him and said, "Do you believe in the Son of Man?"
He answered and said,
"Who is he, sir, that I may believe in him?"
Jesus said to him,
"You have seen him,
and the one speaking with you is he."
He said,
"I do believe, Lord," and he worshiped him.
Then Jesus said,
"I came into this world for judgment,
so that those who do not see might see,
and those who do see might become blind."

Some of the Pharisees who were with him heard this
and said to him, "Surely we are not also blind, are we?"
Jesus said to them,
"If you were blind, you would have no sin;
but now you are saying, 'We see,' so your sin remains."

*or*

John 9:1, 6-9, 13-17, 34-38; L31A

As Jesus passed by he saw a man blind from birth.
He spat on the ground and made clay with the saliva,
and smeared the clay on his eyes, and said to him,
"Go wash in the Pool of Siloam"—which means Sent—.
So he went and washed, and came back able to see.

His neighbors and those who had seen him earlier as a beggar said,
"Isn't this the one who used to sit and beg?"
Some said, "It is,"
but others said, "No, he just looks like him."
He said, "I am."

They brought the one who was once blind to the Pharisees.
Now Jesus had made clay and opened his eyes on a sabbath.
So then the Pharisees also asked him how he was able to see.
He said to them,
"He put clay on my eyes, and I washed, and now I can see."
So some of the Pharisees said,
"This man is not from God,
because he does not keep the sabbath."
But others said,
"How can a sinful man do such signs?"
And there was a division among them.
So they said to the blind man again,
"What do you have to say about him,
since he opened your eyes?"
He said, "He is a prophet."

They answered and said to him,
"You were born totally in sin,
and are you trying to teach us?"
Then they threw him out.

When Jesus heard that they had thrown him out,
he found him and said, "Do you believe in the Son of Man?"
He answered and said,
"Who is he, sir, that I may believe in him?"
Jesus said to him,
"You have seen him,
and the one speaking with you is he."
He said,
"I do believe, Lord," and he worshiped him.

## Gospel (cont.)
John 12:20-33; L35B

The crowd there heard it and said it was thunder;
 but others said, "An angel has spoken to him."
Jesus answered and said,
 "This voice did not come for my sake but for yours.
Now is the time of judgment on this world;
 now the ruler of this world will be driven out.
And when I am lifted up from the earth,
 I will draw everyone to myself."
He said this indicating the kind of death he would die.

### FIRST READING
Ezek 37:12-14

Thus says the Lord GOD:
 O my people, I will open your graves
 and have you rise from them,
 and bring you back to the land of Israel.
Then you shall know that I am the LORD,
 when I open your graves and have you rise
  from them,
 O my people!
I will put my spirit in you that you may live,
 and I will settle you upon your land;
 thus you shall know that I am the LORD.
I have promised, and I will do it, says the
 LORD.

### RESPONSORIAL PSALM
Ps 130:1-2, 3-4, 5-6, 7-8

R℘. (7) With the Lord there is mercy and
 fullness of redemption.

Out of the depths I cry to you, O LORD;
 LORD, hear my voice!
Let your ears be attentive
 to my voice in supplication.

R℘. With the Lord there is mercy and fullness
 of redemption.

If you, O LORD, mark iniquities,
 LORD, who can stand?
But with you is forgiveness,
 that you may be revered.

R℘. With the Lord there is mercy and fullness
 of redemption.

I trust in the LORD;
 my soul trusts in his word.
More than sentinels wait for the dawn,
 let Israel wait for the LORD.

R℘. With the Lord there is mercy and fullness
 of redemption.

For with the LORD is kindness
 and with him is plenteous redemption;
and he will redeem Israel
 from all their iniquities.

R℘. With the Lord there is mercy and fullness
 of redemption.

### SECOND READING
Rom 8:8-11

Brothers and sisters:
Those who are in the flesh cannot please God.
But you are not in the flesh;
 on the contrary, you are in the spirit,
 if only the Spirit of God dwells in you.
Whoever does not have the Spirit of Christ
 does not belong to him.
But if Christ is in you,
 although the body is dead because of sin,
 the spirit is alive because of righteousness.
If the Spirit of the One who raised Jesus from
  the dead dwells in you,
 the One who raised Christ from the dead
 will give life to your mortal bodies also,
 through his Spirit dwelling in you.

## Gospel
John 11:1-45; L34A

Now a man was ill, Lazarus from Bethany,
    the village of Mary and her sister Martha.
Mary was the one who had anointed the Lord with perfumed oil
    and dried his feet with her hair;
    it was her brother Lazarus who was ill.
So the sisters sent word to Jesus saying,
    "Master, the one you love is ill."
When Jesus heard this he said,
    "This illness is not to end in death,
    but is for the glory of God,
    that the Son of God may be glorified through it."
Now Jesus loved Martha and her sister and Lazarus.
So when he heard that he was ill,
    he remained for two days in the place where he was.
Then after this he said to his disciples,
    "Let us go back to Judea."
The disciples said to him,
    "Rabbi, the Jews were just trying to stone you,
    and you want to go back there?"
Jesus answered,
    "Are there not twelve hours in a day?
If one walks during the day, he does not stumble,
    because he sees the light of this world.
But if one walks at night, he stumbles,
    because the light is not in him."
He said this, and then told them,
    "Our friend Lazarus is asleep,
    but I am going to awaken him."
So the disciples said to him,
    "Master, if he is asleep, he will be saved."
But Jesus was talking about his death,
    while they thought that he meant ordinary sleep.
So then Jesus said to them clearly,
    "Lazarus has died.
And I am glad for you that I was not there,
    that you may believe.
Let us go to him."
So Thomas, called Didymus, said to his fellow disciples,
    "Let us also go to die with him."

When Jesus arrived, he found that Lazarus
    had already been in the tomb for four days.
Now Bethany was near Jerusalem, only about two miles away.
And many of the Jews had come to Martha and Mary
    to comfort them about their brother.
When Martha heard that Jesus was coming,
    she went to meet him;
    but Mary sat at home.
Martha said to Jesus,
    "Lord, if you had been here,
    my brother would not have died.
But even now I know that whatever you ask of God,
    God will give you."
Jesus said to her,
    "Your brother will rise."
Martha said to him,
    "I know he will rise,
    in the resurrection on the last day."
Jesus told her,

    "I am the resurrection and the life;
    whoever believes in me, even if he dies, will live,
    and everyone who lives and believes in me will never die.
Do you believe this?"
She said to him, "Yes, Lord.
I have come to believe that you are the Christ, the Son of God,
    the one who is coming into the world."

When she had said this,
    she went and called her sister Mary secretly, saying,
    "The teacher is here and is asking for you."
As soon as she heard this,
    she rose quickly and went to him.
For Jesus had not yet come into the village,
    but was still where Martha had met him.
So when the Jews who were with her in the house comforting her
    saw Mary get up quickly and go out,
    they followed her,
    presuming that she was going to the tomb to weep there.
When Mary came to where Jesus was and saw him,
    she fell at his feet and said to him,
    "Lord, if you had been here,
    my brother would not have died."
When Jesus saw her weeping and the Jews who had come with her
        weeping,
    he became perturbed and deeply troubled, and said,
    "Where have you laid him?"
They said to him, "Sir, come and see."
And Jesus wept.
So the Jews said, "See how he loved him."
But some of them said,
    "Could not the one who opened the eyes of the blind man
    have done something so that this man would not have died?"

So Jesus, perturbed again, came to the tomb.
It was a cave, and a stone lay across it.
Jesus said, "Take away the stone."
Martha, the dead man's sister, said to him,
    "Lord, by now there will be a stench;
    he has been dead for four days."
Jesus said to her,
    "Did I not tell you that if you believe
    you will see the glory of God?"
So they took away the stone.
And Jesus raised his eyes and said,
    "Father, I thank you for hearing me.
I know that you always hear me;
    but because of the crowd here I have said this,
    that they may believe that you sent me."
And when he had said this,
    he cried out in a loud voice,
    "Lazarus, come out!"
The dead man came out,
    tied hand and foot with burial bands,
    and his face was wrapped in a cloth.
So Jesus said to them,
    "Untie him and let him go."

Now many of the Jews who had come to Mary
    and seen what he had done began to believe in him.

## *Gospel*

John 11:3-7, 17, 20-27, 33b-45; L34A

The sisters of Lazarus sent word to Jesus saying,
  "Master, the one you love is ill."
When Jesus heard this he said,
  "This illness is not to end in death,
  but is for the glory of God,
  that the Son of God may be glorified through it."
Now Jesus loved Martha and her sister and Lazarus.
So when he heard that he was ill,
  he remained for two days in the place where he was.
Then after this he said to his disciples,
  "Let us go back to Judea."

When Jesus arrived, he found that Lazarus
  had already been in the tomb for four days.
When Martha heard that Jesus was coming,
  she went to meet him;
  but Mary sat at home.
Martha said to Jesus,
  "Lord, if you had been here,
  my brother would not have died.
But even now I know that whatever you ask of God,
  God will give you."
Jesus said to her,
  "Your brother will rise."
Martha said,
  "I know he will rise,
  in the resurrection on the last day."
Jesus told her,
  "I am the resurrection and the life;
  whoever believes in me, even if he dies, will live,
  and everyone who lives and believes in me will never die.
Do you believe this?"
She said to him, "Yes, Lord.
I have come to believe that you are the Christ, the Son of God,
  the one who is coming into the world."

He became perturbed and deeply troubled, and said,
  "Where have you laid him?"
They said to him, "Sir, come and see."
And Jesus wept.
So the Jews said, "See how he loved him."
But some of them said,
  "Could not the one who opened the eyes of the blind man
  have done something so that this man would not have died?"

So Jesus, perturbed again, came to the tomb.
It was a cave, and a stone lay across it.
Jesus said, "Take away the stone."
Martha, the dead man's sister, said to him,
  "Lord, by now there will be a stench;
  he has been dead for four days."
Jesus said to her,
  "Did I not tell you that if you believe
  you will see the glory of God?"
So they took away the stone.
And Jesus raised his eyes and said,
  "Father, I thank you for hearing me.
I know that you always hear me;
  but because of the crowd here I have said this,
  that they may believe that you sent me."
And when he had said this,
  he cried out in a loud voice,
  "Lazarus, come out!"
The dead man came out,
  tied hand and foot with burial bands,
  and his face was wrapped in a cloth.
So Jesus said to them,
  "Untie him and let him go."

Now many of the Jews who had come to Mary
  and seen what he had done began to believe in him.

## Gospel
Matt 1:16, 18-21, 24a; L543

Jacob was the father of Joseph, the husband of Mary.
Of her was born Jesus who is called the Christ.

Now this is how the birth of Jesus Christ came about.
When his mother Mary was betrothed to Joseph,
    but before they lived together,
    she was found with child through the Holy Spirit.
Joseph her husband, since he was a righteous man,
    yet unwilling to expose her to shame,
    decided to divorce her quietly.
Such was his intention when, behold,
    the angel of the Lord appeared to him in a dream and said,
    "Joseph, son of David,
    do not be afraid to take Mary your wife into your home.
For it is through the Holy Spirit
    that this child has been conceived in her.
She will bear a son and you are to name him Jesus,
    because he will save his people from their sins."
When Joseph awoke,
    he did as the angel of the Lord had commanded him
    and took his wife into his home.

### FIRST READING
2 Sam 7:4-5a, 12-14a, 16

The LORD spoke to Nathan and said:
"Go, tell my servant David,
    'When your time comes and you rest with
        your ancestors,
    I will raise up your heir after you, sprung
        from your loins,
    and I will make his kingdom firm.
It is he who shall build a house for my name.
And I will make his royal throne firm forever.
I will be a father to him,
    and he shall be a son to me.
Your house and your kingdom shall endure
    forever before me;
    your throne shall stand firm forever.'"

### RESPONSORIAL PSALM
Ps 89:2-3, 4-5, 27 and 29

R7. (37) The son of David will live for ever.

The promises of the LORD I will sing forever,
    through all generations my mouth will
        proclaim your faithfulness,
For you have said, "My kindness is
    established forever";
    in heaven you have confirmed your
    faithfulness.

R7. The son of David will live for ever.

"I have made a covenant with my chosen one;
    I have sworn to David my servant:
Forever will I confirm your posterity
    and establish your throne for all
    generations."

R7. The son of David will live for ever.

"He shall say of me, 'You are my father,
    my God, the Rock, my savior.'
Forever I will maintain my kindness toward
    him,
    and my covenant with him stands firm."

R7. The son of David will live for ever.

### SECOND READING
Rom 4:13, 16-18, 22

Brothers and sisters:
It was not through the law
    that the promise was made to Abraham
        and his descendants
    that he would inherit the world,
    but through the righteousness that comes
        from faith.
For this reason, it depends on faith,
    so that it may be a gift,
    and the promise may be guaranteed to all
        his descendants,
    not to those who only adhere to the law
    but to those who follow the faith of
        Abraham,
    who is the father of all of us, as it is
        written,
*I have made you father of many nations.*
He is our father in the sight of God,
    in whom he believed, who gives life to the
        dead
    and calls into being what does not exist.
He believed, hoping against hope,
    that he would become *the father of many*
        *nations,*
    according to what was said, *Thus shall your*
        *descendants be.*
That is why *it was credited to him as*
    *righteousness.*

### Gospel (cont.) at the procession with palms

Some of the bystanders said to them,
"What are you doing, untying the colt?"
They answered them just as Jesus had told them to,
and they permitted them to do it.
So they brought the colt to Jesus
and put their cloaks over it.
And he sat on it.
Many people spread their cloaks on the road,
and others spread leafy branches
that they had cut from the fields.
Those preceding him as well as those following kept crying out:
"Hosanna!
Blessed is he who comes in the name of the Lord!
Blessed is the kingdom of our father David that is to come!
Hosanna in the highest!"

### Gospel at Mass
Mark 14:1–15:47; L38B

The Passover and the Feast of Unleavened Bread
were to take place in two days' time.
So the chief priests and the scribes were seeking a way
to arrest him by treachery and put him to death.
They said, "Not during the festival,
for fear that there may be a riot among the people."

When he was in Bethany reclining at table
in the house of Simon the leper,
a woman came with an alabaster jar of perfumed oil,
costly genuine spikenard.
She broke the alabaster jar and poured it on his head.
There were some who were indignant.
"Why has there been this waste of perfumed oil?
It could have been sold for more than three hundred days' wages
and the money given to the poor."
They were infuriated with her.
Jesus said, "Let her alone.
Why do you make trouble for her?
She has done a good thing for me.
The poor you will always have with you,
and whenever you wish you can do good to them,
but you will not always have me.
She has done what she could.
She has anticipated anointing my body for burial.
Amen, I say to you,
wherever the gospel is proclaimed to the whole world,
what she has done will be told in memory of her."

Then Judas Iscariot, one of the Twelve,
went off to the chief priests to hand him over to them.
When they heard him they were pleased and promised to pay him
money.
Then he looked for an opportunity to hand him over.

On the first day of the Feast of Unleavened Bread,
when they sacrificed the Passover lamb,
his disciples said to him,
"Where do you want us to go
and prepare for you to eat the Passover?"

He sent two of his disciples and said to them,
"Go into the city and a man will meet you,
carrying a jar of water.
Follow him.
Wherever he enters, say to the master of the house,
'The Teacher says, "Where is my guest room
where I may eat the Passover with my disciples?"'
Then he will show you a large upper room furnished and ready.
Make the preparations for us there."
The disciples then went off, entered the city,
and found it just as he had told them;
and they prepared the Passover.

When it was evening, he came with the Twelve.
And as they reclined at table and were eating, Jesus said,
"Amen, I say to you, one of you will betray me,
one who is eating with me."
They began to be distressed and to say to him, one by one,
"Surely it is not I?"
He said to them,
"One of the Twelve, the one who dips with me into the dish.
For the Son of Man indeed goes, as it is written of him,
but woe to that man by whom the Son of Man is betrayed.
It would be better for that man if he had never been born."

While they were eating,
he took bread, said the blessing,
broke it, and gave it to them, and said,
"Take it; this is my body."
Then he took a cup, gave thanks, and gave it to them,
and they all drank from it.
He said to them,
"This is my blood of the covenant,
which will be shed for many.
Amen, I say to you,
I shall not drink again the fruit of the vine
until the day when I drink it new in the kingdom of God."
Then, after singing a hymn,
they went out to the Mount of Olives.

Then Jesus said to them,
"All of you will have your faith shaken, for it is written:
*I will strike the shepherd,*
*and the sheep will be dispersed.*
But after I have been raised up,
I shall go before you to Galilee."
Peter said to him,
"Even though all should have their faith shaken,
mine will not be."
Then Jesus said to him,
"Amen, I say to you,
this very night before the cock crows twice
you will deny me three times."
But he vehemently replied,
"Even though I should have to die with you,
I will not deny you."
And they all spoke similarly.

Then they came to a place named Gethsemane,
and he said to his disciples,
"Sit here while I pray."
He took with him Peter, James, and John,
and began to be troubled and distressed.

Then he said to them, "My soul is sorrowful even to death.
Remain here and keep watch."
He advanced a little and fell to the ground and prayed
    that if it were possible the hour might pass by him;
    he said, "Abba, Father, all things are possible to you.
Take this cup away from me,
    but not what I will but what you will."
When he returned he found them asleep.
He said to Peter, "Simon, are you asleep?
Could you not keep watch for one hour?
Watch and pray that you may not undergo the test.
The spirit is willing but the flesh is weak."
Withdrawing again, he prayed, saying the same thing.
Then he returned once more and found them asleep,
    for they could not keep their eyes open
    and did not know what to answer him.
He returned a third time and said to them,
    "Are you still sleeping and taking your rest?
It is enough. The hour has come.
Behold, the Son of Man is to be handed over to sinners.
Get up, let us go.
See, my betrayer is at hand."

Then, while he was still speaking,
    Judas, one of the Twelve, arrived,
    accompanied by a crowd with swords and clubs
    who had come from the chief priests,
    the scribes, and the elders.
His betrayer had arranged a signal with them, saying,
    "The man I shall kiss is the one;
    arrest him and lead him away securely."
He came and immediately went over to him and said,
    "Rabbi." And he kissed him.
At this they laid hands on him and arrested him.
One of the bystanders drew his sword,
    struck the high priest's servant, and cut off his ear.
Jesus said to them in reply,
    "Have you come out as against a robber,
    with swords and clubs, to seize me?
Day after day I was with you teaching in the temple area,
    yet you did not arrest me;
    but that the Scriptures may be fulfilled."
And they all left him and fled.
Now a young man followed him
    wearing nothing but a linen cloth about his body.
They seized him,
    but he left the cloth behind and ran off naked.

They led Jesus away to the high priest,
    and all the chief priests and the elders and the scribes came together.
Peter followed him at a distance into the high priest's courtyard
    and was seated with the guards, warming himself at the fire.
The chief priests and the entire Sanhedrin
    kept trying to obtain testimony against Jesus
    in order to put him to death, but they found none.
Many gave false witness against him,
    but their testimony did not agree.
Some took the stand and testified falsely against him,
    alleging, "We heard him say,
    'I will destroy this temple made with hands
    and within three days I will build another

not made with hands.'"
Even so their testimony did not agree.
The high priest rose before the assembly and questioned Jesus,
    saying, "Have you no answer?
What are these men testifying against you?"
But he was silent and answered nothing.
Again the high priest asked him and said to him,
    "Are you the Christ, the son of the Blessed One?"
Then Jesus answered, "I am;
    and 'you will see the Son of Man
        seated at the right hand of the Power
        and coming with the clouds of heaven.'"
At that the high priest tore his garments and said,
    "What further need have we of witnesses?
You have heard the blasphemy.
What do you think?"
They all condemned him as deserving to die.
Some began to spit on him.
They blindfolded him and struck him and said to him, "Prophesy!"
And the guards greeted him with blows.

While Peter was below in the courtyard,
    one of the high priest's maids came along.
Seeing Peter warming himself,
    she looked intently at him and said,
    "You too were with the Nazarene, Jesus."
But he denied it saying,
    "I neither know nor understand what you are talking about."
So he went out into the outer court.
Then the cock crowed.
The maid saw him and began again to say to the bystanders,
    "This man is one of them."
Once again he denied it.
A little later the bystanders said to Peter once more,
    "Surely you are one of them; for you too are a Galilean."
He began to curse and to swear,
    "I do not know this man about whom you are talking."
And immediately a cock crowed a second time.
Then Peter remembered the word that Jesus had said to him,
    "Before the cock crows twice you will deny me three times."
He broke down and wept.

As soon as morning came,
    the chief priests with the elders and the scribes,
    that is, the whole Sanhedrin, held a council.
They bound Jesus, led him away, and handed him over to Pilate.
Pilate questioned him,
    "Are you the king of the Jews?"
He said to him in reply, "You say so."
The chief priests accused him of many things.
Again Pilate questioned him,
    "Have you no answer?
See how many things they accuse you of."
Jesus gave him no further answer, so that Pilate was amazed.

Now on the occasion of the feast he used to release to them
    one prisoner whom they requested.
A man called Barabbas was then in prison
    along with the rebels who had committed murder in a rebellion.
The crowd came forward and began to ask him
    to do for them as he was accustomed.

Pilate answered,
   "Do you want me to release to you the king of the Jews?"
For he knew that it was out of envy
   that the chief priests had handed him over.
But the chief priests stirred up the crowd
   to have him release Barabbas for them instead.
Pilate again said to them in reply,
   "Then what do you want me to do
   with the man you call the king of the Jews?"
They shouted again, "Crucify him."
Pilate said to them, "Why? What evil has he done?"
They only shouted the louder, "Crucify him."
So Pilate, wishing to satisfy the crowd,
   released Barabbas to them and, after he had Jesus scourged,
   handed him over to be crucified.

The soldiers led him away inside the palace,
   that is, the praetorium, and assembled the whole cohort.
They clothed him in purple and,
   weaving a crown of thorns, placed it on him.
They began to salute him with, "Hail, King of the Jews!"
   and kept striking his head with a reed and spitting upon him.
They knelt before him in homage.
And when they had mocked him,
   they stripped him of the purple cloak,
   dressed him in his own clothes,
   and led him out to crucify him.

They pressed into service a passer-by, Simon,
   a Cyrenian, who was coming in from the country,
   the father of Alexander and Rufus,
   to carry his cross.

They brought him to the place of Golgotha
   —which is translated Place of the Skull—.
They gave him wine drugged with myrrh,
   but he did not take it.
Then they crucified him and divided his garments
   by casting lots for them to see what each should take.
It was nine o'clock in the morning when they crucified him.
The inscription of the charge against him read,
   "The King of the Jews."
With him they crucified two revolutionaries,
   one on his right and one on his left.
Those passing by reviled him,
   shaking their heads and saying,
   "Aha! You who would destroy the temple
   and rebuild it in three days,
   save yourself by coming down from the cross."
Likewise the chief priests, with the scribes,
   mocked him among themselves and said,
   "He saved others; he cannot save himself.
Let the Christ, the King of Israel,
   come down now from the cross
   that we may see and believe."
Those who were crucified with him also kept abusing him.

At noon darkness came over the whole land
   until three in the afternoon.
And at three o'clock Jesus cried out in a loud voice,
   *"Eloi, Eloi, lema sabachthani?"*
   which is translated,
   "My God, my God, why have you forsaken me?"

Some of the bystanders who heard it said,
   "Look, he is calling Elijah."
One of them ran, soaked a sponge with wine, put it on a reed
   and gave it to him to drink saying,
   "Wait, let us see if Elijah comes to take him down."
Jesus gave a loud cry and breathed his last.

   *Here all kneel and pause for a short time.*

The veil of the sanctuary was torn in two from top to bottom.
When the centurion who stood facing him
   saw how he breathed his last he said,
   "Truly this man was the Son of God!"
There were also women looking on from a distance.
Among them were Mary Magdalene,
   Mary the mother of the younger James and of Joses,
      and Salome.
These women had followed him when he was in Galilee
   and ministered to him.
There were also many other women
   who had come up with him to Jerusalem.

When it was already evening,
   since it was the day of preparation,
   the day before the sabbath, Joseph of Arimathea,
   a distinguished member of the council,
   who was himself awaiting the kingdom of God,
   came and courageously went to Pilate
   and asked for the body of Jesus.
Pilate was amazed that he was already dead.
He summoned the centurion
   and asked him if Jesus had already died.
And when he learned of it from the centurion,
   he gave the body to Joseph.
Having bought a linen cloth, he took him down,
   wrapped him in the linen cloth,
   and laid him in a tomb that had been hewn out of the rock.
Then he rolled a stone against the entrance to the tomb.
Mary Magdalene and Mary the mother of Joses
   watched where he was laid.

*or* Mark 15:1-39; L38B

As soon as morning came,
   the chief priests with the elders and the scribes,
   that is, the whole Sanhedrin, held a council.
They bound Jesus, led him away, and handed him over to Pilate.
Pilate questioned him,
   "Are you the king of the Jews?"
He said to him in reply, "You say so."
The chief priests accused him of many things.
Again Pilate questioned him,
   "Have you no answer?
See how many things they accuse you of."
Jesus gave him no further answer, so that Pilate was amazed.

Now on the occasion of the feast he used to release to them
   one prisoner whom they requested.
A man called Barabbas was then in prison
   along with the rebels who had committed murder in a rebellion.
The crowd came forward and began to ask him
   to do for them as he was accustomed.
Pilate answered,
   "Do you want me to release to you the king of the Jews?"

For he knew that it was out of envy
    that the chief priests had handed him over.
But the chief priests stirred up the crowd
    to have him release Barabbas for them instead.
Pilate again said to them in reply,
    "Then what do you want me to do
    with the man you call the king of the Jews?"
They shouted again, "Crucify him."
Pilate said to them, "Why? What evil has he done?"
They only shouted the louder, "Crucify him."
So Pilate, wishing to satisfy the crowd,
    released Barabbas to them and, after he had Jesus scourged,
    handed him over to be crucified.

The soldiers led him away inside the palace,
    that is, the praetorium, and assembled the whole cohort.
They clothed him in purple and,
    weaving a crown of thorns, placed it on him.
They began to salute him with, "Hail, King of the Jews!"
    and kept striking his head with a reed and spitting upon him.
They knelt before him in homage.
And when they had mocked him,
    they stripped him of the purple cloak,
    dressed him in his own clothes,
    and led him out to crucify him.

They pressed into service a passer-by, Simon,
    a Cyrenian, who was coming in from the country,
    the father of Alexander and Rufus,
    to carry his cross.

They brought him to the place of Golgotha
    —which is translated Place of the Skull—.
They gave him wine drugged with myrrh,
    but he did not take it.
Then they crucified him and divided his garments
    by casting lots for them to see what each should take.

It was nine o'clock in the morning when they crucified him.
The inscription of the charge against him read,
    "The King of the Jews."
With him they crucified two revolutionaries,
    one on his right and one on his left.
Those passing by reviled him,
    shaking their heads and saying,
    "Aha! You who would destroy the temple
    and rebuild it in three days,
    save yourself by coming down from the cross."
Likewise the chief priests, with the scribes,
    mocked him among themselves and said,
    "He saved others; he cannot save himself.
Let the Christ, the King of Israel,
    come down now from the cross
    that we may see and believe."
Those who were crucified with him also kept abusing him.

At noon darkness came over the whole land
    until three in the afternoon.
And at three o'clock Jesus cried out in a loud voice,
    *"Eloi, Eloi, lema sabachthani?"*
    which is translated,
    "My God, my God, why have you forsaken me?"
Some of the bystanders who heard it said,
    "Look, he is calling Elijah."
One of them ran, soaked a sponge with wine, put it on a reed
    and gave it to him to drink saying,
    "Wait, let us see if Elijah comes to take him down."
Jesus gave a loud cry and breathed his last.

*Here all kneel and pause for a short time.*

The veil of the sanctuary was torn in two from top to bottom.
When the centurion who stood facing him
    saw how he breathed his last he said,
    "Truly this man was the Son of God!"

## Gospel (cont.)

John 13:1-15; L39ABC

For he knew who would betray him;
    for this reason, he said, "Not all of you are clean."
So when he had washed their feet
    and put his garments back on and reclined at table again,
    he said to them, "Do you realize what I have done for you?
You call me 'teacher' and 'master,' and rightly so, for indeed I am.
If I, therefore, the master and teacher, have washed your feet,
    you ought to wash one another's feet.
I have given you a model to follow,
    so that as I have done for you, you should also do."

### FIRST READING

Exod 12:1-8, 11-14

The LORD said to Moses and Aaron in the land
        of Egypt,
    "This month shall stand at the head of
        your calendar;
    you shall reckon it the first month of the
        year.
Tell the whole community of Israel:
    On the tenth of this month every one of
        your families
    must procure for itself a lamb, one apiece
        for each household.
If a family is too small for a whole lamb,
    it shall join the nearest household in
        procuring one
    and shall share in the lamb
    in proportion to the number of persons
        who partake of it.
The lamb must be a year-old male and
        without blemish.
You may take it from either the sheep or the
        goats.
You shall keep it until the fourteenth day of
        this month,
    and then, with the whole assembly of Israel
        present,
    it shall be slaughtered during the evening
        twilight.
They shall take some of its blood
    and apply it to the two doorposts and the
        lintel
    of every house in which they partake of
        the lamb.
That same night they shall eat its roasted
        flesh
    with unleavened bread and bitter herbs.

"This is how you are to eat it:
    with your loins girt, sandals on your feet
        and your staff in hand,
    you shall eat like those who are in flight.

It is the Passover of the LORD.
For on this same night I will go through
        Egypt,
    striking down every firstborn of the land,
        both man and beast,
    and executing judgment on all the gods of
        Egypt—I, the LORD!
But the blood will mark the houses where you
        are.
Seeing the blood, I will pass over you;
    thus, when I strike the land of Egypt,
    no destructive blow will come upon you.

"This day shall be a memorial feast for you,
    which all your generations shall celebrate
    with pilgrimage to the LORD, as a perpetual
        institution."

### RESPONSORIAL PSALM

Ps 116:12-13, 15-16bc, 17-18

℟. (cf. 1 Cor 10:16) Our blessing-cup is a
        communion with the Blood of Christ.

How shall I make a return to the LORD
    for all the good he has done for me?
The cup of salvation I will take up,
    and I will call upon the name of the LORD.

℟. Our blessing-cup is a communion with the
        Blood of Christ.

Precious in the eyes of the LORD
    is the death of his faithful ones.
I am your servant, the son of your handmaid;
    you have loosed my bonds.

℟. Our blessing-cup is a communion with the
        Blood of Christ.

To you will I offer sacrifice of thanksgiving,
    and I will call upon the name of the LORD.
My vows to the LORD I will pay
    in the presence of all his people.

℟. Our blessing-cup is a communion with the
        Blood of Christ.

### SECOND READING

1 Cor 11:23-26

Brothers and sisters:
I received from the Lord what I also handed
        on to you,
    that the Lord Jesus, on the night he was
        handed over,
    took bread, and, after he had given thanks,
    broke it and said, "This is my body that is
        for you.
Do this in remembrance of me."
In the same way also the cup, after supper,
        saying,
    "This cup is the new covenant in my blood.
Do this, as often as you drink it, in
        remembrance of me."
For as often as you eat this bread and drink
        the cup,
    you proclaim the death of the Lord until he
        comes.

## Gospel (cont.)

John 18:1–19:42; L40ABC

So the band of soldiers, the tribune, and the Jewish guards seized Jesus,
bound him, and brought him to Annas first.
He was the father-in-law of Caiaphas,
who was high priest that year.
It was Caiaphas who had counseled the Jews
that it was better that one man should die rather than the people.

Simon Peter and another disciple followed Jesus.
Now the other disciple was known to the high priest,
and he entered the courtyard of the high priest with Jesus.
But Peter stood at the gate outside.
So the other disciple, the acquaintance of the high priest,
went out and spoke to the gatekeeper and brought Peter in.
Then the maid who was the gatekeeper said to Peter,
"You are not one of this man's disciples, are you?"
He said, "I am not."
Now the slaves and the guards were standing around a charcoal fire
that they had made, because it was cold,
and were warming themselves.
Peter was also standing there keeping warm.

The high priest questioned Jesus
about his disciples and about his doctrine.
Jesus answered him,
"I have spoken publicly to the world.
I have always taught in a synagogue
or in the temple area where all the Jews gather,
and in secret I have said nothing. Why ask me?
Ask those who heard me what I said to them.
They know what I said."
When he had said this,
one of the temple guards standing there struck Jesus and said,
"Is this the way you answer the high priest?"
Jesus answered him,
"If I have spoken wrongly, testify to the wrong;
but if I have spoken rightly, why do you strike me?"
Then Annas sent him bound to Caiaphas the high priest.

Now Simon Peter was standing there keeping warm.
And they said to him,
"You are not one of his disciples, are you?"
He denied it and said,
"I am not."
One of the slaves of the high priest,
a relative of the one whose ear Peter had cut off, said,
"Didn't I see you in the garden with him?"
Again Peter denied it.
And immediately the cock crowed.

Then they brought Jesus from Caiaphas to the praetorium.
It was morning.
And they themselves did not enter the praetorium,
in order not to be defiled so that they could eat the Passover.
So Pilate came out to them and said,
"What charge do you bring against this man?"
They answered and said to him,
"If he were not a criminal,
we would not have handed him over to you."
At this, Pilate said to them,
"Take him yourselves, and judge him according to your law."

The Jews answered him,
"We do not have the right to execute anyone,"
in order that the word of Jesus might be fulfilled
that he said indicating the kind of death he would die.
So Pilate went back into the praetorium
and summoned Jesus and said to him,
"Are you the King of the Jews?"
Jesus answered,
"Do you say this on your own
or have others told you about me?"
Pilate answered,
"I am not a Jew, am I?
Your own nation and the chief priests handed you over to me.
What have you done?"
Jesus answered,
"My kingdom does not belong to this world.
If my kingdom did belong to this world,
my attendants would be fighting
to keep me from being handed over to the Jews.
But as it is, my kingdom is not here."
So Pilate said to him,
"Then you are a king?"
Jesus answered,
"You say I am a king.
For this I was born and for this I came into the world,
to testify to the truth.
Everyone who belongs to the truth listens to my voice."
Pilate said to him, "What is truth?"

When he had said this,
he again went out to the Jews and said to them,
"I find no guilt in him.
But you have a custom that I release one prisoner to you at Passover.
Do you want me to release to you the King of the Jews?"
They cried out again,
"Not this one but Barabbas!"
Now Barabbas was a revolutionary.

Then Pilate took Jesus and had him scourged.
And the soldiers wove a crown out of thorns and placed it on his head,
and clothed him in a purple cloak,
and they came to him and said,
"Hail, King of the Jews!"
And they struck him repeatedly.
Once more Pilate went out and said to them,
"Look, I am bringing him out to you,
so that you may know that I find no guilt in him."
So Jesus came out,
wearing the crown of thorns and the purple cloak.
And he said to them, "Behold, the man!"
When the chief priests and the guards saw him they cried out,
"Crucify him, crucify him!"
Pilate said to them,
"Take him yourselves and crucify him.
I find no guilt in him."
The Jews answered,
"We have a law, and according to that law he ought to die,
because he made himself the Son of God."
Now when Pilate heard this statement,

he became even more afraid,
and went back into the praetorium and said to Jesus,
"Where are you from?"
Jesus did not answer him.
So Pilate said to him,
"Do you not speak to me?
Do you not know that I have power to release you
and I have power to crucify you?"
Jesus answered him,
"You would have no power over me
if it had not been given to you from above.
For this reason the one who handed me over to you
has the greater sin."
Consequently, Pilate tried to release him; but the Jews cried out,
"If you release him, you are not a Friend of Caesar.
Everyone who makes himself a king opposes Caesar."

When Pilate heard these words he brought Jesus out
and seated him on the judge's bench
in the place called Stone Pavement, in Hebrew, Gabbatha.
It was preparation day for Passover, and it was about noon.
And he said to the Jews,
"Behold, your king!"
They cried out,
"Take him away, take him away! Crucify him!"
Pilate said to them,
"Shall I crucify your king?"
The chief priests answered,
"We have no king but Caesar."
Then he handed him over to them to be crucified.

So they took Jesus, and, carrying the cross himself,
he went out to what is called the Place of the Skull,
in Hebrew, Golgotha.
There they crucified him, and with him two others,
one on either side, with Jesus in the middle.
Pilate also had an inscription written and put on the cross.
It read,
"Jesus the Nazorean, the King of the Jews."
Now many of the Jews read this inscription,
because the place where Jesus was crucified was near the city;
and it was written in Hebrew, Latin, and Greek.
So the chief priests of the Jews said to Pilate,
"Do not write 'The King of the Jews,'
but that he said, 'I am the King of the Jews.'"
Pilate answered,
"What I have written, I have written."

When the soldiers had crucified Jesus,
they took his clothes and divided them into four shares,
a share for each soldier.
They also took his tunic, but the tunic was seamless,
woven in one piece from the top down.
So they said to one another,
"Let's not tear it, but cast lots for it to see whose it will be,"
in order that the passage of Scripture might be fulfilled that says:
*They divided my garments among them,*
*and for my vesture they cast lots.*
This is what the soldiers did.

Standing by the cross of Jesus were his mother
and his mother's sister, Mary the wife of Clopas,
and Mary of Magdala.
When Jesus saw his mother and the disciple there whom he loved
he said to his mother, "Woman, behold, your son."
Then he said to the disciple,
"Behold, your mother."
And from that hour the disciple took her into his home.

After this, aware that everything was now finished,
in order that the Scripture might be fulfilled,
Jesus said, "I thirst."
There was a vessel filled with common wine.
So they put a sponge soaked in wine on a sprig of hyssop
and put it up to his mouth.
When Jesus had taken the wine, he said,
"It is finished."
And bowing his head, he handed over the spirit.

*Here all kneel and pause for a short time.*

Now since it was preparation day,
in order that the bodies might not remain
on the cross on the sabbath,
for the sabbath day of that week was a solemn one,
the Jews asked Pilate that their legs be broken
and that they be taken down.
So the soldiers came and broke the legs of the first
and then of the other one who was crucified with Jesus.
But when they came to Jesus and saw that he was already dead,
they did not break his legs,
but one soldier thrust his lance into his side,
and immediately blood and water flowed out.
An eyewitness has testified, and his testimony is true;
he knows that he is speaking the truth,
so that you also may come to believe.
For this happened so that the Scripture passage might be fulfilled:
*Not a bone of it will be broken.*
And again another passage says:
*They will look upon him whom they have pierced.*

After this, Joseph of Arimathea,
secretly a disciple of Jesus for fear of the Jews,
asked Pilate if he could remove the body of Jesus.
And Pilate permitted it.
So he came and took his body.
Nicodemus, the one who had first come to him at night,
also came bringing a mixture of myrrh and aloes
weighing about one hundred pounds.
They took the body of Jesus
and bound it with burial cloths along with the spices,
according to the Jewish burial custom.
Now in the place where he had been crucified there was a garden,
and in the garden a new tomb, in which no one had yet been buried.
So they laid Jesus there because of the Jewish preparation day;
for the tomb was close by.

## FIRST READING
Isa 52:13–53:12

See, my servant shall prosper,
  he shall be raised high and greatly exalted.
Even as many were amazed at him—
    so marred was his look beyond human
      semblance
    and his appearance beyond that of the sons
      of man—
so shall he startle many nations,
    because of him kings shall stand
      speechless;
for those who have not been told shall see,
    those who have not heard shall ponder it.

Who would believe what we have heard?
  To whom has the arm of the LORD been
    revealed?
He grew up like a sapling before him,
  like a shoot from the parched earth;
there was in him no stately bearing to make
      us look at him,
    nor appearance that would attract us to him.
He was spurned and avoided by people,
    a man of suffering, accustomed to infirmity,
one of those from whom people hide their
      faces,
    spurned, and we held him in no esteem.

Yet it was our infirmities that he bore,
    our sufferings that he endured,
while we thought of him as stricken,
    as one smitten by God and afflicted.
But he was pierced for our offenses,
    crushed for our sins;
upon him was the chastisement that makes
      us whole,
    by his stripes we were healed.
We had all gone astray like sheep,
    each following his own way;
but the LORD laid upon him
    the guilt of us all.

Though he was harshly treated, he submitted
    and opened not his mouth;
like a lamb led to the slaughter
    or a sheep before the shearers,
    he was silent and opened not his mouth.
Oppressed and condemned, he was taken away,
    and who would have thought any more of
      his destiny?
When he was cut off from the land of the
      living,
    and smitten for the sin of his people,
a grave was assigned him among the wicked
    and a burial place with evildoers,
though he had done no wrong
    nor spoken any falsehood.
But the LORD was pleased
    to crush him in infirmity.

If he gives his life as an offering for sin,
    he shall see his descendants in a long life,
    and the will of the LORD shall be
      accomplished through him.

Because of his affliction
    he shall see the light
    in fullness of days;
through his suffering, my servant shall justify
      many,
    and their guilt he shall bear.
Therefore I will give him his portion among
      the great,
    and he shall divide the spoils with the
      mighty,
because he surrendered himself to death
    and was counted among the wicked;
and he shall take away the sins of many,
    and win pardon for their offenses.

## RESPONSORIAL PSALM
Ps 31:2, 6, 12-13, 15-16, 17, 25

℞. (Luke 23:46) Father, into your hands I
  commend my spirit.

In you, O LORD, I take refuge;
  let me never be put to shame.
In your justice rescue me.
Into your hands I commend my spirit;
  you will redeem me, O LORD, O faithful God.

℞. Father, into your hands I commend my
  spirit.

For all my foes I am an object of reproach,
  a laughingstock to my neighbors, and a
      dread to my friends;
  they who see me abroad flee from me.
I am forgotten like the unremembered dead;
  I am like a dish that is broken.

℞. Father, into your hands I commend my
  spirit.

But my trust is in you, O LORD;
  I say, "You are my God.
In your hands is my destiny; rescue me
  from the clutches of my enemies and my
      persecutors."

℞. Father, into your hands I commend my
  spirit.

Let your face shine upon your servant;
  save me in your kindness.
Take courage and be stouthearted,
  all you who hope in the LORD.

℞. Father, into your hands I commend my
  spirit.

## SECOND READING
Heb 4:14-16; 5:7-9

Brothers and sisters:
Since we have a great high priest who has
      passed through the heavens,
  Jesus, the Son of God,
  let us hold fast to our confession.
For we do not have a high priest
  who is unable to sympathize with our
      weaknesses,
  but one who has similarly been tested in
      every way,
  yet without sin.
So let us confidently approach the throne of
      grace
  to receive mercy and to find grace for
      timely help.

In the days when Christ was in the flesh,
  he offered prayers and supplications with
      loud cries and tears
  to the one who was able to save him from
      death,
  and he was heard because of his reverence.
Son though he was, he learned obedience from
      what he suffered;
  and when he was made perfect,
  he became the source of eternal salvation
      for all who obey him.

**FIRST READING**
Gen 1:1–2:2

In the beginning, when God created the
heavens and the earth,
the earth was a formless wasteland, and
darkness covered the abyss,
while a mighty wind swept over the waters.

Then God said,
"Let there be light," and there was light.
God saw how good the light was.
God then separated the light from the
darkness.
God called the light "day," and the darkness
he called "night."
Thus evening came, and morning followed—
the first day.

Then God said,
"Let there be a dome in the middle of the
waters,
to separate one body of water from the
other."
And so it happened:
God made the dome,
and it separated the water above the dome
from the water below it.
God called the dome "the sky."
Evening came, and morning followed—the
second day.

Then God said,
"Let the water under the sky be gathered
into a single basin,
so that the dry land may appear."
And so it happened:
the water under the sky was gathered into
its basin,
and the dry land appeared.
God called the dry land "the earth,"
and the basin of the water he called "the
sea."
God saw how good it was.
Then God said,
"Let the earth bring forth vegetation:
every kind of plant that bears seed
and every kind of fruit tree on earth
that bears fruit with its seed in it."
And so it happened:
the earth brought forth every kind of plant
that bears seed
and every kind of fruit tree on earth
that bears fruit with its seed in it.
God saw how good it was.
Evening came, and morning followed—the
third day.

Then God said:
"Let there be lights in the dome of the sky,
to separate day from night.
Let them mark the fixed times, the days and
the years,

and serve as luminaries in the dome of the
sky,
to shed light upon the earth."
And so it happened:
God made the two great lights,
the greater one to govern the day,
and the lesser one to govern the night;
and he made the stars.
God set them in the dome of the sky,
to shed light upon the earth,
to govern the day and the night,
and to separate the light from the darkness.
God saw how good it was.
Evening came, and morning followed—the
fourth day.

Then God said,
"Let the water teem with an abundance of
living creatures,
and on the earth let birds fly beneath the
dome of the sky."
And so it happened:
God created the great sea monsters
and all kinds of swimming creatures with
which the water teems,
and all kinds of winged birds.
God saw how good it was, and God blessed
them, saying,
"Be fertile, multiply, and fill the water of
the seas;
and let the birds multiply on the earth."
Evening came, and morning followed—the
fifth day.

Then God said,
"Let the earth bring forth all kinds of living
creatures:
cattle, creeping things, and wild animals of
all kinds."
And so it happened:
God made all kinds of wild animals, all
kinds of cattle,
and all kinds of creeping things of the
earth.
God saw how good it was.
Then God said:
"Let us make man in our image, after our
likeness.
Let them have dominion over the fish of the
sea,
the birds of the air, and the cattle,
and over all the wild animals
and all the creatures that crawl on the
ground."
God created man in his image;
in the image of God he created him;
male and female he created them.
God blessed them, saying:
"Be fertile and multiply;
fill the earth and subdue it.
Have dominion over the fish of the sea, the
birds of the air,

and all the living things that move on the
earth."
God also said:
"See, I give you every seed-bearing plant all
over the earth
and every tree that has seed-bearing fruit
on it to be your food;
and to all the animals of the land, all the
birds of the air,
and all the living creatures that crawl on
the ground,
I give all the green plants for food."
And so it happened.
God looked at everything he had made, and he
found it very good.
Evening came, and morning followed—the
sixth day.

Thus the heavens and the earth and all their
array were completed.
Since on the seventh day God was finished
with the work he had been doing,
he rested on the seventh day from all the
work he had undertaken.

*or*

Gen 1:1, 26-31a

In the beginning, when God created the
heavens and the earth,
God said: "Let us make man in our image,
after our likeness.
Let them have dominion over the fish of the
sea,
the birds of the air, and the cattle,
and over all the wild animals
and all the creatures that crawl on the
ground."
God created man in his image;
in the image of God he created him;
male and female he created them.
God blessed them, saying:
"Be fertile and multiply;
fill the earth and subdue it.
Have dominion over the fish of the sea, the
birds of the air,
and all the living things that move on the
earth."
God also said:
"See, I give you every seed-bearing plant all
over the earth
and every tree that has seed-bearing fruit
on it to be your food;
and to all the animals of the land, all the
birds of the air,
and all the living creatures that crawl on
the ground,
I give all the green plants for food."
And so it happened.
God looked at everything he had made, and he
found it very good.

**RESPONSORIAL PSALM**

Ps 104:1-2, 5-6, 10, 12, 13-14, 24, 35

℟. (30) Lord, send out your Spirit, and renew
    the face of the earth.

Bless the LORD, O my soul!
    O LORD, my God, you are great indeed!
You are clothed with majesty and glory,
    robed in light as with a cloak.

℟. Lord, send out your Spirit, and renew the
    face of the earth.

You fixed the earth upon its foundation,
    not to be moved forever;
with the ocean, as with a garment, you
    covered it;
    above the mountains the waters stood.

℟. Lord, send out your Spirit, and renew the
    face of the earth.

You send forth springs into the watercourses
    that wind among the mountains.
Beside them the birds of heaven dwell;
    from among the branches they send forth
        their song.

℟. Lord, send out your Spirit, and renew the
    face of the earth.

You water the mountains from your palace;
    the earth is replete with the fruit of your
        works.
You raise grass for the cattle,
    and vegetation for man's use,
producing bread from the earth.

℟. Lord, send out your Spirit, and renew the
    face of the earth.

How manifold are your works, O LORD!
    In wisdom you have wrought them all—
the earth is full of your creatures.
    Bless the LORD, O my soul!

℟. Lord, send out your Spirit, and renew the
    face of the earth.

*or*

Ps 33:4-5, 6-7, 12-13, 20 and 22

℟. (5b) The earth is full of the goodness of
    the Lord.

Upright is the word of the LORD,
    and all his works are trustworthy.
He loves justice and right;
    of the kindness of the LORD the earth is full.

℟. The earth is full of the goodness of the Lord.

By the word of the LORD the heavens were
    made;
    by the breath of his mouth all their host.
He gathers the waters of the sea as in a flask;
    in cellars he confines the deep.

℟. The earth is full of the goodness of the Lord.

Blessed the nation whose God is the LORD,
    the people he has chosen for his own
        inheritance.
From heaven the LORD looks down;
    he sees all mankind.

℟. The earth is full of the goodness of the Lord.

Our soul waits for the LORD,
    who is our help and our shield.
May your kindness, O LORD, be upon us
    who have put our hope in you.

℟. The earth is full of the goodness of the Lord.

**SECOND READING**

Gen 22:1-18

God put Abraham to the test.
He called to him, "Abraham!"
"Here I am," he replied.
Then God said:
    "Take your son Isaac, your only one, whom
        you love,
    and go to the land of Moriah.
There you shall offer him up as a holocaust
    on a height that I will point out to you."
Early the next morning Abraham saddled his
        donkey,
    took with him his son Isaac and two of his
        servants as well,
    and with the wood that he had cut for the
        holocaust,
    set out for the place of which God had told
        him.

On the third day Abraham got sight of the
        place from afar.
Then he said to his servants:
    "Both of you stay here with the donkey,
    while the boy and I go on over yonder.
We will worship and then come back to you."
Thereupon Abraham took the wood for the
        holocaust
    and laid it on his son Isaac's shoulders,
    while he himself carried the fire and the
        knife.
As the two walked on together, Isaac spoke to
        his father Abraham:
    "Father!" Isaac said.
"Yes, son," he replied.
Isaac continued, "Here are the fire and the
        wood,
    but where is the sheep for the holocaust?"
"Son," Abraham answered,
    "God himself will provide the sheep for the
        holocaust."
Then the two continued going forward.

When they came to the place of which God
        had told him,
    Abraham built an altar there and arranged
        the wood on it.

Next he tied up his son Isaac,
    and put him on top of the wood on the
        altar.
Then he reached out and took the knife to
    slaughter his son.
But the LORD's messenger called to him from
        heaven,
    "Abraham, Abraham!"
"Here I am," he answered.
"Do not lay your hand on the boy," said the
    messenger.
"Do not do the least thing to him.
I know now how devoted you are to God,
    since you did not withhold from me your
        own beloved son."
As Abraham looked about,
    he spied a ram caught by its horns in the
        thicket.
So he went and took the ram
    and offered it up as a holocaust in place of
        his son.
Abraham named the site Yahweh-yireh;
    hence people now say, "On the mountain
        the LORD will see."

Again the LORD's messenger called to
        Abraham from heaven and said:
    "I swear by myself, declares the LORD,
    that because you acted as you did
    in not withholding from me your beloved
        son,
    I will bless you abundantly
    and make your descendants as countless
    as the stars of the sky and the sands of the
        seashore;
    your descendants shall take possession
    of the gates of their enemies,
    and in your descendants all the nations of
        the earth
        shall find blessing—
    all this because you obeyed my command."

*or*

Gen 22:1-2, 9a, 10-13, 15-18

God put Abraham to the test.
He called to him, "Abraham!"
"Here I am," he replied.
Then God said:
    "Take your son Isaac, your only one, whom
        you love,
    and go to the land of Moriah.
There you shall offer him up as a holocaust
    on a height that I will point out to you."

When they came to the place of which God
        had told him,
    Abraham built an altar there and arranged
        the wood on it.
Then he reached out and took the knife to
    slaughter his son.

But the Lord's messenger called to him from
heaven,
"Abraham, Abraham!"
"Here I am," he answered.
"Do not lay your hand on the boy," said the
messenger.
"Do not do the least thing to him.
I know now how devoted you are to God,
since you did not withhold from me your
own beloved son."
As Abraham looked about,
he spied a ram caught by its horns in the
thicket.
So he went and took the ram
and offered it up as a holocaust in place of
his son.

Again the Lord's messenger called to
Abraham from heaven and said:
"I swear by myself, declares the Lord,
that because you acted as you did
in not withholding from me your beloved
son,
I will bless you abundantly
and make your descendants as countless
as the stars of the sky and the sands of the
seashore;
your descendants shall take possession
of the gates of their enemies,
and in your descendants all the nations of
the earth
shall find blessing—
all this because you obeyed my command."

## RESPONSORIAL PSALM
Ps 16:5, 8, 9-10, 11

R̸. (1) You are my inheritance, O Lord.

O Lord, my allotted portion and my cup,
you it is who hold fast my lot.
I set the Lord ever before me;
with him at my right hand I shall not be
disturbed.

R̸. You are my inheritance, O Lord.

Therefore my heart is glad and my soul
rejoices,
my body, too, abides in confidence;
because you will not abandon my soul to the
netherworld,
nor will you suffer your faithful one to
undergo corruption.

R̸. You are my inheritance, O Lord.

You will show me the path to life,
fullness of joys in your presence,
the delights at your right hand forever.

R̸. You are my inheritance, O Lord.

## THIRD READING
Exod 14:15–15:1

The Lord said to Moses, "Why are you crying
out to me?
Tell the Israelites to go forward.
And you, lift up your staff and, with hand
outstretched over the sea,
split the sea in two,
that the Israelites may pass through it on
dry land.
But I will make the Egyptians so obstinate
that they will go in after them.
Then I will receive glory through Pharaoh and
all his army,
his chariots and charioteers.
The Egyptians shall know that I am the Lord,
when I receive glory through Pharaoh
and his chariots and charioteers."

The angel of God, who had been leading
Israel's camp,
now moved and went around behind them.
The column of cloud also, leaving the front,
took up its place behind them,
so that it came between the camp of the
Egyptians
and that of Israel.
But the cloud now became dark, and thus the
night passed
without the rival camps coming any closer
together all night long.
Then Moses stretched out his hand over the
sea,
and the Lord swept the sea
with a strong east wind throughout the
night
and so turned it into dry land.
When the water was thus divided,
the Israelites marched into the midst of the
sea on dry land,
with the water like a wall to their right and
to their left.

The Egyptians followed in pursuit;
all Pharaoh's horses and chariots and
charioteers went after them
right into the midst of the sea.
In the night watch just before dawn
the Lord cast through the column of the
fiery cloud
upon the Egyptian force a glance that
threw it into a panic;
and he so clogged their chariot wheels
that they could hardly drive.
With that the Egyptians sounded the retreat
before Israel,
because the Lord was fighting for them
against the Egyptians.

Then the Lord told Moses, "Stretch out your
hand over the sea,
that the water may flow back upon the
Egyptians,
upon their chariots and their charioteers."
So Moses stretched out his hand over the sea,
and at dawn the sea flowed back to its
normal depth.
The Egyptians were fleeing head on toward
the sea,
when the Lord hurled them into its midst.
As the water flowed back,
it covered the chariots and the charioteers
of Pharaoh's whole army
which had followed the Israelites into the sea.
Not a single one of them escaped.
But the Israelites had marched on dry land
through the midst of the sea,
with the water like a wall to their right and
to their left.
Thus the Lord saved Israel on that day
from the power of the Egyptians.
When Israel saw the Egyptians lying dead on
the seashore
and beheld the great power that the Lord
had shown against the Egyptians,
they feared the Lord and believed in him
and in his servant Moses.

Then Moses and the Israelites sang this song
to the Lord:
I will sing to the Lord, for he is gloriously
triumphant;
horse and chariot he has cast into the sea.

## RESPONSORIAL PSALM
Exod 15:1-2, 3-4, 5-6, 17-18

R̸. (1b) Let us sing to the Lord; he has covered
himself in glory.

I will sing to the Lord, for he is gloriously
triumphant;
horse and chariot he has cast into the sea.
My strength and my courage is the Lord,
and he has been my savior.
He is my God, I praise him;
the God of my father, I extol him.

R̸. Let us sing to the Lord; he has covered
himself in glory.

The Lord is a warrior,
Lord is his name!
Pharaoh's chariots and army he hurled into
the sea;
the elite of his officers were submerged in
the Red Sea.

R̸. Let us sing to the Lord; he has covered
himself in glory.

The flood waters covered them,
  they sank into the depths like a stone.
Your right hand, O Lord, magnificent in
    power,
  your right hand, O Lord, has shattered the
    enemy.

R̶. Let us sing to the Lord; he has covered
  himself in glory.

You brought in the people you redeemed
  and planted them on the mountain of your
    inheritance—
the place where you made your seat, O Lord,
  the sanctuary, Lord, which your hands
    established.
The Lord shall reign forever and ever.

R̶. Let us sing to the Lord; he has covered
  himself in glory.

## FOURTH READING
Isa 54:5-14

The One who has become your husband is
    your Maker;
  his name is the Lord of hosts;
your redeemer is the Holy One of Israel,
  called God of all the earth.
The Lord calls you back,
  like a wife forsaken and grieved in spirit,
  a wife married in youth and then cast off,
  says your God.
For a brief moment I abandoned you,
  but with great tenderness I will take you
    back.
In an outburst of wrath, for a moment
  I hid my face from you;
but with enduring love I take pity on you,
  says the Lord, your redeemer.
This is for me like the days of Noah,
  when I swore that the waters of Noah
  should never again deluge the earth;
so I have sworn not to be angry with you,
  or to rebuke you.
Though the mountains leave their place
  and the hills be shaken,
my love shall never leave you
  nor my covenant of peace be shaken,
  says the Lord, who has mercy on you.
O afflicted one, storm-battered and
    unconsoled,
  I lay your pavements in carnelians,
  and your foundations in sapphires;
I will make your battlements of rubies,
  your gates of carbuncles,
  and all your walls of precious stones.
All your children shall be taught by the Lord,
  and great shall be the peace of your children.

In justice shall you be established,
  far from the fear of oppression,
  where destruction cannot come near you.

## RESPONSORIAL PSALM
Ps 30:2, 4, 5-6, 11-12, 13

R̶. (2a) I will praise you, Lord, for you have
  rescued me.

I will extol you, O Lord, for you drew me clear
  and did not let my enemies rejoice over me.
O Lord, you brought me up from the
    netherworld;
  you preserved me from among those going
    down into the pit.

R̶. I will praise you, Lord, for you have
  rescued me.

Sing praise to the Lord, you his faithful ones,
  and give thanks to his holy name.
For his anger lasts but a moment;
  a lifetime, his good will.
At nightfall, weeping enters in,
  but with the dawn, rejoicing.

R̶. I will praise you, Lord, for you have
  rescued me.

Hear, O Lord, and have pity on me;
  O Lord, be my helper.
You changed my mourning into dancing;
  O Lord, my God, forever will I give you
    thanks.

R̶. I will praise you, Lord, for you have
  rescued me.

## FIFTH READING
Isa 55:1-11

Thus says the Lord:
All you who are thirsty,
  come to the water!
You who have no money,
  come, receive grain and eat;
come, without paying and without cost,
  drink wine and milk!
Why spend your money for what is not bread,
  your wages for what fails to satisfy?
Heed me, and you shall eat well,
  you shall delight in rich fare.
Come to me heedfully,
  listen, that you may have life.
I will renew with you the everlasting covenant,
  the benefits assured to David.
As I made him a witness to the peoples,
  a leader and commander of nations,
so shall you summon a nation you knew not,
  and nations that knew you not shall run
    to you,

because of the Lord, your God,
  the Holy One of Israel, who has glorified
    you.

Seek the Lord while he may be found,
  call him while he is near.
Let the scoundrel forsake his way,
  and the wicked man his thoughts;
let him turn to the Lord for mercy;
  to our God, who is generous in forgiving.
For my thoughts are not your thoughts,
  nor are your ways my ways, says the Lord.
As high as the heavens are above the earth,
  so high are my ways above your ways
  and my thoughts above your thoughts.

For just as from the heavens
  the rain and snow come down
and do not return there
  till they have watered the earth,
  making it fertile and fruitful,
giving seed to the one who sows
  and bread to the one who eats,
so shall my word be
  that goes forth from my mouth;
my word shall not return to me void,
  but shall do my will,
  achieving the end for which I sent it.

## RESPONSORIAL PSALM
Isa 12:2-3, 4, 5-6

R̶. (3) You will draw water joyfully from the
  springs of salvation.

God indeed is my savior;
  I am confident and unafraid.
My strength and my courage is the Lord,
  and he has been my savior.
With joy you will draw water
  at the fountain of salvation.

R̶. You will draw water joyfully from the
  springs of salvation.

Give thanks to the Lord, acclaim his name;
  among the nations make known his deeds,
  proclaim how exalted is his name.

R̶. You will draw water joyfully from the
  springs of salvation.

Sing praise to the Lord for his glorious
    achievement;
  let this be known throughout all the earth.
Shout with exultation, O city of Zion,
  for great in your midst
  is the Holy One of Israel!

R̶. You will draw water joyfully from the
  springs of salvation.

## SIXTH READING
Bar 3:9-15, 32–4:4

Hear, O Israel, the commandments of life:
  listen, and know prudence!
How is it, Israel,
  that you are in the land of your foes,
  grown old in a foreign land,
defiled with the dead,
  accounted with those destined for the
    netherworld?
You have forsaken the fountain of wisdom!
  Had you walked in the way of God,
  you would have dwelt in enduring peace.
Learn where prudence is,
  where strength, where understanding;
that you may know also
  where are length of days, and life,
  where light of the eyes, and peace.
Who has found the place of wisdom,
  who has entered into her treasuries?

The One who knows all things knows her;
  he has probed her by his knowledge—
the One who established the earth for all time,
  and filled it with four-footed beasts;
he who dismisses the light, and it departs,
  calls it, and it obeys him trembling;
before whom the stars at their posts
  shine and rejoice;
when he calls them, they answer, "Here we are!"
  shining with joy for their Maker.
Such is our God;
  no other is to be compared to him:
he has traced out the whole way of
    understanding,
  and has given her to Jacob, his servant,
  to Israel, his beloved son.

Since then she has appeared on earth,
  and moved among people.
She is the book of the precepts of God,
  the law that endures forever;
all who cling to her will live,
  but those will die who forsake her.
Turn, O Jacob, and receive her:
  walk by her light toward splendor.
Give not your glory to another,
  your privileges to an alien race.
Blessed are we, O Israel;
  for what pleases God is known to us!

## RESPONSORIAL PSALM
Ps 19:8, 9, 10, 11

R̖. (John 6:68c) Lord, you have the words of
  everlasting life.

The law of the Lord is perfect,
  refreshing the soul;
the decree of the Lord is trustworthy,
  giving wisdom to the simple.

R̖. Lord, you have the words of everlasting life.

The precepts of the Lord are right,
  rejoicing the heart;
the command of the Lord is clear,
  enlightening the eye.

R̖. Lord, you have the words of everlasting life.

The fear of the Lord is pure,
  enduring forever;
the ordinances of the Lord are true,
  all of them just.

R̖. Lord, you have the words of everlasting life.

They are more precious than gold,
  than a heap of purest gold;
sweeter also than syrup
  or honey from the comb.

R̖. Lord, you have the words of everlasting life.

## SEVENTH READING
Ezek 36:16-17a, 18-28

The word of the Lord came to me, saying:
  Son of man, when the house of Israel lived
    in their land,
  they defiled it by their conduct and deeds.
Therefore I poured out my fury upon them
  because of the blood that they poured out
    on the ground,
  and because they defiled it with idols.
I scattered them among the nations,
  dispersing them over foreign lands;
  according to their conduct and deeds I
    judged them.
But when they came among the nations
    wherever they came,
  they served to profane my holy name,
  because it was said of them: "These are the
    people of the Lord,
  yet they had to leave their land."
So I have relented because of my holy name
  which the house of Israel profaned
  among the nations where they came.
Therefore say to the house of Israel: Thus
    says the Lord God:
  Not for your sakes do I act, house of Israel,
  but for the sake of my holy name,
  which you profaned among the nations to
    which you came.
I will prove the holiness of my great name,
  profaned among the nations,
  in whose midst you have profaned it.
Thus the nations shall know that I am the
    Lord, says the Lord God,
  when in their sight I prove my holiness
    through you.
For I will take you away from among the nations,
  gather you from all the foreign lands,
  and bring you back to your own land.
I will sprinkle clean water upon you
  to cleanse you from all your impurities,
  and from all your idols I will cleanse you.

I will give you a new heart and place a new
    spirit within you,
  taking from your bodies your stony hearts
  and giving you natural hearts.
I will put my spirit within you and make you
    live by my statutes,
  careful to observe my decrees.
You shall live in the land I gave your fathers;
  you shall be my people, and I will be your
    God.

## RESPONSORIAL PSALM
Ps 42:3, 5; 43:3, 4

R̖. (42:2) Like a deer that longs for running
  streams, my soul longs for you, my God.

Athirst is my soul for God, the living God.
  When shall I go and behold the face of God?

R̖. Like a deer that longs for running streams,
  my soul longs for you, my God.

I went with the throng
  and led them in procession to the house of God,
amid loud cries of joy and thanksgiving,
  with the multitude keeping festival.

R̖. Like a deer that longs for running streams,
  my soul longs for you, my God.

Send forth your light and your fidelity;
  they shall lead me on
and bring me to your holy mountain,
  to your dwelling-place.

R̖. Like a deer that longs for running streams,
  my soul longs for you, my God.

Then will I go in to the altar of God,
  the God of my gladness and joy;
then will I give you thanks upon the harp,
  O God, my God!

R̖. Like a deer that longs for running streams,
  my soul longs for you, my God.

*or*

Isa 12:2-3, 4bcd, 5-6

R̖. (3) You will draw water joyfully from the
  springs of salvation.

God indeed is my savior;
  I am confident and unafraid.
My strength and my courage is the Lord,
  and he has been my savior.
With joy you will draw water
  at the fountain of salvation.

R̖. You will draw water joyfully from the
  springs of salvation.

Give thanks to the Lord, acclaim his name;
  among the nations make known his deeds,
  proclaim how exalted is his name.

R̖. You will draw water joyfully from the
  springs of salvation.

Sing praise to the Lord for his glorious
    achievement;
    let this be known throughout all the earth.
Shout with exultation, O city of Zion,
    for great in your midst
    is the Holy One of Israel!

℞. You will draw water joyfully from the
    springs of salvation.

*or*

Ps 51:12-13, 14-15, 18-19

℞. (12a) Create a clean heart in me, O God.

A clean heart create for me, O God,
    and a steadfast spirit renew within me.
Cast me not out from your presence,
    and your Holy Spirit take not from me.

℞. Create a clean heart in me, O God.

Give me back the joy of your salvation,
    and a willing spirit sustain in me.
I will teach transgressors your ways,
    and sinners shall return to you.

℞. Create a clean heart in me, O God.

For you are not pleased with sacrifices;
    should I offer a holocaust, you would not
      accept it.
My sacrifice, O God, is a contrite spirit;
    a heart contrite and humbled, O God, you
      will not spurn.

℞. Create a clean heart in me, O God.

**EPISTLE**
Rom 6:3-11

Brothers and sisters:
Are you unaware that we who were baptized
    into Christ Jesus
    were baptized into his death?
We were indeed buried with him through
    baptism into death,
    so that, just as Christ was raised from the
      dead
    by the glory of the Father,
    we too might live in newness of life.

For if we have grown into union with him
    through a death like his,
    we shall also be united with him in the
      resurrection.
We know that our old self was crucified with
    him,
    so that our sinful body might be done away
      with,
    that we might no longer be in slavery to sin.
For a dead person has been absolved from sin.
If, then, we have died with Christ,
    we believe that we shall also live with him.
We know that Christ, raised from the dead,
    dies no more;
    death no longer has power over him.
As to his death, he died to sin once and for all;
    as to his life, he lives for God.
Consequently, you too must think of
    yourselves as being dead to sin
    and living for God in Christ Jesus.

**RESPONSORIAL PSALM**
Ps 118:1-2, 16-17, 22-23

℞. Alleluia, alleluia, alleluia.

Give thanks to the Lord, for he is good,
    for his mercy endures forever.
Let the house of Israel say,
    "His mercy endures forever."

℞. Alleluia, alleluia, alleluia.

The right hand of the Lord has struck with
    power;
    the right hand of the Lord is exalted.
I shall not die, but live,
    and declare the works of the Lord.

℞. Alleluia, alleluia, alleluia.

The stone which the builders rejected
    has become the cornerstone.
By the Lord has this been done;
    it is wonderful in our eyes.

℞. Alleluia, alleluia, alleluia.

## *Gospel*

Mark 16:1-7; L41B

When the sabbath was over,
    Mary Magdalene, Mary, the mother of James, and Salome
    bought spices so that they might go and anoint him.
Very early when the sun had risen,
    on the first day of the week, they came to the tomb.
They were saying to one another,
    "Who will roll back the stone for us
    from the entrance to the tomb?"
When they looked up,
    they saw that the stone had been rolled back;
    it was very large.

On entering the tomb they saw a young man
    sitting on the right side, clothed in a white robe,
    and they were utterly amazed.
He said to them, "Do not be amazed!
You seek Jesus of Nazareth, the crucified.
He has been raised; he is not here.
Behold the place where they laid him.
But go and tell his disciples and Peter,
    'He is going before you to Galilee;
    there you will see him, as he told you.'"

or, at an afternoon or evening Mass

## *Gospel*

Luke 24:13-35; L46

That very day, the first day of the week,
    two of Jesus' disciples were going
    to a village seven miles from Jerusalem called Emmaus,
    and they were conversing about all the things that had occurred.
And it happened that while they were conversing and debating,
    Jesus himself drew near and walked with them,
    but their eyes were prevented from recognizing him.
He asked them,
    "What are you discussing as you walk along?"
They stopped, looking downcast.
One of them, named Cleopas, said to him in reply,
    "Are you the only visitor to Jerusalem
    who does not know of the things
    that have taken place there in these days?"
And he replied to them, "What sort of things?"
They said to him,
    "The things that happened to Jesus the Nazarene,
    who was a prophet mighty in deed and word
    before God and all the people,
    how our chief priests and rulers both handed him over
    to a sentence of death and crucified him.
But we were hoping that he would be the one to redeem Israel;
    and besides all this,
    it is now the third day since this took place.
Some women from our group, however, have astounded us:
    they were at the tomb early in the morning
    and did not find his body;
    they came back and reported
    that they had indeed seen a vision of angels
    who announced that he was alive.

Then some of those with us went to the tomb
    and found things just as the women had described,
    but him they did not see."
And he said to them, "Oh, how foolish you are!
How slow of heart to believe all that the prophets spoke!
Was it not necessary that the Christ should suffer these things
    and enter into his glory?"
Then beginning with Moses and all the prophets,
    he interpreted to them what referred to him
    in all the Scriptures.
As they approached the village to which they were going,
    he gave the impression that he was going on farther.
But they urged him, "Stay with us,
    for it is nearly evening and the day is almost over."
So he went in to stay with them.
And it happened that, while he was with them at table,
    he took bread, said the blessing,
    broke it, and gave it to them.
With that their eyes were opened and they recognized him,
    but he vanished from their sight.
Then they said to each other,
    "Were not our hearts burning within us
    while he spoke to us on the way and opened the Scriptures to us?"
So they set out at once and returned to Jerusalem
    where they found gathered together
    the eleven and those with them who were saying,
    "The Lord has truly been raised and has appeared to Simon!"
Then the two recounted
    what had taken place on the way
    and how he was made known to them in the breaking of the bread.

## FIRST READING
Acts 10:34a, 37-43

Peter proceeded to speak and said:
"You know what has happened all over Judea,
    beginning in Galilee after the baptism
    that John preached,
    how God anointed Jesus of Nazareth
    with the Holy Spirit and power.
He went about doing good
    and healing all those oppressed by the devil,
    for God was with him.
We are witnesses of all that he did
    both in the country of the Jews and in
        Jerusalem.
They put him to death by hanging him on a tree.
This man God raised on the third day and
        granted that he be visible,
    not to all the people, but to us,
    the witnesses chosen by God in advance,
    who ate and drank with him after he rose
        from the dead.
He commissioned us to preach to the people
    and testify that he is the one appointed by God
    as judge of the living and the dead.
To him all the prophets bear witness,
    that everyone who believes in him
    will receive forgiveness of sins through his
        name."

## RESPONSORIAL PSALM
Ps 118:1-2, 16-17, 22-23

℟. (24) This is the day the Lord has made; let
    us rejoice and be glad.
    *or:*
℟. Alleluia.

Give thanks to the LORD, for he is good,
    for his mercy endures forever.
Let the house of Israel say,
    "His mercy endures forever."

℟. This is the day the Lord has made; let us
    rejoice and be glad.
    *or:*
℟. Alleluia.

"The right hand of the LORD has struck with
        power;
    the right hand of the LORD is exalted.
I shall not die, but live,
    and declare the works of the LORD."

℟. This is the day the Lord has made; let us
    rejoice and be glad.
    *or:*
℟. Alleluia.

The stone which the builders rejected
    has become the cornerstone.
By the LORD has this been done;
    it is wonderful in our eyes.

℟. This is the day the Lord has made; let us
    rejoice and be glad.
    *or:*
℟. Alleluia.

## SECOND READING
1 Cor 5:6b-8

Brothers and sisters:
Do you not know that a little yeast leavens all
        the dough?
Clear out the old yeast,
    so that you may become a fresh batch of
        dough,
    inasmuch as you are unleavened.
For our paschal lamb, Christ, has been
        sacrificed.
Therefore, let us celebrate the feast,
    not with the old yeast, the yeast of malice
        and wickedness,
    but with the unleavened bread of sincerity
        and truth.

*or*

Col 3:1-4

Brothers and sisters:
If then you were raised with Christ, seek what
        is above,
    where Christ is seated at the right hand of
        God.
Think of what is above, not of what is on
        earth.
For you have died, and your life is hidden with
    Christ in God.
When Christ your life appears,
    then you too will appear with him in glory.

## SEQUENCE

*Victimae paschali laudes*
Christians, to the Paschal Victim
    Offer your thankful praises!
A Lamb the sheep redeems;
    Christ, who only is sinless,
    Reconciles sinners to the Father.
Death and life have contended in that combat
        stupendous:
    The Prince of life, who died, reigns
        immortal.
Speak, Mary, declaring
    What you saw, wayfaring.
"The tomb of Christ, who is living,
    The glory of Jesus' resurrection;
Bright angels attesting,
    The shroud and napkin resting.
Yes, Christ my hope is arisen;
    To Galilee he goes before you."
Christ indeed from death is risen, our new life
        obtaining.
    Have mercy, victor King, ever reigning!
    Amen. Alleluia.

# Second Sunday of Easter (or of Divine Mercy), *April 8, 2018*

# Gospel (cont.)
John 20:19-31; L44B

Then he said to Thomas, "Put your finger here and see my hands,
    and bring your hand and put it into my side,
    and do not be unbelieving, but believe."
Thomas answered and said to him, "My Lord and my God!"
Jesus said to him, "Have you come to believe because you have seen me?
Blessed are those who have not seen and have believed."

Now Jesus did many other signs in the presence of his disciples
    that are not written in this book.
But these are written that you may come to believe
    that Jesus is the Christ, the Son of God,
    and that through this belief you may have life in his name.

## The Annunciation of the Lord, *April 9, 2018*

### FIRST READING
Isa 7:10-14; 8:10

The LORD spoke to Ahaz, saying:
Ask for a sign from the LORD, your God;
    let it be deep as the nether world, or high as
        the sky!
But Ahaz answered,
   "I will not ask! I will not tempt the LORD!"
Then Isaiah said:
   Listen, O house of David!
Is it not enough for you to weary people,
    must you also weary my God?
Therefore the Lord himself will give you this
    sign:
   the virgin shall be with child, and bear a
      son,
   and shall name him Emmanuel,
   which means "God is with us!"

### RESPONSORIAL PSALM
Ps 40:7-8a, 8b-9, 10, 11

℟. (8a and 9a) Here I am, Lord; I come to do
   your will.

Sacrifice or offering you wished not,
   but ears open to obedience you gave me.
Holocausts and sin-offerings you sought not;
   then said I, "Behold, I come."

℟. Here I am, Lord; I come to do your will.

"In the written scroll it is prescribed for me,
To do your will, O God, is my delight,
   and your law is within my heart!"

℟. Here I am, Lord; I come to do your will.

I announced your justice in the vast assembly;
   I did not restrain my lips, as you, O LORD,
    know.

℟. Here I am, Lord; I come to do your will.

Your justice I kept not hid within my heart;
   your faithfulness and your salvation I have
    spoken of;
I have made no secret of your kindness and
   your truth
   in the vast assembly.

℟. Here I am, Lord; I come to do your will.

### SECOND READING
Heb 10:4-10

Brothers and sisters:
It is impossible that the blood of bulls and
    goats
   takes away sins.
For this reason, when Christ came into the
    world, he said:

   "Sacrifice and offering you did not desire,
    but a body you prepared for me;
   in holocausts and sin offerings you took no
    delight.
   Then I said, 'As is written of me in the
    scroll,
   behold, I come to do your will, O God.'"

First Christ says, "Sacrifices and offerings,
   holocausts and sin offerings,
   you neither desired nor delighted in."
These are offered according to the law.
Then he says, "Behold, I come to do your will."
He takes away the first to establish the second.
By this "will," we have been consecrated
   through the offering of the Body of Jesus
    Christ once for all.

---

## The Ascension of the Lord, *May 10, 2018 or May 13, 2018*

### SECOND READING
Eph 1:17-23

Brothers and sisters:
May the God of our Lord Jesus Christ, the
    Father of glory,
   give you a Spirit of wisdom and revelation
   resulting in knowledge of him.
May the eyes of your hearts be enlightened,
   that you may know what is the hope that
    belongs to his call,
   what are the riches of glory
   in his inheritance among the holy ones,
   and what is the surpassing greatness of
    his power
   for us who believe,
   in accord with the exercise of his great might,
   which he worked in Christ,
   raising him from the dead
   and seating him at his right hand in the
    heavens,
   far above every principality, authority,
    power, and dominion,
   and every name that is named
   not only in this age but also in the one to
    come.

And he put all things beneath his feet
   and gave him as head over all things to the
    church,
   which is his body,
   the fullness of the one who fills all things in
    every way.

*or*

Eph 4:1-13

Brothers and sisters,
I, a prisoner for the Lord,
   urge you to live in a manner worthy of the
    call you have received,
   with all humility and gentleness, with
    patience,
   bearing with one another through love,
   striving to preserve the unity of the Spirit
   through the bond of peace:
   one body and one Spirit,
   as you were also called to the one hope of
    your call;
   one Lord, one faith, one baptism;
   one God and Father of all,
   who is over all and through all and in all.

But grace was given to each of us
   according to the measure of Christ's gift.
Therefore, it says:
   *He ascended on high and took prisoners*
    *captive;*
   *he gave gifts to men.*
What does "he ascended" mean except that he
   also descended
   into the lower regions of the earth?
The one who descended is also the one who
   ascended
   far above all the heavens,
   that he might fill all things.

And he gave some as apostles, others as
   prophets,
   others as evangelists, others as pastors and
    teachers,
   to equip the holy ones for the work of
    ministry,
   for building up the body of Christ,
   until we all attain the unity of faith
   and knowledge of the Son of God, to
    mature to manhood,
   to the extent of the full stature of Christ.

## The Ascension of the Lord, *May 10, 2018 or May 13, 2018*

### SECOND READING

*or*

Eph 4:1-7, 11-13

Brothers and sisters,
I, a prisoner for the Lord,
    urge you to live in a manner worthy of the
        call you have received,
    with all humility and gentleness, with
        patience,
    bearing with one another through love,
    striving to preserve the unity of the Spirit
through the bond of peace:
one body and one Spirit,
    as you were also called to the one hope of
        your call;
one Lord, one faith, one baptism;
one God and Father of all,
who is over all and through all and in all.

But grace was given to each of us
    according to the measure of Christ's gift.

And he gave some as apostles, others as
    prophets,
    others as evangelists, others as pastors and
        teachers,
    to equip the holy ones for the work of
        ministry,
    for building up the body of Christ,
    until we all attain the unity of faith
and knowledge of the Son of God, to
    mature to manhood,
    to the extent of the full stature of Christ.

## Pentecost Sunday, *May 20, 2018*

### SECOND READING
1 Cor 12:3b-7, 12-13

Brothers and sisters:
No one can say, "Jesus is Lord," except by the
    Holy Spirit.

There are different kinds of spiritual gifts but
    the same Spirit;
    there are different forms of service but the
        same Lord;
    there are different workings but the same
        God
    who produces all of them in everyone.
To each individual the manifestation of the
    Spirit
    is given for some benefit.

As a body is one though it has many parts,
    and all the parts of the body, though many,
        are one body,
    so also Christ.
For in one Spirit we were all baptized into one
    body,
    whether Jews or Greeks, slaves or free
        persons,
    and we were all given to drink of one Spirit.

*or*

Gal 5:16-25

Brothers and sisters, live by the Spirit
    and you will certainly not gratify the desire
        of the flesh.
For the flesh has desires against the Spirit,
    and the Spirit against the flesh;
    these are opposed to each other,
    so that you may not do what you want.
But if you are guided by the Spirit, you are
    not under the law.
Now the works of the flesh are obvious:
    immorality, impurity, lust, idolatry,
    sorcery, hatreds, rivalry, jealousy,
    outbursts of fury, acts of selfishness,
    dissensions, factions, occasions of envy,
    drinking bouts, orgies, and the like.
I warn you, as I warned you before,
    that those who do such things will not
        inherit the kingdom of God.
In contrast, the fruit of the Spirit is love, joy,
    peace,
    patience, kindness, generosity,
    faithfulness, gentleness, self-control.
Against such there is no law.
Now those who belong to Christ Jesus have
    crucified their flesh
    with its passions and desires.
If we live in the Spirit, let us also follow the
    Spirit.

### SEQUENCE

*Veni, Sancte Spiritus*
Come, Holy Spirit, come!
And from your celestial home
    Shed a ray of light divine!
Come, Father of the poor!
Come, source of all our store!
    Come, within our bosoms shine.
You, of comforters the best;
You, the soul's most welcome guest;
    Sweet refreshment here below;
In our labor, rest most sweet;
Grateful coolness in the heat;
    Solace in the midst of woe.
O most blessed Light divine,
Shine within these hearts of yours,
    And our inmost being fill!
Where you are not, we have naught,
Nothing good in deed or thought,
    Nothing free from taint of ill.
Heal our wounds, our strength renew;
On our dryness pour your dew;
    Wash the stains of guilt away:
Bend the stubborn heart and will;
Melt the frozen, warm the chill;
    Guide the steps that go astray.
On the faithful, who adore
And confess you, evermore
    In your sevenfold gift descend;
Give them virtue's sure reward;
Give them your salvation, Lord;
    Give them joys that never end. Amen.
    Alleluia.

## SECOND READING

Heb 9:11-15

Brothers and sisters:
When Christ came as high priest
  of the good things that have come to be,
  passing through the greater and more
    perfect tabernacle
  not made by hands, that is, not belonging to
    this creation,
  he entered once for all into the sanctuary,
  not with the blood of goats and calves
  but with his own blood, thus obtaining
    eternal redemption.
For if the blood of goats and bulls
  and the sprinkling of a heifer's ashes
  can sanctify those who are defiled
  so that their flesh is cleansed,
  how much more will the blood of Christ,
  who through the eternal Spirit offered
    himself unblemished to God,
  cleanse our consciences from dead works
  to worship the living God.

For this reason he is mediator of a new
    covenant:
  since a death has taken place for
    deliverance
  from transgressions under the first
    covenant,
  those who are called may receive the
    promised eternal inheritance.

## OPTIONAL SEQUENCE

*Lauda Sion*

Laud, O Zion, your salvation,
Laud with hymns of exultation,
    Christ, your king and shepherd true:

Bring him all the praise you know,
He is more than you bestow.
    Never can you reach his due.

Special theme for glad thanksgiving
Is the quick'ning and the living
    Bread today before you set:

From his hands of old partaken,
As we know, by faith unshaken,
    Where the Twelve at supper met.

Full and clear ring out your chanting,
Joy nor sweetest grace be wanting,
    From your heart let praises burst:

For today the feast is holden,
When the institution olden
    Of that supper was rehearsed.

Here the new law's new oblation,
By the new king's revelation,
    Ends the form of ancient rite:

Now the new the old effaces,
Truth away the shadow chases,
    Light dispels the gloom of night.

What he did at supper seated,
Christ ordained to be repeated,
    His memorial ne'er to cease:

And his rule for guidance taking,
Bread and wine we hallow, making
    Thus our sacrifice of peace.

This the truth each Christian learns,
Bread into his flesh he turns,
    To his precious blood the wine:

Sight has fail'd, nor thought conceives,
But a dauntless faith believes,
    Resting on a pow'r divine.

Here beneath these signs are hidden
Priceless things to sense forbidden;
    Signs, not things are all we see:

Blood is poured and flesh is broken,
Yet in either wondrous token
    Christ entire we know to be.

Whoso of this food partakes,
Does not rend the Lord nor breaks;
    Christ is whole to all that taste:

Thousands are, as one, receivers,
One, as thousands of believers,
    Eats of him who cannot waste.

Bad and good the feast are sharing,
Of what divers dooms preparing,
    Endless death, or endless life.

Life to these, to those damnation,
See how like participation
    Is with unlike issues rife.

When the sacrament is broken,
Doubt not, but believe 'tis spoken,
    That each sever'd outward token
    doth the very whole contain.

Nought the precious gift divides,
Breaking but the sign betides
    Jesus still the same abides,
    still unbroken does remain.

*The shorter form of the sequence begins here.*

Lo! the angel's food is given
To the pilgrim who has striven;
    See the children's bread from heaven,
    which on dogs may not be spent.

Truth the ancient types fulfilling,
Isaac bound, a victim willing,
    Paschal lamb, its lifeblood spilling,
    manna to the fathers sent.

Very bread, good shepherd, tend us,
Jesu, of your love befriend us,
    You refresh us, you defend us,
    Your eternal goodness send us
In the land of life to see.

You who all things can and know,
Who on earth such food bestow,
    Grant us with your saints, though lowest,
    Where the heav'nly feast you show,
Fellow heirs and guests to be. Amen. Alleluia

## The Most Sacred Heart of Jesus, *June 8, 2018*

### FIRST READING
Hos 11:1, 3-4, 8c-9

Thus says the LORD:
When Israel was a child I loved him,
    out of Egypt I called my son.
Yet it was I who taught Ephraim to walk,
    who took them in my arms;
I drew them with human cords,
    with bands of love;
I fostered them like one
    who raises an infant to his cheeks;
Yet, though I stooped to feed my child,
    they did not know that I was their healer.

My heart is overwhelmed,
    my pity is stirred.
I will not give vent to my blazing anger,
    I will not destroy Ephraim again;
For I am God and not a man,
    the Holy One present among you;
    I will not let the flames consume you.

### RESPONSORIAL PSALM
Isa 12:2-3, 4, 5-6

R̞. (3)You will draw water joyfully from the
    springs of salvation.

God indeed is my savior;
    I am confident and unafraid.
My strength and my courage is the LORD,
    and he has been my savior.
With joy you will draw water
    at the fountain of salvation.

R̞. You will draw water joyfully from the
    springs of salvation.

Give thanks to the LORD, acclaim his name;
    among the nations make known his deeds,
    proclaim how exalted is his name.

R̞. You will draw water joyfully from the
    springs of salvation.

Sing praise to the LORD for his glorious
    achievement;
    let this be known throughout all the earth.
Shout with exultation, O city of Zion,
    for great in your midst
    is the Holy One of Israel!

R̞. You will draw water joyfully from the
    springs of salvation.

### SECOND READING
Eph 3:8-12, 14-19

Brothers and sisters:
To me, the very least of all the holy ones, this
    grace was given,
    to preach to the Gentiles the inscrutable
        riches of Christ,
    and to bring to light for all what is the plan
        of the mystery
    hidden from ages past in God who created
        all things,
    so that the manifold wisdom of God
    might now be made known through the
        church
    to the principalities and authorities in the
        heavens.
This was according to the eternal purpose
    that he accomplished in Christ Jesus our
        Lord,

in whom we have boldness of speech
and confidence of access through faith in
    him.

For this reason I kneel before the Father,
    from whom every family in heaven and on
        earth is named,
    that he may grant you in accord with the
        riches of his glory
    to be strengthened with power through his
        Spirit in the inner self,
    and that Christ may dwell in your hearts
        through faith;
    that you, rooted and grounded in love,
    may have strength to comprehend with all
        the holy ones
    what is the breadth and length and height
        and depth,
    and to know the love of Christ which
        surpasses knowledge,
    so that you may be filled with all the
        fullness of God.

## Tenth Sunday in Ordinary Time, *June 10, 2018*

### Gospel (cont.)
Mark 3:20-35

But no one can enter a strong man's house to plunder his property
    unless he first ties up the strong man.
Then he can plunder the house.
Amen, I say to you,
    all sins and all blasphemies that people utter will be forgiven them.
But whoever blasphemes against the Holy Spirit
    will never have forgiveness,
    but is guilty of an everlasting sin."
For they had said, "He has an unclean spirit."

His mother and his brothers arrived.
Standing outside they sent word to him and called him.
A crowd seated around him told him,
    "Your mother and your brothers and your sisters
    are outside asking for you."

But he said to them in reply,
    "Who are my mother and my brothers?"
And looking around at those seated in the circle he said,
    "Here are my mother and my brothers.
For whoever does the will of God
    is my brother and sister and mother."

## FIRST READING
Acts 12:1-11

In those days, King Herod laid hands upon
 some members of the Church to harm
 them.
He had James, the brother of John, killed by
 the sword,
 and when he saw that this was pleasing to
 the Jews
 he proceeded to arrest Peter also.
—It was the feast of Unleavened Bread.—
He had him taken into custody and put in
 prison
 under the guard of four squads of four
 soldiers each.
He intended to bring him before the people
 after Passover.
Peter thus was being kept in prison,
 but prayer by the Church was fervently
 being made
 to God on his behalf.

On the very night before Herod was to bring
 him to trial,
 Peter, secured by double chains,
 was sleeping between two soldiers,
 while outside the door guards kept watch
 on the prison.
Suddenly the angel of the Lord stood by him,
 and a light shone in the cell.
He tapped Peter on the side and awakened
 him, saying,
 "Get up quickly."
The chains fell from his wrists.
The angel said to him, "Put on your belt and
 your sandals."
He did so.
Then he said to him, "Put on your cloak and
 follow me."
So he followed him out,
 not realizing that what was happening
 through the angel was real;
 he thought he was seeing a vision.
They passed the first guard, then the second,
 and came to the iron gate leading out to the
 city,
 which opened for them by itself.
They emerged and made their way down an
 alley,
 and suddenly the angel left him.
Then Peter recovered his senses and said,
 "Now I know for certain
 that the Lord sent his angel
 and rescued me from the hand of Herod
 and from all that the Jewish people had
 been expecting."

## RESPONSORIAL PSALM
Ps 34:2-3, 4-5, 6-7, 8-9

R̸. (8) The angel of the Lord will rescue those
 who fear him.

I will bless the Lord at all times;
 his praise shall be ever in my mouth.
Let my soul glory in the Lord;
 the lowly will hear me and be glad.

R̸. The angel of the Lord will rescue those
 who fear him.

Glorify the Lord with me,
 let us together extol his name.
I sought the Lord, and he answered me
 and delivered me from all my fears.

R̸. The angel of the Lord will rescue those
 who fear him.

Look to him that you may be radiant with joy,
 and your faces may not blush with shame.
When the poor one called out, the Lord heard,
 and from all his distress he saved him.

R̸. The angel of the Lord will rescue those
 who fear him.

The angel of the Lord encamps
 around those who fear him, and delivers
 them.
Taste and see how good the Lord is;
 blessed the man who takes refuge in him.

R̸. The angel of the Lord will rescue those
 who fear him.

## SECOND READING
2 Tim 4:6-8, 17-18

I, Paul, am already being poured out like a
 libation,
 and the time of my departure is at hand.
I have competed well; I have finished the race;
 I have kept the faith.
From now on the crown of righteousness
 awaits me,
 which the Lord, the just judge,
 will award to me on that day, and not only
 to me,
 but to all who have longed for his
 appearance.

The Lord stood by me and gave me strength,
 so that through me the proclamation might
 be completed
 and all the Gentiles might hear it.
And I was rescued from the lion's mouth.
The Lord will rescue me from every evil threat
 and will bring me safe to his heavenly
 Kingdom.
To him be glory forever and ever. Amen.

## Gospel (cont.)
Mark 5:21-43; L98B

But his disciples said to Jesus,
    "You see how the crowd is pressing upon you,
    and yet you ask, 'Who touched me?'"
And he looked around to see who had done it.
The woman, realizing what had happened to her,
    approached in fear and trembling.
She fell down before Jesus and told him the whole truth.
He said to her, "Daughter, your faith has saved you.
Go in peace and be cured of your affliction."

While he was still speaking,
    people from the synagogue official's house arrived and said,
    "Your daughter has died; why trouble the teacher any longer?"
Disregarding the message that was reported,
    Jesus said to the synagogue official,
    "Do not be afraid; just have faith."
He did not allow anyone to accompany him inside
    except Peter, James, and John, the brother of James.
When they arrived at the house of the synagogue official,
    he caught sight of a commotion,
    people weeping and wailing loudly.
So he went in and said to them,
    "Why this commotion and weeping?
The child is not dead but asleep."
And they ridiculed him.
Then he put them all out.
He took along the child's father and mother
    and those who were with him
    and entered the room where the child was.
He took the child by the hand and said to her, *"Talitha koum,"*
    which means, "Little girl, I say to you, arise!"
The girl, a child of twelve, arose immediately and walked around.
At that they were utterly astounded.
He gave strict orders that no one should know this
    and said that she should be given something to eat.

*or* Mark 5:21-24, 35b-43; L98B

When Jesus had crossed again in the boat
    to the other side,
    a large crowd gathered around him, and he stayed close to the sea.
One of the synagogue officials, named Jairus, came forward.
Seeing him he fell at his feet and pleaded earnestly with him, saying,
    "My daughter is at the point of death.
Please, come lay your hands on her
    that she may get well and live."
He went off with him,
    and a large crowd followed him and pressed upon him.

While he was still speaking, people from the synagogue official's house
        arrived and said,
    "Your daughter has died; why trouble the teacher any longer?"
Disregarding the message that was reported,
    Jesus said to the synagogue official,
    "Do not be afraid; just have faith."
He did not allow anyone to accompany him inside
    except Peter, James, and John, the brother of James.
When they arrived at the house of the synagogue official,
    he caught sight of a commotion,
    people weeping and wailing loudly.
So he went in and said to them,
    "Why this commotion and weeping?
The child is not dead but asleep."
And they ridiculed him.
Then he put them all out.
He took along the child's father and mother
    and those who were with him
    and entered the room where the child was.
He took the child by the hand and said to her, *"Talitha koum,"*
    which means, "Little girl, I say to you, arise!"
The girl, a child of twelve, arose immediately and walked around.
At that they were utterly astounded.
He gave strict orders that no one should know this
    and said that she should be given something to eat.

## Fifteenth Sunday in Ordinary Time, *July 15, 2018*

**SECOND READING**

Eph 1:3-10

Blessed be the God and Father of our Lord
    Jesus Christ,
  who has blessed us in Christ
  with every spiritual blessing in the heavens,
  as he chose us in him, before the foundation
      of the world,
  to be holy and without blemish before him.
In love he destined us for adoption to himself
    through Jesus Christ,
  in accord with the favor of his will,
  for the praise of the glory of his grace
  that he granted us in the beloved.

In him we have redemption by his blood,
    the forgiveness of transgressions,
  in accord with the riches of his grace that
      he lavished upon us.
In all wisdom and insight, he has made
    known to us
  the mystery of his will in accord with his
      favor
  that he set forth in him as a plan for the
      fullness of times,
  to sum up all things in Christ, in heaven
      and on earth.

## Seventeenth Sunday in Ordinary Time, *July 29, 2018*

### *Gospel (cont.)*
John 6:1-15; L110B

Then Jesus took the loaves, gave thanks,
    and distributed them to those who were reclining,
    and also as much of the fish as they wanted.
When they had had their fill, he said to his disciples,
    "Gather the fragments left over,
    so that nothing will be wasted."
So they collected them,
    and filled twelve wicker baskets with fragments
    from the five barley loaves
    that had been more than they could eat.
When the people saw the sign he had done, they said,
    "This is truly the Prophet, the one who is to come into the world."
Since Jesus knew that they were going to come and carry him off
    to make him king,
    he withdrew again to the mountain alone.

## Eighteenth Sunday in Ordinary Time, *August 5, 2018*

### *Gospel (cont.)*
John 6:24-35; L113B

So Jesus said to them,
    "Amen, amen, I say to you,
    it was not Moses who gave the bread from heaven;
    my Father gives you the true bread from heaven.
For the bread of God is that which comes down from heaven
    and gives life to the world."

So they said to him,
    "Sir, give us this bread always."
Jesus said to them,
    "I am the bread of life;
    whoever comes to me will never hunger,
    and whoever believes in me will never thirst."

## Gospel (cont.)

Luke 1:39-56; L622

He has cast down the mighty from their thrones,
  and has lifted up the lowly.
He has filled the hungry with good things,
  and the rich he has sent away empty.
He has come to the help of his servant Israel
  for he has remembered his promise of mercy,
  the promise he made to our fathers,
  to Abraham and his children forever."

Mary remained with her about three months
  and then returned to her home.

### FIRST READING

Rev 11:19a; 12:1-6a, 10ab

God's temple in heaven was opened,
  and the ark of his covenant could be seen
    in the temple.

A great sign appeared in the sky, a woman
    clothed with the sun,
  with the moon under her feet,
  and on her head a crown of twelve stars.
She was with child and wailed aloud in pain
    as she labored to give birth.
Then another sign appeared in the sky;
  it was a huge red dragon, with seven heads
    and ten horns,
  and on its heads were seven diadems.
Its tail swept away a third of the stars in the
    sky
  and hurled them down to the earth.
Then the dragon stood before the woman
    about to give birth,
  to devour her child when she gave birth.
She gave birth to a son, a male child,
  destined to rule all the nations with an iron
    rod.
Her child was caught up to God and his
    throne.
The woman herself fled into the desert
  where she had a place prepared by God.

Then I heard a loud voice in heaven say:
  "Now have salvation and power come,
  and the Kingdom of our God
  and the authority of his Anointed One."

### RESPONSORIAL PSALM

Ps 45:10, 11, 12, 16

℟. (10bc) The queen stands at your right
  hand, arrayed in gold.

The queen takes her place at your right hand
  in gold of Ophir.

℟. The queen stands at your right hand,
  arrayed in gold.

Hear, O daughter, and see; turn your ear,
  forget your people and your father's house.

℟. The queen stands at your right hand,
  arrayed in gold.

So shall the king desire your beauty;
  for he is your lord.

℟. The queen stands at your right hand,
  arrayed in gold.

They are borne in with gladness and joy;
  they enter the palace of the king.

℟. The queen stands at your right hand,
  arrayed in gold.

### SECOND READING

1 Cor 15:20-27

Brothers and sisters:
Christ has been raised from the dead,
  the firstfruits of those who have fallen
    asleep.
For since death came through man,
  the resurrection of the dead came also
    through man.
For just as in Adam all die,
  so too in Christ shall all be brought to life,
  but each one in proper order:
  Christ the firstfruits;
  then, at his coming, those who belong to
    Christ;
  then comes the end,
  when he hands over the Kingdom to his
    God and Father,
  when he has destroyed every sovereignty
  and every authority and power.
For he must reign until he has put all his
    enemies under his feet.
The last enemy to be destroyed is death,
  for "he subjected everything under his feet."

## Twenty-First Sunday in Ordinary Time, August 26, 2018

**SECOND READING**
Eph 5:2a, 25-32

Brothers and sisters:
Live in love, as Christ loved us.
Husbands, love your wives,
    even as Christ loved the church
    and handed himself over for her to sanctify
      her,
    cleansing her by the bath of water with the
      word,
    that he might present to himself the church
      in splendor,
    without spot or wrinkle or any such thing,
    that she might be holy and without blemish.

So also husbands should love their wives as
    their own bodies.
He who loves his wife loves himself.
For no one hates his own flesh
    but rather nourishes and cherishes it,
    even as Christ does the church,
    because we are members of his body.
*For this reason a man shall leave his father*
    *and his mother and be joined to his wife,*
    *and the two shall become one flesh.*
This is a great mystery,
    but I speak in reference to Christ and the
      church.

## Twenty-Second Sunday in Ordinary Time, September 2, 2018

### Gospel (cont.)
Mark 7:1-8, 14-15, 21-23; L125B

He summoned the crowd again and said to them,
    "Hear me, all of you, and understand.
Nothing that enters one from outside can defile that person;
    but the things that come out from within are what defile.

"From within people, from their hearts,
    come evil thoughts, unchastity, theft, murder,
    adultery, greed, malice, deceit,
    licentiousness, envy, blasphemy, arrogance, folly.
All these evils come from within and they defile."

## Twenty-Seventh Sunday in Ordinary Time, October 7, 2018

### Gospel (cont.)
Mark 10:2-16; L140B

He said to them,
    "Whoever divorces his wife and marries another
    commits adultery against her;
    and if she divorces her husband and marries another,
    she commits adultery."

And people were bringing children to him that he might touch them,
    but the disciples rebuked them.
When Jesus saw this he became indignant and said to them,
    "Let the children come to me;
    do not prevent them, for the kingdom of God belongs to such as these.
Amen, I say to you,
    whoever does not accept the kingdom of God like a child
    will not enter it."
Then he embraced them and blessed them,
    placing his hands on them.

*or* Mark 10:2-12; L140B

The Pharisees approached Jesus and asked,
    "Is it lawful for a husband to divorce his wife?"

They were testing him.
He said to them in reply, "What did Moses command you?"
They replied,
    "Moses permitted a husband to write a bill of divorce
    and dismiss her."
But Jesus told them,
    "Because of the hardness of your hearts
    he wrote you this commandment.
But from the beginning of creation, *God made them male and female.*
*For this reason a man shall leave his father and mother*
    *and be joined to his wife,*
    *and the two shall become one flesh.*
So they are no longer two but one flesh.
Therefore what God has joined together,
    no human being must separate."
In the house the disciples again questioned Jesus about this.
He said to them,
    "Whoever divorces his wife and marries another
    commits adultery against her;
    and if she divorces her husband and marries another,
    she commits adultery."

## Gospel (cont.)

Mark 10:17-30; L143B

So Jesus again said to them in reply,
    "Children, how hard it is to enter the kingdom of God!
It is easier for a camel to pass through the eye of a needle
    than for one who is rich to enter the kingdom of God."
They were exceedingly astonished and said among themselves,
    "Then who can be saved?"
Jesus looked at them and said,
    "For human beings it is impossible, but not for God.
All things are possible for God."
Peter began to say to him,
    "We have given up everything and followed you."
Jesus said, "Amen, I say to you,
    there is no one who has given up house or brothers or sisters
    or mother or father or children or lands
    for my sake and for the sake of the gospel
    who will not receive a hundred times more now in this present age:
    houses and brothers and sisters
    and mothers and children and lands,
    with persecutions, and eternal life in the age to come."

*or* Mark 10:17-27

As Jesus was setting out on a journey, a man ran up,
    knelt down before him, and asked him,
    "Good teacher, what must I do to inherit eternal life?"
Jesus answered him, "Why do you call me good?
No one is good but God alone.
You know the commandments: *You shall not kill;*
    *you shall not commit adultery;*
    *you shall not steal;*
    *you shall not bear false witness;*
    *you shall not defraud;*
    *honor your father and your mother."*
He replied and said to him,
    "Teacher, all of these I have observed from my youth."
Jesus, looking at him, loved him and said to him,
    "You are lacking in one thing.
Go, sell what you have, and give to the poor
    and you will have treasure in heaven; then come, follow me."
At that statement his face fell,
    and he went away sad, for he had many possessions.

Jesus looked around and said to his disciples,
    "How hard it is for those who have wealth
    to enter the kingdom of God!"
The disciples were amazed at his words.
So Jesus again said to them in reply,
    "Children, how hard it is to enter the kingdom of God!
It is easier for a camel to pass through the eye of a needle
    than for one who is rich to enter the kingdom of God."
They were exceedingly astonished and said among themselves,
    "Then who can be saved?"
Jesus looked at them and said,
    "For human beings it is impossible, but not for God.
All things are possible for God."

## Twenty-Ninth Sunday in Ordinary Time, *October 21, 2018*

## Gospel

Mark 10:42-45; L146B

Jesus summoned the Twelve and said to them,
    "You know that those who are recognized as rulers over the Gentiles
    lord it over them,
    and their great ones make their authority over them felt.
But it shall not be so among you.
Rather, whoever wishes to be great among you will be your servant;
    whoever wishes to be first among you will be the slave of all.
For the Son of Man did not come to be served
    but to serve and to give his life as a ransom for many."

## FIRST READING
Rev 7:2-4, 9-14

I, John, saw another angel come up from the
    East,
    holding the seal of the living God.
He cried out in a loud voice to the four angels
    who were given power to damage the land
        and the sea,
    "Do not damage the land or the sea or the
        trees
    until we put the seal on the foreheads of
        the servants of our God."
I heard the number of those who had been
    marked with the seal,
    one hundred and forty-four thousand
        marked
    from every tribe of the children of Israel.

After this I had a vision of a great multitude,
    which no one could count,
    from every nation, race, people, and tongue.
They stood before the throne and before the
    Lamb,
    wearing white robes and holding palm
        branches in their hands.
They cried out in a loud voice:

    "Salvation comes from our God,
        who is seated on the throne,
    and from the Lamb."

All the angels stood around the throne
    and around the elders and the four living
        creatures.
They prostrated themselves before the throne,
    worshiped God, and exclaimed:

    "Amen. Blessing and glory, wisdom and
        thanksgiving,
    honor, power, and might
    be to our God forever and ever. Amen."

Then one of the elders spoke up and said to
    me,
    "Who are these wearing white robes, and
        where did they come from?"
I said to him, "My lord, you are the one who
    knows."
He said to me,
    "These are the ones who have survived the
        time of great distress;
    they have washed their robes
    and made them white in the Blood of the
        Lamb."

## RESPONSORIAL PSALM
Ps 24:1bc-2, 3-4ab, 5-6

R̰. (cf. 6) Lord, this is the people that longs to
    see your face.

The LORD's are the earth and its fullness;
    the world and those who dwell in it.
For he founded it upon the seas
    and established it upon the rivers.

R̰. Lord, this is the people that longs to see
    your face.

Who can ascend the mountain of the LORD?
    or who may stand in his holy place?
One whose hands are sinless, whose heart is
    clean,
    who desires not what is vain.

R̰. Lord, this is the people that longs to see
    your face.

He shall receive a blessing from the LORD,
    a reward from God his savior.
Such is the race that seeks him,
    that seeks the face of the God of Jacob.

R̰. Lord, this is the people that longs to see
    your face.

## SECOND READING
1 John 3:1-3

Beloved:
See what love the Father has bestowed on us
    that we may be called the children of God.
Yet so we are.
The reason the world does not know us
    is that it did not know him.
Beloved, we are God's children now;
    what we shall be has not yet been revealed.
We do know that when it is revealed we shall
    be like him,
    for we shall see him as he is.
Everyone who has this hope based on him
    makes himself pure,
    as he is pure.

## FIRST READING
Dan 12:1-3; L1011.7

In those days, I, Daniel, mourned
    and heard this word of the Lord:
At that time there shall arise
    Michael, the great prince,
    guardian of your people;
It shall be a time unsurpassed in distress
    since nations began until that time.
At that time your people shall escape,
    everyone who is found written in the book.

Many of those who sleep in the dust of the
    earth shall awake;
Some shall live forever,
    others shall be an everlasting horror and
    disgrace.
But the wise shall shine brightly
    like the splendor of the firmament,
And those who lead the many to justice
    shall be like the stars forever.

## RESPONSORIAL PSALM
Ps 27:1, 4, 7, and 8b, and 9a, 13-14; L1013.3

R℣. (1a) The Lord is my light and my
        salvation.
    *or:*
R℣. (13) I believe that I shall see the good
        things of the Lord in the land of the
        living.

The LORD is my light and my salvation;
    whom should I fear?
The LORD is my life's refuge;
    of whom should I be afraid?

R℣. The Lord is my light and my salvation.
    *or:*
R℣. I believe that I shall see the good things of
        the Lord in the land of the living.

One thing I ask of the LORD;
    this I seek:
To dwell in the house of the LORD
    all the days of my life,
That I may gaze on the loveliness of the LORD
    and contemplate his temple.

R℣. The Lord is my light and my salvation.
    *or:*
R℣. I believe that I shall see the good things of
        the Lord in the land of the living.

Hear, O LORD, the sound of my call;
    have pity on me and answer me.
Your presence, O LORD, I seek.
    Hide not your face from me.

R℣. The Lord is my light and my salvation.
    *or:*
R℣. I believe that I shall see the good things of
        the Lord in the land of the living.

I believe that I shall see the bounty of the
        LORD
    in the land of the living.
Wait for the LORD with courage;
    be stouthearted, and wait for the LORD.

R℣. The Lord is my light and my salvation.
    *or:*
R℣. I believe that I shall see the good things of
        the Lord in the land of the living.

## SECOND READING
Rom 6:3-9; L1014.3

Brothers and sisters:
Are you unaware that we who were baptized
        into Christ Jesus
    were baptized into his death?
We were indeed buried with him through
        baptism into death,
    so that, just as Christ was raised from the
        dead
    by the glory of the Father,
    we too might live in newness of life.

For if we have grown into union with him
        through a death like his,
    we shall also be united with him in the
        resurrection.
We know that our old self was crucified with
        him,
    so that our sinful body might be done away
        with,
    that we might no longer be in slavery to sin.
For a dead person has been absolved from sin.
If, then, we have died with Christ,
    we believe that we shall also live with him.
We know that Christ, raised from the dead,
        dies no more;
    death no longer has power over him.

## Thirty-Second Sunday in Ordinary Time, *November 11, 2018*

### Gospel
Mark 12:41-44

Jesus sat down opposite the treasury
   and observed how the crowd put money into the treasury.
Many rich people put in large sums.
A poor widow also came and put in two small coins worth a few cents.
Calling his disciples to himself, he said to them,
   "Amen, I say to you, this poor widow put in more
   than all the other contributors to the treasury.
For they have all contributed from their surplus wealth,
   but she, from her poverty, has contributed all she had,
   her whole livelihood."

## Thanksgiving Day, *November 22, 2018*

**FIRST READING**
Sir 50:22-24; L943.2

And now, bless the God of all,
   who has done wondrous things on earth;
Who fosters people's growth from their
     mother's womb,
   and fashions them according to his will!
May he grant you joy of heart
   and may peace abide among you;
May his goodness toward us endure in Israel
   to deliver us in our days.

**RESPONSORIAL PSALM**
Ps 138:1-2a, 2bc-3, 4-5; L945.3

R. (2bc) Lord, I thank you for your
   faithfulness and love.

I will give thanks to you, O LORD, with all of
   my heart,
   for you have heard the words of my mouth;
   in the presence of the angels I will sing
     your praise;
I will worship at your holy temple.

R. Lord, I thank you for your faithfulness and
   love.

I will give thanks to your name,
Because of your kindness and your truth.
When I called, you answered me;
   you built up strength within me.

R. Lord, I thank you for your faithfulness and
   love.

All the kings of the earth shall give thanks to
   you, O LORD,
   when they hear the words of your mouth;
And they shall sing of the ways of the LORD:
   "Great is the glory of the LORD."

R. Lord, I thank you for your faithfulness and
   love.

**SECOND READING**
1 Cor 1:3-9; L944.1

Brothers and sisters:
Grace to you and peace from God our Father
   and the Lord Jesus Christ.

I give thanks to my God always on your
     account
   for the grace of God bestowed on you in
     Christ Jesus,
   that in him you were enriched in every way,
   with all discourse and all knowledge,
   as the testimony to Christ was confirmed
     among you,
   so that you are not lacking in any spiritual
     gift
   as you wait for the revelation of our Lord
     Jesus Christ.
He will keep you firm to the end,
   irreproachable on the day of our Lord Jesus
     Christ.
God is faithful,
   and by him you were called to fellowship
      with his Son, Jesus Christ our Lord.

## Lectionary Pronunciation Guide

| Lectionary Word | Pronunciation |
| --- | --- |
| Aaron | EHR-uhn |
| Abana | AB-uh-nuh |
| Abednego | uh-BEHD-nee-go |
| Abel-Keramin | AY-b'l-KEHR-uh-mihn |
| Abel-meholah | AY-b'l-mee-HO-lah |
| Abiathar | uh-BAI-uh-ther |
| Abiel | AY-bee-ehl |
| Abiezrite | ay-bai-EHZ-rait |
| Abijah | uh-BAI-dzhuh |
| Abilene | ab-uh-LEE-neh |
| Abishai | uh-BIHSH-ay-ai |
| Abiud | uh-BAI-uhd |
| Abner | AHB-ner |
| Abraham | AY-bruh-ham |
| Abram | AY-br'm |
| Achaia | uh-KAY-yuh |
| Achim | AY-kihm |
| Aeneas | uh-NEE-uhs |
| Aenon | AY-nuhn |
| Agrippa | uh-GRIH-puh |
| Ahaz | AY-haz |
| Ahijah | uh-HAI-dzhuh |
| Ai | AY-ee |
| Alexandria | al-ehg-ZAN-dree-uh |
| Alexandrian | al-ehg-ZAN-dree-uhn |
| Alpha | AHL-fuh |
| Alphaeus | AL-fee-uhs |
| Amalek | AM-uh-lehk |
| Amaziah | am-uh-ZAI-uh |
| Amminadab | ah-MIHN-uh-dab |
| Ammonites | AM-uh-naitz |
| Amorites | AM-uh-raits |
| Amos | AY-muhs |
| Amoz | AY-muhz |
| Ampliatus | am-plee-AY-tuhs |
| Ananias | an-uh-NAI-uhs |
| Andronicus | an-draw-NAI-kuhs |
| Annas | AN-uhs |
| Antioch | AN-tih-ahk |
| Antiochus | an-TAI-uh-kuhs |
| Aphiah | uh-FAI-uh |
| Apollos | uh-PAH-luhs |
| Appius | AP-ee-uhs |
| Aquila | uh-KWIHL-uh |
| Arabah | EHR-uh-buh |
| Aram | AY-ram |
| Arameans | ehr-uh-MEE-uhnz |
| Areopagus | ehr-ee-AH-puh-guhs |
| Arimathea | ehr-uh-muh-THEE-uh |
| Aroer | uh-RO-er |

| Lectionary Word | Pronunciation |
| --- | --- |
| Asaph | AY-saf |
| Asher | ASH-er |
| Ashpenaz | ASH-pee-naz |
| Assyria | a-SIHR-ee-uh |
| Astarte | as-TAHR-tee |
| Attalia | at-TAH-lee-uh |
| Augustus | uh-GUHS-tuhs |
| Azariah | az-uh-RAI-uh |
| Azor | AY-sawr |
| Azotus | uh-ZO-tus |
| Baal-shalishah | BAY-uhl-shuh-LAI-shuh |
| Baal-Zephon | BAY-uhl-ZEE-fuhn |
| Babel | BAY-bl |
| Babylon | BAB-ih-luhn |
| Babylonian | bab-ih-LO-nih-uhn |
| Balaam | BAY-lm |
| Barabbas | beh-REH-buhs |
| Barak | BEHR-ak |
| Barnabas | BAHR-nuh-buhs |
| Barsabbas | BAHR-suh-buhs |
| Bartholomew | bar-THAHL-uh-myoo |
| Bartimaeus | bar-tih-MEE-uhs |
| Baruch | BEHR-ook |
| Bashan | BAY-shan |
| Becorath | bee-KO-rath |
| Beelzebul | bee-EHL-zee-buhl |
| Beer-sheba | BEE-er-SHEE-buh |
| Belshazzar | behl-SHAZ-er |
| Benjamin | BEHN-dzhuh-mihn |
| Beor | BEE-awr |
| Bethany | BEHTH-uh-nee |
| Bethel | BETH-el |
| Bethesda | beh-THEHZ-duh |
| Bethlehem | BEHTH-leh-hehm |
| Bethphage | BEHTH-fuh-dzhee |
| Bethsaida | behth-SAY-ih-duh |
| Beth-zur | behth-ZER |
| Bildad | BIHL-dad |
| Bithynia | bih-THIHN-ih-uh |
| Boanerges | bo-uh-NER-dzheez |
| Boaz | BO-az |
| Caesar | SEE-zer |
| Caesarea | zeh-suh-REE-uh |
| Caiaphas | KAY-uh-fuhs |
| Cain | kayn |
| Cana | KAY-nuh |
| Canaan | KAY-nuhn |
| Canaanite | KAY-nuh-nait |
| Canaanites | KAY-nuh-naits |

| Lectionary Word | Pronunciation |
| --- | --- |
| Candace | kan-DAY-see |
| Capernaum | kuh-PERR-nay-uhm |
| Cappadocia | kap-ih-DO-shee-u |
| Carmel | KAHR-muhl |
| carnelians | kahr-NEEL-yuhnz |
| Cenchreae | SEHN-kree-ay |
| Cephas | SEE-fuhs |
| Chaldeans | kal-DEE-uhnz |
| Chemosh | KEE-mahsh |
| Cherubim | TSHEHR-oo-bihm |
| Chislev | KIHS-lehv |
| Chloe | KLO-ee |
| Chorazin | kor-AY-sihn |
| Cilicia | sih-LIHSH-ee-uh |
| Cleopas | KLEE-o-pas |
| Clopas | KLO-pas |
| Corinth | KAWR-ihnth |
| Corinthians | kawr-IHN-thee-uhnz |
| Cornelius | kawr-NEE-lee-uhs |
| Crete | kreet |
| Crispus | KRIHS-puhs |
| Cushite | CUHSH-ait |
| Cypriot | SIH-pree-at |
| Cyrene | sai-REE-nee |
| Cyreneans | sai-REE-nih-uhnz |
| Cyrenian | sai-REE-nih-uhn |
| Cyrenians | sai-REE-nih-uhnz |
| Cyrus | SAI-ruhs |
| Damaris | DAM-uh-rihs |
| Damascus | duh-MAS-kuhs |
| Danites | DAN-aits |
| Decapolis | duh-KAP-o-lis |
| Derbe | DER-bee |
| Deuteronomy | dyoo-ter-AH-num-mee |
| Didymus | DID-I-mus |
| Dionysius | dai-o-NIHSH-ih-uhs |
| Dioscuri | dai-O-sky-ri |
| Dorcas | DAWR-kuhs |
| Dothan | DO-thuhn |
| dromedaries | DRAH-muh-dher-eez |
| Ebed-melech | EE-behd-MEE-lehk |
| Eden | EE-dn |
| Edom | EE-duhm |
| Elamites | EE-luh-maitz |
| Eldad | EHL-dad |
| Eleazar | ehl-ee-AY-zer |
| Eli | EE-lai |
| *Eli Eli Lema Sabachthani* | AY-lee AY-lee luh-MAH sah-BAHK-tah-nee |

| Lectionary Word | Pronunciation | Lectionary Word | Pronunciation | Lectionary Word | Pronunciation |
|---|---|---|---|---|---|
| Eliab | ee-LAI-ab | Gilead | GIHL-ee-uhd | Joppa | DZHAH-puh |
| Eliakim | ee-LAI-uh-kihm | Gilgal | GIHL-gal | Joram | DZHO-ram |
| Eliezer | ehl-ih-EE-zer | Golgotha | GAHL-guh-thuh | Jordan | DZHAWR-dn |
| Elihu | ee-LAI-hyoo | Gomorrah | guh-MAWR-uh | Joseph | DZHO-zf |
| Elijah | ee-LAI-dzhuh | Goshen | GO-shuhn | Joses | DZHO-seez |
| Elim | EE-lihm | Habakkuk | huh-BAK-uhk | Joshua | DZHAH-shou-ah |
| Elimelech | ee-LIHM-eh-lehk | Hadadrimmon | hay-dad-RIHM-uhn | Josiah | dzho-SAI-uh |
| Elisha | ee-LAI-shuh | Hades | HAY-deez | Jotham | DZHO-thuhm |
| Eliud | ee-LAI-uhd | Hagar | HAH-gar | Judah | DZHOU-duh |
| Elizabeth | ee-LIHZ-uh-bth | Hananiah | han-uh-NAI-uh | Judas | DZHOU-duhs |
| Elkanah | el-KAY-nuh | Hannah | HAN-uh | Judea | dzhou-DEE-uh |
| *Eloi Eloi Lama* | AY-lo-ee AY-lo-ee | Haran | HAY-ruhn | Judean | dzhou-DEE-uhn |
| *Sabechthani* | LAH-mah sah- | Hebron | HEE-bruhn | Junia | dzhou-nih-uh |
| | BAHK-tah-nee | Hermes | HER-meez | Justus | DZHUHS-tuhs |
| Elymais | ehl-ih-MAY-ihs | Herod | HEHR-uhd | Kephas | KEF-uhs |
| Emmanuel | eh-MAN-yoo-ehl | Herodians | hehr-O-dee-uhnz | Kidron | KIHD-ruhn |
| Emmaus | eh-MAY-uhs | Herodias | hehr-O-dee-uhs | Kiriatharba | kihr-ee-ath-AHR-buh |
| Epaenetus | ee-PEE-nee-tuhs | Hezekiah | heh-zeh-KAI-uh | Kish | kihsh |
| Epaphras | EH-puh-fras | Hezron | HEHZ-ruhn | Laodicea | lay-o-dih-SEE-uh |
| ephah | EE-fuh | Hilkiah | hihl-KAI-uh | Lateran | LAT-er-uhn |
| Ephah | EE-fuh | Hittite | HIH-tait | Lazarus | LAZ-er-uhs |
| Ephesians | eh-FEE-zhuhnz | Hivites | HAI-vaitz | Leah | LEE-uh |
| Ephesus | EH-fuh-suhs | Hophni | HAHF-nai | Lebanon | LEH-buh-nuhn |
| *Ephphatha* | EHF-uh-thuh | Hor | HAWR | Levi | LEE-vai |
| Ephraim | EE-fray-ihm | Horeb | HAWR-ehb | Levite | LEE-vait |
| Ephrathah | EHF-ruh-thuh | Hosea | ho-ZEE-uh | Levites | LEE-vaits |
| Ephron | EE-frawn | Hur | her | Leviticus | leh-VIH-tih-kous |
| Epiphanes | eh-PIHF-uh-neez | hyssop | HIH-suhp | Lucius | LOO-shih-uhs |
| Erastus | ee-RAS-tuhs | Iconium | ai-KO-nih-uhm | Lud | luhd |
| Esau | EE-saw | Isaac | AI-zuhk | Luke | look |
| Esther | EHS-ter | Isaiah | ai-ZAY-uh | Luz | luhz |
| Ethanim | EHTH-uh-nihm | Iscariot | ihs-KEHR-ee-uht | Lycaonian | lihk-ay-O-nih-uhn |
| Ethiopian | ee-thee-O-pee-uhn | Ishmael | ISH-may-ehl | Lydda | LIH-duh |
| Euphrates | yoo-FRAY-teez | Ishmaelites | ISH-mayehl-aits | Lydia | LIH-dih-uh |
| Exodus | EHK-so-duhs | Israel | IHZ-ray-ehl | Lysanias | lai-SAY-nih-uhs |
| Ezekiel | eh-ZEE-kee-uhl | Ituraea | ih-TSHOOR-ree-uh | Lystra | LIHS-truh |
| Ezra | EHZ-ruh | Jaar | DZHAY-ahr | Maccabees | MAK-uh-beez |
| frankincense | FRANGK-ihn-sehns | Jabbok | DZHAB-uhk | Macedonia | mas-eh-DO-nih-uh |
| Gabbatha | GAB-uh-thuh | Jacob | DZHAY-kuhb | Macedonian | mas-eh-DO-nih-uhn |
| Gabriel | GAY-bree-ul | Jairus | DZH-hr-uhs | Machir | MAY-kihr |
| Gadarenes | GAD-uh-reenz | Javan | DZHAY-van | Machpelah | mak-PEE-luh |
| Galatian | guh-LAY-shih-uhn | Jebusites | DZHEHB-oo-zaits | Magdala | MAG-duh-luh |
| Galatians | guh-LAY-shih-uhnz | Jechoniah | dzhehk-o-NAI-uh | Magdalene | MAG-duh-lehn |
| Galilee | GAL-ih-lee | Jehoiakim | dzhee-HOI-uh-kihm | magi | MAY-dzhai |
| Gallio | GAL-ih-o | Jehoshaphat | dzhee-HAHSH-uh-fat | Malachi | MAL-uh-kai |
| Gamaliel | guh-MAY-lih-ehl | Jephthah | DZHEHF-thuh | Malchiah | mal-KAI-uh |
| Gaza | GAH-zuh | Jeremiah | dzhehr-eh-MAI-uh | Malchus | MAL-kuhz |
| Gehazi | gee-HAY-zai | Jericho | DZHEHR-ih-ko | Mamre | MAM-ree |
| Gehenna | geh-HEHN-uh | Jeroham | dzhehr-RO-ham | Manaen | MAN-uh-ehn |
| Genesis | DZHEHN-uh-sihs | Jerusalem | dzheh-ROU-suh-lehm | Manasseh | man-AS-eh |
| Gennesaret | gehn-NEHS-uh-reht | Jesse | DZHEH-see | Manoah | muh-NO-uh |
| Gentiles | DZHEHN-tailz | Jethro | DZHEHTH-ro | Mark | mahrk |
| Gerasenes | DZHEHR-uh-seenz | Joakim | DZHO-uh-kihm | Mary | MEHR-ee |
| Gethsemane | gehth-SEHM-uh-ne | Job | DZHOB | Massah | MAH-suh |
| Gideon | GIHD-ee-uhn | Jonah | DZHO-nuh | Mattathias | mat-uh-THAI-uhs |

| Lectionary Word | Pronunciation | Lectionary Word | Pronunciation | Lectionary Word | Pronunciation |
|---|---|---|---|---|---|
| Matthan | MAT-than | Parmenas | PAHR-mee-nas | Sabbath | SAB-uhth |
| Matthew | MATH-yoo | Parthians | PAHR-thee-uhnz | Sadducees | SAD-dzhoo-seez |
| Matthias | muh-THAI-uhs | Patmos | PAT-mos | Salem | SAY-lehm |
| Medad | MEE-dad | Peninnah | pee-NIHN-uh | Salim | SAY-lim |
| Mede | meed | Pentecost | PEHN-tee-kawst | Salmon | SAL-muhn |
| Medes | meedz | Penuel | pee-NYOO-ehl | Salome | suh-LO-mee |
| Megiddo | mee-GIH-do | Perez | PEE-rehz | Salu | SAYL-yoo |
| Melchizedek | mehl-KIHZ-eh-dehk | Perga | PER-guh | Samaria | suh-MEHR-ih-uh |
| Mene | MEE-nee | Perizzites | PEHR-ih-zaits | Samaritan | suh-MEHR-ih-tuhn |
| Meribah | MEHR-ih-bah | Persia | PER-zhuh | Samothrace | SAM-o-thrays |
| Meshach | MEE-shak | Peter | PEE-ter | Samson | SAM-s'n |
| Mespotamia | mehs-o-po-TAY-mih-uh | Phanuel | FAN-yoo-ehl | Samuel | SAM-yoo-uhl |
| Micah | MAI-kuh | Pharaoh | FEHR-o | Sanhedrin | san-HEE-drihn |
| Midian | MIH-dih-uhn | Pharisees | FEHR-ih-seez | Sarah | SEHR-uh |
| Milcom | MIHL-kahm | Pharpar | FAHR-pahr | Sarai | SAY-rai |
| Miletus | mai-LEE-tuhs | Philemon | fih-LEE-muhn | saraph | SAY-raf |
| Minnith | MIHN-ihth | Philippi | fil-LIH-pai | Sardis | SAHR-dihs |
| Mishael | MIHSH-ay-ehl | Philippians | fih-LIHP-ih-uhnz | Saul | sawl |
| Mizpah | MIHZ-puh | Philistines | fih-LIHS-tihnz | Scythian | SIH-thee-uihn |
| Moreh | MO-reh | Phinehas | FEHN-ee-uhs | Seba | SEE-buh |
| Moriah | maw-RAI-uh | Phoenicia | fee-NIHSH-ih-uh | Seth | sehth |
| Mosoch | MAH-sahk | Phrygia | FRIH-dzhih-uh | Shaalim | SHAY-uh-lihm |
| myrrh | mer | Phrygian | FRIH-dzhih-uhn | Shadrach | SHAY-drak |
| Mysia | MIH-shih-uh | phylacteries | fih-LAK-ter-eez | Shalishah | shuh-LEE-shuh |
| Naaman | NAY-uh-muhn | Pi-Hahiroth | pai-huh-HAI-rahth | Shaphat | Shay-fat |
| Nahshon | NAY-shuhn | Pilate | PAI-luht | Sharon | SHEHR-uhn |
| Naomi | NAY-o-mai | Pisidia | pih-SIH-dih-uh | Shealtiel | shee-AL-tih-ehl |
| Naphtali | NAF-tuh-lai | Pithom | PAI-thahm | Sheba | SHEE-buh |
| Nathan | NAY-thuhn | Pontius | PAHN-shus | Shebna | SHEB-nuh |
| Nathanael | nuh-THAN-ay-ehl | Pontus | PAHN-tus | Shechem | SHEE-kehm |
| Nazarene | NAZ-awr-een | Praetorium | pray-TAWR-ih-uhm | shekel | SHEHK-uhl |
| Nazareth | NAZ-uh-rehth | Priscilla | PRIHS-kill-uh | Shiloh | SHAI-lo |
| nazirite | NAZ-uh-rait | Prochorus | PRAH-kaw-ruhs | Shinar | SHAI-nahr |
| Nazorean | naz-aw-REE-uhn | Psalm | Sahm | Shittim | sheh-TEEM |
| Neapolis | nee-AP-o-lihs | Put | puht | Shuhite | SHOO-ait |
| Nebuchadnezzar | neh-byoo-kuhd-NEHZ-er | Puteoli | pyoo-TEE-o-lai | Shunammite | SHOO-nam-ait |
| | | Qoheleth | ko-HEHL-ehth | Shunem | SHOO-nehm |
| Negeb | NEH-gehb | qorban | KAWR-bahn | Sidon | SAI-duhn |
| Nehemiah | nee-hee-MAI-uh | Quartus | KWAR-tuhs | Silas | SAI-luhs |
| Ner | ner | Quirinius | kwai-RIHN-ih-uhs | Siloam | sih-LO-uhm |
| Nicanor | nai-KAY-nawr | Raamses | ray-AM-seez | Silvanus | sihl-VAY-nuhs |
| Nicodemus | nih-ko-DEE-muhs | Rabbi | RAB-ai | Simeon | SIHM-ee-uhn |
| Niger | NAI-dzher | Rabbouni | ra-BO-nai | Simon | SAI-muhn |
| Nineveh | NIHN-eh-veh | Rahab | RAY-hab | Sin (desert) | sihn |
| Noah | NO-uh | Ram | ram | Sinai | SAI-nai |
| Nun | nuhn | Ramah | RAY-muh | Sirach | SAI-rak |
| Obed | O-behd | Ramathaim | ray-muh-THAY-ihm | Sodom | SAH-duhm |
| Olivet | AH-lih-veht | Raqa | RA-kuh | Solomon | SAH-lo-muhn |
| Omega | o-MEE-guh | Rebekah | ree-BEHK-uh | Sosthenes | SAHS-thee-neez |
| Onesimus | o-NEH-sih-muhs | Rehoboam | ree-ho-BO-am | Stachys | STAY-kihs |
| Ophir | O-fer | Rephidim | REHF-ih-dihm | Succoth | SUHK-ahth |
| Orpah | AWR-puh | Reuben | ROO-b'n | Sychar | SI-kar |
| Pamphylia | pam-FIHL-ih-uh | Revelation | reh-veh-LAY-shuhn | Syene | sai-EE-nee |
| Paphos | PAY-fuhs | Rhegium | REE-dzhee-uhm | Symeon | SIHM-ee-uhn |
| | | Rufus | ROO-fuhs | synagogues | SIHN-uh-gahgz |

| Lectionary Word | Pronunciation | Lectionary Word | Pronunciation | Lectionary Word | Pronunciation |
|---|---|---|---|---|---|
| Syrophoenician | SIHR-o fee-NIHSH-ih-uhn | Timon | TAI-muhn | Zebedee | ZEH-beh-dee |
| | | Titus | TAI-tuhs | Zebulun | ZEH-byoo-luhn |
| Tabitha | TAB-ih-thuh | Tohu | TO-hyoo | Zechariah | zeh-kuh-RAI-uh |
| *Talitha koum* | TAL-ih-thuh-KOOM | Trachonitis | trak-o-NAI-tis | Zedekiah | zeh-duh-KAI-uh |
| Tamar | TAY-mer | Troas | TRO-ahs | Zephaniah | zeh-fuh-NAI-uh |
| Tarshish | TAHR-shihsh | Tubal | TYOO-b'l | Zerah | ZEE-ruh |
| Tarsus | TAHR-suhs | Tyre | TAI-er | Zeror | ZEE-rawr |
| Tekel | TEH-keel | Ur | er | Zerubbabel | zeh-RUH-buh-behl |
| Terebinth | TEHR-ee-bihnth | Urbanus | er-BAY-nuhs | Zeus | zyoos |
| Thaddeus | THAD-dee-uhs | Uriah | you-RAI-uh | Zimri | ZIHM-rai |
| Theophilus | thee-AH-fih-luhs | Uzziah | yoo-ZAI-uh | Zion | ZAI-uhn |
| Thessalonians | theh-suh-LO-nih-uhnz | Wadi | WAH-dee | Ziph | zihf |
| Theudas | THU-duhs | Yahweh-yireh | YAH-weh-yer-AY | Zoar | ZO-er |
| Thyatira | thai-uh-TAI-ruh | Zacchaeus | zak-KEE-uhs | Zorah | ZAWR-uh |
| Tiberias | tai-BIHR-ih-uhs | Zadok | ZAY-dahk | Zuphite | ZUHF-ait |
| Timaeus | tai-MEE-uhs | Zarephath | ZEHR-ee-fath | | |